Fundamentals OF MANAGEMENT

Essential Concepts and Applications

EDITION
7

Fundamentals
OF
MANAGEMENT
Essential Concepts and Applications

STEPHEN P. ROBBINS

San Diego State University

DAVID A. DECENZO

Coastal Carolina University

MARY COULTER

Missouri State University

Prentice Hall

Boston   Columbus   Indianapolis   New York   San Francisco   Upper Saddle River
Amsterdam   Cape Town   Dubai   London   Madrid   Milan   Munich   Paris   Montreal   Toronto
Delhi   Mexico City   Sao Paulo   Sydney   Hong Kong   Seoul   Singapore   Taipei   Tokyo

Editorial Director: Sally Yagan
Editor in Chief: Eric Svendsen
Acquisitions Editor: Kim Norbuta
Editorial Project Manager: Claudia Fernandes
Media Editor: Denise Vaughn
Editorial Assistant: Meg O'Rourke
Director of Marketing: Patrice Lumumba Jones
Senior Marketing Manager: Nikki Jones
Senior Marketing Assistant: Ian Gold
Senior Managing Editor: Judy Leale
Senior Operations Supervisor: Arnold Vila
Design Development Manager: John Christiana
Art Director: Kathryn Foot
Text and Cover Designer: Kathryn Foot
Manager, Visual Research: Beth Brenzel
Manager, Rights and Permissions: Zina Arabia
Photo Development Editor: Nancy Moudry
Photo Researcher: Sheila Norman
Image Permission Coordinator: Vickie Menanteaux
Manager, Cover Visual Research & Permissions: Karen Sanatar
Media Project Manager: Lisa Rinaldi
Full-Service Project Management: Jen Welsch/BookMasters, Inc.
Composition: Integra Software Services
Printer/Binder: Courier/Kendallville
Cover Printer: Lehigh-Phoenix Color/Hagerstown
Text Font: 10/12 Times New Roman

Credits and acknowledgments borrowed from other sources and reproduced, with permission, in this textbook appear on page 435.

Library of Congress Cataloging-in-Publication Data

Robbins, Stephen P,
   Fundamentals of management : essential concepts and applications/Stephen P. Robbins,
David A. DeCenzo, Mary Coulter.—7th ed.
      p.   cm.
   Includes bibliographical references and index.
   ISBN 978-0-13-610982-2 (pbk. : alk. paper)
   1. Management.   I. DeCenzo, David A.   II. Coulter, Mary K.   III. Title.
HD31.R5643 2011
658—dc22
                                          2009041367

10 9 8 7 6 5 4 3 2

Prentice Hall
is an imprint of

www.pearsonhighered.com

ISBN 10:   0-13-610982-9
ISBN 13: 978-0-13-610982-2

To my wife, Laura

Steve

....

To my family, who continue to be the best support system anyone could have. To Terri, my wife of 27 years, and my children—Mark, Meredith, Gabriella, and Natalie—thank you for showing me what life is really about. Through thick and thin there is one common element—family. What a comfort that brings me.

Dave

....

To my husband, Ron

Mary

Brief Contents

Contents

Part IV Leading 212

A Short Note to Students

Get Experienced!

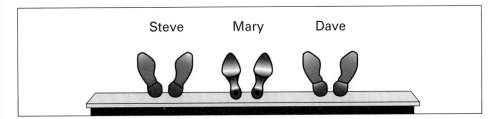

Steve   Mary   Dave

While we have your "first-page" attention, we want to ask you a few important questions.

1. Did you ever wish you could experience a course in a way that best suits your learning style and your schedule?
2. Wouldn't it be nice to take a chapter pretest and find out exactly what you know or don't know?
3. How would you like to create your own study plan, one that lets you monitor your own learning progress, where—at a glance—you could see exactly which topics you need to review?
4. Did you ever wish that you could have this study plan linked to a variety of interactive content to help you learn the material, including a posttest to see if you actually did learn!
5. What about having it all online 24/7?

If you answered *Yes* to any of the above, then **mymanagementlab.com**, the online homework tool that accompanies this book, is for you. It was built with your course and your unique learning style in mind. No complicated registration, no complicated interface, just a straightforward, read it, learn it, and experience it homework tool.

mymanagementlab.com gives you the chance to learn management concepts and principles by creating your own experience.

▶ Read this textbook.
▶ Take a chapter pretest.
▶ Find out exactly where you need to focus your learning.
▶ Review concepts online with interactive simulations, e-book, PowerPoints, and more.
▶ Take a chapter posttest (as many times as you need to, in order to learn the concepts).

Go ahead. Get experienced.

Good luck this semester and we hope you enjoy reading this book as much as we did writing it for you.

Steve Robbins   Mary Coulter   Dave De Cenzo

Preface

You've made a good decision! You're taking a college course . . . maybe more than one. Although it may sometimes feel like you're wasting your time being in college, you're not. Yes, it's expensive. Yes, it's even hard sometimes. But what you're doing now *will* pay off in the long run. In a recent survey of job seekers, a whopping 92 percent said that a major disadvantage in competing for jobs was not having taken college courses. But that won't be you because you *are* enrolled in a college course—the course for which you've purchased this book.

What's New in the Seventh Edition?

You might not think that there could be too much new to put in a book . . . especially a seventh edition! But that's the great thing about a book that discusses managers and management! It's always easy to find new material just by paying attention to what's happening in the news! (Paying attention to the news is a good habit for you to develop, as well!) There are always new issues and ideas confronting managers. Take a look at some of the new "things" we've included in this book:

► **NEW author**
  ► Mary Coulter has joined the author team bringing her extensive experience in the classroom and her "user-friendly" point of view to this edition. Already author of the successful text *Strategic Management in Action, 5e,* Mary has focused on working the new edition into a more engaging, up-to-date, and visual format to motivate students.
► **NEW content and design**
  ► New "Entrepreneurship Module," putting all the information on entrepreneurship in one compact location.
  ► Revamped "Managing Your Career" module now includes a section on challenges of a weak economy.
  ► Revamped "History Module" includes a new visual timeline of the history of management.
  ► New "From the Past to the Present" chapter feature connects management history to the present.
  ► New "Managing Diversity" chapter feature focuses on diversity issues facing new managers.
  ► New "Technology and the Manager's Job" chapter feature discusses how technology is changing the manager's job.
  ► New "And the Survey Says" chapter feature presents survey findings about managers, employees, and workplaces.
  ► New end-of-chapter materials including: self-assessment exercise; "For Your Immediate Action" exercise, simulating a manager's electronic in-box; and new cases.
► **NEW mymanagementlab.com**
  ► mymanagementlab is a powerful online tool that combines assessment, reporting, personalized study, and a complete Robbins ebook to help both students and instructors succeed. In particular, mymanagementlab supports more active learning styles, involving students as they study management and prepare for tests and quizzes. Mymanagementlab also contains key video, testing, and other support resources that offer instructors many ways to enliven their classroom and save time—all in one convenient place.
► **NEW videos**
  ► Up-to-date videos showing management topics in action, as well as access to the complete management video library, will be available at www.managementlab.com. Visit there to gain access and learn more.

▶ Biz Tube—updated in mymanagementlab every month are current and relevant videos with discussion questions for use in class.

▶ Updated company videos addressing specific topics in the book.

▶ **NEW Test Item File**

▶ Completely revised and accuracy-checked test item file, including AASCB tagging and instructor assignment feedback for each question.

▶ **NEW purchasing options**

▶ This book is available in a variety of formats created to meet the needs of students including: Student Value Editions, eBooks, print upgrades, and even the ability to customize materials.

In addition, following is a chapter-by-chapter list of the topic additions and changes in the *Seventh Edition*:

Chapter 1

• New chapter opener—"It's a Good Life"
• New topics—factors reshaping and redefining management, importance of customers and innovation
• New examples

Chapter 2

• New chapter opener—"Extreme Customer Service"
• New topics—what the new economy is like, the financial crisis, the "new" normal, effect of the new economy on organizations, new definitions of global organizations, new discussion of how organizations go global, reorganized discussion of social responsibility, green management, expanded discussion of business ethics, updated discussion of today's workforce, generational differences
• New examples

Chapter 3

• New chapter opener—"Branson Airport"
• New topic—Intuitive decision making
• New examples

Chapter 4

• New chapter opener—"Habitat for Humanity"
• New topics—more coverage of strategic management, setting goals and developing plans, effective planning in dynamic environments
• New examples

Chapter 5

• New chapter opener—"In-N-Out Burger"
• New topics—additional discussion of formalization, reorganized common organization designs, virtual and network organizations, today's organization design challenges, keeping employees connected, global differences, seven dimensions of organizational culture, how employees learn culture, strong cultures
• New examples

Chapter 6

• New chapter opener—"Shedding Workers and Tears"
• New topics—reorganized HRM process, Hugo Munsterberg and I/O psychology, managing downsizing, layoff survivor sickness, controlling HR costs
• New examples

Chapter 7

- New chapter opener—"Methodist Hospital"
- New topics—reorganized discussion of what change is and making changes, new definition of stress
- New examples

Chapter 8

- New chapter opener—"Towels, Severance, and Morale . . . Oh My"
- New topics—workplace misbehavior, employee engagement, generational differences, dealing with negative workplace behaviors
- New examples

Chapter 9

- New chapter opener—"Up to Speed"
- New topics—discussion of groups/group development, major concepts of work groups, what makes teams effective, managing global teams, when teams aren't necessary
- New examples

Chapter 10

- New chapter opener—"Best Buy"
- New topics—revised discussion of what motivation is, moved McCelland's three-needs theory to early theories discussion, goal setting theory, employee recognition programs
- New examples

Chapter 11

- New chapter opener—"Employees First"
- New topics—reorganized into early theories, contingency theories, and contemporary theories
- New examples

Chapter 12

- New chapter opener—"Gossip Girls"
- New topics—Keith Davis's grapevine study, social networks, Net lingo, task, relationship and process conflict
- New examples

Chapter 13

- New chapter opener—"Baggage Blunders"
- New topics—new ethics dilemma, history of benchmarking, balanced scorecard, types of controls, workplace violence
- New examples

Chapter 14

- New chapter opener—"Smooth Ride"
- New topics—Deming's contributions, factory of the future, controlling quality, quality goals
- New examples

What This Course Is About and Why It's Important

This course and this book are about management and managers. Managers are one thing that all organizations—no matter the size, kind, or location—need. And there's no doubt that the world that managers face has changed, is changing, and will continue to change. The dynamic nature of today's organizations means both rewards *and* challenges for the individuals who will be managing those organizations. Management is a dynamic subject, and a management textbook should reflect those changes to help prepare you to manage under the current conditions. Thus, we've written this seventh edition of

Fundamentals of Management to provide you with the best possible understanding of what it means to be a manager confronting change.

What's Expected of You in This Course?

It's simple. Come to class. Read the book. Do your assignments. And . . . study for your exams. If you want to get the most out of the money you've spent for this course and this textbook, that's what you need to do. In addition to writing this book, we teach. And that's what we expect of our students.

Getting the Most Out of Your Textbook: How Can I Get a Good Grade in This Course?

Professors use a textbook because it provides a compact source of information that you need to know about the subject material. Professors like to use this particular textbook because it covers the fundamental (essential) concepts of management and does so with a writing style that readers (that's you) will find interesting and straightforward.

In addition to the discussions and explanations of these management concepts, we provide several ways to help you work to get a good grade in this course. At the end of each chapter, you'll find a "Chapter Summary," which provides you with a brief overview of the chapter material organized by the chapter learning outcomes. In addition to this review, you'll find options for applying what you've learned—reinforcing the concepts and seeing how they're relevant to you right now. The "Understanding the Chapter" material is a great way for you to see if you really do understand the chapter material. Then, take a look at yourself in the "Understanding Yourself" section. Complete the self-assessment exercise to learn more about yourself and what your management style might be like. In the FYIA ("For Your Immediate Action") section, you get to "be" a manager and decide how to respond to an urgent management problem. Then, read through the "Case Application" you'll find at the end of the chapter. These stories come from today's business news and help illustrate the challenges managers face in managing. Your professor may even assign some of these as homework. Finally, utilize the MyManagementLab. It's a great tool and one that will help you learn and understand the management concepts covered in this book and in your class. Good luck in this course! Enjoy and GOOD MANAGING!

Student Supplements

CourseSmart eTextbook

CourseSmart is an exciting new choice for students looking to save money. As an alternative to purchasing the print textbook, you can purchase an electronic version of the same content and save up to 50 percent off the suggested list price of the print text. With a CourseSmart eTextbook, you can search the text, make notes online, print out reading assignments that incorporate lecture notes, and bookmark important passages for later review. For more information, or to purchase access to the CourseSmart eTextbook, visit coursesmart.com.

MyManagementLab mymanagementlab

MyManagementLab (**mymanagementlab.com**) is an easy to use online tool that personalizes course content and provides robust assessment and reporting to measure student and class performance. All the resources you need for course success are in one place—flexible and easily adapted for your course experience. Some of the resources include an e-book version of all chapters, quizzes, video clips, and PowerPoint presentations that engage students while helping them to study independently.

Acknowledgments

Writing and publishing a textbook requires the talents of a number of people whose names never appear on the cover. We'd like to recognize and thank a phenomenal team of talented people who provided their skills and abilities in making this book a reality.

This team includes Kim Norbuta, our acquisitions editor; Judy Leale, our senior managing editor; Nikki Jones, our marketing manager; Claudia Fernandes, our editorial project manager; Kathie Foot, our amazing designer; Eric Svendsen, our editor in chief; Sally Yagan, our editorial director; and Nancy Moudry and Sheila Norman, our gifted photo researchers.

About the Authors

STEPHEN P. ROBBINS received his Ph.D. from the University of Arizona. He previously worked for the Shell Oil Company and Reynolds Metals Company and has taught at the University of Nebraska at Omaha, Concordia University in Montreal, the University of Baltimore, Southern Illinois University at Edwardsville, and San Diego State University. He is currently professor emeritus in management at San Diego State.

Dr. Robbins' research interests have focused on conflict, power, and politics in organizations, behavioral decision making, and the development of effective interpersonal skills. His articles on these and other topics have appeared in such journals as *Business Horizons*, the *California Management Review, Business and Economic Perspectives, International Management, Management Review, Canadian Personnel and Industrial Relations*, and *The Journal of Management Education*.

Dr. Robbins is the world's best-selling textbook author in the areas of management and organizational behavior. His books have sold more than 5 million copies and have been translated into 20 languages. His books are currently used at more than 1,500 U.S. colleges and universities, as well as hundreds of schools throughout Canada, Latin America, Australia, New Zealand, Asia, and Europe.

Dr. Robbins also participates in masters' track competition. Since turning 50 in 1993, he's won 18 national championships and 12 world titles. He is the current world record holder at 100m (12.37) and 200m (25.20) for men 65 and over.

DAVID A. DECENZO (Ph.D., West Virginia University) is president of Coastal Carolina University in Conway, South Carolina. In his capacity as president, Dr. DeCenzo is responsible for the overall vision and leadership of the university. He has been at Coastal since 2002 when he took over leadership of the E. Craig Wall Sr. College of Business. Since then, the college established an economics major and developed an MBA program. During that period, student enrollment and faculty positions nearly doubled. The college also established significant internship opportunities locally, nationally, and internationally in major *Fortune* 100 companies. As provost, Dr. DeCenzo worked with faculty leadership to pass a revised general education core curriculum as well as institute a minimum salary level for the university's faculty members. Before joining the Coastal faculty in 2002, he served as director of partnership development in the College of Business and Economics at Towson University in Maryland. He is an experienced industry consultant, corporate trainer, and public speaker. Dr. DeCenzo is the author of numerous textbooks that are used widely at colleges and universities throughout the United States and the world.

Dr. DeCenzo and his wife, Terri, have four children and reside in Pawleys Island, South Carolina.

MARY COULTER (Ph.D., University of Arkansas) held different jobs including high school teacher, legal assistant, and government program planner before completing her graduate work. She has taught at Drury University, the University of Arkansas, Trinity University, and Missouri State University (since 1983). Dr. Coulter's research interests have focused on competitive strategies for not-for-profit arts organizations and the use of new media in the educational process. Her research on these and other topics has appeared in such journals as *International Journal of Business Disciplines, Journal of Business Strategies, Journal of Business Research, Journal of Nonprofit and Public Sector Marketing*, and *Case Research Journal*. In addition to *Fundamentals of Management*, Dr. Coulter has published other books with Prentice Hall including *Management,* now in its tenth edition; *Strategic Management in Action*, now in its fifth edition; and *Entrepreneurship in Action*, which is in its second edition.

When she's not busy teaching or writing, Dr. Coulter enjoys puttering around in her flower gardens, trying new recipes, reading all different types of books, and enjoying many different activities with Ron, Sarah and James, and Katie and Matt.

CHAPTER

Managers and Management

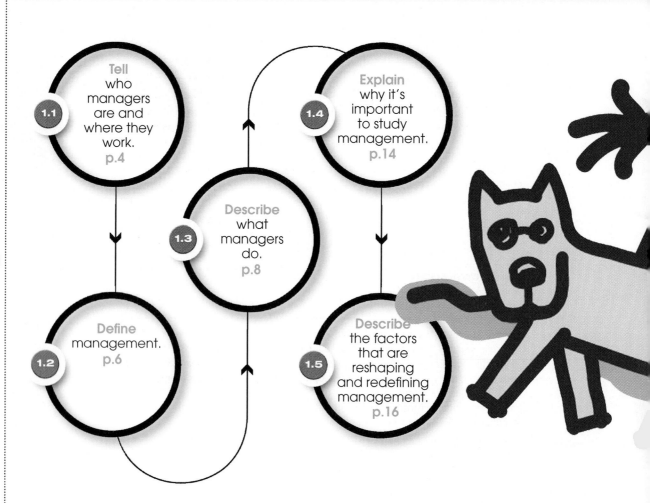

It's a Good Life

Jake and Rocket, a cartoon guy and his cartoon dog, can be found on most of the apparel and other branded products sold by the Life is good company.[1] With his perky beret (or other appropriate head gear), Jake has that contented look of being able to enjoy life as it is and finding reasons to be happy right now. And Rocket? Well, he's just happy to be along for the ride. And what a ride it's been for the two! They've been a part of the company's growth to over $130 million in revenues. Company cofounders and brothers, Bert and John Jacobs (see photo at right) have a personal and business philosophy much like Jake: simplicity, humor, and humility. However, both understand that even with this philosophy, they need to be good managers and they need good managers throughout the organization in order to stay successful.

Bert and John designed their first T-shirts in 1989 and sold them door-to-door in college dorms along the East Coast and in Boston where they'd set up shop using an old card table in locations on one-way streets so they could pick up and move quickly if they needed to. They used this simple sales approach because, like many young entrepreneurs, they couldn't afford required business licenses. Although they met a lot of wonderful people and heard a lot of good stories during those early years, sales weren't that great. As the company legend goes, the brothers "lived on peanut butter and jelly, slept in their beat-up van, and showered when they could." During one of their usual post-sales-trip parties, Bert and John asked some friends for advice on an assortment of images and slogans they had put together. Those friends liked the "Life is good" slogan and a drawing of Jake that had been sketched by John. So Bert and John printed up 48 Jake shirts for a local street fair in Cambridge, Massachusetts. By noon, the 48 shirts were gone, something that had never happened! The brothers were smart enough to recognize that they might be on to something. And, as the old saying goes…the rest is history! Since that momentous day in 1994, they've sold nearly 20 million Life is good T-shirts featuring Jake and Rocket.

Today, Life is good is based in Boston and has a product line of more than 900 items. The company continues to grow around 30 percent to 40 percent annually. Bert and John's style of managing is guided by another of the company's mottoes, "Do what you like. Like what you do." As the company's Web site states, "In addition to knowledge, skills, and experience, we look to hire people who possess the same optimistic outlook on life that Jake has." It's an approach that seems to be working for Bert and John and for Jake and Rocket.

Despite their company's somewhat shaky and uncertain start, Bert and John Jacobs seem to be good examples of successful managers. The key word here is *example*. There's no one universal model of what a successful manager is. Managers today can be under age 18 or over age 80. They may be women as well as men, and they come from all cultures. They manage small businesses, large corporations, government agencies, hospitals, museums, schools, and not-for-profit enterprises. Some hold top-level positions at their companies, some are middle managers, and others are first-line supervisors who directly manage employees. And managers can be found in every country around the world.

This book is about the work that managers like Bert and John Jacobs and the millions of other managers like them do. In this chapter, we introduce you to managers and management: who they are, where they work, what management is, what they do, and why you should spend your time studying management. Finally, we'll look at some factors that are reshaping and redefining management.

Who Are Managers and Where Do They Work?

1.1 Tell who managers are and where they work.

Managers work in organizations. So before we can identify who managers are and what they do, we've got to define what an **organization** is: a deliberate arrangement of people brought together to accomplish some specific purpose. Your college or university is an organization. So are the United Way, your neighborhood convenience store, the Dallas Cowboys football team, fraternities and sororities, the Cleveland Clinic, and globally based Nestlé and Nokia. As an organization, each has three common characteristics. (See Exhibit 1-1.)

What Three Characteristics Do All Organizations Share?

The first characteristic of an organization is that it has a distinct purpose, which is typically expressed in terms of a goal or set of goals. For example, Bob Iger, Disney's president and CEO, has said his company's goal is to "focus on what creates the most value for our shareholders by delivering high-quality creative content and experiences, balancing respect for our legacy with the demand to be innovative, and maintaining the integrity of our people and products."[2] That purpose or goal can only be achieved with people, which is the second common characteristic of organizations. An organization's people make decisions and engage in work activities to make the goal a reality. Finally, the third characteristic is that all organizations develop a deliberate and systematic structure that defines and limits the behavior of its members. Within that structure, rules and regulations might guide what people can or cannot do, some members will supervise other members, work teams might be formed, or job descriptions might be created so organizational members know what they're supposed to do.

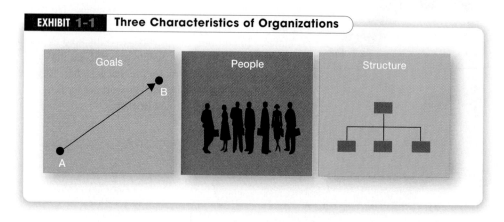

EXHIBIT 1-1 Three Characteristics of Organizations

Goals   People   Structure

A → B

How Are Managers Different from Nonmanagerial Employees?

Although managers work in organizations, not everyone who works in an organization is a manager. For simplicity's sake, we can divide organizational members into two categories: nonmanagerial employees and managers. **Nonmanagerial employees** are people who work directly on a job or task and have no responsibility for overseeing the work of others. The employees who ring up your sale at Home Depot, make your burrito at Chipotle, or process your course registration in your college's registrar's office are all nonmanagerial employees. These nonmanagerial employees may be referred to by names such as associates, team members, contributors, or even employee partners. **Managers**, on the other hand, are individuals in an organization who direct and oversee the activities of other people in the organization. This distinction doesn't mean, however, that managers don't work directly on tasks. Some managers do have work duties not directly related to overseeing the activities of others. For example, regional sales managers for Motorola also have responsibilities in servicing some customer accounts in addition to overseeing the activities of the other sales associates in their territories.

What Titles Do Managers Have?

Identifying exactly who the managers are in an organization isn't difficult, but be aware that they can have a variety of titles. Managers are usually classified as top, middle, or first-line. (See Exhibit 1-2.) **Top managers** are those at or near the top of an organization. Like Bert and John Jacobs, they're responsible for making decisions about the direction of the organization and establishing policies and philosophies that affect all organizational members. Top managers typically have titles such as vice president, president, chancellor, managing director, chief operating officer, chief executive officer, or chairperson of the board. **Middle managers** are those managers found between the lowest and top levels of the organization. These individuals manage other managers and maybe some nonmanagerial employees and are typically responsible for translating the goals set by top managers into specific details that lower-level managers will see get done. Middle managers may have such titles as department or agency head, project leader, unit chief, district manager, division manager, or store manager. **First-line managers** are those individuals responsible for directing the day-to-day activities of nonmanagerial employees. They're often called supervisors, team leaders, coaches, shift managers, or unit coordinators. In

Right or Wrong?

Lying on your résumé.[3] One survey indicated that some 44 percent of people lie about their work history. Another survey found that 93 percent of hiring managers who found a lie on a job candidate's résumé did not hire that person. What if the person lying on a résumé was the top executive? A survey of 358 senior executives and directors at 53 publicly traded companies turned up seven instances of claims of having an academic degree they didn't actually have. Such misstatements have cost the CEOs at Radio Shack, Herbalife, USANA Health Sciences, and MGM Mirage their jobs. Why do you think lying about your academic credentials is considered wrong? What ethical issues does this bring up? Which is worse? Lying about your academic credentials or lying about your work history? Why?

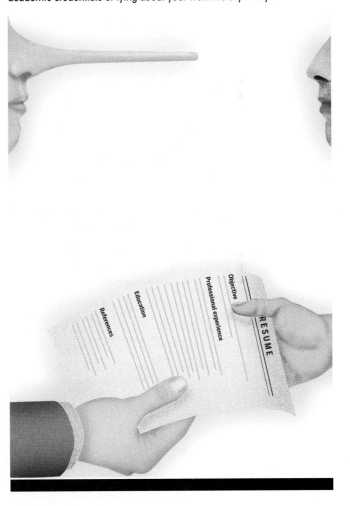

organization
A systematic arrangement of people brought together to accomplish some specific purpose.

nonmanagerial employees
People who work directly on a job or task and have no responsibility for overseeing the work of others.

managers
Individuals in an organization who direct the activities of others.

top managers
Individuals who are responsible for making decisions about the direction of the organization and establishing policies that affect all organizational members.

middle managers
Individuals who are typically responsible for translating goals set by top managers into specific details that lower-level managers will see get done.

first-line managers
Supervisors responsible for directing the day-to-day activities of nonmanagerial employees.

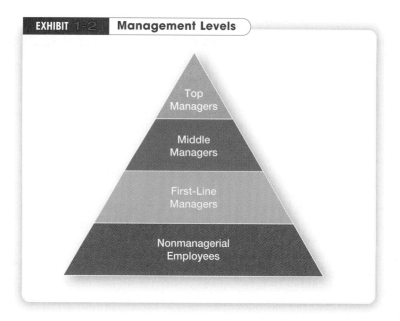

EXHIBIT 1-2   **Management Levels**

Top Managers

Middle Managers

First-Line Managers

Nonmanagerial Employees

your college, for example, department chairpersons would be first-line supervisors overseeing the activities of departmental faculty (nonmanagerial employees).

What Is Management?

Define management.

1.2

Simply speaking, management is what managers do. But that simple statement doesn't tell us much. A better explanation is that **management** is the process of getting things done, effectively and efficiently, with and through other people. We need to look closer at some key words in this definition.

A *process* refers to a set of ongoing and interrelated activities. In our definition of management, it refers to the primary activities or functions that managers perform. We'll explore these functions more in the next section.

Efficiency and effectiveness deal with what we're doing and how we're doing it. **Efficiency** means doing a task correctly ("doing things right") and getting the most output from the least amount of inputs. Because managers deal with scarce inputs—including resources such as people, money, and equipment—they're concerned with the efficient use of those resources. Managers want to minimize resource usage and thus resource costs.

It's not enough, however, just to be efficient. Managers are also concerned with completing activities. In management terms, we call this **effectiveness**. Effectiveness means "doing the right things" by doing those work tasks that help the organization reach its goals. Whereas efficiency is concerned with the *means* of getting things done, effectiveness is concerned with the *ends*, or attainment of organizational goals. (See Exhibit 1-3.)

Although *efficiency* and *effectiveness* are different, they are interrelated. For instance, it's easier to be effective if you ignore efficiency. If Hewlett-Packard disregarded labor and material input costs, it could produce more sophisticated and longer-lasting toner cartridges for its laser printers. Similarly, some government agencies have been regularly criticized for being reasonably effective but extremely inefficient. Our conclusion: Poor management is most often due to both inefficiency and ineffectiveness or to effectiveness achieved without regard for efficiency. Good management is concerned with both attaining goals (effectiveness) and doing so as efficiently as possible.

From the Past to the Present

Where do the terms *management* or *manager* come from?[4] The terms are actually centuries old. One source says that the word *manager* originated in 1588 to describe one who manages. The specific use of the word as "one who conducts a house of business or public institution" is said to have originated in 1705. Another source says that the origin (1555–1565) is from the word *maneggiare*, which meant "to handle or train horses," and was a derivative of the word *mano,* which is from the Latin word for hand, *manus.* That origin arose from the way that horses were guided, controlled, or directed where to go—that is, through using one's hand. As used in the way we've defined it in terms of overseeing and directing organizational members, however, the words *management* and *manager* are more appropriate to the early twentieth-century time period. Peter Drucker, the late management writer, studied and wrote about management for more than 50 years. He said, "When the first business schools in the United States opened around the turn of the twentieth century, they did not offer a single course in management. At about that same time, the word 'management' was first popularized by Frederick Winslow Taylor." Let's look at what he contributed to what we know about management today.

In 1911, Taylor's book *Principles of Scientific Management* was published. Its contents were widely embraced by managers around the world. The book described the theory of **scientific management:** the use of scientific methods to define the "one best way" for a job to be done. Taylor worked at the Midvale and Bethlehem Steel Companies in Pennsylvania. As a mechanical engineer with a Quaker and Puritan background, he was continually appalled by workers' inefficiencies. Employees used vastly different techniques to do the same job. They often "took it easy" on the job, and Taylor believed that worker output was only about one-third of what was possible. Virtually no work standards existed. Workers were placed in jobs with little or no concern for matching their abilities and aptitudes with the tasks they were required to do. Taylor set out to remedy that by applying the scientific method to shop-floor jobs. He spent more than two decades passionately pursuing the "one best way" for such jobs to be done. Based on his groundbreaking studies of manual workers using scientific principles, Taylor became known as the "father" of scientific management. His ideas spread in the United States and to other countries and inspired others to study and develop methods of scientific management. Many of the guidelines and techniques that Taylor and his associates devised for improving production efficiency are still used in organizations today. When managers analyze the basic work tasks that must be performed, use time-and-motion study to eliminate wasted motions, or hire the best-qualified workers for a job, they're using the principles of scientific management.

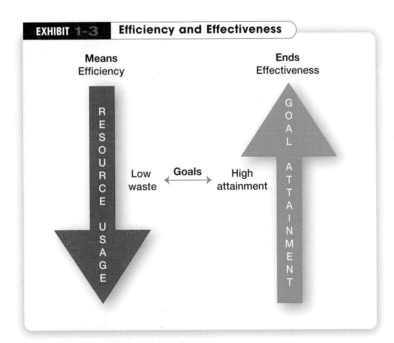

EXHIBIT 1-3 **Efficiency and Effectiveness**

Means
Efficiency

Ends
Effectiveness

RESOURCE USAGE

GOAL ATTAINMENT

Low waste ←— Goals —→ High attainment

---

management
The process of getting things done, effectively and efficiently, through and with other people.

efficiency
Doing things right, or getting the most output from the least amount of inputs.

effectiveness
Doing the right things, or completing activities so that organizational goals are attained.

scientific management
The use of scientific methods to define the "one best way" for a job to be done.

What Do Managers Do?

1.3 Describe what managers do.

Describing what managers do isn't easy because, just as no organizations are alike, neither are managers' jobs. Despite that fact, managers do share some common job elements, whether the manager is a head nurse in the cardiac surgery unit of the Cleveland Clinic overseeing a staff of critical care specialists or the president of O'Reilly Auto Parts establishing goals for the company with over 41,000 team members. Management researchers have developed three approaches to describe what managers do: functions, roles, and skills. Let's look at each.

What Are the Four Management Functions?

According to the functions approach, managers perform certain activities or functions as they direct and oversee others' work. What are these functions? In the early part of the twentieth century, a French industrialist by the name of Henri Fayol proposed that all managers perform five management activities: plan, organize, command, coordinate, and control.[5] Today, these management functions have been condensed to four: planning, organizing, leading, and controlling. (See Exhibit 1-4.) Most management textbooks, this one being no exception, continue to use the four functions approach. Let's look briefly at each function.

Because organizations exist to achieve some purpose, someone has to define that purpose and find ways to achieve it. A manager is that someone and does this by planning. **Planning** includes defining goals, establishing strategy, and developing plans to coordinate activities. Setting goals, establishing strategy, and developing plans ensures that the work to be done is kept in proper focus and helps organizational members keep their attention on what is most important.

EXHIBIT 1-4   Four Management Functions

Planning
Defining goals, establishing strategy, and developing subplans to coordinate activities

Organizing
Determining what needs to be done, how it will be done, and who is to do it

Leading
Directing and coordinating the work activities of an organization's people

Controlling
Monitoring activities to ensure that they are accomplished as planned

Achieving the organization's stated purpose

Managers are also responsible for arranging and structuring work to accomplish the organization's goals. This function is called **organizing**. Organizing includes determining what tasks are to be done and by whom, how tasks are to be grouped, who reports to whom, and where decisions are to be made.

We know that every organization has people. And it's part of a manager's job to direct and coordinate the work activities of those people. This is the **leading** function. When managers motivate employees, direct the activities of others, select the most effective communication channel, or resolve conflicts among members, they're leading.

The fourth and final management function is **controlling**, which involves monitoring, comparing, and correcting work performance. After the goals are set, the plans formulated, the structural arrangements determined, and the people hired, trained, and motivated, there has to be some evaluation to see if things are going as planned. Any significant deviations will require that the manager get work back on track.

Just how well does the functions approach describe what managers do? Is it an accurate description of what managers actually do? Some have argued that it isn't.[6] So, let's look at another perspective on describing what managers do.

What Are Management Roles?

Fayol's original description of management functions wasn't derived from careful surveys of managers in organizations. Rather, it simply represented his observations and experiences in the French mining industry. In the late 1960s, Henry Mintzberg did an empirical study of five chief executives at work.[7] What he discovered challenged long-held notions about the manager's job. For instance, in contrast to the predominant view that managers were reflective thinkers who carefully and systematically processed information before making decisions, Mintzberg found that the managers he studied engaged in a number of varied, unpatterned, and short-duration activities. These managers had little time for reflective thinking because they encountered constant interruptions and their activities often lasted less than nine minutes. In addition to these insights, Mintzberg provided a categorization scheme for defining what managers do based on the managerial roles they use at work. These **managerial roles** referred to specific categories of managerial actions or behaviors expected of a manager. (Think of the different roles you play—such as student, employee, volunteer, bowling team member, sibling, and so forth—and the different things you're expected to do in those roles.)

Mintzberg concluded that managers perform 10 different but interrelated roles. These 10 roles, as shown in Exhibit 1-5, are grouped around interpersonal relationships, the transfer of information, and decision making. The **interpersonal roles** are ones that involve people (subordinates and persons outside the organization) and other duties that are ceremonial and symbolic in nature. The three interpersonal roles are figurehead, leader, and liaison. The **informational roles** involve collecting, receiving, and disseminating information. The three informational roles include monitor, disseminator, and spokesperson. Finally, the **decisional roles** entail making decisions or choices. The four decisional roles are entrepreneur, disturbance handler, resource allocator, and negotiator.

So which approach is better—functions or roles? Although each describes what managers do, the functions approach seems to be the best way of describing the manager's job.

Shortly after ascending from president to chief executive officer of Xerox Corporation, Ursula Burns assumed the important informational roles of monitor and disseminator. She embarked on a 30-day trip to meet with Xerox employees outside the United States, in countries that account for almost one-half of company sales, and to gather information about how to increase customer purchases of Xerox products. Burns transmitted the information she received to other Xerox employees to help them develop plans to restore growth, improve efficiency, and revive sales.

planning
Includes defining goals, establishing strategy, and developing plans to coordinate activities.

organizing
Includes determining what tasks are to be done, who is to do them, how the tasks are to be grouped, who reports to whom, and where decisions are to be made.

leading
Includes motivating employees, directing the activities of others, selecting the most effective communication channel, and resolving conflicts.

controlling
The process of monitoring performance, comparing it with goals, and correcting any significant deviations.

managerial roles
Specific categories of managerial behavior; often grouped under three primary headings: interpersonal relationships, transfer of information, and decision making.

interpersonal roles
Involve people (subordinates and persons outside the organization) and other duties that are ceremonial and symbolic in nature.

informational roles
Involve collecting, receiving, and disseminating information.

decisional roles
Entail making decisions or choices.

EXHIBIT 1-5 **Mintzberg's Managerial Roles**

INTERPERSONAL ROLES

- Figurehead
- Leader
- Liaison

INFORMATIONAL ROLES

- Monitor
- Disseminator
- Spokesperson

DECISIONAL ROLES

- Entrepreneur
- Disturbance handler
- Resource allocator
- Negotiator

Source: Based on Mintzberg, Henry, *The Nature of Managerial Work*, 1st Edition, © 1973.

Its continued popularity is a tribute to its clarity and simplicity. "The classical functions provide clear and discrete methods of classifying the thousands of activities that managers carry out and the techniques they use in terms of the functions they perform for the achievement of goals."[8] However, Mintzberg's roles approach does offer additional insight into what managers do.

What Skills Do Managers Need?

The final approach we're going to look at for describing what managers do is by looking at the skills they need in managing. Robert L. Katz and others have proposed that managers must possess and use four critical management skills in managing.[9]

Conceptual skills are the skills managers use to analyze and diagnose complex situations. They help managers see how things fit together and facilitate making good decisions. **Interpersonal skills** are those skills involved with working well with other people both individually and in groups. Because managers get things done with and through other people, they must have good interpersonal skills to communicate, motivate, mentor, and delegate. Additionally, all managers need **technical skills**, which are the job-specific knowledge and techniques needed to perform work tasks. These abilities are based on specialized knowledge or expertise. For top-level managers, these abilities tend to be related to knowledge of the industry and a general understanding of the organization's processes and products. For middle- and lower-level managers, these abilities are related to the specialized knowledge required in the areas where they work—finance, human resources, marketing, computer systems, manufacturing, information technology, and so forth. Finally, managers need and use **political skills** to build a power base and establish the right connections. Organizations are political arenas in which people compete for resources. Managers who have and know how to use political skills tend to be better at getting resources for their groups. (See the "Developing Your Political Skill" box.)

Is The Manager's Job Universal?

So far, we have discussed the manager's job as if it were a generic activity. That is, a manager is a manager regardless of where he or she manages. If management is truly a generic discipline, then what a manager does should be essentially the same whether he or she is a

Developing Your *Political* Skill

About the Skill

Research has shown that people differ in their political skills.[10] Those who are politically skilled are more effective in their use of influence tactics. Political skill also appears to be more effective when the stakes are high. Finally, politically skilled individuals are able to exert their influence without others detecting it, which is important in being effective so that you're not labeled political. A person's political skill is determined by his or her networking ability, interpersonal influence, social astuteness, and apparent sincerity.

Steps in Practicing the Skill

1 *Develop your networking ability.* A good network can be a very powerful tool. You can begin building a network by getting to know important people in your work area and the organization and then developing relationships with individuals who are in positions of power. Volunteer for committees or offer your help on projects that will be noticed by those in positions of power. Attend important organizational functions so that you can be seen as a team player and someone who's interested in the organization's success. Start a Rolodex file of names of individuals that you meet even if for a brief moment. Then, when you need advice on work, use your connections and network with others throughout the organization.

2 *Work on gaining interpersonal influence.* People will listen to you when they're comfortable and feel at ease around you. Work on your communication skills so that you can communicate easily and effectively with others. Work on developing good rapport with people in all areas and at all levels of your organization. Be open, friendly, and willing to pitch in. The amount of interpersonal influence you have will be affected by how well people like you.

3 *Develop your social astuteness.* Some people have an innate ability to understand people and sense what they're thinking. If you don't have that ability, you'll have to work at developing your social astuteness by doing things such as saying the right things at the right time, paying close attention to people's facial expressions, and by trying to determine if others have hidden agendas.

4 *Be sincere.* Sincerity is important to getting people to want to associate with you. Be genuine in what you say and do. And show a genuine interest in others and their situations.

Practicing the Skill

Select each of the components of political skill and spend one week working on it. Write a brief set of notes describing your experiences—good and bad. Were you able to begin developing a network of people throughout the organization or did you work at developing your social astuteness maybe by starting to recognize and interpret people's facial expressions and the meaning behind those expressions? What could you have done differently to be more politically skilled? Once you begin to recognize what's involved with political skills, you should find yourself becoming more connected and politically adept.

---

top-level executive or a first-line supervisor, in a business firm or a government agency; in a large corporation or a small business; or located in Paris, Texas, or Paris, France. Let's take a closer look at the generic issue.

LEVEL IN THE ORGANIZATION. Although a supervisor in a claims department at Aetna may not do exactly the same things that the president of Aetna does, it doesn't mean that their jobs are inherently different. The differences are of degree and emphasis but not of activity.

As managers move up in the organization, they do more planning and less direct overseeing of others. This distinction is shown in Exhibit 1-6. All managers, regardless of level, make decisions. They do planning, organizing, leading, and controlling activities, but the amount of time they give to each activity is not necessarily constant. In addition, the content of the managerial activities changes with the manager's level. For example, as we'll demonstrate in

---

conceptual skills
A manager's ability to analyze and diagnose complex situations.

interpersonal skills
A manager's ability to work with, understand, mentor, and motivate others, both individually and in groups.

technical skills
Job-specific knowledge and techniques needed to perform work tasks.

political skills
A manager's ability to build a power base and establish the right connections.

EXHIBIT 1-6 **Management Activities by Organizational Level**

First-Level Managers
- Organizing 24%
- Planning 15%
- Controlling 10%
- Leading 51%

Middle Managers
- Organizing 33%
- Planning 18%
- Controlling 13%
- Leading 36%

Top Managers
- Planning 28%
- Organizing 36%
- Controlling 14%
- Leading 22%

Source: Based on T. A. Mahoney, T. H. Jerdee, and S. J. Carroll, "The Job(s) of Management." *Industrial Relations* 4, no. 2 (1965), p. 103.

Chapter 5, top managers are concerned with designing the overall organization's structure, whereas lower-level managers focus on designing the jobs of individuals and work groups.

PROFIT VERSUS NOT-FOR-PROFIT. Does a manager who works for the U.S. Postal Service, the Memorial Sloan-Kettering Cancer Center, or the Red Cross do the same things that a manager in a business firm does? Put another way, is the manager's job the same in both profit and not-for-profit organizations? The answer is, for the most part, yes. All managers make decisions, set goals, create workable organization structures, hire and motivate employees, secure legitimacy for their organization's existence, and develop internal political support in order to implement programs. Of course, the most important difference between the two is how performance is measured. Profit, or the "bottom line," acts as an unambiguous measure of a business organization's effectiveness. No such universal measure is used in not-for-profit organizations. Measuring the performance of schools, museums, government agencies, or charitable organizations is more difficult. But don't interpret this difference to mean that managers in those organizations can ignore the financial side of their operations. Even not-for-profit organizations need to make money to survive. It's just that making a profit for the "owners" of not-for-profit organizations is not the primary focus.

SIZE OF ORGANIZATION. Would you expect the job of a manager in a print shop that employs 12 people to be different from that of a manager who runs a 1,200-person printing plant for the *Washington Times*? This question is best answered by looking at the jobs of managers in small businesses and comparing them with our previous discussion of managerial roles. First, however, let's define a small business.

No commonly agreed-upon definition of a small business is available because different criteria are used to define *small*. For example, an organization can be classified as a small business using such criteria as number of employees, annual sales, or total assets. For our purposes, we'll describe a **small business** as an independent business having fewer than 500 employees and which doesn't necessarily engage in any new or innovative practices and which has relatively little impact on its industry.[11] Now to the question at hand: Is the job of managing a small business different from that of managing a large one? Some differences appear to exist. For example, as illustrated in Exhibit 1-7, the small business manager's most important role is that of spokesperson. He or she spends a great deal of time performing outwardly directed actions such as meeting with customers, arranging financing with bankers, searching for new opportunities, and stimulating

Like other small business managers, Aldo Coffee Company owners Rich and Melanie Westerfield of Pittsburgh search for new opportunities and plan activities for performance improvement. To boost their image as providers of professional service and product knowledge, they invest their time and money in barista training and competitions (shown here). Aldo Coffee Company helps others expand their coffee knowledge and improve their espresso techniques by offering classes to the public and to other restaurants and coffee shops on barista skills, latte art, and coffee tasting and cupping.

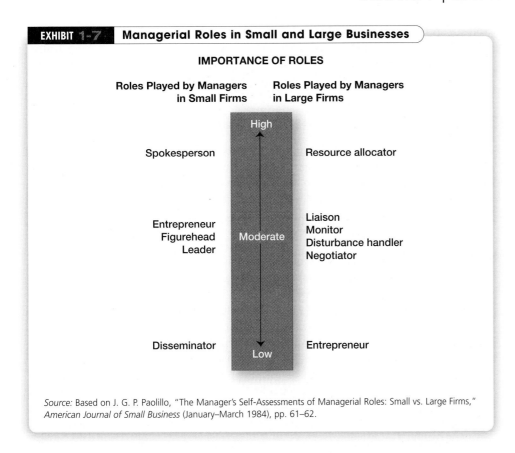

EXHIBIT 1-7   **Managerial Roles in Small and Large Businesses**

IMPORTANCE OF ROLES

Roles Played by Managers in Small Firms | Roles Played by Managers in Large Firms

High

Spokesperson — Resource allocator

Entrepreneur
Figurehead   Moderate
Leader — Liaison / Monitor / Disturbance handler / Negotiator

Disseminator — Entrepreneur

Low

Source: Based on J. G. P. Paolillo, "The Manager's Self-Assessments of Managerial Roles: Small vs. Large Firms," *American Journal of Small Business* (January–March 1984), pp. 61–62.

change. In contrast, the most important concerns of a manager in a large organization are directed internally—deciding which organizational units get what available resources and how much of them. Accordingly, the entrepreneurial role—looking for business opportunities and planning activities for performance improvement—appears to be least important to managers in large firms, especially among first-level and middle managers.

Compared with a manager in a large organization, a small business manager is more likely to be a generalist. His or her job will combine the activities of a large corporation's chief executive with many of the day-to-day activities undertaken by a first-line supervisor. Moreover, the structure and formality that characterize a manager's job in a large organization tend to give way to informality in small firms. Planning is less likely to be a carefully orchestrated ritual. The organization's design will be less complex and structured, and control in the small business will rely more on direct observation than on sophisticated, computerized monitoring systems. Again, as with organizational level, we see differences in degree and emphasis but not in the activities that managers do. Managers in both small and large organizations perform essentially the same activities, but how they go about those activities and the proportion of time they spend on each are different.

MANAGEMENT CONCEPTS AND NATIONAL BORDERS. The last generic issue concerns whether management concepts are transferable across national borders. If managerial concepts were completely generic, they would also apply universally in any country in the world, regardless of economic, social, political, or cultural differences. Studies that have compared managerial practices between countries have not generally supported the universality of management concepts. In Chapter 2, we'll examine some specific differences between countries and describe their effect on managing. At this point, do understand that most of the concepts discussed in the following chapters primarily apply to the United

small business
An independent business having fewer than 500 employees and which doesn't necessarily engage in any new or innovative practices and which has relatively little impact on its industry.

States, Canada, Great Britain, Australia, and other English-speaking countries. Managers should be prepared to modify these concepts if they want to apply them in India, China, Chile, or other countries whose economic, political, social, or cultural environments differ greatly from that of the so-called free-market democracies.

Why Study Management?

You may be wondering why you need to study management. Maybe you're majoring in accounting or marketing or information technology and may not understand how studying management is going to help you in your career. Let's look at some reasons why you may want to understand more about management.

First, all of us have a vested interest in improving the way organizations are managed. Why? Because we interact with them every day of our lives and an understanding of management offers insights into many organizational aspects. When you get your driver's license renewed, are you frustrated that a seemingly simple task takes so long? Were you surprised when well-known businesses you thought would never go bankrupt did go bankrupt or angry when entire industries had to rely on government bailout money to survive changing economic conditions? Are you annoyed when you call an airline three times and its representatives quote three different prices for the same trip? These types of problems can be attributed largely to poor management.

Organizations that are well managed—such as Wal-Mart, Apple, Samsung, McDonald's, Singapore Airlines, and Google—develop a loyal following and find ways to prosper even in economically challenging times. Those that are poorly managed may find themselves with a declining customer base and reduced revenues and may even have to file for bankruptcy protection. For instance, Gimbels, W. T. Grant, Dave & Barry's, Circuit City, Eastern Airlines, and Enron were once thriving corporations. They employed tens of thousands of people and provided goods and services on a daily basis to hundreds of thousands of customers. Today those companies no longer exist. Poor management did them in. You can begin to recognize poor management and know what good managers should be doing by studying management.

The second reason for studying management is the reality that for most of you, once you graduate from college and begin your career, you will either manage or be managed. For those who plan to be managers, an understanding of management forms the foundation on which to build your management skills. For those of you who don't see yourself managing, you're still likely to have to work with managers. Also, assuming that you will have to work for a living and recognizing that you are likely to work in an organization, you'll probably have some managerial responsibilities even if you're not a manager. Our experience tells us that you can gain a great deal of insight into the way your boss (and fellow employees) behave and how organizations function by studying management. Our point is that you don't have to aspire to be a manager to gain something valuable from a course in management.

What Can Students of Management Learn from Other Courses?

College curriculums often lack cohesion and don't seem to make any sense because they're composed of separate and distinct disciplines. So it's sometimes hard for students to see how it all relates and why it's important to study areas outside the business curriculum. Thus, let's briefly look at some of the other disciplines in humanities and social sciences and how they affect management practice.

ANTHROPOLOGY. Anthropology is the study of societies, which helps us learn about human beings and their activities. Anthropologists' work on cultures and environments, for instance, has helped managers better understand differences in fundamental values, attitudes, and behavior between people in different countries and within different organizations.

and the survey says...[12]

35 percent of employees quit their jobs because they were unhappy with management.

69 percent of workers at all levels of the organization said they wouldn't want their boss's job.

2.6 percent of *Fortune* 500 companies have a female CEO.

30 percent of employees asked to characterize their relationship with their boss said "my boss is my friend"; 5 percent said "parent figure."

70 percent of the difference in workplace climate from one organization to another can be attributed to a front-line manager's behavior.

30 percent of white-collar workers think incompetence is what makes for a bad boss.

51 percent of the U.S. population is women; but only 36 percent of managers are women.

91 percent of companies in China have women in senior management positions.

The global financial crisis and the role of competition and free markets have prompted a growing number of multinational firms to locate factories and call centers in the Maghreb, which refers to the four nations in North Africa of Morocco, Algeria, Tunisia, and Libya. Automotive, aviation, electronics, and telecommunication firms are attracted to these countries because of their inexpensive but high-quality labor and growing populations. In this photo, a Moroccan employee works in the French automaker Renault's factory in Casablanca, which exports Logan cars to France and Spain.

ECONOMICS. Economics is concerned with the allocation and distribution of scarce resources. It provides us with an understanding of the changing economy as well as the role of competition and free markets in a global context. For example, why are most athletic shoes made in Asia? Or why does Mexico now have more automobile plants than Detroit? Economists provide the answer to these questions when they discuss comparative advantage. Similarly, an understanding of free trade and protectionist policies is absolutely essential to any manager operating in the global marketplace, and these topics are addressed by economists.

PHILOSOPHY. Philosophy courses inquire into the nature of things, particularly values and ethics. Ethics are standards that govern human conduct. Ethical concerns go directly to the existence of organizations and what constitutes proper behavior within them. For instance, the liberty ethic (John Locke) proposes that freedom, equality, justice, and private property are legal rights; the Protestant ethic (John Calvin) encourages individuals to be frugal, work hard, and attain success; and the market ethic (Adam Smith) argues that the market and competition, not government, should be the sole regulators of economic activity. These ethics have shaped today's organizations by providing a basis for legitimate authority, linking rewards to performance, and justifying the existence of business and the corporate form.

POLITICAL SCIENCE. Political science is the study of the behavior of individuals and groups within a political environment. Specific topics of concern to political scientists include structuring of conflict, allocating power, and manipulating power for individual self-interest.

Management is affected by a nation's form of government—by whether it allows its citizens to hold property, by its citizens' ability to engage in and enforce contracts, and by the appeal mechanisms available to redress grievances. In a democracy, for instance, people typically have the right to private property, the freedom to enter or not enter into contracts, and an appeal system for justice. A nation's stand on property, contracts, and justice, in turn, shapes the type, form, and policies of its organizations.

PSYCHOLOGY. Psychology is the science that seeks to measure, explain, and sometimes change the behavior of humans and other animals. The field of psychology is leading the way in providing managers with insights into human behavior. Today's managers confront both a diverse customer base and a diverse set of employees. Psychologists' efforts to understand gender and cultural diversity provide managers with a better perception of the needs of their changing customer and employee populations. Psychology courses are also relevant to managers in terms of gaining a better understanding of motivation, leadership, trust, employee selection, performance appraisals, and training techniques.

SOCIOLOGY. Sociology is the study of people in relation to their fellow human beings. Here are a few of the sociological issues that have relevance to managers: How are societal changes such as globalization, increasing cultural diversity, changing gender roles, and varying forms of family life affecting organizational practices? What are the implications of schooling practices and education trends on future employees' skills and abilities? How are changing demographics altering customer and employment markets? What will the information age society look like 10 years from now? Answers to questions such as these will have a major effect on how managers operate their businesses.

What Factors Are Reshaping and Redefining Management?

1.5 Describe the factors that are reshaping and redefining management.

At Best Buy's headquarters, more than 60 percent of the 4,000 employees are now judged only on tasks or results. Salaried people put in as much time as it takes to do their work. Those employees report better relationships with family and friends, more company loyalty, and more focus and energy. Productivity has increased by 35 percent. Employees say they don't know whether they work fewer hours—they've stopped counting. Perhaps more important, they're finding new ways to become efficient.[13]

Welcome to the new world of management!

In today's world, managers are dealing with changing workplaces, ethical and trust issues, global economic uncertainties, and changing technology. For example, although people still need to buy food even during a recession, grocery stores are struggling to retain their customer base and to keep costs down. At Publix Super Markets, the large grocery chain in the southeastern United States, everyone, including managers, is looking for ways to better serve customers. The company's president, Todd Jones, who started his career bagging groceries at a Publix in New Smyrna Beach, Florida, is guiding the company through these challenging economic times by keeping everyone's focus—from baggers to checkers to stockers—on exceptional customer service.[14] Or consider the management challenges faced by Roger Oglesby, the publisher and editor of the *Seattle Post-Intelligencer*. His newspaper, like many others, has been struggling to find a way to be successful in an industry that was losing readers and revenues at an alarming rate. The decision was made to go all-digital and in early 2009, the *Seattle Post-Intelligencer* became an Internet-only news source. Difficult actions followed as the news staff was reduced from 165 to about 20 people. As the organization moves forward, other challenges remain—challenges for Oglesby, the manager who needs to plan, organize, lead, and control in this changed environment.[15] Managers everywhere are likely to have to manage in changing circumstances, and the fact is that *how* managers manage is changing. Throughout the rest of this book, we'll be discussing these changes and how they're impacting the way managers plan, organize, lead, and control. We want to highlight two of these changes: the increasing importance of customers and innovation.

Why Are Customers Important to the Manager's Job?

John Chambers, CEO of Cisco Systems, likes to listen to voice mails forwarded to him from dissatisfied customers. He said, "E-mail would be more efficient, but I want to hear the emotion, I want to hear the frustration, I want to hear the caller's level of comfort with the strategy we're employing. I can't get that through e-mail."[16] This is a manager who understands the importance of customers. You need customers. Without them, most organizations would cease to exist. Yet, focusing on the customer has long been thought to be the responsibility of marketing types. "Let the marketers worry about the customers" is how many managers felt. We're discovering, however, that employee attitudes and behaviors play a big role in customer satisfaction.

Managers are recognizing that delivering consistent high-quality customer service is essential for survival and success in today's competitive environment and that employees are an important part of that equation.[17] The implication is clear—they must create a customer responsive organization where employees are friendly and courteous, accessible, knowledgeable, prompt in responding to customer needs, and willing to do what's necessary to please the customer.[18]

Why Is Innovation Important to the Manager's Job?

"Nothing is more risky than not innovating."[19] Innovation means doing things differently, exploring new territory, and taking risks. And innovation isn't just for high-tech or other technologically sophisticated organizations. Innovative efforts can be found in all types of organizations. For instance, the manager of the Best Buy store in Manchester, Connecticut, clearly understood the importance of getting employees to be innovative, a task made particularly challenging because the average Best Buy store is often staffed by young adults in their first or second jobs. "The complexity of the products demands a high level of training, but the many distractions that tempt college-aged employees keep the turnover potential high." However, the manager tackled the problem by getting employees to suggest new ideas. One idea—a "team close," in which employees scheduled to work at the store's closing time, closed the store together and walked out together as a team—has had a remarkable impact on employee attitudes and commitment.[20]

As you can see, being a manager is both challenging and exciting. One thing we know is that managers do matter to organizations. The Gallup Organization, which has polled millions of employees and tens of thousands of managers, has found that the single most important variable in employee productivity and loyalty isn't pay or benefits or workplace environment; it's the quality of the relationship between employees and their direct supervisors.[21] In addition, global consulting firm Watson Wyatt Worldwide found that the way a company manages its people can significantly affect its financial performance.[22] What can we conclude from such reports? That managers *do* matter!

Tony Hsieh, CEO of online shoe and clothing retailer Zappos.com, is a manager who understands the importance of both customers and innovation. In addition to providing customers the best selection of merchandise, the goal of Zappos is to give the best service online. Innovations that help Zappos achieve its goal are free shipping both ways on all purchases, 24/7 call center staffing, and a 365-day return policy. Hsieh offers new customer service reps who complete a four-week paid training period a $2,000 bonus to leave the company if they don't buy into the Zappos culture of service and innovation.

Review and ① Applications

Chapter Summary

1.1 Tell who managers are and where they work. Managers are individuals who work in an organization directing and overseeing the activities of other people. Managers are usually classified as top, middle, or first-line. Organizations, which are where managers work, have three characteristics: goals, people, and a deliberate structure.

1.2 Define management. Management is the process of getting things done, effectively and efficiently, with and through other people.

1.3 Describe what managers do. What managers do can be described using three approaches: functions, roles, and skills. The functions approach says that managers perform four functions: planning, organizing, leading, and controlling. Mintzberg's roles approach says that what managers do is based on the 10 roles they use at work, which are grouped around interpersonal relationships, the transfer of information, and decision making. The skills approach looks at what managers do in terms of the skills they need and use. These four critical skills are conceptual, interpersonal, technical, and political. All managers plan, organize, lead, and control although how they do these and how much they do these may vary according to level in the organization, whether the organization is profit or not-for-profit, the size of the organization, and the geographic location of the organization.

1.4 Explain why it's important to study management. One reason it's important to study management is that all of us interact with organizations daily so we have a vested interest in seeing that organizations are well managed. Another reason is the reality that in your career you will either manage or be managed. By studying management you can gain insights into the way your boss and fellow employees behave and how organizations function.

1.5 Describe the factors that are reshaping and redefining management. In today's world, managers are dealing with changing workplaces, ethical and trust issues, global economic uncertainties, and changing technology. Two areas of critical importance to managers are delivering high-quality customer service and encouraging innovative efforts.

 To check your understanding of learning outcomes **1.1** – **1.5**, go to **mymanagementlab.com** and try the chapter questions.

Understanding the Chapter

1. What is an organization and why are managers important to an organization's success?

2. Are all effective organizations also efficient? Discuss. If you had to choose between being effective or being efficient, which one would you say is more important? Why?

3. Using any of the popular business periodicals (such as *BusinessWeek, Fortune, Wall Street Journal, Fast Company*), find examples of managers doing each of the four management functions. Write up a description and explain how these are examples of that function.

4. Is your course instructor a manager? Discuss in terms of planning, organizing, leading, and controlling. Also discuss using Mintzberg's managerial roles approach.

5. Is there one best "style" of management? Why or why not?

6. Is business management a profession? Why or why not? Do some external research in answering this question.

7. Why are managers important to organizations?

8. Using current business periodicals, find five examples of managers you would describe as *master managers*. Write a paper describing these individuals as managers and why you think they deserve this title.

9. An article by Gary Hamel in the February 2009 issue of *Harvard Business Review* addresses how management must be reinvented to be more relevant to today's world. Get a copy of that article. Choose one of the 25 grand challenges identified. Discuss what it is and what it means for the way that organizations are managed.

Understanding Yourself

How Motivated Am I to Manage?

Not everyone is motivated to perform managerial functions. This self-assessment instrument taps six components that have been found to be related to managerial success, especially in larger organizations. These components include a favorable attitude toward authority, a desire to compete, a desire to exercise power, assertiveness, desire for a distinctive position, and a willingness to engage in repetitive tasks.

INSTRUMENT   Complete this instrument by identifying your degree of agreement or disagreement. Use the following rating scale:

      1 = Strongly disagree

      2 = Moderately disagree

      3 = Slightly disagree

      4 = Neither agree or disagree

      5 = Slightly agree

      6 = Moderately agree

      7 = Strongly agree

1.	I have a generally positive attitude toward those holding positions of authority over me.	1 2 3 4 5 6 7
2.	I enjoy competition and striving to win for myself and my work group.	1 2 3 4 5 6 7
3.	I like to tell others what to do and have no problem with imposing sanctions to enforce my directives.	1 2 3 4 5 6 7
4.	I like being active, assertive, and protecting the members of my work group.	1 2 3 4 5 6 7
5.	I enjoy the idea of standing out from the group, behaving in a unique manner, and being highly visible.	1 2 3 4 5 6 7
6.	I am willing to perform routine, day-to-day administrative tasks and duties.	1 2 3 4 5 6 7

SCORING KEY   To calculate your score, add up your responses to the six items.

ANALYSIS AND INTERPRETATION   Scores on this instrument will range between 6 and 42. Arbitrary cut-offs suggest that scores of 6–18 indicate low motivation to manage; 19–29 is moderate motivation; and 30 and above is high motivation to manage.

What meaning can you draw from your score? It provides you with an idea of how comfortable you would be doing managerial activities. Note, however, that this instrument emphasizes tasks associated with managing in larger and more bureaucratic organizations. A low or moderate score may indicate that you're more suited to managing in a small firm, in a more flexible unstructured organization, or in entrepreneurial situations.

Source: Based on J. B. Miner and N. R. Smith, "Decline and Stabilization of Managerial Motivation over a 20-Year Period," *Journal of Applied Psychology* (June 1982) pp. 297–305; and J. B. Miner, B. Ebrahimi, and J. M. Wachtel, "How Deficiencies in Motivation to Manage Contribute to the United States' Competitiveness Problem (and What Can Be Done About It)," *Human Resource Management* (Fall 1995), pp. 363–86.

FYIA (For Your Immediate Action)

Heartland's Traditional Fragrances

Reply **Reply All** **Forward**

To: Eric Kim, Training Coordinator
From: Helen Merkin, Human Resources Director
Re: **Supervisory Training and Management Certification Program**

As you know, our sales numbers have been growing steadily. Even given the economic uncertainties, we had an 8% increase during the first quarter, a 10% increase during the second, and then, of course, our strong holiday seasonal sales increase of 15%. We do love these numbers, don't we! However, the downside is that these continual sales increases are putting a strain on our manufacturing supervisors. They're challenged to keep our line employees motivated and excited about their jobs. I'm afraid if we don't take some action soon to help train our supervisors in dealing with this demanding pace, our manufacturing employees are likely to get stressed out and we may see product quality go down. And we certainly don't want this to happen since our quality products are what our customers have said they love about us.

There are two issues I'd like for you to look into. One is that I think we need a training program focusing on the skills our supervisors are going to need to be more effective under these conditions. As a first step in developing this program, I'd like you to research and create a list of the skills that you think would be most important for our supervisors to have, together with a justification for why you think these skills are important. Please keep this information under two pages typed.

The second issue I'd like you to address is that I think we need to acknowledge the important role our supervisors play in our company's success by helping them achieve certification that verifies their skills, knowledge, and professionalism. Two certification programs that I'm aware of are the Certified Manager and the Certified Business Manager. I'd like for you to research each of these programs and prepare a bulleted list of what each involves. Keep this information under two pages typed as well.

As we need to start our planning for both of these important initiatives soon, please get your information to me as soon as possible. Once we've had a chance to discuss what you've come up with, we'll be ready to proceed with actually designing some skills training and management certification sessions.

This fictionalized company and message were created for educational purposes only. It is not meant to reflect positively or negatively on management practices by any company that may share this name.

CASE APPLICATION

A NEW WAY OF WORKING

Being efficient and effective isn't important just for the people that managers supervise. It's also important for managers! However, that isn't always easy. A manager's job is varied, complex, and sometimes hectic. Their workdays are filled with tasks, decisions, actions, and interruptions. Just like your work on school projects, managers sometimes find that certain parts of the projects they're working on are boring and monotonous. Wouldn't it be great to have a magic button you could push to get someone else to do that boring, time-consuming stuff? At Pfizer, that "magic button" is a reality for a large number of employees.

As a global pharmaceutical company, Pfizer is continually looking for ways to help employees be more efficient and effective. The company's senior director of organizational effectiveness, Jordan Cohen (pictured above), found that the "Harvard MBA staff we hired to develop strategies and innovate were instead Googling and making PowerPoints." Indeed, internal studies conducted to find out just how much time its valuable talent was spending on menial tasks was startling. The average Pfizer employee was spending 20 percent to 40 percent of his or her time on support work (creating documents, typing notes, doing research, manipulating data, scheduling meetings) and only 60 percent to 80 percent on knowledge work (strategy, innovation, networking, collaborating, critical thinking). And the problem wasn't just at lower levels. Even the highest level employees were affected. Take, for instance, David Cain, an executive director for global engineering. He enjoys his job—assessing environmental real estate risks, managing facilities, and controlling a multimillion-dollar budget. But he didn't so much enjoy having to go through spreadsheets and put together PowerPoints. Now, however, with Pfizer's "magic button," those tasks could be passed off to individuals outside the organization.

PfizerWorks allows employees to shift tedious and time-consuming tasks with the click of a single button on their computer desktop. They describe what they need on an online form, which is then sent to one of two Indian service-outsourcing firms. When a request is received, a team member in India calls the Pfizer employee to clarify what's needed and by when. The team member then e-mails back a cost specification for the requested work. If the Pfizer employee decides to proceed, the costs involved are charged to the employee's department. About this unique arrangement, Cain said that, "He relishes working with what he prefers to call his 'personal consulting organization.'"

How beneficial has PfizerWorks been? It's estimated that 66,500 employee work hours have been saved. What about David Cain's experiences? When he gave the Indian team a complex project researching strategic actions that worked when consolidating company facilities, the team put the report together in a month, something that would have taken him six months to do alone.

Discussion Questions

1. Describe and evaluate what Pfizer is doing with its PfizerWorks.
2. We've defined managers as those individuals in an organization who direct and oversee the activities of other people in the organization. What challenges might there be for managers when those "people" are halfway around the world? How might the four management functions be useful in dealing with those challenges? What skills would managers need to be able to function effectively in this type of arrangement?
3. Do you think that PfizerWorks would work for someone who's a first-line manager? Why or why not?
4. Do you think this arrangement would work for other types of organizations? Why or why not? What types of organizations might it also work for?

Sources: M. Weinstein, "Retrain and Restructure Your Organization," *Training* (May 2009), p. 36; J. McGregor, "The Chore Goes Offshore," *BusinessWeek,* March 23 & 30, 2009, pp. 50–51; "Pfizer: Making It 'Leaner, Meaner, More Efficient,'" *BusinessWeek Online,* March 2, 2009; and A. Cohen, "Scuttling Scut Work," *Fast Company,* February 2008, pp. 42–43.

History Module

A Brief History of Management's Roots

Henry Ford once said, "History is more or less bunk." Well...he was wrong! History is important because it can put current activities in perspective. We propose that you need to know management history because it can help you understand what today's managers do. In this module, you'll find an annotated timeline that discusses key milestones in management theory. Then, in each chapter's "From the Past to the Present" box feature, we highlight a key person and his or her contributions to contemporary management concepts. We believe this approach will help you better understand the origins of many contemporary management concepts.

● Early Management

Management has been practiced a long time. Organized endeavors directed by people responsible for planning, organizing, leading, and controlling activities have existed for thousands of years. Regardless of what these individuals were called, someone had to perform those functions.

3000-2500 BC

The Egyptian pyramids are proof that projects of tremendous scope, employing tens of thousands of people, were completed in ancient times.[1] It took more than 100,000 workers some 20 years to construct a single pyramid. Someone had to plan what was to be done, organize people and materials to do it, make sure those workers got the work done, and impose some controls to ensure that everything was done as planned. That someone was managers.

1400s

At the arsenal of Venice, warships were floated along the canals, and at each stop, materials and riggings were added to the ship.[2] Sounds a lot like a car "floating" along an assembly line, doesn't it? In addition, the Venetians used warehouse and inventory systems to keep track of materials, human resource management functions to manage the labor force (including wine breaks), and an accounting system to keep track of revenues and costs.

1780s – mid-1800s

The **Industrial Revolution** may be the most important pre-twentieth-century influence on management. Why? Because with the industrial age came the birth of the corporation. Now with large efficient factories pumping out products, someone needed to forecast demand, make sure there were adequate supplies of materials, assign tasks to workers, and so forth. Again, that someone was managers! It was indeed an historical event for two reasons: (1) because of all the organizational aspects (hierarchy, control, job specialization, and so forth) that were now a part of the way work was done and (2) because management had now become a necessary component to ensure the success of the enterprise.

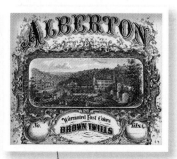

1776

Although this is an important date in U.S. history, it's also important because it's the year when Adam Smith's *Wealth of Nations* was published. In it, he argued the economic advantages of the **division of labor** (or **job specialization**)—

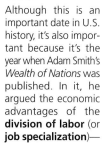

that is, breaking down jobs into narrow, repetitive tasks. Using division of labor, individual productivity could be increased dramatically. Job specialization continues to be a popular way to determine how work gets done in organizations. But as you'll see in Chapter 5, it does have its drawbacks.

○ Classical Approaches

Beginning around the turn of the twentieth century, the discipline of management began to evolve as a unified body of knowledge. Rules and principles were developed that could be taught and used in a variety of settings. These early management proponents were called classical theorists.

1911

That's the year Frederick W. Taylor's *Principles of Scientific Management* was published. His groundbreaking book described a theory of **scientific management**—the use of scientific methods to determine the "one best way" for a job to be done. His theories were widely accepted and used by managers around the world and Taylor (top photo) became known as the "father" of scientific management.[3] Other major contributors to scientific management were Frank and Lillian Gilbreth (early proponents of time-and-motion studies and parents of the large family described in the original book *Cheaper by the Dozen*) and Henry Gantt (whose work on scheduling charts was the foundation for today's project management). Taylor's work is profiled in Chapter 1's "From the Past to the Present" box.

1916 – 1947

Unlike Taylor who focused on an individual production worker's job, Henri Fayol and Max Weber (bottom photo) looked at organizational practices by focusing on what managers do and what constituted good management. This approach is known as **general administrative theory**. Fayol was introduced in Chapter 1 as the person who first identified five management functions. He also identified 14 **principles of management**—fundamental rules of management that could be applied to all organizations. (See exhibit below for a list of these 14 principles.) Weber is known for his description and analysis of bureaucracy, which he believed was an ideal, rational form of organization structure, especially for large organizations.[4] In Chapter 5, we elaborate on these two important management pioneers.

FAYOL'S FOURTEEN PRINCIPLES OF MANAGEMENT

1 **Division of Work.** This principle is the same as Adam Smith's "division of labor." Specialization increases output by making employees more efficient.

2 **Authority.** Managers must be able to give orders. Authority gives them this right. Along with authority, however, goes responsibility. Whenever authority is exercised, responsibility arises.

3 **Discipline.** Employees must obey and respect the rules that govern the organization. Good discipline is the result of effective leadership, a clear understanding between management and workers regarding the organization's rules, and the judicious use of penalties for infractions of the rules.

4 **Unity of Command.** Every employee should receive orders from only one superior.

5 **Unity of Direction.** Each group of organizational activities that have the same objective should be directed by one manager using one plan.

6 **Subordination of Individual Interests to the General Interest.** The interests of any one employee or group of employees should not take precedence over the interests of the organization as a whole.

7 **Remuneration.** Workers must be paid a fair wage for their services.

8 **Centralization.** Centralization refers to the degree to which subordinates are involved in decision making. Whether decision making is centralized (to management) or decentralized (to subordinates) is a question of proper proportion. The task is to find the optimum degree of centralization for each situation.

9 **Scalar Chain.** The line of authority from top management to the lowest ranks represents the scalar chain. Communications should follow this chain. However, if following the chain creates delays, cross-communications can be allowed if agreed to by all parties and if superiors are kept informed. Also called chain of command.

10 **Order.** People and materials should be in the right place at the right time.

11 **Equity.** Managers should be kind and fair to their subordinates.

12 **Stability of Tenure of Personnel.** High employee turnover is inefficient. Management should provide orderly personnel planning and ensure that replacements are available to fill vacancies.

13 **Initiative.** Employees who are allowed to originate and carry out plans will exert high levels of effort.

14 **Esprit de Corps.** Promoting team spirit will build harmony and unity within the organization.

Behavioral Approach ○

The behavioral approach to management focused on the actions of workers. How do you motivate and lead employees in order to get high levels of performance?

Late 1700s – early 1900s

Managers get things done by working with people. Several early management writers recognized how important people are to an organization's success.[5] For instance, Robert Owen, who was concerned about deplorable working conditions, proposed an idealistic workplace. Hugo Munsterberg, a pioneer in the field of industrial psychology, suggested using psychological tests for employee selection, learning theory concepts for employee training, and studies of human behavior for employee motivation. Mary Parker Follett was one of the first to recognize that organizations could be viewed from both individual and group behavior. She thought that organizations should be based on a group ethic rather than on individualism.

1960s – today

An organization's people continue to be an important focus of management research. The field of study that researches the actions (behaviors) of people at work is called **organizational behavior (OB)**. OB researchers do empirical research on human behavior in organizations. Much of what managers do today when managing people—motivating, leading, building trust, working with a team, managing conflict, and so forth—has come out of OB research. These topics are explored in depth in Chapters 8–12.

1924 – mid-1930s

The **Hawthorne studies**, a series of studies that provided new insights into individual and group behavior, were without question the most important contribution to the behavioral approach to management.[6] Conducted at the Hawthorne (Cicero, Illinois) Works of the Western Electric Company, the studies were initially designed as a scientific management experiment. Company engineers wanted to see the effect of various lighting levels on worker productivity. Using control and experimental groups of workers, they expected to find that individual output in the experimental group would be directly related to the intensity of the light. However, much to their surprise, they found that productivity in both groups varied with the level of lighting. Not able to explain it, the engineers called in Harvard professor Elton Mayo. Thus began a relationship that lasted until 1932 and encompassed numerous experiments in the behavior of people at work. What were some of their conclusions? Group pressures can significantly impact individual productivity, and people behave differently when they're being observed. Scholars generally agree that the Hawthorne Studies had a dramatic impact on management beliefs about the role of people in organizations. This led to a new emphasis on the human behavior factor in managing organizations.

1930s – 1950s

The human relations movement is important to management history because its supporters never wavered from their commitment to making management practices more humane. Proponents of this movement uniformly believed in the importance of employee satisfaction—a satisfied worker was believed to be a productive worker.[7] So they offered suggestions like employee participation, praise, and being nice to people to increase employee satisfaction. For instance, Abraham Maslow, a humanistic psychologist, who's best known for his description of a hierarchy of five needs (a well-known theory of employee motivation), said that once a need was substantially satisfied, it no longer served to motivate behavior. Douglas McGregor developed Theory X and Theory Y assumptions, which related to a manager's beliefs about an employee's motivation to work. Even though both Maslow's and McGregor's theories were never fully supported by research, they're important because they represent the foundation from which contemporary motivation theories were developed. Both are described more fully in Chapter 10.

Quantitative Approach

The quantitative approach, which focuses on the application of statistics, optimization models, information models, computer simulations, and other quantitative techniques to management activities, provided tools for managers to make their jobs easier.

1940s

The **quantitative approach** to management—which is the use of quantitative techniques to improve decision making—evolved from mathematical and statistical solutions developed for military problems during World War II. After the war was over, many of these techniques used for military problems were applied to businesses.[8] For instance, one group of military officers, dubbed the "Whiz Kids," joined Ford Motor Company in the mid-1940s and immediately began using statistical methods to improve decision making at Ford. You'll find more information on these quantitative applications in Chapter 14.

1950s

After WW II, Japanese organizations enthusiastically embraced the concepts espoused by a small group of quality experts, the most famous being W. Edwards Deming (photo on right) and Joseph M. Duran. As these Japanese manufacturers began beating U.S. competitors in quality comparisons, Western managers soon took a more serious look at Deming's and Juran's ideas. Their ideas became the basis for **total quality management (TQM)**, which is a management philosophy devoted to continual improvement and responding to customer needs and expectations. We'll look closer at Deming and his beliefs about TQM in Chapter 14.

Contemporary Approaches

Most of the early approaches to management focused on managers' concerns inside the organization. Starting in the 1960s, management researchers began to look at what was happening in the external environment outside the organization.

1960s

Although Chester Barnard, a telephone company executive, wrote in his 1938 book *The Functions of the Executive* that an organization functioned as a cooperative **system**, it wasn't until the 1960s that management researchers began to look more carefully at systems theory and how it related to organizations.[10] The idea of a system is a basic concept in the physical sciences. As related to organizations, a system is a set of interrelated and interdependent parts arranged in a manner that produces a unified whole. Organizations function as open systems, which means they are influenced by and interact with their environment. The exhibit on the right illustrates an organization as an **open system**. A manager has to efficiently and effectively manage all parts of the system in order to achieve established goals.

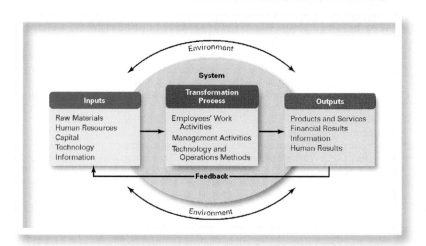

Environment

System

Inputs	Transformation Process	Outputs
Raw Materials	Employees' Work Activities	Products and Services
Human Resources	Management Activities	Financial Results
Capital	Technology and	Information
Technology	Operations Methods	Human Results
Information		

Feedback

Environment

Contemporary Approaches

1960s

Early management theorists proposed management principles that they generally assumed to be universally applicable. Later research found exceptions to many of these principles. The **contingency approach** (or **situational approach**) says that organizations, employees, and situations are different and require different ways of managing. A good way to describe contingency is "if, then." *If* this is the way my situation is, *then* this is the best way for me to manage in this situation. One of the earliest contingency studies was done by Fred Fiedler and looked at what style of leadership was most effective in what situation.[11] Popular contingency variables have been found to include organization size, the routineness of task technology, environmental uncertainty, and individual differences.

1980s – present

Although the dawn of the information age is said to have begun with Samuel Morse's telegraph in 1837, the most dramatic changes in information technology have occurred in the latter part of the twentieth century and have directly affected the manager's job. Managers now may manage employees who are working from home or working halfway around the world. An organization's computing resources used to be mainframe computers locked away in temperature-controlled rooms and only accessed by the experts. Now, practically everyone in an organization is connected—wired or wireless—with devices no larger than the palm of the hand. Just like the impact of the Industrial Revolution in the 1700s on the emergence of management, the information age has brought dramatic changes that continue to influence the way organizations are managed. The impact of information technology on how managers do their work is so profound that we've included in several chapters a boxed feature on "Technology and the Manager's Job".

division of labor
The breakdown of jobs into narrow, repetitive tasks.

Industrial Revolution
The advent of machine power, mass production, and efficient transportation begun in the late eighteenth century in Great Britain.

scientific management
The use of the scientific method to define the one best way for a job to be done.

general administrative theorists
Writers who developed general theories of what managers do and what constitutes good management practice.

principles of management
Fayol's fundamental or universal principles of management practice.

Hawthorne studies
Research done in the late 1920s and early 1930s devised by Western Electric industrial engineers to examine the effect of different work environment changes on worker productivity, which led to a new emphasis on the human factor in the functioning of organizations and the attainment of their goals.

Organizational Behavior (OB)
The field of study that researches the actions (behaviors) of people at work.

quantitative approach
The use of quantitative techniques to improve decision making.

total quality management (TQM)
A management philosophy devoted to continual improvement and responding to customer needs and expectations.

systems approach
An approach to management that views an organization as a system, which is a set of interrelated and interdependent parts arranged in a manner that produces a unified whole.

open systems
Systems that dynamically interact with its environment.

contingency approach (or situational approach)
An approach to management that says that organizations, employees, and situations are different and require different ways of managing.

2

The
Management
Environment

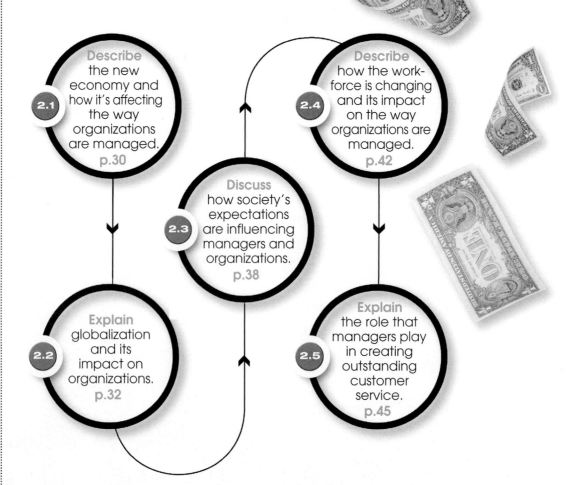

Extreme Customer Service

It's called the $10 test.[1] Managers at a Florida resort hotel felt that the instructional videos they used to train housekeepers on how to quickly and effectively clean guest rooms didn't seem to have a lasting impact. So they began doing surprise inspections evaluating room cleanliness based on the video information. A manager would choose a room that had just been cleaned, place 10 one-dollar bills on the bed, and then go through the room and look for areas not up to cleanliness standards. If, for instance, a hair was found on the bathroom counter or in the tub, the manager would pick up a dollar. Other cleaning "mistakes" also cost a dollar. After the inspection, any money left on the bed was given to the housekeeper as a bonus. At first, the housekeepers resented the "$10 tests" because there wasn't much left after the inspection. However, after doing the "tests" for a time, most of the housekeepers ended up with an extra $9 or $10 and actually started looking forward to the inspections. And managers got what they wanted . . . guest rooms cleaned to an impeccable standard, an important consideration since cleanliness is a critical component in customer satisfaction.

The hospitality industry has been hit hard by the economic turmoil. Not only are families not going on vacation, many companies are curtailing business travel. Hotel occupancy rates were down almost 3 percent in 2008 and forecasted to decline another 2 percent in 2009. Hotel managers recognized that to attract guests and keep them returning, they had to offer exceptional customer service. That's why so many are taking actions to ensure that employees are working efficiently and effectively to provide that service.

For instance, at Hilton Hotels Corporation, its global workforce is undergoing intensive customer service training. "One of the biggest challenges is getting globally dispersed employees to read from the same playbook." Part of its efforts involves translating customized learning material into at least 16, and as many as 27, languages. The company is also using a special **intranet** (a private computer network that uses Internet technology and is accessible only to organizational members) to put service training materials online. Employees use it to quickly review quality and service standards, regardless of their job role or location. Thus, a room service employee in London or in San Francisco can use it to make sure they've fulfilled all required job duties. Also, managers use "brand service cards" to remind their employees of the service standards. Hilton's director of brand education says that the company is "zeroing in on employee behaviors that provide guests with hassle-free, personalized, and informational service." Will it be enough? Although Hilton's managers can't control the external environmental changes, they can control how the company is responding to those changes.

No successful organization, or its managers, can operate without understanding and dealing with the dynamic environment that surrounds it. One of the biggest problems managers make today is failing to adapt to the changing world. As one executive said recently regarding the economic crisis, "I have learned more about management and leadership during the past six months than I had in the previous ten years."[2] Organizations that are bound by tradition and don't (or refuse to) change are less and less likely to survive the turbulence in today's world. To better understand this, we need to look at the important external environmental forces that are impacting the way organizations are managed today. In this chapter, we'll look at those forces, which include the new economy, globalization, society's expectations, the changing workforce, and the expanding role of customer service.

What's the New Economy Like?

Describe the new economy and how it's affecting the way organizations are managed. **2.1**

You know the economic context has changed when you have a company like General Motors in bankruptcy, 9.4 million jobs vanishing in the United States, and an economic vocabulary that includes terminology like *toxic assets*, *collaterized debt obligations*, *TARP*, *bailouts*, *economic stabilization*, *wraparound mortgages*, and *stress tests*. To understand what this new economy is like, we need to look at the changes that have taken place and the impact of those changes on the way that organizations are managed.

How Has the Economy Changed?

During the early 1980s, the U.S. economy was growing and tax rates were low. Individuals had money to spend and took risks by investing in the stock market, buying homes, and starting their own businesses. With all this new economic activity, the economy continued to expand and consumers enjoyed low inflation and interest rates. This "healthy" economy prompted financial institutions to lure consumers with cheap and available money thus encouraging them to spend aggressively, fueling even more economic growth. As one expert said, "For a while, this formula worked."[3] But then as gas prices hit $4 plus per gallon during the summer of 2008, adjustable mortgages adjusted upward with higher monthly payments due, and consumers took on record amounts of debt; those who were teetering on the financial edge found they couldn't keep up. "The financial crisis revealed just how much risk individuals had taken on, wittingly or not."[4] And it wasn't just consumers who were making bad decisions. Many business executives taking advantage of loose government regulations and loose credit made decisions that were too risky especially as economic conditions worsened.

This economic crisis, which began with turmoil in mortgage markets and spread to businesses when broader credit markets collapsed, has been called the worst since the Great Depression. With foreclosures, financial recession, a huge public debt, and widespread social problems from job losses, it's clear that the U.S. and global economic environments have changed and are continuing to change. For instance, the International Monetary Fund forecasted that the global economy would likely contract in 2009 for the first time since World War II and that the recovery would take longer than expected. However, the Organization for Economic Cooperation and Development, an economic organization of 30 industrialized countries, issued a revised forecast of upward growth for its members for the first time in two years.[5]

As this financial mess unfolded during 2008, people got angry at America's business leaders. With massive employee layoffs, plummeting stock values, government bailouts in the billions of dollars, outrageous executive compensation packages (one bank CEO went so far as to suggest that he deserved a $40 million bonus even after his company lost $15 billion in the fourth quarter of 2008), outrageous executive behavior (auto executives who flew to Washington, DC, on corporate jets to ask for billions of dollars in government bailout money), it's understandable that people were mad. But worse than the anger was the aftermath—the lack of trust in business and its leaders. According to a January 2009 survey, trust in U.S. businesses dropped from 58 percent to 38 percent in one year.[6] Rebuilding that confidence is likely to take time and won't be easily earned.

What Will the "New" Normal Be Like?

In the U.S. economic system, which is based mostly on capitalistic principles, trade and industry are controlled privately rather than by the government. But in such a system, as we've seen time and time again, people sometimes make bad, even disastrous, decisions. The esteemed economist John Maynard Keynes once said, "Capitalism is the astounding belief that the most wickedest of men will do the most wickedest of things for the greatest good of everyone."[7] Despite this cynical view, modern capitalism has had a significant impact. It's created "unprecedented wealth in our lifetime, shown its power to lift people out of poverty, and spread a culture of competitive genius."[8] It's also been called the "most productive economic engine invented."[9] Since the early 1900s, the U.S. approach has been the most important model for organizing business activities. It brought the world the corporate model of ownership and organization, large-scale operations based on mass production techniques, open markets, formal organization structures with hierarchies and multiple business divisions, and labor-management collective bargaining. Business organizations in many countries have patterned themselves after this model. However, as the current economic problems show, it's by no means perfect.

Bad business and consumer decisions fueled a global economic crisis that resulted in diluted trust in business leaders, home foreclosures, bank failures, plant closings, and massive employee layoffs that produced long lines of unemployed workers seeking jobs like those shown here at a job fair in New York City. This crisis is expected to change the way managers manage their workforce and businesses operate within a new economic environment of increased government regulation that protects employees and consumers.

Experts believe that once the U.S. economy emerges from recession things won't be the way they were—that there will be a "new" normal. As Timothy Geithner, the U.S. Secretary of the Treasury, said, "Capitalism will be different."[10] How managers manage and the way businesses operate will not be as they've always been. The biggest change is likely to be in the role of government, especially in financial markets and in consumer protection. Since the onset of the financial crisis, the U.S. government has become the nation's biggest mortgage lender, guaranteed more than $3 trillion in money-market mutual-fund assets, taken over and restructured two car companies, taken equity stakes in some 600 banks, lent more than $300 billion to large companies, supported the life-insurance industry, and become a credit source for consumers wanting to buy goods.[11] Also, government spending as a share of the U.S. economy is at levels not seen since World War II. Beyond that, more government intervention is likely to mean more regulations or at the least, increased enforcement and oversight of regulations that are already in place. However, some believe that more governmental oversight isn't the answer. For example, social scientist Amitai Etzioni said, "The world economy consists of billions of transactions every day. There can never be enough inspectors, accountants, customs officers, and police to ensure that all or even most of these transactions are properly carried out. Moreover, those charged with enforcing regulations are themselves not immune to corruption, and hence, they too must be supervised and held accountable to others—who also have to be somehow regulated. The upshot is that regulation cannot be the linchpin of attempts to reform our economy. What is needed is something far more sweeping: for people to internalize a different sense of how one ought to behave, and act on it because they believe

intranet
A private computer network that uses Internet technology and is accessible only to organizational members.

One positive aspect of this new economy comes from the vast possibilities associated with continuing advancements in technology.[12] Technology includes any equipment, tools, or operating methods that are designed to make work more efficient. One area where technology has had an impact is in the process where inputs (labor, raw materials, and the like) are transformed into outputs (goods and services to be sold). In years past, this transformation was usually performed by human labor. With technology, however, human labor has been replaced with electronic and computer equipment. From robots on assembly lines to online banking systems to social networks where employees interact with customers, technology has made the work of creating and delivering goods and services more efficient and effective.

Another area where technology has had a major impact is in information. Information technology (IT) has created the ability to circumvent the physical confines of working only in a specified organizational location. With notebook and desktop computers, fax machines, smartphones, organizational intranets, and other IT tools, organizational members who work mainly with information can do that work from any place at any time.

Finally, technology is also changing the way managers manage, especially in terms of how they interact with employees who may be working anywhere and anytime. Effectively communicating with individuals in remote locations and ensuring that performance goals are being met are challenges that managers must address. Throughout the rest of the book, we'll look at how managers are meeting those challenges in the ways they plan, organize, lead, and control.

it is right."[13] We've also seen a shift in public opinion as more people have expressed concerns about the growing budget deficit and increased government intervention in the economy. In a poll by the *Wall Street Journal,* some 49 percent of the respondents said they had a great deal of concern about a greater government role in the economy and business.[14] So, how is this "new" normal likely to affect businesses and managers?

How Is the New Economy Affecting Organizations?

As we've tried to make clear, it's not going to be "business as usual" for organizations or for managers. Managers will have hard decisions to make about their way of doing business and about an organization's people. These decisions are likely to determine how companies do business globally, how they deal with the expectations of society to act responsibly and ethically, how they treat their workforce, and how they deal with skeptical and demanding consumers. Many of these changes are likely to be broad and sweeping in nature. Since this isn't something we can discuss in a few sentences, the rest of the chapter is devoted to discussing these changes. The new economy has changed the management environment, and it's important that you understand how these changes will affect your organizational and management experiences.

What Is Globalization and How Does It Affect Organizations?

2.2 Explain globalization and its impact on organizations.

An important part of the environment that managers must deal with is globalization. And due to the global economic meltdown, how organizations do business globally has changed. Like the United States, many nations are struggling with rising unemployment, increased government intervention, financial markets in turmoil, and consumer uncertainty and reluctance to spend money. Despite these challenges, globalization isn't about to disappear. Nations and businesses have been trading with each other for centuries through economic ups and downs. Over the last couple of decades, we've seen an explosion of companies operating almost anywhere in the world. National borders mean little when it comes to doing business. Avon, a so-called American company, gets 81 percent of its annual revenues from sales outside the United States. BMW, a German-owned firm, builds cars in South Carolina. McDonald's sells hamburgers in China. Although the world is still a **global village**, how managers do business in that global village is changing. To be effective in this boundaryless world, managers need to adapt to this changed environment, as well as continue to foster an understanding of cultures, systems, and techniques that are different from their own.

What does it mean to be "global?" Organizations are considered global if they exchange goods and services with consumers in other countries. Such marketplace globalization is the most common approach to being global. However, many organizations, especially high-tech organizations, are considered global because they use managerial and technical employee talent from other countries. One factor that affects talent globalization is immigration laws and regulations. Managers must be alert to changes in those laws. Finally, an organization can be considered global if it uses financial sources and resources outside its home country, which is known as financial globalization.[15] As might be expected, the global economic slow-down has severely affected the availability of financial resources globally.

What Are the Different Types of Global Organizations?

In the mid-1960s, **multinational corporations (MNCs)** became commonplace and initiated the rapid growth in international trade that we've seen. MNCs are any type of international company that maintains operations in multiple countries. Today, companies such as Procter & Gamble, Wal-Mart, Exxon, Coca-Cola, and Aflac are among a growing number of U.S.-based firms that get significant portions of their annual revenues from foreign operations.

One type of MNC is a **multidomestic corporation**, which decentralizes management and other decisions to the local country where it's doing business. A multidomestic corporation doesn't attempt to replicate its domestic successes by managing foreign operations from its home country. Instead, local employees typically are hired to manage the business and marketing strategies are tailored to that country's unique characteristics. Many consumer product companies organize their global businesses using this approach because they must adapt their products to meet the needs of local markets. For example, Switzerland-based Nestlé operates as a multidomestic corporation. With operations in almost every country on the globe, its managers are responsible for making sure the company's products fit its consumers wherever they are. In parts of Europe, Nestlé sells products that are not available in the United States or Latin America.

Another type of MNC is a **global corporation**, which centralizes its management and other decisions in the home country. These companies treat the world market as an integrated whole and focus on the need for global efficiency. Although these companies may have considerable global holdings, management decisions with company-wide implications are made from headquarters in the home country. Some examples of global companies include Sony, Deutsche Bank AG, and Merrill Lynch (now a subsidiary of Bank of America).

Other companies use an arrangement that eliminates artificial geographical barriers. This type of MNC is often called a **transnational** or **borderless organization**.[16] For example, IBM dropped its organizational structure based on country and reorganized into industry groups. Ford Motor Company is pursuing the One Ford concept as it integrates its global operations. Another company, Thomson SA, which is legally incorporated in France, has eight major locations around the globe. The CEO said, "we don't want people to think we're based anyplace." [17] Managers choose this approach to increase efficiency and effectiveness in a competitive global marketplace.[18]

technology
Any equipment, tools, or operating methods that are designed to make work more efficient.

global village
Refers to the concept of a boundaryless world where goods and services are produced and marketed worldwide.

multinational corporation (MNC)
Any type of international company that maintains operations in multiple countries.

multidomestic corporation
An MNC that decentralizes management and other decisions to the local country where it's doing business.

global corporation
An MNC that centralizes management and other decisions in the home country.

transnational (borderless) organization
A structural arrangement for global organizations that eliminates artificial geographical barriers.

How Do Organizations Go Global?

When organizations do go global, they often use different approaches. (See Exhibit 2-1.) At first, managers want to get into a global market with minimal investment. At this stage, they may start with **global sourcing** (also called global outsourcing), which is purchasing materials or labor from around the world wherever it is cheapest. The goal: take advantage of lower costs in order to be more competitive. For instance, Massachusetts General Hospital uses radiologists in India to interpret CT scans.[19] Although global sourcing may be the first step to going international for many companies, they often continue using this approach because of the competitive advantages it offers. However, as the current economic crisis accelerated, many organizations reconsidered their decisions to source globally. For instance, Dell, Apple, and American Express are just a few that scaled back some of their offshore customer service operations. One analyst said that companies rethinking their global sourcing decisions are trying to make "choices about the best place to do a given piece of work—be it offshore, onshore, or nearshore. As this transformation occurs, work is being spread throughout the world and companies are globalizing to keep up."[20] When a company wants to take that next step in going global, each successive stage beyond global sourcing requires more investment and thus entails more risk for the organization.

The next step in going global may involve **exporting** the organization's products to other countries—that is, making products domestically and selling them abroad. In addition, an organization might do **importing**, which involves acquiring products made abroad and selling them domestically. Both usually entail minimal investment and risk, which is why many small businesses often use these approaches to doing business globally.

Finally, managers might use **licensing** or **franchising**, which are similar approaches involving one organization giving another organization the right to use its brand name, technology, or product specifications in return for a lump sum payment or a fee usually based on sales. The only difference is that licensing is primarily used by manufacturing organizations that make or sell another company's products, and franchising is primarily used by service organizations that want to use another company's name and operating methods. For example, New Delhi consumers can enjoy Subway sandwiches, Hong Kong

Operating as a global corporation, Tata is an Indian-based conglomerate with 27 companies in seven business sectors ranging from consumer goods to information technology. While decision making is anchored in India, Tata has a presence in every major international market. Company chairman Ratan Tata is shown here at the launch of Tata Motors' new Nano car in Mumbai, India. The Nano, the world's lowest-cost car, is designed to put auto ownership within reach of millions of the world's poor. Tata plans to drive its global business by focusing on innovations like the Nano.

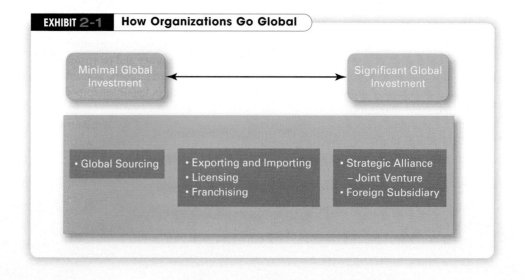

EXHIBIT 2-1 **How Organizations Go Global**

Minimal Global Investment ⟷ Significant Global Investment

- Global Sourcing
- Exporting and Importing
- Licensing
- Franchising
- Strategic Alliance
  – Joint Venture
- Foreign Subsidiary

residents can dine on Shakey's Pizza, and Malaysians can consume Schlotzky's deli sandwiches—all because of *franchises* in these countries. On the other hand, Anheuser-Busch InBev *licensed* the right to brew and market its Budweiser beer to brewers such as Labatt in Canada, Modelo in Mexico, and Kirin in Japan.

Once an organization has been doing business internationally for a while and has gained experience in international markets, managers may decide to make more of a direct investment. One way to do this is through a **global strategic alliance**, which is a partnership between an organization and a foreign company partner or partners in which both share resources and knowledge in developing new products or building production facilities. For example, Honda Motor and General Electric teamed up to produce a new jet engine. A specific type of strategic alliance in which the partners form a separate, independent organization for some business purpose is called a **joint venture**. For example, Hewlett-Packard has had numerous joint ventures with various suppliers around the globe to develop different components for its computer equipment. These partnerships provide a relatively easy way for companies to compete globally.

Finally, managers may choose to directly invest in a foreign country by setting up a **foreign subsidiary** as a separate and independent facility or office. This subsidiary can be managed as a multidomestic organization (local control) or as a global organization (centralized control). As you can probably guess, this arrangement involves the greatest commitment of resources and poses the greatest amount of risk. For instance, United Plastics Group of Westmont, Illinois, built three injection-molding facilities in Suzhou, China. The company's executive vice president for business development says that level of investment was necessary because "it fulfilled our mission of being a global supplier to our global accounts."[21]

Rick Howarth (left) is a manager who understands differences among country cultures. Formerly a chipset plant manager for Intel in China, Howarth is now general and factory manager for Intel's new plant in Ho Chi Minh City, Vietnam. He recognizes that Vietnam's business culture is based on a hierarchical system of power and authority, in contrast to Intel's culture of teamwork. Knowing that Vietnamese youth love American culture, Howarth sponsors team-building exercises like Karaoke Fridays to teach the plant's young workforce how to become team players.

What Do Managers Need to Know About Managing in a Global Organization?

A global world brings new challenges for managers, especially in managing in a country with a different national culture.[22] The specific challenge is recognizing the differences that might exist and finding ways to make interactions effective.

U.S. managers once held (and some still do hold) a rather parochial view of the world of business. **Parochialism** is a narrow focus in which managers see things only through their own eyes and from their own perspectives. They don't recognize that people from other countries have different ways of doing things or that they live differently from Americans. This view can't succeed in a global village—nor is it the dominant view held today. Changing such perceptions requires understanding that countries have different cultures and environments.

global sourcing
Purchasing materials or labor from around the world wherever it is cheapest.

exporting
Making products domestically and selling them abroad.

importing
Acquiring products made abroad and selling them domestically.

licensing
An agreement primarily used by manufacturing businesses in which an organization gives another

the right, for a fee, to make or sell its products, using its technology or product specifications.

franchising
An agreement primarily used by service businesses in which an organization gives another organization the right, for a fee, to use its name and operating methods.

global strategic alliance
A partnership between an organization and a foreign company partner(s) in which resources and knowledge are shared in developing new products or building production facilities.

joint venture
A specific type of strategic alliance in which the partners agree to form a separate, independent organization for some business purpose.

foreign subsidiary
A direct investment in a foreign country that involves setting up a separate and independent facility or office.

parochialism
A narrow focus in which managers see things only through their own eyes and from their own perspective.

All countries have different values, morals, customs, political and economic systems, and laws, all of which can affect how a business is managed. For instance, in the United States, laws guard against employers taking action against employees solely on the basis of their age. Similar laws can't be found in all other countries. Thus, managers must be aware of a country's laws when doing business there.

The most important and challenging differences for managers to understand, however, are those related to a country's social context or culture. For example, status is perceived differently in different countries. In France, status is often the result of factors important to the organization, such as seniority, education, and the like. In the United States, status is more a function of what individuals have accomplished personally. Managers need to understand societal issues (such as status) that might affect business operations in another country and recognize that organizational success can come from a variety of managerial practices. Fortunately, managers have help in this regard stemming from research that has been done on the differences in cultural environments.

HOFSTEDE'S FRAMEWORK. Geert Hofstede's framework is one of the most widely referenced approaches for analyzing cultural variations. His work has had a major impact on what we know about cultural differences among countries and is highlighted in our "From the Past to the Present" box.

GLOBE FINDINGS. Although Hofstede's work has provided the basic framework for differentiating among national cultures, the data are nearly 30 years old. Another more recent

From the Past to the Present

An illuminating study of the differences in cultural environments was conducted by Geert Hofstede in the 1970s and 1980s.[23] He surveyed more than 116,000 IBM employees in 40 countries about their work-related values. He found that managers and employees vary on five value dimensions of national culture:

▶ *Power distance.* The degree to which people in a country accept that power in institutions and organizations is distributed unequally. Ranges from relatively low (low power distance) to extremely unequal (high power distance).

▶ *Individualism versus collectivism.* Individualism is the degree to which people in a country prefer to act as individuals rather than as members of groups. Collectivism is the equivalent of low individualism. Most Asian countries were more collectivistic than individualistic.

▶ *Achievement versus nurturing.* Achievement is the degree to which values such as assertiveness, the acquisition of money and material goods, and competition are important. Nurturing is the degree to which people value relationships and show sensitivity and concern for the welfare of others.

▶ *Uncertainty avoidance.* This is the degree to which people in a country prefer structured over unstructured situations.

▶ *Long-term versus short-term orientation.* People in cultures with long-term orientations look to the future and value thrift and persistence. A short-term orientation values the past and present and emphasizes respect for tradition and fulfilling social obligations.

Here are a few highlights of four of Hofstede's cultural dimensions and how different countries rank on those dimensions:

Examples of Hofstede's Cultural Dimensions

Country	Individualism/ Collectivism	Power Distance	Uncertainty Avoidance	Achievement/ Nurturing[a]
Australia	Individual	Small	Moderate	Strong
Canada	Individual	Moderate	Low	Moderate
England	Individual	Small	Moderate	Strong
France	Individual	Large	High	Weak
Greece	Collective	Large	High	Moderate
Italy	Individual	Moderate	High	Strong
Japan	Collective	Moderate	High	Strong
Mexico	Collective	Large	High	Strong
Singapore	Collective	Large	Low	Moderate
Sweden	Individual	Small	Low	Weak
United States	Individual	Small	Low	Strong
Venezuela	Collective	Large	High	Strong

[a]A weak achievement score is equivalent to high nurturing.

Source: Based on G. Hofstede, "Motivation, Leadership, and Organization: Do American Theories Apply Abroad?" *Organizational Dynamics*, Summer 1980, pp. 42–63.

| EXHIBIT 2-2 | GLOBE Highlights |

DIMENSION	COUNTRIES RATING LOW	COUNTRIES RATING MODERATE	COUNTRIES RATING HIGH
Assertiveness	Sweden New Zealand Switzerland	Egypt Ireland Philippines	Spain United States Greece
Future orientation	Russia Argentina Poland	Slovenia Egypt Ireland	Denmark Canada Netherlands
Gender differentiation	Sweden Denmark Slovenia	Italy Brazil Argentina	South Korea Egypt Morocco
Uncertainty avoidance	Russia Hungary Bolivia	Israel United States Mexico	Austria Denmark Germany
Power distance	Denmark Netherlands South Africa	England France Brazil	Russia Spain Thailand
Individualism/collectivism*	Denmark Singapore Japan	Hong Kong United States Egypt	Greece Hungary Germany
In-group collectivism	Denmark Sweden New Zealand	Japan Israel Qatar	Egypt China Morocco
Performance orientation	Russia Argentina Greece	Sweden Israel Spain	United States Taiwan New Zealand
Humane orientation	Germany Spain France	Hong Kong Sweden Taiwan	Indonesia Egypt Malaysia

*A low score is synonymous with collectivism.

Source: M. Javidan and R. J. House, "Cultural Acumen for the Global Manager: Lessons from Project GLOBE," *Organizational Dynamics* (Spring 2001), pp. 289–305.

research program called **Global Leadership and Organizational Behavior Effectiveness (GLOBE)** is an ongoing cross-cultural investigation of leadership and national culture. Using data from more than 18,000 managers in 62 countries, the GLOBE research team (led by Robert House) has identified nine dimensions on which national cultures differ.[24] (See Exhibit 2-2 for country ratings.)

- ▶ *Assertiveness.* The extent to which a society encourages people to be tough, confrontational, assertive, and competitive versus modest and tender.
- ▶ *Future orientation.* The extent to which a society encourages and rewards future-oriented behavior such as planning, investing in the future, and delaying gratification.
- ▶ *Gender differentiation.* The extent to which a society maximizes gender role differences.
- ▶ *Uncertainty avoidance.* As defined in Hofstede's landmark research, the GLOBE team also defined this term as a society's reliance on social norms and procedures to alleviate the unpredictability of future events.

Global Leadership and Organizational Behavior Effectiveness (GLOBE)
A program that studies cross-cultural leadership behaviors.

Right or Wrong?

"Apple's chief takes a medical leave after months of denial that his health is declining; many feel that because he is so closely linked with the firm's creative vision, Steve Jobs should be required to release more medical information." What do you think? Do the heads of publicly traded firms have a right to medical privacy? What ethical issues might arise in such a situation?[25]

▶ *Power distance.* As in the original research, the GLOBE team defined this as the degree to which members of a society expect power to be unequally shared.

▶ *Individualism/collectivism.* Again, this term was defined similarly to the original research as the degree to which individuals are encouraged by societal institutions to be integrated into groups within organizations and society.

▶ *In-group collectivism.* In contrast to focusing on societal institutions, this dimension encompasses the extent to which members of a society take pride in membership in small groups such as their family and circle of close friends and the organizations in which they are employed.

▶ *Performance orientation.* This dimension refers to the degree to which a society encourages and rewards group members for performance improvement and excellence.

▶ *Humane orientation.* This cultural aspect is the degree to which a society encourages and rewards individuals for being fair, altruistic, generous, caring, and kind to others.

The GLOBE studies confirm that Hofstede's dimensions are still valid, and extend his research rather than replace it. GLOBE's added dimensions provide an expanded and updated measure of countries' cultural differences. It's likely that cross-cultural studies of human behavior and organizational practices will increasingly use the GLOBE dimensions to assess differences between countries.

What Does Society Expect from Organizations and Managers?

2.3 Discuss how society's expectations are influencing managers and organizations.

"Reinserting ethics into business is no mere luxury. It's essential to our survival as a wealth-creating nation."[26] "American companies have adopted a different attitude toward corporate responsibility. They seem to think it's fine for the rest of the world to do it, but it doesn't apply to them."[27] These two quotes reflect a belief that society expects organizations and managers to be responsible and ethical. However, as we saw in the publicized stories of notorious financial scandals at Enron, Bernard Madoff Investment Securities, HealthSouth, and others, managers don't always act responsibly and ethically.

The importance of corporate social responsibility surfaced in the 1960s when social activists questioned the singular economic objective of business. Even today, good arguments can be made for and against businesses being socially responsible. (See Exhibit 2-3.) Yet, arguments aside, times have changed. Managers regularly confront decisions that have a dimension of social responsibility: philanthropy, pricing, employee relations, resource conversation, product quality, and doing business in countries with oppressive governments are just a few. To address these issues, managers may reassess packaging design, recyclability of products, environmental safety practices, outsourcing decisions, foreign supplier practices, employee policies, and the like.

One area where many organizations have become more socially involved is **green management**, which is when managers recognize and consider the impact of their organization and its practices on the natural environment. For instance, Whole Foods Market uses wind energy for all its electricity needs, making it the largest corporate user of renewable energy. At Marriott International's employee cafeteria, plastic and paper containers have been replaced with real plates and compostable potato-based containers called SpudWare.[28] The idea of being environmentally friendly or green affects many aspects of business, from the creation of products and services to use and subsequent

| **EXHIBIT 2-3** | **Arguments For and Against Social Responsibility** |

FOR	AGAINST
Public expectations	**Violation of profit maximization**
Public opinion now supports businesses pursuing economic and social goals.	Business is being socially responsible only when it pursues its economic interests.
Long-run profits	**Dilution of purpose**
Socially responsible companies tend to have more secure long-run profits.	Pursuing social goals dilutes business's primary purpose—economic productivity.
Ethical obligation	**Costs**
Businesses should be socially responsible because responsible actions are the right thing to do.	Many socially responsible actions do not cover their costs and someone must pay those costs.
Public image	**Too much power**
Businesses can create a facorable public image by pursuing social goals.	Businesses have a lot of power already and if they pursue social goals they will have even more.
Better environment	**Lack of skills**
Business involvement can help solve difficult social problems.	Business leaders lack the necessary skills to address social issues.
Discouragement of further governmental regulation	**Lack of accountability**
By becoming socially responsible, businesses can expect less government regulation.	There are no direct lines of accountability for social actions.
Balance of responsibility and power	
Businesses have a lot of power and an equally large amount of responsibility is needed to balance against that power.	
Stockholder interests	
Social responsibility will improve a business's stock price in the long run.	
Possession of resources	
Businesses have the resources to support public and charitable projects that need assistance.	
Superiority of prevention over cures	
Businesses should address social problems before they become serious and costly to correct.	

disposal by consumers. Following green management practices is one way in which organizations can show their commitment to being responsible. In today's world where many individuals have diminishing respect for businesses, few organizations can afford the bad press or potential economic ramifications of being seen as socially irresponsible.

How Can Organizations Demonstrate Socially Responsible Actions?

Few terms have been defined in as many different ways as *social responsibility.* Some of the more popular meanings include profit maximization, going beyond profit making, voluntary activities, and concern for the broader social system.[29] On one side is the classical—or purely economic—view that management's only social responsibility is to maximize profits.[30] On the other side is the socioeconomic position, which holds

green management
When managers recognize and consider the impact of their organization and its practices on the natural environment.

that management's responsibility goes beyond making profits to include protecting and improving society's welfare.[32]

When we talk about **social responsibility**, we mean a business firm's intention, beyond its legal and economic obligations, to do the right things and act in ways that are good for society. Note that this definition assumes that a business obeys the law and pursues economic interests. But also note that this definition views a business as a moral agent. In its effort to do good for society, it must differentiate between right and wrong.

We can understand social responsibility better if we compare it to two similar concepts. **Social obligation** is when a business firm engages in social actions because of its obligation to meet certain economic and legal responsibilities. It does the minimum that the law requires and only pursues social goals to the extent that they contribute to its economic goals. **Social responsiveness** is when a business firm engages in social actions in response to some popular social need. Managers in these companies are guided by social norms and values and make practical, market-oriented decisions about their actions.[33] A U.S. business that meets federal pollution standards or safe packaging regulations is meeting its social obligation because laws mandate these actions. However, when it provides on-site child-care facilities for employees or packages products using recycled paper, it's being socially responsive because working parents and environmentalists have voiced these social concerns and demanded such actions. For many businesses, their social actions are probably better viewed as being socially responsive rather than socially responsible, at least according to our definitions. However, such actions are still good for society. Social responsibility adds an ethical imperative to do those things that make society better and to not do those that could make it worse.

How Can Managers Become More Ethical?

Two weeks after firing seven top managers for failing to meet company standards, Wal-Mart issued an extensive ethics policy for employees. The Gemological Institute of America, which grades diamonds for independent dealers and large retailers, fired four employees and made changes to top management after an internal investigation showed that lab workers took bribes to inflate the quality of diamonds in grading reports.[34] When you hear about such behaviors and actions, you might conclude that businesses aren't ethical. Although that isn't the case, managers do face ethical issues and dilemmas.

Ethics commonly refers to a set of rules or principles that defines right and wrong conduct.[35] Right or wrong behavior, though, may at times be difficult to determine. Most recognize that something illegal is also unethical. But what about questionable "legal" areas or strict organizational policies? For instance, what if you managed an employee who worked all weekend on a rush project and you told him to take off two days sometime later and mark it down as "sick days" because your company had a clear policy that overtime would not be compensated for any reason?[36] Would that be wrong? How will you handle such situations? As managers plan, organize, lead, and control, they must consider ethical dimensions. (See the "Developing Your Ethics Skill" box.)

Exhibit 2-4 presents three views of ethical standards. Regardless of which view you think is most appropriate, whether a manager acts ethically or unethically will depend on several factors. These factors include an individual's morality, values, personality, and experiences; the organization's culture; and the ethical issue being faced.[37] People who lack a strong moral sense are much less likely to do the wrong things if they are constrained by rules, policies, job descriptions, or strong cultural norms that discourage such behaviors. For example, suppose that someone in your class stole the final exam and is selling a copy for $50. You need to do well on the exam or risk failing the course. You suspect that some classmates have bought copies, which could affect any results because your professor grades on a curve. Do you buy a copy because you fear that without it you'll be disadvantaged, do you refuse to buy a copy and try your best, or do you report your knowledge to your instructor?

This example of the final exam illustrates how ambiguity over what is ethical can be a problem for managers. Codes of ethics are popular tools for attempting to reduce that ambiguity.[38] A **code of ethics** is a formal document that states an organization's primary

EXHIBIT 2-4	Three Views of Ethics

Utilitarian view of ethics	Refers to a situation in which decisions are made solely on the basis of their outcomes or consequences. The goal of utilitarianism is to provide the greatest good for the greatest number. On one side, utilitarianism encourages efficiency and productivity and is consistent with the goal of profit maximization. On the other side, however, it can result in biased allocations of resources, especially when some of those affected lack representation or voice.
Rights view of ethics	Refers to a situation in which the individual is concerned with respecting and protecting individual liberties and privileges, including the rights to privacy, freedom of conscience, free speech, and due process. The positive side of the rights perspective is that it protects individuals' freedom and privacy. But it has a negative side in organizations: It can present obstacles to high productivity and efficiency by creating an overly legalistic work climate.
Theory of justice view of ethics	Refers to a situation in which an individual imposes and enforces rules fairly and impartially. A manager would be using a theory of justice perspective in deciding to pay a new entry-level employee $1.50 an hour over the minimum wage because that manager believes that the minimum wage is inadequate to allow employees to meet their basic financial commitments. Imposing standards of justice also comes with pluses and minuses. It protects the interests of those stakeholders who may be underrepresented or lack power, but it can encourage a sense of entitlement that reduces risk taking, innovation, and productivity.

Source: G. F. Cavanaugh, D. J. Moberg, and M. Valasquez, "The Ethics of Organizational Politics,"*Academy of Management Journal* (June 1981), pp. 363–374.

values and the ethical rules it expects managers and nonmanagerial employees to follow. Ideally, these codes should be specific enough to guide organizational members in what they're supposed to do yet loose enough to allow for freedom of judgment. Research shows that 97 percent of organizations with more than 10,000 employees have written codes of ethics. Even in smaller organizations, nearly 93 percent have them.[39] And codes of ethics are becoming more popular globally. Research by the Institute for Global Ethics says that shared values such as honesty, fairness, respect, responsibility, and caring are pretty much universally embraced worldwide.[40]

In isolation, however, ethics codes are not likely to be much more than window dressing—after all even Enron had a code of ethics statement. The effectiveness of such codes depends heavily on whether management supports them and ingrains them into the corporate culture, and how individuals who break the codes are treated.[41] If management considers them to be important, regularly reaffirms their content, follows the rules themselves, and publicly reprimands rule breakers, ethics codes can be a strong foundation for an effective corporate ethics program.[42] And we need to make clear that managers must be good ethical role models both in words *and* more importantly, in actions. What you *do* is far more important than what you *say* in getting employees to act ethically.

social responsibility
A business firm's intention, beyond its legal and economic obligations, to do the right things and act in ways that are good for society.

social obligation
When a business firm engages in social actions because of its obligation to meet certain economic and legal responsibilities.

social responsiveness
When a business firm engages in social actions in response to some popular social need.

ethics
A set of rules or principles that defines right and wrong conduct.

code of ethics
A formal document that states an organization's primary values and the ethical rules it expects managers and nonmanagerial employees to follow.

Developing Your *Ethics* Skill

About the Skill

Making ethical choices often can be difficult for managers. Obeying the law is mandatory, but acting ethically goes beyond mere compliance with the law. It means acting responsibly in those gray areas, where right and wrong are not easily defined. What can you do to enhance your managerial abilities in acting ethically? Here are some guidelines.

Steps in Practicing the Skill

1 *Know your organization's policy on ethics.* Company policies on ethics, if they exist, describe what the organization perceives as ethical behavior and what it expects you to do. This policy will help you to clarify what is permissible and the managerial discretion you have. It becomes YOUR code of ethics.

2 *Understand the ethics policy.* Just having the policy in your hand does not guarantee that it will achieve what it is intended to do. You need to fully understand it. Behaving ethically is rarely a cut-and-dried process, but the policy can act as a guideline and provide a basis from which you act within the organization. Even if a policy does not exist, you can still take several steps before you deal with the ethical dilemma.

3 *Think before you act.* Ask yourself, "Why am I going to do what I'm about to do? What led up to the problem? What is my true intention in taking this action? Is my reason valid? Or are there ulterior motives behind it—such as demonstrating organizational loyalty? Will my action injure someone? Would I disclose to my boss or my family what I'm going to do?" Remember, it's your behavior and your actions. You need to make sure that you're not doing something that will jeopardize your role as a manager, your organization, or your reputation.

4 *Ask yourself what-if questions.* If you're thinking about why you are going to do something, you should also be asking yourself what-if questions. For example, the following questions may help you shape your actions: "What if I make the wrong decision? What will happen to me? To my job? What if my actions were described, in detail, on the local TV news show or in the newspaper? Would it bother or embarrass me or those around me? What if I get caught doing something unethical? Am I prepared to deal with the consequences?"

5 *Seek opinions from others.* If it is something major that you must do, and about which you are uncertain, ask for advice from other managers. Maybe they've been in a similar situation and can share the benefit of their experience. Or maybe they can just listen and act as a sounding board for you.

6 *Do what you truly believe is right.* You have a conscience, and you are responsible for your behavior. Whatever you do, if you truly believe it was the right action to take, then what others say or what the Monday morning quarterbacks say is immaterial. You need to be true to your own internal ethical standards. Ask yourself: "Can I live with what I've done?"

Practicing the Skill

Find a copy of your school's code of conduct or the code of ethics of any organization to which you belong. Or obtain a copy of the code of ethics for a professional organization you hope to join after graduating. Evaluate the code's provisions and policies. Are you uncomfortable with any of the code's provisions? Why? Is any part of the code routinely violated? Why do you think these violations occur? What are the usual consequences of such violations? Do you think these consequences are appropriate?

If you had trouble obtaining the code of conduct, find out why. Under what circumstances is it normally distributed, posted, or otherwise made available to members?

2.4 Describe how the workforce is changing and its impact on the way organizations are managed.

What Is Today's Workforce Like and How Does It Impact the Way Organizations Are Managed?

An important challenge facing today's organizations is adapting to a diverse workforce. **Workforce diversity** refers to ways in which people in a workforce are similar and different from one another in terms of gender, age, race, sexual orientation, ethnicity, cultural background, and physical abilities and disabilities. Until recently, organizations took a "melting pot" approach to diversity. It was assumed that people who were different would somehow automatically want to assimilate. But today's managers find that employees do not set aside their cultural values and lifestyle preferences when they come to work. The challenge for managers, then, is to make their organizations more accommodating to diverse groups of people by addressing different lifestyles, family needs, and work styles. The melting-pot assumption has been replaced by a recognition and celebration of differences.

MANAGING DIVERSITY | The Paradox of Diversity

When organizations bring in diverse individuals and socialize them into the culture, a paradox is created.[43] Managers want the new employees to accept the organization's core cultural values so they don't have a difficult time fitting in or being accepted. At the same time, managers want to openly acknowledge, embrace, and support the diverse perspectives and ideas that the new employees bring to the workplace.

Strong organizational cultures pressure employees to conform, and the range of acceptable values and behaviors is limited—hence the paradox. Organizations hire diverse individuals because of their unique strengths, yet their diverse behaviors and strengths are likely to diminish in strong cultures as people attempt to fit in.

A manager's challenge is to balance two conflicting goals: to encourage employees to accept the organization's dominant values and to encourage employees to accept differences. As the external environment changes and brings about change in an organization, managers need to remember the importance of keeping diversity alive.

What Does the Workforce Look Like Today?

Much of the change in the U.S. workforce over the last 50 years can be attributed to federal legislation enacted in the 1960s that prohibited employment discrimination. With these laws, avenues opened up for minority and female job applicants. These two groups dramatically changed the workplace in the latter half of the twentieth century. Women, in particular, have changed the composition of the workforce as they now hold some 49.1 percent of jobs. And that percentage may increase as some 82 percent of jobs lost during the current economic crisis have been ones held by men. Why the disproportion? Because women tend to be employed in education and health care industries, which are less sensitive to economic ups and downs.[44] If this trend continues, women are set to become the majority group in the workforce.

Workforce trends in the first half of the twenty-first century will be notable for three reasons: (1) changes in racial and ethnic composition, (2) an aging baby boom generation, and (3) an expanding cohort of Gen Y workers. By 2050, Hispanics will grow from today's 13 percent of the workforce to 24 percent; blacks will increase from 12 percent to 14 percent, and Asians will increase from 5 percent to 11 percent. Meanwhile, the labor force is aging. The 55-and-older age group, which currently makes up 13 percent of the workforce, will increase to 20 percent by 2014. However, labor force analysts who had predicted a mass exodus of baby boomers into retirement have pulled back somewhat on those forecasts, especially since many baby boomers lost significant personal financial resources as the economy and stock market floundered. Many baby boomers are postponing retirement until they can better afford it. Another group that's having a significant impact on today's workforce is **Gen Y**, a population group that includes individuals born from about 1978 to 1994. Gen Y has been the fastest-growing segment of the workforce—increasing from 14 percent to over 24 percent. With Gen Y now in the workforce, analysts point to the four generations that are working side-by-side in the workplace including:[45]

▶ The oldest, most experienced workers (those born before 1946)—they make up 6 percent of the workforce.
▶ The baby boomers (those born between 1946 and 1964)—they make up 41.5 percent of the workforce.
▶ Generation X (those born 1965 to 1977)—they make up almost 29 percent of the workforce.
▶ Gen Y (those born 1978 to 1994)—they make up almost 24 percent of the workforce.

workforce diversity
Ways in which people in a workforce are similar and different from one another in terms of gender, age, race, sexual orientation, ethnicity, cultural background, and physical abilities and disabilities.

Gen Y
A population group that includes individuals born from about 1978 to 1994.

How Are Organizations and Managers Adapting to a Changing Workforce?

Since organizations wouldn't be able to do what they're in business to do without employees, managers have to adapt to the changes taking place in the workforce. They're responding with work/life balance programs, contingent jobs, and recognition of generational differences.

WORK/LIFE BALANCE PROGRAMS. The typical employee in the 1960s or 1970s showed up at the workplace Monday through Friday and did his or her job in eight- or nine-hour chunks of time. The workplace and hours were clearly specified. That's not the case anymore for a large segment of the workforce. Employees are increasingly complaining that the line between work and nonwork time has blurred, creating personal conflicts and stress.[46] Several factors have contributed to this blurring between work and personal life. One is that in a world of global business, work never ends. At any time and on any day, for instance, thousands of Caterpillar employees are working somewhere in the company's facilities. The need to consult with colleagues or customers 8 or 10 time zones away means that many employees of global companies are "on call" 24 hours a day. Another factor is that communication technology allows employees to do their work at home, in their cars, or on the beach in Tahiti. Although this capability allows those in technical and professional jobs to do their work anywhere and at anytime, it means there's no escaping from work. Another factor is that as organizations have had to lay off employees during the economic downturn, "surviving" employees have had to work longer hours. It's not unusual for employees to work more than 45 hours a week, and some work more than 50. Finally, fewer families today have a single wage earner. Today's married employee is typically part of a dual-career couple, which makes it increasingly difficult for married employees to find time to fulfill commitments to home, spouse, children, parents, and friends.[47]

More and more, employees recognize that work is squeezing out their personal lives, and they're not happy about it. Today's progressive workplaces must accommodate the varied needs of a diverse workforce. In response, many organizations are offering **family-friendly benefits**, benefits that provide a wide range of scheduling options that allow employees more flexibility at work, accommodating their need for work/life balance. They've introduced programs such as on-site child care, summer day camps, flextime, job sharing, time off for school functions, telecommuting, and part-time employment. Younger people, particularly, put a higher priority on family and a lower priority on jobs and are looking for organizations that give them more work flexibility.[48]

General Mills is a progressive workplace that accommodates the varied needs of a diverse workforce. For working parents, the company provides a variety of family-friendly benefits and programs that help them balance the demands of their jobs and their children. These include flexible work schedules, benefits for birth moms and dads and for adopting parents, and backup child care and sick child care. A child care center for kids from 6 weeks to 16 months old, shown here, is available for employees who work at General Mills' international headquarters in Minneapolis.

CONTINGENT JOBS. "Companies want a workforce they can switch on and off as needed."[49] Although this quote may shock you, the truth is that the labor force already has begun shifting away from traditional full-time jobs toward a **contingent workforce**—part-time, temporary, and contract workers who are available for hire on an as-needed basis. In today's economy, many organizations have responded by converting full-time permanent jobs into contingent jobs. It's predicted that by the end of the next decade the number of contingent employees will have grown to about 40 percent of the workforce. (It's at 30 percent today.)[50] In fact, one compensation and benefits expert says that "a growing number of workers will need to structure their careers around this model."[51] That's likely to include you!

What are the implications for managers and organizations? Since contingent employees are not "employees" in the traditional sense of the word, managing them has its own set of challenges and expectations. Managers must recognize that because contingent workers lack the stability and security of permanent employees, they may not identify with the organization or be as committed or motivated. Managers may need to treat contingent workers differently in terms of practices and policies. However, with good communication and leadership, an organization's contingent employees can be just as valuable a resource to an organization as permanent employees are. Today's managers must recognize that it will be their responsibility to motivate their entire workforce, full-time and contingent, and to build their commitment to doing good work!

GENERATIONAL DIFFERENCES. Managing generational differences presents some unique challenges, especially for baby boomers and Gen Y. Conflicts and resentment can arise over issues ranging from appearance to technology and management style.

What *is* appropriate office attire? That answer may depend on who you ask, but more importantly, it depends on the type of work being done and the size of the organization. To accommodate generational differences in what is considered appropriate, the key is flexibility. For instance, a guideline might be that when an employee is not interacting with someone outside the organization, more casual wear (with some restrictions) is acceptable.

What about technology? Gen Y has grown up with ATMs, DVDs, cell phones, e-mail, texting, laptops, and the Internet. When they don't have information they need, they just enter a few keystrokes to get it. They're content to meet virtually to solve problems, while baby boomers expect important problems to be solved with in-person meetings. Baby boomers complain about Gen Y's inability to focus on one task, while Gen Yers see nothing wrong with multitasking. Again, flexibility and understanding from both is the key in working together effectively and efficiently.

Finally, what about management style? Gen Y employees want bosses who are open minded; experts in their field, even if they aren't tech savvy; organized; teachers, trainers, and mentors; not authoritarian or paternalistic; respectful of their generation; understanding of their need for work/life balance; providing constant feedback; communicating in vivid and compelling ways; and providing stimulating and novel learning experiences.[52]

Because Gen Y employees have a lot to offer organizations in terms of their knowledge, passion, and abilities, managers have to recognize and understand the behaviors of this group in order to create an environment in which work can be done efficiently, effectively, and without disruptive conflict.

How Do Organizations Make the Customer King?

Henry Ford once said his customers could have any color car they wanted—as long as it was black. In contrast, Stew Leonard, Jr., CEO of a large dairy business with stores in southern Connecticut and in New York, says there are only two rules in his business. "Rule 1—the customer is always right. Rule 2—If the customer is ever wrong, reread Rule 1."

Managers in today's organizations are being influenced by the Stew Leonards of the world. They realize that long-term success is primarily achieved by satisfying the customer, because it's the customer who ultimately pays the bills. In today's economic climate, this is even more critical as customers have become increasingly skeptical, cautious, and frugal, even though they have more choices. And, those customers are more difficult to please—demanding quicker service, higher quality, and now especially, more value for their money. Mass customization, toll-free service hotlines, e-commerce

Explain the role that managers play in creating outstanding customer service. 2.5

family-friendly benefits
Benefits that provide a wide range of scheduling options that allow employees more flexibility at work, accommodating their needs for work/life balance.

contingent workforce
Part-time, temporary, and contract workers who are available for hire on an as-needed basis.

Chef David Chang is raising the bar for customer service. At his restaurant Momofuku Ko in New York City, Chang not only cooks and plates customers' food, he also serves the food, recommends wine, confirms reservations, and takes coats. With this intense focus on customers, Chang and other young chefs are reaching for a new level of intimacy with their customers at their upscale dining establishments. Their closeness-to-the-cook services go beyond the intimacy of restaurants that offer patrons chef's tables and open kitchens.

options, and managers obsessed with quality are all responses to the concept that quality is what the customer says it is. To make this a reality, organizations and managers are relying on several activities such as creating a customer-responsive culture, continually improving quality, and reengineering work processes.

Can Organizations Improve Customer Service?

American Express recently turned Joan Weinbel's worst nightmare into a nonevent. At 10 P.M. Joan was home in New Jersey, packing for a weeklong trip, when she suddenly realized she had left her AmEx Gold Card at a restaurant in New York City earlier in the evening. The restaurant was 30 miles away. She had a flight to catch at 7:30 A.M. the next day and she wanted her card for the trip. She called American Express. The phone was quickly answered by a courteous and helpful AmEx customer service representative. He told Ms. Weinbel not to worry. He quickly asked her a few questions and told her "help was on the way." To say she was flabbergasted would be an understatement when her doorbell rang at 11:45 P.M., less than two hours after she had called AmEx. At her door was a courier with her new card. How the company was able to produce the card and get it to her so quickly still puzzles Weinbel. But she said the experience made her a customer for life.

The majority of employees today in developed countries work in service jobs. For instance, some 79 percent of the U.S. labor force is employed in service industries. In Australia, 71 percent work in service industries. In the United Kingdom, Germany, and Japan the percentages are 76, 70, and 73, respectively.[53] Examples of service jobs include technical support representatives, fast-food counter workers, sales clerks, teachers, food servers, nurses, computer repair technicians, front desk clerks, consultants, purchasing agents, credit representatives, financial planners, and bank tellers. The common characteristic of these jobs is that they require substantial interaction with an organization's customers. And because an organization can't exist without customers, management needs to ensure that employees do what it takes to please its customers.

Organizations in service industries also need to include attention to customer needs and requirements in assessing their effectiveness. Why? Because in these types of businesses, a clear chain of cause-and-effect runs from employee attitudes and behavior to customer attitudes and behavior to an organization's revenue and profits. Sears, in fact, carefully documented this chain. The company's executives found that a 5 percent improvement in employee attitudes leads to a 1.3 point increase in customer satisfaction, which in turn translates into a 0.5 percent improvement in revenue growth. More specifically, Sears found that by training employees to improve the employee-customer interaction, it was able to improve customer satisfaction by 4 percent over a 12-month period, which generated an estimated $200 million in additional revenues.[54]

Except for a few researchers' interest in customer satisfaction through improvements in quality, the field of management has generally ignored the customer. Focusing on the customer was thought to be the concern of people who study and practice marketing. But an organization's performance can be improved by showing managers how employee attitudes and behavior are associated with customer satisfaction. Many an organization has failed because its employees failed to please the customer. So management needs to create a customer-responsive culture—where employees are friendly and courteous, accessible, knowledgeable, prompt in responding to customer needs, and willing to do what's necessary to please the customer.

CREATING A CUSTOMER-RESPONSIVE CULTURE. French retailers have a well-established reputation for indifference to customers.[55] Salespeople, for instance, routinely make it clear that their phone conversations should not be interrupted. Just getting any help at all from a salesperson can be a challenge. And no one in France finds it particularly surprising that the owner of a Paris store should complain that he was unable to work on his books all morning because he kept being bothered by customers!

Most organizations today are trying hard to be un-French-like. They're attempting to create a customer-responsive culture because they recognize that it's the path to customer loyalty and long-term profitability. Companies that have created such cultures—Nordstrom, Southwest Airlines, Amazon.com, Publix Supermarkets, American Express, and L.L.Bean—have built a strong and loyal customer base and have generally outperformed their competitors in revenue growth and financial performance. Let's look at the variables that shape customer-responsive cultures and offer some suggestions that managers can follow for creating such cultures.

KEY VARIABLES SHAPING CUSTOMER-RESPONSIVE CULTURES. As shown in Exhibit 2-5, customer-responsive cultures routinely have several variables.[56] First is the type of employees themselves. Successful, service-oriented organizations hire employees who are outgoing and friendly. Second, service employees need to have the freedom to meet changing customer-service requirements. Rigid rules, procedures, and regulations inhibit an employee's ability to do this. Third, employees need to be empowered. **Empowerment** means that employees have decision discretion. In customer service, that means they can do whatever is necessary to please the customer.

Fourth is good listening skills. Employees in customer-responsive cultures have the ability to listen to and understand customers. Finally, customer-responsive cultures have employees who exhibit organizational citizenship behavior. They are conscientious in their desire to please the customer. And they're willing to take the initiative, even when it's outside their normal job requirements, to satisfy a customer's needs.

| EXHIBIT 2-5 | Shaping a Customer-Responsive Culture |

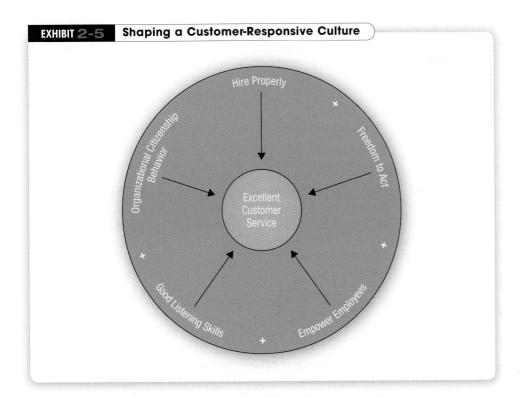

MANAGERIAL ACTIONS THAT ARE NEEDED. Managers can take a number of actions if they want to make their organization's culture more customer responsive. These actions are designed to create employees with the competence, ability, and willingness to solve customer problems as they arise.

- *Selection.* The place to start in building a customer-responsive culture is to hire service-contact people with the personality and attitudes consistent with a high service orientation. Southwest Airlines is a shining example of a company that has focused its hiring process on weeding out job candidates whose personalities aren't people friendly. Job applicants go through an extensive interview process at Southwest where company employees and executives carefully assess whether a candidate has the outgoing and fun-loving personality that it wants in all its employees.

- *Training.* Organizations that are trying to become more customer responsive don't always have the option of hiring all new employees. More typically, management is faced with the challenge of making its current employees more customer focused. In such cases, the emphasis will be on training rather than hiring. Senior executives at companies such as Best Buy, Shell, IBM, and J.P. Morgan have faced this dilemma in the past decade as they attempted to move away from their product focus. The content of these training programs will vary widely but should focus on improving product knowledge, active listening, showing patience, and displaying emotions. Additionally, even new employees who have a customer-friendly attitude may need to understand management's expectations, which means that all new service-contact people should be socialized into the organization's goals and values. Lastly, even the most customer-focused employees can lose direction every once in a while. This issue should be addressed with regular training updates in which the organization's customer-focused values are restated and reinforced.

- *Organizing.* Organization structures need to give employees more control. The primary way to increase control is to reduce rules and regulations. Employees are better able to satisfy customers when they have some control over the service encounter. So management needs to allow employees to adjust their behavior to the changing needs and requests of customers. What customers don't want to hear are responses such as "I can't handle this. You need to talk to someone else" or "I'm sorry, but that's against our company policy."

- *Empowerment.* Empowering employees is a necessary component of a customer-responsive culture because it allows service employees to make on-the-spot decisions to completely satisfy customers.

- *Leadership.* Leaders convey the organization's culture through both what they say and what they do. Effective leaders in customer-responsive cultures deliver by conveying a customer-focused vision and demonstrating by their continual behavior that they are committed to customers.

- *Evaluation.* Employee performance needs to be evaluated on such measures as how they behave or act—on criteria such as effort, commitment, teamwork, friendliness, and the ability to solve customer problems—rather than simply on the measurable outcomes they achieve.

- *Rewards.* Finally, if management wants employees to give good service, it has to reward good service. It needs to provide ongoing recognition to employees who have demonstrated extraordinary effort to please customers and who have been singled out by customers for "going the extra mile." And it needs to make pay and promotions contingent on outstanding customer service.

How Have Organizations Shown Increased Concern with Quality?

Quality management is a departure from early management theories that were based on the belief that low costs were the only road to increased productivity. Managers in both the private and public sectors continue to pursue quality. The generic term that has evolved to describe this pursuit of quality is *quality management* or **continuous improvement**. The revolution was inspired by a small group of quality experts, individuals such as the late

Joseph Juran and the late W. Edwards Deming.[57] For our discussion, we'll focus our attention primarily on Deming's work.

After finding few managers in the United States interested in his ideas, Deming went to Japan in 1950 and began advising many top Japanese managers on ways to improve their production effectiveness. Central to his management methods was the use of statistics to analyze variability in production processes. A well-managed organization, according to Deming, was one in which statistical control reduced variability and resulted in uniform quality and predictable quantity of output. Deming developed a 14-point program for transforming organizations.[58] Today, Deming's original program has been expanded into a philosophy of management that is driven by customer needs and expectations.[59] (See Exhibit 2-6.) Quality management expands the term *customer* beyond the traditional definition to include everyone involved with the organization, either internally or externally, encompassing employees and suppliers as well as the people who buy the organization's products or services. The objective is to create an organization committed to continuous improvement or, as the Japanese call it, **kaizen**.[60]

The term *quality management* may not be as popular as it was 15 years ago. As often happens with new business practices, they can become clichés. However, regardless of the terminology, the elements and the goals of quality management and continuous improvements are still essential characteristics in achieving an effective and lean workplace.[61]

When Will Managers Use Quantum Changes Rather Than Continuous Improvement?

Although continuous improvement methods are useful innovations in many organizations, they generally focus on incremental change. Such action—a constant and permanent search to make things better—is intuitively appealing. Many organizations, however, operate in an environment of rapid and dynamic change. As the elements around them change so quickly, a continuous improvement process may keep them behind the times.

The problem with a focus on continuous improvements is that it may provide a false sense of security. It may make managers feel as if they are actively doing something positive, which is somewhat true. Unfortunately, ongoing incremental change may allow managers to avoid facing up to the possibility that what the organization may really need is radical or quantum change, referred to as **work process engineering**.[62] Continuous change may also

---

EXHIBIT 2-6   Components of Continuous Improvement

1. Intense focus on the *customer*. The customer includes not only outsiders who buy the organization's products or services but also internal customers (such as shipping or accounts payable personnel) who interact with and serve others in the organization.

2. Concern for *continuous improvement*. Continuous improvement is a commitment to never being satisfied. "Very good" is not good enough. Quality can always be improved.

3. Improvement in the *quality of everything* the organization does. Continuous improvement uses a broad definition of quality. It is related not only to the final product but also to how the organization handles deliveries, how rapidly it responds to complaints, how politely the phones are answered, and the like.

4. Accurate *measurement*. Continuous improvement uses statistical techniques to measure every critical variable in the organization's operations. These are compared against standards, or benchmarks, to identify problems, trace them to their roots, and eliminate their causes.

5. *Empowerment of employees*. Continuous improvement involves the people on the line in the improvement process. Teams are widely used in continuous improvement programs as empowerment vehicles for finding and solving problems.

---

continuous improvement
An organization's commitment to continually improving the quality of a product or service.

kaizen
The Japanese term for an organization's commitment to continuous improvement.

work process engineering
Radical or quantum change in an organization.

make managers feel as if they are taking progressive action while, at the same time, avoiding having to implement quantum changes that will threaten organizational members. The incremental approach of continuous improvement, then, may be today's version of rearranging the deck chairs on the *Titanic*.

If you've been reading this chapter carefully, you may be asking yourself, "Aren't these authors contradicting what they said a few paragraphs ago about quality management?" It may appear so, but consider this: Although continuous improvement can often lead to organizational improvements, it may not always be the right approach initially. That's the case if you are producing an improved version of an outdated product. Instead, a complete overhaul might be required. Once these changes are made, then continuous improvement can have its rightful place. Let's see how this process operates.

Assume that you're the manager responsible for implementing design changes in your electronic organizer. If you take the continuous improvement approach, your frame of reference might be an electronic search capability for names and addresses, calendar of tasks, an expanded keyboard function, and the like. Your continuous improvement program may lead you to focus on innovations such as more memory, larger storage capabilities, or longer-lasting batteries. Of course, your electronic organizer may be better than the one you previously made, but is "better" enough? Compare your product with that of a competitor who reengineers the design process. To begin, your competitor poses the following question: How can we design an electronic organizer that is more useful and expandable and provides greater mobility? Starting from scratch and not being constrained by her current manufacturing process, your competitor completes her redesign with something she calls a wireless personal data assistant. Instead of larger and faster capabilities, you're now competing against a technology that may make your product obsolete.

In this theoretical example, both companies made progress. But which company do you believe made the most progress given the dynamic environment they face? Our example demonstrates why companies such as Thermos, Ryder Trucks, and Casio Computer are opting for work process engineering rather than incremental change. It is imperative in today's business environment that all managers consider the challenge of work process engineering in their organizational processes. Why? Because work process engineering can lead to major gains in cost, service, or time, as well as assist an organization in preparing to meet the challenges technology changes bring.

Now, go back and reread the chapter-opening case. This time, as you read it, think about how the managers at the resort hotel in Florida and the managers at Hilton Hotels Corporation have responded to the management environment. Think about how the changed economy, globalization, customer service, and even technology have played a role in actions they've taken and how these external forces will continue to affect how they do what they're in business to do.

Review and ② Applications

Chapter Summary

2.1 **Describe the new economy and how it's affecting the way organizations are managed.** The main characteristic of the new economy is the global economic crisis. Foreclosures, financial recession, a huge public debt, and widespread social problems from job losses are a few of its features. Also, this new economy is characterized by public anger at business leaders, which has led to a lack of trust in business. Experts believe that when the economy emerges from recession, it will be a "new" normal. The biggest change is likely to be in the role of government in financial markets and consumer protection and in increased enforcement and oversight of regulations. This new economy will affect organizations in the way they do business globally, how they deal with the expectations of society to act responsibly and ethically, how they treat their workforce, and how they deal with skeptical and demanding consumers.

2.2 **Explain globalization and its impact on organizations.** Organizations are considered global if they exchange goods and services with consumers in other countries, if they use managerial and technical employee talent from other countries, or if they use financial sources and resources outside their home country. Businesses going global are usually referred to as multinational corporations (MNCs). As an MNC, they may operate as a multidomestic corporation, a global corporation, or a transnational or borderless organization. When a business goes global, they may start with global sourcing, move to exporting or importing, use licensing or franchising, pursue a global strategic alliance, or set up a foreign subsidiary. In doing business globally, managers need to be aware of different laws and political and economic systems. But the biggest challenge is in understanding the different country cultures. Two cross-cultural frameworks that managers can use are Hofstede's and GLOBE.

2.3 **Discuss how society's expectations are influencing managers and organizations.** Society expects organizations and managers to be responsible and ethical. An organization's social involvement can be from the perspective of social obligation, social responsiveness, or social responsibility. Whether a manager behaves ethically depends on several factors including personal morality, values, personality, and experiences; the organization's culture; and the ethical issue being faced. Organizations attempt to reduce the ambiguity over what is ethical by using codes of ethics. However, managers also need to be good ethical role models in words and in actions.

2.4 **Discuss how the workforce is changing and its impact on the way organizations are managed.** The workforce continues to reflect increasing diversity. Other trends include changes in racial and ethnic composition, an aging baby boom generation, and an expanding cohort of Gen Y workers. Organizations and managers are responding with work/life balance programs, contingent jobs, and recognition of generational differences.

2.5 **Explain the role that managers play in creating outstanding customer service.** As customers have become increasingly skeptical, cautious, frugal, and more difficult to please, customer service is ever more critical. To create outstanding customer service, organizations and managers are relying on several activities such as creating a customer-responsive culture, continually improving quality, and reengineering work processes.

Understanding the Chapter

1. How is the new economy affecting what managers do? Find examples in current business periodicals of activities and practices that organizations are using. Discuss them in light of the changed management environment.

2. Describe the shifts in the workforce. What implications have these shifts created for today's managers?

3. What are the managerial implications of Hofstede's research on cultural environments? The GLOBE study?

4. How can managers help employees deal with work/life balance issues?

5. What does social responsibility mean to you personally? Do you think businesses should be socially responsible? Explain.

6. Describe the characteristics and behaviors of someone you consider to be an ethical person. How could the types of decisions and actions this person engages in be encouraged in a workplace?

7. This question was posed in an article in *USA Today*: "Is capitalism going to be the salvation of the world or the cause of its demise?" Discuss.

8. Discuss the implications of hiring contingent workers from the perspectives of the organization and the contingent worker.

Understanding Yourself

Am I Well-Suited for a Career as a Global Manager?

In today's global economy, being a manager often means being a *global* manager. But, unfortunately, not all managers are able to transfer their skills smoothly from domestic environments to global ones. Take this self-assessment to help you determine whether your skills align with those needed to succeed as a global manager.

INSTRUMENT   Indicate the extent to which you agree or disagree with each of the 14 statements in terms of how well they describe you. Use the following rating scale for your responses:

1 = Very strongly disagree

2 = Strongly disagree

3 = Disagree

4 = Neither agree or disagree

5 = Agree

6 = Strongly agree

7 = Very strongly agree

1. When working with people from other cultures, I work hard to understand their perspectives.	1 2 3 4 5 6 7
2. I have a solid understanding of my organization's products and services.	1 2 3 4 5 6 7
3. I am willing to take a stand on issues.	1 2 3 4 5 6 7
4. I have a special talent for dealing with people.	1 2 3 4 5 6 7
5. I can be depended on to tell the truth regardless of circumstances.	1 2 3 4 5 6 7
6. I am good at identifying the most important part of a complex problem or issue.	1 2 3 4 5 6 7
7. I clearly demonstrate commitment to seeing the organization succeed.	1 2 3 4 5 6 7
8. I take personal as well as business risks.	1 2 3 4 5 6 7
9. I have changed as a result of feedback from others.	1 2 3 4 5 6 7
10. I enjoy the challenge of working in countries other than my own.	1 2 3 4 5 6 7
11. I take advantage of opportunities to do new things.	1 2 3 4 5 6 7
12. I find criticism hard to take.	1 2 3 4 5 6 7
13. I seek feedback even when others are reluctant to give it.	1 2 3 4 5 6 7
14. I don't get so invested in things that I cannot change when something doesn't work.	1 2 3 4 5 6 7

SCORING KEY   To calculate your score, add up all your responses, except reverse your score for item 12.

ANALYSIS AND INTERPRETATION   This instrument has been designed to tap dimensions associated with success as a global executive. These include general intelligence, business knowledge, interpersonal skills, commitment, courage, cross-cultural competencies, and the ability to learn from experience.

Total scores will fall between 14 and 98. The higher your score, the greater your potential for success as a global manager. While the authors of this instrument provided no specific cutoffs, it seems reasonable to assume that scores of 70 or higher indicate relatively strong potential for success in a global management position.

Source: Adapted from G. M. Spreitzer, M. W. McCall Jr., and J. D. Mahoney, "Early Identification of International Executive Potential," *Journal of Applied Psychology* (February 1997), pp. 6–29.

FYIA (For Your Immediate Action)

Delaney Environmental Services

Reply   Reply All   Forward

To:	Sandy Burk, Director of Operations
From:	J. Delaney, Managing Director
Subject:	**Global Expansion**

Sandy, as we talked about last week at some length, I think it's important that DES start carefully looking at expanding its global market opportunities. We've developed a successful track record for providing environmental consulting and design services here in San Antonio, and I believe that with our experience we have a lot to offer the Latin American market, particularly in Mexico.

I would like for you to do some research into the problems we might face in moving into the Mexican market. Specifically, I would like for you to cover: (1) cultural differences we would need to consider; (2) the current currency rate of exchange and how it has changed over the last three years; and (3) any legal or political situations we need to be aware of. Since this is just an initial analysis, please keep your report to two pages or less.

CASE APPLICATION

HELD HOSTAGE

Hostage and *manager*. These are not two words that you would usually expect to hear spoken in the same breath. However, during the first few months of 2009, workers at manufacturing facilities of 3M Company (pictured, Luc Rousselet, industrial director of 3M's plant in Pithiviers, France), Sony Corporation, and Caterpillar Inc. in France have taken managers hostage. Why? To negotiate better severance packages and benefits for laid-off employees.

French workers have long been known for their aggressive and radical responses to what they feel is wrong or oppressive treatment. Says one French executive, "Protest is inscribed in the genes of French culture. In the past, peasants protested against their lords. Today the difference is that the lords are chief executives." Protesting French workers have been known to burn piles of tires in city streets or tie up traffic with caravans of farm tractors. In one instance, striking truckers blockaded roads and highways to highlight their campaign for retirement at age 55. The labor blockade worked, as the French government relented when food supplies started to run out. And the tactic of taking the boss hostage has been used previously, as well. For instance, in 1997, workers at the state-run mortgage bank Crédit Foncier de France, took their boss hostage for five days to try and prevent the bank's closing even though it had been losing money. Although kidnapping your boss isn't legal, a French sociologist who surveyed 3,000 companies in 2004 found that 18 of them had experienced an "executive detention" in the prior three years.

The actions being taken by workers, which have been peaceful and more of a symbolic protest, are in response to a continuing economic downturn. Although France isn't in any worse shape than the other big industrialized economies, the country's "strong tradition of egalitarianism triggers strong reactions when people think they are being mistreated or when better-off people appear to flaunt their wealth at a time of general hardship." At Caterpillar's French facility near Grenoble, unhappy workers first went on strike for a day. The next day, they detained the plant director and four other managers for about 24 hours. The managers were released only after the company agreed to resume talks with unions and a government mediator on "how to improve compensation for workers being laid off." The incident at Caterpillar followed others at Sony and 3M, where managers also were held captive by workers angry over being laid off. Although all the hostage-taking incidents were resolved peacefully, some analysts wonder if more violent actions may be in store especially if workers feel they have nothing to lose.

Discussion Questions

1. What's your reaction to these events? Do you think your reaction is influenced by the culture, values, and traditions of the country in which you find yourself? Explain.
2. Look at what Hofstede's and the GLOBE findings say about France. How would you explain these workers' actions given these findings?
3. We've said throughout this chapter that it's important for managers to be aware of external environmental forces. Discuss this in light of these events.
4. What might the French managers have done differently in this situation, especially prior to the point where workers felt they had to make their point by taking them hostage? Explain.
5. Do you think something like this could happen in the United States? Why or why not?

Sources: J. Marquez, "French Hostage Situations Have Some Wondering If U.S. Is Next," *Workforce Management Online,* April 3, 2009; D. Gauthier-Villars and L. Abboud, "In France, Boss Can Become a Hostage," *Wall Street Journal,* April 3, 2009, pp. B1+; L. Abboud and M. Colchester, "French Bosses Besieged as Worker Anger Rises," *Wall Street Journal,* April 1, 2009, pp. B1+; D. Gauthier-Villars, "French Business Leaders Vow to Give Up 'Abusive' Benefits," *Wall Street Journal,* October 8, 2008, p. A14; and F. Coleman, "Take A Hostage, Save Your Job," *U.S. News & World Report,* February 3, 1997, p. 43.

CHAPTER

3

Foundations of Decision Making

learning outcomes

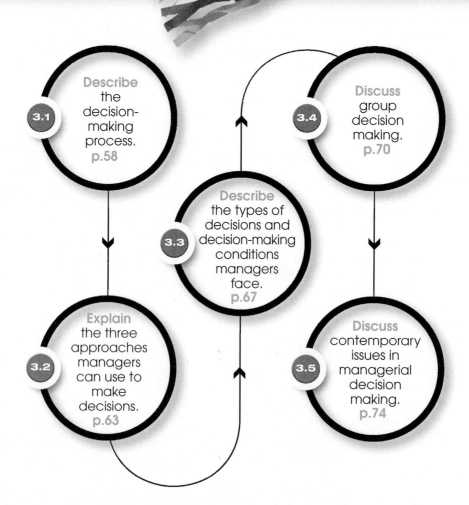

3.1 Describe the decision-making process. p.58

3.2 Explain the three approaches managers can use to make decisions. p.63

3.3 Describe the types of decisions and decision-making conditions managers face. p.67

3.4 Discuss group decision making. p.70

3.5 Discuss contemporary issues in managerial decision making. p.74

With a small year-round population, Branson, Missouri, is in a location not easily accessible by air service.[1] The city, best known for its country music, aging pop-star variety shows, and family-style attractions, also has the kinds of outdoor activities that attracted eight and a half million visitors last year, "earning it the unofficial nickname 'Vegas without the gambling.' " About 95 percent of those visitors come by car or bus. But now it's show time for a new entrant—the Branson Airport. The $155 million airport, which opened in May 2009, is an experiment that many people are watching.

The new airport is generating interest from city governments and the travel industry because it's the nation's first commercial airport built and operated as a private, for-profit business with absolutely no government funding. As one expert said, "...unpretentious little Branson Airport could have an outsize effect it if works. It could turn what now is a mostly regional tourist spot into a national destination for tourists."

Steve Peet, the airport's chief executive admits that he had no idea where Branson was in 2000. But by 2004, he was convinced there was money to be made flying tourists there. He says, "If you were ever going to think about building a private commercial airport, this would be the place to do it. How many more visitors would come here if we made it easier and affordable for them? It seemed like an incredible opportunity." So he decided to build a new commercial airport using private financing a short distance south of Branson's popular theater district. Decisions made by both Peet and Jeff Bourk (pictured), executive director of the airport, have been a big part of turning that dream into reality.

After deciding where to locate the airport, work began on constructing the 7,140-foot runway (which can accommodate most narrow-body jets) and the terminal. Despite all the major decisions, project construction went smoothly. Bourk believed that much of that was due to minimal red tape. Because the airport wasn't using federal assistance, it didn't face the restrictions that accompany taking government money. Thus, it could also pick and choose the airlines it would let in. The airport's owners offered exclusive contracts to AirTran and Sun Country on certain routes to Branson. To attract those providers, the airport agreed to not allow other competitors in. Also, the airport owners kept the airlines' operating costs low since airport employees do much of the work usually done by an airline's ground staff. Peet stated that they *want* the airlines to succeed. "We want to build real service, sustainable service." The airport earns money from landing fees (based on number of passengers, not on weight), aircraft fuel sales, a percentage of every sale at the airport's facility, and a $8.24 fee paid by the city of Branson for each arriving passenger. To reach Peet's goal of 250,000 passengers a year, the airport needs only 685 passengers (five to six planeloads) a day. He says, "What we're doing is going to work."

Making decisions, especially when there are no precedents to guide you, can't be easy. However, that doesn't mean that managers can just forget about or ignore making decisions. Rather, as the decision makers in the chapter-opening story about Branson Airport illustrate, even when decisions are difficult or complex, you gather the best information you can and just do it.

Managers make a lot of decisions—some minor and some major. The overall quality of those decisions goes a long way in determining an organization's success or failure. In this chapter, we examine the basics of decision making.

How Do Managers Make Decisions?

3.1 Describe the decision-making process.

Decision making is typically described as choosing among alternatives, but this view is overly simplistic. Why? Because decision making is a process rather than the simple act of choosing among alternatives. Exhibit 3-1 illustrates the **decision-making process** as a set of eight steps that begins with identifying a problem; it moves through selecting an alternative that can alleviate the problem and concludes with evaluating the decision's effectiveness. This process is as applicable to your decision about what you're going to do on spring break as it is to the decisions Branson Airport executives made as they got the new airport up and running. The process can also be used to describe both individual and group decisions. Let's take a closer look at the process in order to understand what each step entails.

What Defines a Decision Problem?

The decision-making process begins with the identification of a **problem** (step 1) or, more specifically, a discrepancy between an existing and a desired state of affairs.[2] Let's develop an example illustrating this point to use throughout this section. For the sake of simplicity, we'll make the example something to which most of us can relate: the decision to buy a vehicle. Take the case of a new-product manager for the Netherlands-based food company Royal Ahold. The manager spent nearly $6,000 on auto repairs over the past few years, and now the car has a blown engine. Repair estimates indicate that it is not economical to repair the car. Furthermore, convenient public transportation is unavailable.

So now we have a problem that results from the disparity between the manager's need to have a functional vehicle and the fact that her current one isn't working. Unfortunately, this example doesn't tell us much about how managers identify problems. In the real world, most problems don't come with neon signs identifying them as such. A blown engine is a clear signal to the manager that she needs a new vehicle, but few problems

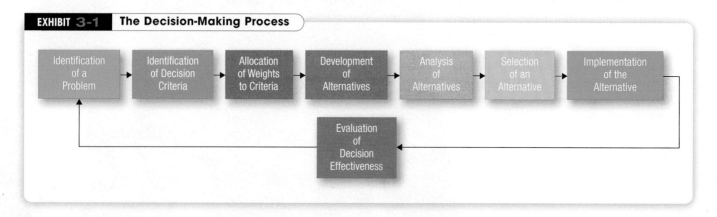

| EXHIBIT 3-1 | The Decision-Making Process |

| Identification of a Problem | Identification of Decision Criteria | Allocation of Weights to Criteria | Development of Alternatives | Analysis of Alternatives | Selection of an Alternative | Implementation of the Alternative |

Evaluation of Decision Effectiveness

are so obvious. Instead, problem identification is sub-jective. Furthermore, the manager who mistakenly solves the wrong problem perfectly is just as likely to perform poorly as the manager who fails to identify the right problem and does nothing. Problem identifi-cation is neither a simple nor an unimportant part of the decision-making process.[3] How do managers become aware they have a discrepancy? They have to make a comparison between the current state of affairs and some standard, which can be past performance, previously set goals, or the performance of some other unit within the organization or in other organizations. In our vehicle-buying example, the standard is a previ-ously set goal—a vehicle that runs.

The steps involved in buying a vehicle provide a good example of the decision-making process, which applies to both individual and group decisions. For this young man, the process starts with a problem: He needs a car to drive to a new job. He identifies decision criteria (price, color, and performance); assigns priorities to the criteria; develops, analyzes, and selects alternatives; implements the alternative; and finally, evaluates the effectiveness of his decision.

What Is Relevant in the Decision-Making Process?

Once a manager has identified a problem that needs attention, the **decision criteria** that will be important in solving the problem must be identified (step 2).

In our vehicle-buying example, the product manager assesses the factors that are relevant in her decision, which might include criteria such as price, model (two door or four door), size (compact or intermediate), manufacturer (Japanese, German, American), optional equipment (automatic transmission, side-protection impact system, leather interior), and repair records. These criteria reflect what she thinks is relevant in her decision. Every decision maker has criteria—whether explicitly stated or not—that guide his or her decision making. Note that in this step in the decision-making process, what is not identified is as important as what is. If the product manager doesn't con-sider fuel economy to be a criterion, then it will not influence her choice of vehicle. Thus, if a decision maker does not identify a particular factor in this second step, it's treated as irrelevant.

How Does the Decision Maker Weight the Criteria and Analyze Alternatives?

The criteria are not all equally important.[4] It's necessary, therefore, to allocate weights to the items listed in step 2 in order to give them their relative priority in the decision (step 3). A simple approach is to give the most important criterion a weight of 10 and then assign weights to the rest against that standard. Thus, in contrast to a criterion that you gave a 5, the highest-rated factor would be twice as important. The idea is to use your personal preferences to assign priorities to the relevant criteria in your decision as well as to indicate their degree of importance by assigning a weight to each. Exhibit 3-2 lists the criteria and weights that our manager developed for her vehicle replacement decision. Price is the most important criterion in her decision, with performance and handling having low weights.

Then the decision maker lists the alternatives that could succeed in resolving the problem (step 4). No attempt is made in this step to appraise these alternatives, only to list them.[5] Let's assume that our manager has identified 12 vehicles as viable choices: Jeep Compass, Ford Focus, Mercedes C230, Pontiac G6, Mazda CX7,

---

decision-making process
A set of eight steps that includes identifying a problem, selecting a solution, and evaluating the effectiveness of the solution.

problem
A discrepancy between an existing and a desired state of affairs.

decision criteria
Factors that are relevant in a decision.

EXHIBIT 3-2 **Important Criteria and Weights in a Car-Buying Decision**

CRITERION	WEIGHT
Price	10
Interior comfort	8
Durability	5
Repair record	5
Performance	3
Handling	1

Dodge Durango, Volvo S60, Isuzu Ascender, BMW 335, Audi A6, Toyota Camry, and Volkswagen Passat.

Once the alternatives have been identified, the decision maker must critically analyze each one (step 5). Each alternative is evaluated by appraising it against the criteria. The strengths and weaknesses of each alternative become evident as they're compared with the criteria and weights established in steps 2 and 3. Exhibit 3-3 shows the assessed values that the manager put on each of her 12 alternatives after she had test driven each vehicle. Keep in mind that the ratings given the 12 vehicles shown in Exhibit 3-3 are based on the assessment made by the new-product manager. Again, we're using a 1-to-10 scale. Some assessments can be achieved in a relatively objective fashion. For instance, the purchase price represents the best price the manager can get from local dealers, and consumer magazines report data from owners on frequency of repairs. However, the assessment of handling is clearly a personal judgment. The point is that most decisions contain judgments. They're reflected in the criteria chosen in step 2, the weights given to the criteria, and the evaluation of alternatives. The influence of personal judgment explains why two vehicle buyers with the same amount of money may look at two totally distinct sets of alternatives or even look at the same alternatives and rate them differently.

Exhibit 3-3 is only an assessment of the 12 alternatives against the decision criteria; it does not reflect the weighting done in step 3. If one choice had scored 10 on every criterion, you wouldn't need to consider the weights. Similarly, if the weights were all equal, you could evaluate each alternative merely by summing up the appropriate lines in Exhibit 3-3.

EXHIBIT 3-3 **Assessment of Possible Car Alternatives**

ALTERNATIVES	INITIAL PRICE	INTERIOR COMFORT	DURABILITY	REPAIR RECORD	PERFORMANCE	HANDLING	TOTAL
Jeep Compass	2	10	8	7	5	5	37
Ford Focus	9	6	5	6	8	6	40
Mercedes C230	8	5	6	6	4	6	35
Pontiac G6	9	5	6	7	6	5	38
Mazda CX7	5	6	9	10	7	7	44
Dodge Durango	10	5	6	4	3	3	31
Volvo S60	4	8	7	6	8	9	42
Isuzu Ascender	7	6	8	6	5	6	38
BMW 335	9	7	6	4	4	7	37
Audi A6	5	8	5	4	10	10	42
Toyota Camry	6	5	10	10	6	6	43
Volkswagen Passat	8	6	6	5	7	8	40

| EXHIBIT 3-4 | Evaluation of Car Alternatives: Assessment Criteria × Criteria Weight |

ALTERNATIVES	INITIAL PRICE [10]		INTERIOR COMFORT [8]		DURABILITY [5]		REPAIR RECORD [5]		PERFORMANCE [3]		HANDLING [1]		TOTAL
Jeep Compass	2	20	10	80	8	40	7	35	5	15	5	5	195
Ford Focus	9	90	6	48	5	25	6	30	8	24	6	6	223
Mercedes C230	8	80	5	40	6	30	6	30	4	12	6	6	198
Pontiac G6	9	90	5	40	6	30	7	35	6	18	5	5	218
Mazda CX7	5	50	6	48	9	45	10	50	7	21	7	7	221
Dodge Durango	10	100	5	40	6	30	4	20	3	9	3	3	202
Volvo S60	4	40	8	64	7	35	6	30	8	24	9	9	202
Isuzu Ascender	7	70	6	48	8	40	6	30	5	15	6	6	209
BMW 335	9	90	7	56	6	30	4	20	4	12	7	7	215
Audi A6	5	50	8	64	5	25	4	20	10	30	10	10	199
Toyota Camry	6	60	5	40	10	50	10	50	6	18	6	6	224
Volkswagen Passat	8	80	6	48	6	30	5	25	7	21	8	8	212

For instance, the Pontiac G6 would have a score of 38, and the Toyota Camry a score of 43. If you multiply each alternative assessment against its weight, you get the figures in Exhibit 3-4. For instance, the Isuzu Ascender scored a 40 on durability, which was determined by multiplying the weight given to durability [5] by the manager's appraisal of Isuzu on this criterion [8]. The sum of these scores represents an evaluation of each alternative against the previously established criteria and weights. Notice that the weighting of the criteria has changed the ranking of alternatives in our example. The Mazda CX7, for example, has gone from first to third. From our analysis, both initial price and interior comfort worked against the Mazda.

What Determines the Best Choice?

Step 6 is the critical act of choosing the best alternative from among those assessed. Since we determined all the pertinent factors in the decision, weighted them appropriately, and identified the viable alternatives, we merely have to choose the alternative that generated the highest score in step 5. In our vehicle example (Exhibit 3-4), the decision maker would choose the Toyota Camry. On the basis of the criteria identified, the weights given to the criteria, and the decision maker's assessment of each vehicle's achievement on the criteria, the Toyota scored highest [224 points] and, thus, became the best alternative.

What Happens in Decision Implementation?

Although the choice process is completed in the previous step, the decision may still fail if it is not implemented properly (step 7). Therefore, this step is concerned with putting the decision into action. **Decision implementation** includes conveying the decision to those affected and getting their commitment to it.[6] As we'll demonstrate later in this chapter, groups or committees can help a manager achieve commitment. The people who must carry out a decision are most likely to enthusiastically endorse the outcome if they participate in the decision-making process.

decision implementation
Putting a decision into action.

What Is the Last Step in the Decision Process?

In the last step in the decision-making process (step 8) managers appraise the result of the decision to see whether it has corrected the problem. Did the alternative chosen in step 6 and implemented in step 7 accomplish the desired result? The evaluation of the results of decisions is detailed in Chapter 13 where we will look at the control function.

What Common Errors Are Committed in the Decision-Making Process?

When managers make decisions, they not only use their own particular style, but may use "rules of thumb" or **heuristics**, to simplify their decision making.[7] Rules of thumb can be useful because they help make sense of complex, uncertain, and ambiguous information. Even though managers may use rules of thumb, that doesn't mean those rules are reliable. Why? Because they may lead to errors and biases in processing and evaluating information. Exhibit 3-5 identifies 12 common decision errors and biases that managers make. Let's look at each.[8]

When decision makers tend to think they know more than they do or hold unrealistically positive views of themselves and their performance, they're exhibiting the *overconfidence bias*. The *immediate gratification bias* describes decision makers who tend to want immediate rewards and to avoid immediate costs. For these individuals, decision choices that provide quick payoffs are more appealing than those in the future. The *anchoring effect* describes when decision makers fixate on initial information as a starting point and then, once set, fail to adequately adjust for subsequent information. First impressions, ideas, prices, and estimates carry unwarranted weight relative to information received later. When decision makers selectively organize and interpret events based on their biased perceptions, they're using the *selective perception bias*. This influences the information they pay attention to, the problems they identify, and the alternatives they develop. Decision makers who seek out information that reaffirms their past choices and discount information that contradicts past judgments exhibit the *confirmation bias*. These people tend to accept at face value information that confirms their preconceived views and are critical and skeptical of information that challenges

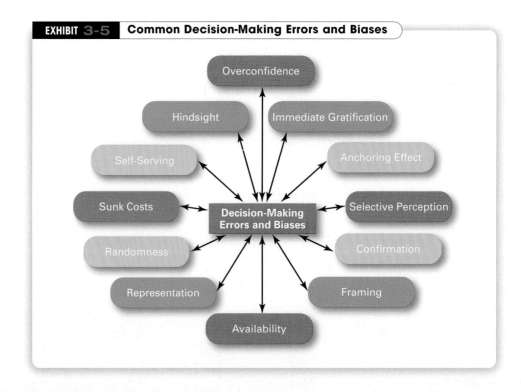

EXHIBIT 3-5 | **Common Decision-Making Errors and Biases**

these views. The *framing bias* is when decision makers select and highlight certain aspects of a situation while excluding others. By drawing attention to specific aspects of a situation and highlighting them, while at the same time downplaying or omitting other aspects, they distort what they see and create incorrect reference points. The *availability bias* is when decisions makers tend to remember events that are the most recent and vivid in their memory. The result? It distorts their ability to recall events in an objective manner and results in distorted judgments and probability estimates. When decision makers assess the likelihood of an event based on how closely it resembles other events or sets of events, that's the *representation bias*. Managers exhibiting this bias draw analogies and see identical situations where they don't exist. The *randomness bias* describes when decision makers try to create meaning out of random events. They

do this because most decision makers have difficulty dealing with chance even though random events happen to everyone and there's nothing that can be done to predict them. The *sunk costs error* is when decision makers forget that current choices can't correct the past. They incorrectly fixate on past expenditures of time, money, or effort in assessing choices rather than on future consequences. Instead of ignoring sunk costs, they can't forget them. Decision makers who are quick to take credit for their successes and to blame failure on outside factors are exhibiting the *self-serving bias*. Finally, the *hindsight bias* is the tendency for decision makers to falsely believe that they would have accurately predicted the outcome of an event once that outcome is actually known.

Like most managers, Carol Bartz, CEO of Yahoo!, Inc., makes decisions within bounded rationality. When she assumed the top job at Yahoo!, Bartz faced the problem of a slump in sales following years of rapid growth. She decided to begin her revitalization plan for Yahoo! by improving the firm's internal functions such as streamlining the management structure, bringing a disciplined approach to product management, and closing down underperforming products like online storage site Yahoo! Briefcase. To make sure that Yahoo! develops products customers want, Bartz formed a Customer Advocacy Group for soliciting direct input and feedback from customers.

Managers can avoid the negative effects of these decision errors and biases by being aware of them and then not using them! Beyond that, managers also should pay attention to "how" they make decisions and try to identify the heuristics they typically use and critically evaluate how appropriate those are. Finally, managers might want to ask those around them to help identify weaknesses in their decision-making style and try to improve on them.

What Are Three Approaches Managers Can Use to Make Decisions?

Explain the three approaches managers can use to make decisions.

3.2

Although everyone in an organization makes decisions, decision making is particularly important to managers. As Exhibit 3-6 shows, it's part of all four managerial functions. In fact, that's why we say that decision making is the essence of management.[9] And that's why managers—as they plan, organize, lead, and control—are called *decision makers*.

The fact that almost everything a manager does involves making decisions doesn't mean that decisions are always time-consuming, complex, or evident to an outside observer. Most decision making is routine. Every day of the year you make a decision about what to eat for dinner. It's no big deal. You've made the decision thousands of times before. It's a pretty simple decision and can usually be handled quickly. It's the type of decision you almost forget *is* a decision. And managers also make dozens of these routine

heuristics
Judgmental shortcuts or "rules of thumb" used to simplify decision making.

| EXHIBIT 3-6 | Decisions Managers May Make |

PLANNING

- What are the organization's long-term objectives?
- What strategies will best achieve those objectives?
- What should the organization's short-term objectives be?
- How difficult should individual goals be?

ORGANIZING

- How many employees should I have report directly to me?
- How much centralization should there be in the organization?
- How should jobs be designed?
- When should the organization implement a different structure?

LEADING

- How do I handle employees who appear to be low in motivation?
- What is the most effective leadership style in a given situation?
- How will a specific change affect worker productivity?
- When is the right time to stimulate conflict?

CONTROLLING

- What activities in the organization need to be controlled?
- How should those activities be controlled?
- When is a performance deviation significant?
- What type of management information system should the organization have?

---

decisions every day, such as, for example, which employee will work what shift next week, what information should be included in a report, or how to resolve a customer's complaint. Keep in mind that even though a decision seems easy or has been faced by a manager a number of times before, it still is a decision. Let's look at three perspectives on how managers make decisions.

What Is the Rational Model of Decision Making?

When Hewlett-Packard (HP) acquired Compaq, the company did no research on how customers viewed Compaq products until "months after then-CEO Carly Fiorina publicly announced the deal and privately warned her top management team that she didn't want to hear any dissent pertaining to the acquisition."[10] By the time they discovered that customers perceived Compaq products as inferior—just the opposite of what customers felt about HP products—it was too late. HP's performance suffered and Fiorina lost her job.

We assume that managers' decision making will be **rational**; that is, they'll make logical and consistent choices to maximize value.[11] After all, managers have all sorts of tools and techniques to help them be rational decision makers. (See the "Technology and the Manager's Job" box for additional information.) But as the HP example illustrates, managers aren't always rational. What does it mean to be a "rational" decision maker?

A rational decision maker would be fully objective and logical. The problem faced would be clear and unambiguous, and the decision maker would have a clear and specific goal and know all possible alternatives and consequences. Finally, making decisions rationally would consistently lead to selecting the alternative that maximizes the likelihood of achieving that goal. These assumptions apply to any decision—personal or managerial. However, for managerial decision making, we need to add one additional assumption— decisions are made in the best interests of the organization. These assumptions of rationality aren't very realistic, but the next concept can help explain how most decisions get made in organizations.

TECHNOLOGY AND THE MANAGER'S JOB

MAKING BETTER DECISIONS WITH TECHNOLOGY

Information technology is providing managers with a wealth of decision-making support, including expert systems, neural networks, groupware, and specific problem-solving software.[12] Expert systems use software programs to encode the relevant experience of an expert and allow a system to act like that expert in analyzing and solving ill-structured problems. The essence of expert systems is that (1) they use specialized knowledge about a particular problem area rather than general knowledge that would apply to all problems, (2) they use qualitative reasoning rather than numerical calculations, and (3) they perform at a level of competence that is higher than that of nonexpert humans. They guide users through problems by asking them a set of sequential questions about the situation and drawing conclusions based on the answers given. The conclusions are based on programmed rules that have been modeled on the actual reasoning processes of experts who have confronted similar problems before. Once in place, these systems allow employees and lower-level managers to make high-quality decisions that previously could have been made only by senior managers.

Neural networks are the next step beyond expert systems. They use computer software to imitate the structure of brain cells and connections among them. Sophisticated robotics use neural networks for their intelligence. Neural networks are able to distinguish patterns and trends too subtle or complex for human beings. For instance, people can't easily assimilate more than two or three variables at once, but neural networks can perceive correlations among hundreds of variables. As a result, they can perform many operations simultaneously, recognizing patterns, making associations, generalizing about problems they haven't been exposed to before, and learning through experience. For instance, most banks today use neural networks to flag potential credit card fraud. In the past they relied on expert systems to track millions of credit card transactions, but these earlier systems could look at only a few factors, such as the size of a transaction. Consequently, thousands of potential defrauding incidents were "flagged," most of which were false positives. Now with neural networks, significantly fewer numbers of cases are being identified as problematic—and it's more likely now that the majority of those identified will be actual cases of fraud. Furthermore, with the neural network system, fraudulent activities on a credit card can be uncovered in a matter of hours, rather than the two to three days it took prior to the implementation of neural networks. This is just one example of the power of IT to enhance an organization's—and its managers'—decision-making capabilities.

What Is Bounded Rationality?

Despite the unrealistic assumptions, managers are expected to act rationally when making decisions.[13] They understand that "good" decision makers are supposed to do certain things and exhibit good decision-making behaviors as they identify problems, consider alternatives, gather information, and act decisively but prudently. When they do so, they show others that they're competent and that their decisions are the result of intelligent deliberation. However, a more realistic approach to describing how managers make decisions is the concept of **bounded rationality**, which says that managers make decisions rationally, but are limited (bounded) by their ability to process information.[14] Because they can't possibly analyze all information on all alternatives, managers **satisfice**, rather than maximize. That is, they accept solutions that are "good enough." They're being rational within the limits (bounds) of their ability to process information. Let's look at an example.

Suppose that you're a finance major and upon graduation you want a job, preferably as a personal financial planner, with a minimum salary of $42,000 and within a

---

rational decision making
Describes choices that are consistent and value-maximizing within specified constraints.

bounded rationality
Making decisions that are rational within the limits of a manager's ability to process information.

satisfice
Accepting solutions that are "good enough."

From the Past to the Present

Herbert A. Simon, who won a Nobel Prize in economics for his work on decision making, was primarily concerned with how people use logic and psychology to make choices.[15] He proposed that individuals were limited in their ability to "grasp the present and anticipate the future," and this bounded rationality made it difficult for them to "achieve the best possible decisions." Thus, people made "good enough" or "satisficing" choices. He went on to describe all administrative activity as group activity in which an organization took some decision-making autonomy from the individual and substituted it for an organizational decision-making process.

Simon believed that such a process was necessary since it was impossible for any single individual to achieve any "high degree of objective rationality."

Simon's important contributions to management thinking came through his belief that to study and understand organizations meant studying the complex network of decisional processes that were inherent. His work in bounded rationality helps us make sense of how managers can behave rationally and still make satisfactory decisions, even given the limits of their capacity to process information.

---

hundred miles of your hometown. You accept a job offer as a business credit analyst—not exactly a personal financial planner but still in the finance field—at a bank 50 miles from home at a starting salary of $38,000. If you had done a more comprehensive job search, you would have discovered a job in personal financial planning at a trust company only 25 miles from your hometown and starting at a salary of $43,000. You weren't a perfectly rational decision maker because you didn't maximize your decision by searching all possible alternatives and then choosing the best. But because the first job offer was satisfactory (or "good enough"), you behaved in a bounded rationality manner by accepting it.

Most decisions that managers make don't fit the assumptions of perfect rationality, so they satisfice. However, keep in mind that their decision making is also likely influenced by the organization's culture, internal politics, power considerations, and by a phenomenon called **escalation of commitment**, which is an increased commitment to a previous decision despite evidence that it may have been wrong.[16] The *Challenger* space shuttle disaster is often used as an example of escalation of commitment. Decision makers chose to launch the shuttle that day even though the decision was questioned by several individuals who believed that it was a bad one. Why would decision makers escalate commitment to a bad decision? Because they don't want to admit that their initial decision may have been flawed. Rather than search for new alternatives, they simply increase their commitment to the original solution.

What Role Does Intuition Play in Managerial Decision Making?

When managers at stapler-maker Swingline saw the company's market share declining, they used a logical scientific approach to address the issue. For three years, they exhaustively researched stapler users before deciding what new products to develop. However, at Accentra, Inc., founder Todd Moses used a more intuitive decision approach to come up with his line of unique PaperPro staplers.[17]

Like Todd Moses, managers often use their intuition to help their decision making. What is **intuitive decision making**? It's making decisions on the basis of experience, feelings, and accumulated judgment. It's been described as "unconscious reasoning."[18] Researchers studying managers' use of intuitive decision making have identified five different aspects of intuition, which are described in Exhibit 3-7.[19] How common is intuitive decision making? One survey found that almost half of the executives surveyed "used intuition more often than formal analysis to run their companies."[20]

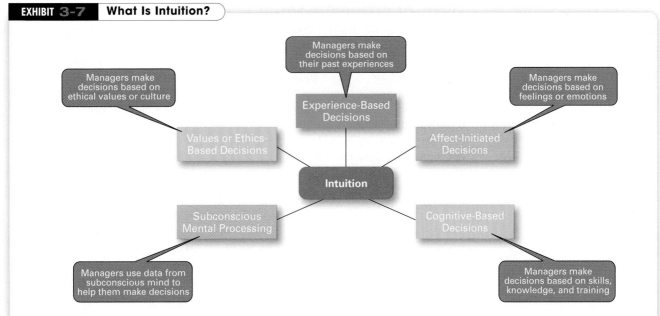

EXHIBIT 3-7 **What Is Intuition?**

Sources: Based on "Exploring Intuition and Its Role in Managerial Decision Making," *Academy of Management Review* (January 2007), pp. 33–54; M. H. Bazerman and D. Chugh, "Decisions Without Blinders," *Harvard Business Review* (January 2006), pp. 88–97; C. C. Miller and R. D. Ireland, "Intuition in Strategic Decision Making: Friend or Foe in the Fast-Paced 21st Century," *Academy of Management Executive* (February 2005), pp. 19–30; E. Sadler-Smith and E. Shefy, "The Intuitive Executive: Understanding and Applying 'Gut Feel' in Decision-Making," *Academy of Management Executive* (November 2004), pp. 76–91; L. A. Burke and J. K. Miller, "Taking the Mystery Out of Intuitive Decision Making, *Academy of Management Executive* (October 1999), pp. 91–99; and W. H. Agor, "The Logic of Intuition: How Top Executives Make Important Decisions," *Organizational Dynamics* (Winter 1986), pp. 5–18.

Intuitive decision making can complement both bounded rationality and rational decision making.[21] First of all, a manager who has had experience with a similar type of problem or situation often can act quickly with what appears to be limited information because of that past experience. In addition, a recent study found that individuals who experienced intense feelings and emotions when making decisions actually achieved higher decision-making performance, especially when they understood their feelings as they were making decisions. The old belief that managers should ignore emotions when making decisions may not be the best advice.[22]

What Types of Decisions and Decision-Making Conditions Do Managers Face?

The types of problems managers face in decision-making situations often determine how a problem is treated. In this section, we present a categorization scheme for problems and for types of decisions. Then we show how the type of decision making a manager uses should reflect the characteristics of the problem.

Describe the types of decisions and decision-making conditions managers face.

3.3

escalation of commitment
An increased commitment to a previous decision despite evidence that it may have been a poor decision.

intuitive decision making
Making decisions on the basis of experience, feelings, and accumulated judgment.

How Do Problems Differ?

Some problems are straightforward. The goal of the decision maker is clear, the problem familiar, and information about the problem easily defined and complete. Examples might include a supplier's tardiness with an important delivery, a customer's wanting to return an Internet purchase, a news program team's having to respond to an unexpected and fast-breaking event, or a university's handling of a student who is applying for financial aid. Such situations are called **structured problems**. They align closely with the assumptions underlying perfect rationality.

Many situations faced by managers, however, are **unstructured problems**. They are new or unusual. Information about such problems is ambiguous or incomplete. Examples of unstructured problems include the decision to enter a new market segment, to hire an architect to design a new office park, or to merge two organizations. So, too, is the decision to invest in a new, unproven technology.

How Does a Manager Make Programmed Decisions?

Just as problems can be divided into two categories, so, too, can decisions. Programmed, or routine, decision making is the most efficient way to handle structured problems. However, when problems are unstructured, managers must rely on nonprogrammed decision making in order to develop unique solutions.

An auto mechanic damages a customer's rim while changing a tire. What does the manager do? Because the company probably has a standardized method for handling this type of problem, it is considered a **programmed decision**. For example, the manager may replace the rim at the company's expense. Decisions are programmed to the extent that they are repetitive and routine and to the extent that a specific approach has been worked out for handling them. Because the problem is well structured, the manager does not have to go to the trouble and expense of an involved decision process. Programmed decision making is relatively simple and tends to rely heavily on previous solutions. The develop-the-alternatives stage in the decision-making process is either nonexistent or given little attention. Why? Because once the structured problem is defined, its solution is usually self-evident or at least reduced to only a few alternatives that are familiar and that have proved successful in the past. In many cases, programmed decision making becomes decision making by precedent. Managers simply do what they and others have done previously in the same situation. The damaged rim does not require the manager to identify and weight decision criteria or develop a long list of possible solutions. Rather, the manager falls back on a systematic procedure, rule, or policy.

Netflix founder and CEO Reed Hastings made a nonprogrammed decision that changed the course of his company—and the movie-rental business. Hastings originally launched Netflix as a movie rental by mail firm that operated much like Blockbuster. While some customers liked the concept, Hastings admitted it wasn't very popular. So he decided to try a more radical approach of a subscription-based service. Hastings' new strategy resulted in Netflix becoming the world's largest online movie rental service with more than 10 million subscribers.

PROCEDURES. A **procedure** is a series of interrelated sequential steps that a manager can use when responding to a well-structured problem. The only real difficulty is identifying the problem. Once the problem is clear, so is the procedure. For instance, a purchasing manager receives a request from computing services for licensing arrangements to install 250 copies of Norton Antivirus Software. The purchasing manager knows that a definite procedure is in place for handling this decision. Has the requisition been properly filled out and approved? If not, one can send the requisition back with a note explaining what is deficient. If the request is complete, the approximate costs are estimated. If the total exceeds $8,500, three bids must be obtained. If the total is $8,500 or less, only one vendor need be identified and the order placed. The decision-making process is merely the execution of a simple series of sequential steps.

RULES. A **rule** is an explicit statement that tells a manager what he or she ought—or ought not—to do. Rules are frequently used by managers who confront a structured problem because they're simple to follow and ensure consistency. In the preceding example, the $8,500 cutoff rule simplifies the purchasing manager's decision about when to use multiple bids.

POLICIES. A third guide for making programmed decisions is a policy. It provides guidelines to channel a manager's thinking in a specific direction. The statement that "we promote from within, whenever possible" is an example of a policy. In contrast to a rule, a policy establishes parameters for the decision maker rather than specifically stating what should or should not be done. It's at this point that one's ethical standards will come into play. As an analogy, think of the Ten Commandments as rules and the U.S. Constitution as policy. The latter requires judgment and interpretation; the former do not.

How Do Nonprogrammed Decisions Differ from Programmed Decisions?

Examples of **nonprogrammed decisions** include deciding whether to acquire another organization, deciding which global markets offer the most potential, or deciding whether to sell off an unprofitable division. Such decisions are unique and nonrecurring. When a manager confronts an unstructured problem, no cut-and-dried solution is available. A custom-made, nonprogrammed response is required.

The creation of a new organizational strategy is a nonprogrammed decision. This decision is different from previous organizational decisions because the issue is new; a different set of environmental factors exists, and other conditions have changed. For example, Amazon.com's Jeff Bezos's strategy to "get big fast" helped the company grow tremendously. But this strategy came at a cost—perennial financial losses. To turn a profit, Bezos made decisions regarding "sorting orders, anticipating demand, more efficient shipping, foreign partnerships, and opening a marketplace allowing other sellers to sell their books at Amazon." As a result, for the first time in company history, Amazon.com earned a profit.[24]

How Are Problems, Types of Decisions, and Organizational Level Integrated?

Exhibit 3-8 describes the relationship among types of problems, types of decisions, and level in the organization. Structured problems are responded to with programmed decision making. Unstructured problems require nonprogrammed decision making. Lower-level

EXHIBIT 3-8 Types of Problems, Types of Decisions, and Organizational Level

Unstructured ↑ Type of Problem ↓ Structured

Nonprogrammed Decisions

Programmed Decisions

Top ↑ Level in Organization ↓ Lower

structured problem
A straightforward, familiar, and easily defined problem.

unstructured problem
A problem that is new or unusual for which information is ambiguous or incomplete.

programmed decision
A repetitive decision that can be handled using a routine approach.

procedure
A series of interrelated, sequential steps used to respond to a structured problem.

rule
An explicit statement that tells employees what can or cannot be done.

policy
A guideline for making decisions.

nonprogrammed decision
A unique and nonrecurring decision that requires a custom-made solution.

managers essentially confront familiar and repetitive problems; therefore, they most typically rely on programmed decisions such as standard operating procedures. However, the problems confronting managers are likely to become less structured as they move up the organizational hierarchy. Why? Because lower-level managers handle the routine decisions themselves and pass upward only decisions that they find unique or difficult. Similarly, managers pass down routine decisions to their employees in order to spend their time on more problematic issues.

Few managerial decisions in the real world are either fully programmed or fully nonprogrammed. Most decisions fall somewhere in between. Few programmed decisions are designed to eliminate individual judgment completely. At the other extreme, even the most unusual situation requiring a nonprogrammed decision can be helped by programmed routines. A final point on this topic is that organizational efficiency is facilitated by programmed decision making—a fact that may explain its wide popularity. Whenever possible, management decisions are likely to be programmed. Obviously, this approach isn't too realistic at the top of the organization, because most of the problems that top-level managers confront are of a nonrecurring nature. However, strong economic incentives motivate them to create policies, standard operating procedures, and rules to guide other lower-level managers.

Programmed decisions minimize the need for managers to exercise discretion. This factor is important because discretion costs money. The more nonprogrammed decision making a manager is required to do, the greater the judgment needed. Because sound judgment is an uncommon quality, it costs more to acquire the services of managers who possess it.

What Decision-Making Conditions Do Managers Face?

When making decisions, managers may face three different conditions: certainty, risk, and uncertainty. Let's look at the characteristics of each.

The ideal situation for making decisions is one of **certainty**, which is a situation where a manager can make accurate decisions because the outcome of every alternative is known. For example, when North Dakota's state treasurer decides where to deposit excess state funds, he knows exactly the interest rate being offered by each bank and the amount that will be earned on the funds. He is certain about the outcomes of each alternative. As you might expect, most managerial decisions aren't like this.

A far more common situation is one of **risk**, conditions in which the decision maker is able to estimate the likelihood of certain outcomes. Under risk, managers have historical data from past personal experiences or secondary information, which lets them assign probabilities to different alternatives.

What happens if you face a decision where you're not certain about the outcomes and can't even make reasonable probability estimates? We call this condition **uncertainty**. Managers do face decision-making situations of uncertainty. Under these conditions, the choice of alternative is influenced by the limited amount of available information and by the psychological orientation of the decision maker.

How Do Groups Make Decisions?

3.4 Discuss group decision making.

Do managers make a lot of decisions in groups? You bet they do! Many decisions in organizations, especially important decisions that have far-reaching effects on organizational activities and personnel, are typically made in groups. It's a rare organization that doesn't at some time use committees, task forces, review panels, work teams, or similar groups as vehicles for making decisions. Why? In many cases, these groups represent the people who will be most affected by the decisions being made. Because of their expertise, these people are often best qualified to make decisions that affect them.

Studies tell us that managers spend a significant portion of their time in meetings. Undoubtedly, a large portion of that time is involved with defining problems, arriving at solutions to those problems, and determining the means for implementing the solutions. It's possible, in fact, for groups to be assigned any of the eight steps in the decision-making process.

What Are the Advantages of Group Decision Making?

Individual and group decisions have their own set of strengths. Neither is ideal for all situations. Let's begin by reviewing the advantages that group decisions have over individual decisions.

Group decisions provide more complete information than do individual ones.[25] There is often truth to the saying that two heads are better than one. A group will bring a diversity of experiences and perspectives to the decision process that an individual acting alone cannot.[26] Groups also generate more alternatives. Because groups have a greater quantity and diversity of information, they can identify more alternatives than can an individual. Quantity and diversity of information are greatest when group members represent different specialties. Furthermore, group decision making increases acceptance of a solution.[27] Many decisions fail after the final choice has been made because people do not accept the solution. However, if the people who will be affected by a certain solution, and who will help implement it, participate in the decision they will be more likely to accept the decision and encourage others to accept it. And, finally, this process increases legitimacy. The group decision-making process is consistent with democratic ideals; therefore, decisions made by groups may be perceived as more legitimate than decisions made by a single person. The fact that the individual decision maker has complete power and has not consulted others can create a perception that a decision was made autocratically and arbitrarily.

MANAGING DIVERSITY | The Value of Diversity in Decision Making

Have you decided what your major is going to be? How did you decide? Do you feel your decision is a good one? Is there anything you could have done differently to make sure that your decision was the best one?[28]

Making good decisions is tough! Managers continuously make decisions—for instance, developing new products, establishing weekly or monthly goals, implementing an advertising campaign, reassigning an employee to a different work group, resolving a customer's complaint, or purchasing new laptops for sales reps. One important suggestion for making better decisions is to tap into the diversity of the work group. Drawing upon diverse employees can prove valuable to a manager's decision making. Why? Diverse employees can provide fresh perspectives on issues. They can offer differing interpretations on how a problem is defined and may be more open to trying new ideas. Diverse employees can be more creative in generating alternatives and more flexible in resolving issues. And getting input from diverse sources increases the likelihood that creative and unique solutions will be generated.

Even though diversity in decision making can be valuable, there are drawbacks. The lack of a common perspective usually means that more time is spent discussing the issues. Communication may be a problem particularly if language barriers are present. In addition, seeking out diverse opinions can make the decision-making process more complex, confusing, and ambiguous. And with multiple perspectives on the decision, it may be difficult to reach a single agreement or to agree on specific actions. Although these drawbacks are valid concerns, the value of diversity in decision making outweighs the potential disadvantages.

Now, about that decision on a major. Did you ask others for their opinions? Did you seek out advice from professors, family members, friends, or coworkers? Getting diverse perspectives on an important decision like this could help you make the best decision! Managers also should consider the value to be gained from diversity in decision making.

What Are the Disadvantages of Group Decision Making?

If groups are so good, how did the phrase "a camel is a racehorse put together by a committee" become so popular? The answer, of course, is that group decisions are not without their drawbacks. First, they're *time-consuming*. It takes time to assemble a group. In addition, the interaction that takes place once the group is in place is frequently inefficient. Groups almost always take more time to reach a solution than an individual would take to make the decision alone. They may also be subject to *minority domination*, where members of a group are never perfectly equal.[29] They may differ in rank in the organization, experience, knowledge about the problem, influence on other members, verbal skills, assertiveness, and the like. This imbalance creates the opportunity for one or more members to dominate others in the group. A minority that dominates a group frequently has an undue influence on the final decision.

Another problem focuses on the *pressures to conform* in groups. For instance, have you ever been in a situation in which several people were sitting around discussing a particular item and you had something to say that ran contrary to the consensus views of the group, but you remained silent? Were you surprised to learn later that others shared your views and also had remained silent? What you experienced is what Irving Janis termed **groupthink**.[30] In this form of conformity, group members withhold deviant, minority, or unpopular views in order to give the appearance of agreement. As a result, groupthink undermines critical thinking in the group and eventually harms the quality of the final decision. And, finally, *ambiguous responsibility* can become a problem. Group members share responsibility, but who is actually responsible for the final outcome?[31] In an individual decision, it's clear who is responsible. In a group decision, the responsibility of any single member is watered down.

Groupthink applies to a situation in which a group's ability to appraise alternatives objectively and arrive at a quality decision is jeopardized. Because of pressures for conformity, groups often deter individuals from critically appraising unusual, minority, or unpopular views. Consequently, an individual's mental efficiency, reality testing, and moral judgment deteriorate. How does groupthink occur? The following are examples of situations in which groupthink is evident:

▶ Group members rationalize any resistance to the assumptions they have made.

▶ Members apply direct pressure on those who momentarily express doubts about any of the group's shared views or who question the validity of arguments favored by the majority.

▶ Those members who have doubts or hold differing points of view seek to avoid deviating from what appears to be group consensus.

▶ An illusion of unanimity is pervasive. If someone does not speak, it is assumed that he or she is in full accord.

Does groupthink really hinder decision making? Yes. Several research studies have found that groupthink symptoms were associated with poorer-quality decision outcomes. But groupthink can be minimized if the group is cohesive, fosters open discussion, and has an impartial leader who seeks input from all members.[32]

When Are Groups Most Effective?

Whether groups are more effective than individuals depends on the criteria you use for defining effectiveness, such as accuracy, speed, creativity, and acceptance. Group decisions tend to be more accurate. On average, groups tend to make better decisions than individuals, although groupthink may occur.[33] However, if decision

Team members at mission control of the Jet Propulsion Laboratory celebrate confirmation of the successful touchdown of NASA's Phoenix Mars Lander on the surface of Mars. The many decisions needed to develop, launch, and operate this project required the collaboration of a large group of science and spacecraft experts. In terms of accuracy, creativity, and acceptance, group decision making is more effective than individual decision making in projects of this magnitude and complexity.

effectiveness is defined in terms of speed, individuals are superior. If creativity is important, groups tend to be more effective than individuals. And if effectiveness means the degree of acceptance the final solution achieves, the nod again goes to the group.

The effectiveness of group decision making is also influenced by the size of the group. The larger the group, the greater the opportunity for heterogeneous representation. On the other hand, a larger group requires more coordination and more time to allow all members to contribute. This factor means that groups probably should not be too large: A minimum of five to a maximum of about fifteen members is best. Groups of five to seven individuals appear to be the most effective. Because five and seven are odd numbers, decision deadlocks are avoided. Effectiveness should not be considered without also assessing efficiency. Groups almost always stack up as a poor second in efficiency to the individual decision maker. With few exceptions, group decision making consumes more work hours than does individual decision making. In deciding whether to use groups, then, primary consideration must be given to assessing whether increases in effectiveness are more than enough to offset the losses in efficiency.

How Can You Improve Group Decision Making?

Three ways of making group decisions more creative are brainstorming, the nominal group technique, and electronic meetings.

WHAT IS BRAINSTORMING? Brainstorming is a relatively simple technique that utilizes an idea-generating process that specifically encourages any and all alternatives while withholding any criticism of those alternatives.[34] In a typical brainstorming session, a half-dozen to a dozen people sit around a table. Of course, technology is changing where that "table" is. The group leader states the problem in a clear manner that is understood by all participants. Members then "freewheel" as many alternatives as they can in a given time. No criticism is allowed, and all the alternatives are recorded for later discussion and analysis.[35] Brainstorming, however, is merely a process for generating ideas. The next method, the nominal group technique, helps groups arrive at a preferred solution.[36]

HOW DOES THE NOMINAL GROUP TECHNIQUE WORK? The nominal group technique restricts discussion during the decision-making process, hence the term. Group members must be present, as in a traditional committee meeting, but they are required to operate independently. They secretly write a list of general problem areas or potential solutions to a problem. The chief advantage of this technique is that it permits the group to meet formally but does not restrict independent thinking, as so often happens in the traditional interacting group.[37]

HOW CAN ELECTRONIC MEETINGS ENHANCE GROUP DECISION MAKING? The most recent approach to group decision making blends the nominal group technique with computer technology and is called the electronic meeting.

Once the technology for the meeting is in place, the concept is simple. Numerous people sit around a table that's empty except for a series of computer terminals. Issues are presented to the participants, who type their responses onto their computer screens. Individual comments, as well as aggregate votes, are displayed on a projection screen in the room.

The major advantages of electronic meetings are anonymity, honesty, and speed.[38] Participants can anonymously type any message they want, and it will flash on the screen

Videoconferencing improves the efficiency of group decision making at Accenture, a global management consulting, technology services, and outsourcing firm. Accenture has offices in more than 200 cities in 52 countries and clients spanning the world's major geographic regions. With such dispersion of employees and customers, videoconferencing enables Accenture to conduct face-to-face meetings while saving the time and costs involved in business travel. This photo shows Jill Smart, Accenture's chief human resources officer, conducting a meeting from her office in Chicago with colleagues working in Atlanta and London.

for all to see with a keystroke. It allows people to be brutally honest with no penalty. And it is fast—chitchat is eliminated, discussions do not digress, and many participants can "talk" at once without interrupting the others.

Electronic meetings are significantly faster and much cheaper than traditional face-to-face meetings.[39] Nestlé, for instance, continues to use the approach for many of its meetings, especially globally focused meetings.[40] However, as with all other forms of group activities, electronic meetings do experience some drawbacks. Those who type quickly can outshine those who may be verbally eloquent but lousy typists; those with the best ideas don't get credit for them; and the process lacks the informational richness of face-to-face oral communication. However, group decision making is likely to include extensive usage of electronic meetings.[41]

A variation of the electronic meeting is the videoconference. By linking together media from different locations, people can have face-to-face meetings even when they are thousands of miles apart. This capability has enhanced feedback among the members, saved countless hours of business travel, and ultimately saved companies such as Nestlé and Logitech hundreds of thousands of dollars. As a result, they're more effective in their meetings and have increased the efficiency with which decisions are made.[42]

3.5 Discuss contemporary issues in managerial decision making.

What Contemporary Decision-Making Issues Do Managers Face?

Today's business world revolves around making decisions, often risky ones, usually with incomplete or inadequate information, and under intense time pressure. Most managers make one decision after another; and as if that weren't challenging enough, more is at stake than ever before. Bad decisions can cost millions. We're going to look at two important issues—national culture and creativity—that managers face in today's fast-moving and global world.

How Does National Culture Affect Managers' Decision Making?

Research shows that, to some extent, decision-making practices differ from country to country.[43] The way decisions are made—whether by group, by team members, participatively, or autocratically by an individual manager—and the degree of risk a decision maker is willing to take are just two examples of decision variables that reflect a country's cultural environment. For example, in India, power distance and uncertainty avoidance (see Chapter 2) are high. There, only very senior-level managers make decisions, and they are likely to make safe decisions. In contrast, in Sweden, power distance and uncertainty avoidance are low. Swedish managers are not afraid to make risky decisions. Senior managers in Sweden also push decisions down in the ranks. They encourage lower-level managers and employees to take part in decisions that affect them. In countries such as Egypt, where time pressures are low, managers make decisions at a slower and more deliberate pace than managers do in the United States. And in Italy, where history and traditions are valued, managers tend to rely on tried and proven alternatives to resolve problems.

Decision making in Japan is much more group oriented than in the United States.[44] The Japanese value conformity and cooperation. Before making decisions, Japanese CEOs collect a large amount of information, which is then used in consensus-forming group decisions called **ringisei**. Because employees in Japanese organizations have high job security, managerial decisions take a long-term perspective rather than focusing on short-term profits, as is often the practice in the United States.

Senior managers in France and Germany also adapt their decision styles to their countries' cultures. In France, for instance, autocratic decision making is widely practiced, and managers avoid risks. Managerial styles in Germany reflect the German culture's concern for structure and order. Consequently, German organizations generally operate under extensive rules and regulations. Managers have well-defined responsibilities and accept that decisions must go through channels.

As managers deal with employees from diverse cultures, they need to recognize common and accepted behavior when asking them to make decisions. Some individuals may not be as comfortable as others with being closely involved in decision making, or they may not be willing to experiment with something radically different. Managers who accommodate the diversity in decision-making philosophies and practices can expect a high payoff if they capture the perspectives and strengths that a diverse workforce offers.

Why Is Creativity Important in Decision Making?

A decision maker needs **creativity**: the ability to produce novel and useful ideas. These ideas are different from what's been done before but are also appropriate to the problem or opportunity presented. Why is creativity important to decision making? It allows the decision maker to appraise and understand the problem more fully, including "seeing" problems others can't see. However, creativity's most obvious value is in helping the decision maker identify all viable alternatives. (See the "Developing Your Creativity Skill" box.)

Most people have creative potential that they can use when confronted with a decision-making problem. But to unleash that potential, they have to get out of the psychological ruts most of us get into and learn how to think about a problem in divergent ways.

We can start with the obvious. People differ in their inherent creativity. Einstein, Edison, Dali, and Mozart were individuals of exceptional creativity. Not surprisingly, exceptional creativity is scarce. A study of lifetime creativity of 461 men and women

Right or Wrong?

The 75 employees of Atomic Games worked nearly four years creating a realistic video game called *Six Days in Fallujah*, "weaving in real war footage and interviews with Marines who had fought there."[45] Now, relatives of dead Marines are angry. Said one mom whose son was killed by a sniper in Fallujah, "By making it something people play for fun, they are trivializing the battle." Company executive Peter Tamte relied on the advice of a number of Fallujah veterans and calls the video game a "documentary-style reconstruction that will be so true to the original battle, gamers will almost feel what it was like to fight in Fallujah in November 2004." What do you think? What ethical issues do you see here? Should the company proceed with the game's release? Why or why not?

ringisei
Japanese consensus-forming group decisions.

creativity
The ability to produce novel and useful ideas.

Developing Your *Creativity* Skill

About the Skill

Creativity is a frame of mind. You need to open your mind to new ideas. Every individual has the ability to be creative, but many people simply don't try to develop that ability. In contemporary organizations, such people may have difficulty achieving success. Dynamic environments and managerial chaos require that managers look for new and innovative ways to attain their goals as well as those of the organization.[46]

Steps in Practicing the Skill

1 Think of yourself as creative. Although it's a simple suggestion, research shows that if you think you can't be creative, you won't be. Believing in yourself is the first step in becoming more creative.

2 Pay attention to your intuition. Every individual's subconscious mind works well. Sometimes answers come to you when least expected. For example, when you are about to go to sleep, your relaxed mind sometimes whispers a solution to a problem you're facing. Listen to that voice. In fact, most creative people keep a notepad near their bed and write down those great ideas when they occur. That way, they don't forget them.

3 Move away from your comfort zone. Every individual has a comfort zone in which certainty exists. But creativity and the known often do not mix. To be creative, you need to move away from the status quo and focus your mind on something new.

4 Engage in activities that put you outside your comfort zone. You not only must think differently; you need to do things differently and, thus, challenge yourself. Learning to play a musical instrument or learning a foreign language, for example, opens your mind to a new challenge.

5 Seek a change of scenery. People are often creatures of habit. Creative people force themselves out of their habits by changing their scenery, which may mean going into a quiet and serene area where you can be alone with your thoughts.

6 Find several right answers. In the discussion of bounded rationality, we said that people seek solutions that are good enough. Being creative means continuing to look for other solutions even when you think you have solved the problem. A better, more creative solution just might be found.

7 Play your own devil's advocate. Challenging yourself to defend your solutions helps you to develop confidence in your creative efforts. Second-guessing yourself may also help you find more creative solutions.

8 Believe in finding a workable solution. Like believing in yourself, you also need to believe in your ideas. If you don't think you can find a solution, you probably won't.

9 Brainstorm with others. Being creative is not a solitary activity. Bouncing ideas off others creates a synergistic effect.

10 Turn creative ideas into action. Coming up with ideas is only half the process. Once the ideas are generated, they must be implemented. Keeping great ideas in your mind or on paper that no one will read does little to expand your creative abilities.

Practicing the Skill

How many words can you make using the letters in the word *brainstorm*? There are at least 95.

found that fewer than 1 percent were exceptionally creative. But 10 percent were highly creative, and about 60 percent were somewhat creative. These findings suggest that most of us have creative potential, if we can learn to unleash it.

Given that most people have the capacity to be at least moderately creative, what can individuals and organizations do to stimulate employee creativity? The best answer to this question lies in the three-component model of creativity based on an extensive body of research.[47] This model proposes that individual creativity essentially requires expertise, creative-thinking skills, and intrinsic task motivation. Studies confirm that the higher the level of each of these three components, the higher the creativity.

Expertise is the foundation of all creative work. Dali's understanding of art and Einstein's knowledge of physics were necessary conditions for them to be able to make creative contributions to their fields. And you wouldn't expect someone with a minimal knowledge of programming to be highly creative as a software engineer. The potential for creativity is enhanced when individuals have abilities, knowledge, proficiencies, and similar expertise in their fields of endeavor.

The second component is *creative-thinking skills*. It encompasses personality characteristics associated with creativity, the ability to use analogies, as well as the talent to see the familiar in a different light. For instance, the following individual traits have been found to be associated with the development of creative ideas: intelligence, independence, self-confidence, risk taking, internal locus of control, tolerance for ambiguity, and perseverance in the face of frustration. The effective use of analogies allows decision makers to apply an idea from one context to another. One of the most famous examples in which analogy resulted in a creative breakthrough was Alexander Graham Bell's observation that it might be possible to take concepts that operate in the ear and apply them to his "talking box." He noticed that the bones in the ear are operated by a delicate, thin membrane. He wondered why, then, a thicker and stronger piece of membrane shouldn't be able to move a piece of steel. Out of that analogy the telephone was conceived. Of course, some people have developed their skill at being able to see problems in a new way. They're able to make the strange familiar and the familiar strange. For instance, most of us think of hens laying eggs. But how many of us have considered that a hen is only an egg's way of making another egg?

The final component in our model is *intrinsic task motivation*—the desire to work on something because it's interesting, involving, exciting, satisfying, or personally challenging. This motivational component is what turns creative *potential* into *actual* creative ideas. It determines the extent to which individuals fully engage their expertise and creative skills. So creative people often love their work, to the point of seeming obsessed. Importantly, an individual's work environment and the organization's culture (we'll look at organization culture in the next chapter) can have a significant effect on intrinsic motivation. Specifically, five organizational factors have been found that can impede your creativity: (1) expected evaluation—focusing on how your work is going to be evaluated; (2) surveillance—being watched while you're working; (3) external motivators—emphasizing external, tangible rewards; (4) competition—facing win–lose situations with your peers; and (5) constrained choices—being given limits on how you can do your work.

Review and ③ Applications

Chapter Summary

3.1 **Describe the decision-making process.** The decision-making process consists of eight steps: (1) identify problem, (2) identify decision criteria, (3) weight the criteria, (4) develop alternatives, (5) analyze alternatives, (6) select alternative, (7) implement alternative, and (8) evaluate decision effectiveness. As managers make decisions, they may use heuristics to simplify the process, which can lead to errors and biases in their decision making. The 12 common decision-making errors and biases include overconfidence, immediate gratification, anchoring, selective perception, confirmation, framing, availability, representation, randomness, sunk costs, self-serving bias, and hindsight.

3.2 **Explain the three approaches managers can use to make decisions.** The first approach is the rational model. The assumptions of rationality are as follows: the problem is clear and unambiguous, a single, well-defined goal is to be achieved, all alternatives and consequences are known, and the final choice will maximize the payoff. The second approach, bounded rationality, says that managers make rational decisions but are bounded (limited) by their ability to process information. In this approach, managers satisfice, which is when decision makers accept solutions that are good enough. Finally, intuitive decision making is making decisions on the basis of experience, feelings, and accumulated judgment.

3.3 **Describe the types of decisions and decision-making conditions managers face.** Programmed decisions are repetitive decisions that can be handled by a routine approach and are used when the problem being resolved is straightforward, familiar, and easily defined (structured). Nonprogrammed decisions are unique decisions that require a custom-made solution and are used when the problems are new or unusual (unstructured) and for which information is ambiguous or incomplete. Certainty is a situation when a manager can make accurate decisions because all outcomes are known. Risk is a situation when a manager can estimate the likelihood of certain outcomes. Uncertainty is a situation where a manager is not certain about the outcomes and can't even make reasonable probability estimates.

3.4 **Discuss group decision making.** Groups offer certain advantages when making decisions—more complete information, more alternatives, increased acceptance of a solution, and greater legitimacy. On the other hand, groups are time-consuming, can be dominated by a minority, create pressures to conform, and cloud responsibility. Three ways of improving group decision making are brainstorming (utilizing an idea-generating process that specifically encourages any and all alternatives while withholding any criticism of those alternatives), the nominal group technique (a technique that restricts discussion during the decision-making process), and electronic meetings (the most recent approach to group decision making, which blends the nominal group technique with sophisticated computer technology).

3.5 **Discuss contemporary issues in managerial decision making.** As managers deal with employees from diverse cultures, they need to recognize common and accepted behavior when asking them to make decisions. Some individuals may not be as comfortable as others with being closely involved in decision making, or they may not be willing to experiment with something radically different. Also, managers need to be creative in their decision making since creativity allows them to appraise and understand the problem more fully, including "seeing" problems that others can't see.

PEARSON **mymanagementlab** To check your understanding of learning outcomes **3.1** – **3.5**, go to **mymanagementlab.com** and try the chapter questions.

Understanding the Chapter

1. Why is decision making often described as the essence of a manager's job?

2. All of us bring biases to the decisions we make. What would be the drawbacks of having biases? Could there be any advantages to having biases? Explain. What are the implications for managerial decision making?

3. "Because managers have software tools to use, they should be able to make more rational decisions." Do you agree or disagree with this statement? Why?

4. Is there a difference between wrong decisions and bad decisions? Why do good managers sometimes make wrong decisions? Bad decisions? How might managers improve their decision-making skills?

5. Describe a decision you've made that closely aligns with the assumptions of perfect rationality. Compare this decision with the process you used to select your college. Did you depart from the rational model in your college decision? Explain.

6. Explain how a manager might deal with making decisions under conditions of uncertainty.

7. Why do you think organizations have increased the use of groups for making decisions? When would you recommend using groups to make decisions?

8. Find two examples each of procedures, rules, and policies. Bring your examples to class and be prepared to share them.

9. Do a Web search on the phrase "dumbest moments in business" and get the most current version of this list. Choose three of the examples and describe what happened. What's your reaction to each example? How could the managers in each have made better decisions?

Understanding Yourself

Am I a Deliberate Decision Maker?

People differ in how they make decisions. Some people prefer to collect information, carefully weigh alternatives, and then select the best option. Others prefer to make a choice as quickly as possible. This self-assessment exercise assesses how deliberate you are when making decisions.

INSTRUMENT   Indicate to what extent the following statements describe you when you make decisions.

> **1** = To a very little extent
> **2** = To a little extent
> **3** = Somewhat
> **4** = To a large extent
> **5** = To a very large extent

1.	I jump into things without thinking.	1	2	3	4	5
2.	I make rash decisions.	1	2	3	4	5
3.	I like to act on a whim.	1	2	3	4	5
4.	I rush into things.	1	2	3	4	5
5.	I don't know why I do some of the things I do.	1	2	3	4	5
6.	I act quickly without thinking.	1	2	3	4	5
7.	I choose my words with care.	1	2	3	4	5

SCORING KEY   To score the measure, first reverse-code items 1, 2, 3, 4, 5, and 6 so that 1 = 5, 2 = 4, 3 = 3, 4 = 2, and 5 = 1. Then, compute the sum of the seven items. Your score will range from 7 to 35.

ANALYSIS AND INTERPRETATION   If you scored at or above 28, you tend to be quite deliberate. If you scored at or below 14, you tend to be more hasty in making decisions. Scores between 14 and 27 reveal a more blended style of decision making.

How should decisions be made? The rational model states that individuals should define the problem, identify what criteria are relevant to making the decision and weigh those criteria according to importance, develop alternatives, and finally evaluate and select the best alternative. Though this sounds like an arduous process, research has shown that the rational model tends to result in better decisions.

If you tend to make decisions on a whim, you may want to be especially careful in auction settings, like those found on eBay. The time pressures involved, along with the emotional arousal that comes with bidding, can result in "auction fever" and suboptimal decisions. Put simply, if you make quick, impulsive decisions, you may pay more than you should have, and that's true not only for buying on eBay, but in other situations as well.

Source: Based on L. R. Goldberg, J. A. Johnson, H. W. Eber, R. Hogan, M. C. Ashton, C. R. Cloninger, and H. G. Gough, "The International Personality Item Pool and the Future of Public-Domain Personality Measures," *Journal of Research in Personality* 40 (2006), pp. 84–96.

FYIA (For Your Immediate Action)

Magic Carpet Software

Reply   Reply All   Forward

To: Rajiv Dutta, Research Manager
From: Amanda Schrenk, Vice President of Operations
Re: **Software Design Decisions**

For some time, I've been aware of a problem in our software design unit. Our diverse pool of extremely talented and skilled designers is, undoubtedly, one of our company's most important assets. However, I'm concerned that our designers' emotional attachment to the software they've created overshadows other important factors that should be considered in the decision whether to proceed with the new product design. At this point, I'm not sure how to approach this issue. The last thing I want to do is stifle their creativity. But I'm afraid if we don't come up with an action plan soon, the problem may get worse.

Please research the role of emotions in decision making. What do the "experts" say? Is it even an issue that we need to be concerned about? What's the best way to deal with it? Please provide me with a one-page bulleted list of the important points you find from your research. And be sure to cite your sources in case I need to do some follow-up.

This fictionalized company and message were created for educational purposes only. It is not meant to reflect positively or negatively on management practices by any company that may share this name.

IN TUNE

The Nazareth, Pennsylvania–based C. F. Martin Guitar Company has been producing acoustic instruments since 1833. Martin's legendary guitars have long been loved by legendary musicians, and a Martin guitar is among the best that money can buy. CEO Christian Frederick Martin IV—better known as Chris—continues to be committed to the guitar maker's craft. Although the company increased sales by 8 percent in 2008 to $93 million, it's facing some serious issues.

Martin Guitar Company is an interesting blend of old and new. Although the equipment and tools may have changed over the years, company employees remain true to the principle of high standards of musical excellence. The company's customers expect exceptional quality. Building a guitar to meet these standards requires considerable attention and patience. Each guitar goes through a series of 60 workstations, with more than 300 distinct production steps. Musician Eric Clapton once said that, "If [I] could be reincarnated as anything, it would be as a Martin guitar." It's not surprising that Martin guitars aren't cheap. Some of its limited-edition guitars made of Brazilian rosewood sell for $100,000 or more. Its more popular models sell for $2,000 to $3,000.

Like many businesses, Martin's sales have dropped off—some 20 percent since fall 2008—as consumer spending nosedived. Guitars aren't exactly necessities and consumers were being extremely cautious in spending. Meanwhile, the company's inventories of its higher-priced guitars ballooned. Chris didn't want to lay off employees, especially since it takes special woodworking skills to make the guitars. "The company figured it is better to find a way to keep workers occupied than face the challenge of having to train new ones after the economy recovered." Chris and his managers came up with a solution: "Copy what many big retailers do by offering a lower-priced alternative." The challenge was how to do that without sacrificing quality or harming its image.

They've been able to do just that by using extreme flexibility and less labor hours on the production line, something the company had to do back in the 1930s during the Great Depression. "The ability to come up with a new design quickly and without tearing apart a production process allowed Martin to get a lower-priced product into stores without a huge investment." Initial reaction to the company's under $1,000 guitar has been promising. The 1 Series guitar was introduced in April 2009 and promptly sold out.

Discussion Questions

1. How do you think good decision making has contributed to the success of this business?
2. A decision to move into a new market as Chris did is a major decision. How could he have used the decision-making process to help him make this decision?
3. What criteria do you think would be most important to Chris as he makes decisions about the company's future?
4. Would you characterize the conditions surrounding C. F. Martin Guitar Company as conditions of certainty, risk, or uncertainty? Explain your choice. How would these conditions affect managerial decision making?

Sources: T. Aeppel, "Guitar Maker Revives No-Frills Act from '30s," *Wall Street Journal*, July 6, 2009, pp. B1+; B. Erdman, "Craft a Product, Not an Excuse," *Brandweek*, June 1, 2009, p. 15; A. Ben-Yehuda, "Instruments of Change," *Billboard*, March 29, 2008, p. 23; and D. Lieberman, "Guitar Sales Jam Despite Music Woes," *USA Today*, December 16, 2002, p. 2B.

4

Foundations of Planning

Building a Future

As many not-for-profit organizations struggle with increasing demand for services and wonder where their next dollar is coming from, one organization is struggling to decide what to do with a $100 million gift from a donor.[1] That's right . . . $100 million! A staggering amount for anyone, but for the organization that was the recipient, it's especially challenging to make sure that the gift is used in the most effective and efficient way possible. The lucky—and deserving—organization? Atlanta-based Habitat for Humanity.

Habitat is a nonprofit, ecumenical Christian housing ministry whose mission is to "eliminate poverty and homelessness from the world and to make decent shelter a matter of conscience and action." The organization was founded by Millard and Linda Fuller in 1976 in Americus, Georgia. More than 300,000 Habitat houses have been built, sheltering more than 1.5 million people around the world. These houses can be found in all 50 states of the United States, the District of Columbia, Guam, Puerto Rico, and more than 90 countries around the world. "Thousands of low-income families have found new hope in this form of affordable housing." And Habitat's approach is simple. Families in need of decent housing apply to local Habitat affiliates. Home owners are chosen based on their level of need, their willingness to become partners in the program, and their ability to repay the loan. And that's the unique thing about Habitat's approach. It's not a giveaway program. Families chosen to become home owners have to make a down payment and monthly mortgage payments, and invest hundreds of hours of their own labor into building their Habitat home and helping build other Habitat houses. Habitat volunteers provide labor and donations of money and materials as well. (Maybe some of you have helped in a Habitat build.)

Now about this $100 million gift. According to the Center on Philanthropy at Indiana University, "It's one of the largest gifts in recent years to a group devoted to social services." The donation came from J. Ronald Terwilliger (pictured above in photo), a former CEO of housing developer Trammell Crow Residential Co., who also has been a long-time member of Habitat's board of directors. He says that "through his work with Habitat and in the private sector, he's witnessed the depths of poverty, seeing people living in cardboard shacks and unspeakable filth, as well as the struggle for middle-class families to find affordable housing." His gift is intended to give people a helping hand . . . a decent, safe clean home. And it's intended to send a message to other philanthropists to "step up their giving." As for Habitat, its CEO, Jonathan Reckford, said, "This is a chance to have a really deep impact." Having that type of impact when the needs now are greater than ever is a definite planning challenge for the organization and its managers.

Habitat for Humanity, like other organizations, has a purpose, people, and a structure to support and enable those people in carrying out that purpose. Now, it also has a $100 million gift to put to good use. Deciding when, where, and how those funds will be used will require thorough and effective planning on the part of the organization's board and managers.

This chapter presents the basics of planning. You'll learn what planning is, how managers do strategic management, and how they set goals and establish plans. Finally, we'll look at some of the contemporary planning issues managers have to deal with.

What Is Planning and Why Do Managers Need to Plan?

4.1 Discuss the nature and purposes of planning.

Planning is often called the primary management function because it establishes the basis for all the other things managers do as they organize, lead, and control. What is meant by the term *planning?* As we said in Chapter 1, planning encompasses defining the organization's objectives or goals, establishing an overall strategy for achieving those goals, and developing a comprehensive hierarchy of plans to integrate and coordinate activities. It's concerned with ends (*what* is to be done) as well as with means (*how* it's to be done).

Planning can be further defined in terms of whether it's *formal* or *informal.* All managers plan, even if it's only informally. In informal planning, very little, if anything, is written down. What is to be accomplished is in the heads of one or a few people. Furthermore, the organization's goals are rarely verbalized. Informal planning generally describes the planning that takes place in many smaller businesses. The owner-manager has an idea of where he or she wants to go and how he or she expects to get there. The planning is general and lacks continuity. Of course, you'll see informal planning in some large organizations, while some small businesses will have sophisticated formal plans.

When we use the term *planning* in this book, we're implying formal planning. In formal planning, specific goals covering a specific time period are defined. These goals are written down and made available to organization members. Using these goals, managers develop specific plans that clearly define the path the organization will take to get from where it is to where it wants to be.

Why Should Managers Formally Plan?

Managers should plan for at least four reasons. (See Exhibit 4-1.) First, planning establishes coordinated effort. It gives direction to managers and nonmanagerial employees. When all organizational members understand where the organization is going and what they must contribute to reach the goals, they can begin to coordinate their activities, thus fostering teamwork and cooperation. On the other hand, a lack of planning can cause organizational members or work units to work against one another and keep the organization from moving efficiently toward its goals.

Second, by forcing managers to look ahead, anticipate change, consider the impact of change, and develop appropriate responses, planning reduces uncertainty. It also clarifies the consequences of the actions managers might take in response to change. Planning, then, is precisely what managers need in a changing environment.

Third, planning reduces overlapping and wasteful activities. Coordination before the fact is likely to uncover waste and redundancy. Furthermore, when means and ends are clear, inefficiencies become obvious.

Finally, planning establishes the goals or standards that facilitate control. If organizational members are unsure of what they are attempting to achieve, how can they assess whether they've achieved it? When managers plan, they develop goals and plans. When they control, they see whether the plans have been carried out and the goals met.

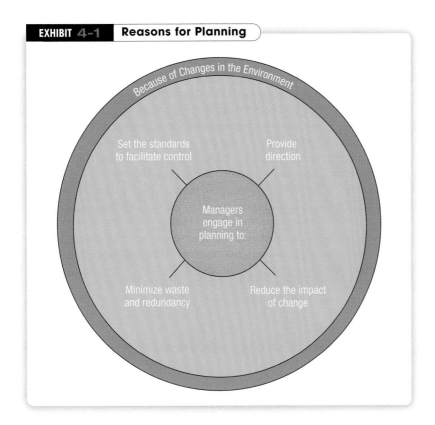

EXHIBIT 4-1 **Reasons for Planning**

Because of Changes in the Environment

Managers engage in planning to:

Set the standards to facilitate control

Provide direction

Minimize waste and redundancy

Reduce the impact of change

If significant deviations are identified, corrective action can be taken. Without planning, there would be no goals against which to measure or evaluate work efforts.

What Are Some Criticisms of Formal Planning?

Although it makes sense for an organization to establish goals and direction, critics have challenged some of the basic assumptions of planning.[2]

1. *Planning may create rigidity.* Formal planning efforts can lock an organization into specific goals to be achieved within specific timetables. Such goals may have been set under the assumption that the environment wouldn't change. Forcing a course of action when the environment is random and unpredictable can be a recipe for disaster. Instead, managers need to remain flexible and not be tied to a course of action simply because it's the plan.

2. *Formal plans can't replace intuition and creativity.* Successful organizations are typically the result of someone's vision, but these visions have a tendency to become formalized as they evolve. If formal planning efforts reduce the vision to a programmed routine, that too can lead to disaster. Planning should enhance and support intuition and creativity, not replace it.

3. *Planning focuses managers' attention on today's competition, not on tomorrow's survival.* Formal planning, especially strategic planning (which we'll discuss shortly), has a tendency to focus on how to best capitalize on existing business opportunities within the industry. Managers may not look at ways to recreate or reinvent the industry. Instead, when managers plan, they should be open to forging into uncharted waters if there are untapped opportunities.

4. *Formal planning reinforces success, which may lead to failure.* The American tradition has been that success breeds success. After all, if it's not broken, don't fix it. Right? Well maybe not! Success may, in fact, breed failure in an uncertain environment. It's hard to change or discard successful plans—to leave the comfort of what works for the uncertainty (and anxiety) of the unknown. Still, managers may need to face that unknown and be open to doing things in new ways to be even more successful.

Does Formal Planning Improve Organizational Performance?

Does it pay to plan? Or have the critics of planning won the debate? Let's look at the evidence.

Contrary to what the critics of planning say, the evidence generally supports the position that organizations should have formal plans. Although most studies that have looked at the relationship between planning and performance have shown generally positive relationships, it would be inaccurate to say that organizations that formally plan always outperform those that don't.[3] On the basis of those studies, what can we conclude?

First, formal planning generally means higher profits, higher return on assets, and other positive financial results. Second, the quality of the planning process and the appropriate implementation of the plan probably contribute more to high performance than does the extent of planning. Finally, in those organizations in which formal planning did not lead to higher performance, the environment was often to blame. For instance, governmental regulations, unforeseen economic challenges, and other environmental constraints reduce the impact of planning on an organization's performance. Why? Because managers will have fewer viable alternatives.

One important aspect of an organization's formal planning is strategic planning, which managers do as part of the strategic management process.

What Do Managers Need to Know About Strategic Management?

4.2 Explain what managers do in the strategic management process.

McDonald's is planning to open another 40 restaurants in India, bringing its total there to almost 200. After much research and customer feedback, Starbucks introduced a new line of healthier and made-from-scratch baked goods (including a gluten-free Valencia Orange Cake with Almonds). Tata Motors Ltd. introduced the Jaguar and Land Rover luxury-car brands in India to compete with BMW, Audi, and Daimler (Mercedes Benz) in attracting the country's growing number of millionaires.[4] These are just a few of the business news stories from a single week, and each one is about a company's strategies. Strategic management is very much a part of what managers do.

What Is Strategic Management?

Strategic management is what managers do to develop an organization's strategies. What are an organization's **strategies**? They're the plans for how the organization will do what it's in business to do, how it will compete successfully, and how it will attract and satisfy its customers in order to achieve its goals.

Why Is Strategic Management Important?

Teen retailer Buckle Inc. hasn't suffered during the economic turmoil that affected many mall-based clothing chains. As one consultant said, "Buckle's sales growth has been going on month after month after month." What's the company's strategy? One important part is its location strategy. Only a few of its some 400 stores are located in states that are suffering the worst from the recession. Another part of its strategy is offering customer perks such as custom pant fittings and free hemming on its jeans. Such "customer-service investments can go a long way in differentiating Buckle in the congested teen market."[5] This company's managers obviously understand why strategic management is important!

Why *is* strategic management so important? One reason is that it can make a difference in how well an organization performs. Why do some businesses succeed and others fail, even when faced with the same environmental conditions? Research has found a generally positive relationship between strategic planning and performance.[6] Those companies that plan strategically appear to have better financial results than those organizations that don't.

Another reason it's important has to do with the fact that managers in organizations of all types and sizes face continually changing situations (recall our discussion in Chapter 2). They cope with this uncertainty by using the strategic management process to examine relevant factors in planning future actions.

Finally, strategic management is important because organizations are complex and diverse. Each part needs to work together to achieve the organization's goals; strategic management helps do this. For example, with more than 2.1 million employees worldwide working in various departments, functional areas, and stores, Wal-Mart uses strategic management to help coordinate and focus employees' efforts on what's important.

Strategic management isn't just for business organizations. Even organizations such as government agencies, hospitals, educational institutions, and social agencies (see the chapter opener on Habitat for Humanity) need strategic management. For example, the skyrocketing costs of a college education, competition from companies offering alternative educational forums, state budgets being slashed because of declining revenues, and cutbacks in federal aid for students and research have led many university administrators to assess their colleges' aspirations and identify a market niche in which they can survive and prosper.

Alibaba.com's strategic plans include reducing the company's reliance on its home market of China by expanding globally. Alibaba.com is an online business-to-business service that targets small and midsize importers and exporters. Company founder and chairman Jack Ma (center) plans to compete successfully by launching local versions of its service worldwide, beginning in Japan, Korea, and India. Alibaba's expansion began in Japan, China's largest trading partner, through a joint venture with Softbank, a Japanese media and telecommunications firm. In this photo, Jack Ma discusses the joint venture at a press conference with the leaders of Softbank and Alibaba Japan.

What Are the Steps in the Strategic Management Process?

The **strategic management process** (see Exhibit 4-2) is a six-step process that encompasses strategy planning, implementation, and evaluation. Although the first four steps describe the planning that must take place, implementation and evaluation are just as important! Even the best strategies can fail if management doesn't implement or evaluate them properly.

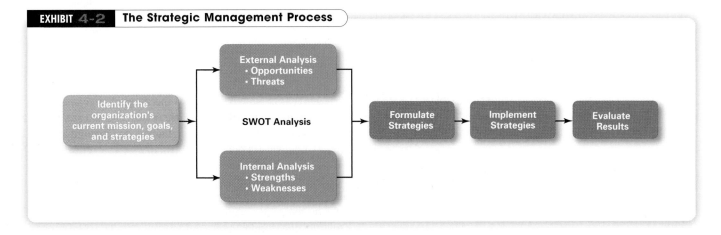

| **EXHIBIT 4-2** | **The Strategic Management Process** |

Identify the organization's current mission, goals, and strategies

External Analysis
• Opportunities
• Threats

SWOT Analysis

Internal Analysis
• Strengths
• Weaknesses

Formulate Strategies → Implement Strategies → Evaluate Results

strategic management
What managers do to develop an organization's strategies.

strategies
Plans for how the organization will do what it's in business to do, how it will compete successfully, and how it will attract its customers in order to achieve its goals.

strategic management process
A six-step process that encompasses strategy planning, implementation, and evaluation.

> **EXHIBIT 4-3** **What a Mission Statement Includes**
>
> **Customers:** Who are the firm's customers?
> **Markets:** Where does the firm compete geographically?
> **Concern for survival, growth, and profitability:** Is the firm committed to growth and financial stability?
> **Philosophy:** What are the firm's basic beliefs, values, and ethical priorities?
> **Concern for public image:** How responsive is the firm to societal and environmental concerns?
> **Products or services:** What are the firm's major products or services?
> **Technology:** Is the firm technologically current?
> **Self-concept:** What are the firm's major competitive advantage and core competencies?
> **Concern for employees:** Are employees a valuable asset of the firm?
>
> *Source:* Based on F. David, *Strategic Management,* 11 ed. (Upper Saddle River, NJ: Prentice Hall, 2007), p. 70.

STEP 1: IDENTIFYING THE ORGANIZATION'S CURRENT MISSION, GOALS, AND STRATEGIES. Every organization needs a **mission**—a statement of its purpose. Defining the mission forces managers to identify what it's in business to do. For instance, the mission of Avon is "To be the company that best understands and satisfies the product, service, and self-fulfillment needs of women on a global level." The mission of Facebook is "a social utility that connects you with the people around you." The mission of the National Heart Foundation of Australia is to "reduce suffering and death from heart, stroke, and blood vessel disease in Australia." These statements provide clues to what these organizations see as their purpose. What should a mission statement include? Exhibit 4-3 describes some typical components.

It's also important for managers to identify the current goals and strategies. Why? So managers have a basis for assessing whether they need to be changed.

STEP 2: DOING AN EXTERNAL ANALYSIS. We discussed the external environment in Chapter 2. Analyzing that environment is a critical step in the strategic management process. Managers do an external analysis so they know, for instance, what the competition is doing, what pending legislation might affect the organization, or what the labor supply is like in locations where it operates. In an external analysis, managers should examine both the specific and general environments to see the trends and changes.

Once they've analyzed the environment, managers need to pinpoint opportunities that the organization can exploit and threats that it must counteract or buffer against. **Opportunities** are positive trends in the external environment; **threats** are negative trends.

STEP 3: DOING AN INTERNAL ANALYSIS. Now we move to the internal analysis, which provides important information about an organization's specific resources and capabilities. An organization's **resources** are its assets—financial, physical, human, and intangible—that it uses to develop, manufacture, and deliver products to its customers. They're "what" the organization has. On the other hand, its **capabilities** are its skills and abilities in doing the work activities needed in its business—"how" it does its work. The major value-creating capabilities of the organization are known as its **core competencies.**[7] Both resources and core competencies determine the organization's competitive weapons.

After completing an internal analysis, managers should be able to identify organizational strengths and weaknesses. Any activities the organization does well or any unique resources that it has are called **strengths.** **Weaknesses** are activities the organization doesn't do well or resources it needs but doesn't possess.

The combined external and internal analyses are called the **SWOT analysis** because it's an analysis of the organization's *s*trengths, *w*eaknesses, *o*pportunities, and *t*hreats. After completing the SWOT analysis, managers are ready to formulate appropriate strategies—that is, strategies that (1) exploit an organization's strengths and external opportunities, (2) buffer or protect the organization from external threats, or (3) correct critical weaknesses.

STEP 4: FORMULATING STRATEGIES. As managers formulate strategies, they should consider the realities of the external environment and their available resources and capabilities and design strategies that will help an organization achieve its goals. There are three main types of strategies managers will formulate: corporate, competitive, and functional. We'll describe each shortly.

STEP 5: IMPLEMENTING STRATEGIES. Once strategies are formulated, they must be implemented. No matter how effectively an organization has planned its strategies, performance will suffer if the strategies aren't implemented properly.

STEP 6: EVALUATING RESULTS. The final step in the strategic management process is evaluating results. How effective have the strategies been at helping the organization reach its goals? What adjustments are necessary? For instance, when Anne Mulcahy, Xerox's former CEO, was first named to that post, she assessed the results of previous strategies and determined that changes were needed. She made strategic adjustments—cutting jobs, selling assets, and reorganizing management—to regain market share and improve her company's bottom line.

What Strategies Do Managers Use?

Strategies need to be formulated for all levels in the organization: corporate, competitive, and functional (see Exhibit 4-4). Let's look closer at each of these types of strategies.

CORPORATE STRATEGY. A **corporate strategy** is an organizational strategy that specifies what businesses a company is in or wants to be in and what it wants to do with those businesses. It's based on the mission and goals of the organization and the roles that each business unit of the organization will play. We can see both of these aspects with PepsiCo, for instance. Its mission is:

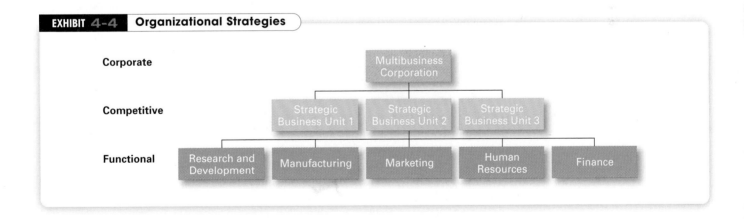

EXHIBIT 4-4 | **Organizational Strategies**

mission
A statement of an organization's purpose.

opportunities
Positive trends in the external environment.

threats
Negative trends in the external environment.

resources
An organization's assets that it uses to develop, manufacture, and deliver products to its customers.

capabilities
An organization's skills and abilities in doing the work activities needed in its business.

core competencies
The major value-creating capabilities of an organization.

strengths
Any activities the organization does well or any unique resources that it has.

weaknesses
Activities the organization doesn't do well or resources it needs but doesn't possess.

SWOT analysis
The combined external and internal analyses.

corporate strategy
An organizational strategy that specifies what businesses a company is in or wants to be in and what it wants to do with those businesses.

Avon Products CEO Andrea Jung formulated a growth strategy of increasing the number of company sales representatives. For Jung, the rising unemployment worldwide due to the global economic downturn presented an opportunity to implement a recruitment plan. She launched the biggest recruiting drive in Avon's history, increasing recruiting advertising 250 percent from the previous year. Advertising messages focused on offering women an economic opportunity in becoming an Avon sales rep. As incentives to join Avon's 5.8 million direct sellers, Jung offered recruits gas money, free online sales training, and a Web site where reps can post questions to financial adviser Suze Orman.

To be the world's premier consumer products company focused on convenient foods and beverages. It pursues that mission with a corporate strategy that has put it in different businesses including PepsiCo International, Frito-Lay North America, PepsiCo Beverages North America, and Quaker Foods North America. The other part of corporate strategy is when top managers decide what to do with those businesses. The three main types of corporate strategies are growth, stability, and renewal.

The Growth Strategy. Even though Wal-Mart is the world's largest retailer, it continues to grow internationally and in the United States. A **growth strategy** is when an organization expands the number of markets served or products offered, either through its current business(es) or through new business(es). Because of its growth strategy, an organization may increase revenues, number of employees, or market share. Organizations grow by using concentration, vertical integration, horizontal integration, or diversification.

An organization that grows using *concentration* focuses on its primary line of business and increases the number of products offered or markets served in this primary business. For instance, Beckman Coulter, Inc., a Fullerton, California-based organization with annual revenues of almost $3.1 billion, has used concentration to become one of the world's largest medical diagnostics and research equipment companies.

A company also might choose to grow by *vertical integration*, either backward, forward, or both. In backward vertical integration, the organization becomes its own supplier so it can control its inputs. For instance, eBay owns an online payment business that helps it provide more secure transactions and control one of its most critical processes. In forward vertical integration, the organization becomes its own distributor and is able to control its outputs. For example, Apple has some 260 retail stores to distribute its products.

In *horizontal integration*, a company grows by combining with competitors. For instance, French cosmetics giant L'Oréal acquired The Body Shop. Horizontal integration has been used in a number of industries in the last few years—financial services, consumer products, airlines, department stores, and software, among others. The U.S. Federal Trade Commission usually scrutinizes these combinations closely to see if consumers might be harmed by decreased competition. Other countries may have similar restrictions. For instance, managers at Oracle Corporation had to get approval from the European Commission, the "watchdog" for the European Union, before it could acquire rival business-software maker PeopleSoft.

Finally, an organization can grow through *diversification*, either related or unrelated. Related diversification is when a company combines with other companies in different, but related, industries. For example, American Standard Companies is in a variety of businesses including bathroom fixtures, air conditioning and heating units, plumbing parts, and pneumatic brakes for trucks. Although this mix of businesses seems odd, the company's "strategic fit" is the efficiency-oriented manufacturing techniques developed in its primary business of bathroom fixtures, which it has transferred to all its other businesses. Unrelated diversification is when a company combines with firms in different and unrelated industries. For instance, the Tata Group of India has businesses in chemicals, communications and IT, consumer products, energy, engineering, materials, and services. Again, an odd mix. But in this case, no strategic fit exists among the businesses.

The Stability Strategy. During periods of economic uncertainty, many companies choose to maintain things as they are. This is a **stability strategy**, which is a corporate strategy in which an organization continues to do what it is currently doing. Examples of this strategy include continuing to serve the same clients by offering the same product or service, maintaining market share, and sustaining the organization's current business operations. The organization doesn't grow, but doesn't fall behind, either.

The Renewal Strategy. In 2008, General Motors lost almost $31 billion after losing $38.7 billion in 2007. Sprint-Nextel lost nearly $2.8 billion, and many financial institutions and real-estate-related companies faced serious financial issues. When an organization is in trouble, something needs to be done. Managers need strategies that address declining performance. These strategies are called **renewal strategies**, of which there are two main types. A *retrenchment strategy* is a short-run renewal strategy used for minor performance problems. This strategy helps it stabilize operations, revitalize organizational resources and capabilities, and prepare to compete once again. When an organization's problems are more serious, more drastic action—the *turnaround strategy*—is needed. Managers do two things for both renewal strategies: cut costs and restructure organizational operations. However, in a turnaround strategy, these measures are more extensive than in a retrenchment strategy.

COMPETITIVE STRATEGY. A **competitive strategy** is a strategy for how an organization will compete in its business(es). For a small organization in only one line of business or a large organization that has not diversified into different products or markets, its competitive strategy describes how it will compete in its primary or main market. For organizations in multiple businesses, however, each business will have its own competitive strategy that defines its competitive advantage, the products or services it will offer, the customers it wants to reach, and the like. For example, the French company LVMH-Moët Hennessy Louis Vuitton SA has different competitive strategies for its businesses, which include Donna Karan fashions, Louis Vuitton leather goods, Guerlain perfume, TAG Heuer watches, Dom Perignon champagne, and other luxury products. When an organization is in several different businesses, those single businesses that are independent and formulate their own competitive strategies are often called **strategic business units (SBUs)**.

The Role of Competitive Advantage. Michelin has mastered a complex technological process for making superior radial tires. Coca-Cola has created the world's most powerful brand using specialized marketing and merchandising capabilities. The Ritz-Carlton hotels have a unique ability to deliver personalized customer service. Each of these companies has created a competitive advantage.

Developing an effective competitive strategy requires an understanding of **competitive advantage**, which is what sets an organization apart; that is, its distinctive edge. That distinctive edge comes from the organization's core competencies by doing something that others cannot do or doing it better than others can do it. For example, Southwest Airlines has a competitive advantage because of its skills at giving passengers what they want—convenient and inexpensive service. Or competitive advantage can come from the company's resources—the organization has something that its competitors do not have. For instance, Wal-Mart's state-of-the-art information system allows it to monitor and

Right or Wrong?

It's one of the Internet's most popular "tests" since it promises to help shave years off your age.[8] Of course, having Oprah's "Dr. Oz" affiliated with it hasn't hurt either! Over 27 million people have taken the RealAge test, which asks some 150 or so questions about lifestyle and family history and reports a "biological age, how young or old your habits make you." The dilemma is that RealAge allows drug companies to send e-mail messages based on those test results. Even though it doesn't give personally identifiable information to the drug companies, what do you think of this? Is it ethical? Why or why not? Should RealAge discontinue the practice? Why or why not?

growth strategy
A corporate strategy in which an organization expands the number of markets served or products offered either through its current business(es) or through new business(es).

stability strategy
A corporate strategy in which an organization continues to do what it is currently doing.

renewal strategy
A corporate strategy that addresses declining organizational performance.

competitive strategy
An organizational strategy for how an organization will compete in its business(es).

strategic business units (SBUs)
An organization's single businesses that are independent and formulate their own competitive strategies.

competitive advantage
What sets an organization apart; its distinctive edge.

control inventories and supplier relations more efficiently than its competitors, which Wal-Mart has turned into a cost advantage.

Choosing a Competitive Strategy. One of the leading researchers in strategy formulation is Michael Porter of Harvard's Graduate School of Business. His competitive strategies framework argues that managers can choose among three generic competitive strategies.[9] According to Porter, no firm can successfully perform at an above-average profitability by trying to be all things to all people. Rather, Porter proposed that managers must choose a competitive strategy that will give it a distinct advantage by capitalizing on the strengths of the organization and the industry it is in. His three competitive strategies are cost leadership, differentiation, and focus.

When an organization competes on the basis of having the lowest costs in its industry, it's following a **cost leadership strategy**. A low-cost leader is highly efficient. Overhead is kept to a minimum, and the firm does everything it can to cut costs. You won't find expensive art or interior décor at offices of low-cost leaders. For example, at Wal-Mart's headquarters in Bentonville, Arkansas, office furnishings are functional, not elaborate, maybe not what you'd expect for the world's largest retailer. Although a low-cost leader doesn't place a lot of emphasis on "frills," its product must be perceived as comparable in quality to that offered by rivals or at least be acceptable to buyers.

A company that competes by offering unique products that are widely valued by customers is following a **differentiation strategy**. Product differences might come from exceptionally high quality, extraordinary service, innovative design, technological capability, or an unusually positive brand image. Practically any successful consumer product or service can be identified as an example of the differentiation strategy; for instance, Nordstrom (customer service), 3M Corporation (product quality and innovative design), Coach (design and brand image), and Apple (product design).

Although these two competitive strategies are aimed at the broad market, the final type of competitive strategy—the **focus strategy**—involves a cost advantage (cost focus) or a differentiation advantage (differentiation focus) in a narrow segment or niche. Segments can be based on product variety, customer type, distribution channel, or geographical location. For example, Denmark's Bang & Olufsen, whose revenues are over $851 million, focuses on high-end audio equipment sales. Whether a focus strategy is feasible depends on the size of the segment and whether the organization can make money serving that segment.

What happens if an organization can't develop a cost or differentiation advantage? Porter called that being *stuck in the middle* and warned that's not a good place to be.

Sustaining Competitive Advantage. Every organization has resources (assets) and capabilities (how work gets done). So what makes some organizations more successful than others? Why do some professional baseball teams consistently win championships or draw large crowds? Why do some organizations have consistent and continuous growth in revenues and profits? Why do some colleges, universities, or departments experience continually increasing enrollments? Why do some companies consistently appear at the

Trader Joe's uses a differentiation focus as its competitive strategy. The company attracts a narrow segment of food shoppers by offering primarily private label brands like the vegetable root chips shown here and many unique food items at affordable prices like Morello cherries from Eastern Europe. Trader Joe's has emerged as one of the most successful niche marketers by holding true to the vision of its founder Joe Coulombe of providing shoppers "a little adventure by stocking items they couldn't find elsewhere at prices that wouldn't empty their wallets."

top of lists ranking the "best," or the "most admired," or the "most profitable"? The answer is that not every organization is able to effectively exploit its resources and to develop the core competencies that can provide it with a competitive advantage. And it's not enough simply to create a competitive advantage. The organization must be able to sustain that advantage; that is, to keep its edge despite competitors' actions or evolutionary changes in the industry. But that's not easy to do! Market instabilities, new technology, and other changes can challenge managers' attempts at creating a long-term, sustainable competitive advantage. However, by using strategic management, managers can better position their organizations to get a sustainable competitive advantage.

FUNCTIONAL STRATEGY. The final type of strategies managers use are the functional strategies, which are the strategies used by an organization's various functional departments to support the competitive strategy. For instance, when Starbucks found itself facing increased competition from the likes of McDonald's and Dunkin' Donuts, it put additional emphasis on its marketing, product research and development, and customer service strategies. We don't cover specific functional strategies here since you'll cover them in other business courses you take.

What Strategic Weapons Do Managers Have?

In today's intensely competitive and chaotic marketplace, organizations are looking for whatever "weapons" they can use to do what they're in business to do and to achieve their goals. Some of these weapons include customer service, employee skills and loyalty, innovation, and quality. We've covered customer service in previous chapters and will discuss employee-related matters in Chapters 6 and 8 through 12. Look for a discussion related to innovation and strategy in the "Technology and the Manager's Job" box. That leaves quality, which we need to look at.

QUALITY AS A STRATEGIC WEAPON. When W. K. Kellogg started manufacturing his cornflake cereal in 1906, his goal was to provide his customers with a high-quality, nutritious product that was enjoyable to eat. That emphasis on quality is still important today. Every Kellogg employee has a responsibility to maintain the high quality of its products.

Many organizations are employing quality practices to build competitive advantage and attract and hold a loyal customer base. If implemented properly, quality can be a way for an organization to create a sustainable competitive advantage.[10] And if a business is able to continuously improve the quality and reliability of its products, it may have a competitive advantage that can't be taken away.[11] Incremental improvement is something that becomes an integrated part of an organization's operations and can develop into a considerable advantage.

How Can Benchmarking Help Promote Quality? Managers in such diverse industries as health care, education, and financial services are discovering what manufacturers have

---

cost leadership strategy
When an organization competes on the basis of having the lowest costs in its industry.

differentiation strategy
When an organization competes on the basis of having unique products that are widely valued by customers.

focus strategy
When an organization competes in a narrow segment or niche with either a cost focus or a differentiation focus.

functional strategies
The strategies used in an organization's various functional departments to support the competitive strategy.

TECHNOLOGY AND THE MANAGER'S JOB

TECHNOLOGY'S ROLE IN COMPANY STRATEGY

How important is IT to a company's strategy?[12] Very important....as two examples will illustrate! Harrah's Entertainment, the world's largest gaming company, is fanatical about customer service, and for good reason. Company research showed that customers who were satisfied with the service they received at a Harrah's casino increased their gaming expenditures by 10 percent, and those who were extremely satisfied increased their gaming expenditures by 24 percent. It discovered this important customer service–expenditures connection because of its incredibly sophisticated information system. But an organization's IT may not always have such a positive payoff as the next example shows! At Prada's Manhattan flagship store, store designers were hoping for a "radically new shopping experience" that combined "cutting-edge architecture and twenty-first-century customer service." Or at least that was the strategy. Prada invested almost one-fourth of the new store's budget into IT, including wireless networks linked to an inventory database. As envisioned, sales staff would roam the store armed with PDAs so they could check whether items were in stock. Even the dressing rooms would have touch screens so customers could do the same. But, the strategy didn't work as planned. The equipment malfunctioned and the staff was overwhelmed with trying to cope with crowds and equipment that didn't work. It's no wonder the multi-million-dollar investment might not have been the best strategy. When an organization's IT "works," it can be a very powerful strategic tool!

long recognized—the benefits of **benchmarking**, which is the search for the best practices among competitors or noncompetitors that lead to their superior performance. The basic idea of benchmarking is that managers can improve quality by analyzing and then copying the methods of the leaders in various fields.

In 1979, Xerox undertook what is widely regarded as the first benchmarking effort in the United States. Until then, the Japanese had been aggressively copying the successes of others by traveling around, watching what others were doing, and then using their new knowledge to improve their products and processes. Xerox's managers couldn't figure out how Japanese manufacturers could sell midsized copiers in the United States for considerably less than Xerox's production costs. So the company's head of manufacturing took a

The Ritz Carlton Hotel Company's approach to quality includes the use of benchmarking practices. In anticipating and responding to evolving customer expectations, the company uses internal and external benchmarking to stimulate new ideas and develop innovative services that create exceptional experiences for guests. One innovation that has become very popular with guests is cooking classes with Ritz-Carlton chefs. Even guests' children between the ages of 7 and 12 can learn culinary skills in the hotel's pastry kitchen. Shown here are kids learning how to make a raspberry tart during a pastry class at the Ritz Carlton in Pasadena, California.

team to Japan to make a detailed study of its competition's costs and processes. The team got most of their information from Xerox's own joint venture partner, Fuji-Xerox, which knew its competition well. What the team found was shocking. Their Japanese rivals were light-years ahead of Xerox in efficiency. Benchmarking those efficiencies was the beginning of Xerox's recovery in the copier field. Today, many organizations use benchmarking practices. For instance, the American Medical Association developed more than 100 standard performance measures to improve medical care. Carlos Ghosn, CEO of Nissan, benchmarked Wal-Mart's operations in purchasing, transportation, and logistics. And Southwest Airlines studied Indy 500 pit crews, who can change a race car's tire in under 15 seconds, to see how their gate crews could make their gate turnaround times even faster.[13]

Once managers have the organization's strategies in place, it's time to set goals and develop plans to pursue those strategies.

How Do Managers Set Goals and Develop Plans?

Compare and contrast approaches to goal setting and planning.

4.3

Planning involves two important aspects: goals and plans. **Goals (objectives)** are desired outcomes or targets. They guide managers' decisions and form the criteria against which work results are measured. **Plans** are documents that outline how goals are going to be met. They usually include resource allocations, budgets, schedules, and other necessary actions to accomplish the goals. As managers plan, they develop both goals and plans.

What Types of Goals Do Organizations Have and How Do They Set Those Goals?

Although it might seem that organizations have a single goal—for businesses, to make a profit and for not-for-profit organizations, to meet the needs of some constituent group(s)—an organization's success can't be determined by a single goal. In reality, all organizations have multiple goals. For instance, businesses may want to increase market share, keep employees motivated, or work toward more environmentally sustainable practices. And a church provides a place for religious practices, but also assists economically disadvantaged individuals in its community and acts as a social gathering place for church members.

TYPES OF GOALS. Most company's goals can be classified as either strategic or financial. Financial goals are related to the financial performance of the organization while strategic goals are related to all other areas of an organization's performance. For instance, McDonald's financial targets include 3 percent to 5 percent average annual sales and revenue growth, 6 percent to 7 percent average annual operating income growth, and returns on invested capital in the high teens.[14] An example of a strategic goal would be the request by Nissan's CEO for the company's GT-R supercar: match or beat the performance of Porsche's 911 Turbo.[15] These goals are **stated goals**—official statements of what an organization says, and what it wants its stakeholders to believe, its goals are. However, stated goals—which can be found in an organization's charter, annual report, public

and the survey says... [16]

relations announcements, or in public statements made by managers—are often conflicting and influenced by what various stakeholders think organizations should do. Such statements can be vague and probably better represent management's public relations skills instead of being meaningful guides to what the organization is actually trying to accomplish. It shouldn't be surprising then to find that an organization's stated goals are often irrelevant to what's actually done. [17]

If you want to know an organization's **real goals**—those goals an organization actually pursues—observe what organizational members are doing. Actions define priorities. Knowing that real and stated goals may differ is important for recognizing what you might otherwise think are inconsistencies.

SETTING GOALS. As we stated earlier, goals provide the direction for all management decisions and actions and form the criterion against which actual accomplishments are measured. Everything organizational members do should be oriented toward achieving goals. These goals can be set either through a process of traditional goal setting or by using management by objectives.

Traditional Goal Setting. In **traditional goal setting**, goals set by top managers flow down through the organization and become subgoals for each organizational area. (See Exhibit 4-5.) This traditional perspective assumes that top managers know what's best because they see the "big picture." And the goals passed down to each succeeding level guide individual employees as they work to achieve those assigned goals. Take a manufacturing business, for example. The president tells the vice president of production what he expects manufacturing costs to be for the coming year and tells the marketing vice president what level he expects sales to reach for the year. These goals are passed to the next organizational level and written to reflect the responsibilities of that level, passed to the next level, and so forth. Then, at some later time, performance is evaluated to determine whether the assigned goals have been achieved. Or that's the way it's supposed to happen. But in reality, it doesn't always do so. Turning broad strategic goals into departmental, team, and individual goals can be a difficult and frustrating process.

Another problem with traditional goal setting is that when top managers define the organization's goals in broad terms—such as achieving "sufficient" profits or increasing "market leadership"—these ambiguous goals have to be made more specific as they flow down through the organization. Managers at each level define the goals and apply their own interpretations and biases as they make them more specific. Clarity is often lost as the goals make their way down from the top of the organization to lower levels. But it doesn't

EXHIBIT 4-5 **Traditional Goal Setting**

"We need to improve the company's performance."

"I want to see a significant improvement in this division's profits."

Top Management's Objective

"Increase profits regardless of the means."

Division Manager's Objective

"Don't worry about quality; just work fast."

Department Manager's Objective

Individual Employee's Objective

have to be that way. For example, at Tijuana-based dj Orthopedics de Mexico, employee teams see the impact of their daily work output on company goals. The company's human resource manager says, "When people get a close connection with the result of their work, when they know every day what they are supposed to do and how they achieved the goals, that makes a strong connection with the company and their job."[18]

When the hierarchy of organizational goals *is* clearly defined, as it is at dj Orthopedics, it forms an integrated network of goals, or a **means-ends chain**. Higher-level goals (or ends) are linked to lower-level goals, which serve as the means for their accomplishment. In other words, the goals achieved at lower levels become the means to reach the goals (ends) at the next level. And the accomplishment of goals at that level becomes the means to achieve the goals (ends) at the next level and on up through the different organizational levels. That's how traditional goal setting is supposed to work.

Management by Objectives. Instead of using traditional goal setting, many organizations use **management by objectives (MBO)**, a process of setting mutually agreed-upon goals and using those goals to evaluate employee performance. If a manager were to use this approach, he or she would sit down with each member of the team and set goals and periodically review whether progress was being made toward achieving those goals. MBO programs have four elements: goal specificity, participative decision making, an explicit time period, and performance feedback.[19] Instead of using goals to make sure

---

From the Past to the Present

Management by objectives (MBO) is not new. The concept goes back over 50 years when Peter Drucker first popularized the term in his 1954 book *The Practice of Management.*[20] Its appeal lies in its emphasis on converting overall objectives into specific objectives for organizational units and individual members.

MBO makes goals operational by a process in which they cascade down through the organization. The organization's overall objectives are translated into specific objectives for each succeeding level—division, departmental, individual—in the organization. The result is a hierarchy that links objectives at one level to those at the next level. For the individual employee, MBO provides specific personal performance objectives. If all the individuals achieve their goals, then the unit's goals will be attained. Likewise, if all the units attain their goals, then the divisional goals will be met until ultimately the organization's overall goals will become a reality.

Does MBO work? Assessing the effectiveness of MBO is a complex task. But goal-setting research can give us some answers. For instance, research has shown that specific, difficult-to-achieve goals produce a higher level of output than do no goals or generalized goals such as "do your best." Also, feedback favorably affects performance because it lets a person know whether his or her level of effort is sufficient or needs to be increased. These findings are consistent with MBO's emphasis on specific goals and feedback. What about participation, though, since MBO strongly advocates that goals be set participatively? Research comparing participatively set goals with assigned goals has not shown any strong or consistent relationship to performance. One critical factor in the success of any MBO program, however, is top management commitment to the process. When top managers had a high commitment to MBO and were personally involved in its implementation, productivity gains were higher than if this commitment was lacking.

---

real goals
Those goals an organization actually pursues as shown by what the organization's members are doing.

traditional goal setting
Goals set by top managers flow down through the organization and become subgoals for each organizational area.

means-end chain
An integrated network of goals in which higher-level goals are linked to lower-level goals, which serve as the means for their accomplishment.

management by objectives (MBO)
A process of setting mutually agreed-upon goals and using those goals to evaluate employee performance.

employees are doing what they're supposed to be doing, MBO uses goals to motivate them as well. The appeal is that it focuses on employees working to accomplish goals they've had a hand in setting.

Studies of actual MBO programs have shown that it can increase employee performance and organizational productivity. For example, one review of MBO programs found productivity gains in almost all of them.[21] But is MBO relevant for today's organizations? If it's viewed as a way of setting goals, then yes, since research shows that goal setting can be an effective approach to motivating employees.[22]

Characteristics of Well-Written Goals. No matter which approach is used, goals have to be written, and some goals are better than others at clearly indicating what the desired outcomes are. Managers should develop well-written goals. Exhibit 4-6 lists the characteristics.[23] With these characteristics in mind, managers are now ready to actually set goals.

Steps in Goal Setting. Managers should follow six steps when setting goals.

1. *Review the organization's mission and employee's key job tasks.* An organization's mission statement will provide an overall guide to what organizational members think is important. Managers should review the mission before writing goals because goals should reflect that mission. In addition, it's important to define what you want employees to accomplish as they do their tasks.
2. *Evaluate available resources.* You don't want to set goals that are impossible to achieve given your available resources. Even though goals should be challenging, they should be realistic. After all, if the resources you have to work with won't allow you to achieve a goal no matter how hard you try or how much effort is exerted, you shouldn't set that goal. That would be like the person with a $50,000 annual income and no other financial resources setting a goal of building an investment portfolio worth $1 million in three years. No matter how hard he or she works at it, it's not going to happen.
3. *Determine the goals individually or with input from others.* The goals reflect desired outcomes and should be congruent with the organizational mission and goals in other organizational areas. These goals should be measurable, specific, and include a time frame for accomplishment.
4. *Make sure goals are well-written and then communicate them to all who need to know.* Writing down and communicating goals forces people to think them through. The written goals also become visible evidence of the importance of working toward something.
5. *Build in feedback mechanisms to assess goal progress.* If goals aren't being met, change them as needed.
6. *Link rewards to goal attainment.* It's natural for employees to ask "What's in it for me?" Linking rewards to goal achievement will help answer that question.

Once the goals have been established, written down, and communicated, managers are ready to develop plans for pursuing the goals.

EXHIBIT 4-6   Well-Written Goals

- Written in terms of outcomes rather than actions
- Measurable and quantifiable
- Clear as to a time frame
- Challenging yet attainable
- Written down
- Communicated to all necessary organizational members

What Types of Plans Do Managers Use and How Do They Develop Those Plans?

Managers need plans to help them clarify and specify how goals will be met. Let's look first at the types of plans managers use.

TYPES OF PLANS. The most popular ways to describe plans are in terms of their *breadth* (strategic versus tactical), *time frame* (long term versus short term), *specificity* (directional versus specific), and *frequency of use* (single use versus standing). As Exhibit 4-7 shows, these types of plans aren't independent. That is, strategic plans are usually long term, directional, and single use. Let's look at each type of plan.

Breadth. **Strategic plans** are those that apply to an entire organization and encompass the organization's overall goals. **Tactical plans** (sometimes referred to as operational plans) specify the details of how the overall goals are to be achieved. When McDonald's founded its Redbox kiosk business, it was the result of strategic planning. Deciding when, where, and how to actually operate the business was the result of tactical plans in marketing, logistics, finance, and so forth.

Time Frame. The number of years used to define short-term and long-term plans has declined considerably due to environmental uncertainty. *Long term* used to mean anything over seven years. Try to imagine what you're likely to be doing in seven years. It seems pretty distant, doesn't it? Now, you can begin to understand how difficult it is for managers to plan that far in the future. Thus, **long-term plans** are now defined as plans with a time frame beyond three years. **Short-term plans** cover one year or less.

Specificity. Intuitively, it would seem that specific plans would be preferable to directional, or loosely guided, plans. **Specific plans** are plans that are clearly defined and leave no room for interpretation. For example, a manager who wants to increase his work unit's output by 8 percent over the next 12 months might establish specific procedures, budget allocations, and work schedules to reach that goal. However, when uncertainty is high and managers must be flexible in order to respond to unexpected changes, they'd likely use **directional plans**, flexible plans that set general guidelines. For example, Sylvia Rhone, president of Motown Records, had a simple goal—to "sign great artists."[24] She could create a specific plan to produce and market 10 albums from new artists this year. Or, she might formulate a directional plan to use a network of people around the world to alert her to new and promising talent so she can increase the number of artists she has under contract. Sylvia, and any manager that engages in planning, must keep in mind that you have to weigh the flexibility of directional plans against the lack of clarity you can get from specific plans.

EXHIBIT 4-7	**Types of Plans**		
Breadth of Use	Time Frame	Specificity	Frequency of Use
Strategic	Long term	Directional	Single use
Tactical	Short term	Specific	Standing

strategic plans
Plans that apply to the entire organization and encompass the organization's overall goals.

tactical plans
Plans that specify the details of how the overall goals are to be achieved.

long-term plans
Plans with a time frame beyond three years.

short-term plans
Plans with a time frame of one year or less.

specific plans
Plans that are clearly defined and leave no room for interpretation.

directional plans
Plans that are flexible and set general guidelines.

Frequency of Use. Some plans that managers develop are ongoing, while others are used only once. A **single-use plan** is a one-time plan specifically designed to meet the needs of a unique situation. For instance, when Dell began developing a pocket-sized device for getting on the Internet, managers used a single-use plan to guide their decisions. In contrast, **standing plans** are ongoing plans that provide guidance for activities performed repeatedly. For example, when you register for classes for the upcoming semester, you're using a standardized registration plan at your college or university. The dates change, but the process works the same way semester after semester.

DEVELOPING PLANS. The process of developing plans is influenced by three contingency factors and by the planning approach followed.

Contingency Factors in Planning. Look back at our chapter-opening case. How will the CEO of Habitat for Humanity go about developing plans for guiding the organization in using this gift? Three contingency factors affect the choice of plans: organizational level, degree of environmental uncertainty, and length of future commitments.[25]

Exhibit 4-8 shows the relationship between a manager's level in the organization and the type of planning done. For the most part, lower-level managers do operational (or tactical) planning while upper-level managers do strategic planning.

The second contingency factor is environmental uncertainty. When uncertainty is high, plans should be specific, but flexible. Managers must be prepared to change or amend plans as they're implemented. For example, at Continental Airlines, the former CEO and his management team established a specific goal of focusing on what customers wanted most—on-time flights—to help the company become more competitive in the highly uncertain airline industry. Because of that uncertainty, the management team identified a "destination, but not a flight plan," and changed plans as necessary to achieve its goal of on-time service.

The last contingency factor also is related to the time frame of plans. The **commitment concept** says that plans should extend far enough to meet those commitments made when the plans were developed. Planning for too long or too short a time period is inefficient and ineffective. We can see the importance of the commitment concept, for example, with the plans that organizations make to increase their computing capabilities. At the data centers where companies' computers are housed, many have found their "power-hungry computers" generate so much heat that their electric bills have skyrocketed because of the increased need for air conditioning.[26] How does this illustrate the commitment concept? As organizations expand their computing technology, they're "committed" to whatever future expenses are generated by that plan. They have to live with the plan and its consequences.

EXHIBIT 4-8 **Planning and Organizational Level**

Strategic Planning

Operational Planning

Top Executives

Middle-Level Managers

First-Level Managers

Developing Your Business Planning Skill

About the Skill

One of the first steps in starting a business is to prepare a business plan.[27] Not only does the business plan aid you in thinking about what you're going to do and how you're going to do it but it also provides a sound basis from which you can obtain funding and resources for your organization.

Steps in Practicing the Skill

1 **Describe your company's background and purpose.** Provide the history of the company. Briefly describe the company's history and what this company does that's unique. Describe what your product or service will be, how you intend to market it, and what you need to bring your product or service to the market.

2 **Identify your short- and long-term goals.** What is your intended goal for this organization? Clearly, for a new company three broad objectives are relevant: creation, survival, and profitability. Specific objectives can include such things as sales, market share, product quality, employee morale, or social responsibility. Identify how you plan to achieve each objective, how you intend to determine whether you met the objective, and when you intend the objective to be met (e.g., short or long term).

3 **Do a thorough market analysis.** You need to convince readers that you understand what you are doing, what your market is, and what competitive pressures you'll face. In this analysis, you'll need to describe the overall market trends, the specific market you intend to compete in, and who the competitors are. In essence, in this section you'll perform your SWOT analysis.

4 **Describe your development and production emphasis.** Explain how you're going to produce your product or service. Include time frames from start to finish. Describe the difficulties you may encounter in this stage as well as how much you believe activities in this stage will cost. Provide an explanation of what decisions (e.g., make or buy?) you will face and what you intend to do.

5 **Describe how you'll market your product or service.** What is your selling strategy? How do you intend to reach your customers? In this section, you'll want to describe your product or service in terms of your competitive advantage and demonstrate how you'll exploit your competitors' weaknesses. In addition to the market analysis, you'll also want to provide sales forecasts in terms of the size of the market, how much of the market you can realistically capture, and how you'll price your product or service.

6 **Put together your financial statements.** What's your bottom line? Investors want to know this information. In the financial section, you'll need to provide projected profit-and-loss statements (income statements) for approximately three to five years. You'll also need to include a cash flow analysis as well as the company's projected balance sheets. In the financial section, you should also give thought to how much start-up costs will be as well as to developing a financial strategy—how you intend to use funds received from a financial institution and how you'll control and monitor the financial well-being of the company.

7 **Provide an overview of the organization and its management.** Identify the key executives, summarizing their education, experience, and any relevant qualifications. Identify their positions in the organization and their job roles. Explain how much salary they intend to earn initially. Identify others who may assist the organization's management (e.g., company lawyer, accountant, board of directors). This section should also include, if relevant, a section on how you intend to deal with employees. For example, how will employees be paid, what benefits will be offered, and how will employee performance be assessed?

8 **Describe the legal form of the business.** Identify the legal form of the business. For example, is it a sole proprietor, a partnership, a corporation? Depending on the legal form, you may need to provide information regarding equity positions, shares of stock issued, and the like.

9 **Identify the critical risks and contingencies facing the organization.** In this section you'll want to identify what you'll do if problems arise. For instance, if you don't meet sales forecasts, what then? Similar responses to such questions as problems with suppliers, inability to hire qualified employees, poor-quality products, and so on should be addressed. Readers want to see if you've anticipated potential problems and if you have contingency plans. This is the what-if section.

10 **Put the business plan together.** Using the information you've gathered from the previous nine steps, it's now time to put the business plan together into a well-organized document. A business plan should contain a cover page that shows the company name,

---

single-use plan
A one-time plan specifically designed to meet the needs of a unique situation.

standing plans
Plans that are ongoing and provide guidance for activities performed repeatedly.

commitment concept
The idea that plans should extend far enough to meet those commitments made when the plans were developed.

address, contact person, and numbers at which the individual can be reached. The cover page should also contain the date the business was established and, if one exists, the company logo. The next page of the business plan should be a table of contents. Here you'll want to list and identify the location of each major section and subsection in the business plan. Remember to use proper outlining techniques. Next comes the executive summary, the first section the readers will actually read. Thus, it's one of the more critical elements of the business plan because if the executive summary is poorly done, readers may not read any further. In a two- to three-page summary, highlight information about the company, its management, its market and competition, the funds requested, how the funds will be used, financial history (if available), financial projections, and when investors can expect to get their money back (called the exit). Next come the main sections of your business plan; that is, the material you've researched and written about in steps 1 through 9. Close out the business plan

with a section that summarizes the highlights of what you've just presented. Finally, if you have charts, exhibits, photographs, tables, and the like, you might want to include an appendix in the back of the business plan. If you do, remember to cross-reference this material to the relevant section of the report.

Practicing the Skill

You have a great idea for a business and need to create a business plan to present to a bank. Choose one of the following products or services and draft the part of your plan that describes how you will price and market it (see step 5).

1 Haircuts at home (you make house calls)
2 Olympic snowboarding computer game
3 Online apartment rental listing
4 Ergonomic dental chair
5 Voice-activated house alarm
6 Customized running shoes

Now choose a different product or service from the list and identify critical risks and contingencies (see step 9).

The global financial crisis and economic slowdown has created a volatile and highly uncertain environment for retailers, even for companies like British retailer Burberry Group PLC that targets the luxury market. In recent years Burberry implemented plans to expand its global reach and now operates more than 300 company-owned stores and shops within high-end department stores around the world. For Angela Ahrendts, CEO of Burberry, flexibility is the key for dealing with dynamic market conditions, especially the downturns in Asia, Europe, and the United States. On a daily basis Burberry monitors global trends and each week adjusts forecasts before making plans to move forward.

Approaches to Planning. Federal, state, and local government officials are working together on a plan to boost populations of wild salmon in the northwestern United States. Managers in the Global Fleet Graphics division of the 3M Company are developing detailed plans to satisfy increasingly demanding customers and to battle more aggressive competitors. Emilio Azcárraga Jean, chairman, president, and CEO of Grupo Televisa, gets input from many different people before setting company goals and then turns over the planning for achieving the goals to various executives. In each of these situations, planning is done a little differently. *How* an organization plans can best be understood by looking at *who* does the planning.

In the traditional approach, planning is done entirely by top-level managers who often are assisted by a **formal planning department**, a group of planning specialists whose sole responsibility is to help write the various organizational plans. Under this approach, plans developed by top level managers flow down through other organizational levels, much like the traditional approach to goal setting. As they flow down through the organization, the plans are tailored to the particular needs of each level. Although this approach makes managerial planning thorough, systematic, and coordinated, all too often the focus is on developing "the plan," a thick binder (or binders) full of meaningless information, that's stuck away on a shelf and never used by anyone for guiding or coordinating work efforts. In fact, in a survey of managers about formal top-down organizational planning processes, over 75 percent said that their company's planning approach was unsatisfactory.[28] A common complaint was that, "plans are documents that you prepare for the corporate planning staff and later forget." Although this traditional top-down approach to planning is used by many organizations, it can be effective only if managers understand the importance of creating documents that organizational members actually use, not documents that look impressive but are never used.

Another approach to planning is to involve more organizational members in the process. In this approach, plans aren't handed down from one level to the next, but instead are developed by organizational members at the various levels and in the various work units to meet their specific needs. For instance, at Dell, employees from production, supply management, and channel management meet weekly to make plans based on current product demand and supply. In addition, work teams set their own daily schedules and track their progress against those schedules. If a team falls behind, team members develop "recovery" plans to try to get back on schedule.[29] When organizational members are more actively involved in planning, they see that the plans are more than just something written down on paper. They can actually see that the plans are used in directing and coordinating work.

What Contemporary Planning Issues Do Managers Face?

We conclude this chapter by addressing two contemporary issues in planning. Specifically, we're going to look at planning effectively in dynamic environments and then at how managers can use environmental scanning, especially competitive intelligence.

Discuss contemporary issues in planning.

4.4

How Can Managers Plan Effectively in Dynamic Environments?

As we saw in the last chapter, the external environment is continually changing. For instance, Wi-Fi has revolutionized all kinds of industries from airlines to automobile manufacturing to supermarkets. Social networking sites are being used by companies for connecting with customers. Amounts spent on eating out instead of cooking at home are predicted to decline. And experts believe that China and India are transforming the twenty-first century global economy.

How can managers effectively plan when the external environment is continually changing? We already discussed uncertain environments as one of the contingency factors that affect the types of plans managers develop. Because dynamic environments are more the norm than the exception, let's look at how they can effectively plan in such environments.

In an uncertain environment, managers should develop plans that are specific, but flexible. Although this may seem contradictory, it's not. To be useful, plans need some specificity, but the plans should not be set in stone. Managers need to recognize that planning is an ongoing process. The plans serve as a road map although the destination may change due to dynamic market conditions. They should be ready to change directions if environmental conditions warrant. This flexibility is particularly important as plans are implemented. Managers need to stay alert to environmental changes that may impact implementation and respond as needed. Keep in mind, also, that even when the environment is highly uncertain, it's important to continue formal planning in order to see any effect on organizational performance. It's the persistence in planning that contributes to significant performance improvement. Why? It seems that, as with most activities, managers "learn to plan" and the quality of their planning improves when they continue to do it.[30] Finally, make the organizational hierarchy flatter to effectively plan in dynamic environments. This means allowing lower organizational levels to set goals and develop plans because there's little time for goals and plans to flow down from the top. Managers should teach their employees how to set goals and to plan and then trust them to do it. And you need look no further than Bangalore, India, to find a company that effectively understands this. Just a decade ago, Wipro Limited was "an anonymous conglomerate selling cooking oil and personal computers, mostly in India." Today, it's a $4.9 billion-a-year

formal planning department
A group of planning specialists whose sole responsibility is to help write the various organizational plans.

environmental scanning
An analysis of the external environment that involves screening large amounts of information to detect emerging trends.

competitive intelligence
A type of environmental scanning that gives managers accurate information about competitors.

global company with most of its business (some 90 percent) coming from information-technology services.[31] Accenture, EDS, IBM, and the big U.S. accounting firms know all too well the competitive threat Wipro represents. Not only are Wipro's employees economical, they're knowledgeable and skilled. And they play an important role in the company's planning. Since the information services industry is continually changing, employees are taught to analyze situations and to define the scale and scope of a client's problems in order to offer the best solutions. These employees are the ones on the front line with the clients and it's their responsibility to establish what to do and how to do it. It's an approach that positions Wipro for success no matter how the industry changes.

How Can Managers Use Environmental Scanning?

A manager's analysis of the external environment may be improved by **environmental scanning**, which involves screening large amounts of information to detect emerging trends. One of the fastest-growing forms of environmental scanning is **competitive intelligence**, which is accurate information about competitors that allows managers to anticipate competitors' actions rather than merely react to them.[32] It seeks basic information about competitors: Who are they? What are they doing? How will what they're doing affect us?

Many who study competitive intelligence suggest that much of the competitor-related information managers need to make crucial strategic decisions is available and accessible to the public.[33] In other words, competitive intelligence isn't organizational espionage. Advertisements, promotional materials, press releases, reports filed with government agencies, annual reports, want ads, newspaper reports, information on the Internet, and industry studies are readily accessible sources of information. Specific information on an industry and associated organizations is increasingly available through electronic databases. Managers can literally tap into this wealth of competitive information by purchasing access to databases. Attending trade shows and debriefing your own sales staff also can be good sources of information on competitors. In addition, many organizations even regularly buy competitors' products and ask their own employees to evaluate them to learn about new technical innovations.[34]

In a changing global business environment, environmental scanning and obtaining competitive intelligence can be quite complex, especially since information must be gathered from around the world. However, managers could subscribe to news services that review newspapers and magazines from around the globe and provide summaries to client companies.

Managers do need to be careful about the way information, especially competitive intelligence, is gathered to prevent any concerns about whether it's legal or ethical. For instance, Starwood Hotels recently sued Hilton Hotels alleging that two former employees stole trade secrets and helped Hilton develop a new line of luxury, trendy hotels designed to appeal to a young demographic.[35] The court filing said, "This is the clearest imaginable case of corporate espionage, theft of trade secrets, unfair competition, and computer fraud." Competitive intelligence becomes illegal corporate spying when it involves the theft of proprietary materials or trade secrets by any means. The Economic Espionage Act makes it a crime in the United States to engage in economic espionage or to steal a trade secret.[36] Difficult decisions about competitive intelligence arise because often there's a fine line between what's considered *legal and ethical* and what's considered *legal but unethical*. Although the top manager at one competitive intelligence firm contends that 99.9 percent of intelligence gathering is legal, there's no question that some people or companies will go to any lengths—some unethical—to get information about competitors.[37]

Review and  Applications

Chapter Summary

4.1 **Discuss the nature and purposes of planning.** As the primary management function, planning establishes the basis for all the other things that managers do. The planning we're concerned with is formal planning; that is, specific goals covering a specific time period are defined and written down and specific plans are developed to make sure those goals are met. There are four reasons why managers should plan: (1) it establishes coordinated efforts, (2) it reduces uncertainty, (3) it reduces overlapping and wasteful activities, and (4) it establishes the goals or standards that are used in controlling work. Although criticisms have been directed at planning, the evidence generally supports the position that organizations benefit from formal planning.

4.2 **Explain what managers do in the strategic management process.** Managers develop the organization's strategies in the strategic management process, which is a six-step process encompassing strategy planning, implementation, and evaluation. The six steps are as follows: (1) Identify the organization's current mission, goals, and strategies; (2) Do an external analysis; (3) Do an internal analysis—steps 2 and 3 together are called SWOT analysis; (4) Formulate strategies; (5) Implement strategies; and (6) Evaluate results. The end result of this process is a set of corporate, competitive, and functional strategies that allow the organization to do what it's in business to do and to achieve its goals.

4.3 **Compare and contrast approaches to goal setting and planning.** Most company's goals are classified as either strategic or financial. We can also look at goals as either stated or real. In traditional goal setting, goals set by top managers flow down through the organization and become subgoals for each organizational area. Organizations could also use management by objectives, which is a process of setting mutually agreed-upon goals and using those goals to evaluate employee performance. Plans can be described in terms of their breadth, time frame, specificity, and frequency of use. Plans can be developed by a formal planning department or by involving more organizational members in the process.

4.4 **Discuss contemporary issues in planning.** One contemporary planning issue is planning in dynamic environments, which usually means developing plans that are specific but flexible. Also, it's important to continue planning even when the environment is highly uncertain. Finally, because there's little time in a dynamic environment for goals and plans to flow down from the top, lower organizational levels should be allowed to set goals and develop plans. Another contemporary planning issue is using environmental scanning to help do a better analysis of the external environment. One form of environmental scanning, competitive intelligence, can be especially helpful in finding out what competitors are doing.

PEARSON mymanagementlab   To check your understanding of learning outcomes **4.1** – **4.4**, go to **mymanagementlab.com** and try the chapter questions.

Understanding the Chapter

1. Contrast formal with informal planning. Discuss why planning is beneficial.

2. Describe in detail the six-step strategic management process.

3. What is a SWOT analysis and why is it important to managers?

4. Organizations that fail to plan are planning to fail. Do you agree or disagree with this statement? Explain your position.

5. Under what circumstances do you believe MBO would be most useful? Discuss.

6. Find examples in current business periodicals of each of Porter's generic strategies. Name the company, describe the strategy being used, and explain why it's an example of that strategy. Be sure to cite your sources.

7. "The primary means of sustaining a competitive advantage is to adjust faster to the environment than your competitors do." Do you agree or disagree with this statement? Explain your position.

8. First we had the bird flu. Now, the H1N1 flu pandemic has been in the news recently. How could organizations be prepared for an outbreak of H1N1 flu or some new unknown flu strain or medical crisis? What types of planning would they need to do? Now, take a specific organization (your college or university, your place of employment, or some business organization) and describe all the possible organizational areas that might be impacted and the plans that organization would need to have in place to be prepared.

9. Do a personal SWOT analysis. Assess your personal strengths and weaknesses (skills, talents, abilities). What are you good at? What are you not so good at? What do you enjoy doing? Not enjoy doing? Then, identify career opportunities and threats by researching job prospects in the industry you're interested in. Look at trends and projections. You might want to check out the information the Bureau of Labor Statistics provides on job prospects. Once you have all this information, write a specific career action plan. Outline five-year career goals and what you need to do to achieve those goals.

Understanding Yourself

What Are My Course Performance Goals?

INSTRUMENT   Using the following scale, select the answer for each of the 12 statements that best expresses why you study for a course.

1 = Never
2 = Rarely
3 = Sometimes
4 = Often
5 = Always

I study because:

1. I want to be praised by my professors and parents.	1	2	3	4	5
2. I want to be noticed by my friends.	1	2	3	4	5
3. I don't want my classmates to make fun of me.	1	2	3	4	5
4. I don't want to be disliked by a professor.	1	2	3	4	5
5. I want people to see how smart I am.	1	2	3	4	5
6. I wish to get better grades than my peers.	1	2	3	4	5
7. I want to get good grades.	1	2	3	4	5
8. I want to be proud of getting good grades.	1	2	3	4	5
9. I don't want to fail final exams.	1	2	3	4	5
10. I wish to be admitted to graduate school.	1	2	3	4	5
11. I want to get a good job in the future.	1	2	3	4	5
12. I want to attain status in the future.	1	2	3	4	5

SCORING KEY   Total up the number of 4 and 5 responses. This will be between zero and 12.

ANALYSIS AND INTERPRETATION   What drives you to study? What goals are you trying to achieve? This questionnaire measures goal orientation as related to your course work.

There are no "right" goals. But having clear goals can help you better understand your studying behavior. If you had no responses in the 4 or 5 categories, your course performance is likely to suffer because you have no strong reasons for studying. This suggests a need for you to reassess your goals and consider what you want from your course work. If you had a number of responses in the 4 or 5 categories, you appear to have specific goals that will motivate you to study and achieve high performance.

Source: Based on T. Hayamizu and B. Weiner, "A Test of Dweck's Model of Achievement Goals as Related to Perceptions of Ability," *Journal of Experimental Education*, vol. 59, 1991, pp. 226–34. Modified per C. Dupeyrat and E. V. Smith Jr., "Toward Establishing a Unified Metric for Performance and Learning Goal Orientations," *Journal of Applied Measurement*, vol. 2, no. 4, 2001, pp. 312–36.

FYIA (For Your Immediate Action)

People Power²

Reply   Reply All   Forward

To: Alpha Team members
From: Eric Smallwood, Alpha Team Leader
Subject: **Goals for developing new training module**

Hey Alpha Team! Great job! We've been chosen to develop People Power's new Internet training module. The overall goal is to come up with a training module that helps people learn how to research information on the Internet. The sales reps say we've already had several requests from our corporate clients for this type of training program. That means we're on a fast-track development schedule.

I'm asking each of you to identify two or three specific goals for each of the three stages of the project: (1) researching our customers' needs, (2) researching the Internet for specific information sources and techniques we want to teach in our training modules, and (3) designing and writing the actual training modules. Please have these written by next   week. We'll have a team meeting to share ideas and finalize the specific project goals. Then . . . it will be time to get to work!

This fictionalized company and message were created for educational purposes only. It is not meant to reflect positively or negatively on management practices by any company that may share this name.

CASE APPLICATION

MANAGING THE MAGIC

Magic happens at the happiest place on earth. At least that's what the folks at the Walt Disney Company (Disney) work hard to make us believe. However, the difficult business climate in 2008 and 2009 challenged Disney, as it did many other well-managed companies. CEO Bob Iger and his top management team are working hard to conjure up their own magic; that is, to find the best way to strategically maneuver the company to prosper despite the environmental uncertainties.

Disney has had a long record of successes and the "Disney Difference" is noticeably apparent. What is the Disney Difference? It's "high-quality creative content, backed up by a clear strategy for maximizing that content's value across platforms and markets." From books, toys, and games to online media, soundtracks, and DVDs, Disney exploits its rich legacy of products through quality creative content and exceptional storytelling. Some of these products include, among many others, *The Lion King, Toy Story, The Jungle Book, Cars,* Disney-ABC Television, and ESPN programming. Although Disney is a U.S.-based company, its businesses span the globe with operations in North America, Europe, Asia Pacific, and Latin America. Its latest push is Russia, a large untapped media market, where it's planning a broadcast version of the Disney Channel. The president of Walt Disney International says, "We believe there is vast growth to come out of this market, despite the near-term economic turmoil." The company is also funding a $452 million expansion of the Disneyland theme park in Hong Kong in hopes of boosting poor attendance figures. One of the new themed areas called Grizzly Trail is "set in an American frontier gold-mining town and features a roller coaster patterned after a runaway mine train." Despite its magical touch, just a few short years ago, Disney wasn't such a happy place.

When Bob Iger was named CEO in 2005, analysts believed that the Disney brand had become dated. And, there was this sense that Disney's target audience was young and that its products couldn't possibly be of interest to older kids. Iger, who views himself as the steward of the entire Disney brand, immediately recognized the importance of leveraging the company's vast media content on different platforms. His strategic approach had been working well until the economy slowed and the decline in global consumer spending made things even more precarious. Now, Iger and his management team will have to use all the strategic tools they have to guide the company and keep the magic coming.

Discussion Questions

1. What is the Disney Difference and how will it affect the company's corporate, competitive, and functional strategies?

2. What challenges do you think Disney might face in doing business in Russia? How could Iger and his top management team use planning to best prepare for those challenges?

3. With the announced expansion of Disney's Hong Kong Disneyland, what goals might the company set? What type of planning will be necessary?

4. How might Iger and his top management team use the strategic management process to "keep the magic coming" in the current economic climate?

Sources: C. Yung and J. Ng, "In Asia, Disney's World Will Get Bigger," *Wall Street Journal,* July 1, 2009, p. B5; P. Sanders, "Disney Profit Falls Sharply but Clouds Are Parting," *Wall Street Journal,* May 6, 2009, p. B1; R. Siklos, "Bob Iger Rocks Disney," *CNN Online,* http://www.cnnmoney.com (January 5, 2009); B. Barnes, "Disney Plans a Channel for Russian TV," *New York Times Online,* December 17, 2008; P. Sanders, "Disney Net Slips as Slump Hits Home," *Wall Street Journal,* November 17, 2008, p. B1; R. Siklos, "Q&A: The Iger Difference," *Fortune,* April 28, 2008, pp. 90–94; R. Grover, "A Star Is Born, Disney Style," *BusinessWeek,* April 21, 2008, pp. 50–51; and The Walt Disney Company *2007 Fact Book,* http://corporate. disney.go.com/investors/fact_books.html.

Entrepreneurship Module
Managing Entrepreneurial Ventures

Viking Ranges are loved by serious cooks—professionals and amateurs. The company that makes the kitchen appliances was founded in 1986 in Greenwood, Mississippi, by Fred Carl Jr. Today, the company employs more than 1,000 local residents and has annual sales of about $300 million. Viking also recently "opened an 87,000 square foot manufacturing plant and a separate distribution center to handle its expansion into premium appliances, cookware, and cutlery." Carl also founded 16 Viking Cooking Schools, which attract more than 70,000 students annually. Fred Carl is an entrepreneur. And Viking Range is an entrepreneurial success story.

In this module we're going to look at the activities of entrepreneurs like Fred Carl. We'll start by looking at the context of entrepreneurship and then examine entrepreneurship from the perspective of the four managerial functions.

What Is Entrepreneurship?

Entrepreneurship is the process of starting new businesses, generally in response to opportunities. For instance, Fred Carl saw an opportunity to create an appliance that combined the best features of commercial and residential ranges.

Many people think that entrepreneurial ventures and small businesses are the same, but they're not. Entrepreneurs create **entrepreneurial ventures**—organizations that pursue opportunities, are characterized by innovative practices, and have growth and profitability as their main goals. On the other hand, a **small business** is an independent business having fewer than 500 employees that doesn't necessarily engage in any new or innovative practices and that has relatively little impact on its industry. A small business isn't necessarily entrepreneurial because it's small. To be entrepreneurial means that the business is innovative and seeking out new opportunities. Even though entrepreneurial ventures may start small, they pursue growth. Some new small firms may grow, but many remain small businesses, by choice or by default.

Who's Starting Entrepreneurial Ventures?

"Call them accidental entrepreneurs, unintended entrepreneurs, or forced entrepreneurs." As the unemployment rate hovers around double digits, many corporate "refugees" are becoming entrepreneurs. These individuals are looking to entrepreneurship, not because they sense some great opportunity, but because there are no jobs. The Index of Entrepreneurial Activity by the Kauffman Foundation showed a slight increase in the number of

entrepreneurship
The process of starting new businesses, generally in response to opportunities.

entrepreneurial ventures
Organizations that pursue opportunities, are characterized by innovative practices, and have growth and profitability as their main goals.

small business
An independent business having fewer than 500 employees that doesn't necessarily engage in any new or innovative practices and that has relatively little impact on its industry.

new businesses formed in 2008. The report found that "the patterns provided some early evidence that 'necessity' entrepreneurship is increasing and 'opportunity' entrepreneurship is decreasing." But "accidental or by design," entrepreneurship is on the rise again.

As many entrepreneurs (successful and not-so-successful) would attest, being an entrepreneur isn't easy. According to the Small Business Administration, only two-thirds of new businesses survive at least two years. The survival rate falls to 44 percent at four years, and to 31 percent at seven years. But the interesting thing is that entrepreneurial venture survival rates are about the same in economic expansions and recessions.

What Do Entrepreneurs Do?

Describing what entrepreneurs do isn't an easy or simple task! No two entrepreneurs' work activities are exactly alike. In a general sense, entrepreneurs create something new, something different. They search for change, respond to it, and exploit it.

Initially, an entrepreneur is engaged in assessing the potential for the entrepreneurial venture and then dealing with start-up issues. In exploring the entrepreneurial context, entrepreneurs gather information, identify potential opportunities, and pinpoint possible competitive advantage(s). Then, armed with this information, an entrepreneur researches the venture's feasibility—uncovering business ideas, looking at competitors, and exploring financing options.

After looking at the potential of the proposed venture and assessing the likelihood of pursuing it successfully, an entrepreneur proceeds to plan the venture. This includes such activities as developing a viable organizational mission, exploring organizational culture issues, and creating a well-thought-out business plan. Once these planning issues have been resolved, the entrepreneur must look at organizing the venture, which involves choosing a legal form of business organization, addressing other legal issues such as patent or copyright searches, and coming up with an appropriate organizational design for structuring how work is going to be done.

Only after these start-up activities have been completed is the entrepreneur ready to actually launch the venture. This involves setting goals and strategies, and establishing the technology-operations methods, marketing plans, information systems, financial-accounting systems, and cash flow management systems.

Once the entrepreneurial venture is up and running, the entrepreneur's attention switches to managing it. What's involved with actually managing the entrepreneurial venture? An important activity is managing the various processes that are part of every business: making decisions, establishing action plans, analyzing external and internal environments, measuring and evaluating performance, and making needed changes. Also, the entrepreneur must perform activities associated with managing people including selecting and hiring, appraising and training, motivating, managing conflict, delegating tasks, and being an effective leader. Finally, the entrepreneur must manage the venture's growth including such activities as developing and designing growth strategies, dealing with crises, exploring various avenues for financing growth, placing a value on the venture, and perhaps even eventually exiting the venture.

What Planning Do Entrepreneurs Need to Do?

Planning is important to entrepreneurial ventures. Once a venture's feasibility has been thoroughly researched, an entrepreneur then must look at planning the venture. The most important thing that an entrepreneur does in planning the venture is developing a **business plan**—a written document that summarizes a business opportunity and defines and articulates how the identified opportunity is to be seized and exploited. A written business plan can range from basic to thorough. The most basic type of business plan would simply include an *executive summary,* sort of a mini–business plan that's no longer than two pages. A *synopsis*-type plan is a little more involved. It's been described as an "executive summary on steroids." In addition to the executive summary, it includes a business proposal that explains why the idea is relevant to potential investors. A *summary business plan* includes an executive summary and a page or so of explanation of each of the key components of a business plan. A *full business plan* is the traditional business plan, which we describe fully next. Finally, an *operational business plan* is the most detailed (50 or more pages) since it's used by ventures that are already operating with an existing strategy. It's often used to "plan the business" but also can be used to raise additional money or to attract potential acquirers. It's important for entrepreneurs to know which type of business plan they need for their purposes.

What's in a Full Business Plan?

For many would-be entrepreneurs, developing and writing a business plan seems like a daunting task. However, a good business plan is valuable. It pulls together all the elements of the entrepreneur's vision into a single coherent document. The business plan requires careful planning and creative thinking. But if done well, it can be a convincing document that serves many functions. It serves as a blueprint and road map for operating the business. And the business plan is a "living" document, guiding organizational decisions and actions throughout the life of the business, not just in the start-up stage.

If an entrepreneur has completed a feasibility study, much of the information included in it becomes the basis for the business plan. A good business plan covers six major areas: executive summary, analysis of opportunity, analysis of the context, description of the business, financial data and projections, and supporting documentation.

EXECUTIVE SUMMARY. The executive summary summarizes the key points that the entrepreneur wants to make about the proposed entrepreneurial venture. These might include a brief mission statement; primary goals; brief history of the entrepreneurial venture, maybe in the form of a timeline; key people involved in the venture; nature of the business; concise product or service descriptions; brief explanations of market niche, competitors, and competitive advantage; proposed strategies; and selected key financial information.

ANALYSIS OF OPPORTUNITY. In this section of the business plan, an entrepreneur presents the details of the perceived opportunity. Essentially, this means (1) sizing up the market by describing the demographics of the target market, (2) describing and evaluating industry trends, and (3) identifying and evaluating competitors.

ANALYSIS OF THE CONTEXT. Whereas the opportunity analysis focuses on the opportunity in a specific industry and market, the context analysis takes a much broader perspective. Here, the entrepreneur describes the broad external changes and trends taking place in the economic, political-legal, technological, and global environments.

DESCRIPTION OF THE BUSINESS. In this section, an entrepreneur describes how the entrepreneurial venture is going to be organized, launched, and managed. It includes a thorough description of the mission statement; a description of the desired organizational culture; marketing plans including overall marketing strategy, pricing, sales tactics, service-warranty policies, and advertising and promotion tactics; product development plans such as an explanation of development status, tasks, difficulties and risks, and anticipated costs; operational plans including a description of proposed geographic location, facilities and needed improvements, equipment, and work flow; human resource plans including a description of key management persons, composition of board of directors including their background experience and skills, current and future staffing needs, compensation and benefits, and training needs; and an overall schedule and timetable of events.

business plan
A written document that summarizes a business opportunity and defines and articulates how the identified opportunity is to be seized and exploited.

FINANCIAL DATA AND PROJECTIONS. Every effective business plan contains financial data and projections. Although the calculations and interpretation may be difficult, they are absolutely critical. No business plan is complete without financial information. Financial plans should cover at least three years and contain projected income statements, pro forma cash flow analysis (monthly for the first year and quarterly for the next two), pro forma balance sheets, breakeven analysis, and cost controls. If major equipment or other capital purchases are expected, the items, costs, and available collateral should be listed. All financial projections and analyses should include explanatory notes, especially where the data seem contradictory or questionable.

SUPPORTING DOCUMENTATION. This *is* an important component of an effective business plan. The entrepreneur should back up his or her descriptions with charts, graphs, tables, photographs, or other visual tools. In addition, it might be important to include information (personal and work-related) about the key participants in the entrepreneurial venture.

Just as the idea for an entrepreneurial venture takes time to germinate, so does the writing of a good business plan. It's important for an entrepreneur to put serious thought and consideration into the plan. It's not an easy thing to do. However, the resulting document should be valuable in current and future planning efforts.

What Issues Are There in Organizing an Entrepreneurial Venture?

Once the start-up and planning issues for the entrepreneurial venture have been addressed, the entrepreneur is ready to begin organizing the entrepreneurial venture. The main organizing issues an entrepreneur must address include the legal forms of organization, organizational design and structure, and human resource management.

What Are the Legal Forms of Organization for Entrepreneurial Ventures?

The first organizing decision that an entrepreneur must make is a critical one. It's the form of legal ownership for the venture. The two primary factors affecting this decision are taxes and legal liability. An entrepreneur wants to minimize the impact of both of these factors. The right choice can protect the entrepreneur from legal liability as well as save tax dollars, in both the short run and the long run.

There are three basic ways to organize an entrepreneurial venture: sole proprietorship, partnership, and corporation. However, when you include the variations of these basic organizational alternatives, you end up with six possible choices, each with its own tax consequences, liability issues, and pros and cons. These six choices are sole proprietorship, general partnership, limited liability partnership (LLP), C corporation, S corporation, and limited liability company (LLC).

The decision regarding the legal form of organization is important because it has significant tax and liability consequences. Although the legal form of organization can be changed, it's not easy to do. An entrepreneur needs to think carefully about what's important, especially in the areas of flexibility, taxes, and amount of personal liability in choosing the best form of organization.

What Type of Organizational Structure Should Entrepreneurial Ventures Use?

The choice of an appropriate organizational structure is also an important decision when organizing an entrepreneurial venture. At some point, successful entrepreneurs find that they can't do everything. They need people. The entrepreneur must then decide on the most appropriate structural arrangement for effectively and efficiently carrying out the organization's activities. Without a suitable type of organizational structure, an entrepreneurial venture may soon find itself in a chaotic situation.

In many small firms, the organizational structure tends to evolve with very little intentional and deliberate planning by the entrepreneur. For the most part, the structure may be very simple—one person does whatever is needed. As an entrepreneurial venture grows and the entrepreneur finds it increasingly difficult to go it alone, employees are brought on board to perform certain functions or duties that the entrepreneur can't handle. As the company continues to grow, these individuals tend to perform those same functions. Soon, each functional area may require managers and employees.

As the venture evolves to a more deliberate structure, an entrepreneur faces a whole new set of challenges. All of a sudden, he or she must share decision-making and operating responsibilities. This is typically one of the most difficult things for an entrepreneur to do— letting go and allowing someone else to make decisions. *After all*, he or she reasons, *How can anyone know this business as well as I do?* Also, what might have been a fairly informal, loose, and flexible atmosphere that worked well when the organization was small may no longer be effective. Many entrepreneurs are greatly concerned about keeping that "small company" atmosphere alive even as the venture grows and evolves into a more structured arrangement. But having a structured organization doesn't necessarily mean giving up flexibility, adaptability, and freedom. In fact, the structural design may be as fluid as the entrepreneur feels comfortable with and yet still have the rigidity it needs to operate efficiently.

Organizational design decisions in entrepreneurial ventures also revolve around the six elements of organizational structure discussed in Chapter 5: work specialization, departmentalization, chain of command, span of control, amount of centralization-decentralization, and amount of formalization. Decisions about these six elements will determine whether an entrepreneur designs a more mechanistic or organic organizational structure. When would each be preferable? A mechanistic structure would be preferable when cost efficiencies are critical to the venture's competitive advantage; when more control over employees' work activities is important; if the venture produces standardized products in a routine fashion; and when the external environment is relatively stable and certain. An organic structure would be most appropriate when innovation is critical to the organization's competitive advantage; for smaller organizations where rigid approaches to dividing and coordinating work aren't necessary; if the organization produces customized products in a flexible setting; and where the external environment is dynamic, complex, and uncertain.

What Human Resource Management (HRM) Issues Must Entrepreneurs Deal With?

As an entrepreneurial venture grows, additional employees must be hired to perform the increased workload. As employees are brought on board, two HRM issues of particular importance are employee recruitment and employee retention.

An entrepreneur wants to ensure that the venture has the people to do the required work. Recruiting new employees is one of the biggest challenges that entrepreneurs face. In fact, the ability of small firms to successfully recruit appropriate employees is consistently rated as one of the most important factors influencing organizational success.

Entrepreneurs, particularly, look for high-potential people who can perform multiple roles during various stages of venture growth. They look for individuals who "buy into" the venture's entrepreneurial culture—individuals who have a passion for the business. Unlike their corporate counterparts who often focus on filling a job by matching a person to the job requirements, entrepreneurs look to fill in critical skills gaps. They're looking for people who are exceptionally capable and self-motivated, flexible, multiskilled, and who can help grow the entrepreneurial venture. While corporate managers tend to focus on using traditional HRM practices and techniques, entrepreneurs are more concerned with matching characteristics of the person to the values and culture of the organization; that is, they focus on matching the person to the organization.

Getting competent and qualified people into the venture is just the first step in effectively managing the human resources. An entrepreneur wants to keep the people he or she has hired and trained. A unique and important employee retention issue entrepreneurs must deal with is compensation. Whereas traditional organizations are more likely to view compensation from the perspective of monetary rewards (base pay, benefits, and incentives), smaller entrepreneurial firms are more likely to view compensation from a total rewards perspective. For these firms, compensation encompasses psychological rewards, learning opportunities, and recognition in addition to monetary rewards (base pay and incentives).

What Issues Do Entrepreneurs Face in Leading an Entrepreneurial Venture?

Leading is an important function of entrepreneurs. As an entrepreneurial venture grows and people are brought on board, an entrepreneur takes on a new role—that of a leader. In this section, we want to look at what's involved with that. First, we're going to look at the unique personality characteristics of entrepreneurs. Then we're going to discuss the important role entrepreneurs play in motivating employees through empowerment and leading the venture and employee teams.

What Type of Personality Do Entrepreneurs Have?

Think of someone you know who is an entrepreneur. Maybe it's someone you personally know or maybe it's someone like Bill Gates of Microsoft. How would you describe this person's personality? One of the most researched areas of entrepreneurship has been the search to determine what—if any—psychological characteristics entrepreneurs have in common, what types of personality traits entrepreneurs have that might distinguish them from nonentrepreneurs, and what traits entrepreneurs have that might predict who will be a successful entrepreneur.

Is there a classic "entrepreneurial personality"? Although trying to pinpoint specific personality characteristics that all entrepreneurs share has the same problem as identifying the trait theories of leadership—that is, being able to identify specific personality traits that *all* entrepreneurs share—this hasn't stopped entrepreneurship researchers from listing common traits. For instance, one list of personality characteristics included the following: high level of motivation, abundance of self-confidence, ability to be involved for the long term, high energy level, persistent problem solver, high degree of initiative, ability to set goals, and moderate risk-taker. Another list of characteristics of "successful" entrepreneurs included high energy level, great persistence, resourcefulness, the desire and ability to be self-directed, and relatively high need for autonomy.

Another development in defining entrepreneurial personality characteristics was the proactive personality scale to predict an individual's likelihood of pursuing entrepreneurial ventures. The **proactive personality** is a personality trait describing those individuals who are more prone to take actions to influence their environment—that is, they're more proactive. Obviously, an entrepreneur is likely to exhibit proactivity as he or she searches for opportunities and acts to take advantage of those opportunities. Various items on the proactive personality scale were found to be good indicators of a person's likelihood of becoming an entrepreneur, including gender, education, having an entrepreneurial parent, and possessing a proactive personality. In addition, studies have shown that entrepreneurs have greater risk propensity than do managers. However, this propensity is moderated by the entrepreneur's primary goal. Risk propensity is greater for entrepreneurs whose primary goal is growth versus those whose focus is on producing family income.

proactive personality
A personality trait describing those individuals who are more prone to take actions to influence their environment.

Understanding Yourself

Am I Likely to Become an Entrepreneur?

This instrument assesses proactive personality. That is, it identifies differences among people in the extent to which they take action to influence their environment. Proactive personalities identify opportunities and act on them; they show initiative, take action, and persevere until they bring about change. Research finds that the proactive personality is positively associated with entrepreneurial intentions.

INSTRUMENT Respond to each of the 17 statements using the following rating scale:

1 = Strongly disagree
2 = Moderately disagree
3 = Slightly disagree
4 = Neither agree or disagree
5 = Slightly agree
6 = Moderately agree
7 = Strongly agree

1. I am constantly on the lookout for new ways to improve my life. 1 2 3 4 5 6 7
2. I feel driven to make a difference in my community, and maybe the world. 1 2 3 4 5 6 7
3. I tend to let others take the initiative to start new projects. 1 2 3 4 5 6 7
4. Wherever I have been, I have been a powerful force for constructive change. 1 2 3 4 5 6 7
5. I enjoy facing and overcoming obstacles to my ideas. 1 2 3 4 5 6 7
6. Nothing is more exciting than seeing my ideas turn into reality. 1 2 3 4 5 6 7
7. If I see something I don't like, I fix it. 1 2 3 4 5 6 7
8. No matter what the odds, if I believe in something I will make it happen. 1 2 3 4 5 6 7
9. I love being a champion for my ideas, even against others' opposition. 1 2 3 4 5 6 7
10. I excel at identifying opportunities. 1 2 3 4 5 6 7
11. I am always looking for better ways to do things. 1 2 3 4 5 6 7
12. If I believe in an idea, no obstacle will prevent me from making it happen. 1 2 3 4 5 6 7
13. I love to challenge the status quo. 1 2 3 4 5 6 7
14. When I have a problem, I tackle it head-on. 1 2 3 4 5 6 7
15. I am great at turning problems into opportunities. 1 2 3 4 5 6 7
16. I can spot a good opportunity long before others can. 1 2 3 4 5 6 7
17. If I see someone in trouble, I help out in any way I can. 1 2 3 4 5 6 7

SCORING KEY To calculate your proactive personality score, add up your responses to all statements except item 3. For item 3, reverse your score.

ANALYSIS AND INTERPRETATION Your total score will range from 17 to 119. The higher your score, the stronger your proactive personality. For instance, scores above 85 indicate fairly high proactivity. Although a number of factors have been found to be associated with becoming an entrepreneur, a high score on this questionnaire suggests you have strong inclinations toward becoming an entrepreneur.

Sources: T. S. Bateman and J. M. Crant, "The Proactive Component of Organizational Behavior: A Measure and Correlates," *Journal of Organizational Behavior* (March 1993), pp. 103–18; and J. M. Crant, "The Proactive Personality Scale as a Predictor of Entrepreneurial Intentions," *Journal of Small Business Management* (July 1996), pp. 42–49.

How Can Entrepreneurs Motivate Employees?

When you're motivated to do something, don't you find yourself energized and willing to work hard at doing whatever it is you're excited about? Wouldn't it be great if all of a venture's employees were energized, excited, and willing to work hard at their jobs? Having motivated employees is an important goal for any entrepreneur, and employee empowerment is an important motivational tool entrepreneurs can use.

Although it's not easy for entrepreneurs to do, employee empowerment—giving employees the power to make decisions and take actions on their own—is an important motivational approach. Why? Because successful entrepreneurial ventures must be quick and nimble, ready to pursue opportunities and go off in new directions. Empowered employees can provide that flexibility and speed. When employees are empowered, they often display stronger work motivation, better work quality, higher job satisfaction, and lower turnover.

Empowerment is a philosophical concept that entrepreneurs have to "buy into." It doesn't come easily. In fact, it's hard for many entrepreneurs to do. Their life is tied up in the business. They've built it from the ground up. But continuing to grow the entrepreneurial venture is eventually going to require handing over more responsibilities to employees. How can entrepreneurs empower employees? For many entrepreneurs, it's a gradual process.

Entrepreneurs can begin by using participative decision making in which employees provide input into decisions. Although getting employees to participate in decisions isn't quite taking the full plunge into employee empowerment, at least it's a way to begin tapping into the collective array of employees' talents, skills, knowledge, and abilities.

Another way to empower employees is through delegation—the process of assigning certain decisions or specific job duties to employees. By delegating decisions and duties, the entrepreneur is turning over the responsibility for carrying them out.

When an entrepreneur is finally comfortable with the idea of employee empowerment, fully empowering employees means redesigning their jobs so they have discretion over the way they do their work. It's allowing employees to do their work effectively and efficiently by using their creativity, imagination, knowledge, and skills.

If an entrepreneur implements employee empowerment properly—that is, with complete and total commitment to the program and with appropriate employee training—results can be impressive for the entrepreneurial venture and for the empowered employees. The business can enjoy significant productivity gains, quality improvements, more satisfied customers, increased employee motivation, and improved morale. Employees can enjoy the opportunities to do a greater variety of work that is more interesting and challenging.

How Can Entrepreneurs Be Leaders?

The last topic we want to discuss in this section is the role of an entrepreneur as a leader. In this role, the entrepreneur has certain leadership responsibilities in leading the venture and in leading employee work teams.

Today's successful entrepreneur must be like the leader of a jazz ensemble known for its improvisation, innovation, and creativity. Max DePree, former head of Herman Miller, Inc., a leading office furniture manufacturer known for its innovative leadership approaches, said it best in his book, *Leadership Jazz:* "Jazz band leaders must choose the music, find the right musicians, and perform—in public. But the effect of the performance depends on so many things—the environment, the volunteers playing the band, the need for everybody to perform as individuals and as a group, the absolute dependence of the leader on the members of the band, the need for the followers to play well. . . . The leader of the jazz band has the beautiful opportunity to draw the best out of the other musicians. We have much to learn from jazz band leaders, for jazz, like leadership, combines the unpredictability of the future with the gifts of individuals."

The way an entrepreneur leads the venture should be much like the jazz leader—drawing the best out of other individuals, even given the unpredictability of the situation. One way an entrepreneur does this is through the vision he or she creates for the organization. In fact, the driving force through the early stages of the entrepreneurial venture is often the visionary leadership of the entrepreneur. The entrepreneur's ability to articulate a coherent, inspiring, and attractive vision of the future is a key test of his or her leadership. But if an entrepreneur can do this, the results can be worthwhile. A study contrasting visionary and nonvisionary companies showed that visionary companies outperformed the nonvisionary ones by six times on standard financial criteria, and their stocks outperformed the general market by 15 times.

Many organizations—entrepreneurial and otherwise—are using employee work teams to perform organizational tasks, create new ideas, and resolve problems. The three most common types of employee work teams in entrepreneurial ventures are empowered teams (teams that have the authority to plan and implement process improvements), self-directed teams (teams that are nearly autonomous and responsible for many managerial activities), and cross-functional teams (work teams composed of individuals from various specialties who work together on various tasks).

Developing and using teams is necessary because technology and market demands are forcing entrepreneurial ventures to make products faster, cheaper, and better. Tapping into the collective wisdom of a venture's employees and empowering them to make decisions just may be one of the best ways to adapt to change. In addition, a team culture can improve the overall workplace environment and morale. For team efforts to work, however, entrepreneurs must shift from the traditional command-and-control style to a coach-and-collaboration style.

What Controlling Issues Do Entrepreneurs Face?

Entrepreneurs must look at controlling their venture's operations in order to survive and prosper in both the short run and long run. The unique control issues that face entrepreneurs include managing growth, managing downturns, exiting the venture, and managing personal life choices and challenges.

How Is Growth Managed?

Growth is a natural and desirable outcome for entrepreneurial ventures. Growth is what distinguishes an entrepreneurial venture. Entrepreneurial ventures pursue growth. Growing slowly can be successful, but so can rapid growth.

Growing successfully doesn't occur randomly or by luck. Successfully pursuing growth typically requires an entrepreneur to manage all the challenges associated with growing. This entails planning, organizing, and controlling for growth.

How Are Downturns Managed?

Although organizational growth is a desirable and important goal for entrepreneurial ventures, what happens when things don't go as planned—when the growth strategies don't result in the intended outcomes and, in fact, result in a decline in performance? There are challenges, as well, in managing the downturns.

Nobody likes to fail, especially entrepreneurs. However, when an entrepreneurial venture faces times of trouble, what can be done? How can downturns be managed successfully? The first step is recognizing that a crisis is brewing. An entrepreneur should be alert to the warning signs of a business in trouble. Some signals of potential performance decline include inadequate or negative cash flow, excess number of employees, unnecessary and cumbersome administrative procedures, fear of conflict and taking risks, tolerance of work incompetence, lack of a clear mission or goals, and ineffective or poor communication within the organization.

Although an entrepreneur hopes to never have to deal with organizational downturns, declines, or crises, there may come a time when he or she must do just that. After all, nobody likes to think about things going bad or taking a turn for the worse. But that's exactly what the entrepreneur should do—think about it *before* it happens. It's important to have an up-to-date plan for covering crises. It's like mapping exit routes from your home in case of a fire. An entrepreneur wants to be prepared before an emergency hits. This plan should focus on providing specific details for controlling the most fundamental and critical aspects of running the venture—cash flow, accounts receivable, costs, and debt. Beyond having a plan for controlling the venture's critical inflows and outflows, other actions would involve identifying specific strategies for cutting costs and restructuring the venture.

What's Involved with Exiting the Venture?

Getting out of an entrepreneurial venture may seem to be a strange thing for entrepreneurs to do. However, there may come a point when the entrepreneur decides it's time to move on. That decision may be based on the fact that the entrepreneur hopes to capitalize financially on the investment in the venture—called **harvesting**—or that the entrepreneur is facing serious organizational performance problems and wants to get out, or even on the entrepreneur's desire to focus on other pursuits (personal or business). The issues involved with exiting the venture include choosing a proper business valuation method and knowing what's involved in the process of selling a business.

Although the hardest part of preparing to exit a venture may involve valuing it, other factors are also important. These include being prepared, deciding who will sell the business, considering the tax implications, screening potential buyers, and deciding whether to tell employees before or after the sale. The process of exiting the entrepreneurial venture should be approached as carefully as the process of launching it. If the entrepreneur is selling the venture on a positive note, he or she wants to realize the value built up in the business. If the venture is being exited because of declining performance, the entrepreneur wants to maximize the potential return.

Why Is It Important to Think About Managing Personal Challenges as an Entrepreneur?

Being an entrepreneur is extremely exciting and fulfilling, yet extremely demanding. There are long hours, difficult demands, and high stress. Yet, there are many rewards to being an entrepreneur as well. In this section, we want to look at how entrepreneurs can make it work—that is, how can they be successful and effectively balance the demands of their work and personal lives?

Entrepreneurs are a special group. They're focused, persistent, hardworking, and intelligent. Because they put so much of themselves into launching and growing their entrepreneurial ventures, many may neglect their personal lives. Entrepreneurs often have to make sacrifices to pursue their entrepreneurial dreams. However, they can make it work. They can balance their work and personal lives. But how?

One of the most important things an entrepreneur can do is *become a good time manager*. Prioritize what needs to be done. Use a planner (daily, weekly, monthly) to help schedule priorities. Some entrepreneurs don't like taking the time to plan or prioritize, or they think it's a ridiculous waste of time. Yet identifying the important duties and distinguishing them from those that aren't so important actually makes an entrepreneur more efficient and effective. In addition, part of being a good time manager is delegating those decisions and actions the entrepreneur doesn't have to be personally involved in to trusted employees. Although it may be hard to let go of some of the things they've always done, entrepreneurs who delegate effectively will see their personal productivity levels rise.

Another suggestion for finding that balance is to *seek professional advice* in those areas of business where it's needed. Although entrepreneurs may be reluctant to spend scarce cash, the time, energy, and potential problems saved in the long run are well worth the investment. Competent professional advisers can provide entrepreneurs with information to make more intelligent decisions. Also, it's important to *deal with conflicts* as they arise. This includes both workplace and family conflicts. If an entrepreneur doesn't deal with conflicts, negative feelings are likely to crop up and lead to communication breakdowns. When communication falls apart, vital information may get lost, and people (employees *and* family members) may start to assume the worst. It can turn into a nightmare situation that feeds upon itself. The best strategy is to deal with conflicts as they come up. Talk, discuss, argue (if you must), but an entrepreneur shouldn't avoid the conflict or pretend it doesn't exist.

Another suggestion for achieving that balance between work and personal life is to *develop a network of trusted friends and peers*. Having a group of people to talk with is a good way for an entrepreneur to think through problems and issues. The support and encouragement offered by these people can be an invaluable source of strength for an entrepreneur.

Finally, *recognize when your stress levels are too high*. Entrepreneurs *are* achievers. They like to make things happen. They thrive on working hard. Yet, too much stress can lead to significant physical and emotional problems. Entrepreneurs have to learn when stress is overwhelming them and to do something about it. After all, what's the point of growing and building a thriving entrepreneurial venture if you're not around to enjoy it?

Sources: "Entrepreneurship Module" based on: M. Meece, "On to Plan B: Starting a Business," *New York Times Online,* August 23, 2009; D. Holthouse, "Well Done: How Viking Range Got Started: An Interview with Fred Carl Jr.," *CNNMoney.com,* August 19, 2009; "Frequently Asked Questions," *U.S. Small Business Administration,* http://www.sba.gov/advo (September 2008); D. E. Gumpert, "The Right Business Plan for the Job," *BusinessWeek Online,* January 7, 2008; W. H. Stewart, "Risk Propensity Differences Between Entrepreneurs and Managers: A Meta-Analytic Review," *Journal of Applied Psychology* (February 2001), pp. 145–53; I. O. Williamson, "Employer Legitimacy and Recruitment Success in Small Businesses," *Entrepreneurship Theory and Practice* (Fall 2000), pp. 27–42; R. L. Heneman, J. W. Tansky, and S. M. Camp, "Human Resource Management Practices in Small and Medium-Sized Enterprises: Unanswered Questions and Future Research Perspectives," *Entrepreneurship Theory and Practice* (Fall 2000), pp. 11–26; T. L. Hatten, *Small Business: Entrepreneurship and Beyond* (Upper Saddle River, NJ: Prentice Hall, 1997), p. 5; L. W. Busenitz, "Research on Entrepreneurial Alertness," *Journal of Small Business Management* (October 1996), pp. 35–44; J. M. Crant, "The Proactive Personality Scale as Predictor of Entrepreneurial Intentions," *Journal of Small Business Management* (July 1996), pp. 42–49; J. C. Collins and J. I. Porras, *Built to Last: Successful Habits of Visionary Companies* (New York: Harper Business, 1994); M. Depree, *Leadership Jazz* (New York: Currency Doubleday, 1992), pp. 8–9; P. B. Robinson, D. V. Simpson, J. C. Huefner, and H. K. Hunt, "An Attitude Approach to the Prediction of Entrepreneurship," *Entrepreneurship Theory and Practice* (Summer 1991), pp. 13–31; P. F. Drucker, *Innovation and Entrepreneurship: Practice and Principles* (New York: Harper & Row, 1985); and J. W. Carland, F. Hoy, W. R. Boulton, and J. C. Carland, "Differentiating Entrepreneurs from Small Business Owners: A Conceptualization," *Academy of Management Review* 9, no. 2 (1984), pp. 354–59.

harvesting
Exiting a venture when an entrepreneur hopes to capitalize financially on the investment in the venture.

CHAPTER

5

Organizational Structure and Culture

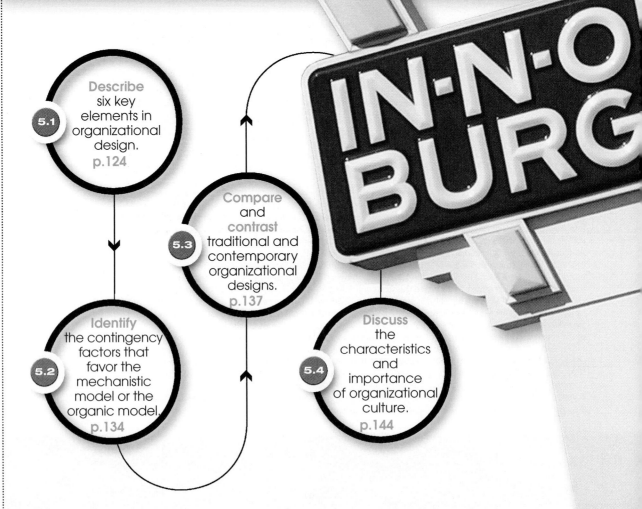

The Fanatical Burger Business

"Businesses, if they are lucky, can have a lot in common with cults. Apple Computer, Harley-Davidson and Trader Joe's are all examples of companies that inspire fanatical loyalty in their customers."[1] Another company that would definitely be on such a list is In-N-Out Burger. The popular burger places, located primarily in California, have many fans, including celebrities. Part of the allure is the company's food. Just four items: hamburgers, cheeseburgers, the Double-Double (double hamburger patties and double slices of cheese), and fries. And since the company does not use microwaves, heat lamps, or freezers, the food is fresh and delicious. But the food isn't the only secret to its success. It's the culture that founders Harry and Esther Snyder instilled in their company.

Harry was fond of saying, "Do one thing and do it the best you can." From the company's beginnings in 1948, he obsessed over quality. He believed that "running a successful fast-food business wasn't about cutting corners or using the right equipment. What it boiled down to was the people on the front lines." His hope was that his associates (what Harry and Esther called their employees) would work hard, save money, and move on. After Harry's death in 1976, his son Rich became president. Although he shared his father's beliefs on quality, he differed from his philosophy on people. Rich said, "Why let good people move on when you can use them to help your company grow?"

Rich understood the importance of training and established In-N-Out University to train managers and reinforce the company's focus on quality, cleanliness, and service. Teams of field specialists go to store locations to motivate and instruct associates. New trainees are videotaped and their performance is critiqued, again with the intent of arming them with the best information and skills.

Despite the dreary and sometimes demeaning work, all associates are made to feel that they're important to the company and are given opportunities to advance. "Rich wanted each associate to understand the job and how he or she could do it better." He viewed his position in the organizational hierarchy differently than most top-level managers. He thought of his job as "the point at the bottom of an inverted triangle. He was there to support everyone in the company." Rich died in a tragic plane crash in 1993. However, his people philosophy lives on.

One result of having a culture that recognizes the value of people and that treats associates with special care and concern is that In-N-Out has one of the lowest employee turnover rates in the industry. Industry-wide, only about half of all fast-food workers stay beyond one year with the numbers tumbling to just 25 percent at two years and 12 percent at three, but at In-N-Out, managers' typical tenure is 14 years. Part-time associates remain, on average, for two years. So within an organization where the top manager viewed himself at the bottom of the pyramid and where the culture was one of quality, loyalty, and respect, having a cult-like status isn't at all surprising.

In this chapter, we present the basics of organizational structure and design and explore aspects of organizational culture. We define the concepts and their key components and how managers use these to create a structured environment in which organizational members can do their work efficiently and effectively, like that at In-N-Out Burger.

Once the organization's goals, plans, and strategies are in place, managers must develop a structure that will best facilitate the attainment of those goals. Recall from Chapter 1 that we defined **organizing** as the function of management that creates the organization's structure. When managers develop or change the organization's structure, they're engaging in **organizational design**. This process involves making decisions about how specialized jobs should be, the rules to guide employees' behaviors, and at what level decisions are to be made. Although organizational design decisions are typically made by top-level managers, it's important for all to understand the process. Why? Because each of us works in some type of organization structure, and we need to know how and why things get done. In addition, given the changing environment and the need for organizations to adapt, we should begin understanding what tomorrow's structures may look like.

What Are the Six Key Elements in Organizational Design?

5.1 Describe six key elements in organizational design.

Few topics in management have undergone as much change in the past few years as that of organizing and organizational structure. Managers are reevaluating traditional approaches and exploring new structural designs that best support and facilitate employees' doing the organization's work— designs that can achieve efficiency but are also flexible.

The basic concepts of organizational design formulated by management writers like Henri Fayol and Max Weber offered structural principles for managers to follow. Almost 80 years have passed since many of those principles were originally proposed. Given that length of time and all the changes that have taken place, you'd think that those principles would be pretty worthless today. Surprisingly, they're not. For the most part, they still provide valuable insights into designing effective and efficient organizations. Of course, we've also gained a great deal of knowledge over the years as to their limitations. In the following sections, we discuss the six basic elements of organizational structure: work specialization, departmentalization, authority and responsibility, span of control, centralization versus decentralization, and formalization.

What Is Work Specialization?

At the Wilson Sporting Goods factory in Ada, Ohio, workers make every football used in the National Football League and most of those used in college and high school football games. To meet daily output goals, the workers specialize in job tasks such as molding, stitching and sewing, lacing, and so forth.[2] This is an example of **work specialization**, which is dividing work activities into separate job tasks. Individual employees "specialize" in doing part of an activity rather than the entire activity in order to increase work output. It's also known as division of labor.

Work specialization makes efficient use of the diversity of skills that workers have. In most organizations, some tasks require highly developed skills; others can be performed by employees with lower skill levels. If all workers were engaged in all the steps of, say, a manufacturing process, all would need the skills necessary to perform both the most demanding and the least demanding jobs. Thus, except when performing the most highly skilled or highly sophisticated tasks, employees would be working below their skill levels. In addition, skilled workers are paid more than unskilled workers, and, because wages tend to reflect the highest level of skill, all workers would be paid at highly skilled rates to do easy tasks—an inefficient use of resources. This concept explains why you rarely find a cardiac surgeon closing up a patient after surgery. Instead, doctors doing their residencies in open-heart surgery and learning the skill usually stitch and staple the patient after the surgeon has finished the surgery.

Early proponents of work specialization believed that it could lead to great increases in productivity. At the beginning of the twentieth century, that generalization was reasonable. Because specialization was not widely practiced, its introduction almost always generated higher productivity, but a good thing can be carried too far. At some point, the human diseconomies from division of labor surface as boredom, fatigue, stress, low productivity, poor quality, increased absenteeism, and high turnover exceed the economic advantages (see Exhibit 5-1).[3]

These women manually weld the top connections of photovoltaic modules that will be assembled with other components by different employees to produce photovoltaic panels for solar energy production. The job of welding at the Fluitecnik factory in Moura, Portugal, illustrates work specialization, as these women perform one part of an activity on the production line rather than the entire activity. Also known as division of labor, work specialization increases employee output, allowing this factory to produce an average of 320 photovoltaic panels a day.

WHAT IS TODAY'S VIEW OF SPECIALIZATION? Most managers today see work specialization as an important organizing mechanism because it helps employees be more efficient. For example, McDonald's uses high specialization to get its products made and delivered to customers efficiently. However, managers also have to recognize its limitations. That's why companies such as Avery-Dennison, Ford Australia, Hallmark, and American Express use minimal work specialization and instead give employees a broad range of tasks to do.

EXHIBIT 5-1 **Economies and Diseconomies of Work Specialization**

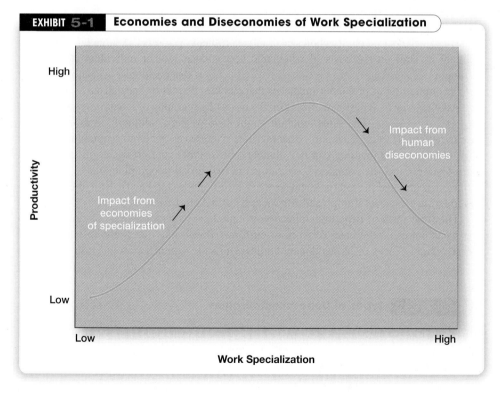

organizing
The function of management that creates the organization's structure.

organizational design
When managers develop or change the organization's structure.

work specialization
Dividing work activities into separate job tasks; also called division of labor.

What Is Departmentalization?

Early management writers argued that after deciding what job tasks will be done by whom, common work activities needed to be grouped back together so work gets done in a coordinated and integrated way. How jobs are grouped together is called **departmentalization**. There are five common forms of departmentalization (see Exhibit 5-2) although an organization may use its own unique classification. No single method of departmentalization was advocated by the early writers. The method or methods used should reflect the grouping that would best contribute to the attainment of the goals of the organization and the individual units.

HOW ARE ACTIVITIES GROUPED? One of the most popular ways to group activities is by functions performed or **functional departmentalization**. A manager might organize the workplace by separating engineering, accounting, information systems, human resources, and purchasing specialists into departments. Functional departmentalization can be used in all types of organizations. Only the functions change to reflect the organization's objectives and activities. The major advantage to functional departmentalization is the achievement of economies of scale by placing people with common skills and specializations into common units.

Product departmentalization focuses attention on major product areas in the corporation. Each product is under the authority of a senior manager who is a specialist in, and is responsible for, everything having to do with his or her product line. One company that uses product departmentalization is L.A. Gear. Its structure is based on its varied product lines, which include women's footwear, men's footwear, and apparel and accessories. If an organization's activities were service related rather than product related, as are those of L.A. Gear, each service would be autonomously grouped. The advantage of product grouping is that it increases accountability for product performance, because all activities related to a specific product are under the direction of a single manager.

The particular type of customer an organization seeks to reach can also dictate employee grouping. The sales activities in an office supply firm, for instance, can be divided into three departments that serve retail, wholesale, and government customers. A large law office can segment its staff on the basis of whether it serves corporate or individual clients. The assumption underlying **customer departmentalization** is that customers in each department have a common set of problems and needs that can best be met by specialists.

Another way to departmentalize is on the basis of geography or territory—**geographic departmentalization**. The sales function might have western, southern, midwestern, and eastern regions. If an organization's customers are scattered over a large geographic area, this form of departmentalization can be valuable. For instance, the organization structure of Coca-Cola reflects the company's operations in two broad geographic areas—the North American sector and the international sector (which includes the Pacific Rim, the European Community, Northeast Europe and Africa, and Latin America).

The final form of departmentalization is called **process departmentalization**, which groups activities on the basis of work or customer flow—like that found in many states' motor vehicle offices or in health care clinics. Units are organized around common skills

EXHIBIT 5-2	**Types of Departmentalization**
• **Functional**	Groups employees based on work performed (e.g., engineering, accounting, information systems, human resources)
• **Product**	Groups employees based on major product areas in the corporation (e.g., women's footwear, men's footwear, and apparel and accessories)
• **Customer**	Groups employees based on customers' problems and needs (e.g., wholesale, retail, government)
• **Geographic**	Groups employees based on location served (e.g., North, South, Midwest, East)
• **Process**	Groups employees based on the basis of work or customer flow (e.g., testing, payment)

needed to complete a certain process. If you've ever been to a state motor vehicle office to get a driver's license, you've probably experienced process departmentalization. With separate departments to handle applications, testing, information and photo processing, and payment collection, customers "flow" through the various departments in sequence to get their licenses.

WHAT IS TODAY'S VIEW OF DEPARTMENTALIZATION? Most large organizations continue to use most or all of the departmental groups suggested by the early management writers. Black & Decker, for instance, organizes its divisions along functional lines, its manufacturing units around processes, its sales around geographic regions, and its sales regions around customer groupings. A recent trend is the use of **cross-functional teams**, which are teams made up of individuals from various departments and that cross traditional departmental lines.

Also, today's competitive environment has refocused the attention of management on its customers. To better monitor the needs of customers and to be able to respond to changes in those needs, many organizations give greater emphasis to customer departmentalization. Finally, we also see more organizations using teams especially as tasks have become more complex and diverse skills are needed to accomplish those tasks. Nearly all *Fortune* 500 firms use teams of some type.[4] We'll cover teams more thoroughly in Chapter 9.

What Are Authority and Responsibility?

To understand authority and responsibility, you also have to be familiar with the **chain of command**, the line of authority extending from upper organizational levels to lower levels, which clarifies who reports to whom. Managers need to consider it when organizing work because it helps employees with questions such as "Who do I report to?" or "Who do I go to if I have a problem?" So, what *are* authority and responsibility?

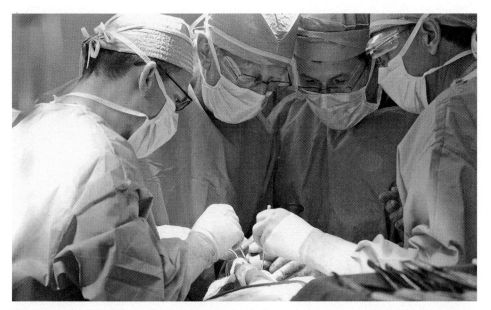

A recent trend in organizations is the use of cross-functional teams. Hospitals, for example, are using cross-functional teams that consist of individuals from various departments and that cross department lines. Shown here is a cross-functional surgical transplant team at Brigham and Women's Hospital in Boston, Massachusetts. The team includes seven plastic surgeons, an ear, nose, and throat surgeon, nurses, residents, and anesthesiologists who worked for 17 hours in performing a partial face transplant.

departmentalization
How jobs are grouped together.

functional departmentalization
Grouping activities by functions performed.

product departmentalization
Grouping activities by major product areas.

customer departmentalization
Grouping activities by customer.

geographic departmentalization
Grouping activities on the basis of geography or territory.

process departmentalization
Grouping activities on the basis of work or customer flow.

cross-functional teams
Teams made up of individuals from various departments and that cross traditional departmental lines.

chain of command
The line of authority extending from upper organizational levels to lower levels, which clarifies who reports to whom.

Authority refers to the rights inherent in a managerial position to give orders and expect the orders to be obeyed. Authority was a major concept discussed by the early management writers as they viewed it as the glue that held an organization together.[5] It was delegated downward to lower-level managers, giving them certain rights while prescribing certain limits within which to operate. Each management position had specific inherent rights that incumbents acquired from the position's rank or title. Authority, therefore, is related to one's position within an organization and has nothing to do with the personal characteristics of an individual manager. The expression "The king is dead; long live the king" illustrates the concept. Whoever is "king" acquires the rights inherent in the king's position. When a position of authority is vacated, the person who has left the position no longer has any authority. The authority remains with the position and its new incumbent.

When managers delegate authority, they must allocate commensurate **responsibility** That is, when employees are given rights, they also assume a corresponding obligation to perform. And they should be held accountable for their performance! Allocating authority without responsibility and accountability creates opportunities for abuse. Likewise, no one should be held responsible or accountable for something over which he or she has no authority.

WHAT ARE THE DIFFERENT TYPES OF AUTHORITY RELATIONSHIPS? The early management writers distinguished between two forms of authority: line authority and staff authority. **Line authority** entitles a manager to direct the work of an employee. It is the employer–employee authority relationship that extends from the top of the organization to the lowest echelon, according to the chain of command, as shown in Exhibit 5-3. As a link in the chain of command, a manager with line authority has the right to direct the work of employees and to make certain decisions without consulting anyone. Of course, in the chain of command, every manager is also subject to the direction of his or her superior.

Keep in mind that sometimes the term *line* is used to differentiate line managers from staff managers. In this context, *line* refers to managers whose organizational function contributes directly to the achievement of organizational objectives. In a manufacturing firm, line managers are typically in the production and sales functions, whereas managers in human resources and payroll are considered staff managers with staff authority. Whether

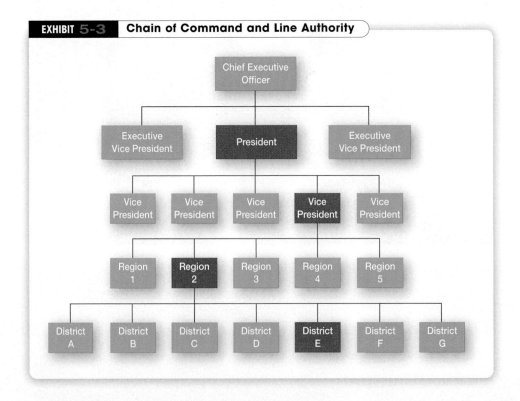

EXHIBIT 5-3 | **Chain of Command and Line Authority**

a manager's function is classified as line or staff depends on the organization's objectives. For example, at Staff Builders, a supplier of temporary employees, interviewers have a line function. Similarly, at the payroll firm of ADP, payroll is a line function.

As organizations get larger and more complex, line managers find that they do not have the time, expertise, or resources to get their jobs done effectively. In response, they create **staff authority** functions to support, assist, advise, and generally reduce some of their informational burdens. The hospital administrator cannot effectively handle the purchasing of all the supplies the hospital needs, so she creates a purchasing department, a staff department. Of course, the head of the purchasing department has line authority over the purchasing agents who work for him. The hospital administrator might also find that she is overburdened and needs an assistant. In creating the position of her assistant, she has created a staff position. Exhibit 5-4 illustrates line and staff authority.

WHAT IS UNITY OF COMMAND? An employee who has to report to two or more bosses might have to cope with conflicting demands or priorities.[6] Accordingly, the early writers believed that each employee should report to only one manager, a term called **unity of command**. In those rare instances when the unity of command had to be violated, a clear separation of activities and a supervisor responsible for each was always explicitly designated.

Unity of command was logical when organizations were relatively simple. Under some circumstances it is still sound advice and organizations continue to adhere to it. But advances in technology, for instance, allow access to organizational information that was once accessible only to top managers. Moreover, with computers, employees can communicate with anyone else in the organization without going through the formal communication channels of the chain of command. As such, in some instances, strict adherence to the unity of command creates a degree of inflexibility that may hinder an organization's performance.

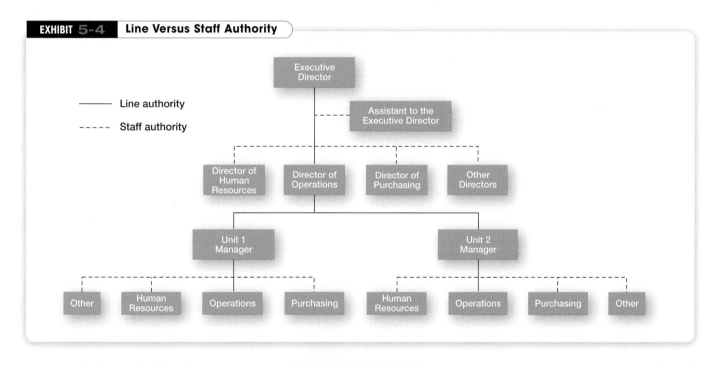

EXHIBIT 5-4   Line Versus Staff Authority

—— Line authority

- - - - Staff authority

HOW DOES TODAY'S VIEW OF AUTHORITY AND RESPONSIBILITY DIFFER FROM THE HISTORICAL VIEW? The early management writers were enamored of authority. They assumed that the rights inherent in one's formal position in an organization were the sole source of influence, and they believed that managers were all-powerful. This assumption might have been true 60 or even 30 years ago. Organizations were simpler. Staff was less important. Managers were only minimally dependent on technical specialists. Under such conditions, influence is the same as authority. And the higher a manager's position in the organization, the more influence he or she had. However, those conditions no longer exist. Researchers and practitioners of management now recognize that you don't have to be a manager to have power and that power is not perfectly correlated with one's level in the organization.

Authority is an important concept in organizations, but an exclusive focus on authority produces a narrow, unrealistic view of influence. Today, we recognize that authority is but one element in the larger concept of power.

HOW DO AUTHORITY AND POWER DIFFER? Authority and power are often considered the same thing, but they're not. Authority is a right. Its legitimacy is based on an authority figure's position in the organization. Authority goes with the job. **Power**, on the other hand, refers to an individual's capacity to influence decisions. Authority is part of the larger concept of power. That is, the formal rights that come with an individual's position in the organization are just one means by which an individual can affect the decision process.

Exhibit 5-5 visually depicts the difference between authority and power. The two-dimensional arrangement of boxes in part A portrays authority. The area in which the

---

EXHIBIT 5-5 | **Authority Versus Power**

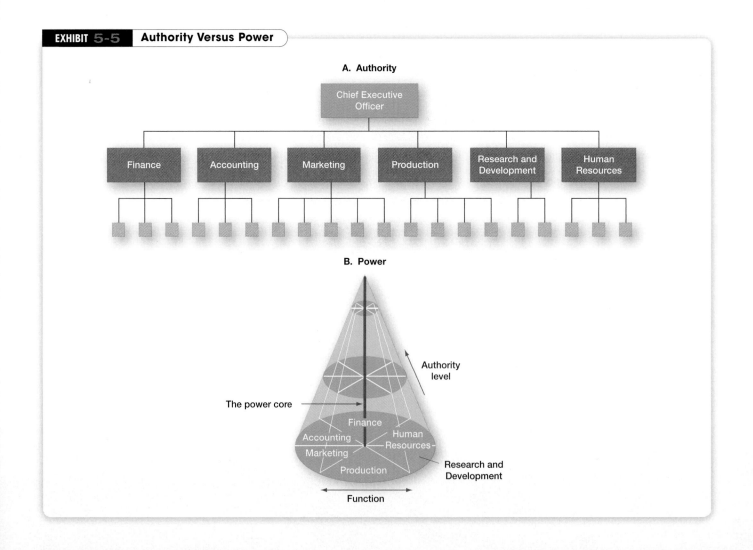

authority applies is defined by the horizontal dimension. Each horizontal grouping represents a functional area. The influence one holds in the organization is defined by the vertical dimension in the structure. The higher one is in the organization, the greater one's authority.

Power, on the other hand, is a three-dimensional concept (the cone in part B of Exhibit 5-5). It includes not only the functional and hierarchical dimensions but also a third dimension called centrality. Although authority is defined by one's vertical position in the hierarchy, power is made up of both one's vertical position and one's distance from the organization's power core or center.

Think of the cone in Exhibit 5-5 as an organization. The center of the cone is the power core. The closer you are to the power core, the more influence you have on decisions. The existence of a power core is, in fact, the only difference between A and B in Exhibit 5-5. The vertical hierarchy dimension in A is merely one's level on the outer edge of the cone. The top of the cone corresponds to the top of the hierarchy, the middle of the cone to the middle of the hierarchy, and so on. Similarly, the functional groups in A become wedges in the cone. Each wedge represents a functional area.

The cone analogy explicitly acknowledges two facts: (1) The higher one moves in an organization (an increase in authority), the closer one moves to the power core; and (2) it is not necessary to have authority in order to wield power because one can move horizontally inward toward the power core without moving up. For instance, assistants often are powerful in a company even though they have little authority. As gatekeepers for their bosses, these assistants have considerable influence over whom their bosses see and when they see them. Furthermore, because they're regularly relied upon to pass information on to their bosses, they have some control over what their bosses hear. It's not unusual for a $105,000-a-year middle manager to tread carefully in order not to upset the boss's $45,000-a-year administrative assistant. Why? Because the assistant has power. This individual may be low in the authority hierarchy but close to the power core.

Likewise, low-ranking employees who have relatives, friends, or associates in high places might also be close to the power core. So, too, are employees with scarce and important skills. The lowly production engineer with 20 years of experience in a company might be the only one in the firm who knows the inner workings of all the old production machinery. When pieces of this old equipment break down, only this engineer understands how to fix them. Suddenly, the engineer's influence is much greater than it would appear from his or her level in the vertical hierarchy. What do these examples tell us about power? They indicate that power can come from different areas (see "Developing Your Power Base Skill"). French and Raven identified five sources, or bases, of power: coercive, reward, legitimate, expert, and referent.[7] We summarize them in Exhibit 5-6.

EXHIBIT 5-6   **Types of Power**

Coercive power	Power based on fear.
Reward power	Power based on the ability to distribute something that others value.
Legitimate power	Power based on one's position in the formal hierarchy.
Expert power	Power based on one's expertise, special skill, or knowledge.
Referent power	Power based on identification with a person who has desirable resources or personal traits.

---

power
An individual's capacity to influence decisions.

Developing Your *Power Base* Skill

About the Skill

One of the more difficult aspects of power is acquiring it.[8] For some individuals, power comes naturally, and for others, it's a function of the job they hold. But what can an individual do to develop power? The answer is respect others, build power relationships, develop associations, control important information, gain seniority, and build power in stages.

Steps in Practicing the Skill

1 Respect others. One of the most crucial aspects of developing power is to treat others the way you would like to be treated. That sentence may be a cliché, but it holds a key understanding. If others don't respect you, your power will generally be limited. Sure, they may do the things you ask, but only because of the authority of your position. People need to know that you're genuine, which is conveyed through respecting others. In today's world, with the great diversity that exists, you must be sensitive to others' needs. Failure to do so may only lead to problems, most of which can be avoided if you see the good in people and realize that most people try their best and want to do a good job.

2 Build power relationships. People who possess power often associate with others who have power. It appears to be a natural phenomenon—birds of a feather do flock together! You need to identify these people and model their behavior. The idea is that you want to make yourself visible to powerful people and let them observe you in a number of situations.

3 Develop associations. We learn at an early age that there is strength in numbers. In the "power" world, this tenet also applies. By associating with others, you become part of a group in which all the members' energies are brought together to form one large base of power. Often called coalitions, these groups form to influence some event.

4 Control important information. Get yourself into a position that gives you access to information other people perceive as important. Access to information is especially critical in a world where people's lives depend so much on information processing. One of the greatest means of developing this power is to continue to learn. Finding new approaches to solving old problems or creating a special process are ways of gaining a level of expertise that can make you indispensable to the organization.

5 Gain seniority. Seniority is somewhat related to controlling information. Power can be gained by simply having been around for a long time. People will often respect individuals who have lived through the ups and downs of an organization. Their experience gives them a perspective or information that newcomers don't have.

6 Build power in stages. No one goes from being powerless one moment to being powerful the next. That simply doesn't occur. Power comes in phases. As you build your power, remember, it will start off slowly. You will be given opportunities to demonstrate that you can handle the power. After each test you pass, you'll more than likely be given more power.

Practicing the Skill

Margaret is a supervisor in the Internet sales division of a large clothing retailer. She has let it be known that she is devoted to the firm and plans to build her career there. Margaret is hardworking and reliable, has volunteered for extra projects, has taken in-house development courses, and joined a committee dedicated to improving employee safety on the job. She undertook an assignment to research ergonomic office furniture for the head of the department and gave up several lunch hours to consult with the head of human resources about her report. Margaret filed the report late, but she excused herself by explaining that her assistant lost several pages that she had to redraft over the weekend. The report was well received, and several of Margaret's colleagues think she should be promoted when the next opening arises.

Evaluate Margaret's skill in building a power base. What actions has she taken that are helpful to her in reaching her goal? Is there anything she should have done differently?

What Is Span of Control?

How many employees can a manager efficiently and effectively supervise? This question of **span of control** received a great deal of attention from early management writers. Although early writers came to no consensus on a specific number, most favored small spans—typically no more than six workers—in order to maintain close control.[9] However, several writers did acknowledge level in the organization as a contingency variable. They argued that as a manager rises in an organization, he or she has to deal with a greater number of unstructured problems, so top managers need a smaller span than do middle managers, and middle managers require a smaller span than do supervisors. Over the last decade, however, we've seen some change in theories about effective spans of control.[10]

Many organizations are increasing their spans of control. The span for managers at such companies as General Electric and Kaiser Aluminum has expanded significantly in the past decade. It has also expanded in the federal government, where efforts to increase the span of control are being implemented to save time in making decisions.[11] The span of control is increasingly being determined by looking at contingency variables. It's obvious that the more training and experience employees have, the less direct supervision they need. Managers who have well-trained and experienced employees can function with a wider span. Other contingency variables that determine the appropriate span include similarity of employee tasks, the complexity of those tasks, the physical proximity of employees, the degree to which standardized procedures are in place, the sophistication of the organization's management information system, the strength of the organization's value system, and the preferred managing style of the manager.[12]

How Do Centralization and Decentralization Differ?

One of the questions that needs to be answered when organizing is "At what level are decisions made?" **Centralization** is the degree to which decision making takes place at upper levels of the organization. **Decentralization** is the degree to which lower-level managers provide input or actually make decisions. Centralization-decentralization is not an either-or concept. Rather, it's a matter of degree. What we mean is that no organization is completely centralized or completely decentralized. Few, if any, organizations could effectively function if all their decisions were made by a select few people (centralization) or if all decisions were pushed down to the level closest to the problems (decentralization). Let's look, then, at how the early management writers viewed centralization as well as at how it exists today.

Early management writers proposed that centralization in an organization depended on the situation.[13] Their goal was the optimum and efficient use of employees. Traditional organizations were structured in a pyramid, with power and authority concentrated near the top of the organization. Given this structure, historically centralized decisions were the most prominent, but organizations today have become more complex and responsive to dynamic changes in their environments. As such, many managers believe that decisions need to be made by those individuals closest to the problems, regardless of their organizational level. In fact, the trend over the past several decades—at least in U.S. and Canadian organizations—has been a movement toward more decentralization in organizations.[14]

WHAT IS TODAY'S VIEW OF CENTRALIZATION-DECENTRALIZATION? Today, managers often choose the amount of centralization or decentralization that will allow them to best implement their decisions and achieve organizational goals.[15] What works in one organization, however, won't necessarily work in another, so managers must determine the amount of decentralization for each organization and work units within it. You may also recall that in Chapter 2 we discussed empowering employees and delegating to them the authority to make decisions on those things that affect their work and to change the way that they think about work. That's decentralization. Notice, however, that it doesn't imply that top-level managers no longer make decisions.

Decentralization is at work at Wegmans grocery stores, where employees are empowered to make decisions about things that affect their work and that please their customers. The company delegates to employees the authority to make on-the-spot decisions without consulting their immediate supervisors. By creating an environment where employees are not burdened by hierarchies, Wegmans enables them to be passionate about customer service so that no shopper leaves a store unhappy. Shown here is an employee at a Wegmans store in Pittsford, New York, helping a customer put groceries in her car and putting a smile on her face.

What Is Formalization?

Formalization refers to how standardized an organization's jobs are and the extent to which employee behavior is guided by rules and procedures. In highly formalized organizations, there are

---

span of control
The number of employees a manager can efficiently and effectively supervise.

centralization
The degree to which decision making takes place at upper levels of the organization.

decentralization
The degree to which lower-level managers provide input or actually make decisions.

formalization
How standardized an organization's jobs are and the extent to which employee behavior is guided by rules and procedures.

explicit job descriptions, numerous organizational rules, and clearly defined procedures covering work processes. Employees have little discretion over what's done, when it's done, and how it's done. However, where formalization is low, employees have more discretion in how they do their work. Early management writers expected organizations to be fairly formalized, as formalization went hand-in-hand with bureaucratic-style organizations.

WHAT IS TODAY'S VIEW OF FORMALIZATION? Although some formalization is necessary for consistency and control, many organizations today rely less on strict rules and standardization to guide and regulate employee behavior. For instance, consider the following situation:

> It is 2:37 P.M. and a customer at a branch of a large national drug store chain is trying to drop off a roll of film for same-day developing. Store policy states that film must be dropped off by 2:00 P.M. for this service. The clerk knows that rules like this are supposed to be followed. At the same time, he wants to be accommodating to the customer, and he knows that the film could, in fact, be processed that day. He decides to accept the film, and in so doing, to violate the policy. He just hopes that his manager does not find out.[16]

Has this employee done something wrong? He did "break" the rule. But by "breaking" the rule, he actually brought in revenue and provided good customer service. Considering there are numerous situations where rules may be too restrictive, many organizations have allowed employees some latitude, giving them sufficient autonomy to make those decisions that they feel are best under the circumstances. It doesn't mean throwing out all organizational rules because there always *will* be rules that are important for employees to follow— and these rules should be explained so employees understand why it's important to adhere to them. But for other rules, employees may be given some leeway.[17]

5.2 Identify the contingency factors that favor the mechanistic model or the organic model.

What Contingency Variables Affect Structural Choice?

The most appropriate structure to use will depend on contingency factors. In this section, we address two generic organization structure models and then look at the more popular contingency variables—strategy, size, technology, and environment.

How Is a Mechanistic Organization Different from an Organic Organization?

Exhibit 5-7 describes two organizational forms.[18] The **mechanistic organization** (or bureaucracy) was the natural result of combining the six elements of structure. Adhering to the chain-of-command principle ensured the existence of a formal hierarchy of authority, with each person controlled and supervised by one superior. Keeping the span of control small at increasingly higher levels in the organization created tall, impersonal structures. As the distance between the top and the bottom of the organization expanded, top management would increasingly impose rules and regulations. Because top managers couldn't control lower-level activities through direct observation and ensure the use of standard practices, they substituted rules and regulations. The early management writers' belief in a high degree of work specialization created jobs that were simple, routine, and standardized. Further specialization through the use of departmentalization increased impersonality and the need for multiple layers of management to coordinate the specialized departments.

The **organic organization** is a highly adaptive form that is as loose and flexible as the mechanistic organization is rigid and stable. Rather than having standardized jobs and regulations, the organic organization's loose structure allows it to change rapidly as required.[19] It has division of labor, but the jobs people do are not standardized. Employees tend to be professionals who are technically proficient and trained to handle diverse problems. They need few formal rules and little direct supervision because their training has instilled in them standards of professional conduct. For instance, a petroleum engineer

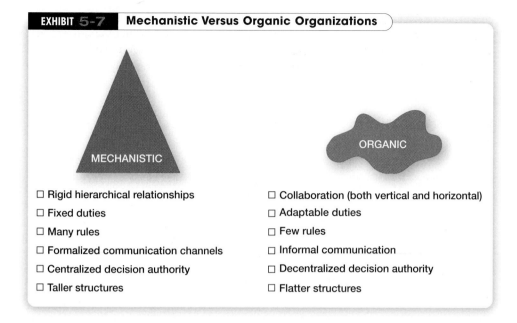

EXHIBIT 5-7 **Mechanistic Versus Organic Organizations**

MECHANISTIC

ORGANIC

- ☐ Rigid hierarchical relationships
- ☐ Fixed duties
- ☐ Many rules
- ☐ Formalized communication channels
- ☐ Centralized decision authority
- ☐ Taller structures

- ☐ Collaboration (both vertical and horizontal)
- ☐ Adaptable duties
- ☐ Few rules
- ☐ Informal communication
- ☐ Decentralized decision authority
- ☐ Flatter structures

doesn't need to be given procedures on how to locate oil sources miles offshore. The engineer can solve most problems alone or after conferring with colleagues. Professional standards guide his or her behavior. The organic organization is low in centralization so that the professional can respond quickly to problems and because top-level managers cannot be expected to possess the expertise to make necessary decisions.

Top managers typically put a great deal of thought into designing an appropriate structure. What that appropriate structure is depends on four contingency variables: the organization's strategy, size, technology, and degree of environmental uncertainty. Let's look at these contingency variables.

How Does Strategy Affect Structure?

An organization's structure should facilitate goal achievement. Because goals are an important part of the organization's strategies, it's only logical that strategy and structure are closely linked. Alfred Chandler initially researched this relationship.[20] He studied several large U.S. companies and concluded that changes in corporate strategy led to changes in an organization's structure that supported the strategy. Specifically, he found that organizations usually begin with a single product or line. The simplicity of the strategy required only a simple or loose form of structure to execute it. As such, decisions could be centralized in the hands of a single senior manager, and complexity and formalization were low. However, as organizations grew, their strategies become more ambitious and elaborate.

Research has shown that certain structural designs work best with different organizational strategies.[21] For instance, the flexibility and free-flowing information of the organic structure works well when an organization is pursuing meaningful and unique innovations. The mechanistic organization with its efficiency, stability, and tight controls works best for companies wanting to tightly control costs.

How Does Size Affect Structure?

There's considerable evidence that an organization's size affects its structure.[22] Large organizations—typically considered to be those with more than 2,000 employees—tend to have more specialization, departmentalization, centralization, and rules and regulations than

mechanistic organization
A bureaucratic organization; a structure that's high in specialization, formalization, and centralization.

organic organization
A structure that's low in specialization, formalization, and centralization.

do small organizations. However, once an organization grows past a certain size, size has less influence on structure. Why? Essentially, once there are around 2,000 employees, it's already fairly mechanistic. Adding another 500 employees won't impact the structure much. On the other hand, adding 500 employees to an organization that has only 300 employees is likely to make it more mechanistic.

How Does Technology Affect Structure?

Every organization uses some form of technology to convert its inputs into outputs. For instance, workers at Whirlpool's Brazilian facility build microwave ovens and air conditioners on a standardized assembly line. Employees at FedEx Kinko's produce custom design and print jobs for individual customers. And employees at Bayer's facility in Pakistan make pharmaceutical products using a continuous-flow production line. The initial research on technology's effect on structure can be traced to Joan Woodward.[23] For more information on her ground-breaking work, see the "From the Past to the Present" box.

How Does the Environment Affect Structure?

In Chapter 2, we discussed the organization's environment as a constraint on managerial discretion. It also has a major effect on an organization's structure. Essentially, mechanistic organizations are most effective in stable environments. Organic organizations are best matched with dynamic and uncertain environments.

The evidence on the environment–structure relationship helps to explain why so many managers have restructured their organizations to be lean, fast, and flexible.[24] Global competition, accelerated product innovation by all competitors, knowledge management, and increased demands from customers for higher quality and faster deliveries are examples

---

From the Past to the Present

Joan Woodward, a British management scholar, studied small manufacturing firms in southern England to determine the extent to which structural design elements were related to organizational success.[25] She couldn't find any consistent pattern until she divided the firms into three distinct technologies that had increasing levels of complexity and sophistication. The first category, **unit production**, described the production of items in units or small batches. The second category, **mass production**, described large-batch manufacturing. Finally, the third and most technically complex group, **process production**, included continuous-process production. A summary of her findings regarding technology and appropriate organizational structure is shown in Exhibit 5-8.

Woodward's study of technology and organizational structure is one of the earliest studies of contingency theory. Her answer to the "it depends on" question would be that appropriate organizational design depends on what the organization's technology is. Other more recent studies also have shown that organizations adapt their structures to their technology depending on how routine their technology is for transforming inputs into outputs. In general, the more routine the technology, the more mechanistic the structure can be, and organizations with more nonroutine technology are more likely to have organic structures.

EXHIBIT 5-8	Woodward's Findings on Technology and Structure		
	UNIT PRODUCTION	**MASS PRODUCTION**	**PROCESS PRODUCTION**
Structural characteristics:	Low vertical differentiation	Moderate vertical differentiation	High vertical differentiation
	Low horizontal differentiation	High horizontal differentiation	Low horizontal differentiation
	Low formalization	High formalization	Low formalization
Most effective structure:	Organic	Mechanistic	Organic

of dynamic environmental forces.[26] Mechanistic organizations tend to be ill equipped to respond to rapid environmental change. As a result, managers, such as those at Samsung Electronics, are redesigning their organizations in order to make them more organic.[27]

What Are Some Common Organizational Designs?

In making structural decisions, managers have some common designs from which to choose: traditional ones and more contemporary ones. Let's look at some of the various types of organizational designs.

Compare and contrast traditional and contemporary organizational designs.

5.3

What Traditional Organizational Designs Can Managers Use?

When designing a structure, managers may choose one of the traditional organizational designs. These structures—simple, functional, and divisional—tend to be more mechanistic in nature. (See Exhibit 5-9 for a summary of the strengths and weaknesses of each.)

WHAT IS THE SIMPLE STRUCTURE? Most companies start as entrepreneurial ventures using a **simple structure**, which is an organizational design with low departmentalization, wide spans of control, authority centralized in a single person, and little formalization.[28] The simple structure is most widely used in smaller businesses and its strengths should be obvious. It's fast, flexible, and inexpensive to maintain, and accountability is clear. However, it becomes increasingly inadequate as an organization grows, because its few policies or rules to guide operations and its high centralization result in information overload at the top. As size increases, decision making becomes slower and can eventually come to a standstill as the single executive tries to continue making all the decisions. If the structure is not changed and adapted to its size, the firm can lose momentum and is likely to eventually fail. The simple structure's other weakness is that it's risky: Everything depends on one person. If anything happens to the owner-manager, the organization's information and decision-making center is lost. As employees are added, however, most

---

EXHIBIT 5-9 | **Traditional Organization Designs**

Simple Structure

- **Strengths:** Fast; flexible; inexpensive to maintain; clear accountability.
- **Weaknesses:** Not appropriate as organization grows; reliance on one person is risky.

Functional Structure

- **Strengths:** Cost-saving advantages from specialization (economies of scale, minimal duplication of people and equipment); employees are grouped with others who have similar tasks.
- **Weaknesses:** Pursuit of functional goals can cause managers to lose sight of what's best for the overall organization; functional specialists become insulated and have little understanding of what other units are doing.

Divisional Structure

- **Strengths:** Focuses on results—division managers are responsible for what happens to their products and services.
- **Weaknesses:** Duplication of activities and resources increases costs and reduces efficiency.

---

unit production
The production of items in units or small batches.
mass production
Large-batch manufacturing.

process production
Continuous flow of products being produced.

simple structure
An organizational design with low departmentalization, wide spans of control, authority centralized in a single person, and little formalization.

small businesses don't remain as simple structures. The structure tends to become more specialized and formalized. Rules and regulations are introduced, work becomes specialized, departments are created, levels of management are added, and the organization becomes increasingly bureaucratic. Two of the most popular bureaucratic design options grew out of functional and product departmentalizations and are called the functional and divisional structures.

WHAT IS THE FUNCTIONAL STRUCTURE?   A **functional structure** is an organizational design that groups similar or related occupational specialties together. You can think of this structure as functional departmentalization applied to the entire organization. For example, Revlon, Inc., is organized around the functions of operations, finance, human resources, and product research and development.

The strength of the functional structure lies in the advantages that accrue from work specialization. Putting like specialties together results in economies of scale, minimizes duplication of personnel and equipment, and makes employees comfortable and satisfied because it gives them the opportunity to talk the same language as their peers. The most obvious weakness of the functional structure, however, is that the organization frequently loses sight of its best interests in the pursuit of functional goals. No one function is totally responsible for results, so members within individual functions become insulated and have little understanding of what people in other functions are doing.

WHAT IS THE DIVISIONAL STRUCTURE?   The **divisional structure** is an organizational structure made up of separate business units or divisions.[29] In this structure, each division has limited autonomy, with a division manager who has authority over his or her unit and is responsible for performance. In divisional structures, however, the parent corporation typically acts as an external overseer to coordinate and control the various divisions, and often provides support services such as financial and legal. Health care giant Johnson & Johnson, for example, has three divisions: pharmaceuticals, medical devices and diagnostics, and consumer products. In addition, it has several subsidiaries that also manufacture and market diverse health care products.

The chief advantage of the divisional structure is that it focuses on results. Division managers have full responsibility for a product or service. The divisional structure also frees the headquarters staff from being concerned with day-to-day operating details so that they can pay attention to long-term and strategic planning. The major disadvantage of the divisional structure is duplication of activities and resources. Each division, for instance, may have a marketing research department. If there weren't any divisions, all of an organization's marketing research might be centralized and done for a fraction of the cost that divisionalization requires. Thus, the divisional form's duplication of functions increases the organization's costs and reduces efficiency.

What Contemporary Organizational Designs Can Managers Use?

Managers are finding that the traditional designs often aren't appropriate for today's increasingly dynamic and complex environment. Instead, organizations need to be lean, flexible, and innovative; that is, more organic. So managers are finding creative ways to structure and organize work and are using designs such as team-based structures, matrix and project structures, and boundaryless structures.[30] (See Exhibit 5-10 for a summary of these designs.)

WHAT ARE TEAM STRUCTURES?   Larry Page and Sergey Brin, cofounders of Google, have created a corporate structure that "tackles most big projects in small, tightly focused teams."[31] A **team structure** is one in which the entire organization is made up of work teams that do the organization's work.[32] In this structure, employee empowerment is crucial because there is no line of managerial authority from top to bottom. Rather, employee teams design and do work in the way they think is best, but are also held responsible for all

EXHIBIT 5-10	Contemporary Organization Designs

Team Structure
- **What it is:** — A structure in which the entire organization is made up of work groups or teams.
- **Advantages:** Employees are more involved and empowered. Reduced barriers among functional areas.
- **Disadvantages:** No clear chain of command. Pressure on teams to perform.

Matrix-Project Structure
- **What it is:** Matrix is structure that assigns specialists from different functional areas to work on projects but who return to their areas when the project is completed. Project is a structure in which employees continuously work on projects. As one project is completed, employees move on to the next project.
- **Advantages:** Fluid and flexible design that can respond to environmental changes. Faster decision making.
- **Disadvantages:** Complexity of assigning people to projects. Task and personality conflicts.

Boundaryless Structure
- **What it is:** A structure that is not defined by or limited to artificial horizontal, vertical, or external boundaries; includes *virtual* and *network* types of organizations.
- **Advantages:** Highly flexible and responsive. Utilizes talent wherever it's found.
- **Disadvantages:** Lack of control. Communication difficulties.

work performance results in their respective areas. In large organizations, the team structure complements what is typically a functional or divisional structure. This allows the organization to have the efficiency of a bureaucracy while providing the flexibility of teams. For instance, companies such as Amazon, Boeing, Hewlett-Packard, Louis Vuitton, Motorola, and Xerox extensively use employee teams to improve productivity.

Although team structures have been positive, simply arranging employees into teams is not enough. Employees must be trained to work on teams, receive cross-functional skills training, and be compensated accordingly. Without a properly implemented team-based pay plan, many of the benefits of a team structure may be lost.[33]

WHAT ARE MATRIX AND PROJECT STRUCTURES? In addition to team-based structures, other popular contemporary designs are the matrix and project structures. The **matrix structure** assigns specialists from different functional departments to work on projects led by a project manager. When employees finish work on an assigned project, they go back to their functional departments. One unique aspect of this design is that it creates a *dual chain of command* since employees in a matrix organization have two managers: their functional area manager and their product or project manager, who share authority. (See Exhibit 5-11.) The project manager has authority over the functional members who are part of his or her project team in areas related to the project's goals. However, any decisions about promotions, salary recommendations, and annual performance reviews typically remain the functional manager's responsibility. To work effectively, both

functional structure
An organizational design that groups similar or related occupational specialties together.

divisional structure
An organizational structure made up of separate business units or divisions.

team structure
A structure in which the entire organization is made up of work teams.

matrix structure
A structure in which specialists from different functional departments are assigned to work on projects led by a project manager.

EXHIBIT 5-11 | Sample Matrix Structure

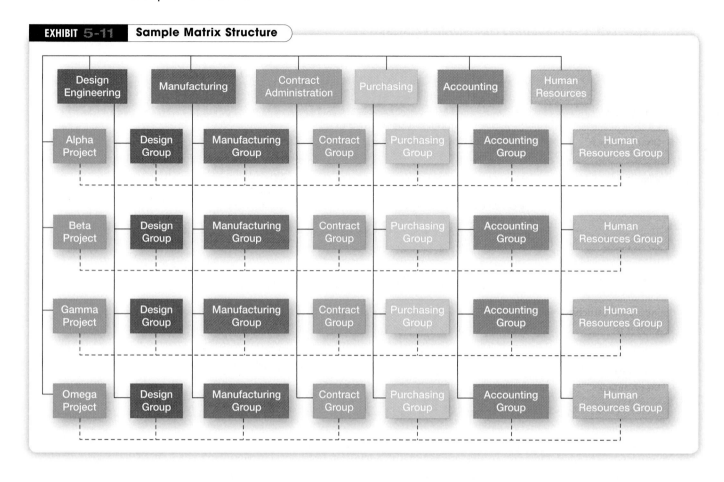

managers have to communicate regularly, coordinate work demands on employees, and resolve conflicts together.

The primary strength of the matrix is that it can facilitate coordination of a multiple set of complex and interdependent projects while still retaining the economies that result from keeping functional specialists grouped together. The major disadvantages of the matrix are the confusion it creates and its propensity to foster power struggles. When you dispense with the chain of command and unity of command principles, you significantly increase ambiguity. Confusion can arise over who reports to whom. The confusion and ambiguity, in turn, are what trigger the power struggles.

Instead of a matrix structure, many organizations are using a **project structure**, in which employees continuously work on projects. Unlike the matrix structure, a project structure has no formal departments where employees return at the completion of a project. Instead, employees take their specific skills, abilities, and experiences to other projects. Also, all work in project structures is performed by teams of employees. For instance, at design firm IDEO, project teams form, disband, and form again as the work requires. Employees "join" project teams because they bring needed skills and abilities to that project. Once a project is completed, however, they move on to the next one.[34]

Project structures tend to be more flexible organizational designs. The major advantage of that is that employees can be deployed rapidly to respond to environmental changes. Also, there's no departmentalization or rigid organizational hierarchy to slow down making decisions or taking action. In this structure, managers serve as facilitators, mentors, and coaches. They eliminate or minimize organizational obstacles and ensure that teams have the resources they need to effectively and efficiently complete their work. The two major disadvantages of the project structure are the complexity of assigning people to projects and the inevitable task and personality conflicts that arise.

WHAT IS A BOUNDARYLESS ORGANIZATION? Another contemporary organizational design is the **boundaryless organization**, which is an organization whose design is not defined by, or limited to, the horizontal, vertical, or external boundaries imposed by a predefined structure.[35] Former GE chairman Jack Welch coined the term because he wanted to eliminate vertical and horizontal boundaries within GE and break down external barriers between the company and its customers and suppliers. Although the idea of eliminating boundaries may seem odd, many of today's most successful organizations are finding that they can operate most effectively by remaining flexible and *un*structured: that the ideal structure for them is *not* having a rigid, bounded, and predefined structure.[36]

What do we mean by "boundaries"? There are two types: (1) *internal*—the horizontal ones imposed by work specialization and departmentalization and the vertical ones that separate employees into organizational levels and hierarchies; and (2) *external*—the boundaries that separate the organization from its customers, suppliers, and other stakeholders. To minimize or eliminate these boundaries, managers might use virtual or network structural designs.

A **virtual organization** consists of a small core of full-time employees and outside specialists temporarily hired as needed to work on projects.[37] An example is StrawberryFrog, a global advertising agency with offices in Amsterdam, New York, Mumbai, and Saõ Paulo. It does its work with a minimal administrative staff but engages a global network of freelancers who are assigned client work. By relying on these freelancers, the company enjoys a network of talent without all the unnecessary overhead and structural complexity.[38] The inspiration for this structural approach comes from the film industry. There, people are essentially "free agents" who move from project to project applying their skills—directing, talent casting, costuming, makeup, set design, and so forth—as needed.

Another structural option for managers wanting to minimize or eliminate organizational boundaries is a **network organization**, which is one that uses its own employees to do some work activities and networks of outside suppliers to provide other needed product components or work processes.[39] This organizational form is sometimes called a modular organization by manufacturing firms.[40] This structural approach allows organizations to concentrate on what they do best by contracting out other activities to companies that do those activities best. Many companies are using such an approach for certain organizational work activities. For instance, the head of development for Boeing's 787 airplane manages thousands of employees and some 100 suppliers at more than 100 sites in different countries.[41] Sweden's Ericsson contracts its manufacturing and even some of its research and development to more cost-effective contractors in New Delhi, Singapore, California, and other global

In using a network organization structure to develop its new 787 Dreamliner aircraft, The Boeing Company performed some work activities while an international team of top aerospace companies helped develop the plane by providing other product components, work processes, or services. Boeing outsourced the production of about 70 percent of the plane's components. For example, the Italian firm Alenia Aeronautica produced the plane's rear fuselage and horizontal stabilizer, and Tokyo-based Mitsubishi Motors Corporation created the wings. All of Boeing's suppliers are connected virtually at 135 sites around the world.

project structure
A structure in which employees continuously work on projects.

boundaryless organization
An organization whose design is not defined by, or limited to, boundaries imposed by a predefined structure.

virtual organization
An organization that consists of a small core of full-time employees and outside specialists temporarily hired as needed to work on projects.

network organization
An organization that uses its own employees to do some work activities and networks of outside suppliers to provide other needed product components or work processes.

locations.[42] And at Penske Truck Leasing, dozens of business processes such as securing permits and titles, entering data from drivers' logs, and processing data for tax filings and accounting have been outsourced to Mexico and India.[43]

What Are Today's Organizational Design Challenges?

As managers look for organizational designs that will best support and facilitate employees doing their work efficiently and effectively, there are certain challenges with which they must contend. These include keeping employees connected, managing global structural issues, and building a learning organization.

HOW DO YOU KEEP EMPLOYEES CONNECTED? Many organizational design concepts were developed during the twentieth century when work tasks were fairly predictable and constant, most jobs were full-time and continued indefinitely, and work was done at an employer's place of business under a manager's supervision.[44] That's not what it's like in many organizations today, as you saw in our preceding discussion of virtual and network organizations. A major structural design challenge for managers is finding a way to keep widely dispersed and mobile employees connected to the organization. The "Technology and the Manager's Job" box describes ways that information technology can help.

HOW DO GLOBAL DIFFERENCES AFFECT ORGANIZATIONAL STRUCTURE? Are there global differences in organizational structures? Are Australian organizations structured like those in the United States? Are German organizations structured like those in France or Mexico? Given the global nature of today's business environment, this is an issue with which managers need to be familiar. Researchers have concluded that the structures and strategies of organizations worldwide are similar, "while the behavior within them is maintaining its cultural uniqueness."[45] What does this mean for designing effective and efficient structures? When designing or changing structure, managers may need to think about the

TECHNOLOGY AND THE MANAGER'S JOB

TECHNOLOGY'S IMPACT ON ORGANIZATIONAL DESIGN

It's fair to say that the world of work will never be like it was 10 years ago.[46] IT has opened up new possibilities for employees to do their work in locations as remote as Patagonia or in the middle of downtown Seattle. Although organizations have always had employees who traveled to distant corporate locations to take care of business, these employees no longer have to find the nearest pay phone or wait to get back to "the office" to see what problems have cropped up. Instead, mobile computing and communication have given organizations and employees ways to stay connected and to be more productive. Let's look at some of the technologies that are changing the way work is done.

▶ Handheld devices with e-mail, calendars, and contacts can be used anywhere there's a wireless network. And these devices can be used to log into corporate databases and company intranets.

▶ Employees can videoconference using broadband networks and Webcams.

▶ Many companies are giving employees key fobs with constantly changing encryption codes that allow them to log onto the corporate network to access e-mail and company data from any computer hooked up to the internet.

▶ Cell phones switch seamlessly between cellular networks and corporate Wi-Fi connections.

The biggest issue in doing work anywhere, anytime is security. Companies must protect their important and sensitive information. However, software and other disabling devices have minimized security issues considerably. Even insurance providers are more comfortable giving their mobile employees access to information. For instance, Health Net Inc. gives BlackBerrys to many of its managers so they can tap into customer records from anywhere. As one tech company CEO said, "Companies now can start thinking about innovative apps [applications] they can create and deliver to their workers anywhere."

cultural implications of certain design elements. For instance, one study showed that formalization—rules and bureaucratic mechanisms—may be more important in less economically developed countries and less important in more economically developed countries where employees may have higher levels of professional education and skills.[47] Other structural design elements may be affected by cultural differences as well.

HOW DO YOU BUILD A LEARNING ORGANIZATION? Doing business in an intensely competitive global environment, British retailer Tesco realized how important it was for its stores to run well behind the scenes. And it does so using a proven "tool" called Tesco in a Box, which promotes consistency in operations as well as being a way to share innovations. Tesco is an example of a **learning organization**, an organization that has developed the capacity to continuously learn, adapt, and change.[48] The concept of a learning organization doesn't involve a specific organizational design per se, but instead describes an organizational mind-set or philosophy that has significant design implications. In a learning organization, employees are practicing knowledge management by continually acquiring and sharing new knowledge and are willing to apply that knowledge in making decisions or performing their work. Some organizational design theorists even go so far as to say that an organization's ability to learn and to apply that learning as they perform the organization's work may be the only sustainable source of competitive advantage.

What would a learning organization look like? As you can see in Exhibit 5-12, the important characteristics of a learning organization revolve around organizational design, information sharing, leadership, and culture. Let's take a closer look at each.

What types of organizational design elements would be necessary for learning to take place? In a learning organization, it's critical for members to share information and collaborate on work activities throughout the entire organization—across different functional

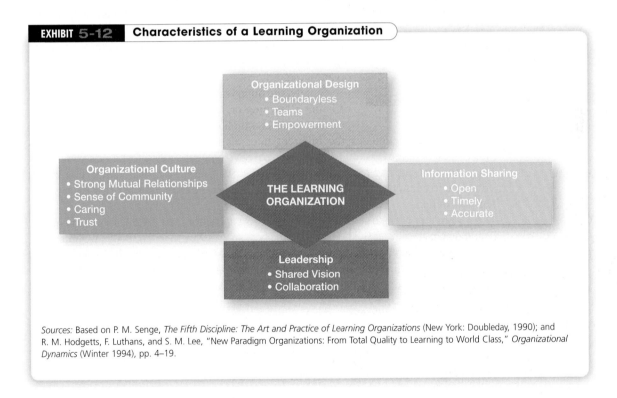

EXHIBIT 5-12 **Characteristics of a Learning Organization**

Organizational Design
• Boundaryless
• Teams
• Empowerment

Organizational Culture
• Strong Mutual Relationships
• Sense of Community
• Caring
• Trust

THE LEARNING ORGANIZATION

Information Sharing
• Open
• Timely
• Accurate

Leadership
• Shared Vision
• Collaboration

Sources: Based on P. M. Senge, *The Fifth Discipline: The Art and Practice of Learning Organizations* (New York: Doubleday, 1990); and R. M. Hodgetts, F. Luthans, and S. M. Lee, "New Paradigm Organizations: From Total Quality to Learning to World Class," *Organizational Dynamics* (Winter 1994), pp. 4–19.

learning organization
An organization that has developed the capacity to continuously learn, adapt, and change.

Right or Wrong?

It was dubbed the "miracle on the Hudson."[49] The ditching of US Airways Flight 1549 in the Hudson River a short time after take-off due to engine failure. But now, the passengers who "suffered real losses and injuries" are being denied compensation because "they are widely perceived as having been saved from sudden, violent death by their heroic and quick-thinking flight crew." Although luggage and other personal belongings that have been found have been returned to passengers, the insurance company is playing hardball on nonrecovered items because airline liability insurance looks for negligence on the part of an airline and "if there's no negligence, then there's no liability, and no obligation to pay claims." What do you think? The insurance company is acting legally, but is it being ethical? Are there other alternatives that might be more ethical?

specialties and even at different organizational levels—through minimizing or eliminating the existing structural and physical boundaries. In this type of boundaryless environment, employees are free to work together and collaborate in doing the organization's work the best way they can, and to learn from each other. Because of this need to collaborate, teams also tend to be an important feature of a learning organization's structural design. Employees work in teams on whatever activities need to be done, and these employee teams are empowered to make decisions about doing their work or resolving issues. Empowered employees and teams have little need for "bosses" who direct and control. Instead, managers serve as facilitators, supporters, and advocates for employee teams.

Learning can't take place without information. For a learning organization to "learn," information must be shared among members; that is, organizational employees must engage in knowledge management by sharing information openly, in a timely manner, and as accurately as possible. Because few structural and physical barriers exist in a learning organization, the environment is conducive to open communication and extensive information sharing.

Leadership plays an important role as an organization moves toward becoming a learning organization. What should leaders do in a learning organization? One of their most important functions is facilitating the creation of a shared vision for the organization's future and then keeping organizational members working toward that vision. In addition, leaders should support and encourage the collaborative environment that's critical to learning. Without strong and committed leadership throughout the organization, it would be extremely difficult to be a learning organization.

Finally, the organizational culture is an important aspect of being a learning organization. A learning organization's culture is one in which everyone agrees on a shared vision and everyone recognizes the inherent interrelationships among the organization's processes, activities, functions, and external environment. It also fosters a strong sense of community, caring for each other, and trust. In a learning organization, employees feel free to communicate openly, share, experiment, and learn without fear of criticism or punishment.

No matter what structural design managers choose for their organizations, the design should help employees do their work in the best, most efficient and effective way they can. The structure needs to help, not hinder, organizational members as they carry out the organization's work. After all, the structure is simply a means to an end. Another factor that affects the way work gets done within an organization is its culture, the topic we're going to look at next.

5.4 Discuss the characteristics and importance of organizational culture.

What Is an Organization's Culture and Why Is It Important?

Each of us has a unique personality—traits and characteristics that influence the way we act and interact with others. When we describe someone as warm, open, relaxed, shy, or aggressive, we're describing personality traits. An organization, too, has a personality, which we call its *culture.*

What Is Organizational Culture?

Organizational culture has been described as the shared values, principles, traditions, and ways of doing things that influence the way organizational members act. In most organizations, these shared values and practices have evolved over time and determine, to a large extent, how "things are done around here."[50]

Our definition of culture implies three things. First, culture is a *perception*. It's not something that can be physically touched or seen, but employees perceive it on the basis of what they experience within the organization. Second, organizational culture is *descriptive*. It's concerned with how members perceive the culture, not with whether they like it. Finally, even though individuals may have different backgrounds or work at different organizational levels, they tend to describe the organization's culture in similar terms. That's the *shared* aspect of culture.

HOW CAN CULTURE BE ASSESSED? Research suggests there are seven dimensions that describe an organization's culture.[51] These dimensions (shown in Exhibit 5-13) range from low to high, meaning it's not very typical of the culture (low) or is very typical of the culture (high). Describing an organization using these seven dimensions gives a composite picture of the organization's culture. In many organizations, one cultural dimension often is emphasized more than the others and essentially shapes the organization's personality and the way organizational members work. For instance, at Sony Corporation the focus is product innovation (innovation and risk taking). The company "lives and breathes" new product development, and employees'

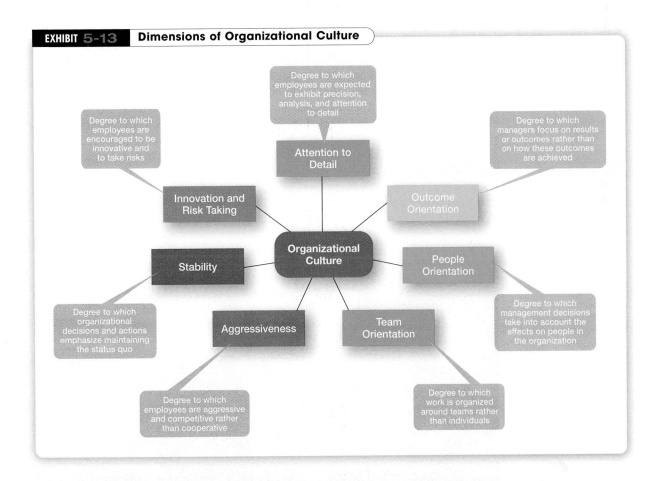

EXHIBIT 5-13   **Dimensions of Organizational Culture**

Degree to which employees are expected to exhibit precision, analysis, and attention to detail

Degree to which employees are encouraged to be innovative and to take risks

Degree to which managers focus on results or outcomes rather than on how these outcomes are achieved

Attention to Detail

Innovation and Risk Taking

Outcome Orientation

Stability

Organizational Culture

People Orientation

Degree to which organizational decisions and actions emphasize maintaining the status quo

Aggressiveness

Team Orientation

Degree to which management decisions take into account the effects on people in the organization

Degree to which employees are aggressive and competitive rather than cooperative

Degree to which work is organized around teams rather than individuals

organizational culture
The shared values, principles, traditions, and ways of doing things that influence the way organizational members act.

work behaviors support that goal. In contrast, Southwest Airlines has made its employees a central part of its culture (people orientation) and shows this through the way it treats them.

WHERE DOES AN ORGANIZATION'S CULTURE COME FROM? An organization's culture usually reflects the vision or mission of the organization's founders. Because the founders had the original idea, they also have biases on how to carry out the idea. They are not constrained by previous customs or ideologies. The founders establish the early culture by projecting an image of what the organization should be and what its values are. The small size of most new organizations also helps the founders impose their vision on all organization members. An organization's culture, then, results from the interaction between (1) the founders' biases and assumptions and (2) what the first employees learn subsequently from their own experiences. For example, the founder of IBM, Thomas Watson, established a culture based on "pursuing excellence, providing the best customer service, and respect for employees." Ironically, some 85 years later, in an effort to revitalize the ailing IBM, CEO Louis Gerstner enhanced that culture with his strong, "customer-oriented sensibility," recognizing the urgency the marketplace imposes on having customers' expectations met. And at Southwest Airlines, former CEO Herb Kelleher reinforced the company's "people culture" by implementing certain practices—such as compensation and benefits that are above industry averages—to make employees happy.

HOW DO EMPLOYEES LEARN THE CULTURE? Employees "learn" an organization's culture in a number of ways. The most common are stories, rituals, material symbols, and language.

Organizational *stories* typically contain a narrative of significant events or people including such things as the organization's founders, rule breaking, reactions to past mistakes, and so forth.[52] For instance, managers at Nike feel that stories told about the company's past help shape the future. Whenever possible, corporate "storytellers" (senior executives) explain the company's heritage and tell stories that celebrate people getting things done. When they tell the story of how cofounder Bill Bowerman (now deceased) went to his workshop and poured rubber into his wife's waffle iron to create a better running shoe, they're celebrating and promoting Nike's spirit of innovation. These company stories provide examples that people can learn from.[53] At the 3M Company, the product innovation stories are legendary. There's the story about the 3M scientist who spilled chemicals on her tennis shoe and came up with Scotchgard. Then, there's the story about Art Fry, a 3M researcher, who wanted a better way to mark the pages of his church hymnal and invented the Post-it Note. These stories reflect what made 3M great and what it will take to continue that success.[54] To help employees learn the culture, organizational stories anchor the present

When Wal-Mart founder Sam Walton saw employees at a Korean tennis ball factory meet each morning for a company cheer and calisthenics, he liked the idea so much that when he arrived home he wrote the Wal-Mart cheer—"Give me a W, give me an A..." that spells the company name and ends with "Who's number one? The customer! Always!" For Walton, the ritual cheer is a way for employees to show pride in the company and how much they value their customers. Today the Wal-Mart cheer is delivered by associates in many different languages around the world. In this photo, employees in Shanghai, China, begin their work day with the ritual cheer.

in the past, provide explanations and legitimacy for current practices, exemplify what is important to the organization, and provide compelling pictures of an organization's goals.[55]

Corporate *rituals* are repetitive sequences of activities that express and reinforce the important values and goals of the organization.[56] The "Passing of the Pillars" is an important ritual at Boston Scientific's facility near Minneapolis. When someone has a challenging assignment, they're "awarded" a two-foot-high plaster of Paris pillar to show that they've got support from all their colleagues.

When you walk into different businesses, do you get a "feel" for what type of work environment it is—formal, casual, fun, serious, and so forth? These reactions demonstrate the power of *material symbols* or *artifacts* in creating an organization's personality.[57] The layout of an organization's facilities, how employees dress, the types of automobiles provided to top executives, and the availability of corporate aircraft are examples of material symbols. Others include the size of offices, the elegance of furnishings, executive "perks" (extra benefits provided to managers such as health club memberships, use of company-owned facilities, and so forth), employee fitness centers or on-site dining facilities, and reserved parking spaces for certain employees. At WorldNow, an important material symbol is an old dented drill that the founders purchased for $2 at a thrift store. The drill symbolizes the company's culture of "drilling down to solve problems." When an employee is presented with the drill in recognition of outstanding work, he or she is expected to personalize the drill in some way and devise a new rule for caring for it. One employee installed a Bart Simpson trigger; another made the drill wireless by adding an antenna. The company's "icon" carries on the culture even as the organization evolves and changes.[58] Material symbols convey to employees who is important and the kinds of behavior (for example, risk taking, conservative, authoritarian, participative, individualistic, and so forth) that are expected and appropriate.

Many organizations and units within organizations use *language* as a way to identify and unite members of a culture. By learning this language, members attest to their acceptance of the culture and their willingness to help preserve it. At Cranium, a Seattle board game company, "chiff" is used to remind employees of the need to be incessantly innovative in everything they do. "Chiff" stands for "clever, high-quality, innovative, friendly, fun."[59] Over time, organizations often develop unique terms to describe equipment, key personnel, suppliers, customers, processes, or products related to its business. New employees are frequently overwhelmed with acronyms and jargon that, after a short period of time, become a natural part of their language. Once learned, this language acts as a common denominator that bonds members.

How Does Culture Influence Structure?

An organization's culture may have an effect on its structure, depending on how strong, or weak, the culture is. **Strong cultures**—those in which the key values are deeply held and widely shared—have a greater influence on employees than do weaker cultures. The more employees accept the organization's key values and the greater their commitment to those values, the stronger the culture is. Most organizations have moderate to strong cultures; that is, there is relatively high agreement on what's important, what defines "good" employee behavior, what it takes to get ahead, and so forth. The stronger a culture becomes, the more it affects the way managers plan, organize, lead, and control.[61]

Also, in organizations with a strong culture, that culture can substitute for the rules and regulations that formally guide employees. In essence, strong cultures can create predictability, orderliness, and consistency without the need for written documentation. Therefore, the stronger an organization's culture, the less managers need to be concerned with developing formal rules and regulations. Instead, those guides will be internalized in employees when they accept the organization's culture. If, on the other hand, an organization's culture is weak—if no dominant shared values are present—its effect on structure is less clear.

and the survey says...[60]

 51 percent of white-collar workers say that teleworking is a good idea.

 41 percent of workers say they can go only 30 minutes without checking their e-mail.

 68 percent of organizations say they've increased centralization in the last five years.

 55 percent of workers believe that their work quality is perceived the same when working remotely as when working in the office.

 42 percent of U.S. companies offer some form of telework arrangement.

 80 percent of workers believe that lack of respect and courtesy is a serious problem in the workplace.

 60 percent of those same workers believe the problem of workplace incivility is getting worse.

strong cultures
Organizational cultures in which the key values are deeply held and widely shared.

Review and ⑤ Applications

Chapter Summary

5.1 **Describe six key elements in organizational design.** The first element, *work specialization*, refers to dividing work activities into separate job tasks. The second, *departmentalization,* is how jobs are grouped together, which can be one of five types: functional, product, customer, geographic, or process. The third—*authority, responsibility, and power*—all have to do with getting work done in an organization. Authority refers to the rights inherent in a managerial position to give orders and expect those orders to be obeyed. Responsibility refers to the obligation to perform when authority has been delegated. Power is the capacity of an individual to influence decisions and is not the same as authority. The fourth, *span of control*, refers to the number of employees a manager can efficiently and effectively manage. The fifth, *centralization and decentralization*, deals with where the majority of decisions are made—at upper organizational levels or pushed down to lower-level managers. The sixth, *formalization*, describes how standardized an organization's jobs are and the extent to which employees' behavior is guided by rules and procedures.

5.2 **Identify the contingency factors that favor the mechanistic model or the organic model.** A *mechanistic* organizational design is quite bureaucratic whereas an *organic* organizational design is more fluid and flexible. The *strategy*-determines-structure factor says that as organizational strategies move from single product to product diversification, the structure will move from organic to mechanistic. As an organization's *size* increases, so does the need for a more mechanistic structure. The more nonroutine the *technology*, the more organic a structure should be.

Finally, stable *environments* are better matched with mechanistic structures, but dynamic ones fit better with organic structures.

5.3 **Compare and contrast traditional and contemporary organizational designs.** Traditional structural designs include simple, functional, and divisional. A *simple structure* is one with low departmentalization, wide spans of control, authority centralized in a single person, and little formalization. A *functional structure* is one that groups similar or related occupational specialties together. A *divisional structure* is one made up of separate business units or divisions. Contemporary structural designs include *team-based structures* (the entire organization is made up of work teams); *matrix and project structures* (where employees work on projects for short periods of time or continuously); and *boundaryless organizations* (where the structural design is free of imposed boundaries). A boundaryless organization can either be a virtual or a network organization.

5.4 **Discuss the characteristics and importance of organizational culture.** Organizational culture refers to the shared values, principles, traditions, and ways of doing things that influence the way organizational members act. Cultures are assessed using seven dimensions: attention to detail, outcome orientation, people orientation, team orientation, aggressiveness, stability, and innovation and risk taking. The culture comes from the founders but is learned by employees through stories, rituals, material symbols, and language. Strong cultures—those in which the key values are deeply held and widely shared—have more of an impact on how organizations are structured and on the way work is done.

 mymanagementlab To check your understanding of learning outcomes **5.1** – **5.4**, go to **mymanagementlab.com** and try the chapter questions.

Understanding the Chapter

1. Describe what is meant by the term *organizational design.*

2. Can an organization's structure be changed quickly? Why or why not? Should it be changed quickly? Why or why not?

3. "An organization can have no structure." Do you agree or disagree with this statement? Explain.

4. With the availability of information technology that allows employees to work anywhere, anytime, is organizing still an important managerial function? Why or why not?

5. Researchers are now saying that efforts to simplify work tasks actually have negative results for both companies and their employees. Do you agree? Why or why not?

6. Classrooms have cultures. Describe your class culture using Exhibit 5-13. How does it affect your instructor? How does it affect you?

7. Draw an organization chart of an organization with which you're familiar (where you work, a student organization to which you belong, your college or

university, etc.). Be very careful in showing the departments (or groups) and especially be careful to get the chain of command correct. Be prepared to share your chart with the class.

8. Pick two organizations that you interact with frequently (as an employee or as a customer) and assess their culture according to the cultural dimensions shown in Exhibit 5-13.

Understanding Yourself

What Type of Organization Structure Do I Prefer?

In what type of structure—mechanistic or organic—will you be most comfortable working? Mechanistic structures are characterized by extensive departmentalization, high formalization, a limited information network, and centralization. In contrast organic structures are flat, use cross-hierarchical and cross-functional teams, have low formalization, possess a comprehensive information network, and rely on participative decision making.

INSTRUMENT   Respond to each of the 15 statements by using one of the following numbers:

  1 = Strongly disagree

  2 = Disagree somewhat

  3 = Undecided

  4 = Agree somewhat

  5 = Strongly agree

I prefer to work in an organization where:

1.	Goals are defined by those at higher levels.	1	2	3	4	5
2.	Clear job descriptions exist for every job.	1	2	3	4	5
3.	Top management makes important decisions.	1	2	3	4	5
4.	Promotions and pay increases are based as much on length of service as on level of performance.	1	2	3	4	5
5.	Clear lines of authority and responsibility are established.	1	2	3	4	5
6.	My career is pretty well planned out for me.	1	2	3	4	5
7.	I have a great deal of job security.	1	2	3	4	5
8.	I can specialize.	1	2	3	4	5
9.	My boss is readily available.	1	2	3	4	5
10.	Organization rules and regulations are clearly specified.	1	2	3	4	5
11.	Information rigidly follows the chain of command.	1	2	3	4	5
12.	There is a minimal number of new tasks for me to learn.	1	2	3	4	5
13.	Work groups incur little turnover in members.	1	2	3	4	5
14.	People accept authority of a leader's position.	1	2	3	4	5
15.	I am part of a group whose training and skills are similar to mine.	1	2	3	4	5

SCORING KEY   To calculate your score, add up your responses to all 15 items.

ANALYSIS AND INTERPRETATION   Scores above 60 suggest that you prefer a mechanistic design. Scores below 45 indicate a preference for an organic design. Scores between 45 and 60 suggest no clear preference.

Since the trend in recent years has been toward more organic designs, you're likely to find a good organizational match if you score low on this instrument. But there are few, if any, pure organic structures. So very low scores may also mean that you're likely to be frustrated by what you perceive as overly rigid structures of rules, regulations, and boss-centered leadership. In general, however, low scores indicate that you prefer small, innovative, flexible, team-oriented organizations. And high scores indicate a preference for stable, rule-oriented, more bureaucratic organizations.

Source: Based on J. F. Veiga and J. N. Yanouzas, *The Dynamics of Organization Theory: Gaining a Macro Perspective* (St. Paul, MN: West, 1979), pp. 158–60.

FYIA (For Your Immediate Action)

Ontario Electronics Ltd.

Reply   Reply All   Forward

To:	Claude Fortier, Special Assistant to the President
From:	Ian Campbell, President
Subject:	**Learning Organizations**

First of all, thanks for keeping everything "going" while I was at the annual meeting of the Canadian Electronics Manufacturers Industry Association last week. Our luncheon speaker on the final day talked about how important it is for organizations to be responsive to customer and marketplace needs. One of the approaches she discussed for doing this was becoming a learning organization. I came away from this talk convinced that our company's future may well depend on how well we're able to "learn."

I'd like you to find some current information on learning organizations. Although I'm sure you'll be able to find numerous articles about the topic, limit your report to five of what you consider to be the best sources of information on the topic. Write a one-paragraph summary for each of these five articles, being sure to note all the bibliographic information in case we need to find the article later.

I'd like for our executive team to move on this idea fairly quickly, so please have your report back to me by the end of the week.

This fictionalized company and message were created for educational purposes only. It is not meant to reflect positively or negatively on management practices by any company that may share this name.

CASE APPLICATION

UNCONVENTIONAL DESIGN

Danish company Bang & Olufsen (B&O) is known globally for its high-end audio and video equipment. Many of its incredibly beautiful and artistic products—most of which are made in Denmark—are part of the collection at New York's Museum of Modern Art. Needless to say, product design is critically important to B&O. What's even more unique than its futuristic products, however, is the company's approach to the design process, which is a critical strategic capability of the organization. CEO Kalle Hvidt Nielsen says, "Our mission is to make complex technology very simple to use."

Unlike the conventional design approach used by most organizations in which marketing employees conduct consumer market research and then decide design direction, B&O uses contract designers, not organizational design employees, to create the company's products. And these designers have been empowered to veto any product they don't like. The company's lead designer, David Lewis, has freelanced for the company since the early 1960s. He spends just two or three days per month at the company's headquarters in Struer and says that, "It's a great, concentrated way of working…I see things in a different way because I am not at all part of the system here." Lewis and his team of six designers, who all are external freelancers, don't ever meet.

The design process isn't really a process. Lewis says that, "Every time we design a new product, it's like starting all over. Time frames, technology, and demands are different each time." However, he and his team do have an approach. They don't use sketches; they model the new product out of cardboard, pieces of paper, little bits of plastic, or whatever's on hand. Working like a sculptor, the team builds the model. They stand around it, talk about it, and modify it as needed. Once the model is complete, Lewis takes it to headquarters where company executives can see what the design is about. And being able to see and feel the new product in three dimensions, it's easy for top-level decision makers to see all the details and really feel the design.

Giving such power to individuals who aren't employees would frighten most managers. However, it works well for B&O. This "business-by-genius model depends on the instincts of a handful of quirky and creative individuals and the ability of executives to manage them."

Discussion Questions

1. Describe and evaluate what B&O is doing.
2. What structural implications—good and bad—does this approach have? (Think in terms of the six organizational design elements.)
3. Do you think this arrangement would work for other types of organizations? Why or why not?
4. The B&O design approach depends on "the ability of executives to manage" the designers. What abilities would managers need in managing in this type of organizational design?
5. What role do you think organizational structure plays in an organization's strategic capabilities, especially in innovation efforts?

Sources: D. A. Keeps, "Out-of-the-Box Offices," *Fortune,* January 19, 2009, pp. 45–50; D. Steinbom, "Talking About Design: An Interview with David Lewis," *Wall Street Journal,* June 23, 2008, p. R6; D. Steinbom, "A Speaker That Was Decades in the Making," *Wall Street Journal,* June 23, 2008, p. R6; and J. Greene, "Where Designers Rule," *BusinessWeek,* November 5, 2007, pp. 46–51.

6

Managing Human Resources

learning outcomes

6.1 **Describe** the key components of the HRM process and what influences it. p.154

6.2 **Discuss** the tasks associated with identifying and selecting competent employees. p.158

6.3 **Explain** how employees are provided with needed skills and knowledge. p.166

6.4 **Describe** strategies for retaining competent, high-performing employees. p.169

6.5 **Discuss** contemporary issues in managing human resources. p.173

Shedding Workers and Tears

It's probably one of the hardest things that a manager may have to do.[1] Telling an employee that he or she is being laid off. And some 7.2 million Americans who have been laid off since the economic recession began in early 2008 have been given that news by someone. In smaller businesses, it's especially difficult to do because it's often more personal and employees are more like family. In carrying out such an assignment, managers may fear that employees will get highly emotional or angry, although those reactions don't happen often. Such reactions are more likely when workers have no notice that layoffs are coming. That's when the situation can become very raw as those being laid off respond with expressions of shock and disbelief and sometimes crying.

At Ram Tool, a small family-owned manufacturing company in Grafton, Wisconsin, the task fell to Shelly Polum (see photo on right), the company's vice president of administration. After the nine-member management team met to consider which employees would be laid off, Shelly had to inform four workers that they were being let go. "When it was over, trying to maintain her composure, she rushed back to her office and shut the door quickly. Then she sank to the floor and burst into tears."

At Shuqualak Lumber in Shuqualak, Mississippi, vice president Charlie Thomas started his speech to employees announcing that nearly a quarter of them were going to be laid off. He had to stop to go back to his office and regain his composure. He says, "I couldn't get it out. It just killed me." And it's not just American managers facing the emotional challenge of laying off employees.

In Ditzingen, Germany, at TRUMPF, a laser machine tools manufacturer, company president Nicola Leibinger-Kammüller says, "The responsibility I have for our employees is what is dearest to my heart." However, the worldwide economic recession has severely impacted the company's exports and revenues and TRUMPF executives are contemplating employee layoffs for the first time in 20 years. Says Leibinger-Kammüller, "What vexes me day and night is the idea that I would have to lay people off."

Studies of managers involved with layoffs have shown that those who must tell people they've been laid off also experience stress, poor sleep, and even health problems. In one study, managers called the layoffs "gut-wrenching" and "devastating." And these problems often can linger. In that same study, those managers had mostly regained their emotional health up to six years after the layoffs, but were still more likely than other managers to have stress-related health problems.

Managers who've had to deal several times with telling employees they're laid off say that, "It gets a little easier with experience." They soon learned how to tell people in the least hurtful way and to emphasize that it was the job that was being eliminated. However, one manager who has laid off several dozen workers during her 25 years at Union Oil Company says, "It's not that you ever lose the butterflies in your stomach or that sinking feeling, but you get better at handling it as something that is not personal."

With the organization's structure in place, managers have to find people to fill the jobs that have been created or to remove people from the jobs if business circumstances require that. That's where human resource management (HRM) comes in. It's an important task that involves having the right number of the right people in the right place at the right time. In this chapter, we'll look at the process managers use to do just that. In addition, we'll look at some contemporary HRM issues facing managers.

What Is the Human Resource Management Process and What Influences It?

6.1 Describe the key components of the HRM process and what influences it.

The quality of an organization is to a large degree determined by the quality of the people it employs. Success for most organizations depends on finding the employees with the skills to successfully perform the tasks required to attain the company's strategic goals. Staffing and human resource management decisions and methods are critical to ensuring that the organization hires and keeps the right people.

Some of you may be thinking, "Sure, personnel decisions are important. But aren't most of them made by people who specifically handle human resource issues?" It's true that, in many organizations, a number of the activities grouped under the label **human resource management (HRM)** are done by specialists. In other cases, HRM activities may be outsourced to companies, domestic or global. Not all managers have HRM staff support, though. Many small business managers, for instance, frequently must do their own hiring without the assistance of HRM specialists. Even managers in larger organizations are often involved in recruiting candidates, reviewing application forms, interviewing applicants, orienting new employees, making decisions about employee training, providing career advice to employees, and evaluating employees' performance. So, even if an organization provides HRM support activities, every manager is involved with human resource decisions in his or her unit.[2]

Exhibit 6-1 introduces the key components of an organization's HRM process. It represents eight activities (the gold boxes) that, if properly executed, will staff an organization with competent, high-performing employees who are capable of sustaining their performance level over the long term.

After an organization's strategy has been established and the organization structure designed, it's time to add the people. That's one of the most critical roles for HRM and one that has increased the importance of human resource managers to the organization. The first three activities in the HRM process represent employment planning: the addition of staff through recruitment, the reduction in staff through downsizing, and selection. When executed properly, these steps lead to the identification and selection of competent employees and assist organizations in achieving their strategic directions.

Once you select competent people, you need to help them adapt to the organization and ensure that their job skills and knowledge are kept current. These next two activities in the HRM process are accomplished through orientation and training. The last steps in the HRM process are designed to identify performance goals, correct performance problems if necessary, and help employees sustain a high level of performance over their entire work life. The activities involved include performance appraisal, and compensation and benefits. HRM also includes safety and health issues, but we're not covering those topics in this book.

Notice in Exhibit 6-1 that the entire process is influenced by the external environment. Many of the factors introduced in Chapter 2 directly affect all management practices, but their effect is felt the most in managing the organization's human resources, because whatever happens to an organization ultimately influences what happens to its employees. So, before we review the HRM process, let's examine one primary environmental force that affects it—the legal environment, and especially, employment and discrimination laws.

EXHIBIT 6-1 **The Human Resource Management Process**

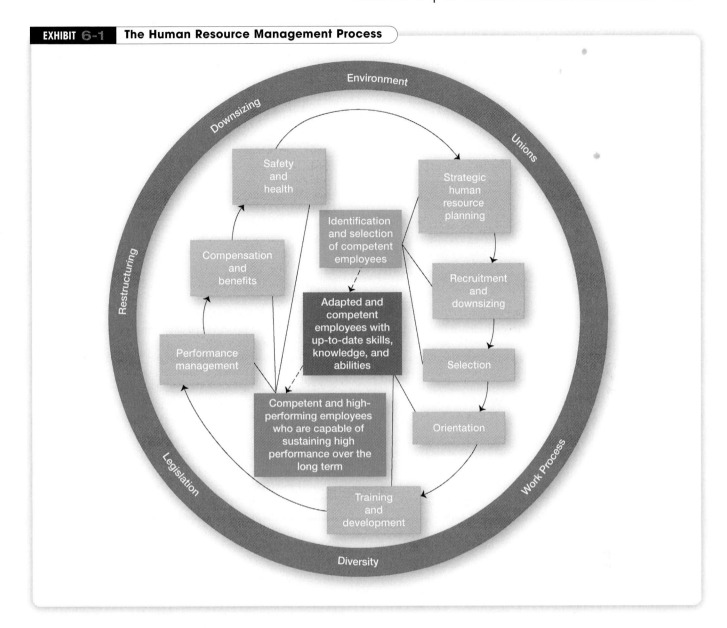

What Is the Legal Environment of HRM?

HRM practices are governed by laws, which vary from country to country. Within countries, state or provincial and local regulations further influence specific practices. Consequently, it's impossible to provide you with all the information you need about the relevant regulatory environment. As a manager, it will be important for you to know what you can and cannot do, legally.

WHAT ARE THE PRIMARY U.S. LAWS AFFECTING HRM? Since the mid-1960s, the federal government in the United States has greatly expanded its influence over HRM by enacting a number of laws and regulations (see Exhibit 6-2 for examples). Although we've not seen

human resource management (HRM)
The management function concerned with getting, training, motivating, and keeping competent employees.

| EXHIBIT 6-2 | Major U.S. Federal HRM Laws |

YEAR	LAW OR REGULATION	DESCRIPTION
1963	Equal Pay Act	Prohibits pay differences based on sex for equal work
1964 (amended, in 1972)	Civil Rights Act, Title VII	Prohibits discrimination based on race, color, religion, national origin or sex
1967 (amended in 1978)	Age Discrimination in Employment Act	Prohibits age discrimination against employees between 40 and 65 years of age
1973	Vocational Rehabilitation Act	Prohibits discrimination on the basis of physical or mental disabilities
1974	Privacy Act	Gives employees the legal right to examine letters of reference concerning them
1978	Pregnancy Discrimination Act, Title VII	Prohibits dismissal because of pregnancy alone and protects job security during maternity leaves
1978	Mandatory Retirement Act	Prohibits the forced retirement of most employees before the age of 70; later amended to eliminate upper limit
1986	Immigration Reform and Control Act	Prohibits unlawful employment of aliens and unfair immigration-related employment practices
1988	Polygraph Protection Act	Limits an employer's ability to use lie detectors
1988	Worker Adjustment and Retraining Notification Act	Requires employers to provide 60 days' notice before a facility closing or mass layoff
1990	Americans with Disabilities Act	Prohibits employers from discriminating against and requires reasonable accommodation of essentially qualified individuals with physical or mental disabilities or the chronically ill
1991	Civil Rights Act	Reaffirms and tightens prohibition of discrimination; permits individuals to sue for punitive damages in cases of intentional discrimination
1993	Family and Medical Leave Act	Permits employees in organizations with 50 or more workers to take up to 12 weeks of unpaid leave each year for family or medical reasons
2002	Sarbanes–Oxley Act	Establishes requirements for proper financial record keeping for public companies and penalties for noncompliance
2007	Federal Minimum Wage Bill	Increases federal minimum wage rates—$5.85 summer of 2007; $6.55 summer of 2008; and $7.25 in summer 2009
2009	Lilly Ledbetter Fair Pay Act	Changes the statute of limitations on pay discrimination to 180 days from each paycheck

many laws enacted recently at the federal level, many state laws have been passed that add to the provisions of the federal laws. For instance, in many states today, it's illegal to discriminate against an individual based on sexual orientation. As a result, today's employers must ensure that equal employment opportunities exist for job applicants and current employees. Decisions regarding who will be hired, for example, or which employees will be chosen for a management training program must be made without regard to race, sex, religion, age, color, national origin, or disability. Exceptions can occur only when special circumstances exist. For instance, a community fire department can deny employment to a firefighter applicant who is confined to a wheelchair, but if that same individual is applying for a desk job, such as a fire department dispatcher, the disability cannot be used as a reason to deny employment. The issues involved, however, are rarely that clear-cut. For example, employment laws protect most employees whose religious beliefs require a specific style of dress—robes, long shirts, long hair, and the like. However, if the specific style of dress may be hazardous or unsafe in the work setting (e.g., when operating machinery), a company could refuse to hire a person who would not adopt a safer dress code.

Trying to balance the "shoulds and should nots" of these laws often falls within the realm of **affirmative action programs**. Many organizations operating in the United States have affirmative action programs to ensure that decisions and practices enhance the employment, upgrading, and retention of members from protected groups such as minorities and

From the Past to the Present

Hugo Munsterberg was a pioneer in the field of industrial psychology and is "generally credited with creating the field."[3] As an admirer of Frederick W. Taylor and the scientific management movement, Munsterberg stated that "Taylor had introduced most valuable suggestions which the industrial world cannot ignore." Drawing on Taylor's works, Munsterberg stressed "the importance of efficiently using workers to achieve economic production." His research and work in showing organizations ways to improve the performance and well-being of workers was fundamental to the emerging field of management in the early 1900s.

Today, industrial-organizational psychology is defined as the scientific study of the workplace. Industrial-organizational (I/O) psychologists use scientific principles and research-based designs to generate knowledge about workplace issues. (Check out the Society for Industrial and Organizational Psychology at www.siop.org.) They study organizational topics such as job performance, job analysis, performance appraisal, compensation, work/life balance, work sample tests, employee training, employment law, personnel recruitment and selection, and so forth. Their research has contributed much to the field that we call human resource management. And all of this is due to the early work done by Hugo Munsterberg.

---

females. That is, the organization refrains from discrimination and actively seeks to enhance the status of members from protected groups.

U.S. managers are not completely free to choose whom they hire, promote, or fire. Although these regulations have significantly helped to reduce employment discrimination and unfair employment practices, they have, at the same time, reduced management's discretion over HR decisions.

ARE HRM LAWS THE SAME GLOBALLY? HRM laws aren't the same globally. You need to know the laws and regulations that apply in your locale. To illustrate our point that laws and regulations shape HRM practices, we highlight some of the federal legislation in countries such as Canada, Mexico, Australia, and Germany.

Canadian laws pertaining to HRM practices closely parallel those in the United States. The Canadian Human Rights Act prohibits discrimination on the basis of race, religion, age, marital status, sex, physical or mental disability, or national origin. This act governs practices throughout the country. Canada's HRM environment, however, is somewhat different from that in the United States in that it involves more decentralization of lawmaking to the provincial level. For example, discrimination on the basis of language is not prohibited anywhere in Canada except in Quebec.

In Mexico, employees are more likely to be unionized than they are in the United States. Labor matters in Mexico are governed by the Mexican Federal Labor Law. One hiring law states that an employer has 28 days to evaluate a new employee's work performance. After that period, the employee is granted job security and termination is quite difficult and expensive. Those who violate the Mexican Federal Labor Law are subject to severe penalties, including criminal action that can result in steep fines and even jail sentences for employers who fail to pay, for example, the minimum wage.

Australia's discrimination laws were not enacted until the 1980s, and generally apply to discrimination and affirmative action for women. Yet, gender opportunities for women in Australia appear to lag behind those in the United States. In Australia, however, a significant proportion of the workforce is unionized. The higher percentage of unionized workers has placed increased importance on industrial relations specialists in Australia, and reduced

affirmative action programs
Programs that ensure that decisions and practices enhance the employment, upgrading, and retention of members of protected groups.

the control of line managers over workplace labor issues. However, in 1997, Australia over-hauled its labor and industrial relations laws with the objective of increasing productivity and reducing union power. The Workplace Relations Bill gives employers greater flexibil-ity to negotiate directly with employees on pay, hours, and benefits. It also simplifies fed-eral regulation of labor-management relations.

Our final example, Germany, is similar to most Western European countries when it comes to HRM practices. Legislation requires companies to practice representative partic-ipation, in which the goal is to redistribute power within the organization, putting labor on a more equal footing with the interests of management and stockholders. The two most common forms of representative participation are work councils and board representatives. **Work councils** link employees with management. They are groups of nominated or elected employees who must be consulted when management makes decisions involving personnel. **Board representatives** are employees who sit on a company's board of directors and repre-sent the interest of the firm's employees.

Discuss the tasks associated with identifying and selecting competent employees.

6.2

How Do Managers Identify and Select Competent Employees?

Every organization needs people to do whatever work is necessary for doing what the organization is in business to do. How do organizations get those people? And more importantly what can they do to ensure they get competent, talented people? This first phase of the HRM process involves three tasks: employment planning, recruitment and downsizing, and selection.

What Is Employment Planning?

In the first four months of 2009, Boeing cut more than 3,000 jobs, mostly from its commer-cial airplanes unit. During the same time, it added 106 employees to its defense unit and was looking for several hundred more.[4] Like most companies, Boeing was juggling its supply of human resources to meet demand.

Employment planning is the process by which managers ensure that they have the right number and kinds of people in the right places at the right times, people who are capable of effectively and efficiently completing those tasks that will help the organization achieve its overall goals. Employment planning, then, translates the organization's mission and goals into an HR plan that will allow the organization to achieve those goals. The process can be condensed into two steps: (1) assessing current human resources and future human resource needs, and (2) developing a plan to meet those needs.

HOW DOES AN ORGANIZATION CONDUCT AN EMPLOYEE ASSESSMENT? Managers begin by reviewing the current human resource status. This review is typically done by gen-erating a **human resource inventory**. It's not difficult to generate an inventory in most organizations since the information for it is derived from forms completed by employees. Such inventories might list the name, education, training, prior employment, languages spo-ken, capabilities, and specialized skills of each employee in the organization. This inventory allows managers to assess what talents and skills are currently available in the organization.

Another part of the current assessment is **job analysis**. Whereas the human resources inventory is concerned with telling management what individual employees can do, job analy-sis is more fundamental. It's typically a lengthy process, one in which workflows are analyzed and skills and behaviors that are necessary to perform jobs are identified. For instance, what does an international reporter who works for the *Wall Street Journal* do? What minimal knowl-edge, skills, and abilities are necessary for the adequate performance of this job? How do the job requirements for an international reporter compare with those for a domestic reporter or for a newspaper editor? Job analysis can answer these questions. Ultimately, the purpose of job analysis is to determine the kinds of skills, knowledge, and attitudes needed to successfully per-form each job. This information is then used to develop or revise job descriptions and job specifications.

A **job description** is a written statement that describes the job—what a job holder does, how it's done, and why it's done. It typically portrays job content, environment, and conditions of employment. The **job specification** states the minimum qualifications that a person must possess to perform a given job successfully. It focuses on the person and identifies the knowledge, skills, and attitudes needed to do the job effectively. The job description and job specification are important documents when managers begin recruiting and selecting. For instance, the job description can be used to describe the job to potential candidates. The job specification keeps the manager's attention on the list of qualifications necessary for an incumbent to perform a job and assists in determining whether candidates are qualified. Furthermore, hiring individuals on the basis of the information contained in these two documents helps ensure that the hiring process does not discriminate.

HOW ARE FUTURE EMPLOYEE NEEDS DETERMINED? Future human resource needs are determined by the organization's strategic direction. Demand for human resources (employees) is a result of demand for the organization's products or services. On the basis of an estimate of total revenue, managers can attempt to establish the number and mix of people needed to reach that revenue. In some cases, however, the situation may be reversed. When particular skills are necessary and in scarce supply, the availability of needed human resources determines revenues. For example, managers of an upscale chain of assisted-living retirement facilities who find themselves with abundant business opportunities are limited in building revenues by their ability to locate and hire a qualified nursing staff to fully meet the needs of the residents. In most cases, however, the overall organizational goals and the resulting revenue forecast provide the major input in determining the organization's HR requirements.

After it has assessed both current capabilities and future needs, managers are able to estimate shortages—both in number and in kind—and to highlight areas in which the organization is overstaffed. A plan can then be developed that matches these estimates with forecasts of future labor supply. Employment planning not only guides current staffing needs but also projects future employee needs and availability.

HOW DO ORGANIZATIONS RECRUIT EMPLOYEES? Once managers know their current staffing levels—whether understaffed or overstaffed—they can begin to do something about it. If one or more vacancies exist, they can use the information gathered through job analysis to guide them in **recruitment**—that is, the process of locating, identifying, and attracting capable applicants. On the other hand, if employment planning indicates a surplus, managers will want to reduce the labor supply within the organization and will initiate downsizing or restructuring activities.

WHERE DOES A MANAGER RECRUIT APPLICANTS? Applicants can be found by using several sources, including the Internet. Exhibit 6-3 offers some guidance. The source that's used should reflect the local labor market, the type or level of position, and the size of the organization.

An organization's strategic direction determines its future human resource needs. Following Target Corporation's growth strategy, the discount retailer plans to add about 100 stores a year through 2011, although the actual number may fluctuate depending on economic conditions. Each of Target's three different store formats requires a different number of employees: general merchandise from 100 to 250; general merchandise with an expanded food format from100 to 250; and Super Target with full grocery, deli, and bakery from 200 to 300. Knowing the number of planned stores and the type of format helps Target managers determine its human resource needs.

work councils
Groups of nominated or elected employees who must be consulted when management makes decisions involving personnel.

board representatives
Employees who sit on a company's board of directors and represent the interest of employees.

employment planning
The process by which managers ensure they have the right numbers and kinds of people in the right places at the right time.

human resource inventory
A report listing important information about employees such as name, education, training, skills, languages spoken, and so forth.

job analysis
An assessment that defines jobs and the behaviors necessary to perform them.

job description
A written statement that describes a job.

job specification
A written statement of the minimum qualifications that a person must possess to perform a given job successfully.

recruitment
Locating, identifying, and attracting capable applicants.

| EXHIBIT 6-3 | Recruiting Sources |

SOURCE	ADVANTAGE	DISADVANTAGE
Internal searches	Low cost; build employee morale; candidates are familiar with organization	Limited supply; may not increase proportion of protected group employees
Advertisements	Wide distribution can be targeted to specific groups	Generate many unqualified candidates
Employee referrals	Knowledge about the organization provided by current employees; can generate strong candidates because a good referral reflects on the recommender	May not increase the diversity and mix of employees
Public employment agencies	Free or nominal cost	Candidates tend to be lower skilled, although some skilled employees available
Private employment agencies	Wide contacts; careful screening; short-term guarantees often given	High cost
School placement	Large, centralized body of candidates	Limited to entry-level positions
Temporary help services	Fill temporary needs	Expensive
Employee leasing and independent contractors	Fill temporary needs but usually for more specific, longer-term projects	Little commitment to an organization other than current project

Do certain recruiting sources produce superior applicants? The answer is generally yes. The majority of studies have found that employee referrals generally produce the best applicants.[5] The explanation for this finding is intuitively logical. First, applicants referred by current employees are prescreened by those employees. Because the recommenders know both the job and the person being recommended, they tend to refer well-qualified applicants.[6] Second, because current employees often feel that their reputation in the organization is at stake with a referral, they tend to make referrals only when they are reasonably confident that the referral won't make them look bad. However, managers shouldn't always opt for the employee-referred applicant since such referrals may not increase the diversity and mix of employees.

How Does a Manager Handle Layoffs?

In the past decade, and especially during the last year, most global organizations, as well as many government agencies and small businesses, have been forced to shrink the size of their workforce or restructure their skill composition. Downsizing has become a relevant strategy for meeting the demands of a dynamic environment.

WHAT ARE DOWNSIZING OPTIONS? Obviously, people can be fired, but other restructuring choices may be more beneficial to the organization. Exhibit 6-4 summarizes a manager's major downsizing options. Keep in mind that, regardless of the method chosen, employees may suffer. We discuss downsizing more fully—for both victims and survivors—later in this chapter.

How Do Managers Select Job Applicants?

Once the recruiting effort has developed a pool of applicants, the next step in the HRM process is to determine who is best qualified for the job. In essence, then, the **selection process** is a prediction exercise: It seeks to predict which applicants will be "successful" if hired; that is, who will perform well on the criteria the organization uses to evaluate its

EXHIBIT 6-4	Downsizing Options

OPTION	DESCRIPTION
Firing	Permanent involuntary termination
Layoffs	Temporary involuntary termination; may last only a few days or extend to years
Attrition	Not filling openings created by voluntary resignations or normal retirements
Transfers	Moving employees either laterally or downward; usually does not reduce costs but can reduce intraorganizational supply–demand imbalances
Reduced workweeks/ furloughs	Having employees work fewer hours per week, share jobs, or perform their jobs on a part-time basis
Early retirements	Providing incentives to older and more-senior employees for retiring before their normal retirement date
Job sharing	Having employees, typically two part-timers, share one full-time position

employees. In filling a network administrator position, for example, the selection process should be able to predict which applicants will be capable of properly installing, debugging, and managing the organization's computer network. For a position as a sales representative, it should predict which applicants will be successful at generating high sales volumes. Consider, for a moment, that any selection decision can result in four possible outcomes. As shown in Exhibit 6-5, two outcomes would indicate correct decisions, and two would indicate errors.

A decision is correct (1) when the applicant who was predicted to be successful (was accepted) and later proved to be successful on the job, or (2) when the applicant who was predicted to be unsuccessful (was rejected) and, if hired, would not have been able to do the job. In the former case, we have successfully accepted; in the latter case, we have successfully rejected. Problems occur, however, when we reject applicants who, if hired, would have

EXHIBIT 6-5	Selection Decision Outcomes

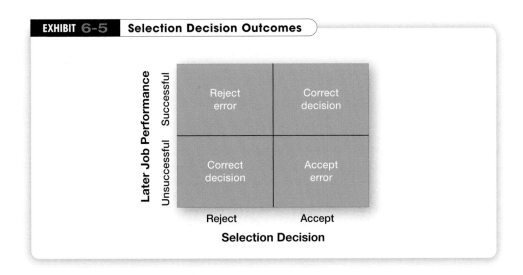

selection process
Screening job applicants to ensure that the most appropriate candidates are hired.

performed successfully on the job (called *reject errors*) or accept those who subsequently perform poorly (*accept errors*). These problems are, unfortunately, far from insignificant. A generation ago, reject errors only meant increased selection costs because more applicants would have to be screened. Today, selection techniques that result in reject errors can open the organization to charges of employment discrimination, especially if applicants from protected groups are disproportionately rejected. Accept errors, on the other hand, have obvious costs to the organization, including the cost of training the employee, the costs generated or profits forgone because of the employee's incompetence, and the cost of severance and the subsequent costs of additional recruiting and selection screening. The major intent of any selection activity is, therefore, to reduce the probability of making reject errors or accept errors while increasing the probability of making correct decisions. We do this by using selection procedures that are both reliable and valid.

WHAT IS RELIABILITY? Reliability addresses whether a selection device measures the same characteristic consistently. For example, if a test is reliable, any individual's score should remain fairly stable over time, assuming that the characteristics it is measuring are also stable. The importance of reliability should be self-evident. No selection device can be effective if it's low in reliability. Using such a device would be the equivalent of weighing yourself every day on an erratic scale. If the scale is unreliable—randomly fluctuating, say, 10 to 15 pounds every time you step on it—the results will not mean much. To be effective predictors, selection devices must possess an acceptable level of consistency.

WHAT IS VALIDITY? Any selection device that a manager uses—such as application forms, tests, interviews, or physical examinations—must also demonstrate **validity**. Validity is based on a proven relationship between the selection device used and some relevant measure. For example, we mentioned earlier a firefighter applicant who was wheelchair bound. Because of the physical requirements of a firefighter's job, someone confined to a wheelchair would be unable to pass the physical endurance tests. In that case, denying employment could be considered valid, but requiring the same physical endurance tests for the dispatching job would not be job related. Federal law prohibits managers from using any selection device that cannot be shown to be directly related to successful job performance. That constraint goes for entrance tests, too; managers must be able to demonstrate that, once on the job, individuals with high scores on such a test outperform individuals with low scores. Consequently, the burden is on the organization to verify that any selection device it uses to differentiate applicants is related to job performance.

MANAGING DIVERSITY | Diversity and Discrimination

Data released by the Equal Employment Opportunity Commission in early 2009 stated that more people experienced workplace discrimination in 2008 than ever before.[7] More than 95,400 job-bias claims were filed, an increase of 15 percent over the previous year. All major categories of workplace discrimination saw increases although age and retaliation claims increased the most. Charges of age discrimination jumped by 28.7 percent, while complaints about retaliation were up 22.6 percent. The acting chairperson of the agency said, "The EEOC has not seen an increase of this magnitude in charges filed for many years. While we do not know if this signifies a trend, it is clear that employment discrimination remains a persistent problem."

What seems to be driving these numbers? The major reason, according to analysts, is likely to be the current economic conditions. "The economy is in meltdown mode and from the point of view of the company, if you lay off an older worker, the cost savings are greater than if you lay off a younger worker." However, another reason, experts believe, is a greater awareness of EEOC policy. That can be considered a sign of the impact that equal employment opportunity advocates have had.

Managers have the responsibility of ensuring that their HRM policies and practices don't violate discrimination laws and regulations. It's especially critical in today's environment where employees are facing stress and uncertainty over personal and work issues.

HOW EFFECTIVE ARE TESTS AND INTERVIEWS AS SELECTION DEVICES? Managers can use a number of selection devices to reduce accept and reject errors. The best-known devices include written and performance-simulation tests and interviews. Let's briefly review each device, giving particular attention to its validity in predicting job performance.

Typical *written tests* include tests of intelligence, aptitude, ability, and interest. Such tests have long been used as selection devices, although their popularity has run in cycles. Written tests were widely used after World War II, but beginning in the late 1960s, they fell out of favor. They were frequently characterized as discriminatory, and many organizations could not validate that their written tests were job related. Today, written tests have made a comeback although most of them are now Internet based.[8] Managers are increasingly aware that poor hiring decisions are costly and that properly designed tests can reduce the likelihood of making such decisions. In addition, the cost of developing and validating a set of written tests for a specific job has declined significantly.

A review of the evidence finds that tests of intellectual ability, spatial and mechanical ability, perceptual accuracy, and motor ability are moderately valid predictors for many semiskilled and unskilled operative jobs in industrial organizations.[9] However, an enduring criticism of written tests is that intelligence and other tested characteristics can be somewhat removed from the actual performance of the job itself.[10] For example, a high score on an intelligence test is not necessarily a good indicator that the applicant will perform well as a computer programmer. This criticism has led to an increased use of *performance-simulation tests*.

What better way to find out whether an applicant for a technical writing position at Google can write technical manuals than to ask him or her to do it? That's why there's an increasing interest in **performance-simulation tests**. Undoubtedly, the enthusiasm for these tests lies in the fact that they're based on job analysis data and, therefore, should more easily meet the requirement of job relatedness than do written tests. Performance-simulation tests are made up of actual job behaviors rather than substitutes. The best-known performance-simulation tests are work sampling (a miniature replica of the job) and assessment centers (simulating real problems one may face on the job). The former is suited to persons applying for routine jobs, the latter to managerial personnel.

The advantage of performance simulation over traditional testing methods should be obvious. Because its content is essentially identical to job content, performance simulation should be a better predictor of short-term job performance and should minimize potential employment discrimination allegations. Additionally, because of the nature of their content and the methods used to determine content, well-constructed performance-simulation tests are valid predictors.

The *interview*, along with the application form, is an almost universal selection device. Few of us have ever gotten a job without undergoing one or more interviews. The irony of this is that the value of an interview as a selection device has been the subject of considerable debate.[11]

Interviews can be reliable and valid selection tools, but too often they're not. When interviews are structured and well organized, and when interviewers are held to

The job interview is an almost universal selection device. Air China used professional job interviewers for the process of selecting 300 new stewardesses. Formal, structured, and well organized, the interviews evaluated candidates on their proficiency in English and knowledge of the airline and the industry. In China, the behavioral interview is prevalent, with candidates being carefully observed on how they behave. Interviewers look for behaviors such as speaking with a calm voice, never speaking or acting in an aggressive manner, maintaining good posture, showing modesty and respect for seniority and rank, demonstrating good etiquette, never sitting down unless invited to, and never interrupting the interviewer.

---

reliability
The degree to which a selection device measures the same thing consistently.

validity
The proven relationship between a selection device and some relevant criterion.

performance-simulation tests
Selection devices based on actual job behaviors.

relevant questioning, interviews are effective predictors.[12] But those conditions don't characterize many interviews. The typical interview in which applicants are asked a varying set of essentially random questions in an informal setting often provides little in the way of valuable information.

All kinds of potential biases can creep into interviews if they're not well structured and standardized. To illustrate, a review of the research leads us to the following conclusions:

▶ Prior knowledge about the applicant will bias the interviewer's evaluation.
▶ The interviewer tends to hold a stereotype of what represents a good applicant.
▶ The interviewer tends to favor applicants who share his or her own attitudes.
▶ The order in which applicants are interviewed will influence evaluations.
▶ The order in which information is elicited during the interview will influence evaluations.
▶ Negative information is given unduly high weight.
▶ The interviewer may make a decision concerning the applicant's suitability within the first four or five minutes of the interview.
▶ The interviewer may forget much of the interview's content within minutes after its conclusion.
▶ The interview is most valid in determining an applicant's intelligence, level of motivation, and interpersonal skills.
▶ Structured and well-organized interviews are more reliable than unstructured and unorganized ones.[13]

What can managers do to make interviews more valid and reliable? A number of suggestions have been made over the years. We list some in the "Developing Your Interviewing Skill" box.

One last modification to interviews that's now popular is the behavioral or situation interview.[14] In this type of interview, applicants are observed not only for what they say, but also how they behave. Applicants are presented with situations—often complex problems involving role playing—and are asked to "deal" with the situation. This type of interview provides an opportunity for interviewers to see how a potential employee will behave and how he or she will react under stress. Proponents of behavioral interviewing indicate such a process is much more indicative of an applicant's performance than simply having the individual tell the interviewer what he or she has done. In fact, research in this area indicates that behavioral interviews are nearly eight times more effective for predicting successful job performance.[15]

HOW CAN YOU "CLOSE THE DEAL"? Interviewers who treat the recruiting and hiring of employees as if the applicants must be sold on the job and exposed only to an organization's positive characteristics are likely to have a workforce that is dissatisfied and prone to high turnover.[16]

During the hiring process, every job applicant acquires a set of expectations about the company and about the job for which he or she is interviewing. When the information an applicant receives is excessively inflated, a number of things happen that have potentially negative effects on the company. First, mismatched applicants are less likely to withdraw from the search process. Second, because inflated information builds unrealistic expectations, new employees are likely to become quickly dissatisfied and to resign prematurely. Third, new hires are prone to become disillusioned and less committed to the organization when they face the unexpected harsh realities of the job. In many cases, these individuals feel that they were misled during the hiring process and may become problem employees.

To increase job satisfaction among employees and reduce turnover, managers should consider a **realistic job preview (RJP)**.[17] An RJP includes both positive and negative information about the job and the company. For example, in addition to the positive comments typically expressed in the interview, the applicant is told of the less attractive aspects of the job. For instance, he or she might be told that there are limited opportunities to talk to coworkers during work hours, that chances of being promoted are slim, or that work

Developing Your *Interviewing* Skill

About the Skill

Every manager needs to develop his or her interviewing skills. The following discussion highlights the key behaviors associated with this skill.

Steps in Practicing the Skill

1 **Review the job description and job specification.** Reviewing pertinent information about the job provides valuable information about how to assess the candidate. Furthermore, relevant job requirements help to eliminate interview bias.

2 **Prepare a structured set of questions to ask all applicants for the job.** By having a set of prepared questions, you ensure that the information you wish to elicit is attainable. Furthermore, if you ask all applicants similar questions, you're better able to compare their answers against a common base.

3 **Before meeting an applicant, review his or her application form and résumé.** Doing so helps you to create a complete picture of the applicant in terms of what is represented on the résumé or application and what the job requires. You will also begin to identify areas to explore in the interview. That is, areas that are not clearly defined on the résumé or application but that are essential for the job will become a focal point of your discussion with the applicant.

4 **Open the interview by putting the applicant at ease and by providing a brief preview of the topics to be discussed.** Interviews are stressful for job applicants. By opening with small talk (e.g., the weather), you give the person time to adjust to the interview setting. By providing a preview of topics to come, you're giving the applicant an agenda that helps the individual begin framing what he or she will say in response to your questions.

5 **Ask your questions and listen carefully to the applicant's answers.** Select follow-up questions that naturally flow from the answers given. Focus on the responses as they relate to information you need to ensure that the applicant meets your job requirements. Any uncertainty you may still have requires a follow-up question to probe further for the information.

6 **Close the interview by telling the applicant what's going to happen next.** Applicants are anxious about the status of your hiring decision. Be honest with the applicant regarding others who will be interviewed and the remaining steps in the hiring process. If you plan to make a decision in two weeks or so, let the individual know what you intend to do. In addition, tell the applicant how you will let him or her know about your decision.

7 **Write your evaluation of the applicant while the interview is still fresh in your mind.** Don't wait until the end of your day, after interviewing several applicants, to write your analysis of each one. Memory can fail you. The sooner you complete your write-up after an interview, the better chance you have of accurately recording what occurred in the interview.

Practicing the Skill

Review and update your résumé. Then have several friends critique it who are employed in management-level positions or in management training programs. Ask them to explain their comments and make any changes to your résumé that they think will improve it. Now inventory your interpersonal and technical skills and any practical experiences that do not show up in your résumé. Draft a set of leading questions you would like to be asked in an interview that would give you a chance to discuss the unique qualities and attributes you could bring to the job.

hours fluctuate so erratically that employees may be required to work during what are usually off hours (nights and weekends). Research indicates that applicants who have been given a realistic job preview hold lower and more realistic job expectations for the jobs they will be performing and are better able to cope with the frustrating elements of the job than are applicants who have been given only inflated information. The result is fewer unexpected resignations by new employees. For managers, realistic job previews offer a major insight into the HRM process. That is, it's just as important to *retain* good

realistic job preview (RJP)
A preview of a job that provides both positive and negative information about the job and the company.

people as it is to *hire* them in the first place. Presenting only positive job aspects to an applicant may initially entice him or her to join the organization, but it may be a decision that both parties quickly regret.

Explain how employees are provided with needed skills and knowledge.

6.3

How Are Employees Provided with Needed Skills and Knowledge?

If we've done our recruiting and selecting properly, we should have hired competent individuals who can perform successfully on the job. But successful performance requires more than possessing certain skills. New hires must be acclimated to the organization's culture and be trained and given the knowledge to do the job in a manner consistent with the organization's goals. To achieve this, HRM uses orientation and training.

How Are New Hires Introduced to the Organization?

Once a job candidate has been selected, he or she needs to be introduced to the job and organization. This introduction is called **orientation**.[18] The major goals of orientation are to reduce the initial anxiety all new employees feel as they begin a new job; to familiarize new employees with the job, the work unit, and the organization as a whole; and to facilitate the outsider–insider transition. *Job orientation* expands on the information the employee obtained during the recruitment and selection stages. The new employee's specific duties and responsibilities are clarified as well as how his or her performance will be evaluated. Orientation is also the time to correct any unrealistic expectations new employees might hold about the job. *Work unit orientation* familiarizes an employee with the goals of the work unit, makes clear how his or her job contributes to the unit's goals, and provides an introduction to his or her coworkers. *Organization orientation* informs the new employee about the organization's goals, history, philosophy, procedures, and rules. This information includes relevant HR policies such as work hours, pay procedures, overtime requirements, and benefits. A tour of the organization's physical facilities is often part of this orientation.

Managers have an obligation to make the integration of a new employee into the organization as smooth and anxiety-free as possible. Successful orientation, whether formal or informal, results in an outsider–insider transition that makes the new member feel comfortable and fairly well-adjusted, lowers the likelihood of poor work performance, and reduces the probability of a surprise resignation by the new employee only a week or two into the job.[19]

TECHNOLOGY AND THE MANAGER'S JOB

HR AND IT

HR has gone digital.[20] Using software that automates many basic HR processes associated with recruiting, selecting, orienting, training, appraising performance, and storing and retrieving employee information, HR departments have cut costs and optimized service. The main area where IT has had a significant impact is in training.

In a survey by the American Society for Training and Development, 95 percent of the responding companies reported using some form of e-learning. Using technology to deliver needed knowledge, skills, and attitudes has had many benefits. As one researcher said, "The ultimate purpose of e-learning is not to reduce the cost of training, but to improve the way your organization does business." And in many instances, it seems to do that! For example, when Hewlett-Packard looked at how its customer service was affected by a blend of e-learning and other instructional methods, rather than just classroom training, it found that "sales representatives were able to answer questions more quickly and accurately, enhancing customer-service provider relations." And Unilever found that after e-learning training for sales employees, sales increased by several million dollars.

What Is Employee Training?

On the whole, planes don't cause airline accidents, people do. Most collisions, crashes, and other airline mishaps—nearly three-quarters of them—result from errors by the pilot or air traffic controller, or from inadequate maintenance. Weather and structural failures typically account for the remaining accidents.[21] We cite these statistics to illustrate the importance of training in the airline industry. Such maintenance and human errors could be prevented or significantly reduced by better employee training, as shown by the amazing "landing" of US Airways Flight 1549 in the Hudson River in January 2009 with no loss of life. Pilot Captain Chesley Sullenberger attributed the positive outcome to the extensive and intensive training that all pilots and flight crews undergo.[22]

Employee training is a learning experience that seeks a relatively permanent change in employees by improving their ability to perform on the job. Thus, training involves changing skills, knowledge, attitudes, or behavior.[23] This change may involve what employees know, how they work, or their attitudes toward their jobs, coworkers, managers, and the organization. It's been estimated, for instance, that U.S. business firms spend billions each a year on formal courses and training programs to develop workers' skills.[24] Managers, of course, are responsible for deciding when employees are in need of training and what form that training should take.

Determining training needs typically involves answering several questions. If some of these questions sound familiar, you've been paying close attention. It's precisely the type of analysis that takes place when managers develop an organizational structure to achieve their strategic goals—only now the focus is on the people.[25]

The leading questions in Exhibit 6-6 suggest the kinds of signals that can warn a manager when training may be necessary. The more obvious ones are related directly to productivity. Indications that job performance is declining include decreases in production numbers, lower quality, more accidents, and higher scrap or rejection rates. Any of these outcomes might suggest that worker skills need to be fine-tuned. Of course, we're assuming that an employee's performance decline is in no way related to lack of effort. Managers, too, must also recognize that training may be required because the workplace is constantly evolving. Changes imposed on employees as a result of job redesign or a technological breakthrough also require training.

Customer service training for new employees of Seven and I Holdings, Japan's largest retail group, includes teaching recruits how to assist blind, disabled, and elderly customers. Trainees also learn sign language so they can communicate with hearing-impaired shoppers. This training is a learning experience designed to permanently change employees' abilities to perform on the job. It involves changing their skills in learning proper techniques in helping customers and changing their attitudes in making them aware of and more sensitive to the special needs of shoppers who require assistance.

HOW ARE EMPLOYEES TRAINED? Most training takes place on the job. Why? It's simple and it usually costs less. However, on-the-job training can disrupt the workplace and result in an increase in errors while learning takes place. Also, some skill training is too complex to learn on the job and must take place outside the work setting.

Many different types of training methods are available. For the most part, we can classify them as on-the-job or off-the-job training. The more popular training methods are summarized in Exhibit 6-7.

HOW CAN MANAGERS ENSURE THAT TRAINING IS WORKING? It's easy to develop a new training program, but if training efforts aren't evaluated, any can be rationalized. It would be nice if all companies could boast the returns on investments in training that Neil Huffman Auto Group executives do; they claim they receive $230 in increased productivity for every dollar spent on training.[26] But such a claim cannot be made unless training is properly evaluated.

EXHIBIT 6-6 Determining Whether Training Is Needed

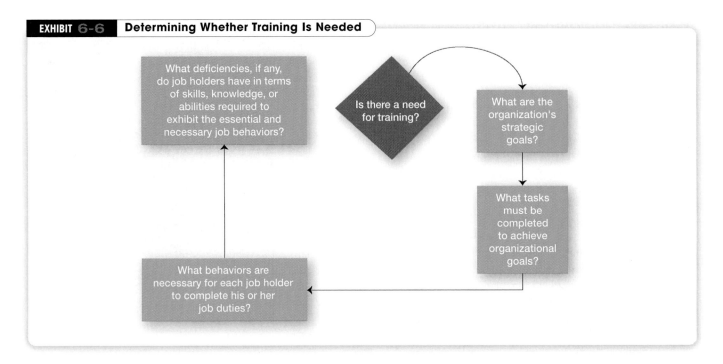

How are training programs typically evaluated? The following approach is probably generalizable across organizations: Several managers, representatives from HRM, and a group of workers who have recently completed a training program are asked for their opinions. If the comments are generally positive, the program may get a favorable evaluation and it's continued until someone decides, for whatever reason, that it should be eliminated or replaced.

Such reactions from participants or managers, while easy to acquire, are the least valid. Their opinions are heavily influenced by factors that may have little to do with the training's effectiveness—difficulty, entertainment value, or the personality characteristics of the instructor. However, trainees' reactions to the training may, in fact, provide

EXHIBIT 6-7 Typical Training Methods

SAMPLE ON-THE-JOB TRAINING METHODS	
Job rotation	Lateral transfers allowing employees to work at different jobs. Provides good exposure to a variety of tasks.
Understudy assignments	Working with a seasoned veteran, coach, or mentor. Provides support and encouragement from an experienced worker. In the trades industry, this may also be an apprenticeship.

SAMPLE OFF-THE-JOB TRAINING METHODS	
Classroom lectures	Lectures designed to convey specific technical, interpersonal, or problem-solving skills.
Films and videos	Using media to explicitly demonstrate technical skills that are not easily presented by other training methods.
Simulation exercises	Learning a job by actually performing the work (or its simulation). May include case analyses, experiential exercises, role-playing, and group interaction.
Vestibule training	Learning tasks on the same equipment that one actually will use on the job but in a simulated work environment.

feedback on how worthwhile the participants viewed the training to be. Beyond general reactions, however, training must also be evaluated in terms of how much the participants learned; how well they are using their new skills on the job (did their behavior change?); and whether the training program achieved its desired results (reduced turnover, increased customer service, etc.).[27]

How Do Organizations Retain Competent, High-Performing Employees?

Describe strategies for retaining competent, high-performing employees.

6.4

Once an organization has invested significant dollars in recruiting, selecting, orienting, and training employees, it wants to keep them, especially the competent, high-performing ones! Two HRM activities that play a role in this are managing employee performance and developing an appropriate compensation and benefits program.

What Is a Performance Management System?

It's important for managers to get their employees to achieve performance levels that the organization considers desirable. How do managers ensure that employees are performing as well as they're supposed to? In organizations, the formal means of assessing the work of employees is through a systematic performance appraisal process.

A **performance management system** is a process of establishing performance standards and evaluating performance in order to arrive at objective human resource decisions—such as pay increases and training needs—as well as to provide documentation to support any personnel actions. But how do you evaluate an employee's performance? We list specific appraisal techniques in Exhibit 6-8.

The *written essay* requires no complex forms or extensive training to complete. However, a "good" or "bad" appraisal may be determined as much by the evaluator's writing skill as

---

EXHIBIT 6-8 | **Performance Appraisal Methods**

METHOD	ADVANTAGE	DISADVANTAGE
Written essay	Simple to use	More a measure of evaluator's writing ability than of employee's actual performance
Critical incidents	Rich examples; behaviorally based	Time-consuming; lack quantification
Graphic rating scales	Provide quantitative data; less time-consuming than others	Do not provide depth of job behavior assessed
BARS	Focus on specific and measurable job behaviors	Time-consuming; difficult to develop measures
Multiperson	Compares employees with one another	Unwieldy with large number of employees
MBO	Focuses on end goals; results oriented	Time-consuming
360° appraisal	More thorough	Time-consuming

---

performance management system
A system that establishes performance standards that are used to evaluate employee performance.

by the employee's actual level of performance. The use of *critical incidents* focuses the evaluator's attention on critical or key behaviors. The appraiser writes down anecdotes describing whatever the employee did that was especially effective or ineffective. The key here is that specific behaviors are cited, not vaguely defined personality traits. One of the oldest and most popular methods of appraisal is by *graphic rating scales*. This method lists a set of performance factors such as quantity and quality of work, job knowledge, cooperation, loyalty, attendance, honesty, and initiative. The evaluator then goes down the list and rates each factor on an incremental scale. An approach that has received renewed attention involves *behaviorally anchored rating scales (BARS)*.[28] These scales combine major elements from the critical incident and graphic rating scale approaches. The appraiser rates an employee according to items along a numerical scale, but the items are examples of actual behavior on a given job rather than general descriptions or traits.[29]

Finally, an appraisal device that seeks performance feedback from such sources as the person being rated, bosses, peers, team members, customers, and suppliers has become popular in organizations. It's called the **360-degree appraisal**.[30] It's being used in approximately 90 percent of *Fortune* 1000 firms, including such companies as Otis Elevator, DuPont, Nabisco, Pfizer, ExxonMobil, Cook Children's Health Care System, General Electric, UPS, and Nokia.[31]

In today's dynamic organizations, traditional performance evaluation systems may be archaic.[32] Downsizing has given supervisors greater responsibility and more employees who report directly to them. Accordingly, it may be next to impossible for supervisors to have extensive job knowledge of each of their employees. Furthermore, the growth of project teams and employee involvement places the responsibility for evaluation where people are better able to make accurate assessments.[33]

The 360-degree feedback process also has some positive benefits for development concerns.[34] Many managers simply do not know how their employees view them and the work they have done. Research studies into the effectiveness of 360-degree performance appraisals report positive results including more accurate feedback, empowering employees, reducing the subjective factors in the evaluation process, and developing leadership in an organization.[35]

SHOULD PEOPLE BE COMPARED TO ONE ANOTHER OR AGAINST A SET OF STANDARDS?
The methods previously identified have one thing in common. They require us to evaluate employees on the basis of how well their performance matches established or absolute criteria. Multiperson comparisons, on the other hand, compare one person's performance with that of one or more individuals. These are relative, not absolute, measuring devices.

The three most popular forms of this method are group-order ranking, individual ranking, and paired comparison.

The *group-order ranking* requires the evaluator to place employees into a particular classification such as "top fifth" or "second fifth." If a rater has 20 employees, only four can be in the top fifth, and, of course, four must be relegated to the bottom fifth. The *individual ranking* approach requires the evaluator to list the employees in order from highest to lowest. Only one can be "best." In an appraisal of 30 employees, the difference between the first and second employee is assumed to be the same as that between the twenty-first and twenty-second. Even though some employees may be closely grouped, no ties are allowed. In the *paired comparison* approach, each employee is compared with every other employee in the comparison group and rated as either the superior or weaker member of the pair. After all paired comparisons are made, each employee is assigned a summary ranking based on the number of superior scores he or she achieved. Although this approach ensures that each employee is compared against every other employee, it can become unwieldy when large numbers of employees are being assessed.

WHAT ABOUT MBO AS AN APPRAISAL APPROACH? We introduced management by objectives during our discussion of planning in Chapter 4. However, MBO is also a mechanism for appraising performance.

At one time renowned for its excellent customer service, Home Depot had fallen in customer satisfaction surveys to one of the worst performing firms in the retail industry. In repairing its damaged reputation, Home Depot listed customer service as its number one strategic priority. One way that Home Depot is implementing the customer focus is by replacing its traditional performance evaluation system with a system that evaluates store employees almost entirely on how well they treat customers and satisfy their needs.

Employees are evaluated by how well they accomplish a specific set of objectives that are critical to the successful completion of their jobs. As you'll recall from our discussion in Chapter 4, these objectives need to be tangible, verifiable, and measurable. MBO's popularity among managerial personnel is probably due to its focus on end goals. Managers tend to emphasize such results-oriented outcomes as profit, sales, and costs. This emphasis meshes with MBO's concern with quantitative measures of performance. Because MBO emphasizes ends rather than means, this appraisal method allows managers to choose the best path for achieving their goals.

What Happens If an Employee's Performance Is Not Up to Par?

So far this discussion has focused on the performance management system. But what if an employee is not performing in a satisfactory manner? What can you do?

If, for some reason, an employee is not meeting his or her performance goals, a manager needs to find out why. If it's because the employee is mismatched for the job (a hiring error) or because he or she does not have adequate training, the fix is relatively simple. The manager can either reassign the individual to a job that better matches his or her skills or train the employee to do the job more effectively. If the problem is associated with an employee's lack of desire to do the job, not with his or her abilities, it becomes a **discipline** problem. In that case, a manager can try counseling and, if necessary, take disciplinary action such as verbal and written warnings, suspensions, and even terminations.

Employee counseling is a process designed to help employees overcome performance-related problems. Rather than viewing the performance problem from a punitive standpoint (discipline), employee counseling attempts to uncover why employees have lost their desire or ability to work productively. More importantly, it's designed to find ways to fix the problem. In many cases, employees don't go from being productive one day to being unproductive the next. Rather, the change happens gradually and may be a function of what's occurring in their personal lives. Employee counseling attempts to assist employees in getting help to resolve whatever is bothering them. The premise behind employee counseling is fairly simple: It's beneficial to both the organization and the employee. Just as it's costly to have an employee quit shortly after being hired, it's costly to fire someone. The time spent recruiting and selecting, orienting, training, and developing employees translates into money. If, however, an organization can help employees overcome personal problems and get them back on the job quickly, it can avoid these costs. But make no mistake about it, employee counseling is not intended to lessen the effect of an employee's poor performance, nor is it intended to reduce his or her responsibility to change inappropriate work behavior. If the employee can't or won't accept help, then disciplinary actions must be taken.

How Are Employees Compensated?

Executives at Discovery Communications Inc. had an employee morale problem on their hands. Many of the company's top performers were making the same salaries as the poorer performers, and the company's compensation program didn't allow for giving raises to people who stayed in the same position. The only way for managers to reward the top performers was to give them a bonus or promote them to another position. Executives were discovering that not only was that unfair, it was counterproductive. So they overhauled the program.[37]

and the survey says...[36]

39 percent of employees look for a positive attitude when hiring seasonal employees.

75 percent of layoff survivors say that their individual productivity has declined.

50 percent of managers recognize the value of hiring people different from themselves and do what they can to meet this goal.

26 percent of interviewers say that the best way to "blow" your interview is by not learning about the job or organization.

94 percent of participants in classroom training said that e-learning was convenient; 90 percent viewed it as a time-saver.

34 percent of U.S. employees say they've heard a sexually inappropriate comment at work.

52.4 percent of HR executives say their companies have frozen or cut salaries to save money instead of firing employees.

360-degree appraisal
An appraisal device that seeks feedback from a variety of sources for the person being rated.

discipline
Actions taken by a manager to enforce an organization's standards and regulations.

employee counseling
A process designed to help employees overcome performance-related problems.

Although there are exceptions, most of us work for money. What our jobs pay and what benefits we get fall under the heading of compensation and benefits. Determining levels of compensation isn't easy. However, most of us expect to receive appropriate compensation from our employer. Developing an effective and appropriate compensation system is an important part of the HRM process.[38] It can help attract and retain competent and talented individuals who help an organization accomplish its mission and goals. In addition, an organization's compensation system has been shown to have an impact on its strategic performance.[39] Managers must develop a compensation system that reflects the changing nature of work and the workplace in order to keep people motivated.

HOW ARE PAY LEVELS DETERMINED? How does management decide who gets paid $15.85 an hour and who receives $325,000 a year? The answer lies in **compensation administration**. The goals of compensation administration are to design a cost-effective pay structure that will attract and retain competent employees and to provide an incentive for these individuals to exert high energy levels at work. Compensation administration also attempts to ensure that pay levels, once determined, will be perceived as fair by all employees. Fairness means that the established pay levels are adequate and consistent for the demands and requirements of the job. Therefore, the primary determination of pay is the kind of job an employee performs. Different jobs require different kinds and levels of skills, knowledge, and abilities, and these factors vary in their value to the organization. So, too, do the responsibility and authority of various positions. In short, the higher the skills, knowledge, and abilities—and the greater the authority and responsibility—the higher the pay.

So, how do managers determine who gets paid what? Several factors influence the compensation and benefit packages that different employees receive. Exhibit 6-9 summarizes these factors, which are job-based and business- or industry-based. One factor that's critical is the organization's philosophy toward compensation. Some organizations, for instance,

EXHIBIT 6-9 **What Determines Pay and Benefits?**

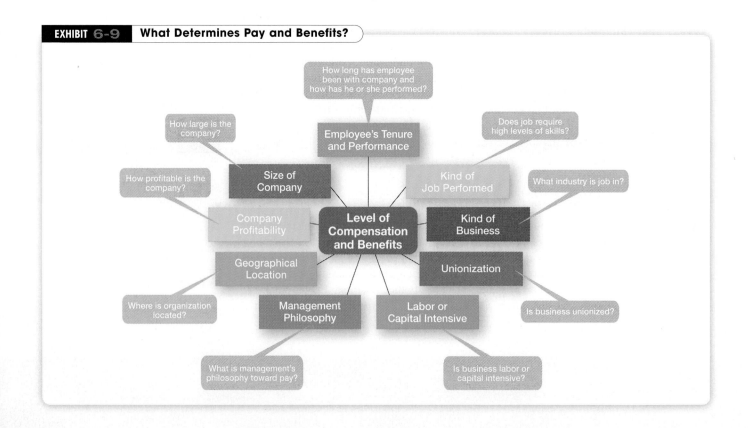

don't pay employees any more than they have to. In the absence of a union contract that stipulates wage levels, those organizations only have to pay minimum wage for most of their jobs. On the other hand, some organizations are committed to a compensation philosophy of paying their employees at or above area wage levels in order to emphasize that they want to attract and keep the best pool of talent.

Many organizations are using alternative approaches to determine compensation including skill-based pay and variable pay. **Skill-based pay** systems reward employees for the job skills and competencies they can demonstrate. Under this type of pay system, an employee's job title doesn't define his or her pay category, skills do.[40] Research shows that these types of pay systems tend to be more successful in manufacturing organizations than in service organizations and in organizations pursuing technical innovations.[41] On the other hand, many organizations use **variable pay** systems, in which an individual's compensation is contingent on performance—90 percent of U.S. organizations use variable pay plans, and 81 percent of Canadian and Taiwanese organizations do.[42]

WHY DO ORGANIZATIONS OFFER EMPLOYEE BENEFITS? When an organization designs its overall compensation package, it has to look further than just an hourly wage or annual salary. It has to take into account another element, **employee benefits**, which are nonfinancial rewards designed to enrich employees' lives. They have grown in importance and variety over the past several decades. Once viewed as "fringes," today's benefit packages reflect efforts to provide something that each employee values.

The benefits offered by an organization vary widely in scope. Most organizations are legally required to provide Social Security and workers' and unemployment compensation, but organizations may also provide an array of benefits such as paid time off from work, life and disability insurance, retirement programs, and health insurance.[43] The costs of some of these, such as retirement and health insurance benefits, may be paid by both the employer and the employee, although as you'll see in the next section, organizations are cutting back or putting stipulations on these two costly benefits.

What Contemporary HRM Issues Face Managers?

We'll conclude this chapter by looking at several HR issues facing today's managers including downsizing, workforce diversity, sexual harassment, workplace spirituality, and HR costs.

Discuss contemporary issues in managing human resources.

6.5

How Can Managers Manage Downsizing?

Downsizing is the planned elimination of jobs in an organization. Because downsizing typically involves shrinking the organization's workforce, it's an important issue in HRM. (Take another look at the chapter-opening story.) When an organization has too many employees—which may happen when it's faced with an economic crisis, declining market share, too aggressive growth, or when it's been poorly managed—one option for improving profits is to eliminate some of those excess workers. Over the last 18 months, many well-known companies have gone through several rounds of downsizing—Boeing, Volkswagen,

Right or Wrong?

A report released by The Corporate Library says that many CEOs who voluntarily didn't take their salary for a year or only took a $1 in pay were actually well compensated.[45] Such action by a CEO is usually intended to convey concern and commitment, but in many cases, it may have been largely a symbolic action. In 41 companies where the CEO had either no base salary or a salary of $1 for the year and no cash bonus, 21 received some form of "all other compensation." In 18 instances of these "dollar CEOs," the individuals received a combined $6 billion in company stock alone. What do you think of this? What do such actions convey to employees? To stockholders? To the general public?

Microsoft, Dell, General Motors, Unisys, Siemens, Merck, Toyota, among others. How can managers best manage a downsized workplace?

After downsizing, disruptions in the workplace and in employees' personal lives are to be expected. Stress, frustration, anxiety, and anger are typical reactions of both individuals being laid off and the job survivors. And it may surprise you to learn that both victims and survivors experience those feelings.[44] Many organizations have done a fairly good job of helping layoff victims by offering a variety of job-help services, psychological counseling, support groups, severance pay, extended health insurance benefits, and detailed communications. Although some individuals react negatively to being laid off (the worst cases involve individuals returning to their former organization and committing a violent act), the assistance offered reveals that the organization does care about its former employees. The layoff victims get to start over with a clean slate and a clear conscience. Survivors don't. Unfortunately, too often, little is done for the "survivors" who retain their jobs and have the task of keeping the organization going or even of revitalizing it.

A new syndrome seems to be popping up in organizations: **layoff-survivor sickness**, a set of attitudes, perceptions, and behaviors of employees who survive involuntary staff reductions.[46] Symptoms include job insecurity, perceptions of unfairness, guilt, depression, stress from increased workload, fear of change, loss of loyalty and commitment, reduced effort, and an unwillingness to do anything beyond the required minimum.

To address survivor syndrome, managers may want to provide opportunities for employees to talk to counselors about their guilt, anger, and anxiety.[47] Group discussions can also provide an opportunity for the survivors to vent their feelings. Some organizations have used downsizing as the spark to implement increased employee participation programs such as empowerment and self-managed work teams. In short, to keep morale and productivity high, managers should make every attempt to ensure that those individuals still working in the organization know that they're valuable and much-needed resources. Exhibit 6-10 summarizes some ways that managers can reduce the trauma associated with downsizing.[48]

How Can Workforce Diversity Be Managed?

We're discussing the changing makeup of the workforce in several places in this book, mostly through our "Managing Diversity" boxes. But workforce diversity also affects such basic HRM concepts as recruitment, selection, and orientation.[49]

EXHIBIT 6-10	**Tips for Managing Downsizing**

- Communicate openly and honestly:
  - ▶ Inform those being let go as soon as possible
  - ▶ Tell surviving employees the new goals and expectations
  - ▶ Explain impact of layoffs
- Follow any laws regulating severance pay or benefits
- Provide support/counseling for surviving employees
- Reassign roles according to individuals' talents and backgrounds
- Focus on boosting morale:
  - ▶ Offer individualized reassurance
  - ▶ Continue to communicate, especially one-on-one
  - ▶ Remain involved and available

Improving workforce diversity requires managers to widen their recruiting net. For example, the popular practice of relying on current employee referrals as a source of new job applicants tends to produce candidates who have similar characteristics to those of present employees. So managers have to look for applicants in places where they haven't typically looked before. To increase diversity, managers are increasingly turning to nontraditional recruitment sources such as women's job networks, over-50 clubs, urban job banks, disabled people's training centers, ethnic newspapers, and gay rights organizations. This type of outreach should enable an organization to broaden its pool of applicants.

Once a diverse set of applicants exists, efforts must be made to ensure that the selection process does not discriminate. Moreover, applicants need to be made comfortable with the organization's culture and be made aware of management's desire to accommodate their needs. For instance, at TGI Friday's, company managers work diligently to accommodate differences and create workplace choices for a diverse workforce; so, too, do companies such as Johnson & Johnson, Ernst & Young, Marriott International, IBM, and Bank of America.[50]

Finally, orientation is often difficult for women and minorities. Many organizations, such as Lotus and Hewlett-Packard, provide special workshops to raise diversity consciousness among current employees as well as programs for new employees that focus on diversity issues. The thrust of these efforts is to increase individual understanding of the differences each of us brings to the workplace. A number of companies also have special mentoring programs to deal with the reality that lower-level female and minority managers have few role models with whom to identify.[51]

What Is Sexual Harassment?

Sexual harassment is a serious issue in both public and private sector organizations. More than 12,000 complaints are filed with the EEOC each year,[52] with more than 15 percent of the complaints filed by males.[53] Settlements in some of these cases incurred a substantial cost to the companies in terms of litigation. It's estimated that sexual harassment is the single largest financial risk facing companies today—and can result in upward of a 30 percent decrease in a company's stock price.[54] At Mitsubishi, for example, the company paid out more than $34 million to 300 women for the rampant sexual harassment to which they were exposed.[55] But it's more than just jury awards. Sexual harassment results in millions lost in absenteeism, low productivity, and turnover.[56] Sexual harassment, furthermore, is not just a U.S. phenomenon. It's a global issue. For instance, sexual harassment charges have been filed against employers in such countries as Japan, Australia, Netherlands, Belgium, New Zealand, Sweden, Ireland, and Mexico.[57] Even though discussions of sexual harassment cases often focus on the large awards granted by a court, employers face other concerns. Sexual harassment creates an unpleasant work environment for organization members and undermines their ability to perform their jobs. But just what is sexual harassment?

Any unwanted activity of a sexual nature that affects an individual's employment can be regarded as **sexual harassment**. It can occur between members of the opposite or of the same sex—between employees of the organization or between employee and nonemployee.[58] Although such an activity has been generally protected under Title VII (sex discrimination) in the United States, in recent years this problem has gained more recognition. By most accounts, prior to the mid-1980s, occurrences were generally viewed as isolated incidents, with the individual committing the act being solely responsible (if at all) for his or her actions.[59] Since the beginning of the twenty-first century, however, charges of sexual harassment have continued to appear in the headlines on an almost regular basis.

layoff-survivor sickness
A set of attitudes, perceptions, and behaviors of employees who survive layoffs.

sexual harassment
Any unwanted action or activity of a sexual nature that explicitly or implicitly affects an individual's employment, performance, or work environment.

Much of the problem associated with sexual harassment is determining what constitutes this illegal behavior.[60] In 1993, the EEOC cited three situations in which sexual harassment can occur. In these instances, verbal or physical conduct toward an individual:

1. Creates an intimidating, offensive, or hostile environment.
2. Unreasonably interferes with an individual's work.
3. Adversely affects an employee's employment opportunities.

For many organizations, it's the offensive or hostile environment issue that's problematic.[61] What constitutes such an environment? Challenging hostile environment situations gained much support from the Supreme Court case of *Meritor Savings Bank v. Vinson*.[62] This case stemmed from a situation in which Ms. Vinson initially refused the sexual advances of her boss. However, out of fear of reprisal, she ultimately conceded. But according to court records, it didn't stop there. Vinson's boss continued to harass Vinson, subjecting her to severe hostility that affected her job.[63] In addition to supporting hostile environment claims, the *Meritor* case also identified employer liability; that is, in sexual harassment cases, an organization can be held liable for sexual harassment actions by its managers, employees, and even customers![64]

Although the *Meritor* case has implications for organizations, how do organizational members determine whether something is offensive? For instance, does sexually explicit language in the office create a hostile environment? How about off-color jokes? Pictures of women totally undressed? The answer is it could! It depends on the people in the organization and the environment in which they work. The point here is that we all must be attuned to what makes fellow employees uncomfortable—and if we don't know, then we should ask! Organizational success will, in part, reflect how sensitive each employee is toward another in the company. At DuPont, for example, the corporate culture and diversity programs are designed to eliminate sexual harassment through awareness and respect for all individuals.[65] It means understanding one another and, most importantly, respecting others' rights. Similar programs exist at FedEx, General Mills, and Levi-Strauss, among other companies.

If sexual harassment carries with it potential costs to the organization, what can a company do to protect itself?[66] The courts want to know two things—did the organization know about, or should it have known about, the alleged behavior? And what did managers do to stop it?[67] With the number and dollar amounts of the awards today, it's even more important for organizations and managers to educate all employees on sexual harassment matters and to have mechanisms available to monitor employees. Furthermore, "victims" no longer have to prove that their psychological well-being is seriously affected. The U.S. Supreme Court ruled in 1993, in the case of *Harris v. Forklift Systems, Inc.*, that victims do not have to suffer substantial mental distress to receive a jury award. Furthermore, in June 1998, the Supreme Court ruled that sexual harassment may have occurred even if the employee had not experienced any "negative" job repercussions. In this case, Kimberly Ellerth, a marketing assistant at Burlington Industries, filed harassment charges against her boss because he "touched her, suggested she wear shorter skirts, and told her during a business trip that he could make her job 'very hard or very easy.'" When Ellerth refused, the harasser never "punished" her; in fact, she even received a promotion during the time the harassment was ongoing. What the Supreme Court's decision in this case indicates is that "harassment is defined by the ugly behavior of the manager, not by what happened to the worker subsequently."[68]

Finally, in a sexual harassment matter, managers must remember that the harasser may have rights, too.[69] No action should be taken against someone until a thorough investigation has been conducted. Furthermore, the results of the investigation should be reviewed by an independent and objective individual before any action against the alleged harasser is taken. Even then, the harasser should be given an opportunity to respond to the allegation and have

Orientation training for cadets of the United States Air Force Academy emphasizes the academy's zero-tolerance policy for assault and harassment misconduct. Recognizing that the academy fostered a culture and climate that tolerated sexual assault and harassment, an Air Force team was formed to identify weak points that needed correction and to recommend ways to improve the environment. Changes made based on the recommendations include the establishment of clear sexual-assault and harassment reporting procedures and formation of a new academy response team to review alleged offenses.

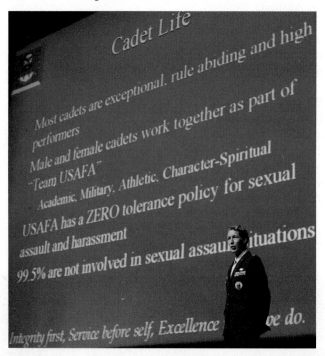

Cadet Life

Most cadets are exceptional, rule abiding and high performers

Male and female cadets work together as part of "Team USAFA"

Academic, Military, Athletic, Character-Spiritual

USAFA has a ZERO tolerance policy for sexual assault and harassment

99.5% are not involved in sexual assault situations

Integrity first, Service before self, Excellence ... we do.

a disciplinary hearing if desired. Additionally, an avenue for appeal should also exist for the alleged harasser—an appeal heard by someone at a higher level of management who is not associated with the case.

What Is Workplace Spirituality?

What do organizations such as Southwest Airlines, Tom's of Maine, Herman Miller, or Hewlett-Packard have in common? Among other characteristics, they're among a growing number of organizations that have embraced workplace spirituality.

Workplace spirituality is not about organized religious practices.[70] It's not about theology or about one's spiritual leader. Rather, **workplace spirituality** is about recognizing that employees have an inner life that nourishes and is nourished by meaningful work that takes place in the context of an organizational community.[71] Organizations that promote a spiritual culture recognize that employees have both a mind and a spirit, seek to find meaning and purpose in their work, and desire to connect with other employees and be part of a community.

WHY THE EMPHASIS ON SPIRITUALITY IN TODAY'S ORGANIZATIONS? Historical management models had no room for spirituality.[72] These models typically focused on organizations that were efficiently run without feelings toward others. Similarly, concern about an employee's inner life had no role in managing organizations. But just as we've come to realize that the study of emotions improves our understanding of how and why people act the way they do in organizations, an awareness of spirituality can help one better understand employee work behavior in the twenty-first-century organization.

WHAT DOES A SPIRITUAL ORGANIZATION LOOK LIKE? The concept of spirituality draws on the ethics, values, motivation, work/life balance, and leadership elements of an organization. Spiritual organizations are concerned with helping employees develop and reach their full potential. They're also concerned with addressing problems created by work/life conflicts.

What differentiates spiritual organizations from their nonspiritual counterparts? Although research is fairly new in this arena, several characteristics tend to be associated with a spiritual organization.[73] We list them in Exhibit 6-11.

EXHIBIT 6-11	Characteristics of a Spiritual Organization

CHARACTERISTIC	DESCRIPTION
Strong sense of purpose	Organizational members know why the organization exists and what it values.
Focus on individual development	Employees are valuable and need to be nurtured to help them grow; this characteristic also includes a sense of job security.
Trust and openness	Organizational member relationships are characterized by mutual trust, honesty, and openness.
Employee empowerment	Employees are allowed to make work-related decisions that affect them, highlighting a strong sense of delegation of authority.
Toleration of employee expression	The organizational culture encourages employees to be themselves and to express their moods and feelings without guilt or fear of reprimand.

workplace spirituality
A spiritual culture where organizational values promote a sense of purpose through meaningful work that takes place in the context of community.

Although workplace spirituality has generated some interest in many organizations, it's not without its critics. Those who argue against spirituality in organizations typically focus on two issues. First is the question of legitimacy. Specifically, do organizations have the right to impose spiritual values on their employees? Second is the question of economics. Are spirituality and profits compatible? Let's briefly look at these issues.

The potential for an emphasis on spirituality to make some employees uneasy is clear. Critics argue that organizations have no business imposing spiritual values on employees. This criticism is undoubtedly valid when spirituality is defined as bringing religion and God into the workplace.[74] However, the criticism appears less stinging when the goal is limited to helping employees find meaning in their work lives.

The issue of whether spirituality and profits are compatible goals is certainly relevant for anyone in business. The evidence, although limited, indicates that the two may be compatible. Several studies show that organizations that have introduced spirituality into the workplace have witnessed improved productivity, reduced turnover, greater employee satisfaction, and increased organizational commitment.[75]

WHAT DOES HRM HAVE TO DO WITH SPIRITUALITY? Ironically, introducing spirituality into the organization is nothing new for HR. In actuality, many of the areas that HRM addresses, and has done so for many years, are many of the same things that support spirituality.[76] For instance, matters such as work/life balances, proper selection of employees, setting performance goals, and rewarding people for the work they do, are all components of making the organization more "spiritual." In fact, as you review the characteristics of a spiritual organization, in every case, HRM is either the leader in making such things happen, or is the vehicle by which the organization helps employees understand their responsibilities and offers the requisite training to make things happen. In the end, it's HRM that will make the workplace a supportive work environment, one where communication abounds and employees feel free to express themselves.

How and Why Are Organizations Controlling HR Costs?

HR costs are skyrocketing, especially those associated with employee health care and employee pensions. Organizations are looking for ways to control these costs.

WHAT ABOUT EMPLOYEE HEALTH CARE COSTS? Employees at Aetna can earn financial incentives up to $345 a year for participating in weight-management and fitness classes. Some 80 percent of employees at Fairview Health Services in Minneapolis participate in a comprehensive health-management program. Employees of King County in Seattle get health insurance discounts if they do not smoke, are not overweight, and do not speed when driving. At Alaska Airlines, employees must abide by a no-smoking policy, and new hires must submit to a urine test to prove they're tobacco-free.[77] All these examples illustrate how companies are trying to control skyrocketing employee health care costs. Since 2002, health care costs have risen an average of 15 percent a year and are expected to double by the year 2016 from the $2.2 trillion spent in 2007.[78] And smokers cost companies even more—about 25 percent more for health care than nonsmokers do.[79] However, the biggest health care cost for companies is obesity—an estimated $45 billion a year in medical expenditures and absenteeism.[80] A study of manufacturing organizations found that presenteeism, which is defined as employees not performing at full capacity, was 1.8 percent higher for workers with moderate to severe obesity than for all other employees.[81] The reason for the lost productivity is likely the result of reduced mobility because of body size or pain problems such as arthritis. Is it any wonder that organizations are looking for ways to control their health care costs? How? First, many organizations are providing opportunities for employees to lead healthy lifestyles. From financial incentives to company-sponsored health and wellness programs, the goal is to limit rising health care costs. About 41 percent of companies use some type of positive incentives aimed at encouraging healthy behavior, up from 34 percent in 1996.[82] Another recent study indicated that nearly 90 percent of companies surveyed planned to aggressively promote healthy lifestyles to their employees during the next three to five years.[83] Many are starting sooner: Google, Yamaha Corporation of America, Caterpillar, and others are putting health food in company break rooms, cafeterias, and vending machines; providing deliveries of fresh organic fruit; and putting "calorie taxes" on fatty foods.[84] In the case of smokers, however, some companies have taken a more aggressive stance by increasing the amount smokers pay for health insurance or by firing them if they refuse to stop smoking.

WHAT ABOUT EMPLOYEE PENSION PLAN COSTS? The other area where organizations are looking to control costs is employee pension plans. Corporate pensions have been around since the nineteenth century.[85] But the days when companies could afford to give employees a broad-based pension that provided them a guaranteed retirement income have changed. Pension commitments have become such an enormous burden that companies can no longer afford them. In fact, the corporate pension system has been described as "fundamentally broken."[86] It's not just struggling companies that have eliminated employee pension plans. Lots of reasonably sound companies—for instance, NCR, FedEx, Lockheed Martin, and Motorola—no longer provide pensions. Even IBM, which closed its pension plan to new hires in December 2004, told employees that their pension benefits would be frozen.[87] Obviously, the pension issue is one that directly affects HR decisions. On the one hand, organizations want to attract talented, capable employees by offering them desirable benefits such as pensions. But on the other hand, organizations have to balance that with the costs of providing such benefits.

Review and ⑥ Applications

Chapter Summary

6.1 **Describe the key components of the human resource management process and the important influences on that process.** The HRM process consists of eight activities that will staff an organization with competent, high-performing employees who are capable of sustaining their performance level over the long term. The first three HR activities involve employment planning and include recruitment, downsizing, and selection. The next two steps involve helping employees adapt to the organization and ensuring that their skills and knowledge are kept current, and include the HR activities of orienting and training. The last steps involve identifying performance goals, correcting performance problems, and helping employees sustain high levels of performance. These are done using the HR activities of performance appraisal, compensation and benefits, and safety and health. The main influences on the HRM process are legal although other environmental conditions such as restructuring, downsizing, diversity, and so forth can impact it as well.

6.2 **Discuss the tasks associated with identifying and selecting competent employees.** The first task is employment planning, which involves job analysis and

the creation of job descriptions and job specifications. Then, if job needs are indicated, recruitment involves attempts to develop a pool of potential job candidates. Downsizing is used to reduce the labor supply. Selection involves determining who is best qualified for the job. Selection devices need to be both reliable and valid. Managers may want to give potential employees a realistic job preview.

6.3 **Explain how employees are provided with needed skills and knowledge.** New hires must be acclimated to the organization's culture and be trained and given the knowledge to do the job in a manner consistent with the organization's goals. Orientation—job, work unit, and organizational—provides new employees with information to introduce them to the job. Training is used to help employees improve their ability to perform on the job.

6.4 **Describe strategies for retaining competent, high-performing employees.** Two HRM activities that play a role in this are managing employee performance and developing an appropriate compensation and benefits program. Managing employee performance involves establishing performance standards and then appraising performance to see if those standards have been met. There are various performance appraisal techniques managers can use. If an employee's performance is not up to par, managers need to assess why and take action. Compensation and benefits programs can help attract and retain competent and talented individuals. Managers have to determine who gets paid what and what benefits will be offered.

6.5 **Discuss contemporary issues in managing human resources.** Downsizing is the planned elimination of jobs and must be managed from the perspective of

layoff victims and job survivors. Workforce diversity must be managed through HRM activities including recruitment, selection, and orientation. Sexual harassment is a significant concern of organizations and managers, which mean programs and mechanisms must be in place to educate all employees about it. Workplace spirituality involves attempts by organizations to make work more meaningful to employees. Finally, organizations are looking for ways to control HR costs, especially health care costs and pension costs.

 **PEARSON mymanagementlab** To check your understanding of learning outcomes **6.1** – **6.5**, go to **mymanagementlab.com** and try the chapter questions.

Understanding the Chapter

1. How does HRM affect all managers?

2. Should an employer have the right to choose employees without governmental interference? Support your position.

3. Some critics claim that corporate HR departments have outlived their usefulness and are not there to help employees but to shield the organization from legal problems. What do you think? What benefits are there to having a formal HRM process? What drawbacks?

4. Do you think it's ethical for a prospective employer to delve into an applicant's life by means of interviews, tests, and background investigations? What if those investigations involved looking at your Facebook page or personal blogs? Explain your position.

5. Discuss the advantages and drawbacks of the various recruiting sources.

6. Discuss the advantages and drawbacks of the various selection devices.

7. What are the benefits and drawbacks of realistic job previews? (Consider this question from both the perspective of the organization *and* the perspective of a potential employee.)

8. What, in your view, constitutes sexual harassment? Describe how companies can minimize sexual harassment in the workplace.

9. Research your chosen career by finding out what it's going to take to be successful in this career in terms of education, skills, experience, and so forth. Write a personal career guide that details this information.

Understanding Yourself

How Much Do I Know About HRM?

This scale measures how much you know about human resource management. Although it assesses your knowledge of some key findings within the HRM field, there are many other important things to know.

INSTRUMENT   Below are a number of statements about research findings in human resource management. For each statement, indicate whether you think it is true or false.

> **0** = False
> **1** = True

1.	Most managers give employees lower performance appraisals than they objectively deserve.	**0** **1**
2.	Poor performers are generally more realistic about their performance than good performers are.	**0** **1**
3.	Despite the popularity of drug testing, there is no clear evidence that applicants who score positive on drug tests are any less reliable or less productive employees.	**0** **1**
4.	Most people over-evaluate how well they perform on the job.	**0** **1**
5.	The most important determinant of how much training employees actually use on their jobs is how much they learned during training.	**0** **1**
6.	The most valid employment interviews are designed around each candidate's unique background.	**0** **1**
7.	Although there are "integrity tests" that try to predict whether someone will steal, be absent, or otherwise take advantage of an employer, they don't work well in practice because so many people lie on them.	**0** **1**
8.	On average, conscientiousness is a better predictor of job performance than is intelligence.	**0** **1**
9.	Most employees prefer to be paid on the basis of individual performance rather than on team or organizational performance.	**0** **1**
10.	There is a positive relationship between the proportion of managers receiving organizationally based pay incentives and company profitability.	**0** **1**

SCORING KEY   To score the measure, compare your answers to the correct answers, which are as follows: (1) False, (2) False, (3) False, (4) True, (5) False, (6) False, (7) False, (8) False, (9) True, and (10) True. Matches should be counted as one. Compute the number of correct responses. Scores will range from zero (all responses incorrect) to 10 (all responses correct).

ANALYSIS AND INTERPRETATION   If you didn't achieve a high score, don't worry just yet. These questions were given to nearly 1,000 HR professionals in a variety of organizations. These professionals had an average of 14 years of work experience in HRM. How did they do? On some of the questions (such as, "Most managers give employees lower performance appraisals than they objectively deserve"), the vast majority gave the correct answer (which is false, by the way). On other questions, however, a much smaller percentage gave the correct answer. For example, for the statement: "On average, conscientiousness is a better predictor of job performance than is intelligence," only 18 percent of the HR professionals gave the correct response (false)!

Why the discrepancies? There are several reasons. It could be that practicing HR professionals are unaware of research findings, either because they don't have time to read academic journals (or textbooks), or because the journals are so technically complex that it's difficult to extract the main findings. It also could be that practicing professionals are aware of the research findings but choose not to utilize them because of factors such as political reasons, organizational inertia, or aversion to risk. In any event, closing the gap between research and practice is likely to be beneficial, as research has indicated that organizations that implement effective HRM practices perform better than those that don't.

Source: Based on S. L. Rynes, A. E. Colbert, and K. G. Brown, "HR Professionals' Beliefs About Effective Human Resource Practices: Correspondence Between Research and Practice," *Human Resource Management* (Summer, 2002), pp. 149–74.

FYIA (For Your Immediate Action)

Western Montana Power & Light

Reply   Reply All   Forward

To:	Sandra Gillies, Director of Human Resources
From:	William Munroney, CEO
Re:	**Sexual Harassment**

Sandra, I think we might have a problem. It appears that some of our employees aren't clear about the practices and actions that do or do not constitute sexual harassment. We can't have any ambiguity or uncertainty about this, as you know. We need to immediately develop a training program for all our employees and develop a workable procedure to handle any complaints that might arise.

I want to make the issue of sexual harassment the primary topic at next month's executive board meeting. To facilitate discussion, I'd like for you to write a working paper (no longer than two pages in length) describing (1) the content of an initial two-hour employee workshop on sexual harassment and (2) an appropriate procedure that all employees could follow if they believe that they have been the victims of sexual harassment.

This fictionalized company and message were created for educational purposes only. It is not meant to reflect positively or negatively on management practices by any company that may share this name.

BUSTED

Like many companies today, Scotts Miracle-Gro is facing the dilemma of persuading employees to take better care of themselves without diminishing employee morale or getting hit with employee lawsuits. It's on the leading edge of companies looking to monitor and change employee behavior. But sometimes that edge can be razor sharp.

Scotts' CEO Jim Hagedorn (in photo) acknowledges that his company's wellness program is controversial. In 2000, he, like many other CEOs, watched as his company's health care costs skyrocketed. No help was in sight from either the government or from the health insurance industry, and the company's employees were "bingeing on health care." By February 2003, workers' health care insurance premiums had doubled and employee morale had plummeted. Following his usual tell-it-like-it-is style, Hagedorn confronted the issue head-on with employees. He wanted them to know what they were up against—20 percent of the company's net profits were going to health care. The company's health-risk assessment showed that half of the 6,000 employees were overweight or morbidly obese and a quarter of them smoked. After seeing a CNN program late one night where a doctor was arguing that employers needed to get serious about employee obesity, smoking, and diabetes, Hagedorn knew what he had to do. Despite the late hour, he immediately called his HR chief and told her that he wanted to ban smoking and tackle obesity.

Getting that done wasn't so easy. The legal department worried that the plan might violate federal laws. Other advisors told Hagedorn not to do it or that he was moving too fast. But he wasn't easily dissuaded. He found a law firm that helped determine that in 21 states (including the company's home base in Ohio) it wasn't illegal to hire and fire people based on their smoking habits. Hagedorn also implemented a company-wide wellness program but realized that he needed a third-party to run it so managers couldn't discriminate against employees based on their health.

Today, Scotts' employees are encouraged to take exhaustive health-risk assessments. Those who don't, pay $40 a month more in premiums. All employees are assigned a health coach, who works closely with those who are moderate to high risk. Those who don't comply pay an additional $67 a month on top of the $40. Many employees find the policy "intrusive." Hagedorn hasn't budged. He's adamant about bringing down health care costs and getting employees all the help they need to be healthy and lead healthier lives. One employee who was fired on his 30th birthday because he failed a drug test for nicotine is suing the company. (The lawsuit is still proceeding through the courts system.) However, another employee who was prodded by his health coach to see a doctor had his life saved when surgeons found a 95 percent blockage in his heart that would have killed him within five days without the stents that were inserted.

Discussion Questions

1. What do you think about Hagedorn's approach to controlling employee health care costs? Do you agree with it? Why or why not?

2. What benefits/drawbacks are there to this type of wellness program for (a) employees and (b) the company?

3. Research company wellness programs. What types of things are companies doing to encourage employee wellness? Are there any things that you found that you might recommend that Hagedorn implement? Describe.

Sources: L. Alderman, "Getting Healthy, with a Little Help from the Boss," *New York Times Online,* May 23, 2009; P. B. Kavilanz, "Unhealthy Habits Cost You More at Work," *CNNMoney.com,* March 24, 2009; M. Freudenheim, "Seeking Savings, Employers Help Smokers Quit," *New York Times Online,* October 26, 2007; and M. Conlin, "Get Healthy or Else," *BusinessWeek,* February 26, 2007, pp. 58–69.

Career Module
Building Your Career

The term *career* has several meanings. In popular usage, it can mean advancement ("she is on a management career track"), a profession ("he has chosen a career in accounting"), or a lifelong sequence of jobs ("his career has included 12 jobs in six organizations"). For our purposes, we define a **career** as the sequence of work positions held by a person during his or her lifetime. Using this definition, it's apparent that we all have, or will have, a career. Moreover, the concept is as relevant to unskilled laborers as it is to software designers or physicians. But career development isn't what it used to be!

What Was Career Development Like, Historically?

Although career development has been an important topic in management courses for years, there have been some dramatic changes in the concept. Career development programs used to be designed to help employees advance their work lives within a specific organization. The focus of such programs was to provide employees the information, assessment, and training needed to help them realize their career goals. Career development was also a way for organizations to attract and retain highly talented people. This approach has all but disappeared in today's workplace. Now, organizations that have such traditional career programs are few and far between. Downsizing, restructuring, and other organizational adjustments have brought us to one significant conclusion about career development: You—not the organization—will be responsible for designing, guiding, and developing your own career.

What Is Career Development Like, Now?

This idea of increased personal responsibility for one's career has been described as a **boundaryless career**. The challenge is that there are few hard-and-fast rules to guide you.

One of the first decisions you have to make is career choice. The optimum choice is one that offers the best match between what you want out of life and your interests, your abilities and personality, and market opportunities. Good career choices should result in a series of jobs that give you an opportunity to be a good performer, make you want to maintain your commitment to your career, lead to highly satisfying work, and give you the proper balance between work and personal life. A good career match, then, is one in which you are able to develop a positive self-concept, to do work that you think is important, and to lead the kind of life you desire. In a recent survey by Capital One Financial Corporation, 66 percent of college graduates said that a comprehensive benefits package (including, for example, health care, 401(k) program, child care, and domestic partner benefits) was the most important factor in their job search. Starting salary ranked second at 64 percent, with job location

career
The sequence of work positions held by a person during his or her lifetime.

boundaryless career
When an individual takes personal responsibility for his or her own career.

ranked third at 60 percent. Today's college grads are also looking to be rewarded or compensated (with comp time or matching donations, for instance) for their volunteer and philanthropic activities.

Once you've identified a career choice, it's time to initiate the job search. However, we aren't going to get into the specifics of job hunting, writing a résumé, or interviewing successfully, although those things are important. Let's fast-forward through all that and assume that your job search was successful. It's time to go to work! How do you survive and excel in your career?

How Can I Have a Successful Career?

What can you do to improve your chances for career success? You're already doing the *most* important thing: You're getting a college education! It's the surest way to increase your lifetime earnings. Currently, the average high school graduate earns $27,915 a year. His or her counterpart with a college degree earns $51,206. College graduates earn, on average, $800,000 more than high school graduates over their working career. Investing in your education and training is one of the best investments you'll make in your lifetime. What *else* can you do? Here are some suggestions based on extensive research into career management:

Assess Your Personal Strengths and Weaknesses

Where do your natural talents lie? What can you do, relative to others, that gives you a competitive advantage? Are you particularly good with numbers? Have strong people skills? Good with your hands? Write better than most people? Everyone has some things that they do better than others and some things where they're weak. Play to your strengths.

Identify Market Opportunities

Where are tomorrow's job opportunities? Regardless of your strengths, certain job categories are likely to decline in the coming decades—for instance, bank tellers, small farmers, movie projectionists, travel agents, and secretaries. In contrast, there are likely to be abundant opportunities created by an increasingly aging society, continued emphasis on technology, increased spending on education and training, and concern with personal security. This is likely to create excellent opportunities for jobs in gerontological counseling, network administration, training consultants, and security-alarm installers.

Take Responsibility for Managing Your Own Career

Historically, companies tended to assume responsibility for their employees' careers. Today, this is the exception rather than the rule. Employees are increasingly expected to take responsibility for their own careers.

Think of your careers as your business and you're its CEO. To survive, you have to monitor market forces, head off competitors, and be ready to quickly take advantage of opportunities when they surface. You have to protect your career from harm and position yourself to benefit from changes in the environment.

Develop Your Interpersonal Skills

Interpersonal skills, especially the ability to communicate, top the list of almost every employer's "must have" skills. Whether it's getting a new job or a promotion, strong interpersonal skills are likely to give you a competitive edge.

Practice Makes Perfect

There's an increasing amount of evidence indicating that super-high achievers aren't fundamentally different from the rest of us. They just work harder and smarter. It's been found, based on studies of world-class performers in music, sports, chess, science, and business, that people like Tiger Woods, Mozart, and Bill Gates put in about 10,000 hours (or 10 years at 1,000 hours a year) of persistent, focused training and experience before they hit their peak performance level. If you want to excel in any field, you should expect to have to put in a lot of deliberate practice—consistently engaging in repeated activity specifically designed to improve performance beyond your current comfort and ability level.

Stay Up-to-Date

In today's dynamic world, skills can become obsolete quickly. To keep your career on track, you need to make learning a lifetime commitment. You should be continually "going to school"—if not taking formal courses, then reading books and journals to ensure that you don't get caught with obsolete skills.

Network

Networking refers to creating and maintaining beneficial relationships with others in order to accomplish your goals. It helps to have friends in high places. It also helps to have contacts who can keep you informed of changes that are going on in your organization and in your industry. Go to conferences. Maintain contact with former college friends and alumni. Get involved in community activities. Cultivate a broad set of relationships. And in today's increasingly interconnected world, join online business networking groups like LinkedIn, spoke, and Talkbiznow.

Stay Visible

Networking can increase your visibility. So, too, can writing articles in your professional journals, teaching classes or giving talks in your area of expertise, attending conferences and professional meetings, and making sure your accomplishments are properly promoted. You increase your mobility and value in the marketplace by keeping visible.

Seek a Mentor

Employees with mentors are likely to have enhanced mobility, increased knowledge of the organization's inside workings, greater access to senior executives, increased satisfaction, and increased visibility. For women and minorities, having mentors has been shown to be particularly helpful in promoting career advancement and success.

Leverage Your Competitive Advantage

Develop skills that will give you a competitive advantage in the marketplace. Especially focus on skills that are important to employers, skills that are scarce, and areas where you have limited competition. Try to avoid a worst-case scenario: You have a job that anyone can learn in 30 minutes. Remember that the harder it is for you to learn and develop a highly prized skill, the harder it'll also be for others to acquire it. Generally speaking, the more training necessary to do a job and the fewer people who have that training, the greater your security and influence.

Here's an insight from many years as a student and a professor: To succeed in school, you have to be a generalist and excel at everything. For instance, to earn a 4.0 GPA, you need to be a star in English, math, science, geography, languages, etc. The "real world," on the other hand, rewards specialization. You don't have to be good at everything. You just need to be good at something that others aren't and that society values. You can be lousy in math or science and still be a very successful opera singer, artist, salesperson, or writer. You don't have to excel in English to be a computer programmer or electrician. The secret to life success is identifying your comparative advantage and then developing it. And, as we've noted previously, you need to invest approximately 10,000 hours in honing your skills to achieve optimum proficiency.

Don't Shun Risks

Don't be afraid to take risks, especially when you're young and you don't have much to lose. Going back to school, moving to a new state or country, or quitting a job to start your own business can be the decision that will set your life in a completely new direction. Great accomplishments almost always require taking the path less traveled; and the road to nowhere is paved with fears of the unknown.

It's OK to Change Jobs

Past generations often believed "you don't leave a good job." That advice no longer applies. In today's fast-changing job market, staying put often only means that you're staying behind. Employers no longer expect long-term loyalty. And to keep your skills fresh, your income increasing, and your job tasks interesting, it will be increasingly likely that you'll need to change employers.

Opportunities, Preparation, and Luck = Success

Successful people are typically ambitious, intelligent, and hardworking. But they are also lucky. It's not by happenchance that many of the biggest technology success stories—Bill Gates and Paul Allen at Microsoft, Steve Jobs at Apple, Scott McNealy at Sun Microsystems, Eric Schmidt at Novell and Goggle—were born in a narrow three-year period between June 1953 and March 1956. They were smart. They were interested in computers and technology. But they were also lucky. They reached their teens and early 20s in 1975—at the dawn of the personal computer age. Those people with similar interests and talents but born in the mid-1940s were likely to have joined a firm like IBM out of college and been enamored with mainframe computers. Had they been born in the early 1960s, they would have missed getting in on the ground floor of the revolution.

Success is a matter of matching up opportunities, preparation, and luck. It's been suggested that few of us get more than a couple of special opportunities in our lifetime. If you're lucky, you will recognize those opportunities, have made the proper preparations, and then act on them.

You can't control when you were born, where you were born, your parents' finances, or the like. Those are the luck factors. But what you can control is your preparation and willingness to act when opportunity knocks.

Sources: "Managing Your Career Module" based on: J. H. Greenhaus, V. M. Godstalk, and G. A. Callahan, *Career Management*, 3rd ed. (Cincinnati, OH: South–Western, 2000); K. A. Ericsson, "Deliberate Practice and the Modifiability of Body and Mind," *International Journal of Sports Psychology* (January–March 2007), pp. 4–34; J. P. Newport, "Mastery, Just 10,000 Hours Away," *Wall Street Journal*, March 14–15, 2009, p. W6; "Capital One Survey Highlights What Today's College Graduates Want from Employers," http://www.businesswire.com (June 10, 2008); M. Gladwell, *Outliers: The Story of Success* (New York: Little, Brown, 2008); R. N. Boles, *What Color Is Your Parachute? 2009: A Practical Manual for Job-Hunters and Career-Changers* (Berkeley, CA: Ten Speed Press, 2009); D. E. Super and D. T. Hall, "Career Development: Exploration and Planning," in M. R. Rosenzweig and L.W. Porter (eds.), *Annual Review of Psychology*, vol. 29 (Palo Alto, CA: Annual Reviews, 1978), p. 334; and M. B. Arthur and D. M. Rousseau, *The Boundaryless Career: A New Employment Principle for a New Organizational Era* (New York: Oxford University Press, 1996).

Understanding Yourself

How Confident Am I in My Abilities to Succeed?

As we indicated earlier, you have to work at being successful. One personal characteristic that can affect your chances at being successful includes how confident you are in you abilities to succeed.

INSTRUMENT Indicate the extent to which you agree or disagree with each of the following statements using the scale below.

1 = Strongly disagree

2 = Disagree

3 = Neutral

4 = Agree

5 = Strongly agree

1.	I am strong enough to overcome life's struggles.	1	2	3	4	5
2.	At root, I am a weak person.	1	2	3	4	5
3.	I can handle the situations that life brings.	1	2	3	4	5
4.	I usually feel that I am an unsuccessful person.	1	2	3	4	5
5.	I often feel that there is nothing that I can do well.	1	2	3	4	5
6.	I feel competent to deal effectively with the real world.	1	2	3	4	5
7.	I often feel like a failure.	1	2	3	4	5
8.	I usually feel I can handle the typical problems that come up in life.	1	2	3	4	5

SCORING KEY To score the measure, first reverse-code items 2, 4, 5, and 7 so that 1 = 5, 2 = 4, 3 = 3, 4 = 2, and 5 = 1. Then add up all your responses.

ANALYSIS AND INTERPRETATION Your score on this measure can range from 8 to 40. The higher your score, the more confidence you have in yourself to be successful. Confidence has an influence on many things we do. People who are confident have high self-efficacy that generalizes across a variety of situations. They believe that they have the capability to mobilize the motivation and resources required to perform successfully on different tasks or in different jobs. Ultimately, this confidence translates into better performance. Why? One reason is that successful individuals set more goals for themselves, are more committed to their goals, and even persist in achieving their goals in the face of failure. In fact, when individuals who are confident about themselves are given negative feedback (say, by a supervisor), they respond by *increasing* their effort and motivation. Perhaps not surprisingly, individuals with such positive self-concepts are more satisfied with their jobs and obtain higher levels of career success.

If you don't have a great deal of confidence in yourself, there are several ways to increase it. One was is to simply gain experience with tasks that you are less confident about. Another way is to watch someone else, such as a friend, perform the task. For instance, if you don't have confidence in your ability to hit a tennis ball, first observing someone else do it is likely to boost your confidence. Finally, being persuaded by someone else that you can do something (think motivational speaker) helps to increase the efficacy of individuals to perform a given task.

Source: T. A. Judge, E. A. Locke, C. C. Durham, and A. N. Kluger, "Dispositional Effects on Job and Life Satisfaction: The Role of Core Evaluations," *Journal of Applied Psychology* 83 (1998), pp. 17–34.

7

Managing Change and Innovation

Dr. Kanter

INTOUCH HEALTH.

Technology Transformers

Imagine lying as a patient in a hospital bed and being visited by a 5-foot robot.[1] You might attribute such a "vision" to too many drugs or too little sleep. But in Methodist Hospital in Houston, that 5-foot robot isn't a vision. It's real. The robot, which looks like "an oversize carpet cleaner with a computer monitor stuck on top," visits patients, being guided remotely by a patient's doctor from a command center on another floor. With this type of technology, especially in a critical care unit, a medical team can do its rounds and "read" vital signs and "see" how patients are doing without disturbing or distressing them.

Robots roaming hospital hallways aren't the only technological advancements transforming how medical centers and health care systems work. Radio-frequency ID tags keep track of doctors, nurses, and pieces of equipment in real time, leading to faster emergency response times. "Smart beds automatically transfer patients' breathing and heart rates to their charts," quickly alerting nurses to potential or developing problems. And one of the biggest technological changes is in medical records information keeping. Rather than having massive numbers of paper-based files, health care organizations are moving toward completely digital medical records. But the rate of change has been slow. Currently, only 1.5 percent of private hospitals have a comprehensive electronic medical records system in all clinical units. Only 7.6 percent have a basic system in at least one unit. Yet, it's a major change with significant promise. "Putting patient records into digital form . . . can provide a wealth of information about which treatments work and which don't, and speed diagnosis and medical care."

The investment that hospitals and other health care organizations are making in technology has basically two goals: (1) to improve medical care and reduce error rates, and (2) to minimize patient stress, which encourages healing. "Ironically, one of the most anticipated developments is that technology will allow hospitals to keep people out of them." The vice president of the innovation and technology group at Kaiser Permanente's Sidney R. Garfield Health Care Innovation Center says, "By 2015, the home will be the hub of health care." And such changes are already taking place. In many rural areas of the United States where specialized medical care is scarce, telemedicine is in place to cover the gaps. For instance, 31 hospitals in remote locations in Michigan use robots, similar to the one described earlier, for diagnosis and follow-up. Robots are even found in operating rooms—the "assembly line" of a health care system—just as they are in other organization's assembly lines, *and* for the same reasons: quality control and cost control.

In an industry where you'd expect up-to-date technology, the changes in the way health care organizations do their work haven't been occurring as rapidly as you might think. However, technological changes will continue to transform the industry and the organizations and the people who make it work.

Change is a constant for organizations and thus for managers. Large companies, small businesses, entrepreneurial start-ups, universities, hospitals, and even the military are changing the way they do things. Although change has always been a part of the manager's job, it's become even more so in recent years. And because change can't be eliminated, managers must learn how to manage it successfully. In this chapter, we're going to look at organizational change efforts, the ways that managers can deal with the stress that exists in organizations, and how managers can stimulate innovation in their organizations.

What Is Change and How Do Managers Deal with It?

7.1 Define organizational change and compare and contrast views on the change process.

If it weren't for change, a manager's job would be relatively easy. Planning would be easier because tomorrow would be no different from today. The issue of organizational design would be solved because the environment would be free from uncertainty and there would be no need to adapt. Similarly, decision making would be dramatically simplified because the outcome of each alternative could be predicted with near pinpoint accuracy. It would also simplify the manager's job if competitors never introduced new products or services, if customers didn't make new demands, if government regulations were never modified, if technology never advanced, or if employees' needs always remained the same. But that's not the way it is.

Change is an organizational reality. Most managers, at one point or another, will have to change some things in their workplace. We classify these changes as **organizational change**, which is any alteration of an organization's people, structure or technology. (See Exhibit 7-1.) Let's look more closely at each of these three areas.

Changing *structure* includes any alteration in authority relationships, coordination mechanisms, degree of centralization, job design, or similar organization structure variables. For instance, in previous chapters, we've mentioned that work process engineering, restructuring, and empowering result in decentralization, wider spans of control, reduced work specialization, and work teams. These structural components give employees the authority and means to implement process improvements. For instance, the creation of work teams that cut across departmental lines allows those people who understand a problem best to solve that problem. In addition, cross-functional work teams encourage cooperative problem solving rather than "us versus them" situations. All of these may involve some type of structural change.

Changing *technology* encompasses modifications in the way work is done or the methods and equipment used. One organizational area, in particular, where managers deal with changing technology is continuous improvement initiatives, which are directed at developing flexible processes to support better-quality operations. Employees committed

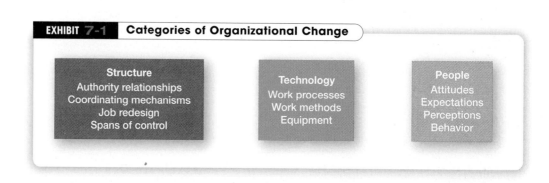

EXHIBIT 7-1 **Categories of Organizational Change**

Structure	Technology	People
Authority relationships	Work processes	Attitudes
Coordinating mechanisms	Work methods	Expectations
Job redesign	Equipment	Perceptions
Spans of control		Behavior

to continuous improvements are constantly looking for things to fix. Thus, work processes must be adaptable to continual change and fine-tuning. Such adaptability requires an extensive commitment to educating and training workers. Employees need skills training in problem solving, decision making, negotiation, statistical analysis, and team-building, and they must be able to analyze and act on data. For example, Herman Miller, Inc., used both technology and employee training to achieve its market-leading position in the office furniture industry.[2]

Changes in *people* refer to changes in employee attitudes, expectations, perceptions, or behaviors. The human dimension of change requires a workforce that's committed to quality and continuous improvement. Again, proper employee education and training are needed, as is a performance evaluation and reward system that supports and encourages those improvements. For example, successful programs put quality goals into bonus plans for executives and incentives for employees.

Why Do Organizations Need to Change?

In Chapter 2 we pointed out that both external and internal forces constrain managers. These same forces also bring about the need for change. Let's briefly review these factors.

WHAT EXTERNAL FORCES CREATE A NEED TO CHANGE? The external forces that create the need for organizational change come from various sources. In recent years, the *marketplace* has affected firms such as AT&T and Lowe's because of new competition. AT&T, for example, faces competition from local cable companies and from free Internet services such as Skype. Lowe's, too, must now contend with a host of aggressive competitors such as Home Depot and Menard's. *Government laws and regulations* are also an impetus for change. For example, when the Americans with Disabilities Act was signed into law, thousands of businesses were required to widen doorways, reconfigure restrooms, and add ramps. Even today, organizations continue to deal with the requirements of improving accessibility for the disabled.

Technology also creates the need for organizational change. Our chapter opening case perfectly illustrates how changing technology can impact organizations. The Internet has changed the way we get information, how products are sold, and how we get our work done. Technological advancements have created significant economies of scale for many organizations. For instance, technology allows Scottrade to offer its clients the opportunity to make online trades without a broker. The assembly line in many industries has also undergone dramatic change as employers replace human labor with technologically advanced mechanical robots. Also, the fluctuation in *labor markets* forces managers to initiate changes. For example, the shortage of registered nurses in the United States has led many hospital administrators to redesign nursing jobs and to alter their rewards and benefits packages for nurses, as well as join forces with local universities to address the nursing shortage.

As the news headlines remind us, *economic* changes affect almost all organizations. For instance, prior to the mortgage market meltdown, low interest rates led to significant growth in the housing market. This growth meant more jobs, more employees hired, and significant increases in sales in other businesses that supported the building industry. However, as the economy soured, it had the opposite effect on the housing industry and other industries as credit markets dried up and businesses found it difficult to get the capital they needed to operate. And although it's been almost a decade since 9/11, the airline industry is still dealing with the organizational changes forced on them by increased security measures and other environmental factors such as high fuel costs.

organizational change
Any alteration of an organization's people, structure, or technology.

WHAT INTERNAL FORCES CREATE A NEED TO CHANGE? Internal forces can also create the need for organizational change. These internal forces tend to originate primarily from the internal operations of the organization or from the impact of external changes. (It's also important to recognize that these changes are a normal part of the organizational life cycle.)[3]

When managers redefine or modify an organization's *strategy*, that action often introduces a host of changes. For example, when Nokia brings in new equipment, that's an internal force for change. Because of this action, employees may face job redesign, undergo training to operate the new equipment, or be required to establish new interaction patterns within their work groups. Another internal force for change is that the *composition of an organization's workforce* changes in terms of age, education, gender, nationality, and so forth. A stable organization in which managers have been in their positions for years might need to restructure jobs in order to retain more ambitious employees by affording them some upward mobility. The compensation and benefits systems might also need to be reworked to reflect the needs of a diverse workforce and market forces in which certain skills are in short supply. *Employee attitudes*, such as increased job dissatisfaction, may lead to increased absenteeism, resignations, and even strikes. Such events will, in turn, often lead to changes in organizational policies and practices.

Who Initiates Organizational Change?

Organizational changes need a catalyst. People who act as catalysts and assume the responsibility for managing the change process are called **change agents**.[4]

Any manager can be a change agent. When we talk about organizational change, we assume that it's initiated and carried out by a manager within the organization. However, the change agent could be a nonmanager—for example, an internal staff specialist or an outside consultant whose expertise is in change implementation. For major systemwide changes, an organization will often hire outside consultants to provide advice and assistance. Because these consultants come from the outside, they offer an objective perspective that insiders usually lack. However, the problem is that outside consultants may not understand the organization's history, culture, operating procedures, and personnel. They're also prone to initiating more drastic changes than insiders—which can be either a benefit or a disadvantage—because they don't have to live with the repercussions after the change is implemented. In contrast, internal managers who act as change agents may be more thoughtful (and possibly more cautious) because they must live with the consequences of their actions (see "Developing Your Change Management Skill").

Developing Your *Change Management* Skill

About the Skill

Managers play an important role in organizational change. That is, they often serve as a catalyst for the change—a change agent. However, managers may find that change is resisted by employees. After all, change represents ambiguity and uncertainty, or it threatens the status quo. How can this resistance to change be effectively managed? Here are some suggestions.[5]

Steps in Practicing the Skill

1 **Assess the climate for change.** One major factor in why some changes succeed while others fail is the readiness for change. Assessing the climate for change

involves asking several questions. The more affirmative answers you get, the more likely it is that change efforts will succeed. Here are some guiding questions:

a. Is the sponsor of the change high enough in the organization to have power to effectively deal with resistance?

b. Is senior management supportive of the change and committed to it?

c. Do senior managers convey the need for change, and is this feeling shared by others in the organization?

d. Do managers have a clear vision of how the future will look after the change?

e. Are objective measures in place to evaluate the change effort and have reward systems been explicitly designed to reinforce them?

f. Is the specific change effort consistent with other changes going on in the organization?

g. Are managers willing to sacrifice their personal self-interests for the good of the organization as a whole?

h. Do managers pride themselves on closely monitoring changes and actions by competitors?

i. Are managers and employees rewarded for taking risks, being innovative, and looking for new and better solutions?

j. Is the organizational structure flexible?

k. Does communication flow both down and up in the organization?

l. Has the organization successfully implemented changes in the past?

m. Are employees satisfied with and do they trust management?

n. Is a high degree of interaction and cooperation typical between organizational work units?

o. Are decisions made quickly and do they take into account a wide variety of suggestions?

2 **Choose an appropriate approach for managing the resistance to change.** In this chapter, six strategies are suggested for dealing with resistance to change—education and communication, participation, facilitation and support, negotiation, manipulation and co-optation, and coercion. Review Exhibit 7–3 (p. 200) for the advantages and disadvantages and when it is best to use them.

3 **During the time the change is being implemented and after the change is completed, communicate with employees regarding what support you may be able to provide.** Your employees need to know that you are there to support them during change efforts. Be prepared to offer the assistance that may be necessary to help them enact the change.

Practicing the Skill

Read through the following scenario. Write down some notes about how you would handle the situation described. Be sure to refer to the three suggestions for managing resistance to change.

You're the nursing supervisor at a community hospital employing both emergency room and floor nurses. Each of these teams of nurses tends to work almost exclusively with others doing the same job. In your professional reading, you've come across the concept of cross-training nursing teams and giving them more varied responsibilities, which in turn has been shown to improve patient care while lowering costs. You call the two team leaders, Sue and Scott, into your office to discuss your plan to have the nursing teams move to this approach. To your surprise, they're both opposed to the idea. Sue says she and the other emergency room nurses feel they're needed in the ER, where they fill the most vital role in the hospital. They work special hours when needed, do whatever tasks are required, and often work in difficult and stressful circumstances. They think the floor nurses have relatively easy jobs for the pay they receive. Scott, leader of the floor nurses team, tells you that his group believes the ER nurses lack the special training and extra experience that the floor nurses bring to the hospital. The floor nurses claim they have the heaviest responsibilities and do the most exacting work. Because they have ongoing contact with the patients and their families, they believe they shouldn't be pulled away from vital floor duties to help ER nurses complete their tasks. Now . . . what would you do?

How Does Organizational Change Happen?

We often use two metaphors to clarify the change process.[6] The **"calm waters" metaphor** envisions the organization as a large ship crossing a calm sea. The ship's captain and crew know exactly where they're going because they've made the trip many times before. Change surfaces as the occasional storm, a brief distraction in an otherwise calm and predictable trip. In the **"white-water rapids" metaphor**, the organization is seen as a small raft navigating a raging river with uninterrupted white-water rapids. Aboard the raft are half a dozen people who have never worked together

---

change agents
People who act as change catalysts and assume the responsibility for managing the change process.

"calm waters" metaphor of change
A description of organizational change that likens that change to a large ship making a predictable trip across a calm sea and experiencing an occasional storm.

"white-water rapids" metaphor of change
A description of organizational change that likens that change to a small raft navigating a raging river.

before, who are totally unfamiliar with the river, who are unsure of their eventual destination, and who, as if things weren't bad enough, are traveling at night. In the white-water rapids metaphor, change is a natural state and managing change is a continual process.

These two metaphors present distinctly different approaches to understanding and responding to change. Let's take a closer look at each one.

WHAT IS THE "CALM WATERS" METAPHOR? Until recently, the "calm waters" metaphor dominated the thinking of practicing managers and academics. The prevailing model for handling change in such circumstances is best illustrated in Kurt Lewin's three-step description of the change process.[7] (See Exhibit 7-2.)

According to Lewin, successful change requires unfreezing the status quo, changing to a new state, and freezing the new change to make it permanent. The status quo can be considered an equilibrium state. Unfreezing is necessary to move from this equilibrium. It can be achieved in one of three ways:

► The driving forces, which direct behavior away from the status quo, can be increased.
► The restraining forces, which hinder movement from the existing equilibrium, can be decreased.
► The two approaches can be combined.

Once the situation has been unfrozen, the change itself can be implemented. However, the mere introduction of change doesn't ensure that it will take hold. The new situation, therefore, needs to be frozen so that it can be sustained over time. Unless this last step is done, it's likely that the change will be short-lived and employees will revert to the previous equilibrium state. The objective of freezing the entire equilibrium state, then, is to stabilize the new situation by balancing the driving and restraining forces.

Note how Lewin's three-step process treats change as a break in the organization's equilibrium state.[8] The status quo has been disturbed, and change is necessary to establish a new equilibrium state. This view might have been appropriate to the relatively calm environment that most organizations faced in the 1950s, 1960s, and early 1970s, but the calm waters metaphor is increasingly obsolete as a description of the kinds of "seas" that current managers have to navigate. (See the "From the Past to the Present" box for more information on Lewin and his organizational research.)

WHAT IS THE "WHITE-WATER RAPIDS" METAPHOR? Susan Whiting is chairman of Nielsen Media Research, the company best known for its television ratings, which are frequently used to determine how much advertisers pay for TV commercials. The media research business isn't what it used to be, however, as the Internet, video on demand, cell phones, iPods, digital video recorders, and other changing technologies have made data

EXHIBIT 7-2 **The Three-Step Change Process**

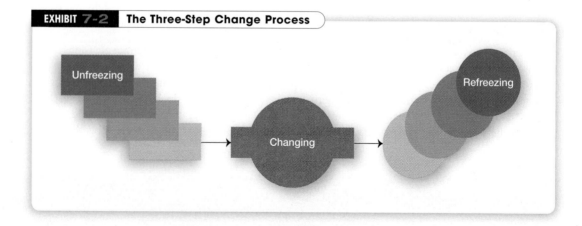

"There is nothing so practical as a good theory."

"If you want truly to understand something, try to change it."

These two quotes by Kurt Lewin provide unique insights into who he was and how he approached studying management.[9] Lewin, who's often called the father of modern social psychology (a discipline that uses scientific methods to "understand and explain how the thought, feeling, and behavior of individuals are influenced by the actual, imagined, or implied presence of other human beings"), made his name in management circles through his studies of group dynamics. His approach was based on the belief that "group behavior is an intricate set of symbolic interactions and forces that not only affect group structure but also modify individual behavior."

One of his research studies that looked at modifying family food habits during World War II provided new and important insights into introducing change. He found that "changes were more easily induced through group decision making than through lectures and individual appeals." So what did this mean? His findings suggested that changes would be more readily accepted when people felt they had an opportunity to be involved in the change rather than when they were simply asked or told to change. That's an important lesson for any manager, even today, to learn and apply.

Finally, another of Lewin's major contributions was the idea of force field analysis, a framework for looking at the factors (forces) that influenced a situation. Those forces could either be *driving* movement toward a goal or *blocking* movement toward a goal. When you view this idea in terms of managing change, you can see how this process also could contribute to understanding the dynamics of what makes change work and how managers can overcome resistance to change; that is, increase the driving forces, decrease the blocking forces, or both.

collection much more challenging. Whiting says, "If you look at a typical week I have, it's a combination of trying to lead a company in change in an industry in change."[10] That's a pretty accurate description of what change is like in our second change metaphor—white-water rapids. It's also consistent with a world that's increasingly dominated by information, ideas, and knowledge.[11]

To get a feeling of what managing change might be like in a white-water rapids environment, consider attending a college that had the following rules: Courses vary in length. When you sign up, you don't know how long a course will run. It might go for 2 weeks or 30 weeks. Furthermore, the instructor can end a course at any time with no prior warning. If that isn't challenging enough, the length of the class changes each time it meets: Sometimes the class lasts 20 minutes; other times it runs for 3 hours. And the time of the next class meeting is set by the instructor during this class. There's one more thing. All exams are unannounced, so you have to be ready for a test at any time. To succeed in this type of environment, you'd have to respond quickly to changing conditions. Students who were overly structured or uncomfortable with change wouldn't succeed.

DOES EVERY MANAGER FACE A WORLD OF CONSTANT AND CHAOTIC CHANGE? No, not every manager faces such a world. However, the number who don't is dwindling. The stability and predictability of the calm waters metaphor don't exist. Disruptions in the status quo are not occasional and temporary, and they are not followed by a return to calm waters. Many managers never get out of the rapids. Like Susan Whiting, described previously, they face constant forces in the environment (external *and* internal) that bring about the need for organizational change.

HOW DO ORGANIZATIONS IMPLEMENT PLANNED CHANGES? We know that most changes employees experience in an organization don't happen by chance. Often managers make a concerted effort to alter some aspect of the organization. Whatever happens—in terms of structure or technology—ultimately affects organizational members. Efforts to assist organizational members with a planned change are referred to as **organization development (OD)**.

organization development (OD)
Efforts that assist organizational members with a planned change by focusing on their attitudes and values.

In facilitating long-term, organization-wide changes, OD focuses on constructively changing the attitudes and values of organization members so that they can more readily adapt to and be more effective in achieving the new directions of the organization.[12] When OD efforts are planned, organization leaders are, in essence, attempting to change the organization's culture.[13] However, a fundamental issue of OD is its reliance on employee participation to foster an environment in which open communication and trust exist.[14] Persons involved in OD efforts acknowledge that change can create stress for employees. Therefore, OD attempts to involve organizational members in changes that will affect their jobs and seeks their input about how the change is affecting them (just as Lewin suggested).

Any organizational activity that assists with implementing planned change can be viewed as an OD technique. However, the more popular OD efforts in organizations rely heavily on group interactions and cooperation and include survey feedback, process consultation, team-building, and intergroup development.

Survey feedback efforts are designed to assess employee attitudes about and perceptions of the change they are encountering. Employees are generally asked to respond to a set of specific questions regarding how they view such organizational aspects as decision making, leadership, communication effectiveness, and satisfaction with their jobs, coworkers, and management.[15] The data a change agent obtains are used to clarify problems that employees may be facing. As a result of this information, the change agent takes some action to remedy the problems.

In **process consultation**, outside consultants help managers to perceive, understand, and act on process elements with which they must deal.[16] These elements might include, for example, workflow, informal relationships among unit members, and formal communications channels. Consultants give managers insight into what is going on. It's important to recognize that consultants are not there to solve these problems. Rather, they act as coaches to help managers diagnose the interpersonal processes that need improvement. If managers, with the consultants' help, cannot solve the problem, the consultants will often help managers find experts who can.

Organizations are made up of individuals working together to achieve some goals. Because organizational members must frequently interact with peers, a primary function of OD is to help them become a team. **Team-building** is generally an activity that helps work groups set goals, develop positive interpersonal relationships, and clarify the roles and responsibilities of each team member. It's not always necessary to address each area because the group may be in agreement and understand what's expected of it. The primary focus of team-building is to increase members' trust and openness toward one another.[17]

Members of the Florida State University football team participate in team-building exercises before the beginning of their season. To foster teamwork, the players participate in several different games before competing in a paint ball competition. While strength and conditioning exercises are important aspects of players' physical training, team-building exercises are important for increasing players' trust and openness toward one another and for developing skills that contribute to positive interpersonal relationships.

Whereas team-building focuses on helping a work group become more cohesive, **intergroup development** attempts to achieve the same results among different work groups. That is, intergroup development attempts to change attitudes, stereotypes, and perceptions that one group may have toward another group. In doing so, better coordination among the various groups can be achieved.

How Do Managers Manage Resistance to Change?

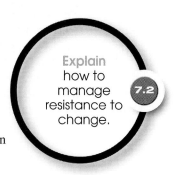

Explain how to manage resistance to change.

7.2

Managers should be motivated to initiate change because they're concerned with improving their organization's effectiveness. But change isn't easy in any organization. It can be disruptive and scary. Organizations, and people within them, can build up inertia that causes them to resist any change, even if the change might be beneficial. In this section, we review why people in organizations resist change and what can be done to lessen that resistance.

Why Do People Resist Organizational Change?

It's often said that most people hate any change that doesn't jingle in their pockets. This resistance to change is well documented.[18] Why *do* people resist organizational change? The main reasons include uncertainty, habit, concern over personal loss, and the belief that the change is not in the organization's best interest.[19]

Change replaces the known with uncertainty. No matter how much you may dislike attending college (or certain classes), at least you know what's expected of you. When you leave college for the world of full-time employment, you'll trade the known for the unknown. Employees in organizations are faced with similar uncertainty. For example, when quality control methods based on statistical models are introduced into manufacturing plants, many quality control inspectors have to learn the new methods. Some may fear that they'll be unable to do so and may develop a negative attitude toward the change or behave poorly if required to use them.

Another cause of resistance is that we do things out of habit. Every day when you go to school or work you probably go the same way, if you're like most people. We're creatures of habit. Life is complex enough—we don't want to have to consider the full range of options for the hundreds of decisions we make every day. To cope with this complexity, we rely on habits or programmed responses. But when confronted with change, our tendency to respond in our accustomed ways becomes a source of resistance.

The third cause of resistance is the fear of losing something already possessed. Change threatens the investment you've already made in the status quo. The more that people have invested in the current system, the more they resist change. Why? They fear losing status, money, authority, friendships, personal convenience, or other economic benefits that they value. This helps explain why older workers tend to resist change more than younger workers since they generally have more invested in the current system and more to lose by changing.

A final cause of resistance is a person's belief that the change is incompatible with the goals and interests of the organization. For instance, an employee who believes that a

---

survey feedback
A method of assessing employees' attitudes toward and perceptions of a change.

process consultation
Using outside consultants to assess organizational processes such as workflow, informal intra-unit relationships, and formal communication channels.

team-building
Using activities to help work groups set goals, develop positive interpersonal relationships, and clarify the roles and responsibilities of each team member.

intergroup development
Activities that attempt to make several work groups more cohesive.

proposed new job procedure will reduce product quality can be expected to resist the change. This type of resistance can actually be beneficial to the organization if expressed in a positive way.

What Are Some Techniques for Reducing Resistance to Organizational Change?

When managers see resistance to change as dysfunctional, what can they do? Several strategies have been suggested in dealing with resistance to change. These approaches include education and communication, participation, facilitation and support, negotiation, manipulation and co-optation, and coercion. These tactics are summarized here and described in Exhibit 7-3. Managers should view these techniques as tools and use the most appropriate one depending on the type and source of the resistance.

Education and communication can help reduce resistance to change by helping employees see the logic of the change effort. This technique, of course, assumes that much of the resistance lies in misinformation or poor communication.

Participation involves bringing those individuals directly affected by the proposed change into the decision-making process. Their participation allows these individuals to express their feelings, increase the quality of the process, and increase employee commitment to the final decision.

Facilitation and support involve helping employees deal with the fear and anxiety associated with the change effort. This help may include employee counseling, therapy, new skills training, or a short paid leave of absence.

Negotiation involves exchanging something of value for an agreement to lessen the resistance to the change effort. This resistance technique may be quite useful when the resistance comes from a powerful source.

Manipulation and co-optation refers to covert attempts to influence others about the change. It may involve twisting or distorting facts to make the change appear more attractive.

Finally, *coercion* can be used to deal with resistance to change. Coercion involves the use of direct threats or force against the resisters.

EXHIBIT 7-3 | **Techniques for Reducing Resistance to Change**

TECHNIQUE	WHEN USED	ADVANTAGE	DISADVANTAGE
Education and communication	When resistance is due to misinformation	Clear up misunderstandings	May not work when mutual trust and credibility are lacking
Participation	When resisters have the expertise to make a contribution	Increase involvement and acceptance	Time-consuming; has potential for a poor solution
Facilitation and support	When resisters are fearful and anxiety ridden	Can facilitate needed adjustments	Expensive; no guarantee of success
Negotiation	When resistance comes from a powerful group	Can "buy" commitment	Potentially high cost; opens doors for others to apply pressure too
Manipulation and co-optation	When a powerful group's endorsement is needed	Inexpensive, easy way to gain support	Can backfire, causing change agent to lose credibility
Coercion	When a powerful group's endorsement is needed	Inexpensive, easy way to gain support	May be illegal; may undermine change agent's credibility

What Reaction Do Employees Have to Organizational Change?

Describe what managers need to know about employee stress. **7.3**

For many employees, change creates stress. A dynamic and uncertain environment characterized by restructurings, downsizings, empowerment, and personal-life matters has caused large numbers of employees to feel overworked and "stressed out." In this section, we'll review specifically what is meant by the term *stress*, what the symptoms of stress are, what causes stress, and what managers can do to reduce anxiety.

What Is Stress?

Stress is the adverse reaction people have to excessive pressure placed on them from extraordinary demands, constraints, or opportunities.[21] Stress isn't always bad. Although it's often discussed in a negative context, stress can be positive, especially when it offers a potential gain. For instance, functional stress allows an athlete, stage performer, or employee to perform at his or her highest level at crucial times.

However, stress is more often associated with constraints and demands. A constraint prevents you from doing what you desire; demands refer to the loss of something desired. When you take a test at school or have your annual performance review at work, you feel stress because you confront opportunity, constraints, and demands. A good performance review may lead to a promotion, greater responsibilities, and a higher salary. But a poor review may keep you from getting a promotion. An extremely poor review might lead to your being fired.

One other thing to understand about stress is that just because the conditions are right for stress to surface doesn't always mean it will. Two conditions are necessary for *potential* stress to become *actual* stress.[22] First, there must be uncertainty over the outcome, and second, the outcome must be important.

What Are the Symptoms of Stress?

We see stress in a number of ways. For instance, an employee who is experiencing high stress may become depressed, accident prone, or argumentative; may have difficulty making routine decisions; may be easily distracted, and so on. As Exhibit 7-4 shows, stress

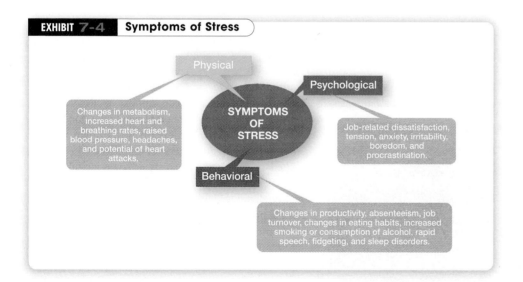

EXHIBIT 7-4 Symptoms of Stress

SYMPTOMS OF STRESS

Physical
Changes in metabolism, increased heart and breathing rates, raised blood pressure, headaches, and potential of heart attacks.

Psychological
Job-related dissatisfaction, tension, anxiety, irritability, boredom, and procrastination.

Behavioral
Changes in productivity, absenteeism, job turnover, changes in eating habits, increased smoking or consumption of alcohol, rapid speech, fidgeting, and sleep disorders.

stress
The adverse reaction people have to excessive pressure placed on them from extraordinary demands, constraints, or opportunities.

symptoms can be grouped under three general categories: physical, psychological, and behavioral. All of these can significantly affect an employee's work.

Too much stress can also have tragic consequences. In Japan, there's a stress phenomenon called **karoshi** (pronounced kah-roe-she), which is translated literally as "death from overwork." During the late 1980s, "several high-ranking Japanese executives still in their prime years suddenly died without any previous sign of illness."[23] As public concern increased, even the Japanese Ministry of Labour got involved, and it now publishes statistics on the number of karoshi deaths. As Japanese multinational companies expand operations to China, Korea, and Taiwan, it's feared that the karoshi culture may follow.

What Causes Stress?

Stress can be caused by personal factors and by job-related factors called **stressors**. Clearly, change of any kind—personal or job-related—has the potential to cause stress as it can involve demands, constraints, or opportunities. Organizations have no shortage of factors that can cause stress. Pressures to avoid errors or complete tasks in a limited time period, changes in the way reports are filed, a demanding supervisor, and unpleasant coworkers are a few examples. Let's look at five categories of organizational stressors: task, role, and interpersonal demands; organization structure; and organizational leadership.

Task demands are factors related to an employee's job. They include the design of a person's job (autonomy, task variety, degree of automation), working conditions, and the physical work layout. Work quotas can put pressure on employees when their "outcomes" are perceived as excessive.[24] The more interdependence between an employee's tasks and the tasks of others, the more potential stress there is. *Autonomy*, on the other hand, tends to lessen stress. Jobs in which temperatures, noise, or other working conditions are dangerous or undesirable can increase anxiety. So, too, can working in an overcrowded room or in a visible location where interruptions are constant.

Role demands relate to pressures placed on an employee as a function of the particular role he or she plays in the organization. **Role conflicts** create expectations that may be hard to reconcile or satisfy. **Role overload** is experienced when the employee is expected to do more than time permits. **Role ambiguity** is created when role expectations are not clearly understood and the employee is not sure what he or she is to do.

Interpersonal demands are pressures created by other employees. Lack of social support from colleagues and poor interpersonal relationships can cause considerable stress, especially among employees with a high social need.

Organization structure can increase stress. Excessive rules and an employee's lack of opportunity to participate in decisions that affect him or her are examples of structural variables that might be potential sources of stress.

Organizational leadership represents the supervisory style of the organization's managers. Some managers create a culture characterized by tension, fear, and anxiety. They establish unrealistic pressures to perform in the short run, impose excessively tight controls, and routinely fire employees who don't measure up. This style of leadership flows down through the organization and affects all employees.

Personal factors that can create stress include family issues, personal economic problems, and inherent personality characteristics. Because employees bring their personal problems to work with them, a full understanding of employee stress requires a manager to be understanding of these personal factors.[25] Evidence also indicates that employees' personalities have an effect on how susceptible they are to stress. The most commonly used labels for these personality traits are Type A and Type B.

Type A personality is characterized by chronic feelings of a sense of time urgency, an excessive competitive drive, and difficulty accepting and enjoying leisure time.

Wang Zhiqian stands before the Airbus A320 aircraft she will fly as the first female pilot for Sichuan Airlines, a regional Chinese carrier. As a commercial airline pilot, Zhiqian has a career that ranks high on the list of the most stressful jobs. Task demands make commercial pilots' jobs very stressful because pilots are responsible for the lives of their passengers and crews every time they fly. In the event of an emergency, pilots must handle unexpected and rapidly changing situations from poor weather conditions to equipment malfunctions.

The opposite of Type A is **Type B personality**. Type Bs never suffer from time urgency or impatience. Until quite recently, it was believed that Type As were more likely to experience stress on and off the job. A closer analysis of the evidence, however, has produced new conclusions. Studies show that only the hostility and anger associated with Type A behavior are actually associated with the negative effects of stress. And Type Bs are just as susceptible to the same anxiety-producing elements. For managers, what is important is to recognize that Type A employees are more likely to show symptoms of stress, even if organizational and personal stressors are low.

How Can Stress Be Reduced?

As mentioned earlier, not all stress is dysfunctional. Since stress can never be totally eliminated from a person's life, managers want to reduce the stress that leads to dysfunctional work behavior. How? Through controlling certain organizational factors to reduce job-related stress, and to a more limited extent, offering help for personal stress.

Things that managers can do in terms of job-related factors begin with employee selection. Managers need to make sure that an employee's abilities match the job requirements. When employees are in over their heads, their stress levels typically will be high. A realistic job preview during the selection process can minimize stress by reducing ambiguity over job expectations. Improved organizational communications will keep ambiguity-induced stress to a minimum. Similarly, a performance planning program such as MBO will clarify job responsibilities, provide clear performance goals, and reduce ambiguity through feedback. Job redesign is also a way to reduce stress. If stress can be traced to boredom or to work overload, jobs should be redesigned to increase challenge or to reduce the workload. Redesigns that increase opportunities for employees to participate in decisions and to gain social support also have been found to lessen stress.[27] For instance, at U.K. pharmaceutical maker GlaxoSmithKline, a team-resilience program in which employees can shift assignments depending on people's workload and deadlines has helped reduce work-related stress by 60 percent.[28]

No matter what you do to eliminate organizational stressors, some employees will still be "stressed out." And stress from an employee's personal life raises two problems. First, it's difficult for the manager to control directly. Second, there are ethical considerations. Specifically, does the manager have the right to intrude—even in the most subtle ways—in an employee's personal life? If a manager believes it's ethical and the employee is receptive, there are a few approaches the manager can consider.

To help deal with these issues, many companies offer employee assistance and wellness programs.[29] These employer-sponsored programs are designed to assist employees in areas where they might be having difficulties such as financial planning, legal matters, health, fitness, or stress.[30]

Right or Wrong?

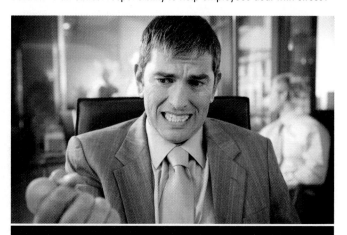

One in five companies offers some form of stress management program.[26] Although such programs are available, many employees may choose not to participate. They may be reluctant to ask for help, especially if a major source of that stress is job insecurity. After all, there's still a stigma associated with stress. Employees don't want to be perceived as being unable to handle the demands of their job. Although they may need stress management now more than ever, few employees want to admit that they're stressed. What can be done about this paradox? Do organizations even *have* an ethical responsibility to help employees deal with stress?

---

karoshi
A Japanese term that refers to a sudden death caused by overworking.

stressors
Factors that cause stress.

role conflicts
Work expectations that are hard to satisfy.

role overload
Having more work to accomplish than time permits.

role ambiguity
When role expectations are not clearly understood.

Type A personality
People who have a chronic sense of urgency and an excessive competitive drive.

Type B personality
People who are relaxed and easygoing and accept change easily.

Contemporary **employee assistance programs (EAPs)** are extensions of programs that began in U.S. companies in the 1940s.[31] Companies such as DuPont, Standard Oil, and Kodak recognized that a number of their employees were experiencing problems with alcohol. Formal programs were implemented on the company's site to educate these workers about the dangers of alcohol and to help them overcome their addiction. The rationale for these programs, which still holds today, is getting a productive employee back on the job as quickly as possible. An organization also can benefit in terms of a return on investment. It's estimated that U.S. companies spend almost $1 billion each year on EAP programs. Studies suggest that most of these companies save up to $5 to $16 for every EAP dollar spent.[32] That's a significant return on investment!

In addition to EAP, many organizations are implementing wellness programs. A **wellness program** is designed to keep employees healthy.[33] These programs vary and may focus on such things as smoking cessation, weight control, stress management, physical fitness, nutrition education, high-blood-pressure control, violence protection, work team problem intervention, and so on.[34] Wellness programs are designed to help cut employer health costs and to lower absenteeism and turnover by preventing health-related problems.[35]

How Can Managers Encourage Innovation in an Organization?

7.4 Discuss techniques for stimulating innovation.

"The way you will thrive in this environment is by innovating—innovating in technologies, innovating in strategies, innovating in business models."[36] That's the message IBM's CEO Sam Palmisano delivered to an audience of executives at an innovation-themed leadership conference. And how true it is! Success in business today demands innovation. Such is the rallying cry of today's managers! In the dynamic, chaotic world of global competition, organizations must create new products and services and adopt state-of-the-art technology if they're going to compete successfully.[37]

What companies come to mind when you think of successful innovators? Maybe Sony Corporation, with its MiniDisks, PlayStations, AIBO robot pets, Cyber-shot digital cameras, and MiniDV Handycam camcorders. Maybe Toyota with its continual advancements in product and manufacturing process designs. What's the secret to the success of these innovator champions? What can other managers do to make their organizations more innovative? In the following pages, we'll try to answer those questions as we discuss the factors behind innovation.

How Are Creativity and Innovation Related?

Creativity refers to the ability to combine ideas in a unique way or to make unusual associations between ideas.[38] A creative organization develops unique ways of working or novel solutions to problems. For instance, at Mattel, company officials introduced "Project Platypus," a special group that brings people from all disciplines—engineering, marketing, design, and sales—and tries to get them to "think outside the box" in order to "understand the sociology and psychology behind children's play patterns." To help make this kind of thinking happen, team members embarked on such activities as imagination exercises, group crying, and stuffed-bunny throwing. What does throwing stuffed bunnies have to do with creativity? It's part of a juggling lesson where team members tried to learn to juggle two balls and a stuffed bunny. Most people can easily learn to juggle two balls but can't let go of that third object. Creativity, like juggling, is learning to let go—that is, to "throw the bunny."[39] But creativity by itself isn't enough. The outcomes of the creative process need to be turned into useful products or work methods, which is defined as **innovation**. Thus, the innovative organization is characterized by its ability to channel creativity into useful outcomes. When managers talk about changing an organization to make it more creative, they usually mean they want to stimulate and nurture innovation.

What's Involved in Innovation?

Some people believe that creativity is inborn; others believe that with training, anyone can be creative. The latter group views creativity as a fourfold process consisting of perception, incubation, inspiration, and innovation.[40]

Perception involves the way you see things. Being creative means seeing things from a unique perspective. One person may see solutions to a problem that others cannot or will not see at all. The movement from perception to reality, however, doesn't occur instantaneously. Instead, ideas go though a process of *incubation*. Sometimes employees need to sit on their ideas, which doesn't mean sitting and doing nothing. Rather, during this incubation period, employees should collect massive amounts of data that are stored, retrieved, studied, reshaped, and finally molded into something new. During this period, it's common for years to pass. Think for a moment about a time you struggled for an answer on a test. Although you tried hard to jog your memory, nothing worked. Then suddenly, like a flash of light, the answer popped into your head. You found it! *Inspiration* in the creative process is similar. Inspiration is the moment when all your efforts successfully come together.

Although inspiration leads to euphoria, the creative work isn't complete. It requires an innovative effort. *Innovation* involves taking that inspiration and turning it into a useful product, service, or way of doing things. Thomas Edison is often credited with saying that "Creativity is 1 percent inspiration and 99 percent perspiration." That 99 percent, or the innovation, involves testing, evaluating, and retesting what the inspiration found. It's usually at this stage that an individual involves others more in what he or she has been working on. Such involvement is critical because even the greatest invention may be delayed, or lost, if an individual cannot effectively deal with others in communicating and achieving what the creative idea is supposed to do.

How Can a Manager Foster Innovation?

The systems model (inputs → transformation process → outputs) can help us understand how organizations become more innovative.[41] If an organization wants innovative products and work methods (*outputs*), it has to take its *inputs* and *transform* them into those outputs. Those *inputs* include creative people and groups within the organization. But as we said earlier, having creative people isn't enough. The *transformation process* requires having the right environment to turn those inputs into innovative products or work methods. This "right" environment—that is, an environment that stimulates innovation—includes three variables: the organization's structure, culture, and human resource practices. (See Exhibit 7-5.)

HOW DO STRUCTURAL VARIABLES AFFECT INNOVATION? Research into the effect of structural variables on innovation shows five things.[42] First, an organic-type structure positively influences innovation. Because this structure is low in formalization, centralization, and work specialization, it facilitates the flexibility and sharing of ideas that are critical to innovation. Second, the availability of plentiful resources provides a key building block for innovation. With an abundance of resources, managers can afford to purchase innovations, can afford the cost of instituting innovations, and can absorb failures. Third, frequent communication between organizational units helps break down barriers to innovation.[43] Cross-functional teams, task forces, and other such organizational designs facilitate interaction across departmental lines and are widely used in innovative organizations. Fourth, innovative organizations try to minimize extreme time pressures on creative activities

employee assistance programs (EAPs)
Programs offered by organizations to help employees overcome personal and health-related problems.

wellness programs
Programs offered by organizations to help employees prevent health problems.

creativity
The ability to combine ideas in a unique way or to make unusual associations between ideas.

innovation
The process of taking a creative idea and turning it into a useful product, service, or method of operation.

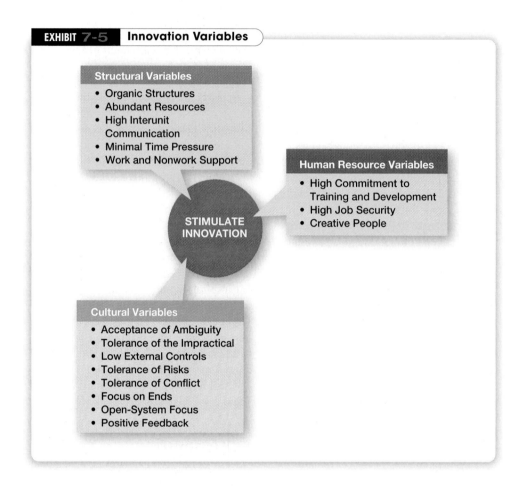

EXHIBIT 7-5   Innovation Variables

Structural Variables
- Organic Structures
- Abundant Resources
- High Interunit Communication
- Minimal Time Pressure
- Work and Nonwork Support

STIMULATE INNOVATION

Human Resource Variables
- High Commitment to Training and Development
- High Job Security
- Creative People

Cultural Variables
- Acceptance of Ambiguity
- Tolerance of the Impractical
- Low External Controls
- Tolerance of Risks
- Tolerance of Conflict
- Focus on Ends
- Open-System Focus
- Positive Feedback

despite the demands of white-water rapids environments. Although time pressures may spur people to work harder and may make them feel more creative, studies show that it actually causes them to be less creative.[44] Finally, studies have shown that an employee's creative performance was enhanced when an organization's structure explicitly supported creativity. Beneficial kinds of support included things like encouragement, open communication, readiness to listen, and useful feedback.[45]

HOW DOES AN ORGANIZATION'S CULTURE AFFECT INNOVATION? Innovative organizations tend to have similar cultures.[46] They encourage experimentation; reward both successes and failures; and celebrate mistakes. An innovative organization is likely to have the following characteristics.

▶ *Accept ambiguity.* Too much emphasis on objectivity and specificity constrains creativity.

▶ *Tolerate the impractical.* Individuals who offer impractical, even foolish, answers to what-if questions are not stifled. What at first seems impractical might lead to innovative solutions.

▶ *Keep external controls minimal.* Rules, regulations, policies, and similar organizational controls are kept to a minimum.

▶ *Tolerate risk.* Employees are encouraged to experiment without fear of consequences should they fail. Mistakes are treated as learning opportunities.

▶ *Tolerate conflict.* Diversity of opinions is encouraged. Harmony and agreement between individuals or units are *not* assumed to be evidence of high performance.

▶ *Focus on ends rather than means.* Goals are made clear, and individuals are encouraged to consider alternative routes toward meeting the goals. Focusing on ends suggests that there might be several right answers to any given problem.

▶ *Use an open-system focus.* Managers closely monitor the environment and respond to changes as they occur. For example, at Starbucks, product development depends on "inspiration field trips to view customers and trends." Michelle Gass, now the company's executive vice president of marketing, "took her team to Paris, Düsseldorf, and London to visit local Starbucks and other restaurants to get a better sense of local cultures, behaviors, and fashions." She says, "You come back just full of different ideas and different ways to think about things than you would had you read about it in a magazine or e-mail."[47]

▶ *Provide positive feedback.* Managers provide positive feedback, encouragement, and support so employees feel that their creative ideas receive attention. For instance, at Research In Motion, Mike Lazaridis, president and co-CEO says, "I think we have a culture of innovation here, and [engineers] have absolute access to me. I live a life that tries to promote innovation."[48]

WHAT HUMAN RESOURCE VARIABLES AFFECT INNOVATION? In this category, we find that innovative organizations actively promote the training and development of their members so their knowledge remains current; offer their employees high job security to reduce the fear of getting fired for making mistakes; and encourage individuals to become **idea champions**, actively and enthusiastically supporting new ideas, building support, overcoming resistance, and ensuring that innovations are implemented. Research finds that idea champions have common personality characteristics: extremely high self-confidence, persistence, energy, and a tendency toward risk taking. They also display characteristics associated with dynamic leadership. They inspire and energize others with their vision of the potential of an innovation and through their strong personal conviction in their mission. They're also good at gaining the commitment of others to support their mission. In addition, idea champions have jobs that provide considerable decision-making discretion. This autonomy helps them introduce and implement innovations in organizations.[49]

Innovation is paramount at Facebook, and the company's culture stimulates the process of taking a creative idea and turning it into useful products and services. Like other innovative organizations, Facebook encourages experimentation and tolerance of conflict and risk and keeps rules and regulations at a minimum. The company insists that employees act like pioneers, asking questions no one has asked before and identifying new opportunities. At Facebook, part of the innovative process involves cutting loose and having fun, such as the employee shown here taking a brief break from work to play.

idea champions
Individuals who actively and enthusiastically support new ideas, build support for, overcome resistance to, and ensure that innovations are implemented.

Review and ⑦ Applications

Chapter Summary

7.1 **Define organizational change and compare and contrast views on the change process.** Organizational change is any alteration of an organization's people, structure, or technology. The "calm waters" metaphor of change suggests that change is an occasional disruption in the normal flow of events and can be planned and managed as it happens using Lewin's three-step change process (unfreezing, changing, and freezing). The "white-water rapids" view of change suggests that change is ongoing, and managing it is a continual process.

7.2 **Explain how to manage resistance to change.** People resist change because of uncertainty, habit, concern about personal loss, and the belief that a change is not in the organization's best interests. Techniques for managing resistance to change include education and communication (educating employees about and communicating to them the need for the change), participation (allowing employees to participate in the change process), facilitation and support (giving employees the support they need to implement the change), negotiation (exchanging something of value to reduce resistance), manipulation and co-optation (using negative actions to influence), selecting people who are open to and accept change, and coercion (using direct threats or force).

7.3 **Describe what managers need to know about employee stress.** Stress is the adverse reaction people have to excessive pressure placed on them from extraordinary demands, constraints, or opportunities.

The symptoms of stress can be physical, psychological, or behavioral. Stress can be caused by personal factors and by job-related factors. To help employees deal with stress, managers can address job-related factors by making sure an employee's abilities match the job requirements, improve organizational communications, use a performance planning program, or redesign jobs. Addressing personal stress factors is trickier, but managers could offer employee counseling, time management programs, and wellness programs.

7.4 **Discuss techniques for stimulating innovation.** Creativity is the ability to combine ideas in a unique way or to make unusual associations between ideas. Innovation is turning the outcomes of the creative process into useful products or work methods. An innovative environment encompasses structural, cultural, and human resource variables.

Important structural variables include an organic-type structure, abundant resources, frequent communication between organizational units, minimal time pressure, and support. Important cultural variables include accept ambiguity, tolerate the impractical, keep external controls minimal, tolerate risk, tolerate conflict, focus on ends not means, use an open-system focus, and provide positive feedback. Important human resource variables include high commitment to training and development, high job security, and encouraging individuals to be idea champions.

PEARSON
mymanagementlab To check your understanding of learning outcomes **7.1** – **7.4**, go to **mymanagementlab.com** and try the chapter questions.

Understanding the Chapter

1. Why is managing change an integral part of every manager's job?

2. Describe Lewin's three-step change process. How is it different from the change process needed in the white-water rapids metaphor of change?

3. How are opportunities, constraints, and demands related to stress? Give an example of each.

4. Organizations typically have limits to how much change they can absorb. As a manager, what signs would you look for that might suggest your organization has exceeded its capacity to change?

5. Why is organization development planned change? Explain how planned change is important for organizations in today's dynamic environment.

6. How do creativity and innovation differ? Give an example of each.

7. Research information on how to be a more creative person. Write down suggestions in a bulleted list format and be prepared to present your information in class.

8. How does an innovative culture make an organization more effective? Do you think an innovative culture could ever make an organization less effective? Why or why not?

9. When you find yourself experiencing dysfunctional stress, write down what's causing the stress, what stress symptoms you're exhibiting, and how you're dealing with the stress. Keep this information in a journal and evaluate how well your stress reducers are working and how you could handle stress better. Your goal is to get to a point where you recognize that you're stressed and can take positive actions to deal with the stress.

Understanding Yourself

Am I Burned Out?

Burnout is when you've reached an overwhelming level of chronic and long-term stress. It can lead to exhaustion and diminished interest in activities, both work and personal. This instrument was designed to provide insights into whether you're suffering from burnout.

INSTRUMENT   Respond to each of the 21 items using the following scale:

1 = Never
2 = Once in a while
3 = Rarely
4 = Sometimes
5 = Often
6 = Usually
7 = Always

How often do you have any of the following experiences?

		1	2	3	4	5	6	7
1.	Being tired	1	2	3	4	5	6	7
2.	Feeling depressed	1	2	3	4	5	6	7
3.	Having a good day	1	2	3	4	5	6	7
4.	Being physically exhausted	1	2	3	4	5	6	7
5.	Being emotionally exhausted	1	2	3	4	5	6	7
6.	Being happy	1	2	3	4	5	6	7
7.	Being "wiped out"	1	2	3	4	5	6	7
8.	"Can't take it anymore"	1	2	3	4	5	6	7
9.	Being unhappy	1	2	3	4	5	6	7
10.	Feeling run-down	1	2	3	4	5	6	7
11.	Feeling trapped	1	2	3	4	5	6	7
12.	Feeling worthless	1	2	3	4	5	6	7
13.	Being weary	1	2	3	4	5	6	7
14.	Being troubled	1	2	3	4	5	6	7
15.	Feeling disillusioned and resentful	1	2	3	4	5	6	7
16.	Being weak and susceptible to illness	1	2	3	4	5	6	7
17.	Feeling hopeless	1	2	3	4	5	6	7
18.	Feeling rejected	1	2	3	4	5	6	7
19.	Feeling optimistic	1	2	3	4	5	6	7
20.	Feeling energetic	1	2	3	4	5	6	7
21.	Feeling anxious	1	2	3	4	5	6	7

SCORING KEY   To calculate your burnout score, add up your score for items 3, 6, 19, and 20. Then subtract that total from 32. To this number, add your direct scores for the remaining 17 items. Finally, divide this combined number by 21.

ANALYSIS AND INTERPRETATION   Your burnout score will be somewhere between 1 and 7. The higher your number, the closer you are to burnout. The authors claim that scores below 3 indicate few signs of burnout. Scores between 3 and 4 suggest the need to examine your work life and reevaluate priorities with the intent of making changes. If your score is higher than 4, you are experiencing a number of signs associated with burnout. You need to take some action to address your problems. Scores above 5 indicate an acute state, requiring immediate professional attention.

Source: A. Pines and E. Aronson, "Why Managers Burn Out," *Sales & Marketing Management* (February 1989), p. 38.

FYIA (For Your Immediate Action)

Performance Pros

Reply   Reply All   Forward

To:	Tina Sanchez, HR Director
From:	Aaron Scott, President
Subject:	**Employee Stress Management Program**

Well, Tina, we've made it through the initial phases of our restructuring efforts. The changes haven't been easy on any of us. But we've still got a long way to go, and that's where I need your assistance. To help minimize the pressures on our software developers and sales staff, I think we need to develop an employee stress management program that we could implement immediately. Our finances are such that we don't have a lot of excess funds available to spend on fitness equipment, so you're going to have to work within that constraint. Could you put together a brief (no more than one page) outline of what you think this program should include? Also, note the benefits you think each of your suggestions would provide. I'd like some time to review your suggestions over the weekend, so please get me your report as soon as possible.

This fictionalized company and message were created for educational purposes only. It is not meant to reflect positively or negatively on management practices by any company that may share this name.

TREASURE FROM TRASH

Eighteen thousand expired cans of sardines. A complete McDonald's McHappy Land play set. Fifty garden gnomes. That's just a sampling of some of the weird stuff that 1-800-GOT-JUNK? customers have asked the uniformed people in the freshly scrubbed blue trucks to haul away. Based in Vancouver, British Columbia, Brian Scudamore, company founder and CEO says, "With a vision of creating the 'FedEx' of junk removal, I dropped out of university with just one year left to become a full-time JUNKMAN! Yes, my father, a liver transplant surgeon, was not impressed to say the least." By the end of 2008, however, the company had over 340 franchises in the United States, Canada, and Australia, and system-wide revenues of over $125 million.

Scudamore's company has been described as a "curious hybrid" that blends the old and new economies. Although its product—hauling trash—has been done for hundreds of years, it relies heavily on sophisticated information technology and has the kind of organizational culture that most people associate with high-tech start-ups.

Information systems and technology have been important to the company's growth. Scudamore says, "It has allowed us to expand all over North America. Our system has made the process easier." The company's call center does all the booking and dispatching for franchise partners. They also use the proprietary intranet to access schedules, customer information, real-time reports, and so forth. Needless to say, the company's franchise partners tend to be pretty tech-savvy.

In addition, the company's culture is a unique blend of fun and seriousness. There's a quote posted in the head office that says "It's all about people." And those four simple words sum up Scudamore's philosophy: Find the right people and treat them right. Since 2004, the company has been ranked by *BC Business* magazine as one of the best companies to work for in British Columbia. Grizzly, Scudamore's dog, comes to the office every day and helps employees relieve stress by playing catch anytime, anywhere. Each morning at exactly 10:55, all employees at headquarters meet for a five-minute huddle, where they share good news, announcements, metrics, and problems they're encountering. Visitors to the office are also expected to join in. The open-concept floor plan encourages communication among all levels of staff—from top to bottom, and embodies the importance of the team environment.

Discussion Questions

1. Do you think 1-800-GOT-JUNK? faces more of a calm waters or white-water rapids environment? Explain.

2. What external and internal forces might create the need for the company to change? Be specific in describing these.

3. Using Exhibit 7-5, how could Brian Scudamore stimulate and nurture innovation at headquarters and with company franchisees?

4. What could other organizations learn about managing change, stress, and innovation from 1-800-GOT-JUNK?

Sources: B. Scudamore, "All You Need Is Tough Love," *Profit,* December 2008/January 2009, p. 19; "Best Places to Work," *BC Business,* December 2008, p. 85; P. Severinson, "Interview with Launi Skinner," *BC Business,* September 2008, pp. 155–156; J. Straczewski, "Turning Up the Heat: Seeking a Solution to the Energy Price Squeeze," *Franchising World,* September 2008, pp. 40–43; S. Kilcarr, "Small Players, Big Ideas," *Waste Age,* September 2008, pp. 44–50; "Honor Roll," *Entrepreneur,* July 2008, p. 100; J. Johnson, "1-800-Got Growth," *Waste News,* June 9, 2008, p. 3; B. Scudamore, "Changing of the Guard," *Profit,* June 2008, p. 22; J. Hainsworth, *The Associated Press,* "Canadian Company Finds Treasure in People's Trash," *Springfield, Missouri News-Leader,* April 24, 2006, p. 5B; and G. Stoller, "Rubbish Boy Turned Junk into His Career," *USA Today,* June 13, 2005, p. 7B.

8 CHAPTER

Foundations of Individual Behavior

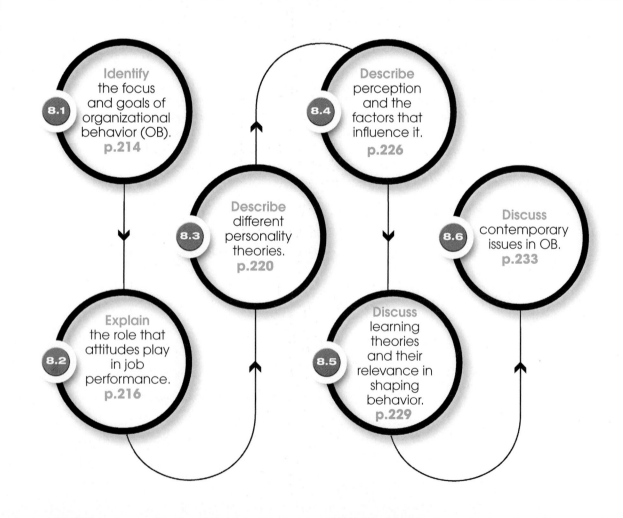

8.1 Identify the focus and goals of organizational behavior (OB). **p.214**

8.2 Explain the role that attitudes play in job performance. **p.216**

8.3 Describe different personality theories. **p.220**

8.4 Describe perception and the factors that influence it. **p.226**

8.5 Discuss learning theories and their relevance in shaping behavior. **p.229**

8.6 Discuss contemporary issues in OB. **p.233**

Towels, Severance, and Morale...Oh My

Like many revolts, it began with something simple.[1] At Microsoft, it was the vanishing towels. For employees who biked to work through the often-drizzly weather in Seattle, the provided towels had become an entitlement. However, one day when employees came to work, the towels were gone . . . pulled without notice from the locker rooms in the company's underground garage. The company's human resources manager thought removing the towels, which had been done as a cost-saving measure, "wouldn't even be a blip." But it was. Irate employees waged war on company message boards and blogs. One post fumed, "It is a dark and dreary day at One Microsoft Way. Do yourself a favor and stay away." The intensity of the comments shocked senior executives. The towel fiasco, in conjunction with a languishing stock price and a little bit of "Google envy," suggested a serious morale problem and a need to bring in a new face to HR. Lisa Brummel (see photo below), a successful Microsoft product development manager with no HR experience, was tapped to become the new HR chief. Her mandate: Improve the mood around here. And Lisa, who had always been a strong people leader, stepped up to do just that.

In addition to reinstating the towels (a no-brainer), Lisa looked for other ways that the company could reshape HR at Microsoft. And in doing so, she brought a unique and insightful understanding of human behavior. One thing she did was to introduce innovative office designs that allowed employees to reconfigure their workspaces for the task they were working on. The customized workspaces included options such as sliding doors, movable walls, and features that made the space seem more like an urban loft than an office. When beginning a workspace redesign, "employees are first divided into four worker types: providers (the godfathers of work groups), travelers (the types who work anywhere but work), concentrators (head-down, always-at-work types), and orchestrators (the company's natural diplomats)." Based on their "type," employees then pick the kind of workspace that works best for them. By allowing their creative, quirky, and talented people freedom to design their workspaces, the company was able to give them some control over their chaotic and often hectic environment.

With Lisa at the helm of HR, the company has made progress in its people policies. Yet, sometimes a decision coming out of One Microsoft Way (company headquarters) still makes you scratch your head and wonder why. The most recent was when 25 recently laid-off employees were asked to return an overpayment of severance pay. The amount, a small sum, amounted to about $5,000 per employee. But by asking for this money back, this billion-dollar organization didn't send a very good message, especially when trying to improve morale and keep employees excited and engaged with their work. Once again, Lisa stepped up. She made the calls to the employees involved and said that the company hadn't handled the situation in a "thoughtful manner" and the money was theirs to keep. Like any successful manager, Lisa recognizes the importance of people skills.

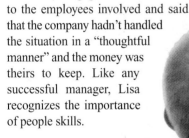

Lisa Brummel had a bit of a people challenge! Like her, most managers want employees with the right attitudes and personality. They want people who show up and work hard, get along with coworkers and customers, have good attitudes, and exhibit good work behaviors in other ways. But as you're probably already aware, people don't always behave like that "ideal" employee. They post critical comments in blogs. They complain over missing towels. People differ in their behaviors and even the same person can behave one way one day and a completely different way another day. For instance, haven't you seen family members, friends, or coworkers behave in ways that prompted you to wonder: Why did they do that? In this chapter, we look at four psychological aspects—attitudes, personality, perception, and learning—and demonstrate how these things can help managers understand the behavior of those people with whom they have to work. We conclude the chapter by looking at contemporary behavioral issues facing managers.

What Are the Focus and Goals of Organizational Behavior?

8.1 Identify the focus and goals of organizational behavior (OB).

The material in this and the next four chapters draws heavily on the field of study that's known as *organizational behavior (OB)*. Although it's concerned with the subject of **behavior**—that is, the actions of people— **organizational behavior** is the study of the actions of people at work.

One of the challenges in understanding organizational behavior is that it addresses issues that aren't obvious. Like an iceberg, OB has a small visible dimension and a much larger hidden portion. (See Exhibit 8-1.) What we see when we look at an organization is its visible aspects: strategies, goals, policies and procedures, structure, technology, formal authority relationships, and chain of command. But under the surface are other elements that managers need to understand—elements that also influence how employees behave at work. As we'll show, OB provides managers with considerable insights into these important, but hidden, aspects of the organization.

EXHIBIT 8-1   **Organization as Iceberg**

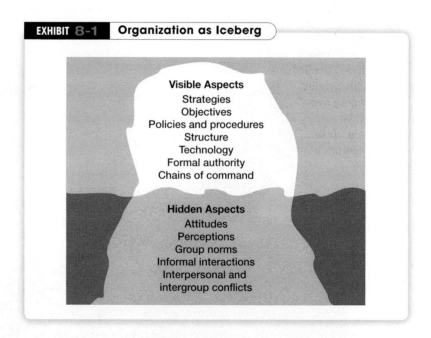

Visible Aspects
Strategies
Objectives
Policies and procedures
Structure
Technology
Formal authority
Chains of command

Hidden Aspects
Attitudes
Perceptions
Group norms
Informal interactions
Interpersonal and
intergroup conflicts

What Is the Focus of OB?

Organizational behavior focuses on three major areas. First, OB looks at *individual behavior*. Based predominantly on contributions from psychologists, this area includes such topics as attitudes, personality, perception, learning, and motivation. Second, OB is concerned with *group behavior*, which includes norms, roles, team building, leadership, and conflict. Our knowledge about groups comes basically from the work of sociologists and social psychologists. Finally, OB also looks at *organizational* aspects including structure, culture, and human resource policies and practices. We've addressed organizational aspects in previous chapters. In this chapter, we'll look at individual behavior and in the following chapter, at group behavior.

What Are the Goals of Organizational Behavior?

The goals of OB are to *explain, predict,* and *influence* behavior. Managers need to be able to *explain* why employees engage in some behaviors rather than others, *predict* how employees will respond to various actions and decisions, and *influence* how employees behave.

What employee behaviors are we specifically concerned with explaining, predicting, and influencing? Six important ones have been identified: employee productivity, absenteeism, turnover, organizational citizenship behavior (OCB), job satisfaction, and workplace misbehavior. **Employee productivity** is a performance measure of both work efficiency and effectiveness. Managers want to know what factors will influence the efficiency and effectiveness of employees. **Absenteeism** is the failure to show up for work. It's difficult for work to get done if employees don't show up. Studies have shown that unscheduled absences cost companies around $660 per employee per year.[2] Although absenteeism can't be totally eliminated, excessive levels have a direct and immediate impact on the organization's functioning. **Turnover** is the voluntary and involuntary permanent withdrawal from an organization. It can be a problem because of increased recruiting, selection, and training costs and work disruptions. Just like absenteeism, managers can never eliminate turnover, but it is something they want to minimize, especially among high-performing employees. **Organizational citizenship behavior** is discretionary behavior that's not part of an employee's formal job requirements, but which promotes the effective functioning of the organization.[3] Examples of good OCB include helping others on one's work team, volunteering for extended job activities, avoiding unnecessary conflicts, and making constructive statements about one's work group and the organization. Organizations need individuals who will do more than their usual job duties, and the evidence indicates that organizations that have such employees outperform those that don't.[4] However, there are drawbacks to OCB as employees may experience work overload, stress, and work/life conflicts.[5] **Job satisfaction** refers to an employee's general attitude toward his or her job. Although job satisfaction is an attitude rather than a behavior, it's an outcome that concerns many managers because satisfied employees are more

Mitsue Endo's job at Japan's Keihin Express Railway is helping lost customers find their way and resolving ticket problems at a Tokyo station used by 250,000 riders each day. Before beginning work, she uses a "smile" machine, a laptop computer with a digital camera mounted on top that instantly gives her a smile score. Although the smile test is optional and smiling is not part of Endo's formal job description, she uses it to improve her interactions with rushed and often agitated passengers. Endo believes that presenting a happy face is a constructive behavior that creates a more relaxed environment for customers and sheds a positive light on her company's goal of improving customer service.

---

behavior
The actions of people.
organizational behavior
The study of the actions of people at work.
employee productivity
A performance measure of both work efficiency and effectiveness.

absenteeism
The failure to show up for work.
turnover
Voluntary and involuntary permanent withdrawal from an organization.

organizational citizenship behavior
Discretionary behavior that's not part of an employee's formal job requirements, but which promotes the effective functioning of the organization.
job satisfaction
An employee's general attitude toward his or her job.

likely to show up for work, have higher levels of performance, and stay with an organization. **Workplace misbehavior** is any intentional employee behavior that is potentially harmful to the organization or individuals within the organization. Workplace misbehavior shows up in organizations in four ways: deviance, aggression, antisocial behavior, and violence.[6] Such behaviors can range from playing loud music just to irritate coworkers to verbal aggression to sabotaging work, all of which can create havoc in any organization. In the following pages, we'll address how an understanding of four psychological factors—employee attitudes, personality, perception, and learning—can help us predict and explain these employee behaviors.

What Role Do Attitudes Play in Job Performance?

8.2 Explain the role that attitudes play in job performance.

Attitudes are evaluative statements, either favorable or unfavorable, concerning objects, people, or events. They reflect how an individual feels about something. When a person says, "I like my job," he or she is expressing an attitude about work.

What Are the Three Components of an Attitude?

To better understand attitude, we need to look at its three components: cognition, affect, and behavior.[7] The **cognitive component** of an attitude is made up of the beliefs, opinions, knowledge, and information held by a person. For example, shortly after the September 11, 2001, attacks on the World Trade Center and the Pentagon, Congress spent weeks debating whether airport baggage screeners should be federal employees. Some claimed the current private airport screeners were adequately doing their jobs, even though evidence presented during the debate showed that knives, pepper spray, and a loaded gun were missed by airport screeners.[8] The belief held by some congressional leaders that private screeners were effective is an example of cognition. The **affective component** is the emotional or feeling part of an attitude. This component would be reflected in the statement, "I don't *like* Erica because she smokes." Cognition and affect can lead to behavioral outcomes. The **behavioral component** of an attitude refers to an intention to behave in a certain way toward someone or something. So, to continue our example, I might choose to avoid Erica because of my feelings about her. Looking at attitudes as being made up of three components—cognition, affect, and behavior—helps to illustrate the complexity of attitudes. For the sake of clarity, keep in mind that the term usually refers only to the affective component.

What Attitudes Might Employees Hold?

Naturally, managers are not interested in every attitude an employee might hold. Rather, they're specifically interested in job-related attitudes, and the three most important and most studied are job satisfaction, job involvement, and organizational commitment.[9] Job satisfaction is an employee's general attitude toward his or her job. When people speak of employee attitudes, more often than not they mean job satisfaction. **Job involvement** is the degree to which an employee identifies with his or her job, actively participates in it, and considers his or her job performance important for self-worth. Finally, **organizational commitment** represents an employee's orientation toward the organization in terms of his or her loyalty to, identification with, and involvement in the organization.

A new concept associated with job attitudes that's generating widespread interest is **employee engagement**, which is when employees are connected to, satisfied with, and enthusiastic about their jobs.[10] Highly engaged employees are passionate about and deeply connected to their work. Disengaged employees have essentially "checked out" and don't care. They show up for work, but have no energy or passion for it. Exhibit 8-2 lists the key engagement factors found in a global study of over 12,000 employees.

There are benefits to having highly engaged employees. First, highly engaged employees are two-and-a-half times more likely to be top performers than their less-engaged

| EXHIBIT 8-2 | Key Employee Engagement Factors |

Globally, respect ranks as the no. 1 factor contributing to employee engagement.

	GLOBAL	CHINA	FRANCE	GERMANY	INDIA	JAPAN	U.K.	U.S.
Respect	125	121	133	129	104	90	144	122
Type of Work	112	75	138	113	116	107	122	112
Work/Life Balance	112	98	133	106	97	119	119	111
Provide Good Service to Customers	108	108	110	108	103	79	122	107
Base Pay	108	113	110	105	103	140	117	114
People You Work With	107	96	105	131	98	107	120	104
Benefits	94	127	81	110	94	75	76	112
Long-Term Career Potential	92	91	89	77	108	94	88	92
Learning and Development	91	83	67	80	98	86	85	82
Flexible Working	87	85	77	92	80	88	83	88
Promotion Opportunities	85	92	79	83	113	92	68	80
Variable Pay/Bonus	80	111	77	65	86	123	56	75

Note: Scores near 100 are middle importance, scores below 100 are less important, scores above 100 are more important.
Source: Mercer; *IndustryWeek,* April 2008, p. 24.

coworkers. In addition, companies with highly engaged employees have higher retention rates, which help keep recruiting and training costs low. And both of these outcomes—higher performance and lower costs—contribute to superior financial performance.[11]

Do an Individual's Attitude and Behavior Need to Be Consistent?

Did you ever notice how people change what they say so that it doesn't contradict what they do? Perhaps a friend of yours had consistently argued that American-manufactured cars were poorly built and that he'd never own anything but a foreign import. Then his parents gave him a late model American-made car, and suddenly they weren't so bad. Or, when going through sorority rush, a new freshman believes that sororities are good and that pledging a sorority is important. If she's not accepted by a sorority, however, she may say, "I recognized that sorority life isn't all it's cracked up to be, anyway."

Research generally concludes that people seek consistency among their attitudes and between their attitudes and their behavior.[12] Individuals try to reconcile differing attitudes and align their attitudes and behavior so that they appear rational and consistent. They do so by altering either the attitudes or the behavior or by developing a rationalization for the discrepancy.

workplace misbehavior
Any intentional employee behavior that is potentially harmful to the organization or individuals within the organization.

attitudes
Evaluative statements, either favorable or unfavorable, concerning objects, people, or events.

cognitive component
The part of an attitude made up of the beliefs, opinions, knowledge, and information held by a person.

affective component
The part of an attitude that's the emotional or feeling part.

behavioral component
The part of an attitude that refers to an intention to behave in a certain way toward someone or something.

job involvement
The degree to which an employee identifies with his or her job, actively participates in it, and considers his or her job performance important for self-worth.

organizational commitment
An employee's orientation toward the organization in terms of his or her loyalty to, identification with, and involvement in the organization.

employee engagement
When employees are connected to, satisfied with, and enthusiastic about their jobs.

What Is Cognitive Dissonance Theory?

Can we assume from this consistency principle that an individual's behavior can always be predicted if we know his or her attitude on a subject? The answer isn't a simple "yes" or "no." Why? Cognitive dissonance theory.

Cognitive dissonance theory, proposed by Leon Festinger in the 1950s, sought to explain the relationship between attitudes and behavior.[13] **Cognitive dissonance** is any incompatibility or inconsistency between attitudes or between behavior and attitudes. The theory argued that inconsistency is uncomfortable and that individuals will try to reduce the discomfort and thus, the dissonance.

Of course, no one can avoid dissonance. You know you should floss your teeth every day, but you don't do it. There's an inconsistency between attitude and behavior. How do people cope with cognitive dissonance? The theory proposed that how hard we'll try to reduce dissonance is determined by three things: (1) the *importance* of the factors creating the dissonance, (2) the degree of *influence* the individual believes he or she has over those factors, and (3) the *rewards* that may be involved in dissonance.

If the factors creating the dissonance are relatively unimportant, the pressure to correct the inconsistency will be low. However, if those factors are important, individuals may change their behavior, conclude that the dissonant behavior isn't so important, change their attitude, or identify compatible factors that outweigh the dissonant ones.

How much influence individuals believe they have over the factors also affects their reaction to the dissonance. If they perceive the dissonance is something about which they have no choice, they won't be receptive to attitude change or feel a need to do so. If, for example, the dissonance-producing behavior was required as a result of a manager's order, the pressure to reduce dissonance would be less than if the behavior had been performed voluntarily. Although dissonance exists, it can be rationalized and justified by the need to follow the manager's orders—that is, the person had no choice or control.

Finally, rewards also influence the degree to which individuals are motivated to reduce dissonance. Coupling high dissonance with high rewards tends to reduce the discomfort by motivating the individual to believe that there is consistency.

Let's look at an example. If the factors creating dissonance are relatively unimportant, the pressure to correct any imbalance would be low. However, say that a corporate manager, Tracey Ford, believes strongly that no company should lay off employees. Unfortunately, Tracey is placed in the position of having to make decisions that would trade off her company's strategic direction against her convictions on layoffs. She knows that, because of restructuring in the company, some jobs may no longer be needed, and the layoffs are in the best economic interest of her firm. What will she do? Undoubtedly, Tracey is experiencing a high degree of cognitive dissonance. Because of the *importance* of the issues in this example, we cannot expect her to ignore the inconsistency. To deal with her dilemma, she can follow several steps. She can change her behavior (lay off employees). Or she can reduce dissonance by concluding that the dissonant behavior is not so important after all ("I've got to make a living, and in my role as a decision maker, I often have to place the good of my company above that of individual organizational members"). A third alternative would be for Tracey to change her attitude ("There is nothing wrong in laying off employees"). Still another choice would be to seek out more consonant elements to outweigh the dissonant ones ("The long-term benefits to the surviving employees from our restructuring more than offset the costs associated with the retrenchment effort").

The *degree of influence* that individuals such as Tracey Ford believe they have over the elements also will

Cognitive dissonance refers to an inconsistency between attitudes and behaviors. For example, most people may believe that they are safe drivers, yet many may create potentially unsafe road conditions by driving and texting at the same time. To reduce the dissonance, these drivers may either stop their habit of driving and texting, or they may rationalize that driving and texting doesn't really pose any threat to others' safety, that they are in control of the situation, or that everyone else is doing the same thing.

have an impact on how they react to the dissonance. If they perceive the dissonance to be uncontrollable—something about which they have no choice—they are less likely to feel a need for an attitude change. If, for example, the dissonance-producing behavior were required by the boss's directive, the pressure to reduce dissonance would be less than if the behavior were performed voluntarily. Dissonance would exist, but it could be rationalized and justified. This is why it's so critical in today's organizations for leaders to establish the ethical culture. Without their influence and support, reducing dissonance toward ethical behaviors is lessened.[14] *Rewards* also influence the degree to which individuals are motivated to reduce dissonance. High dissonance, when accompanied by high rewards, tends to reduce the tension inherent in the dissonance. The reward reduces dissonance by adding to the consistency side of the individual's balance sheet.

These moderating factors suggest that although individuals experience dissonance, they will not necessarily move directly toward consistency, that is, toward reducing the dissonance. If the issues underlying the dissonance are of minimal importance, if an individual perceives that the dissonance is externally imposed and is substantially uncontrollable, or if rewards are significant enough to offset the dissonance, the individual will not be under great tension to reduce the dissonance.[16]

How Can an Understanding of Attitudes Help Managers Be More Effective?

Managers should be interested in their employees' attitudes because they influence behavior. Satisfied and committed employees, for instance, have lower rates of turnover and absenteeism. If managers want to keep resignations and absences down—especially among their more productive employees—they'll want to do things that generate positive job attitudes.

Whether satisfied workers are productive workers is a debate that's been going on for almost 80 years. After the Hawthorne Studies, managers believed that happy workers were productive workers. Since it's not been easy to determine whether job satisfaction "caused" job productivity or vice versa, some management researchers felt that belief was generally wrong. However, we can say with some certainty that the correlation between satisfaction and productivity is fairly strong.[17] Satisfied employees do perform better on the job. So managers should focus on those factors that have been shown to be conducive to high levels of employee job satisfaction: making work challenging and interesting, providing equitable rewards, and creating supportive working conditions and supportive colleagues.[18] These factors are likely to help employees be more productive.

Managers should also survey employees about their attitudes. As one study put it, "A sound measurement of overall job attitude is one of the most useful pieces of information an organization can have about its employees."[19]

Finally, managers should know that employees will try to reduce dissonance. If employees are required to do things that appear inconsistent to them or that are at odds with their attitudes, managers should remember that pressure to reduce the dissonance is not as strong when the employee perceives that the dissonance is externally imposed and uncontrollable. It's also decreased if rewards are significant enough to offset the dissonance. So the manager might point to external forces such as competitors, customers, or other factors when explaining the need to perform some work that the individual may have some dissonance about. Or the manager can provide rewards that an individual desires.

cognitive dissonance
Any incompatibility or inconsistency between attitudes or between behavior and attitudes.

What Do Managers Need to Know About Personality?

8.3 Describe different personality theories.

"Let's face it, dating is a drag. There was a time when we thought the computer was going to make it all better . . . But most of us learned the hard way that finding someone who shares our love of film noir and obscure garage bands does not a perfect match make."[20] Using in-depth personality assessment and profiling, Chemistry.com is trying to do something about making the whole dating process better.

Personality. We all have one. Some of us are quiet and passive; others are loud and aggressive. When we describe people using terms such as *quiet, passive, loud, aggressive, ambitious, extroverted, loyal, tense,* or *sociable,* we're describing their personalities. An individual's **personality** is a unique combination of emotional, thought, and behavioral patterns that affect how a person reacts to situations and interacts with others. Personality is most often described in terms of measurable traits that a person exhibits. We're interested in looking at personality because just like attitudes, it too affects how and why people behave the way they do.

Can Personality Predict Behavior?

Literally dozens of traits are attributed to an individual's behavior. So too are personality types as they show how people interact with one another and how they solve problems. Through the years, researchers attempted to focus specifically on which personality types and personality traits would identify information about the individual. Two of these efforts have been widely recognized—the Myers-Briggs Type Indicator® and the Big Five model of personality.

WHAT IS THE MYERS-BRIGGS TYPE INDICATOR? One of the more widely used methods of identifying personalities is the **Myers-Briggs Type Indicator (MBTI®)**. The MBTI® assessment uses four dichotomies of personality to identify 16 different personality types based on the responses to an approximately 100-item questionnaire. More than 2 million individuals take the MBTI® assessment each year in the United States alone. It's used in such companies as Apple, Honda, AT&T, Exxon, 3M, as well as many hospitals, educational institutions, and the U.S. Armed Forces.

The 16 personality types are based on the four dichotomies shown in Exhibit 8-3. That is, the MBTI® assessment dichotomies include Extraversion versus Introversion (EI), Sensing versus Intuition (SN), Thinking versus Feeling (TF), and Judging versus Perceiving (JP). The EI scale describes an individual's orientation toward the external world of the environment (E) or the inner world of ideas and experiences (I). The Sensing–Intuition scale indicates an individual's preference for gathering data while focusing on a standard routine based on factual data (S) to focusing on the big picture and making connections among the facts (N). Thinking–Feeling reflects one's preference for making decisions in a logical and analytical manner (T) or on the basis of values and beliefs and the effects the decision will have on others (F). The Judging–Perceiving scale reflects an attitude toward how one deals with the external world—either in a planned and orderly way (J) or preferring to remain flexible and spontaneous (P).[21]

How could the MBTI® assessment help managers? Proponents of the instrument believe that it's important to know these personality types because they influence the way people interact and solve problems.[22] For example, if your boss is an Intuition type and you're a Sensing type, you'll deal with information in different ways. An Intuition preference indicates your boss is one who prefers gut reactions, whereas you, as a Sensing type, prefer to deal with the facts. To work well with your boss, you have to present more than just facts about a situation—you'll also have to discuss your gut feeling about the situation. The MBTI® assessment has also been found to be useful in focusing on growth orientations for entrepreneurial types as well as profiles supporting emotional intelligence (something we'll look at shortly).[23]

EXHIBIT 8-3 Examples of MBTI® Types

		SENSING TYPES S		INTUITIVE TYPES N	
		THINKING T	FEELING F	FEELING F	THINKING T
INTROVERTS I	**JUDGING J**	**ISTJ** Quiet, serious, dependable, practical, matter-of-fact. Value traditions and loyalty.	**ISFJ** Quiet, friendly, responsible, thorough, considerate. Strive to create order and harmony.	**INFJ** Seek meaning and connection in ideas. Committed to firm values. Organized and decisive in implementing vision.	**INTJ** Have original minds and great drive for their ideas. Skeptical and independent. Have high standards of competence for self and others.
	PERCEIVING P	**ISTP** Tolerant and flexible. Interested in cause and effect. Value efficiency.	**ISFP** Quiet, friendly, sensitive. Like own space. Dislike disagreements and conflicts.	**INFP** Idealistic, loyal to their values. Seek to understand people and help them fulfill their potential.	**INTP** Seek logical explanations. Theoretical and abstract over social interactions. Skeptical, sometimes critical. Analytical.
EXTROVERTS E	**PERCEIVING P**	**ESTP** Flexible and tolerant. Focus on here and now. Enjoy material comforts. Learn best by doing.	**ESFP** Outgoing, friendly. Enjoy working with others. Spontaneous. Learn best by trying a new skill with other people.	**ENFP** Enthusiastic, imaginative. Want a lot of affirmation. Rely on verbal fluency and ability to improvise.	**ENTP** Quick, ingenious, stimulating. Adept at generating conceptual possibilities and analyzing them strategically. Bored by routine.
	JUDGING J	**ESTJ** Practical, realistic, matter-of-fact, decisive. Focus on getting efficient results. Forceful in implementing plans.	**ESFJ** Warmhearted, cooperative. Want to be appreciated for who they are and for what they contribute.	**ENFJ** Warm, responsive, responsible. Attuned to needs of others. Sociable, facilitate others, provide inspirational leadership.	**ENTJ** Frank, decisive, assume leadership. Enjoy long-term planning and goal setting. Forceful in presenting ideas.

Source: Further information is available at www.cpp.com where you will find the full range of Introduction to Type® titles along with other products that allow you to expand your knowledge and applications of your MBTI® type. Modified and reproduced by special permission of the Publisher, CPP, Inc., Mountain View, CA 94043, from Introduction to Type®, Sixth Edition by Isabel Briggs Myers. Copyright 1998 by Peter B. Myers and Katharine D. Myers. All rights reserved. Further reproduction is prohibited without the Publisher's written consent.

WHAT IS THE BIG FIVE MODEL OF PERSONALITY? Another way of viewing personality is through a five-factor model of personality—more typically called the **Big Five model**.[24] The Big Five factors are:

1. **Extraversion** A personality dimension that describes the degree to which someone is sociable, talkative, and assertive.
2. **Agreeableness** A personality dimension that describes the degree to which someone is good-natured, cooperative, and trusting.
3. **Conscientiousness** A personality dimension that describes the degree to which someone is responsible, dependable, persistent, and achievement oriented.
4. **Emotional stability** A personality dimension that describes the degree to which someone is calm, enthusiastic, and secure (positive) or tense, nervous, depressed, and insecure (negative).
5. **Openness to experience** A personality dimension that describes the degree to which someone is imaginative, artistically sensitive, and intellectual.

The Big Five model provides more than just a personality framework. Research has shown that important relationships exist between these personality dimensions and job performance.[25] For example, one study reviewed five categories of occupations: professionals (e.g., engineers, architects, attorneys), police, managers, sales, and semiskilled and skilled employees.[26] Job performance was defined in terms of employee performance ratings, training competency, and personnel data such as salary level. The results of the study showed that conscientiousness predicted job performance for all five occupational groups.[27] Predictions for the other personality dimensions depended on the situation and the occupational group. For example, extraversion predicted performance in managerial and sales positions, in which high social interaction is necessary.[28] Openness to experience was found to be important in predicting training competency. Ironically, emotional security was not positively related to job performance. Although it would seem logical that calm and secure workers would be better performers, that wasn't the case. Perhaps it's a function of the likelihood that emotionally stable workers often keep their jobs and emotionally unstable people may not. Given that all those participating in the study were employed, the variance on that dimension was probably small.

WHAT IS EMOTIONAL INTELLIGENCE? People who understand their own emotions and are good at reading others' emotions may be more effective in their jobs. That, in essence, is the theme of the underlying research on emotional intelligence.[29]

Emotional intelligence (EI) refers to an assortment of noncognitive skills, capabilities, and competencies that influences a person's ability to cope with environmental demands and pressures.[30] It's composed of five dimensions:

▶ *Self-awareness.* Being aware of what you're feeling.
▶ *Self-management.* The ability to manage your own emotions and impulses.
▶ *Self-motivation.* The ability to persist in the face of setbacks and failures.
▶ *Empathy.* The ability to sense how others are feeling.
▶ *Social skills.* The ability to handle the emotions of others.

Right or Wrong?

It's been called the "desperation hustle."[32] Employees who are "anxious about layoffs want to look irreplaceable." So they clean up their act. Those who might not have paid much attention to their manner of dress now do. Those who were mouthy and argumentative are now quiet and compliant. Those who used to "watch the clock" are now the last to leave. The fear is there and it's noticeable. "Managing that fear can be challenging." What ethical issues might arise for both employees and for managers? How could managers approach these circumstances ethically?

Several studies suggest that EI may play an important role in job performance.[31] For instance, one study looked at the characteristics of Bell Lab engineers who were rated as stars by their peers. The scientists concluded that these stars were better at relating to others. That is, it was EI, not academic IQ, that characterized high performers. A second study of Air Force recruiters generated similar findings: Top-performing recruiters exhibited high levels of EI. Using these findings, the Air Force revamped its selection criteria. A follow-up investigation found that future hires who had high EI scores were 2.6 times more successful than those with low scores. Organizations such as American Express have found that implementing emotional intelligence programs has helped increase its effectiveness; other organizations also found similar results that emotional intelligence contributes to team effectiveness.[33] For instance, at Cooperative Printing in Minneapolis, a study of its 45 employees concluded that EI skills were twice as important in "contributing to excellence as intellect and expertise alone."[34] A poll of human resources managers asked this question: How important is it for your workers to demonstrate EI to move up the corporate ladder? Forty percent of the managers replied "very important." Another 16 percent said moderately important. Other studies also indicated that emotional intelligence can be beneficial to quality improvements in contemporary organizations.[35]

The implications from the initial EI evidence is that employers should consider emotional intelligence as a criterion in their selection process—especially for those jobs that demand a high degree of social interaction.[36]

Can Personality Traits Predict Practical Work-Related Behaviors?

Five specific personality traits have proven most powerful in explaining individual behavior in organizations. These are locus of control, Machiavellianism, self-esteem, self-monitoring, and risk propensity.

Who controls an individual's behavior? Some people believe that they control their own fate. Others see themselves as pawns of fate, believing that what happens to them in their lives is due to luck or chance. The **locus of control** in the first case is internal. In the second case, it's external; these people believe that their lives are controlled by outside forces.[37] A manager might also expect to find that externals blame a poor performance evaluation on their boss's prejudice, their coworkers, or other events outside their control, whereas "internals" explain the same evaluation in terms of their own actions.

The second characteristic is called **Machiavellianism ("Mach")** after Niccolo Machiavelli, who provided instruction in the sixteenth century on how to gain and manipulate power. An individual who is high in Machiavellianism is pragmatic, maintains emotional distance, believes that ends can justify means,[38] and is found to have beliefs that are less ethical.[39] The philosophy "if it works, use it" is consistent with a high Mach perspective. Do high Machs make good employees? That answer depends on the type of job and whether you consider ethical implications in evaluating performance. In jobs that require bargaining skills (a labor negotiator) or that have substantial rewards for winning (a commissioned salesperson), high Machs are productive. In jobs in which ends do not justify the means or that lack absolute standards of performance, it's difficult to predict the performance of high Machs.

People differ in the degree to which they like or dislike themselves. This trait is called **self-esteem (SE)**.[40] The research on SE offers some interesting insights into organizational behavior. For example, SE is directly related to expectations for success. High SEs believe that they possess the ability to succeed at work. Individuals with high SE will take more risks in job selection and are more likely to choose unconventional jobs than are people with low SE.[41] The most common finding on self-esteem is that low SEs are more susceptible to external influence than are high SEs. Low SEs are dependent on positive evaluations from others. As a result, they're more likely to seek approval from others and more prone to conform to the beliefs and behaviors of those they respect than are high SEs. In managerial positions, low SEs will tend to be concerned with pleasing others and, therefore, will be less likely to take unpopular stands than will high SEs. Not surprisingly, self-esteem has also been found to be related to job satisfaction. A number of studies confirm that high SEs are more satisfied with their jobs than are low SEs.

Another personality trait researchers have identified is called **self-monitoring**.[42] Individuals high in self-monitoring can show considerable adaptability in adjusting their behavior to external, situational factors.[43] They're highly sensitive to external cues and can behave differently in different situations. High self-monitors are capable of presenting striking contradictions between their public persona and their private selves. Low self-monitors can't alter their behavior. They tend to display their true dispositions and attitudes in every situation; hence, they exhibit high behavioral consistency between who they are and what they do. Evidence suggests that high self-monitors tend to pay closer attention to the behavior of others and are more capable of conforming than are low self-monitors.[44] We might also hypothesize that high self-monitors will be more successful in managerial positions that require individuals to play multiple, and even contradicting, roles.

The final personality trait influencing worker behavior reflects the willingness to take chances—the propensity for *risk taking*. A preference to assume or avoid risk has been shown to have an impact on how long it takes individuals to make a decision and how much

emotional intelligence (EI)
The ability to notice and to manage emotional cues and information.

locus of control
The degree to which people believe they control their own fate.

Machiavellianism ("Mach")
A measure of the degree to which people are pragmatic, maintain emotional distance, and believe that ends justify means.

self-esteem (SE)
An individual's degree of like or dislike for himself or herself.

self-monitoring
A personality trait that measures the ability to adjust behavior to external situational factors.

information they require before making their choice. For instance, in one classic study, 79 managers worked on a simulated human resource management exercise that required them to make hiring decisions.[45] High risk-taking managers made more rapid decisions and used less information in making their choices than did the low risk-taking managers. Interestingly, the decision accuracy was the same for both groups.

Although it's generally correct to conclude that managers in organizations are risk averse, especially in large companies and government bureaus,[46] individual differences are still found on this dimension.[47] As a result, it makes sense to recognize these differences and even to consider aligning risk-taking propensity with specific job demands. For instance, a high risk-taking propensity may lead to effective performance for a stock trader in a brokerage firm since this type of job demands rapid decision making. The same holds true for the entrepreneur.[48] On the other hand, this personality characteristic might prove a major obstacle to accountants performing auditing activities, which might be better done by someone with a low risk-taking propensity.

How Do We Match Personalities and Jobs?

Obviously, individual personalities differ. So, too, do jobs. How do we match the two? The best-documented personality-job fit theory was developed by psychologist John Holland.[49] His theory states that an employee's satisfaction with his or her job, as well as his or her likelihood of leaving that job, depends on the degree to which the individual's personality matches the job environment. Holland identified six basic personality types as shown in Exhibit 8-4.

Holland's theory proposes that satisfaction is highest and turnover lowest when personality and occupation are compatible.[50] Social individuals should be in "people" type jobs, and so forth. The key points of this theory are that (1) there do appear to be intrinsic differences in personality among individuals; (2) there are different types of jobs; and (3) people in job environments compatible with their personality types should be more satisfied and less likely to resign voluntarily than should people in incongruent jobs.

Do Personality Attributes Differ Across Cultures?

Do personality frameworks, like the Big Five model, transfer across cultures? Are dimensions like locus of control relevant in all cultures? Let's try to answer these questions.

The five personality factors studied in the Big Five model appear in almost all cross-cultural studies.[51] This includes a wide variety of diverse cultures such as China, Israel, Germany, Japan,

---

EXHIBIT 8-4   Holland's Personality-Job Fit

TYPE	CHARACTERISTICS	PERSONALITY SAMPLE OCCUPATIONS
Realistic Prefers physical activities that require skill, strength, and coordination	Shy, genuine, persistent, stable, conforming, practical	Mechanic, drill-press operator, assembly-line worker, farmer
Investigative Prefers activities involving thinking, organizing, and understanding	Analytical, original, curious, independent	Biologist, economist, mathematician, reporter
Social Prefers activities that involve helping and developing others	Sociable, friendly, cooperative, understanding	Social worker, teacher, counselor, clinical psychologist
Conventional Prefers rule-regulated, orderly, and unambiguous activities	Conforming, efficient, practical, unimaginative, inflexible	Accountant, corporate manager, bank teller, file clerk
Enterprising Prefers verbal activities where there are opportunities to influence others and attain power	Self-confident, ambitious, energetic, domineering	Lawyer, real estate agent, public relations specialist, small business manager
Artistic Prefers ambiguous and unsystematic activities that allow creative expression	Imaginative, disorderly, idealistic, emotional, impractical	Painter, musician, writer, interior decorator

Source: Reproduced by special permission of the publisher, Psychological Assessment Resources, Inc., *Making Vocational Choices*, 3rd ed., copyright 1973, 1985, 1992, 1997 by Psychological Assessment Resources, Inc. All rights reserved.

Spain, Nigeria, Norway, Pakistan, and the United States. Differences are found in the emphasis on dimensions. Chinese, for example, use the category of conscientiousness more often and use the category of agreeableness less often than do Americans. But there is a surprisingly high amount of agreement, especially among individuals from developed countries. As a case in point, a comprehensive review of studies covering people from the European Community found that conscientiousness was a valid predictor of performance across jobs and occupational groups.[52] This is exactly what U.S. studies have found.

We know that there are certainly no common personality types for a given country. You can, for instance, find high risk takers and low risk takers in almost any culture. Yet a country's culture influences the *dominant* personality characteristics of its people. We can see this effect of national culture by looking at one of the personality traits we just discussed: locus of control.

National cultures differ in terms of the degree to which people believe they control their environment. For instance, North Americans believe that they can dominate their environment; other societies, such as those in Middle Eastern countries, believe that life is essentially predetermined. Notice how closely this distinction parallels the concept of internal and external locus of control. On the basis of this particular cultural characteristic, we should expect a larger proportion of internals in the U.S. and Canadian workforces than in the workforces of Saudi Arabia or Iran.

As we have seen throughout this section, personality traits influence employees' behavior. For global managers, understanding how personality traits differ takes on added significance when looking at it from the perspective of national culture.

How Can an Understanding of Personality Help Managers Be More Effective?

Over 62 percent of companies are using personality tests when recruiting and hiring.[53] And that's where the major value in understanding personality differences probably lies. Managers are likely to have higher-performing and more-satisfied employees if consideration is given to matching personalities with jobs. In addition, compatibility leads to other benefits. By recognizing that people approach problem solving, decision making, and job interactions differently, a manager can better understand why, for instance, an employee is uncomfortable with making quick decisions or why an employee insists on gathering as much information as possible before addressing a problem. Or, for instance, managers can expect that individuals with an external locus of control may be less satisfied with their jobs than those with an internal locus and also that they may be less willing to accept responsibility for their actions.

Matching personality types to compatible jobs leads to more satisfied employees. According to Holland's personality job-fit theory, people with a "social" preference like activities that involve helping and developing others. Teachers and aides at the early childhood learning center shown here understand the physical and emotional needs of their energetic three-year-old students. They enjoy leading the youngsters in recreational activities that develop the kids' physical skills and in exploratory and educational procedures that stimulate and develop their mental abilities.

8.4 Describe perception and the factors that influence it.

What Is Perception and What Influences It?

Perception is a process by which we give meaning to our environment by organizing and interpreting sensory impressions. Research on perception consistently demonstrates that individuals may look at the same thing yet perceive it differently. One manager, for instance, can interpret the fact that her assistant regularly takes several days to make important decisions as evidence that the assistant is slow, disorganized, and afraid to make decisions. Another manager with the same assistant might interpret the same tendency as evidence that the assistant is thoughtful, thorough, and deliberate.

The first manager would probably evaluate her assistant negatively; the second manager would probably evaluate the person positively. The point is that none of us sees reality. We interpret what we see and call it reality. And, of course, as the example shows, we behave according to our perceptions.

What Influences Perception?

How do we explain the fact that Cathy, a marketing supervisor for a large commercial petroleum products organization, age 52, noticed Bill's nose ring during his employment interview, and Sean, a human resources recruiter, age 23, didn't? A number of factors operate to shape and sometimes distort perception. These factors can reside in the perceiver, in the object or target being perceived, or in the context of the situation in which the perception is made.

When an individual looks at a target and attempts to interpret what he or she sees, that individual's personal characteristics will heavily influence the interpretation. These personal characteristics include attitudes, personality, motives, interests, past experiences, and expectations. The characteristics of the target being observed can also affect what is perceived. Loud people are more likely than quiet people to be noticed in a group. So, too, are extremely attractive or unattractive individuals. Because targets are not looked at in isolation, the relationship of a target to its background also influences perception (see Exhibit 8-5 for an example), as does our tendency to group close things and similar things together.

The context in which we see objects or events is also important. The time at which an object or event is seen can influence attention, as can location, lighting, temperature, and any number of other situational factors.

How Do Managers Judge Employees?

Much of the research on perception is directed at inanimate objects. Managers, though, are more concerned with human beings. Our perceptions of people differ from our perceptions of such inanimate objects as computers, robots, or buildings because we make inferences about the actions of people that we don't, of course, make about inanimate objects. When we observe people, we attempt to develop explanations of why they behave

EXHIBIT 8-5 Perceptual Challenges—What Do You See?

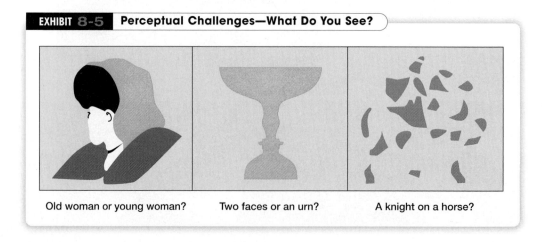

Old woman or young woman?   Two faces or an urn?   A knight on a horse?

in certain ways. Our perception and judgment of a person's actions, therefore, will be significantly influenced by the assumptions we make about the person's internal state. Many of these assumptions have led researchers to develop attribution theory.

WHAT IS ATTRIBUTION THEORY? Attribution theory has been proposed to explain how we judge people differently depending on what meaning we attribute to a given behavior.[54] Basically, the theory suggests that when we observe an individual's behavior, we attempt to determine whether it was internally or externally caused. Internally caused behavior is believed to be under the control of the individual. Externally caused behavior results from outside causes; that is, the person is seen as having been forced into the behavior by the situation. That determination, however, depends on three factors: distinctiveness, consensus, and consistency.

Distinctiveness refers to whether an individual displays a behavior in many situations or whether it is particular to one situation. Is the employee who arrived late to work today also the person coworkers see as a goof-off? What we want to know is whether this behavior is unusual. If it is, the observer is likely to give the behavior an external attribution. If this action is not unique, it will probably be judged as internal.

If everyone who is faced with a similar situation responds in the same way, we can say the behavior shows *consensus*. Our tardy employee's behavior would meet this criterion if all employees who took the same route to work today were also late. If consensus is high, you would be expected to give an external attribution to the employee's tardiness, whereas if other employees who took the same route made it to work on time, you would conclude the reason to be internal.

Finally, a manager looks for *consistency* in an employee's actions. Does the individual engage in the behaviors regularly and consistently? Does the employee respond the same way over time? Coming in 10 minutes late for work is not perceived in the same way if, for one employee, it represents an unusual case (she hasn't been late for several months), but for another it is part of a routine pattern (he is late two or three times a week). The more consistent the behavior, the more the observer is inclined to attribute it to internal causes.

Exhibit 8-6 summarizes the key elements in attribution theory. It would tell us, for instance, that if an employee, Mr. Flynn, generally performs at about the same level on other related tasks as he does on his current task (low distinctiveness), if other employees frequently perform differently—better or worse—than Mr. Flynn does on that current task (low consensus), and if Mr. Flynn's performance on this current task is consistent over time (high consistency), his manager or anyone else who is judging Mr. Flynn's work is likely to hold him primarily responsible for his task performance (internal attribution).

CAN ATTRIBUTIONS BE DISTORTED? One of the more interesting findings drawn from attribution theory is that errors or biases distort attributions. For instance, substantial evidence supports the hypothesis that when we make judgments about the behavior of other people, we have a tendency to underestimate the influence of external factors and overestimate the influence of internal or personal factors.[55] This fundamental attribution error can explain why a sales manager may be prone to attribute the poor performance of her sales agents to laziness rather than to the innovative product line introduced by a competitor. Individuals also tend to attribute their own successes to internal factors such as ability or effort while putting the blame for failure on external factors such as luck. This self-serving bias suggests that feedback provided to employees in performance reviews will be predictably distorted by them, whether it is positive or negative.

---

perception
A process by which we give meaning to our environment by organizing and interpreting sensory impressions.

attribution theory
A theory used to explain how we judge people differently, based on what meaning we attribute to a given behavior.

fundamental attribution error
The tendency to underestimate the influence of external factors and overestimate the influence of internal factors when making judgments about the behavior of others.

self-serving bias
The tendency for individuals to attribute their successes to internal factors while putting the blame for failures on external factors.

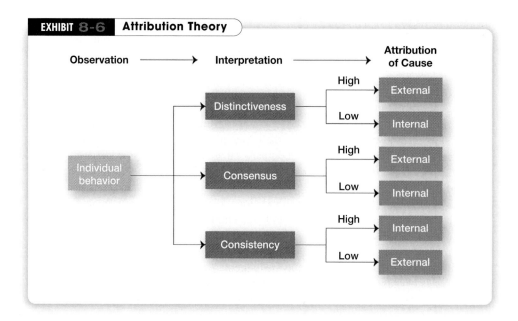

EXHIBIT 8-6 | **Attribution Theory**

All of us, managers included, use a number of shortcuts to judge others. These short-cuts can be particularly critical with diverse workforces. See the "Managing Diversity" box for more information.

How Can an Understanding of Perception Help Managers Be More Effective?

Managers need to recognize that their employees react to perceptions, not to reality. So whether a manager's appraisal of an employee's performance is actually objective and unbiased or whether the organization's wage levels are among the highest in the community is less relevant

---

 MANAGING DIVERSITY | All About Shortcuts

Perceiving and interpreting people's behavior is a lot of work, so we use shortcuts to make the task more manageable.[56] Perceptual shortcuts can be valuable as they let us make accurate perceptions quickly and provide valid data for making predictions. However, they aren't perfect. They can and do get us into trouble. (See Exhibit 8-7 for a summary description of the perceptual shortcuts.)

Individuals can't assimilate all they observe, so they're selective in their perception. They absorb bits and pieces. These bits and pieces are not chosen randomly; rather, they're selectively chosen depending on the interests, background, experience, and attitudes of the observer. **Selective perception** allows us to "speed read" others but not without the risk of drawing an inaccurate picture.

It's easy to judge others if we assume that they're similar to us. In **assumed similarity**, or the "like me" effect, the observer's perception of others is influenced more by the observer's own characteristics than by those of the person observed. For example, if you want challenges and responsibility in your job, you'll assume that others want the same. People who assume that others are like them can, of course, be right, but not always.

When we judge someone on the basis of our perception of a group he or she is part of, we're using the shortcut called **stereotyping**. For instance, "Married people are more stable employees than single persons" or "Older employees are absent more often from work" are examples of stereotyping. To the degree that a stereotype is based on fact, it may produce accurate judgments. However, many stereotypes aren't factual and distort our judgment.

When we form a general impression about a person on the basis of a single characteristic, such as intelligence, sociability, or appearance, we're being influenced by the **halo effect**. This effect frequently occurs when students evaluate their classroom instructor. Students may isolate a single trait such as enthusiasm and allow their entire evaluation to be slanted by the perception of this one trait. An instructor may be quiet, assured, knowledgeable, and highly qualified, but if his classroom teaching style lacks enthusiasm, he might be rated lower on a number of other characteristics.

When dealing with a diverse workforce, managers (and others) first have to be aware of when they're using a perceptual shortcut. And secondly, they have to ensure that the shortcut isn't distorting what they're perceiving and thus believing about an individual or a situation.

EXHIBIT 8-7 **Perceptual Shortcuts**

SHORTCUT	WHAT IT IS	DISTORTION
Selectivity	People assimilate certain bits and pieces of what they observe depending on their interests, background, experience, and attitudes	"Speed reading" others may result in an inaccurate picture of them
Assumed similarity	People assume that others are like them	May fail to take into account individual differences, resulting in incorrect similarities
Stereotyping	People judge others on the basis of their perception of a group to which the others belong	May result in distorted judgments because many stereotypes have no factual foundation
Halo effect	People form an impression of others on the basis of a single trait	Fails to take into account the total picture of what an individual has done

than what employees perceive them to be. If individuals perceive appraisals to be biased or wage levels as low, they'll behave as if those conditions actually exist. Employees organize and interpret what they see, so there is always the potential for perceptual distortion. The message is clear: Pay close attention to how employees perceive both their jobs and management actions. Remember, the valuable employee who quits because of an inaccurate perception is just as great a loss to an organization as the valuable employee who quits for a valid reason.

How Do Learning Theories Explain Behavior?

The last individual behavior concept we're going to look at is learning. It's included for the obvious reason that almost all behavior is learned. If we want to explain, predict, and influence behavior, we need to understand how people learn.

Discuss learning theories and their relevance in shaping behavior.

8.5

The psychologists' definition of learning is considerably broader than the average person's view that "it's what we do in school." Learning occurs all the time as we continuously learn from our experiences. A workable definition of **learning** is any relatively permanent change in behavior that occurs as a result of experience. Two learning theories help us understand how and why individual behavior occurs.

What Is Operant Conditioning?

Operant conditioning argues that behavior is a function of its consequences. People learn to behave to get something they want or to avoid something they don't want. Operant behavior is voluntary or learned behavior, not reflexive or unlearned behavior. The tendency to repeat learned behavior is influenced by reinforcement or lack of reinforcement that happens as a result of the behavior. Reinforcement strengthens a behavior and increases the likelihood that it will be repeated. Lack of reinforcement weakens a behavior and lessens the likelihood that it will be repeated.

selective perception
The tendency for people to only absorb parts of what they observe, allowing them to "speed read" others.

assumed similarity
An observer's perception of others is influenced more by the observer's own characteristics than by those of the person observed.

stereotyping
When we judge someone on the basis of our perception of a group he or she is part of.

halo effect
When we form a general impression of a person on the basis of a single characteristic.

learning
A relatively permanent change in behavior that occurs as a result of experience.

operant conditioning
A theory of learning that says behavior is a function of its consequences.

---

o **From the Past to the Present** **o**

Why does hearing Christmas carols evoke pleasant memories of childhood?[57] *Classical conditioning theory* would say it's because the songs are associated with a festive holiday spirit and make us remember all the fun and excitement. Classical conditioning can also explain why a scheduled visit by the "top brass" brings flurried activities of cleaning, straightening, and rearranging at a local outlet of a major retail company. However, classical conditioning is a passive theory. Something happens, and we react in a specific way. As such, it can explain simple reflexive behavior. But most behavior by people at work is voluntary rather than reflexive; that is, employees *choose* to arrive at work on time, ask their boss for help with some problem, or "goof off" when no one is watching. A better explanation for behavior is operant conditioning.

Operant conditioning says that people behave the way they do so they can get something they want or avoid something they don't want. It's voluntary or learned behavior, not reflexive or unlearned behavior. And Harvard psychologist

B. F. Skinner first identified the process of operant conditioning. He argued that creating pleasing consequences to follow specific forms of behavior would increase the frequency of that behavior. Skinner demonstrated that people will most likely engage in desired behaviors if they're positively reinforced for doing so; that rewards are most effective if they immediately follow the desired response (behavior); and that behavior that is not rewarded or is punished is less likely to be repeated. For example, a professor places a mark by a student's name each time the student makes a contribution to class discussions. Operant conditioning would argue that this practice is motivating because it conditions a student to expect a reward (earning class credit) each time she demonstrates a specific behavior (speaking up in class). Operant conditioning can be seen in work settings as well. And smart managers quickly recognize that they can use operant conditioning to shape employees' behaviors to get work done in the most effective and efficient manner possible.

o

B. F. Skinner's research widely expanded our knowledge of operant conditioning.[58] Behavior is assumed to be determined from without—that is, *learned*—rather than from within—reflexive or unlearned. Skinner argued that people will most likely engage in desired behaviors if they are positively reinforced for doing so, and rewards are most effective if they immediately follow the desired response. In addition, behavior that isn't rewarded or is punished, is less likely to be repeated. (For more information about Skinner's contributions, see the "From the Past to the Present" box.)

You see examples of operant conditioning everywhere. Any situation in which it's either explicitly stated or implicitly suggested that reinforcement (rewards) is contingent on some action on your part is an example of operant conditioning. Your instructor says that if you want a high grade in this course, you must perform well on tests by giving correct answers. A salesperson working on commission knows that earning a sizable income is contingent upon generating high sales in his or her territory. Of course, the linkage between behavior and reinforcement can also work to teach the individual to behave in ways that work against the best interests of the organization. Assume that your boss tells you that if you'll work overtime during the next three-week busy season, you'll be compensated for it at the next performance appraisal. Then, when performance appraisal time comes, you are given no positive reinforcements (such as being praised for pitching in and helping out when needed). What will you do the next time your boss asks you to work overtime? You'll probably refuse. Your behavior can be explained by operant conditioning: If a behavior isn't positively reinforced, the probability that the behavior will be repeated declines.

What Is Social Learning Theory?

Some 60 percent of the Radio City Rockettes have danced in prior seasons. The veterans help newcomers with "Rockette style"—where to place their hands, how to hold their hands, how to keep up stamina, and so forth.[59]

As the Rockettes are well aware, individuals can also learn by observing what happens to other people and just by being told about something as well as by direct experiences. Much of what we have learned comes from watching others (models)—parents, teachers, peers, television and movie actors, managers, and so forth. This view that we can learn both through observation and direct experience is called **social learning theory**.[60]

The influence of others is central to the social learning viewpoint. The amount of influence that these models have on an individual is determined by four processes:

1. *Attentional processes.* People learn from a model when they recognize and pay attention to its critical features. We're most influenced by models who are attractive, repeatedly available, thought to be important, or seen as similar to us.
2. *Retention processes.* A model's influence will depend on how well the individual remembers the model's action, even after the model is no longer readily available.
3. *Motor reproduction processes.* After a person has seen a new behavior by observing the model, the watching must become doing. This process then demonstrates that the individual can actually do the modeled activities.
4. *Reinforcement processes.* Individuals will be motivated to exhibit the modeled behavior if positive incentives or rewards are provided. Behaviors that are reinforced will be given more attention, learned better, and performed more often.

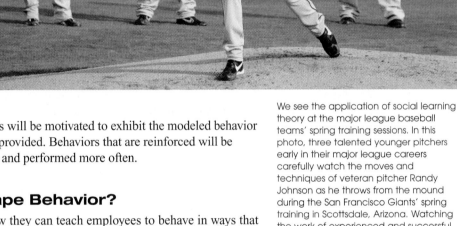

We see the application of social learning theory at the major league baseball teams' spring training sessions. In this photo, three talented younger pitchers early in their major league careers carefully watch the moves and techniques of veteran pitcher Randy Johnson as he throws from the mound during the San Francisco Giants' spring training in Scottsdale, Arizona. Watching the work of experienced and successful players like Johnson and then practicing the skills they observed helps younger players learn how to fine-tune their techniques.

How Can Managers Shape Behavior?

Managers should be concerned with how they can teach employees to behave in ways that most benefit the organization.[61] Thus, managers will often attempt to mold individuals by guiding their learning in graduated steps. This process is called **shaping behavior** (see the "Developing Your Shaping Behavior Skill" box).

Consider the situation in which an employee's behavior is significantly different from that desired by management. If management reinforced the individual only when he or she showed desirable responses, little reinforcement might happen at all.

We shape behavior by systematically reinforcing each successive step that moves the individual closer to the desired response. If an employee who has continually been 30 minutes late for work arrives only 20 minutes late, we can reinforce this improvement. Reinforcement would increase as responses more closely approximate the desired behavior.

Four ways can be used to shape behavior: positive reinforcement, negative reinforcement, punishment, or extinction. When a response is followed with something pleasant, such as when a manager praises an employee for a job well done, it's called *positive reinforcement.* Rewarding a response with the termination or withdrawal of something pleasant is called *negative reinforcement.* Managers who habitually criticize their employees for taking extended coffee breaks are using negative reinforcement. The only way these employees can stop the criticism is to shorten their breaks. *Punishment* penalizes undesirable behavior. Suspending an employee for two days without pay for showing up drunk is an example of punishment. Eliminating any reinforcement that is maintaining a behavior is called *extinction.* When a behavior isn't reinforced, it gradually disappears. Managers who wish to discourage employees from continually asking distracting or irrelevant questions in

social learning theory
A theory of learning that says people can learn through observation and direct experience.

shaping behavior
The process of guiding learning in graduated steps, using reinforcement or lack of reinforcement.

Developing Your *Shaping Behavior* Skill

About the Skill

In today's dynamic work environments, learning is continual. But this learning shouldn't be done in isolation or without any guidance. Most employees need to be shown what's expected of them on the job. As a manager, you must teach your employees the behaviors that are most critical to their, and the organization's, success.

Steps in Practicing the Skill

1   **Identify the critical behaviors that have a significant impact on an employee's performance.** Not everything employees do on the job is equally important in terms of performance outcomes. A few critical behaviors may, in fact, account for the majority of one's results. These high impact behaviors need to be identified.

2   **Establish a baseline of performance.** A baseline is obtained by determining the number of times the identified behaviors occur under the employee's present job conditions.

3   **Analyze the contributing factors to performance and their consequences.** A number of factors, such as the norms of a group, may be contributing to the baseline performance. Identify these factors and their effect on performance.

4   **Develop a shaping strategy.** The change that may occur will entail changing some element of performance—structure, processes, technology, groups, or the task. The purpose of the strategy is to strengthen the desirable behaviors and weaken the undesirable ones.

5   **Apply the appropriate strategy.** Once the strategy has been developed, it needs to be implemented. In this step, an intervention occurs.

6   **Measure the change that has occurred.** An intervention should produce the desired results in performance behaviors. Evaluate the number of times the identified behaviors now occur. Compare these with the baseline evaluation in step 2.

7   **Reinforce desired behaviors.** If an intervention has been successful and the new behaviors are producing the desired results, maintain these behaviors through reinforcement mechanisms.

Practicing the Skill

a.   Imagine that your assistant is ideal in all respects but one—he or she is hopeless at taking phone messages for you when you're not in the office. You're often in training sessions and the calls are sales leads you want to follow up, so you have identified taking accurate messages as a high impact behavior for your assistant.

b.   Focus on steps 3 and 4, and devise a way to shape your assistant's behavior. Identify some factors that might contribute to his or her failure to take messages—these could range from a heavy workload to a poor understanding of the task's importance (you can rule out insubordination). Then develop a shaping strategy by determining what you can change—the available technology, the task itself, the structure of the job, or some other element of performance.

c.   Now plan your intervention and take a brief meeting with your assistant in which you explain the change you expect. Recruit a friend to help you role-play your intervention. Do you think you would succeed in a real situation?

meetings can eliminate that behavior by ignoring those employees when they raise their hands to speak. Soon, the behavior will be diminished.

Both positive and negative reinforcement result in learning. They strengthen a desired response and increase the probability of repetition. Both punishment and extinction also result in learning; however, they weaken behavior and tend to decrease its subsequent frequency.

How Can an Understanding of Learning Help Managers Be More Effective?

Employees are going to learn on the job. The only issue is whether managers are going to manage their learning through the rewards they allocate and the examples they set, or allow it to occur haphazardly. If marginal employees are rewarded with pay raises and promotions, they will have little reason to change their behavior. In fact, productive employees, who see marginal performance rewarded, might change their behavior. If managers want behavior A, but reward behavior B, they shouldn't be surprised to find employees' learning to engage in behavior B. Similarly, managers should expect that employees will look to them as models. Managers who are consistently late to work, or take two hours for lunch, or help themselves to company office supplies for personal use should expect employees to read the message they are sending and model their behavior accordingly.

What Contemporary OB Issues Face Managers?

By this point, you're probably well aware of why managers need to understand how and why employees behave the way they do. We conclude this chapter by looking at two OB issues having a major influence on managers' jobs today.

Discuss contemporary issues in OB.

8.6

How Do Generational Differences Affect the Workplace?

They're young, smart, brash. They wear flip-flops to the office or listen to iPods at their desk. They want to work, but don't want work to be their life. This is Generation Y, some 70 million of them, many who are embarking on their careers, taking their place in an increasingly multigenerational workplace.[62]

JUST WHO IS GEN Y? There's no consensus about the exact time span that Gen Y comprises, but most definitions include those individuals born from about 1982 to 1997. One thing is for sure—they're bringing new attitudes with them to the workplace. Gen Yers have grown up with an amazing array of experiences and opportunities. And they want their work life to provide that as well, as shown in Exhibit 8-8. For instance, Stella Kenyi, who is passionately interested in international development, was sent by her employer, the National Rural Electric Cooperative Association, to Yai, Sudan, to survey energy use.[63] At Best Buy's corporate offices, Beth Trippie, a senior scheduling specialist, feels that as long as the results are there, why should it matter how it gets done. She says, "I'm constantly playing video games, on a call, doing work, and the thing is, all of it gets done, and it gets done well."[64] And Katie Patterson, an assistant account executive in Atlanta says, "We are willing and not afraid to challenge the status quo. An environment where creativity and independent thinking are looked upon as a positive is appealing to people my age. We're very independent and tech savvy."[65]

EXHIBIT 8-8 Gen Y Workers

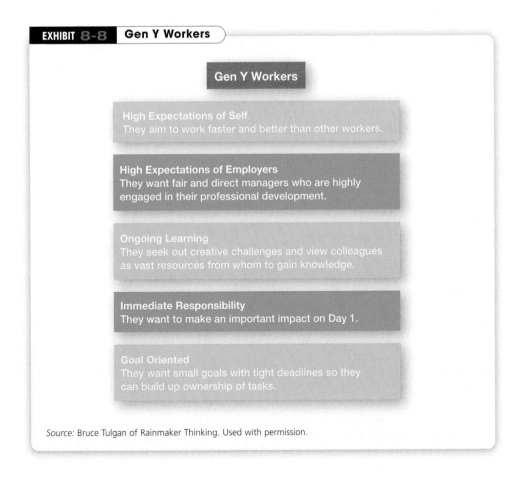

Gen Y Workers

High Expectations of Self
They aim to work faster and better than other workers.

High Expectations of Employers
They want fair and direct managers who are highly engaged in their professional development.

Ongoing Learning
They seek out creative challenges and view colleagues as vast resources from whom to gain knowledge.

Immediate Responsibility
They want to make an important impact on Day 1.

Goal Oriented
They want small goals with tight deadlines so they can build up ownership of tasks.

Source: Bruce Tulgan of Rainmaker Thinking. Used with permission.

DEALING WITH THE MANAGERIAL CHALLENGES. Managing Gen Y workers presents some unique challenges. Conflicts and resentment can arise over issues such as appearance, technology, and management style.

How flexible must an organization be in terms of "appropriate" office attire? It may depend on the type of work being done and the size of the organization. There are many organizations where jeans, T-shirts, and flip-flops are acceptable. However, in other settings, employees are expected to dress more conventionally. But even in those more conservative organizations, one possible solution to accommodate the more casual attire preferred by Gen Y is to be more flexible in what's acceptable. For instance, the guideline might be that when the person is not interacting with someone outside the organization, more casual wear (with some restrictions) can be worn.

What about technology? This is a generation that has lived much of their lives with ATMs, DVDs, cell phones, e-mail, texting, laptops, and the Internet. When they don't have information they need, they just simply enter a few keystrokes to get it. Having grown up with technology, Gen Yers tend to be totally comfortable with it. They're quite content to meet virtually to solve problems, while bewildered baby boomers expect important problems to be solved with an in-person meeting. Baby boomers complain about Gen Yers' inability to focus on one task, while Gen Yers see nothing wrong with multitasking. Again, flexibility from both is the key.

Finally, what about managing Gen Yers? Like the old car advertisement that used to say, "this isn't your father's car," we can say that "this isn't your father's or mother's way of managing." Gen Y employees want bosses who are open minded; experts in their field, even if they aren't tech-savvy; organized; teachers, trainers, and mentors; not authoritarian or paternalistic; respectful of their generation; understanding of their need for work/life balance; providing constant feedback; communicating in vivid and compelling ways; and providing stimulating and novel learning experiences.[66]

Gen Y employees have a lot to offer organizations in terms of their knowledge, passion, and abilities. Managers, however, have to recognize and understand the behaviors of this group in order to create an environment in which work can be accomplished efficiently, effectively, and without disruptive conflict.

How Do Managers Deal with Negative Behavior in the Workplace?

Jerry notices the oil is low in his forklift but continues to drive it until it overheats and can't be used. After enduring 11 months of repeated insults and mistreatment from her supervisor, Maria quits her job. An office clerk slams her keyboard and then shouts profanities whenever her computer freezes up. Rudeness, hostility, aggression, and other forms of workplace negativity have become all too common in today's organizations. In a survey of U.S. employees, 10 percent said

It's not surprising that eBay's young employees rank the company as one of the best places to work for millennials. eBay's culture of fun, casual dress, and flexible work schedules that provide for a work/life balance appeal to Generation Y employees like those shown here at eBay's office in Milan, Italy. The company's young workers say that their managers give them job responsibility quickly, generous recognition for their achievements, and learning opportunities that advance their professional career development.

they witnessed rudeness daily within their workplaces and 20 percent said that they personally were direct targets of incivility at work at least once a week. In a survey of Canadian workers, 25 percent reported seeing incivility daily and 50 percent said they were the direct targets at least once per week.[67] And it's been estimated that negativity costs the U.S. economy some $300 billion a year.[68] What can managers do to manage negative behavior in the workplace?

The main thing is to recognize that it's there. Pretending that negative behavior doesn't exist or ignoring such misbehaviors will only confuse employees about what is expected and acceptable behavior. Although there's some debate among researchers about the preventive or responsive actions to negative behaviors, in reality, both are needed.[69] Preventing negative behaviors by carefully screening potential employees for certain personality traits and responding immediately and decisively to unacceptable negative behaviors can go a long way toward managing negative workplace behaviors. But it's also important to pay attention to employee attitudes since negativity will show up there as well. As we said earlier, when employees are dissatisfied with their jobs, they *will* respond somehow.

Review and ⑧ Applications

Chapter Summary

8.1 **Identify the focus and goals of organizational behavior (OB).** OB focuses on three areas: individual behavior, group behavior, and organizational aspects. The goals of OB are to explain, predict, and influence employee behavior. Six important employee behaviors are as follows: Employee productivity is a performance measure of both efficiency and effectiveness. Absenteeism is the failure to report to work. Turnover is the voluntary and involuntary permanent withdrawal from an organization. Organizational citizenship behavior (OCB) is discretionary behavior that's not part of an employee's formal job requirements but which promotes the effective functioning of an organization. Job satisfaction is an individual's general attitude toward his or her job. Workplace misbehavior is any intentional employee behavior that's potentially harmful to the organization or individuals within the organization.

8.2 **Explain the role that attitudes play in job performance.** Attitudes are evaluative statements concerning people, objects, or events. The cognitive component of an attitude refers to the beliefs, opinions, knowledge, or information held by a person. The affective component is the emotional or feeling part of an attitude. The behavioral component refers to an intention to behave in a certain way toward someone or something.

There are four job-related attitudes: job satisfaction, job involvement, organizational commitment, and employee engagement. Job satisfaction refers to a person's general attitude toward his or her job. Job involvement is the degree to which an employee identifies with his or her job, actively participates in it, and considers his or her job performance to be important to his or her self-worth. Organizational commitment is the degree to which an employee identifies with a particular organization and its goals and wishes to maintain membership in that organization. Employee engagement is when employees are connected to, satisfied with, and enthused about their jobs.

According to cognitive dissonance theory, individuals try to reconcile attitude and behavior inconsistencies by altering their attitudes, altering their behavior, or rationalizing the inconsistency.

8.3 **Describe different personality theories.** The MBTI® measures four dichotomies: social interaction, preference for gathering data, preference for decision making, and style of making decisions. The Big Five model consists of five personality traits: extraversion, agreeableness, conscientiousness, emotional stability, and openness to experience. Another way to view personality is through the five personality traits that help explain individual behavior in organizations: locus of control, Machiavellianism, self-esteem, self-monitoring, and risk-taking.

Finally, how a person responds emotionally and how they deal with their emotions is a function of personality. A person who is emotionally intelligent has the ability to notice and to manage emotional cues and information.

8.4 **Describe perception and the factors that influence it.** Perception is how we give meaning to our environment by organizing and interpreting sensory impressions.

Attribution theory helps explain how we judge people differently. It depends on three factors. Distinctiveness is whether an individual displays different behaviors in different situations (that is, is the behavior unusual). Consensus is whether others facing a similar situation respond in the same way. Consistency is when a person engages in behaviors regularly and consistently. Whether these three factors are high or low helps managers determine whether employee behavior is attributed to external or internal causes.

The fundamental attribution error is the tendency to underestimate the influence of external factors and overestimate the influence of internal factors. The self-serving bias is the tendency to attribute our own successes to internal factors and to put the blame for personal failure on external factors. Shortcuts used in judging others are selective perception, assumed similarity, stereotyping, and the halo effect.

 8.5 Discuss learning theories and their relevance in shaping behavior. Operant conditioning argues that behavior is a function of its consequences. Social learning theory says that individuals learn by observing what happens to other people and by directly experiencing something.

Managers can shape behavior by using positive reinforcement (reinforcing a desired behavior by giving something pleasant), negative reinforcement (reinforcing a desired response by withdrawing something unpleasant), punishment (eliminating undesirable behavior by applying penalties), or extinction (not reinforcing a behavior to eliminate it).

 Discuss contemporary issues in OB. The challenge of managing Gen Y workers is that they bring new attitudes to the workplace. The main challenges are over issues such as appearance, technology, and management style.

Workplace misbehavior can be dealt with by recognizing that it's there; carefully screening potential employees for possible negative tendencies; and most importantly, by paying attention to employee attitudes through surveys about job satisfaction and dissatisfaction.

 To check your understanding of learning outcomes – , go to **mymanagementlab.com** and try the chapter questions.

Understanding the Chapter

1. How is an organization like an iceberg? Use the iceberg metaphor to describe the field of organizational behavior.

2. Does the importance of knowledge of OB differ based on a manager's level in the organization? If so, how? If not, why not? Be specific.

3. Clarify how individuals reconcile inconsistencies between attitudes and behaviors.

4. Describe what is meant by the term *emotional intelligence.* Provide an example of how it's used in contemporary organizations.

5. "Instead of worrying about job satisfaction, companies should be trying to create environments where performance is enabled." What do you think this statement means? Explain. What's your reaction to this statement? Do you agree? Disagree? Why?

6. How might a manager use personality traits to improve employee selection in his department? Emotional intelligence? Discuss.

7. Describe the implications of social learning theory for managing people at work.

8. A Gallup Organization survey shows that most workers rate having a caring boss even higher than they value money or fringe benefits. How should managers interpret this information? What are the implications?

9. Write down three attitudes you have. Identify the cognitive, affective, and behavioral components of those attitudes.

Understanding Yourself

What's My Basic Personality?

The five-factor model of personality—often referred to as the Big Five—has an impressive body of research suggesting that five basic personality dimensions underlie human behavior. This self-assessment exercise will give you an indication of what *your* personality is like according to the Big Five model.

INSTRUMENT   Listed on the next page is a set of 15 adjective pairs. For each, select the number along the scale (you must choose a whole number) that most closely describes you or your preferences.

1. Quiet	1	2	3	4	5	Talkative
2. Tolerant	1	2	3	4	5	Critical
3. Disorganized	1	2	3	4	5	Organized
4. Tense	1	2	3	4	5	Calm
5. Imaginative	1	2	3	4	5	Conventional
6. Reserved	1	2	3	4	5	Outgoing
7. Uncooperative	1	2	3	4	5	Cooperative
8. Unreliable	1	2	3	4	5	Dependable
9. Insecure	1	2	3	4	5	Secure
10. New	1	2	3	4	5	Familiar
11. Sociable	1	2	3	4	5	Loner
12. Suspicious	1	2	3	4	5	Trusting
13. Undirected	1	2	3	4	5	Goal-oriented
14. Enthusiastic	1	2	3	4	5	Depressed
15. Change	1	2	3	4	5	Status-quo

SCORING KEY   To calculate your personality score, add up your points as follows (reverse scoring those items marked with an asterisk):

Items 1, 6, and 11*:	This is your extraversion score.
Items 2*, 7, and 12:	This is your agreeableness score.
Items 3, 8, and 13:	This is your conscientiousness score.
Items 4, 9, and 14*:	This is your emotional stability score.
Items 5*, 10*, and 15*:	This is your openness-to-experience score.

ANALYSIS AND INTERPRETATION

Extraversion—high scores indicate you're an extravert; low scores indicate you're an introvert.

Agreeableness—high scores indicate you value harmony; low scores indicate you prefer having your say or way on issues.

Conscientiousness—high scores indicate that you pursue fewer goals in a purposeful way; lower scores indicate that you're more easily distracted, pursue many goals, and are more hedonistic.

Emotional stability—high scores indicate positive emotional stability; low scores indicate negative emotional stability.

Openness to experience—high scores indicate you have a wide range of interests and a fascination with novelty and innovation; low scores indicate you're more conventional and find comfort in the familiar.

What defines a high or low score? No definite cutoffs are available. However, reasonable cutoffs for each dimension would be 12–15 points = high; 7–11 = moderate; and 3–6 = low.

What are the implications of some of your scores? Studies on the Big Five model suggest that individuals who are dependable, reliable, thorough, organized, able to plan, and persistent (that is, high on conscientiousness) tend to have higher job performance, no matter the occupation. High scores on extraversion indicate you may be suited to a managerial or sales position. Also, high scores on openness-to-experience are a good predictor of your ability to achieve significant benefits from training efforts.

Sources: Based on O. P. John, "The 'Big Five' Factor Taxonomy: Dimensions of Personality in the Natural Language and in Questionnaires," in L.A. Pervin (ed.), *Handbook of Personality Theory and Research* (New York: Guilford Press, 1990), pp. 66–100; and D. L. Formy-Duval, J. E. Williams, D. J. Patterson, and E. E. Fogle, "A 'Big Five' Scoring System for the Item Pool of the Adjective Check List," *Journal of Personality Assessment* 65, (1995), pp. 59–76.

Wood Designs Plus

Reply   Reply All   Forward

To: Ted Sigler, Director of HR
From: Michelle DePriest, President
Re: **Hiring**

Ted, as we discussed last Friday, our manufacturing operations have grown to the point where we need to add a couple of people to our executive team; specifically, a corporate controller and a national sales director. The controller will be responsible for establishing operational and financial standards (in other words, a lot of number-crunching using financial and manufacturing statistics) for our various work units. The national sales director will be responsible for working closely with our sales staff to further develop long-lasting and mutually beneficial relationships with our customers.

I recall something from a management class I took in college that certain personality types fit best with certain types of jobs. Could you do some research on this topic for me? Write up a short report (no more than a page) describing the personality type that might be an appropriate match for each of these new positions. Get this to me by the end of the week.

This fictionalized company and message were created for educational purposes only. It is not meant to reflect positively or negatively on management practices by any company that may share this name.

ODD COUPLES

A 29-year-old and a 68-year-old. How much could they possibly have in common? And what could they learn from each other? At Randstad USA's Manhattan office, such employee pairings are common. One such pair of colleagues sits inches apart facing each other. "They hear every call the other makes. They read every e-mail the other sends or receives. Sometimes they finish each other's sentences."

Randstad Holding NV, a Dutch company, has used this pairing idea since its founding over 40 years ago. The founder's motto was "Nobody should be alone." The original intent was to boost productivity by having sales agents share one job and trade off job responsibilities. Today, these partners in the home office have an arrangement where one is in the office one week while the other one is out making sales calls, then the next week, they switch. The company brought its partner arrangement to the United States in the late 1990s. But when it began recruiting new employees, the vast majority of whom were in their twenties, it realized the challenges and the potential of pairing different generations together. "Knowing that these Gen Yers need lots of attention in the workplace, Randstad executives figured that if they shared a job with someone whose own success depended on theirs, they were certain to get all the nurturing they required."

Randstad doesn't just simply pair up people and hope it works. There's more to it than that! The company looks for people who will work well with others by conducting extensive interviews and requiring job applicants to shadow a sales agent for half a day. "One question Randstad asks is: What's your most memorable moment while being on a team? If they respond: When I scored the winning touchdown, that's a deal killer. Everything about our organization is based on the team and group." When a new hire is paired with an experienced agent, both individuals have some adjusting. One of the most interesting elements of Randstad's program is that neither person is "the boss." And both are expected to teach the other.

Discussion Questions

1. What topics of individual behavior do you see in this case? Explain.
2. What do you think about this pairing-up idea? Would you be comfortable with such an arrangement? Why or why not?
3. What personality traits would be most needed for this type of work arrangement? Why?
4. What types of issues might a Gen Y employee and an older, more-experienced employee face? How could two people in such a close-knit work arrangement deal with those issues? That is, how could both make the adjustment easier?
5. Design an employee attitude survey for Randstad's employees.

Sources: G. Mijuk, "Tough Times for Temp Agencies Likely to Prompt Consolidation," *Wall Street Journal,* March 17, 2009, p. B7; M. Laff, "Gen Y Proves Loyalty in Economic Downturn," *T&D,* December 2008, p. 18; and S. Berfield, "Bridging the Generation Gap," *BusinessWeek,* September 17, 2007, pp. 60–61.

Understanding Groups and Managing Work Teams

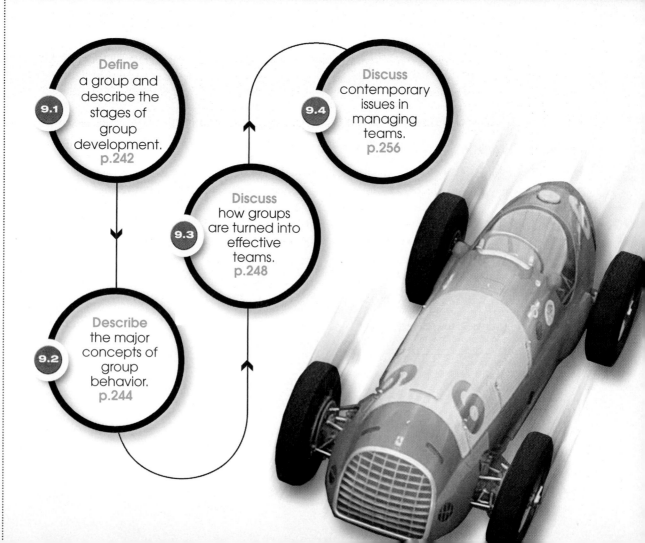

Up to Speed

Imagine working for an organization that employs more than 2,700 individuals with each one having the identical focus.[1] Imagine, too, that company managers in this organization want you to work hard *and* be the best at what you do. If you're employed by Ferrari S.p.A., such realities aren't hard to imagine. When most people hear the name *Ferrari*, they think of expensive, super-fast sports cars. That reputation for speed is why Ferraris continue to be well-known and respected in racing groups around the world. The Italian company was founded by Enzo Ferrari in 1928, and even in its early days, racing was an important part of the Ferrari legend. Today, Luca Cordero (photo on right), president and managing director of the company, believes that his employees truly make a difference in producing one of the world's greatest sports cars. He recognizes that to be the best, he needs employees who understand how to work together and how to achieve common goals. At Ferrari, employee teams combine their efforts to produce an outstanding automobile, with quality befitting its iconic reputation. You won't find traditional assembly lines in the Ferrari factory, nor will you find production quotas. With prices for a Ferrari starting at $140,000, auto assembly time isn't measured in seconds. Rather, team tasks often last more than 90 minutes for each portion of a car. Then the team proudly passes its finished work to the next team so its work can begin. Average time to manufacture one car: three days. The company produces around 6,000 Ferraris in any one year, although the company hopes to boost that number to 10,000 cars by 2010. To achieve that goal, the company is expanding current capacity although its singular focus on quality and teamwork won't change.

Employees at Ferrari truly enjoy being part of a team. They say that working toward a common goal is one of the most satisfying elements in their jobs. They also appreciate what the company does for them. They enjoy a state-of-the-art fitness center, annual physicals at the company's on-site clinic, an employee cafeteria, and home-based training for employees to learn English. They feel as if Cordero and his team treat them as associates, not just as cogs in the Ferrari wheel. As one employee stated, "For many of us working for Ferrari is like working in the Vatican." Recently, the company won an award for Best Place to Work in Europe. The prize resulted from the company's "Formula-1-inspired workplace initiative called Formula Uomo," which took the principles of Ferrari's success in Formula 1 racing and applied them to the workplace. The main thrust was recognizing its people as the "fulcrum of the company's work system."

Is the team concept at Ferrari working? By all accounts, yes. The company has achieved over $2.3 billion in sales. And more importantly, the car still retains its appeal as one of the best and most desired in the world. Although profits have been nominal during the global economic downturn, there are always going to be customers who want to own the car with the rearing-horse logo.

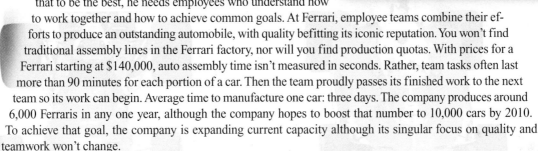

Like company executives at Ferrari, managers today believe that the use of teams allows their organizations to increase sales or produce better products faster and at lower costs. Although the effort to create teams isn't always successful, well-planned teams can reinvigorate productivity and better position an organization to deal with a rapidly changing environment.

You've probably had a lot of experience working in groups—class project teams, maybe an athletic team, a fund-raising committee, or even a sales team at work. Work teams are one of the realities—and challenges—of managing in today's dynamic global environment. Many organizations have made the move to restructure work around teams rather than individuals. Why? What do these teams look like? And how can managers build effective teams? These are some of the questions we'll be answering in this chapter. Before we can understand teams, however, we first need to understand some basics about groups and group behavior.

What Is a Group and What Stages of Development Do Groups Go Through?

9.1 Define a group and describe the stages of group development.

Each person in the group had his or her assigned role: The Spotter, The Back Spotter, The Gorilla, and the Big Player. For over 10 years, this group—former MIT students who were members of a secret Black Jack Club—used their extraordinary mathematical abilities, expert training, teamwork, and interpersonal skills to take millions of dollars from some of the major casinos in the United States.[2] Although most groups aren't formed for such dishonest purposes, the success of this group at its task was impressive. Managers would like their work groups to be successful at their tasks also. The first step is understanding what a group is and how groups develop.

What Is a Group?

A **group** is defined as two or more interacting and interdependent individuals who come together to achieve specific goals. *Formal groups* are work groups that are defined by the organization's structure and have designated work assignments and specific tasks directed at accomplishing organizational goals. Exhibit 9-1 provides some examples. *Informal groups* are social groups. These groups occur naturally in the workplace and tend to form around friendships and common interests. For example, five employees from different departments who regularly eat lunch together are an informal group.

EXHIBIT 9-1 **Examples of Formal Work Groups**

- **Command groups**—Groups that are determined by the organization chart and composed of individuals who report directly to a given manager.
- **Task groups**—Groups composed of individuals brought together to complete a specific job task; their existence is often temporary because when the task is completed, the group disbands.
- **Cross-functional teams**—Groups that bring together the knowledge and skills of individuals from various work areas or groups whose members have been trained to do each other's jobs.
- **Self-managed teams**—Groups that are essentially independent and that, in addition to their own tasks, take on traditional managerial responsibilities, such as hiring, planning and scheduling, and evaluating performance.

EXHIBIT 9-2	Stages of Group Development

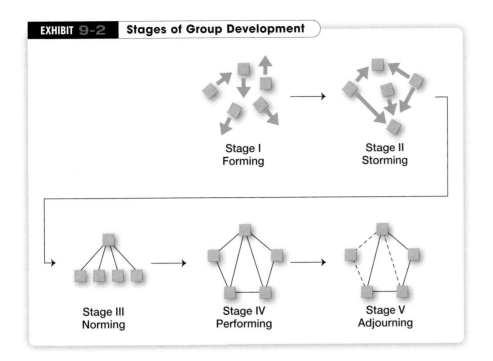

What Are the Stages of Group Development?

Research shows that groups develop through five stages.[3] As shown in Exhibit 9-2, these five stages are: *forming, storming, norming, performing,* and *adjourning.*

The **forming** stage has two phases. The first occurs as people join the group. In a formal group, people join because of some work assignment. Once they've joined, the second phase begins: defining the group's purpose, structure, and leadership. This phase involves a great deal of uncertainty as members "test the waters" to determine what types of behavior are acceptable. This stage is complete when members begin to think of themselves as part of a group.

The **storming** stage is appropriately named because of the intragroup conflict. There's conflict over who will control the group and what the group needs to be doing. When this stage is complete, there will be a relatively clear hierarchy of leadership and agreement on the group's direction.

The **norming** stage is one in which close relationships develop and the group becomes cohesive. There's now a strong sense of group identity and camaraderie. This stage is complete when the group structure solidifies and the group has assimilated a common set of expectations (or norms) regarding member behavior.

Sibyl Goldman, a Yahoo! entertainment group vice president, leads an "omg" Web site meeting at Yahoo!'s offices in Santa Monica, California. This meeting is an example of the performing stage of group development. With an established strong sense of group identity and camaraderie, the group focuses on its task of presenting celebrity news stories in a light and positive way along with galleries of photos and exclusive videos. For permanent work groups such as the "omg" staff, performing is the last stage in the group development process.

group
Two or more interacting and interdependent individuals who come together to achieve specific goals.

forming stage
The first stage of group development in which people join the group and then define the group's purpose, structure, and leadership.

storming stage
The second stage of group development, which is characterized by intragroup conflict.

norming stage
The third stage of group development, which is characterized by close relationships and cohesiveness.

and the survey says...[4]

85 percent of *Fortune* 1000 companies used team- or group-based pay to some degree in 2005.

83 percent of respondents identified teams as a key ingredient to organizational success.

33 percent of females wanted more face-to-face group meetings.

27 percent of males wanted more face-to-face group meetings.

10 to 12: the average number of production workers per team.

40 percent of senior executives said that meeting deadlines was the most important characteristic of a good team player.

37 percent of workers feel more productive in a small group.

69 percent of workers said their teams were not given enough resources.

The fourth stage is **performing**. The group structure is in place and accepted by group members. Their energies have moved from getting to know and understand each other to working on the group's task. This is the last stage of development for permanent work groups. However, for temporary groups—project teams, task forces, or similar groups that have a limited task to do—the final stage is **adjourning**. In this stage, the group prepares to disband. Attention is focused on wrapping up activities instead of task performance. Group members react in different ways. Some are upbeat, thrilled about the group's accomplishments. Others may be sad over the loss of camaraderie and friendships.

Many of you have probably experienced these stages as you've worked on a group project for a class. Group members are selected or assigned and then meet for the first time. There's a "feeling out" period to assess what the group is going to do and how it's going to be done. This is usually followed by a battle for control: Who's going to be in charge? Once this issue is resolved and a "hierarchy" agreed on, the group identifies specific work that needs to be done, who's going to do each part, and dates by which the assigned work needs to be completed. General expectations are established. These decisions form the foundation for what you hope will be a coordinated group effort culminating in a project that's been done well. Once the project is complete and turned in, the group breaks up. Of course, some groups don't get much beyond the forming or storming stages. These groups may have serious interpersonal conflicts, turn in disappointing work, and get lower grades.

Does a group become more effective as it progresses through the first four stages? Some researchers say yes, but it's not that simple.[5] That assumption may be generally true, but what makes a group effective is a complex issue. Under some conditions, high levels of conflict are conducive to high levels of group performance. There might be situations in which groups in the storming stage outperform those in the norming or performing stages. Also, groups don't always proceed sequentially from one stage to the next. Sometimes, groups are storming and performing at the same time. Groups even occasionally regress to previous stages. Therefore, don't assume that all groups precisely follow this process or that performing is always the most preferable stage. Think of this model as a general framework that underscores the fact that groups are dynamic entities and managers need to know the stage a group is in so they can understand the problems and issues that are most likely to surface.

9.2 Describe the major concepts of group behavior.

What Are the Major Concepts of Group Behavior?

The basic foundation for understanding group behavior includes roles, norms and conformity, status systems, group size, and group cohesiveness. Let's take a closer look at each of those aspects.

What Are Roles?

We introduced the concept of roles in Chapter 1 when we discussed what managers do. Of course, managers aren't the only individuals in an organization who have roles. The concept of roles applies to all employees in organizations and to their lives outside the organization as well.

A **role** refers to behavior patterns expected of someone who occupies a given position in a social unit. Individuals play multiple roles, adjusting their roles to the group to which they belong at the time. In an organization, employees attempt to determine what behaviors are expected of them. They read their job descriptions, get suggestions from their bosses, and watch what their coworkers do. An individual who's confronted by divergent role expectations experiences role conflict. Employees in organizations often face such role conflicts. The credit manager expects her credit analysts to process a minimum of 30 applications a week, but the work group pressures members to restrict output to 20 applications a week so that everyone has work to do and no one gets laid off. A newly hired college instructor's colleagues want him to give out only a few high grades in order to maintain the department's reputation for high standards, whereas students want him to give out lots of high grades to enhance their grade point averages. To the degree that the instructor sincerely seeks to satisfy the expectations of both his colleagues and his students, he faces role conflict.

How Do Norms and Conformity Affect Group Behavior?

All groups have established **norms**, acceptable standards that are shared by the group's members. Norms dictate output levels, absenteeism rates, promptness or tardiness, the amount of socializing allowed on the job, and so on. Norms, for example, dictate the dress code of customer service representatives at a credit card processing company. Most workers who have little direct customer contact come to work dressed casually. However, on occasion, a newly hired employee will come to work dressed in a suit. Those who do are teased and pressured until their dress conforms to the group's standard.

Although each group has its own unique set of norms, common classes of norms appear in most organizations. These norms focus on effort and performance, dress, and loyalty. Probably the most widespread norms are related to levels of *effort and performance*. Work groups typically provide their members with explicit cues on how hard to work, what level of output to have, when to look busy, when it's acceptable to goof off, and the like. These norms are extremely powerful in affecting an individual employee's performance. They're so powerful that performance predictions based solely on an employee's ability and level of personal motivation often prove wrong.

Some organizations have formal *dress codes*—even describing what's considered acceptable for corporate casual dress. However, even in the absence of codes, norms frequently develop to dictate the kind of clothing that should be worn to work. College seniors, when interviewing for their first postgraduate job, pick up this norm quickly. Every spring, on college campuses around the country, students interviewing for jobs can be spotted; they're the ones walking around in the dark gray or blue pinstriped suits. They're enacting the dress norms they've learned are expected in professional positions. Of course, acceptable dress in one organization will be different from another's norms.

Few managers appreciate employees who ridicule the organization. Similarly, professional employees and those in the executive ranks recognize that most employers view persons who actively look for another job unfavorably. People who are unhappy know that they should keep their job searches secret. These examples demonstrate that *loyalty norms* are widespread in organizations. This concern for demonstrating loyalty, by the way, often explains why ambitious aspirants to top management positions willingly take work home at night, come in on weekends, and accept transfers to cities in which they would otherwise prefer not to live. Because individuals desire acceptance by the groups to which they belong, they're susceptible to conformity pressures. The impact of group pressures for

Right or Wrong?

You've been hired as a summer intern in the events planning department of a public relations firm in Dallas. After working there about a month, you conclude that the attitude in the office is "anything goes." Employees know that supervisors won't discipline them for ignoring company rules. For example, employees turn in expense reports, but the process is a joke. Nobody submits receipts to verify reimbursement and nothing is ever said. In fact, when you tried to turn in your receipts with your expense report, you were told, "Nobody else turns in receipts and you don't really need to either." Although the employee handbook says that receipts are required for reimbursement, you know that no expense check has ever been denied because of failure to turn in a receipt. Also, your coworkers use company phones for personal long-distance calls even though that's also prohibited by the employee handbook. And one of the permanent employees told you to "help yourself" to any paper, pens, or pencils you might need here or at home. What are the norms of this group? Suppose that you were the supervisor in this area. How would you go about changing the norms?

---

performing stage
The fourth stage of group development, when the group is fully functional and works on the group task.

adjourning stage
The final stage of group development for temporary groups, during which groups prepare to disband.

role
Behavior patterns expected of someone who occupies a given position in a social unit.

norms
Standards or expectations that are accepted and shared by a group's members.

○ **From the Past to the Present** ○

Does the desire to be accepted as a part of a group leave one susceptible to conforming to the group's norms? Will the group exert pressure that's strong enough to change a member's attitude and behavior? According to the research by Solomon Asch, the answer appears to be yes.[6]

Asch's study involved groups of seven or eight people who sat in a classroom and were asked to compare two cards held by an investigator. One card had one line; the other had three lines of varying length. As shown in Exhibit 9-3, one of the lines on the three-line card was identical to the line on the one-line card. The difference in line length was quite obvious; under ordinary conditions, subjects made errors of less than 1 percent. The object was to announce aloud which of the three lines matched the single line. But what happens if all the members of the group begin to give incorrect answers? Will the pressure to conform cause the unsuspecting subject (USS) to alter his or her answers to align with those of the others? That's what Asch wanted to know. He arranged the group so that the USS was unaware that the experiment was fixed. The seating was prearranged so that the USS was the last to announce his or her decision.

The experiment began with two sets of matching exercises. All the subjects gave the right answers. On the third set, however, the first subject gave an obviously wrong answer—for example, saying "C" in Exhibit 9-3. The next subject gave the same wrong answer, and so did the others, until it was the unsuspecting subject's turn. He knew that "B" was the same as "X" but everyone else said "C." The decision confronting the USS was this: Do you publicly state a perception that differs from the preannounced position of the others? Or do you give an answer that you strongly believe to be incorrect in order to have your response agree with the other group members? Asch's subjects conformed in about 35 percent of many experiments and many trials. That is, the subjects gave answers that they knew were wrong but were consistent with the replies of other group members.

For managers, the Asch study provides considerable insight into group behaviors. The tendency, as Asch showed, is for individual members to go along with the pack. To diminish the negative aspects of conformity, managers should create a climate of openness in which employees are free to discuss problems without fear of retaliation.

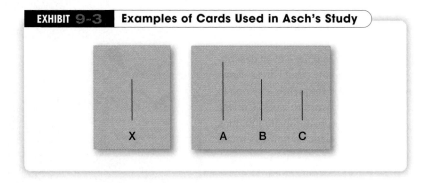

EXHIBIT 9-3 **Examples of Cards Used in Asch's Study**

---

conformity on an individual member's judgment and attitudes was demonstrated in the classic studies by Solomon Asch.[7] Asch's results suggest that group norms press us toward conformity. We desire to be one of the group and to avoid being visibly different. We can generalize this finding to say that when an individual's opinion of objective data differs significantly from that of others in the group, he or she feels extensive pressure to align his or her opinion to conform with those of the others (see our previous discussion on groupthink, p. 72). The "From the Past to the Present" box has additional background information on Asch's contributions to group theory.

What Is Status and Why Is It Important?

Status is a prestige grading, position, or rank within a group. As far back as scientists have been able to trace human groupings, they've found status hierarchies: tribal chiefs and their followers, nobles and peasants, the haves and the have-nots. Status systems are important factors in understanding behavior. Status is a significant motivator that has behavioral consequences when individuals see a disparity between what they perceive their status to be and what others perceive it to be.

Status may be informally conferred by characteristics such as education, age, skill, or experience. However, anything can have status value if others in the group admire it. Of course, just because status is informal doesn't mean that it's unimportant or that there's disagreement on who has it or who doesn't. Members of groups have no problem placing people into status categories, and they usually agree about who's high, low, and in the middle.

It's important for employees to believe that the organization's formal status system is congruent. That is, there should be equity between the perceived ranking of an individual and the status symbols he or she is given by the organization. For instance, incongruence may occur when a supervisor earns less than his or her employees or when a desirable office is occupied by a lower-ranking individual. Employees may view such cases as a disruption to the general pattern of order and consistency in the organization.

Does Group Size Affect Group Behavior?

The size of a group affects that group's behavior. However, that effect depends on what criteria you're looking at.[8]

The evidence indicates, for instance, that small groups complete tasks faster than larger ones. However, if a group is engaged in problem solving, large groups consistently get better marks than their smaller counterparts. Translating these results into specific numbers is a bit trickier, but we can offer some parameters. Large groups—with a dozen or more members—are good for gaining diverse input. Thus, if the goal of the group is to find facts, larger groups should be more effective. On the other hand, smaller groups are better at doing something productive with those facts. Groups of approximately five to seven members tend to act more effectively.

One of the more disturbing findings is that, as groups get incrementally larger, the contribution of individual members often tends to lessen. That is, although the total productivity of a group of four is generally greater than that of a group of three, the individual productivity of each group member declines as the group expands. Thus, a group of four will tend to produce at a level of less than four times the average individual performance. The best explanation for this reduction of effort is that dispersion of responsibility encourages individuals to slack off; a behavior referred to as **social loafing**.[9] When the results of the group can't be attributed to any single person, the relationship between an individual's input and the group's output is clouded. In such situations, individuals may be tempted to become "free riders" and coast on the group's efforts. In other words, efficiency is reduced when individuals think that their contributions cannot be measured. The obvious conclusion from this finding is that managers who use work groups should also provide a means by which individual efforts can be identified.

Group cohesiveness, the degree to which group members are attracted to each other and share goals, was high for the cast and crew of *Wushu: The Young Generation*. Everyone involved in the film, from the executive producer and kung fu star Jackie Chan to the young actors, was focused on the goal of introducing an authentic representation of wushu, a martial arts form that combines exercise, the performing arts, and competitive sports. Authenticity included filming the movie in a real martial arts school in China today and presenting the skills of the young actors, all of whom are martial arts students who perform the action scenes themselves. Shown here at a press conference for the film are Chan with the film's production team members and the young actors and actresses.

status
A prestige grading, position, or rank within a group.

social loafing
The tendency for individuals to expend less effort when working collectively than when working individually.

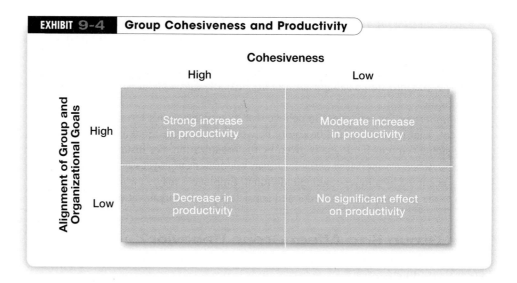

EXHIBIT 9-4   Group Cohesiveness and Productivity

Cohesiveness

	High	Low
High	Strong increase in productivity	Moderate increase in productivity
Low	Decrease in productivity	No significant effect on productivity

Alignment of Group and Organizational Goals

Are Cohesive Groups More Effective?

Intuitively, it makes sense that groups that experience a lot of internal disagreement and lack of cooperation are less effective than are groups in which individuals generally agree, cooperate, and like each other. Research has looked at **group cohesiveness**, the degree to which members are attracted to one another and share the group's goals. The more that members are attracted to one another and the more that a group's goals align with each individual's goals, the greater the group's cohesiveness.

Previous research has generally shown that highly cohesive groups are more effective than are those with less cohesiveness, but the relationship between cohesiveness and effectiveness is more complex.[10] A key moderating variable is the degree to which the group's attitude aligns with its formal goals or those of the larger organization.[11] The more cohesive a group is, the more its members will follow its goals. If these goals are favorable (for instance, high output, quality work, cooperation with individuals outside the group), a cohesive group is more productive than a less cohesive group. But if cohesiveness is high and attitudes are unfavorable, productivity decreases. If cohesiveness is low and goals are supported, productivity increases, but not as much as when both cohesiveness and support are high. When cohesiveness is low and goals are not supported, cohesiveness has no significant effect on productivity. These conclusions are summarized in Exhibit 9-4.

How Are Groups Turned into Effective Teams?

9.3 Discuss how groups are turned into effective teams.

When companies like W. L. Gore, Volvo, and Kraft Foods introduced teams into their production processes, it made news because no one else was doing it. Today, it's just the opposite—the organization that *doesn't* use teams would be newsworthy. It's estimated that some 80 percent of *Fortune* 500 companies have at least half of their employees on teams. And over 70 percent of U.S. manufacturers use work teams.[12] Teams are likely to continue to be popular. Why? Research suggests that teams typically outperform individuals when the tasks being done require multiple skills, judgment, and experience.[13] Organizations are using team-based structures because they've found that teams are more flexible and responsive to changing events than are traditional departments or other permanent work groups. Teams have the ability to quickly assemble, deploy, refocus, and disband. In this section, we'll discuss what a work team is, the different types of teams that organizations might use, and how to develop and manage work teams.

Aren't Work Groups and Work Teams the Same?

At this point, you may be asking yourself: Aren't teams and groups the same thing? No. In this section, we clarify the difference between a work group and a work team.[14]

Most of you are probably familiar with teams especially if you've watched or participated in organized sports events. Work *teams* do differ from work *groups* and have their own unique traits (see Exhibit 9-5). Work groups interact primarily to share information and to make decisions to help each member do his or her job more efficiently and effectively. There's no need or opportunity for work groups to engage in collective work that requires joint effort. On the other hand, **work teams** are groups whose members work intensely on a specific, common goal using their positive synergy, individual and mutual accountability, and complementary skills.

These descriptions should help clarify why so many organizations have restructured work processes around teams. Managers are looking for that positive synergy that will help the organization improve its performance.[15] The extensive use of teams creates the potential for an organization to generate greater outputs with no increase in (or even fewer) inputs. For example, until the economic downturn hit, investment teams at Wachovia's Asset Management Division (which is now a part of Wells Fargo & Company) were able to significantly improve investment performance. As a result, these teams helped the bank improve its Morningstar financial rating.[16]

Recognize, however, that such increases are simply "potential." Nothing inherently magical in the creation of work teams guarantees that this positive synergy and its accompanying productivity will occur. Accordingly, merely calling a group a team doesn't automatically increase its performance.[17] As we show later in this chapter, successful or high-performing work teams have certain common characteristics. If managers hope to gain increases in organizational performance, it will need to ensure that its teams possess those characteristics.

What Are the Different Types of Work Teams?

Teams can do a variety of things. They can design products, provide services, negotiate deals, coordinate projects, offer advice, and make decisions.[18] For instance, at Rockwell Automation's facility in North Carolina, teams are used in work process optimization projects. At Arkansas-based Acxiom Corporation, a team of human resource professionals planned and implemented a cultural change. And every summer weekend at any NASCAR race, you can see work teams in action during drivers' pit stops.[19] The four most common types of work

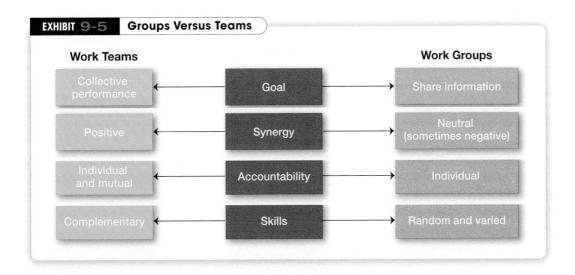

EXHIBIT 9-5 **Groups Versus Teams**

Work Teams		Work Groups
Collective performance	Goal	Share information
Positive	Synergy	Neutral (sometimes negative)
Individual and mutual	Accountability	Individual
Complementary	Skills	Random and varied

group cohesiveness
The degree to which group members are attracted to one another and share the group's goals.

work teams
Groups whose members work intensely on specific, common goals using their positive synergy, individual and mutual accountability, and complementary skills.

One of the most popular types of work teams is the problem-solving team. The employees shown here are members of a Customer Support Team at AhnLab, Inc., a leading Web security firm in Seoul, South Korea, that develops security solutions for information networks and provides security consulting services. Members of the team use their positive synergy in working on the common goal of solving customer problems such as cyber attacks that slow Web sites.

teams are problem-solving teams, self-managed work teams, cross-functional teams, and virtual teams.

When work teams first became popular, most were **problem-solving teams**, which are teams from the same department or functional area involved in efforts to improve work activities or to solve specific problems. Members share ideas or offer suggestions on how work processes and methods can be improved. However, these teams are rarely given the authority to implement any of their suggested actions.

Although problem-solving teams were helpful, they didn't go far enough in getting employees involved in work-related decisions and processes. This led to another type of team, a **self-managed work team**, which is a formal group of employees who operate without a manager and are responsible for a complete work process or segment. A self-managed team is responsible for getting the work done *and* for managing themselves. This usually includes planning and scheduling of work, assigning tasks to members, collective control over the pace of work, making operating decisions, and taking action on problems. For instance, teams at Corning have no shift supervisors and work closely with other manufacturing divisions to solve production-line problems and coordinate deadlines and deliveries. The teams have the authority to make and implement decisions, finish projects, and address problems.[20] Other organizations such as Xerox, Boeing, PepsiCo, and Hewlett-Packard also use self-managed teams. It's estimated that about 30 percent of U.S. employers now use this form of team; and among large firms, the number is probably closer to 50 percent.[21] Most organizations that use self-managed teams find them to be effective.[22]

The third type of team is the **cross-functional team**, which we introduced in Chapter 5 and defined as a work team composed of individuals from various specialties. Many organizations use cross-functional teams. For example, ArcelorMittal, the world's largest steel company, uses cross-functional teams of scientists, plant managers, and salespeople to review and monitor product innovations.[23] The concept of cross-functional teams is even being applied in health care. For instance, at Suburban Hospital in Bethesda, Maryland, intensive care unit (ICU) teams composed of a doctor trained in intensive care medicine, a pharmacist, a social worker, a nutritionist, the chief ICU nurse, a respiratory therapist, and a chaplain meet daily with every patient's bedside nurse to discuss and debate the best course of treatment. The hospital credits this team care approach with reducing errors, shortening the amount of time patients spent in ICU, and improving communication between families and the medical staff.[24]

TECHNOLOGY AND THE MANAGER'S JOB

IT AND TEAMS

Work teams need information to do their work. With work teams often being not just steps away, but continents away from each other, it's important to have a way for team members to communicate and collaborate. That's where IT comes in. Technology has enabled greater online communication and collaboration within teams of all types.[25]

The idea of technologically aided collaboration actually originated with online search engines. The Internet itself was initially intended as a way for groups of scientists and researchers to share information. Then, as more and more information was put "on the Web," users relied on a variety of search engines to help them find that information. Now, we see many examples of collaborative technologies such as wiki pages, blogs, and even multiplayer virtual reality games.

Today, online collaborative tools have given work teams more efficient and effective ways to get work done. For instance, engineers at Toyota use collaborative communication tools to share process improvements and innovations. They have developed a "widely disseminated, collectively owned pool of common knowledge, which drives innovation at a speed few other corporate systems can match." And there's no disputing the successes Toyota has achieved. Managers everywhere should look to the power of IT to help work teams improve the way work gets done.

The final type of team is the **virtual team**, which is a team that uses technology to link physically dispersed members in order to achieve a common goal. For instance, a virtual team at Boeing-Rocketdyne played a pivotal role in developing a radically new product.[26] Another company, Decision Lens, uses a virtual team environment to generate and evaluate creative ideas.[27] In a virtual team, members collaborate online with tools such as wide-area networks, videoconferencing, fax, e-mail, or Web sites where the team can hold online conferences.[28] Virtual teams can do all the things that other teams can—share information, make decisions, and complete tasks; however, they lack the normal give-and-take of face-to-face discussions. That's why virtual teams tend to be more task-oriented—especially if the team members have never personally met.

What Makes a Team Effective?

Much research has been done on what it is that makes a team effective.[29] Out of these efforts, we now have a fairly focused model identifying those characteristics.[30] Exhibit 9-6 summarizes what we currently know about what makes a team effective. As we look at this model, keep in mind two things. First, teams differ in form and structure. This model attempts to generalize across all

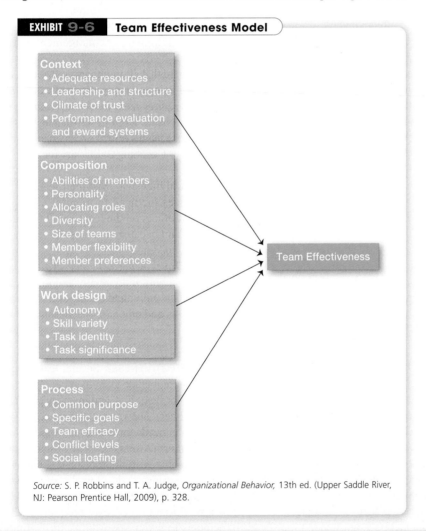

EXHIBIT 9-6   Team Effectiveness Model

Context
- Adequate resources
- Leadership and structure
- Climate of trust
- Performance evaluation and reward systems

Composition
- Abilities of members
- Personality
- Allocating roles
- Diversity
- Size of teams
- Member flexibility
- Member preferences

Work design
- Autonomy
- Skill variety
- Task identity
- Task significance

Process
- Common purpose
- Specific goals
- Team efficacy
- Conflict levels
- Social loafing

→ Team Effectiveness

Source: S. P. Robbins and T. A. Judge, *Organizational Behavior,* 13th ed. (Upper Saddle River, NJ: Pearson Prentice Hall, 2009), p. 328.

problem-solving teams
A team from the same department or functional area that's involved in efforts to improve work activities or to solve specific problems.

self-managed work team
A type of work team that operates without a manager and is responsible for a complete work process or segment.

cross-functional team
Teams made up of individuals from various departments and that cross traditional departmental lines.

virtual team
A type of work team that uses technology to link physically dispersed members in order to achieve a common goal.

teams, so you should only use it as a guide.[31] Secondly, the model assumes that managers have already determined that teamwork is preferable to individual work. Creating "effective" teams in situations in which individuals can do the job better would be wasted effort.

One thing we need to clarify first before looking at the model is what we mean by team effectiveness. Typically, it includes objective measures of a team's productivity, managers' ratings of the team's performance, and aggregate measures of member satisfaction. As you can see from the model, there are four key components of effective teams including the context, the team's composition, work design, and process variables.

WHAT FACTORS IN THE CONTEXT APPEAR TO MAKE A TEAM EFFECTIVE? Four contextual factors appear to be most significantly related to team performance. These include adequate resources, leadership and structure, a climate of trust, and performance evaluation and reward systems.

As part of the larger organization system, a team relies on resources outside the group to sustain it. If it doesn't have *adequate resources*, the team's ability to perform its job effectively is reduced. This factor appears to be so important to team performance that one research study concluded that "perhaps one of the most important characteristics of an effective work group is the support the group receives from the organization."[32] Resources can include timely information, proper equipment, encouragement, adequate staffing, and administrative assistance.

If a team can't agree on who is to do what or ensure that all members contribute equally in sharing the work load, it won't function properly. Agreeing on the specifics of work and how all the team members' individual skills fit together requires *team leadership and structure*. This can come from the organization or from the team itself. Even in self-managed teams, a manager's job is to be more of a coach by supporting the team's efforts and managing outside (rather than inside) the team. See the "Developing Your Coaching Skill" box for more information on coaching skills.

Members of effective teams *trust* each other. And they also trust their leaders.[33] Why is trust important? It facilitates cooperation, reduces the need to monitor each other's behavior, and bonds members around the belief that others on the team won't take advantage of them. Trusting the team leader is also important because it means the team is willing to accept and commit to the leader's goals and decisions.

The final contextual factor of an effective team is a *performance evaluation and reward system*. Team members have to be accountable both individually and jointly. So, in addition to evaluating and rewarding employees for their individual contributions, managers should consider group-based appraisals, profit-sharing, and other approaches that reinforce team effort and commitment.

WHAT TEAM COMPOSITION FACTORS LEAD TO EFFECTIVENESS? Several team composition factors are important to a team's effectiveness. These include team member abilities, personality, role allocation, diversity, size of teams, member flexibility, and member preferences.

Part of a team's performance depends on its members' *knowledge, skills, and abilities*.[34] Research has shown that to perform effectively, a team needs three different types of skills. First, it needs people with technical expertise. Next, it needs members with problem-solving and decision-making skills. Finally, a team needs people with interpersonal skills. A team can't achieve its performance potential if it doesn't have or can't develop all these skills. And the right mix of these skills is also critical. Too much of one at the expense of another will lead to lower team performance. However, a team doesn't necessarily need all these skills immediately. It's not uncommon for team members to take responsibility for learning the skills in which the group is deficient. That way a team can achieve its full potential.

As we saw in the last chapter, *personality* significantly influences individual behavior. It's also true for team behavior. Research has shown that three of the Big Five dimensions are relevant to team effectiveness.[35] For instance, high levels of both conscientiousness and openness-to-experience tend to lead to higher team performance. Agreeableness also appears to matter. And teams that had one or more highly disagreeable members performed poorly. Maybe you've had that not-so-good experience in group projects that you've been part of!

Developing Your *Coaching* Skill

About the Skill

Effective managers are increasingly being described as coaches rather than bosses. Just like coaches, they're expected to provide instruction, guidance, advice, and encouragement to help team members improve their job performance.

Steps in Practicing the Skill

1 **Analyze ways to improve the team's performance and capabilities.** A coach looks for opportunities for team members to expand their capabilities and improve performance. How? You can use the following behaviors. Observe your team members' behaviors on a day-to-day basis. Ask questions of them: Why do you do a task this way? Can it be improved? What other approaches might be used? Show genuine interest in team members as individuals, not merely as employees. Respect them individually. Listen to each employee.

2 **Create a supportive climate.** It's the coach's responsibility to reduce barriers to development and to facilitate a climate that encourages personal performance improvement. How? You can use the following behaviors. Create a climate that contributes to a free and open exchange of ideas. Offer help and assistance. Give guidance and advice when asked. Encourage your team. Be positive and upbeat. Don't use threats. Ask, "What did we learn from this that can help us in the future?" Reduce obstacles. Assure team members that you value their contribution to the team's goals. Take personal responsibility for the outcome, but don't rob team members of their full responsibility. Validate team members' efforts when they succeed. Point to what was missing when they fail. Never blame team members for poor results.

3 **Influence team members to change their behavior.** The ultimate test of coaching effectiveness is whether an employee's performance improves. You must encourage ongoing growth and development. How can you do this? Try the following behaviors. Recognize and reward small improvements and treat coaching as a way of helping employees to continually work toward improvement. Use a collaborative style by allowing team members to participate in identifying and choosing among improvement ideas. Break difficult tasks down into simpler ones. Model the qualities that you expect from your team. If you want openness, dedication, commitment, and responsibility from your team members, demonstrate these qualities yourself.

Practicing the Skill

Collaborative efforts are more successful when every member of the group or team contributes a specific role or task toward the completion of the goal. To improve your skill at nurturing team effort, choose two of the following activities and break each one into at least six to eight separate tasks or steps. Be sure to indicate which steps are sequential, and which can be done simultaneously with others. What do you think is the ideal team size for each activity you choose?

a. Making an omelet
b. Washing the car
c. Creating a computerized mailing list
d. Designing an advertising poster
e. Planning a ski trip
f. Restocking a supermarket's produce department

Nine potential team *roles* have been identified. (See Exhibit 9-7.) High-performing work teams have people to fill all these roles and have selected people to fulfill these roles based on their skills and preferences.[36] On many teams, individuals may play multiple roles. It's important for managers to understand the individual strengths a person will bring to a team and select team members with those strengths in mind to ensure that these roles are filled.

Team *diversity* is another factor that can influence team effectiveness. Although many of us hold the optimistic view that diversity is desirable, research seems to show the opposite. One review found that "Studies on diversity in teams from the last 50 years have shown that surface-level social-category differences such as race/ethnicity, gender, and age tend to . . . have negative effects" on the performance of teams.[37] However, there is some evidence showing that the disruptive effects of diversity decline over time, although little evidence exists that diverse teams perform better eventually. The "Managing Diversity" box describes some of the challenges managers face in managing diverse teams.

What *size* should a work team be in order to be effective? At Amazon.com, work teams have considerable autonomy to innovate and to investigate ideas. And Jeff Bezos, founder and

EXHIBIT 9-7 **Team Member Roles**

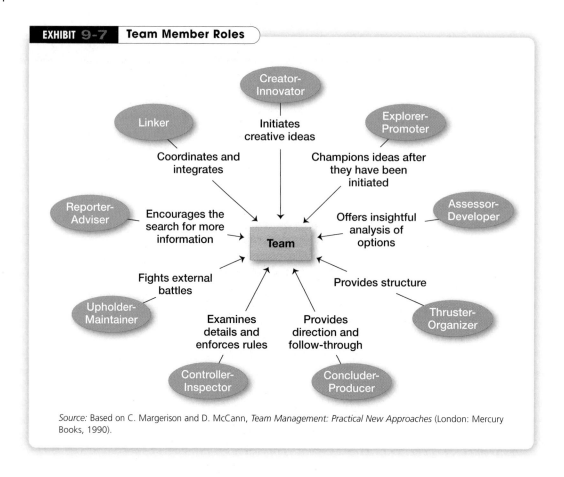

Source: Based on C. Margerison and D. McCann, *Team Management: Practical New Approaches* (London: Mercury Books, 1990).

CEO, uses a "two-pizza" philosophy; that is, a team should be small enough that it can be fed with two pizzas. This "two-pizza" philosophy usually limits groups to five to seven people, depending, of course, on team member appetites![38] Generally speaking, the most effective teams have five to nine members. And experts suggest using the smallest number of people who can do the task.

MANAGING DIVERSITY | The Challenge of Managing Diverse Work Teams

Managing teams composed of people who are similar isn't always easy. But add in diverse members and it can be even more challenging! However, the benefits from the diverse perspectives, skills, and abilities are worth it.[39] Four interpersonal factors are important for meeting the challenge of coordinating a diverse work team: understanding, empathy, tolerance, and communication.

You know that people aren't the same, yet they need to be treated fairly and equitably. And differences (cultural, physical, or other) can cause people to behave in different ways. You need to understand and accept these differences and encourage each team member to do the same.

Empathy is closely related to understanding. As a team leader, you should try to understand others' perspectives. Put yourself in their place and encourage team members to empathize as well. For instance, suppose an Asian woman joins a team of Caucasian and Hispanic men. They can make her feel more welcome and comfortable by identifying with how she might feel. Is she excited or disappointed about her new work assignment? What were

her previous work experiences? How can they help her feel more comfortable? By empathizing with her, existing team members can work together better as an effective group.

Tolerance is another important interpersonal consideration. Just because you understand that people are different and you empathize with them doesn't mean that it's any easier to accept different perspectives or behaviors. But it's important to be tolerant and open-minded about different values, attitudes, and behaviors.

Finally, open and two-way communication is important to managing a diverse team. Diversity problems may intensify if people are afraid or unwilling to openly discuss issues that concern them. If a person wants to know whether a certain behavior is offensive to someone else, it's best to ask. Likewise, a person who is offended by another's behavior should explain his or her concerns and ask that person to stop. Such communication exchanges can be positive when they're handled in a nonthreatening, low-key, and friendly manner.

Team *member preferences* need to be considered. Why? Some people just prefer not to work on teams. Given the option, many employees will opt not to be part of a team. When people who would prefer to work alone are forced on a team, it creates a direct threat to the team's morale and to individual member satisfaction.[40]

HOW DOES WORK DESIGN AFFECT TEAM EFFECTIVENESS? Effective teams need to work together and take collective responsibility for completing tasks. An effective team must be more than a "team in name only."[41] Important work design elements include *autonomy*, using a *variety of skills*, being able to complete a *whole and identifiable* task or product, and working on a task or project that has a *significant impact* on others. Research indicates that these characteristics enhance team member motivation and increase team effectiveness.[42]

WHAT TEAM PROCESSES ARE RELATED TO TEAM EFFECTIVENESS? Five team process variables have been shown to be related to team effectiveness. These include a common purpose, specific team goals, team efficacy, managed conflict, and minimal social loafing.

An effective team has a *common plan and purpose*. This common purpose provides direction, momentum, and commitment for team members.[43] Members of successful teams put a lot of time and effort into discussing, shaping, and agreeing on a purpose that belongs to them both individually and as a team.

Teams also need *specific goals*. Such goals facilitate clear communication and help teams maintain their focus on getting results.

Team efficacy describes when teams believe in themselves and believe they can succeed.[44] Effective teams have confidence in themselves and in their members.

Effective teams need some *conflict*. Conflict on a team isn't necessarily bad and can actually improve team effectiveness.[45] But, it has to be the right kind of conflict. Relationship conflicts—those based on interpersonal incompatibilities, tension, and autonomy toward others—are almost always dysfunctional. However, task conflicts—those based on disagreements about task content—can be beneficial because they may stimulate discussion, promote critical assessment of problems and options, and can lead to better team decisions.

Finally, effective teams work to minimize the tendency for *social loafing*, which we discussed earlier in this chapter. Successful teams make members individually and jointly accountable for the team's purpose, goals, and approach.[46]

Effective teams have a common plan and purpose that provide direction, momentum, and commitment for team members. The goal of "The Elvis Hit Making Team" was to bring back Elvis Presley's famous Memphis rock sound. Dedicated to accomplish this goal, musicians, such as the members of the New York String Section shown here, vocal groups, bands, and composers who created the original Memphis sound reunited in a historical music project that took place in recording studios throughout America during a ten-year period. The team members effectively worked together to accomplish their goal of bringing back the Memphis sound by releasing a CD titled "The End: A New Beginning."

How Can a Manager Shape Team Behavior?

There are several things managers can do to shape a team's behavior including proper selection, employee training, and rewarding the appropriate team behaviors. Let's look at each.

WHAT ROLE DOES SELECTION PLAY? Some individuals already possess the interpersonal skills to be effective team players. When hiring team members, managers should check whether applicants have the technical skills required to successfully perform the job *and* whether they can fulfill team roles.

Some applicants may have been socialized around individual contributions and, consequently, lack team skills, which could also be true for some current employees being moved into teams due to organizational restructuring. When faced with this, a manager can do several things. First, and most obvious, if team skills are woefully lacking, don't hire the person. If successful performance is going to require interaction, not hiring the individual is appropriate. On the other hand, an applicant who has some basic skills can be hired on a probationary basis and required to undergo training to shape him or her into a team player. If the skills aren't learned or practiced, then the individual may have to be let go.

CAN INDIVIDUALS BE TRAINED TO BE TEAM PLAYERS? Performing well in a team involves a set of behaviors.[47] As we discussed in the preceding chapter, new behaviors *can* be learned. Even people who feel strongly about the importance of individual accomplishment can be trained to become team players. Training specialists can conduct exercises so employees can experience what teamwork is all about. The workshops can cover such topics as team problem solving, communications, negotiations, conflict resolution, and coaching skills. It's not unusual, too, for these individuals to be exposed to the stages of team development that we discussed earlier.[48] At Verizon Communications, for example, trainers focus on how a team goes through various stages before it gels. And employees are reminded of the importance of patience, because teams take longer to do some things— such as make decisions—than do employees acting alone.[49]

WHAT ROLE DO REWARDS PLAY IN SHAPING TEAM PLAYERS? An organization's reward system needs to encourage cooperative efforts rather than competitive ones. For instance, Lockheed Martin's aeronautics division organized its 20,000-plus employees into teams. Rewards are structured to return a percentage increase in the bottom line to the team members on the basis of achievements of the team's performance goals.

Promotions, pay raises, and other forms of recognition should be given to employees who are effective collaborative team members. Taking this approach doesn't mean that individual contribution is ignored, but rather that it's balanced with selfless contributions to the team. Examples of behaviors that should be rewarded include training new colleagues, sharing information with teammates, helping resolve team conflicts, and mastering new skills in which the team is deficient.[50] Finally, managers can't forget the inherent rewards that employees can receive from teamwork. Work teams provide camaraderie. It's exciting and satisfying to be an integral part of a successful team. The opportunity to engage in personal development and to help teammates grow can be a satisfying and rewarding experience for employees.[51]

What Current Issues Do Managers Face in Managing Teams?

9.4 Discuss contemporary issues in managing teams.

Few trends have influenced how work gets done in organizations as much as the use of work teams. The shift from working alone to working on teams requires employees to cooperate with others, share information, confront differences, and sublimate personal interests for the greater good of the team. Managers can build effective teams by understanding what influences performance and satisfaction. However, managers also face some current challenges in managing teams, including those associated with managing global teams and with understanding when teams aren't the answer.

What's Involved with Managing Global Teams?

Two characteristics of today's organizations are obvious: they're global and work is increasingly done by teams. This means that any manager is likely to have to manage a global team. What do we know about managing global teams? We know there are both drawbacks and benefits in using global teams (see Exhibit 9-8). What are some of the challenges associated with managing global teams?

HOW DO TEAM COMPOSITION FACTORS AFFECT MANAGING A GLOBAL TEAM? In global organizations, understanding the relationship between team effectiveness and team composition is more challenging because of the unique cultural characteristics represented by members of a global team. In addition to recognizing team members' abilities, skills, knowledge, and personality, managers need to be familiar with and clearly understand the cultural characteristics of the groups and the group members they manage.[52] For instance, is the global team from a culture in which uncertainty avoidance is high? If so, members will not be comfortable dealing with unpredictable and ambiguous tasks. Also, as managers work with global teams, they need to be aware of the potential for stereotyping, which can lead to problems.

HOW DOES TEAM STRUCTURE AFFECT MANAGING A GLOBAL TEAM? Some of the structural areas where we see differences in managing global teams include conformity, status, social loafing, and cohesiveness.

Are conformity findings generalizable across cultures? Research suggests that Asch's findings are culture-bound.[53] For instance, as might be expected, conformity to social norms tends to be higher in collectivistic cultures than in individualistic cultures. Despite this, however, groupthink tends to be less of a problem in global teams because members are less likely to feel pressured to conform to the ideas, conclusions, and decisions of the group.[54]

Also, the importance of status varies between cultures. The French, for example, are extremely status conscious. Also, countries differ on the criteria that confer status. For instance, in Latin America and Asia, status tends to come from family position and formal roles held in organizations. In contrast, while status is important in countries like the United States and Australia, it tends to be less "in your face." And it tends to be given based on accomplishments rather than on titles and family history. Managers must understand who and what holds status when interacting with people from a culture different from their own. An American manager who doesn't understand that office size isn't a measure of a Japanese executive's position or who fails to grasp the importance the British

---

EXHIBIT 9-8   Global Teams

DRAWBACKS	BENEFITS
• Disliking team members	• Greater diversity of ideas
• Mistrusting team members	• Limited groupthink
• Stereotyping	• Increased attention on understanding others' ideas, perspectives, etc.
• Communication problems	
• Stress and tension	

Source: Based on N. Adler, *International Dimensions of Organizational Behavior,* 4th ed. (Cincinnati, OH: Southwestern Cengage Publishing, 2002), pp 141–47.

According to Hofstede's cross-cultural characteristics, India ranks high in power distance and low in uncertainty avoidance. Thus, managers of this Microsoft team in India might expect that team members would be more accepting of a manager's authority but also have high tolerance for unstructured, unclear, and unpredictable situations. It's important for team managers to know and understand the cultural characteristics of team members in order to help that team be most effective.

place on family genealogy and social class is likely to unintentionally offend others and lessen his or her interpersonal effectiveness.

Social loafing has a Western bias. It's consistent with individualistic cultures, like the United States and Canada, which are dominated by self-interest. It's not consistent with collectivistic societies, in which individuals are motivated by group goals. For instance, in studies comparing employees from the United States with employees from the People's Republic of China and Israel (both collectivistic societies), the Chinese and Israelis showed no propensity to engage in social loafing. In fact, they actually performed better in a group than when working alone.[55]

Cohesiveness is another group structural element where managers may face special challenges. In a cohesive group, members are unified and "act as one." There's a great deal of camaraderie and group identity is high. In global teams, however, cohesiveness is often more difficult to achieve because of higher levels of "mistrust, miscommunication, and stress."[56]

HOW DO TEAM PROCESSES AFFECT MANAGING A GLOBAL TEAM? The processes that global teams use to do their work can be particularly challenging for managers. For one thing, communication issues often arise because not all team members may be fluent in the team's working language. This can lead to inaccuracies, misunderstandings, and inefficiencies.[57] However, research has also shown that a multicultural global team is better able to capitalize on the diversity of ideas represented if a wide range of information is used.[58]

Managing conflict in global teams isn't easy, especially when those teams are virtual teams. Conflict can interfere with how information is used by the team. However, research shows that in collectivistic cultures, a collaborative conflict management style can be most effective.[59]

When Are Teams Not the Answer?

Teamwork takes more time and often more resources than does individual work.[60] Teams require managers to communicate more, manage conflicts, and run meetings. So, the benefits of using teams need to exceed the costs. And that's not always the case![61] In the rush to use teams, some managers have introduced them into situations in which it would have been better to have individuals do the work. So before rushing into implementing teams, just because everyone's talking about their popularity, you should carefully evaluate whether the work requires or will benefit from a collective effort.

How do you know whether work is better done individually or by a group? Three "tests" have been suggested.[62] First, can the work be done better by more than one person? Task complexity would be a good indicator of a need for different perspectives. Simple tasks that don't require diverse input are probably better done by individuals. Second, does the work create a common purpose or set of goals for the people in the group that's more than the sum of individual goals? For instance, many car dealerships use teams to link customer-service personnel, mechanics, parts specialists, and sales representatives. Such teams can better meet the goal of outstanding customer satisfaction. The final test to assess whether teams or individuals are better suited for doing work is to look at the interdependence of the individuals. Using teams makes sense when there's interdependence between tasks; that is, when the success of everyone depends on the success of each person *and* the success of each person depends on the others. For example, soccer is an obvious team sport. Success requires a lot of coordination between interdependent players. On the other hand, swim teams aren't really teams, except on relays. They're groups of individuals, performing individually, whose total performance is merely the sum of their individual performances.

Review and  Applications

Chapter Summary

9.1 **Define a group and describe the stages of group development.** A group is two or more interacting and interdependent individuals who come together to achieve specific goals. Formal groups are work groups that are defined by the organization's structure and have designated work assignments and specific tasks directed at accomplishing organizational goals. Informal groups are social groups.

The forming stage consists of two phases: joining the group and defining the group's purpose, structure, and leadership. The storming stage is one of intragroup conflict over who will control the group and what the group will be doing. The norming stage is when close relationships and cohesiveness develop as norms are determined. The performing stage is when group members began to work on the group's task. The adjourning stage is when the group prepares to disband.

9.2 **Describe the major concepts of group behavior.** A role refers to a set of behavior patterns expected of someone occupying a given position in a social unit. At any given time, employees adjust their role behaviors to the group of which they are a part. Norms are standards shared by group members. They informally convey to employees which behaviors are acceptable and which are unacceptable. Status is another factor to know since status can be a significant motivator and it needs to be congruent. Also, group size affects group behavior in a number of ways. Smaller groups are generally faster at completing tasks than are larger ones. However, larger groups are frequently better at fact finding because of their diversified input. As a result, larger groups are generally better at problem solving. Finally, group cohesiveness is important because of its impact on a group's effectiveness at achieving its goals.

9.3 **Discuss how groups are turned into effective teams.** Effective teams have common characteristics. They have adequate resources, effective leadership, a climate of trust, and a performance evaluation and reward system that reflects team contributions. These teams have individuals with technical expertise as well as problem-solving, decision-making, and interpersonal skills and the right traits, especially conscientiousness and openness to new experiences. Effective teams also tend to be small, preferably of diverse backgrounds. They have members who fill role demands and who prefer to be part of a team. And the work that members do provides freedom and autonomy, the opportunity to use different skills and talents, the ability to complete a whole and identifiable task or product, and work that has a substantial impact on others. Finally, effective teams have members who believe in the team's capabilities and are committed to a common plan and purpose, specific team goals, a manageable level of conflict, and a minimal degree of social loafing.

9.4 **Discuss contemporary issues in managing teams.** The challenges of managing global teams can be seen in the team composition factors, especially the diverse cultural characteristics; in team structure, especially conformity, status, social loafing, and cohesiveness; and in team processes, especially with communication and managing conflict; and the manager's role in making it all work.

Managers also need to know when teams are not the answer. They can do this by assessing whether the work can be done better by more than one person; by whether the work creates a common purpose or set of goals for the members of the team; and by the amount of interdependence among team members.

PEARSON mymanagementlab To check your understanding of learning outcomes **9.1** – **9.4**, go to mymanagementlab.com and try the chapter questions.

Understanding the Chapter

1. Think of a group to which you belong (or have belonged). Trace its development through the stages of group development as shown in Exhibit 9-2. How closely did its development parallel the group development model? How might the group development model be used to improve this group's effectiveness?

2. Contrast (a) self-managed and cross-functional teams and (b) virtual and face-to-face teams.

3. How do you explain the popularity of work teams in countries such as the United States and Canada, whose national cultures place a high value on individualism?

4. "All work teams are work groups, but not all work groups are work teams." Do you agree or disagree with this statement? Discuss.

5. Would you prefer to work alone or as part of a team? Why? Support your response with data from the self-

assessment exercise included in the "Understanding Yourself" section.

6. "To have a successful team, first find a great leader." What do you think of this statement? Do you agree? Why or why not?

7. What traits do you think good team players have? Do some research to answer this question and write a short report detailing your findings using a bulleted list format.

8. Do some research on diverse teams and write a short report contrasting the pros and cons of diverse teams.

Understanding Yourself

What's My Attitude Toward Working in Groups?

One thing is for certain about organizations these days: more and more work is being performed by teams. So, it's quite likely that you'll be part of a team at some point if you've not already been so.

Teams comprised of members who enjoy being part of a group can be quite effective. However, research has indicated that as little as one person with a negative attitude toward working in groups can hurt team performance. Why? Team members with negative attitudes can increase interpersonal conflict among group members, harming cohesiveness and team processes. Team morale and satisfaction are lowered, and performance ultimately declines.

INSTRUMENT   Using the scale below, indicate the extent to which you agree or disagree with each of the following statements about your feelings toward working in groups or teams.

> **1** = Strongly disagree
> **2** = Disagree
> **3** = Neutral
> **4** = Agree
> **5** = Strongly agree

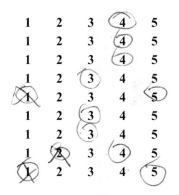

1. I don't miss group meetings or team practices.   1 2 3 ④ 5
2. I enjoy being part of a group.   1 2 3 ④ 5
3. I support my teammates or fellow group members.   1 2 3 ④ 5
4. I feel I must respect the decisions made by my group.   1 2 ③ 4 5
5. I am not good at working with a group.   ①̸ 2 3 4 ⑤
6. I prefer to do everything alone.   1 2 ③ 4 5
7. I work best when I am alone.   1 2 ③ 4 5
8. I keep to myself.   1 ②̸ 3 ④ 5
9. I don't think it's important to socialize with others.   ①̸ 2 3 4 ⑤

SCORING KEY   To score the measure, first reverse-code items 5, 6, 7, 8, and 9 so that 1 = 5, 2 = 4, 3 = 3, 4 = 2, and 5 = 1. Then, compute the sum of the nine items. Scores will range from 9 to 45.

ANALYSIS AND INTERPRETATION   This measure assesses your attitude toward working in groups. Scores at or above 36 indicate that you enjoy working in groups and that you are a "team player." Scores at or below 18 indicate the opposite—that you prefer to work alone and do not enjoy being part of a team. Scores between 18 and 36 indicate no particularly strong feelings either way.

If you scored low on this measure and find yourself on a team at some point, try to see the benefits of teamwork. Not only is work shared among individuals, but teams also can facilitate feelings of inclusion and camaraderie among team members. Remember to be patient, however. Although teams often outperform individuals working by themselves (especially on complex tasks that require multiple skills and experience), they tend to take longer to reach decisions.

Source: L. R. Goldberg, J. A. Johnson, H. W. Eber, R. Hogan, M. C. Ashton, C. R. Cloninger, and H. G. Gough, "The International Personality Item Pool and the Future of Public-Domain Personality Measures," *Journal of Research in Personality* (40) (2006), 84–96.

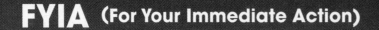

FYIA (For Your Immediate Action)

Colorado State High School Sports Association

Reply   Reply All   Forward

To:	Eric Gershman, Manager, Program Infractions Investigations
From:	Audrey Costa, Director of Association Services
Subject:	**Conflicts on Investigation Teams**

Eric, we've got a potentially big problem on our hands. I've been receiving complaints that the members of the five-person investigation teams we're sending out to high schools to investigate allegations of rules infractions are having conflicts. Because these team members have to work closely together in interviewing people, interpreting the rules, and writing up reports, I'm worried that this conflict may be hurting the quality of the team's investigation process. We've got to address this problem immediately in order to protect our reputation for being fair and reasonable in our rules enforcement. Please send me a bulleted list (no longer than a page) describing how you're going to address this problem and get it to me as soon as possible. Once I've had a chance to look it over, we'll get together to discuss it.

This fictionalized company and message were created for educational purposes only. It is not meant to reflect positively or negatively on management practices by any company that may share this name.

MIXING IT UP

How do you combine two packaged-food companies, both with very well-known household brand names, and make it work? That's the challenge managers at General Mills faced when it acquired Pillsbury. The company's chief learning officer, Kevin Wilde (standing at left in the photo), said, "Let's get the best out of both of our marketing organizations. And let's not stop there." So they decided to identify, share, and integrate the best practices from both companies. And employee teams played a major role in how the company proceeded.

An intensive training program called "Brand Champions" was created and launched. The program was designed not just for marketing specialists, but for all employees from different functional areas who worked on particular brands. These cross-functional teams attended the in-house training together as a unified group. According to one of the program developers (Beth Gunderson, seated in the photo), specific benefits of including these teams soon became evident. "A person from human resources, for instance, would ask a provocative question precisely because she wasn't a marketer. And you'd see the look on the marketers' faces: Whoa, I never thought of that." It helped employees understand and appreciate different perspectives.

Another benefit of including people from different functions was improved communication throughout the company. People were no longer griping about what other functional areas were doing. Employees began to understand how the other functional areas worked and how each area's contribution was important to the overall success of the company.

The training program has been so successful that now General Mills' production plants have asked for a mini-version of the course. "They want to understand the language marketers speak and why things are done as they are." Oh . . . and one other example of how successful the program has been. Betty Crocker is well-known for packaged cake mixes, but less so for cookie mixes. Inspired by input from the group, the cookie-mix team decided to go after scratch bakers. (These are people who bake from scratch rather than from a boxed mix. As one person said, they were "taking on grandma.") The cookie mixes were reformulated and now the brand owns 90 percent of the dry cookie mix category.

Discussion Questions

1. What benefits did the cross-functional teams bring to General Mills?
2. What challenges would there be in creating an effective cross-functional team? How could managers deal with these challenges?
3. Explain how roles, norms, status, group size, and cohesiveness might affect these teams.
4. Explain how each of the characteristics of effective teams (see Exhibit 9-6) would be important for an effective cross-functional team.

Sources: Based on L. Gratton and T. J. Erickson, "8 Ways to Build Collaborative Teams," *Harvard Business Review* (November 2007), pp. 100–109; and J. Gordon, "Building Brand Champions," *Training* (January/February 2007), pp. 14–17.

10

Motivating and Rewarding Employees

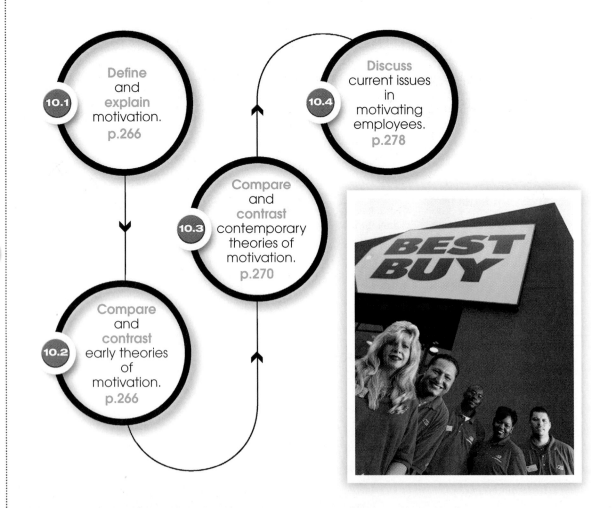

Best Practices at Best Buy

Do traditional workplaces reward long hours instead of efficient hours? Wouldn't it make more sense to have a workplace in which "people can do whatever they want, whenever they want, as long as the work gets done?" Well, that's the approach that Best Buy is taking.[1] And this radical workplace experiment, which obviously has many implications for employee motivation, has been an interesting and enlightening journey for the company.

In 2002, then-CEO Brad Anderson (now the company's vice chairman) introduced a carefully crafted program called ROWE (Results-Only Work Environment). ROWE was the inspiration of two HRM managers at Best Buy, Cali Ressler and Jody Thompson (in photo below), who had been given the task of taking a flexible work program that was in effect at corporate headquarters in Minnesota and developing it for everyone in the company. Ressler and Thompson said, "We realized that the flexible work program was successful as employee engagement was up, productivity was higher, but the problem was the participants were being viewed as 'not working.' " And that's a common reaction from managers who don't really view flexible work employees as "really working because they aren't in the office working traditional hours." The two women set about to change that by creating a program in which "everyone would be evaluated solely on their results, not on how long they worked."

The first thing to understand about ROWE is that it's not about schedules. Instead, it's about changing the work culture of an organization, which is infinitely more difficult than changing schedules. With Anderson's blessing and support, they embarked on this journey to overhaul the company's corporate workplace.

The first step in implementing ROWE was a culture audit at company headquarters, which helped them establish a baseline for how employees perceived their work environment. After four months, the audit was repeated. During this time, Best Buy executives were being educated about ROWE and what it was all about. Obviously, it was important to have their commitment to the program. The second phase involved explaining the ROWE philosophy to all the corporate employees and training managers on how to maintain control in a ROWE workplace. In the third phase, work unit teams were free to figure out how to implement the changes. Each team found a different way to keep the flexibility from spiraling into chaos. For instance, the public relations team got pagers to make sure someone was always available in an emergency. Some employees in the finance department use software that turns voice mail into e-mail files accessible from anywhere, making it easier for them to work at home. Four months after ROWE was implemented, Ressler and Thompson followed up with another culture check to see how everyone was doing.

So what's the bottom line for Best Buy? From 2005 to 2007, productivity jumped 41 percent and voluntary turnover fell to 8 percent from 12 percent. And employees say that the freedom has changed their lives. "They don't know if they work fewer hours—they've stopped counting—but they are more productive." As Ressler and Thompson stated, "Work isn't a place you go—it's something you do."

Successful managers understand that what motivates them personally may have little or no effect on others. Just because you're motivated by being part of a cohesive work team, don't assume everyone is. Or just because you're motivated by your job doesn't mean that everyone is. Effective managers who get employees to put forth maximum effort know how and why those employees are motivated and tailor motivational practices to satisfy their needs and wants. Motivating and rewarding employees is one of the most important and challenging activities that managers do. To get employees to put forth maximum work effort, managers need to know how and why they're motivated. That's what we discuss in this chapter.

What Is Motivation?

10.1 Define and explain motivation.

Several CEOs were attending a meeting where the topic was "What do employees want?"[2] Each CEO took turns describing the benefits they provided and how they gave out free M&Ms every Wednesday and offered their employees stock options and free parking spaces. However, the meeting's main speaker made the point that "employees don't want M&Ms; they want to love what they do." Half expecting his audience to laugh, the speaker was pleasantly surprised as the CEOs stood up one-by-one to agree. They all recognized that "the value in their companies comes from the employees who are motivated to be there."

These CEOs understand how important employee motivation is. Like them, all managers need to be able to motivate their employees. That requires understanding what motivation is. Let's begin by pointing out what motivation is not. Why? Because many people incorrectly view motivation as a personal trait; that is, they think some people are motivated and others aren't. Our knowledge of motivation tells us that we can't label people that way because individuals differ in motivational drive and their overall motivation varies from situation to situation. For instance, you're probably more motivated in some classes than in others.

Motivation refers to the process by which a person's efforts are energized, directed, and sustained toward attaining a goal.[3] This definition has three key elements: energy, direction, and persistence.[4]

The *energy* element is a measure of intensity or drive. A motivated person puts forth effort and works hard. However, the quality of the effort must be considered as well as its intensity. High levels of effort don't necessarily lead to favorable job performance unless the effort is channeled in a *direction* that benefits the organization. Effort that's directed toward, and consistent with, organizational goals is the kind of effort we want from employees. Finally, motivation includes a *persistence* dimension. We want employees to persist in putting forth effort to achieve those goals.

Motivating high levels of employee performance is an important organizational concern, and managers keep looking for answers. For instance, a recent Gallup poll found that a large majority of U.S. employees—some 73 percent—are not excited about their work. As the researchers stated, "These employees are essentially 'checked out.' They're sleepwalking through their workday, putting time, but not energy or passion, into their work."[5] It's no wonder then that both managers and academics want to understand and explain employee motivation.

What Do the Early Theories of Motivation Say?

10.2 Compare and contrast early theories of motivation.

The 1950s and 1960s were a fruitful time for the development of motivation concepts. Four specific theories formulated during this period are probably still the best-known explanations of employee motivation although they've been criticized and questioned. These include the hierarchy of needs theory, Theories X and Y, the two-factor theory, and the three-needs theory. Although more valid explanations of motivation have been developed, you should know these early theories for at least two reasons. First, they represent the foundation from which contemporary theories grew. Second, practicing managers regularly use these theories and their terminology in explaining employee motivation. Let's take a look at them.

What Is Maslow's Hierarchy of Needs Theory?

Having a car to get to work is a necessity for many workers. When two crucial employees of Taleo/Vurv Technology in Jacksonville, Florida, had trouble getting to work, the owner decided to buy two inexpensive used cars for the employees. He said, "I felt that they were good employees and a valuable asset to the company." One of the employees who got one of the cars said, "It wasn't the nicest car. It wasn't the prettiest car. But boy did my overwhelming feeling of dread go from that to enlightenment. The 80-hour weeks we worked after that never meant anything. It was give and take. I was giving and the company was definitely giving back."[7] This company understood employee needs (reliable transportation being an essential need for employees to be able to get to work) and their impact on motivation. The first motivation theory we're going to look at addresses employee needs.

The best-known motivation theory is probably Abraham Maslow's **hierarchy of needs theory**.[8] Maslow was a psychologist who proposed that within every person is a hierarchy of five needs:

1. **Physiological needs:** Food, drink, shelter, sex, and other physical requirements.
2. **Safety needs:** Security and protection from physical and emotional harm, as well as assurance that physical needs will continue to be met.
3. **Social needs:** Affection, belongingness, acceptance, and friendship.
4. **Esteem needs:** Internal esteem factors such as self-respect, autonomy, and achievement and external esteem factors such as status, recognition, and attention.
5. **Self-actualization needs:** Growth, achieving one's potential, and self-fulfillment; the drive to become what one is capable of becoming.

Maslow argued that each level in the needs hierarchy must be substantially satisfied before the next need becomes dominant (see Exhibit 10-1). An individual moves up the needs

and the survey says... [6]

40 percent of workers cited "lack of recognition" as a key reason for leaving a job.

42 percent of administrative professionals prefer verbal forms of recognition.

76 percent of organizations say flextime boosts employee morale.

75 percent of Gen Y workers say that they expect to work for two to five employers during their lifetime.

22 percent of U.S. workers say they "live to work" rather than "work to live."

16 percent of French workers say they "live to work."

15 percent of German and U.K. workers say they "live to work."

#1 reason why people leave a company is a bad relationship with their boss.

| EXHIBIT 10-1 | Maslow's Hierarchy of Needs |

Source: *Motivation and Personality*, 2nd ed., by A. H. Maslow, 1970. Reprinted by permission of Prentice Hall, Inc., Upper Saddle River, New Jersey.

---

motivation
The process by which a person's efforts are energized, directed, and sustained toward attaining a goal.

hierarchy of needs theory
Maslow's theory that there is a hierarchy of five human needs: physiological, safety, social, esteem, and self-actualization.

Linda Lang, chief executive officer of the Jack in the Box fast food chain, is a Theory Y manager. She has a positive view of human nature and assumes that people enjoy work and accept responsibility. Lang fosters a team approach and encourages employees to contribute to decision making. Describing her management style as collaborative rather than directive, Lang motivates employees by giving them responsibility and challenging jobs, and establishing good group relationships. In this photo, Lang visits with an employee in the company's "Innovation Center," a test kitchen where employees work on procedures for preparing their products.

hierarchy from one level to the next. In addition, Maslow separated the five needs into higher and lower levels. Physiological and safety needs were considered *lower-order needs*; social, esteem, and self-actualization needs were considered *higher-order needs*. Lower-order needs are predominantly satisfied externally while higher-order needs are satisfied internally.

How does Maslow's theory explain motivation? Managers using Maslow's hierarchy to motivate employees do things to satisfy employees' needs. But the theory also says that once a need is substantially satisfied, an individual isn't motivated to satisfy that need. Therefore, to motivate someone, you need to understand what need level that person is on in the hierarchy and focus on satisfying needs at or above that level.

Maslow's need theory has received wide recognition, especially among practicing managers. Its popularity probably can be attributed to the theory's intuitive logic and ease of understanding.[9] But Maslow provided no empirical support for his theory, and several studies that sought to validate it could not.[10]

What Are McGregor's Theory X and Theory Y?

"If you're not a fan of in-your-face management, don't work here." That's how one manufacturing plant manager described his managerial style.[11] And it's a perfect description of what Douglas McGregor called a Theory X manager.

Douglas McGregor is best known for proposing two assumptions about human nature: Theory X and Theory Y.[12] Very simply, **Theory X** is a negative view of people that assumes workers have little ambition, dislike work, want to avoid responsibility, and need to be closely controlled to work effectively. **Theory Y** is a positive view that assumes employees enjoy work, seek out and accept responsibility, and exercise self-direction. McGregor believed that Theory Y assumptions should guide management practice and proposed that participation in decision making, responsible and challenging jobs, and good group relations would maximize employee motivation.

Unfortunately, there's no evidence to confirm that either set of assumptions is valid or that being a Theory Y manager is the only way to motivate employees. For instance, Jen-Hsun Huang, founder of NVIDIA Corporation, an innovative and successful microchip manufacturer, has been known to use both reassuring hugs and tough love in motivating employees. But he has little tolerance for screw-ups. "In one legendary meeting, he's said to have ripped into a project team for its tendency to repeat mistakes. 'Do you suck?' he asked the stunned employees. 'Because if you suck, just get up and say you suck.'"[13] His message, delivered in classic Theory X style, was that if you need help, ask for it. It's a harsh approach, but it worked.

What Is Herzberg's Two-Factor Theory?

Frederick Herzberg's **two-factor theory** (also called motivation-hygiene theory) proposes that intrinsic factors are related to job satisfaction, while extrinsic factors are associated with job dissatisfaction.[14] Herzberg wanted to know when people felt exceptionally good (satisfied) or bad (dissatisfied) about their jobs. (These findings are shown in Exhibit 10-2.) He concluded that the replies people gave when they felt good about their jobs were significantly different from the replies they gave when they felt badly. Certain characteristics were consistently related to job satisfaction (factors on the left side of the exhibit), and others to job dissatisfaction (factors on the right side). When people felt good about their work, they tended to cite intrinsic factors arising from the job itself such as achievement, recognition, and responsibility. On the other hand, when they were dissatisfied, they tended to cite extrinsic factors arising from the job context such as company policy and administration, supervision, interpersonal relationships, and working conditions.

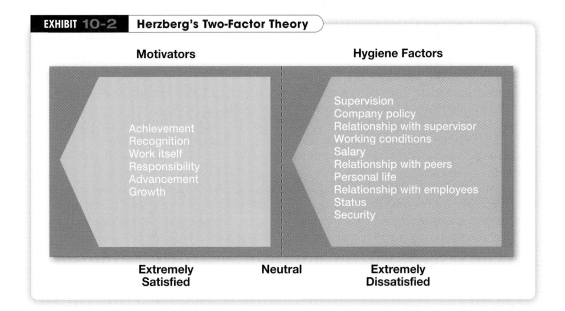

EXHIBIT 10-2 Herzberg's Two-Factor Theory

Motivators

Hygiene Factors

Achievement
Recognition
Work itself
Responsibility
Advancement
Growth

Supervision
Company policy
Relationship with supervisor
Working conditions
Salary
Relationship with peers
Personal life
Relationship with employees
Status
Security

Extremely
Satisfied

Neutral

Extremely
Dissatisfied

In addition, Herzberg believed that the data suggested that the opposite of satisfaction was not dissatisfaction, as traditionally had been believed. Removing dissatisfying characteristics from a job would not necessarily make that job more satisfying (or motivating). As shown in Exhibit 10-3, Herzberg proposed that a dual continuum existed: The opposite of "satisfaction" is "no satisfaction," and the opposite of "dissatisfaction" is "no dissatisfaction."

Again, Herzberg believed that the factors that led to job satisfaction were separate and distinct from those that led to job dissatisfaction. Therefore, managers who sought to eliminate factors that created job dissatisfaction could keep people from being dissatisfied but not necessarily motivate them. The extrinsic factors that create job dissatisfaction were called **hygiene factors**. When these factors are adequate, people won't be dissatisfied, but

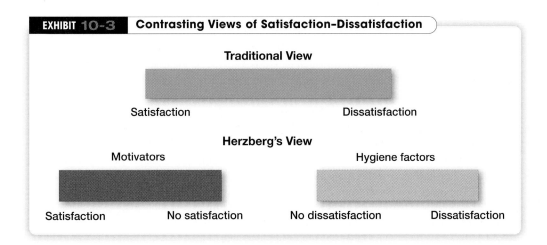

EXHIBIT 10-3 Contrasting Views of Satisfaction–Dissatisfaction

Traditional View

Satisfaction   Dissatisfaction

Herzberg's View

Motivators   Hygiene factors

Satisfaction   No satisfaction   No dissatisfaction   Dissatisfaction

Theory X
The assumption that employees dislike work, are lazy, avoid responsibility, and must be coerced to work.

Theory Y
The assumption that employees are creative, enjoy work, seek responsibility, and can exercise self-direction.

two-factor theory
Herzberg's motivation theory, which proposes that intrinsic factors are related to job satisfaction and motivation, whereas extrinsic factors are associated with job dissatisfaction.

hygiene factors
Factors that eliminate job dissatisfaction but don't motivate.

● From the Past to the Present ●

Deciding how work tasks should be performed has long been of interest to managers.[15] From scientific management's attempts to find the "one best way" to do work to the Hawthorne Studies that attempted to unravel patterns of human behavior at work, researchers have been curious about the ideal approach to work design. In the 1950s, Frederick Herzberg and his associates began research to "discover the importance of attitudes toward work and the experiences both good and bad, that workers reported." He wanted to know the kinds of things that made people at their work happy and satisfied or unhappy and dissatisfied. What he discovered changed the way we view job design. The fact that job dissatisfaction and job satisfaction were the results of different aspects of the work environment was critical. Herzberg's two-factor theory gave practicing managers insights into both job context and job content. And if you wanted to motivate employees, you'd better focus more on the job content aspects (the motivators) than on the job context aspects (the hygiene factors).

In addition, Herzberg's research stimulated additional interest in work design. The Job Characteristics model, for one, built upon Herzberg's findings in identifying the five core job dimensions, especially autonomy. As managers and organizations continue to search for work designs that will energize and engage employees, Herzberg's study of when people felt good and felt bad at work continues as a classic.

---

they won't be satisfied (or motivated) either. To motivate people, Herzberg suggested emphasizing **motivators**, the intrinsic factors having to do with the job itself.

Herzberg's theory enjoyed wide popularity from the mid-1960s to the early 1980s, despite criticisms of his procedures and methodology. Although some critics said his theory was too simplistic, it has influenced how we currently design jobs.

What Is McClelland's Three-Needs Theory?

David McClelland and his associates proposed the **three-needs theory**, which says there are three acquired (not innate) needs that are major motives in work.[16] These three needs include the **need for achievement (nAch)**, which is the drive to succeed and excel in relation to a set of standards; the **need for power (nPow)**, which is the need to make others behave in a way that they would not have behaved otherwise; and the **need for affiliation (nAff)**, which is the desire for friendly and close interpersonal relationships. Of these three needs, the need for achievement has been researched the most.

People with a high need for achievement are striving for personal achievement rather than for the trappings and rewards of success. They have a desire to do something better or more efficiently than it's been done before.[17] They prefer jobs that offer personal responsibility for finding solutions to problems, in which they can receive rapid and unambiguous feedback on their performance in order to tell whether they're improving, and in which they can set moderately challenging goals. High achievers avoid what they perceive to be very easy or very difficult tasks. Also, a high need to achieve doesn't necessarily lead to being a good manager, especially in large organizations. That's because high achievers focus on their *own* accomplishments while good managers emphasize helping *others* accomplish their goals.[18] McClelland showed that employees can be trained to stimulate their achievement need by being in situations where they have personal responsibility, feedback, and moderate risks.[19]

The other two needs in this theory haven't been researched as extensively as the need for achievement. However, we do know that the best managers tend to be high in the need for power and low in the need for affiliation.[20]

How Do the Contemporary Theories Explain Motivation?

10.3 Compare and contrast contemporary theories of motivation.

The theories we look at in this section represent current explanations of employee motivation. Although these theories may not be as well known as those we just discussed, they are supported by research.[21] These contemporary motivation approaches include goal-setting theory, job design theory, equity theory, and expectancy theory.

What Is Goal-Setting Theory?

Before a big assignment or major class project presentation, has a teacher ever encouraged you to "Just do your best"? What does that vague statement, "do your best," mean? Would your performance on a class project have been higher had that teacher said you needed to score a 93 percent to keep your A in the class? Research on goal-setting theory addresses these issues, and the findings, as you'll see, are impressive in terms of the effect that goal specificity, challenge, and feedback have on performance.[22]

There is substantial research support for **goal-setting theory**, which says that specific goals increase performance and that difficult goals, when accepted, result in higher performance than do easy goals. What does goal-setting theory tell us?

First, working toward a goal is a major source of job motivation. Studies on goal setting have demonstrated that specific and challenging goals are superior motivating forces.[23] Such goals produce a higher output than does the generalized goal of "do your best." The specificity of the goal itself acts as an internal stimulus. For instance, when a sales rep commits to making eight sales calls daily, this intention gives him a specific goal to try to attain.

Next, will employees try harder if they have the opportunity to participate in the setting of goals? Not always. In some cases, participatively set goals elicit superior performance; in other cases, individuals performed best when their manager assigned goals. However, participation is probably preferable to assigning goals when employees might resist accepting difficult challenges.[24]

Finally, we know that people will do better if they get feedback on how well they're progressing toward their goals because feedback helps identify discrepancies between what they've done and what they want to do. But all feedback isn't equally effective. Self-generated feedback—where an employee monitors his or her own progress—has been shown to be a more powerful motivator than feedback coming from someone else.[25]

Working toward a goal is a major source of motivation for Mary Kay Cosmetics' independent beauty consultants. They set their own specific sales goals for achieving different categories of rewards. In this photo, Sean Key, vice president of sales development for Mary Kay, celebrates the accomplishment of LaChelle Seleski, who set a challenging sales goal that motivated her to produce a high output for becoming a career car program qualifier. Starting her Mary Kay business as a college student, Seleski has consistently set and met ambitious sales goals and has earned the use of five Mary Kay career cars.

---

motivators
Intrinsic factors that have to do with the job itself and serve to motivate individuals.

three-needs theory
McClelland's theory, which says that three acquired (not innate) needs—achievement, power, and affiliation—are major motives at work.

need for achievement (nAch)
The drive to succeed and excel in relation to a set of standards.

need for power (nPow)
The need to make others behave in a way that they would not have behaved otherwise.

need for affiliation (nAff)
The desire for friendly and close interpersonal relationships.

goal-setting theory
The proposition that specific goals increase performance and that difficult goals, when accepted, result in higher performance than do easy goals.

Three other contingencies besides feedback influence the goal-performance relationship: goal commitment, adequate self-efficacy, and national culture.

First, goal-setting theory assumes that an individual is committed to the goal. Commitment is most likely when goals are made public, when the individual has an internal locus of control, and when the goals are self-set rather than assigned.[26]

Next, **self-efficacy** refers to an individual's belief that he or she is capable of performing a task.[27] The higher your self-efficacy, the more confidence you have in your ability to succeed in a task. So, in difficult situations, we find that people with low self-efficacy are likely to reduce their effort or give up altogether, whereas those with high self-efficacy will try harder to master the challenge.[28] In addition, individuals with high self-efficacy seem to respond to negative feedback with increased effort and motivation, whereas those with low self-efficacy are likely to reduce their effort when given negative feedback.[29]

Finally, the value of goal-setting theory depends on the national culture. It's well adapted to North American countries because its main ideas align reasonably well with those cultures. It assumes that subordinates will be reasonably independent (not a high score on power distance), that people will seek challenging goals (low in uncertainty avoidance), and that performance is considered important by both managers and subordinates (high in assertiveness). Don't expect goal setting to lead to higher employee performance in countries where the cultural characteristics aren't like this.

Exhibit 10-4 summarizes the relationships among goals, motivation, and performance. Our overall conclusion is that the intention to work toward hard and specific goals is a powerful motivating force. Under the proper conditions, it can lead to higher performance. However, there is no evidence that such goals are associated with increased job satisfaction.[30]

How Does Job Design Influence Motivation?

Because managers want to motivate individuals on the job, we need to look at ways to design motivating jobs. If you look closely at what an organization is and how it works, you'll find that it's composed of thousands of tasks. These tasks are, in turn, aggregated into jobs. We use the term **job design** to refer to the way tasks are combined to form complete jobs. The jobs that people perform in an organization should not evolve by chance. Managers should design jobs deliberately and thoughtfully to reflect the demands of the changing environment, the organization's technology, and employees' skills, abilities, and preferences.[31] When jobs are designed like that, employees are motivated to work hard. What are the ways that managers can design motivating jobs?[32] We can answer that with the **job characteristics model (JCM)** developed by J. Richard Hackman and Greg R. Oldham.[33]

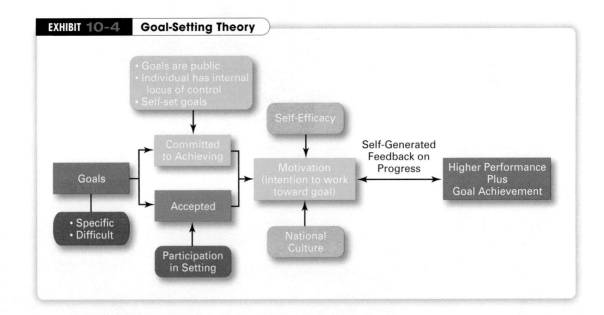

EXHIBIT 10-4   **Goal-Setting Theory**

According to Hackman and Oldham, any job can be described in terms of the following five core job dimensions:

1. ***Skill variety.*** The degree to which the job requires a variety of activities so the worker can use a number of different skills and talents
2. ***Task identity.*** The degree to which the job requires completion of a whole and identifiable piece of work
3. ***Task significance.*** The degree to which the job affects the lives or work of other people
4. ***Autonomy.*** The degree to which the job provides freedom, independence, and discretion to the individual in scheduling the work and in determining the procedures to be used in carrying it out
5. ***Feedback.*** The degree to which carrying out the work activities required by the job results in the individual's obtaining direct and clear information about the effectiveness of his or her performance

Exhibit 10-5 presents the model. Notice how the first three dimensions—skill variety, task identity, and task significance—combine to create meaningful work. What we mean is that if these three characteristics exist in a job, we can predict that the person will view his or her job as being important, valuable, and worthwhile. Notice, too, that jobs that possess autonomy give the job incumbent a feeling of personal responsibility for the results and that, if a job provides feedback, the employee will know how effectively he or she is performing.

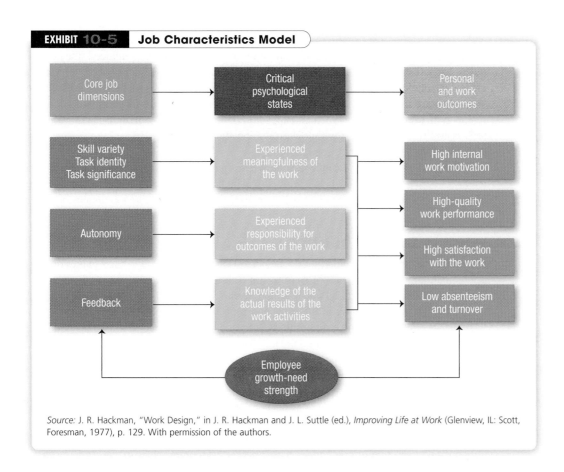

EXHIBIT 10-5 **Job Characteristics Model**

Source: J. R. Hackman, "Work Design," in J. R. Hackman and J. L. Suttle (ed.), *Improving Life at Work* (Glenview, IL: Scott, Foresman, 1977), p. 129. With permission of the authors.

self-efficacy
An individual's belief that he or she is capable of performing a task.

job design
The way tasks are combined to form complete jobs.

job characteristics model (JCM)
A framework for analyzing and designing jobs that identifies five core job dimensions, their interrelationships, and their impact on outcomes.

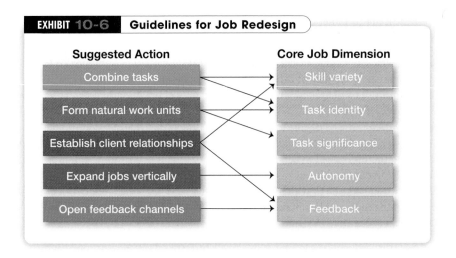

EXHIBIT 10-6 **Guidelines for Job Redesign**

Suggested Action
- Combine tasks
- Form natural work units
- Establish client relationships
- Expand jobs vertically
- Open feedback channels

Core Job Dimension
- Skill variety
- Task identity
- Task significance
- Autonomy
- Feedback

From a motivational point of view, the JCM suggests that internal rewards are obtained when an employee *learns* (knowledge of results through feedback) that he or she *personally* (experienced responsibility through autonomy of work) has performed well on a task that he or she *cares* about (experienced meaningfulness through skill variety, task identity, and/or task significance). The more these three conditions characterize a job, the greater the employee's motivation, performance, and satisfaction and the lower his or her absenteeism and the likelihood of resigning. As the model shows, the links between the job dimensions and the outcomes are moderated by the strength of the individual's growth need (the person's desire for self-esteem and self-actualization). Individuals are more likely to experience the critical psychological states and respond positively when their jobs include the core dimensions than are individuals with a low growth need. This distinction may explain the mixed results with **job enrichment** (vertical expansion of a job by adding planning and evaluation responsibilities): Individuals with low growth need don't tend to achieve high performance or satisfaction by having their jobs enriched.

The JCM provides significant guidance to managers for job design for both individuals and teams.[34] The suggestions shown in Exhibit 10-6, which are based on the JCM, specify the types of changes in jobs that are most likely to improve in each of the five core job dimensions.

What Is Equity Theory?

Do you ever wonder what kind of grade the person sitting next to you in class makes on a test or on a major class assignment? Most of us do! Being human, we tend to compare ourselves with others. If someone offered you $50,000 a year on your first job after graduating from college, you'd probably jump at the offer and report to work enthusiastic, ready to tackle whatever needed to be done, and certainly satisfied with your pay. How would you react, though, if you found out a month into the job that a coworker—another recent graduate, your age, with comparable grades from a comparable school, and with comparable work experience—was getting $55,000 a year? You'd probably be upset! Even though in absolute terms, $50,000 is a lot of money for a new graduate to make (and you know it!), that suddenly isn't the issue. Now you see the issue as what you believe is *fair*—what is *equitable*. The term *equity* is related to the concept of fairness and equitable treatment compared with others who behave in similar ways. There's considerable evidence that employees compare themselves to others and that inequities influence how much effort employees exert.[35]

Equity theory, developed by J. Stacey Adams, proposes that employees compare what they get from a job (outcomes) in relation to what they put into it (inputs) and then compare their inputs-outcomes ratio with the inputs-outcomes ratios of relevant others (Exhibit 10-7). If an employee perceives her ratio to be equitable in comparison to those of relevant others, there's no problem. However, if the ratio is inequitable, she views herself as underrewarded or overrewarded. When inequities occur, employees attempt to do something about it.[36] The result might

---

EXHIBIT 10-7	Equity Theory Relationships

PERCEIVED RATIO COMPARISON*	EMPLOYEE'S ASSESSMENT
$\dfrac{\text{Outcomes A}}{\text{Inputs A}} < \dfrac{\text{Outcomes B}}{\text{Inputs B}}$	Inequity (underrewarded)
$\dfrac{\text{Outcomes A}}{\text{Inputs A}} = \dfrac{\text{Outcomes B}}{\text{Inputs B}}$	Equity
$\dfrac{\text{Outcomes A}}{\text{Inputs A}} > \dfrac{\text{Outcomes B}}{\text{Inputs B}}$	Inequity (overrewarded)

*Person A is the employee, and Person B is a relevant other or referent.

---

be lower or higher productivity, improved or reduced quality of output, increased absenteeism, or voluntary resignation.

The **referent**—the other persons, systems, or selves individuals compare themselves against in order to assess equity—is an important variable in equity theory.[37] Each of the three referent categories is important. The "persons" category includes other individuals with similar jobs in the same organization but also includes friends, neighbors, or professional associates. Based on what they hear at work or read about in newspapers or trade journals, employees compare their pay with that of others. The "system" category includes organizational pay policies, procedures, and allocation. The "self" category refers to inputs-outcomes ratios that are unique to the individual. It reflects past personal experiences and contacts and is influenced by criteria such as past jobs or family commitments.

Originally, equity theory focused on **distributive justice**, which is the perceived fairness of the amount and allocation of rewards among individuals. More recent research has focused on looking at issues of **procedural justice**, which is the perceived fairness of the process used to determine the distribution of rewards. This research shows that distributive justice has a greater influence on employee satisfaction than procedural justice, while procedural justice tends to affect an employee's organizational commitment, trust in his or her boss, and intention to quit.[38] What are the implications for managers? They should consider openly sharing information on how allocation decisions are made, follow consistent and unbiased procedures, and engage in similar practices to increase the perception of procedural justice. By increasing the perception of procedural justice, employees are likely to view their bosses and the organization as positive even if they're dissatisfied with pay, promotions, and other personal outcomes.

Right or Wrong?

The 14-member investment and operations staff of the Missouri State Employees' Retirement System (MOSERS) received almost $300,000 in bonuses in 2008 even though the pension fund lost almost $1.8 billion.[39] One person, the organization's chief investment officer, received over a third of that amount. Organization officials said the payments were based on the fund outperforming the market and that by setting goals and awarding bonuses, they can retain talented employees and improve performance. The state's governor called the bonuses "unconscionable." What do you think? What ethical issues do you see in this situation? What would you do?

How Does Expectancy Theory Explain Motivation?

The most comprehensive explanation of how employees are motivated is Victor Vroom's **expectancy theory**.[40] Although the theory has its critics,[41] most research evidence supports it.[42]

Expectancy theory states that an individual tends to act in a certain way based on the expectation that the act will be followed by a given outcome and on the attractiveness of that outcome to the individual. It includes three variables or relationships (see Exhibit 10-8):

1. *Expectancy* or *effort-performance linkage* is the probability perceived by the individual that exerting a given amount of effort will lead to a certain level of performance.
2. *Instrumentality* or *performance-reward linkage* is the degree to which the individual believes that performing at a particular level is instrumental in attaining the desired outcome.
3. *Valence* or *attractiveness of reward* is the importance that the individual places on the potential outcome or reward that can be achieved on the job. Valence considers both the goals and needs of the individual.

This explanation of motivation might sound complicated, but it really isn't. It can be summed up in the questions: How hard do I have to work to achieve a certain level of performance, and can I actually achieve that level? What reward will performing at that level of performance get me? How attractive is the reward to me, and does it help me achieve my own personal goals? Whether you are motivated to put forth effort (that is, to work hard) at any given time depends on your goals and your perception of whether a certain level of performance is necessary to attain those goals. Let's look at an example. Your third author had a student many years ago who went to work for IBM as a sales rep. Her favorite work "reward" was having an IBM corporate jet fly into Springfield, Missouri, to pick up her best customers and her and take them for a weekend of golfing at some fun location. But to get that particular "reward," she had to achieve a certain level of performance, which involved exceeding her sales goals by a specified percentage. How hard she was willing to work (that is, how motivated she was to put forth effort) was dependent on the level of performance that had to be met and the likelihood that if she achieved at that level of performance she would receive that reward. Since she "valued" that reward, she always worked hard to exceed her sales goals. And the performance-reward linkage was clear because her hard work and performance achievements were always rewarded by the company with the reward she valued (access to a corporate jet).

The key to expectancy theory is understanding an individual's goal and the linkage between effort and performance, between performance and rewards, and finally, between rewards and individual goal satisfaction. It emphasizes payoffs, or rewards. As a result, we have to believe that the rewards an organization is offering align with what the individual wants. Expectancy theory recognizes that there is no universal principle for explaining what motivates individuals and thus stresses that managers understand why employees view certain outcomes

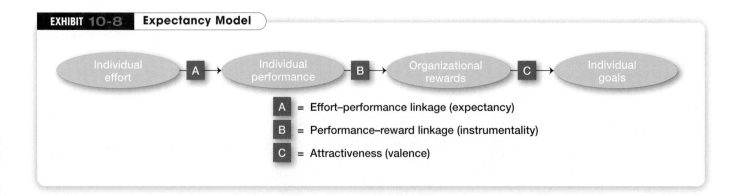

EXHIBIT 10-8 **Expectancy Model**

A = Effort–performance linkage (expectancy)

B = Performance–reward linkage (instrumentality)

C = Attractiveness (valence)

as attractive or unattractive. After all, we want to reward individuals with those things they value positively. Also, expectancy theory emphasizes expected behaviors. Do employees know what is expected of them and how they'll be evaluated? Finally, the theory is concerned with perceptions. Reality is irrelevant. An individual's own perceptions of performance, reward, and goal outcomes, not the outcomes themselves, will determine his or her motivation (level of effort).

How Can We Integrate the Contemporary Motivation Theories?

Many of the ideas underlying the contemporary motivation theories are complementary, and you'll understand better how to motivate people if you see how the theories fit together.[43] Exhibit 10-9 presents a model that integrates much of what we know about

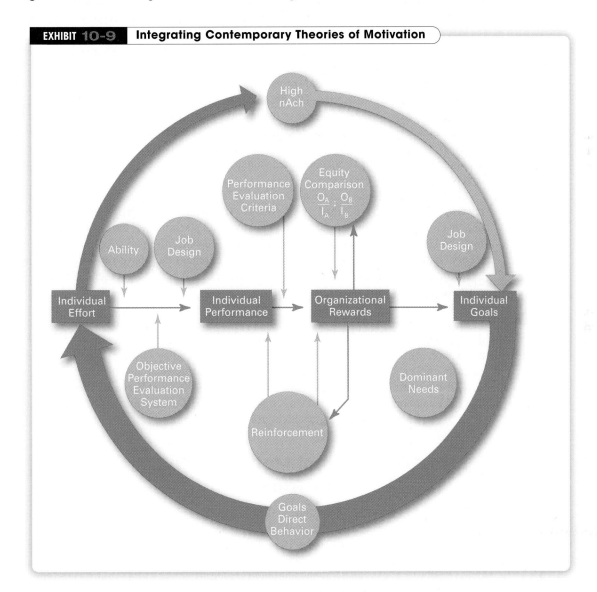

EXHIBIT 10-9 | **Integrating Contemporary Theories of Motivation**

motivation. Its basic foundation is the expectancy model. Let's work through the model, starting on the left.

The individual effort box has an arrow leading into it. This arrow flows from the individual's goals. Consistent with goal-setting theory, this goals-effort link is meant to illustrate that goals direct behavior. Expectancy theory predicts that an employee will exert a high level of effort if he or she perceives that there is a strong relationship between effort and performance, performance and rewards, and rewards and satisfaction of personal goals. Each of these relationships is, in turn, influenced by certain factors. You can see from the model that the level of individual performance is determined not only by the level of individual effort but also by the individual's ability to perform and by whether the organization has a fair and objective performance evaluation system. The performance-reward relationship will be strong if the individual perceives that it is performance (rather than seniority, personal favorites, or some other criterion) that is rewarded. The final link in expectancy theory is the rewards-goal relationship. The traditional need theories come into play at this point. Motivation would be high to the degree that the rewards an individual received for his or her high performance satisfied the dominant needs consistent with his or her individual goals.

A closer look at the model also shows that it considers the achievement-need, reinforcement, equity, and JCM theories. The high achiever isn't motivated by the organization's assessment of his or her performance or organizational rewards; hence the jump from effort to individual goals for those with a high nAch. Remember that high achievers are internally driven as long as the jobs they're doing provide them with personal responsibility, feedback and moderate risks. They're not concerned with the effort-performance, performance-reward, or rewards-goals linkages.

Reinforcement theory is seen in the model by recognizing that the organization's rewards reinforce the individual's performance. If managers have designed a reward system that is seen by employees as "paying off" for good performance, the rewards will reinforce and encourage continued good performance. Rewards also play a key part in equity theory. Individuals will compare the rewards (outcomes) they have received from the inputs or efforts they made with the inputs-outcomes ratio of relevant others. If inequities exist, the effort expended may be influenced.

Finally, the JCM is seen in this integrative model. Task characteristics (job design) influence job motivation at two places. First, jobs that are designed around the five job dimensions are likely to lead to higher actual job performance because the individual's motivation will be stimulated by the job itself—that is, they will increase the linkage between effort and performance. Second, jobs that are designed around the five job dimensions also increase an employee's control over key elements in his or her work. Therefore, jobs that offer autonomy, feedback, and similar task characteristics help to satisfy the individual goals of employees who desire greater control over their work.

What Current Motivation Issues Do Managers Face?

Discuss current issues in motivating employees.

Understanding and predicting employee motivation is one of the most popular areas in management research. We've introduced you to several motivation theories. However, even current studies of employee motivation are influenced by some significant workplace issues—cross-cultural challenges, motivating unique groups of workers, and designing appropriate rewards programs.

How Does Country Culture Affect Motivation Efforts?

In today's global business environment, managers can't automatically assume that motivational programs that work in one geographic location are going to work in others. Most current motivation theories were developed in the United States by Americans and about Americans.[44] Maybe the most blatant pro-American characteristic in these theories

Most motivational theories were developed in the United States, where cultural characteristics favor individualism and a high achievement need. Motivating employees in countries with these cultural characteristics differs from motivating workers in countries such as China that value relationships and collectivism. For the Chinese factory workers shown here, taking a break from work to laugh and visit with coworkers and to soak their feet in tubs of traditional herbal medicine may be the motivators that satisfy their physiological, safety, and social needs.

is the strong emphasis on individualism and achievement. For instance, both goal-setting and expectancy theories emphasize goal accomplishment as well as rational and individual thought. Let's look at the motivation theories to see if there's any cross-cultural transferability.

Maslow's need hierarchy argues that people start at the physiological level and then move progressively up the hierarchy in order. This hierarchy, if it has any application at all, aligns with American culture. In countries like Japan, Greece, and Mexico, where uncertainty avoidance characteristics are strong, security needs would be on top of the need hierarchy. Countries that score high on nurturing characteristics—Denmark, Sweden, Norway, the Netherlands, and Finland—would have social needs on top.[45] We would predict, for instance, that group work will be more motivating when the country's culture scores high on the nurturing criterion.

Another motivation concept that clearly has an American bias is the achievement need. The view that a high achievement need acts as an internal motivator presupposes two cultural characteristics—a willingness to accept a moderate degree of risk (which excludes countries with strong uncertainty avoidance characteristics) and a concern with performance (which applies almost singularly to countries with strong achievement characteristics). This combination is found in Anglo-American countries like the United States, Canada, and Great Britain.[46] On the other hand, these characteristics are relatively absent in countries such as Chile and Portugal.

Equity theory has a relatively strong following in the United States. That's not surprising given that U.S.-style reward systems are based on the assumption that workers are highly sensitive to equity in reward allocations. In the United States, equity is meant to closely link pay to performance. However, recent evidence suggests that in collectivist cultures, especially in the former socialist countries of Central and Eastern Europe, employees expect rewards to reflect their individual needs as well as their performance.[47] Moreover, consistent with a legacy of communism and centrally planned economies, employees exhibited a greater "entitlement" attitude—that is, they expected outcomes to be greater than their inputs.[48] These findings suggest that U.S.-style pay practices may need to be modified in some countries in order to be perceived as fair by employees.

Despite these cross-cultural differences in motivation, don't assume there are no cross-cultural consistencies, because there are some. For instance, the desire for interesting work seems important to almost all workers, regardless of their national culture. In a study of seven countries, employees in Belgium, Britain, Israel, and the United States ranked "interesting work" number one among 11 work goals. It was ranked either second or third in Japan, the Netherlands, and Germany.[49] Similarly, in a study comparing job-preference outcomes among graduate students in the United States, Canada, Australia, and Singapore, growth, achievement, and responsibility were rated the top three and had identical rankings.[50] Both studies suggest some universality to the importance of intrinsic factors identified by Herzberg in his two-factor theory. Another recent study examining workplace motivation trends in Japan also seems to indicate that Herzberg's model is applicable to Japanese employees.[51]

How Can Managers Motivate Unique Groups of Workers?

Motivating employees has never been easy! Employees come into organizations with different needs, personalities, skills, abilities, interests, and aptitudes. They have different expectations of their employers and different views of what they think their employer has a right to expect of them. And they vary widely in what they want from their jobs. For instance, some employees get more satisfaction out of their personal interests and pursuits and only want a weekly paycheck—nothing more. They're not interested in making their work more challenging or interesting or in "winning" performance contests. Others derive a great deal of satisfaction in

Developing Your *Motivating Employees* Skill

About the Skill

Because a simple, all-encompassing set of motivational guidelines is not available, the following suggestions draw on the essence of what we know about motivating employees.

Steps in Practicing the Skill

1 **Recognize individual differences.** Almost every contemporary motivation theory recognizes that employees are not homogeneous. They have different needs. They also differ in terms of attitudes, personality, and other important individual variables.

2 **Match people to jobs.** A great deal of evidence shows the motivational benefits of carefully matching people to jobs. People who lack the necessary skills to perform successfully will be at a disadvantage.

3 **Use goals.** You should ensure that employees have hard, specific goals and feedback on how well they're doing in pursuit of those goals. In many cases, these goals should be participatively set.

4 **Ensure that goals are perceived as attainable.** Regardless of whether goals are actually attainable, employees who see goals as unattainable will reduce their effort. Be sure, therefore, that employees feel confident that increased efforts can lead to achieving performance goals.

5 **Individualize rewards.** Because employees have different needs, what acts as a reinforcer for one may not do so for another. Use your knowledge of employee differences to individualize the rewards over which you have control. Some of the more obvious rewards that you can allocate include pay, promotions, autonomy, and the opportunity to participate in goal setting and decision making.

6 **Link rewards to performance.** You need to make rewards contingent on performance. Rewarding factors other than performance will only reinforce the importance of those other factors. Key rewards such as pay increases and promotions should be given for the attainment of employees' specific goals.

7 **Check the system for equity.** Employees should perceive that rewards or outcomes are equal to the inputs given. On a simplistic level, experience, ability, effort, and other obvious inputs should explain differences in pay, responsibility, and other obvious outcomes.

8 **Don't ignore money.** It's easy to get so caught up in setting goals, creating interesting jobs, and providing opportunities for participation that you forget that money is a major reason why most people work. Thus, the allocation of performance-based wage increases, piece-work bonuses, employee stock ownership plans, and other pay incentives are important in determining employee motivation.

their jobs and are motivated to exert high levels of effort. Given these differences, how can managers do an effective job of motivating the unique groups of employees found in today's workforce? One thing is to understand the motivational requirements of these groups including diverse employees, professionals, and contingent workers.

MOTIVATING A DIVERSE WORKFORCE. To maximize motivation among today's workforce, managers need to think in terms of *flexibility*. For instance, studies tell us that men place more importance on having autonomy in their jobs than do women. In contrast, the opportunity to learn, convenient and flexible work hours, and good interpersonal relations are more important to women.[52] Having the opportunity to be independent and to be exposed to different experiences is important to Gen Y employees whereas older workers may be more interested in highly structured work opportunities.[53] Managers need to recognize that what motivates a single mother with two dependent children who's working full time to support her family may be very different from the needs of a single part-time employee or an older employee who is working only to supplement his or her retirement income. A diverse array of rewards is needed to motivate employees with such diverse needs. Many of the work/life balance programs (see Chapter 2) that organizations have implemented are a response to the varied needs of a diverse workforce. In addition, many organizations have developed flexible work arrangements that recognize different needs. These types of programs may become even more popular as employers look for ways to help employees cope with high fuel prices. For instance, a **compressed workweek** is a workweek where employees work longer hours per day but fewer days per week. The most common arrangement is four 10-hour days (a 4-40 program). However, organizations could design whatever schedules they wanted to fit employees' needs. Another alternative is **flexible work hours** (also known as **flextime**), which is a scheduling system in which employees are required to work a specific number of hours a week but are free to vary those hours within certain limits. In a flextime schedule, there are certain common core hours when all employees are required to be on the job, but starting, ending, and lunch-hour times are flexible. According to a survey by Hewitt Associates, 75 percent of large companies now offer flextime benefits. Another survey by Watson Wyatt of mid- and large-sized companies found that flexible work schedules was the most commonly offered benefit.[54]

In Great Britain, McDonald's is experimenting with an unusual program—dubbed the Family Contract—to reduce absenteeism and turnover at some of its restaurants. Under this Family Contract, employees from the same immediate family can fill in for one another for any work shift without having to clear it first with their manager.[55] This type of job scheduling, which can be effective in motivating a diverse workforce, is called **job sharing**—the practice of having two or more people split a full-time job. Although something like McDonald's Family Contract may be appropriate for a low-skilled job, other organizations might offer job sharing to professionals who want to work but don't want the demands and hassles of a full-time position. For instance, at Ernst & Young, employees in many of the company's locations can choose from a variety of flexible work arrangements including job sharing.

Another alternative made possible by information technology is **telecommuting**. Here, employees work at home but are linked by technology to the workplace. It's

---

compressed workweek
A workweek in which employees work longer hours per day but fewer days per week.

flexible work hours (flextime)
A scheduling system in which employees are required to work a certain number of hours per week but are free, within limits, to vary the hours of work.

job sharing
When two or more people split (share) a full-time job.

telecommuting
A job approach in which employees work at home but are linked by technology to the workplace.

MANAGING DIVERSITY | Developing Employee Potential: The Bottom Line of Diversity

One of a manager's more important goals is helping employees develop their potential.[56] This is particularly important in managing talented diverse employees who can bring new perspectives and ideas to the business but who may find that the workplace environment is not as conducive as it could be to accepting and embracing these different perspectives. For instance, managers at Bell Labs have worked hard to develop an environment in which the ideas of diverse employees are encouraged openly.

What can managers do to ensure that their diverse employees have the opportunity to develop their potential? One thing they can do is make sure that diverse role models are in leadership positions so that others see the opportunities to grow and advance. Giving motivated, talented, hard-working, and enthusiastic diverse employees opportunities to excel in decision-making roles can be a powerful motivator to other diverse employees to work hard to develop their own potential. A mentoring program

in which diverse employees are given the opportunity to work closely with organizational leaders can be a powerful tool. At Silicon Graphics, for instance, new employees become part of a mentoring group called "Horizons." Through this mentoring group, diverse employees have the opportunity to observe and learn from key company decision makers.

Another way for managers to develop the potential of their diverse employees is to offer developmental work assignments that provide a variety of learning experiences in different organizational areas. Employees who are provided the opportunity to learn new processes and new technology are more likely to excel at their work and to stay with the company. These types of developmental opportunities are particularly important for diverse employees because it empowers them with tools that are critical to professional development.

estimated that some 12 percent (and maybe even as high as 15 percent) of the U.S. workforce is part of this "distributed workforce."[57] For example, around 40 percent of IBM's workforce has no physical office space. The number is even higher for Sun Microsystems where nearly 50 percent of employees work off-site.[58] Since many jobs can be done at off-site locations, this approach might be close to the ideal job for many people as there is no commuting, the hours are flexible, there's freedom to dress as you please, and there are little or no interruptions from colleagues. However, keep in mind that not all employees embrace the idea of telecommuting. Some workers relish the informal interactions at work that satisfy their social needs as well as being a source of new ideas.

Do flexible work arrangements motivate employees? Although such arrangements might seem highly motivational, both positive and negative relationships have been found. For instance, a recent study looking at the impact of telecommuting on job satisfaction found that job satisfaction initially increased as the extent of telecommuting increased, but as the number of hours spent telecommuting increased, job satisfaction started to level off, decreased slightly, and then stabilized.[59]

MOTIVATING PROFESSIONALS. In contrast to a generation ago, the typical employee today is more likely to be a professional with a college degree than a blue-collar factory worker. What special concerns should managers be aware of when trying to motivate a team of engineers at Intel's India Development Center, software designers at SAS Institute in North Carolina, or a group of consultants at Accenture in Singapore?

Professionals are different from nonprofessionals.[60] They have a strong and long-term commitment to their field of expertise. To keep current in their field, they need to regularly update their knowledge, and because of their commitment to their profession they rarely define their workweek as 8 A.M. to 5 P.M. five days a week.

What motivates professionals? Money and promotions typically are low on their priority list. Why? They tend to be well paid and enjoy what they do. In contrast, job challenge tends to be ranked high. They like to tackle problems and find solutions. Their chief reward is the work itself. Professionals also value support. They want others to think that what they're working on is important. That may be true for all employees, but professionals tend to be focused on their work as their central life interest, whereas nonprofessionals typically have other interests outside of work that can compensate for needs not met on the job.

MOTIVATING CONTINGENT WORKERS. As full-time jobs have been eliminated through downsizing and other organizational restructurings, the number of openings for part-time, contract, and other forms of temporary work have increased. Contingent workers don't have the security or stability that permanent employees have, and they don't identify with the organization or display the commitment that other employees do. Temporary workers also typically get little or no benefits such as health care or pensions.[61]

There's no simple solution for motivating contingent employees. For that small set of individuals who prefer the freedom of their temporary status, the lack of stability may not be an issue. In addition, temporariness might be preferred by highly compensated physicians, engineers, accountants, or financial planners who don't want the demands of a full-time job. But these are the exceptions. For the most part, temporary employees are not temporary by choice.

What will motivate involuntarily temporary employees? An obvious answer is the opportunity to become a permanent employee. In cases in which permanent employees are selected from a pool of temps, the temps will often work hard in hopes of becoming permanent. A less obvious answer is the opportunity for training. The ability of a temporary employee to find a new job is largely dependent on his or her skills. If an employee sees that the job he or she is doing can help develop marketable skills, then motivation is increased. From an equity standpoint, when temps work alongside permanent employees who earn more and get benefits too for doing the same job, the performance of temps is likely to suffer. Separating such employees or perhaps minimizing interdependence between them might help managers counteract potential problems.[62]

How Can Managers Design Appropriate Rewards Programs?

Blue Cross of California, one of the nation's largest health insurers, pays bonuses to doctors serving its health maintenance organization members based on patient satisfaction and other quality standards. FedEx's drivers are motivated by a pay system that rewards them for timeliness and how much they deliver.[63] There's no doubt that employee rewards programs play a powerful role in motivating appropriate employee behavior. Some of the more popular rewards programs include open-book management, employee recognition, and pay-for-performance.

HOW CAN OPEN-BOOK MANAGEMENT PROGRAMS MOTIVATE EMPLOYEES? Within 24 hours after managers of the Heavy Duty Division of Springfield Remanufacturing Company (SRC) gather to discuss a multipage financial document, every plant employee will have seen the same information. If the employees can meet shipment goals, they'll all share in a large year-end bonus.[64] Many organizations of various sizes involve their employees in workplace decisions by opening up the financial statements (the "books"). They share that information so that employees will be motivated to make better decisions about their work and better able to understand the implications of what they do, how they do it, and the ultimate impact on the bottom line. This approach is called **open-book management** and many organizations are using it.[65] At Best Buy, the

open-book management
A motivational approach in which an organization's financial statements (the "books") are shared with all employees.

USAA chief executive Josue Robles, Jr., personally thanked employees during a celebration after the firm was ranked number one for customer service by *Business Week* magazine. Personal recognition is a powerful tool in motivating employees at USAA, a financial services provider for the military community. Employees are recognized frequently for educational achievements and community and customer service during breakfasts, luncheons, and parties; through articles in USAA's weekly newsletter; and during the firm's weekly television program. The company gives employees "thank you" note stationery so they can express their appreciation and gratitude to coworkers for their help at work.

"Donuts with Darren" sessions (held when Darren Jackson was the company's chief financial officer) were so popular that more than 600 employees regularly took part. His presentations covered the financials and the basics of finance.[66]

The goal of open-book management is to get employees to think like an owner by seeing the impact their decisions have on financial results. Since many employees don't have the knowledge or background to understand the financials, they have to be taught how to read and understand the organization's financial statements. Once employees have this knowledge, however, managers need to regularly share the numbers with them. By sharing this information, employees begin to see the link between their efforts, level of performance, and operational results.

HOW CAN MANAGERS USE EMPLOYEE RECOGNITION PROGRAMS? **Employee recognition programs** consist of personal attention and expressions of interest, approval, and appreciation for a job well done.[67] They can take numerous forms. For instance, Kelly Services introduced a new version of its points-based incentive system to better promote productivity and retention among its employees. The program, called Kelly Kudos, gives employees more choices of awards and allows them to accumulate points over a longer time period. It's working. Participants generate three times more revenue and hours than employees not receiving points.[68] Most managers, however, use a far more informal approach. For example, when Julia Stewart, currently the president and CEO of IHOP International, was president of Applebee's Restaurants, she would frequently leave sealed notes on the chairs of employees after everyone had gone home.[69] These notes explained how important Stewart thought the person's work was or how much she appreciated the completion of a project. Stewart also relied heavily on voice mail messages left after office hours to tell employees how appreciative she was for a job well done. And recognition doesn't have to come only from managers. Some 35 percent of companies encourage coworkers to recognize peers for outstanding work efforts.[70] For instance, managers at Yum! Brands Inc. (the Kentucky-based parent of food chains Taco Bell, KFC, and Pizza Hut) were looking for ways to reduce employee turnover. They found a successful customer-service program involving peer recognition at KFC restaurants in Australia. Workers there spontaneously rewarded fellow workers with "Champs cards, an acronym for attributes such as cleanliness, hospitality, and accuracy." Yum! implemented the program in other restaurants around the world, and credits the peer recognition with reducing hourly employee turnover from 181 percent to 109 percent.[71]

A recent survey of organizations found that 84 percent had some type of program to recognize worker achievements.[72] And do employees think these programs are important? You bet! A survey of a wide range of employees asked them what they considered the most powerful workplace motivator. Their response? Recognition, recognition, and more recognition![73]

Consistent with reinforcement theory (see Chapter 8), rewarding a behavior with recognition immediately following that behavior is likely to encourage its repetition. And recognition can take many forms. You can personally congratulate an employee in private for a good job. You can send a handwritten note or e-mail message acknowledging something positive that the employee has done. For employees with a strong need for social acceptance, you can publicly recognize accomplishments. To enhance group cohesiveness and motivation, you can celebrate team successes. For instance, you can do something as simple as throw a pizza party to celebrate a team's accomplishments. Some of these things may seem simple, but they can go a long way in showing employees they're valued.

HOW CAN MANAGERS USE PAY-FOR-PERFORMANCE TO MOTIVATE EMPLOYEES?

Here's a survey statistic that may surprise you: Forty percent of employees see no clear link between performance and pay.[74] You have to think: What are the companies where these employees work paying for? They're obviously not clearly communicating performance expectations.[75] **Pay-for-performance programs** are variable compensation plans that pay employees on the basis of some performance measure.[76] Piece-rate pay plans, wage incentive plans, profit-sharing, and lump-sum bonuses are examples. What differentiates these forms of pay from more traditional compensation plans is that instead of paying a person for time on the job, pay is adjusted to reflect some performance measure. These performance measures might include such things as individual productivity, team or work group productivity, departmental productivity, or the overall organization's profit performance.

Pay-for-performance is probably most compatible with expectancy theory. Individuals should perceive a strong relationship between their performance and the rewards they receive for motivation to be maximized. If rewards are allocated only on nonperformance factors—such as seniority, job title, or across-the-board pay raises—then employees are likely to reduce their efforts. From a motivation perspective, making some or all an employee's pay conditional on some performance measure focuses his or her attention and effort toward that measure, then reinforces the continuation of the effort with a reward. If the employee, team, or organization's performance declines, so does the reward. Thus, there's an incentive to keep efforts and motivation strong.

Pay-for-performance programs are popular. Some 80 percent of large U.S. companies have some form of variable pay plan.[77] These types of pay plans have also been tried in other countries such as Canada and Japan. About 30 percent of Canadian companies and 22 percent of Japanese companies have company-wide pay-for-performance plans.[78]

Do pay-for-performance programs work? For the most part, studies seem to indicate that they do. For instance, one study found that companies that used pay-for-performance programs performed better financially than those that did not.[79] Another study showed that pay-for-performance

Pfizer, the largest research-based pharmaceutical company in the world, uses a pay-for-performance compensation system to recognize the hard work, effort, and commitment of employees like the scientists shown here in a cancer research laboratory. Part of the company's performance-related pay program includes merit-based pay and an annual bonus as a percentage of an employee's salary. For Pfizer, pay for performance reflects the high value the company places on its employees in achieving its mission of being a global leader in health care.

employee recognition programs
Programs that consist of personal attention and expressions of interest, approval, and appreciation for a job well done.

pay-for-performance programs
Variable compensation plans that pay employees on the basis of some performance measure.

programs with outcome-based incentives had a positive impact on sales, customer satisfaction, and profits.[80] If an organization uses work teams, managers should consider group-based performance incentives that will reinforce team effort and commitment. But whether these programs are individual based or team based, managers need to ensure that they're specific about the relationship between an individual's pay and his or her expected level of appropriate performance. Employees must clearly understand exactly how performance—theirs and the organization's—translates into dollars on their paychecks.[81]

A FINAL NOTE ON EMPLOYEE REWARDS PROGRAMS. During times of economic and financial uncertainty, managers' abilities to recognize and reward employees are often severely constrained. It's hard to keep employees productive during challenging times, even though it's especially critical. It's not surprising, then, that employees feel less connected to their work. In fact, a recent study by the Corporate Executive Board found that declining employee engagement has decreased overall productivity by 3 to 5 percent.[82] But there are actions managers can take to maintain and maybe even increase employees' motivation levels. One is to clarify each person's role in the organization. Show them how their efforts are contributing to improving the company's overall situation. It's also important to keep communication lines open and use two-way exchanges between top-level managers and employees to soothe fears and concerns. The key with taking any actions is continuing to show workers that the company cares about them. As we said at the beginning of the chapter, the value in companies comes from employees who are motivated to be there. Managers have to give employees a reason to want to be there.

Review and Applications

Chapter Summary

 Define and explain motivation. Motivation is the process by which a person's efforts are energized, directed, and sustained toward attaining a goal.

The *energy* element is a measure of intensity or drive. The high level of effort needs to be *directed* in ways that help the organization achieve its goals. Employees must *persist* in putting forth effort to achieve those goals.

 Compare and contrast early theories of motivation. According to Maslow's theory, individuals move up the hierarchy of five needs (physiological, safety, social, esteem, and self-actualization) as needs are substantially satisfied. A need that's substantially satisfied no longer motivates.

A Theory X manager believes that people don't like to work or won't seek out responsibility so they have to be threatened and coerced to work. A Theory Y manager assumes that people like to work and seek out responsibility, so they will exercise self-motivation and self-direction.

Herzberg's two-factor theory proposed that intrinsic factors associated with job satisfaction were what motivated people. Extrinsic factors associated with job dissatisfaction simply kept people from being dissatisfied.

McClelland's three-needs theory proposed three acquired needs that are major motives in work need for achievement, need for affiliation, and need for power.

 Compare and contrast contemporary theories of motivation. Goal-setting theory says that specific goals increase performance and difficult goals, when accepted, result in higher performance than do easy goals. Important points in goal-setting theory include intention to work toward a goal is a major source of job motivation; specific hard goals produce higher levels of output than generalized goals; participation in setting goals is probably preferable to assigning goals, but not always; feedback guides and motivates behavior, especially self-generated feedback; and contingencies that affect goal setting include goal commitment, self-efficacy, and national culture.

The job characteristics model says there are five core job dimensions (skill variety, task identity, task significance, autonomy, and feedback) that are used to design motivating jobs.

Equity theory focuses on how employees compare their inputs-outcomes ratios to relevant others' ratios. A perception of inequity will cause an employee to do something about it. Procedural justice has a greater influence on employee satisfaction than does distributive justice.

Expectancy theory says that an individual tends to act in a certain way based on the expectation that the act will be followed by a desired outcome. Expectancy is the effort-performance linkage (how much effort do I need to exert to achieve a certain level of performance); instrumentality is the performance-reward linkage (achieving at a certain level of performance will get me what reward); and valence is the attractiveness of the reward (is the reward what I want).

10.4 **Discuss current issues in motivating employees.** Most motivational theories were developed in the United States and have a North American bias. Some theories (Maslow's need hierarchy, achievement need, and equity theory) don't work well for other cultures. However, the desire for interesting work seems important to all workers and Herzberg's motivator (intrinsic) factors may be universal.

Managers face challenges in motivating unique groups of workers. A diverse workforce is looking for flexibility. Professionals want job challenge and support, and are motivated by the work itself. Contingent workers want the opportunity to become permanent or to receive skills training.

Open-book management is when financial statements (the books) are shared with employees who have been taught what they mean. Employee recognition programs consist of personal attention, approval, and appreciation for a job well done. Pay-for-performance programs are variable compensation plans that pay employees on the basis of some performance measure.

 To check your understanding of learning outcomes – , go to **mymanagementlab.com** and try the chapter questions.

Understanding the Chapter

1. Most of us have to work for a living, and a job is a central part of our lives. So why do managers have to worry so much about employee motivation issues?

2. Contrast lower-order and higher-order needs in Maslow's needs hierarchy.

3. What role would money play in (a) the hierarchy of needs theory, (b) two-factor theory, (c) equity theory, (d) expectancy theory, and (e) motivating employees with a high nAch?

4. What are some of the possible consequences of employees perceiving an inequity between their inputs and outcomes and those of others?

5. What are some advantages of using pay-for-performance programs to motivate employee performance? Are there drawbacks? Explain.

6. Many job design experts who have studied the changing nature of work say that people do their best work when they're motivated by a sense of purpose rather than by the pursuit of money. Do you agree? Explain your position. What are the implications for managers?

7. Could managers use any of the motivation theories or approaches to encourage and support workforce diversity efforts? Explain.

8. Can an individual be too motivated? Discuss.

9. Do some additional research on ROWE discussed in the chapter opener. Write up your findings in a report. Be sure to cite your information.

Understanding Yourself

What Are My Dominant Needs?

This instrument was designed to deal with flaws in previous attempts to measure four individual needs: achievement, affiliation, autonomy, and power. These are defined as follows:

> Achievement—The desire to excel and to improve on past performance.
> Affiliation—The desire to interact socially and to be accepted by others.
> Autonomy—The desire to be self-directed.
> Power—The desire to influence and direct others.

INSTRUMENT This test contains 20 statements that may describe you and the types of things you may like to do. For each statement, indicate your agreement or disagreement using the following scale:

> **1** = Strongly disagree
> **2** = Disagree
> **3** = Neither agree nor disagree
> **4** = Agree
> **5** = Strongly agree

1.	I try to perform my best at work.	1	2	3	4	5
2.	I spend a lot of time talking to other people.	1	2	3	4	5
3.	I would like a career where I have very little supervision.	1	2	3	4	5
4.	I would enjoy being in charge of a project.	1	2	3	4	5
5.	I am a hard worker.	1	2	3	4	5
6.	I am a "people" person.	1	2	3	4	5
7.	I would like a job where I can plan my work schedule myself.	1	2	3	4	5
8.	I would rather receive orders than give them.	1	2	3	4	5
9.	It is important to me to do the best job possible.	1	2	3	4	5
10.	When I have a choice, I try to work in a group instead of by myself.	1	2	3	4	5
11.	I would like to be my own boss.	1	2	3	4	5
12.	I seek an active role in the leadership of a group.	1	2	3	4	5

13.	I push myself to be "all that I can be."	1 2 3 4 5
14.	I prefer to do my work and let others do theirs.	1 2 3 4 5
15.	I like to work at my own pace on job tasks.	1 2 3 4 5
16.	I find myself organizing and directing the activities of others.	1 2 3 4 5
17.	I try very hard to improve on my past performance at work.	1 2 3 4 5
18.	I try my best to work alone on a work assignment.	1 2 3 4 5
19.	In my work projects, I try to be my own boss.	1 2 3 4 5
20.	I strive to be "in command" when I am working in a group.	1 2 3 4 5

SCORING KEY   Add up items 1, 5, 9, 13, and 17. These represent your achievement score. The affiliation score is made up of items 2, 6, 10, 14, and 18 (reverse score 14 and 18). The autonomy score is items 3, 7, 11, 15, and 19. The power score is items 4 (reverse score), 8, 12, 16, and 20. Scores for each will range from 5 to 25.

ANALYSIS AND INTERPRETATION   The higher a score, the more dominant that need is for you. For comparative purposes, the researchers used this test with approximately 350 college graduates who averaged 28 years of age. Their average scores were 22.6 for achievement; 16.1 for affiliation; 20.0 for autonomy; and 17.7 for power.

Source: T. M. Heckert, G. Cuneio, A. P. Hannah, P. J. Adams, H. E. Droste, M. A. Mueller, H. A. Wallis, C. M. Griffin, and L. L. Roberts, "Creation of a New Needs Assessment Questionnaire," *Journal of Social Behavior and Personality* (March 2000), pp. 121–36.

FYIA (For Your Immediate Action)

La Mexican Kitchen

Reply   Reply All   Forward

To: Linda Bustamante, Operations Manager
From: Matt Perkins, Shift Supervisor
Re: **Staff Turnover**

HELP! We've been having a difficult time keeping our food servers for any length of time. It seems like I just get them trained and they leave. And we both know that our servers are a key element in our company's commitment to excellent customer service. We can have the best food in town (and do!) but if our servers aren't motivated to provide excellent service, we won't have any customers.

    Although these positions pay minimum wage, you and I both know a motivated server can make additional money from tips. But it seems that this isn't enough to motivate them to stay. So what would you recommend? Could you jot down some ideas about how to better motivate our food servers and send those to me? Thanks!

This fictionalized company and message were created for educational purposes only. It is not meant to reflect positively or negatively on management practices by any company that may share this name.

SEARCHING FOR?

It gets over 777,000 applicants a year. And it's no wonder! With a massage every other week, on-site laundry, swimming pool and spa, free delicious all-you-can-eat gourmet meals, what more could an employee want? Sounds like an ideal job, doesn't it? However, at Google, many people are demonstrating by their decisions to leave the company that all those perks (and these are just a few) aren't enough to keep them there. As one analyst said, "Yes, Google's making gobs of money. Yes, it's full of smart people. Yes, it's a wonderful place to work. So why are so many people leaving?"

Google has been in the top 10 list of "Best Companies to Work For" by *Fortune* magazine for three years running and was number one on the list for two of those three years. But make no mistake. Google's executives decided to offer all these fabulous perks for several reasons: to attract the best knowledge workers it can in an intensely competitive, cutthroat market; to help employees work long hours and not have to deal with time-consuming personal chores; to show employees they're valued; and to have employees remain Googlers (the name used for employees) for many years. But a number of Googlers have jumped ship and given up these fantastic benefits to go out on their own.

For instance, Sean Knapp and two colleagues, brothers Bismarck and Belsasar Lepe, came up with an idea on how to handle Web video. They left Google, or as one person put it, "expelled themselves from paradise to start their own company." When the threesome left the company, Google really wanted them and their project to stay. Google offered them a "blank check." But the trio realized they would do all the hard work and Google would own the product. So off they went, for the excitement of a start-up.

If this were an isolated occurrence, it would be easy to write off. But it's not. Other talented Google employees have done the same thing. In fact, there are so many of them who have left that they've formed an informal alumni club of ex-Googlers turned entrepreneurs.

Discussion Questions

1. What's it like to work at Google? (Hint: Go to Google's Web site and click on "About Google." Find the section on Jobs at Google and go from there.) What's your assessment of the company's work environment?

2. Google is doing a lot for its employees, but obviously not enough to retain several of its talented employees. Using what you've learned from studying the various motivation theories, what does this situation tell you about employee motivation?

3. What do you think is Google's biggest challenge in keeping employees motivated?

4. If you were managing a team of Google employees, how would you keep them motivated?

Sources: R. Levering and M. Moskowitz, "And the Winners Are…" *Fortune*, February 2, 2009, pp. 67+; A. Lashinsky, "Where Does Google Go Next?" *CNNMoney.com*, May 12, 2008; K. Hafner, "Google Options Make Masseuse a Multimillionaire," *New York Times Online*, November 12, 2007; Q. Hardy, "Close to the Vest," *Forbes*, July 2, 2007, pp. 40–42; K. J. Delaney, "Start-Ups Make Inroads with Google's Work Force," *Wall Street Journal Online*, June 28, 2007; and "Perk Place: The Benefits Offered by Google and Others May Be Grand, but They're All Business," *Knowledge @ Wharton*, http://knowledge.wharton.upenn.edu/article (March 21, 2007).

11

Leadership and Trust

learning outcomes

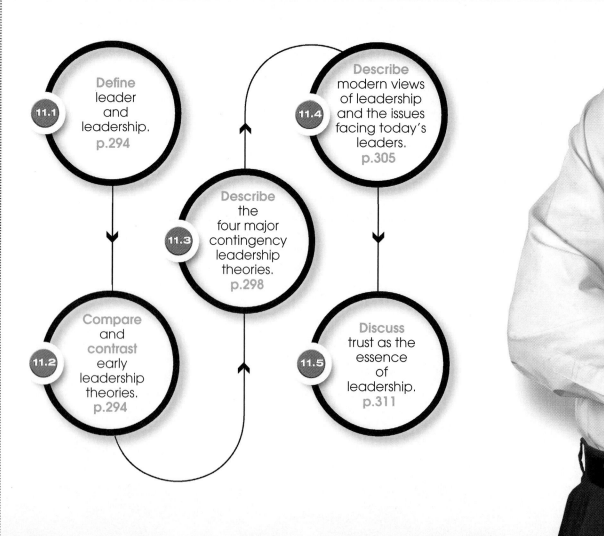

11.1 Define leader and leadership. p.294

11.2 Compare and contrast early leadership theories. p.294

11.3 Describe the four major contingency leadership theories. p.298

11.4 Describe modern views of leadership and the issues facing today's leaders. p.305

11.5 Discuss trust as the essence of leadership. p.311

Employees First

It might seem kind of strange to be talking about putting employees first in a chapter on leadership. However, at HCL Technologies, the "employee first" philosophy has helped catapult the company from peripheral player to center stage in the intensely competitive IT industry.[1]

HCL Technologies is headquartered in the world's largest democracy, so it's quite fitting that the Noida, India–based company is attempting a radical experiment in workplace democracy. CEO Vineet Nayar is committed to creating a company where the job of company leaders is to enable people to find their own destiny by gravitating to their strengths. His goals for the "Employee First" program include creating a unique employee experience, inverting the organizational structure, and increasing transparency. The workplace reforms the company implemented involved better communication with the CEO and a pay scheme that gives workers more job security. A major part of the workplace changes was this pay scheme, which the company referred to as "trust pay." Unlike the standard IT industry practice of having 30 percent of its engineers' pay variable (that is, dependent on performance), the company decided to pay higher fixed salaries that included all of what would have been the variable component—essentially trusting that employees would deliver performance meriting that pay. These changes have helped the company grow and, more importantly, become a talent magnet. (The company's attrition rate dropped to below 15 percent.) And in 2008, HCL won an award for its innovative workforce management approaches.

How does Nayar view leadership? Although he believes that the command-and-control dictatorship approach is the easiest management style, he also thinks it's not the most productive. In his corporate democracy, employees can write a "trouble ticket" on anyone in the company. Anyone with trouble tickets has to respond, just as if it was a customer who had problems and needed some response. Nayar also believes that leaders should be open to criticism. He volunteered to share the information from his 360-degree performance feedback for all employees to see. One year, his team of 81 managers who rated him gave him a 3.6 out of 5 for how well he keeps projects running on schedule, one of his lowest scores—and everyone at HCL was able to see the score. Nayar's scores, along with ratings for the company's top 20 managers, are published on the company's intranet for any employee to see. Employees also can see their own supervisor's scores. Although a lot of people said he was crazy for publicizing managers' "grades" and communicating his own weaknesses, Nayar believed that it was a good way to increase his accountability as a leader to his employees. Such an environment requires a lot of trust between leaders and followers.

Vineet Nayar is a good example of what it takes to be an effective leader in today's organizations. He has created a workplace environment in which employees feel like they're heard and trusted. It's important for managers in all organizations to be seen as effective leaders. Why is leadership so important? Because it's the leaders in organizations who make things happen. But what makes leaders different from nonleaders? What's the most appropriate style of leadership? What makes leaders effective? These are just some of the topics we're going to address in this chapter.

Who Are Leaders, and What Is Leadership?

11.1 Define leader and leadership.

Let's begin by clarifying who leaders are and what leadership is. Our definition of a **leader** is someone who can influence others and who has managerial authority. **Leadership** is a process of leading a group and influencing that group to achieve its goals. It's what leaders do.

Are all managers leaders? Because leading is one of the four management functions, yes, ideally, all managers *should* be leaders. Thus, we're going to study leaders and leadership from a managerial perspective.[2] However, even though we're looking at these from a managerial perspective, we're aware that groups often have informal leaders who emerge. Although these informal leaders may be able to influence others, they have not been the focus of most leadership research and are not the types of leaders we're studying in this chapter.

Leaders and leadership, like motivation, are organizational behavior topics that have been researched a lot. Most of that research has been aimed at answering the question: "What is an effective leader?" We'll begin our study of leadership by looking at some early leadership theories that attempted to answer that question.

What Do Early Leadership Theories Tell Us About Leadership?

11.2 Compare and contrast early leadership theories.

People have been interested in leadership since they started coming together in groups to accomplish goals. However, it wasn't until the early part of the twentieth century that researchers actually began to study it. These early leadership theories focused on the *leader* (trait theories) and how the *leader interacted* with his or her group members (behavioral theories).

What Traits Do Leaders Have?

Ask the average person on the street what comes to mind when he or she thinks of leadership. You're likely to get a list of qualities such as intelligence, charisma, decisiveness, enthusiasm, strength, bravery, integrity, and self-confidence. These responses represent, in essence, **trait theories of leadership**. The search for traits or characteristics that differentiate leaders from nonleaders dominated early leadership research efforts. If the concept of traits were valid, all leaders would have to possess specific characteristics.

However, despite the best efforts of researchers, it proved impossible to identify a set of traits that would *always* differentiate a leader (the person) from a nonleader. Maybe it was a bit optimistic to think that there could be consistent and unique traits that would apply universally to all effective leaders, no matter whether they were in charge of Toyota Motor Corporation, the Moscow Ballet, the country of Brazil, a local collegiate chapter of Alpha Chi Omega, or Ted's Malibu Surf Shop. However, later attempts to identify traits consistently associated with *leadership* (the process, not the person) were more successful. The seven traits shown to be associated with effective leadership are described briefly in Exhibit 11-1.[3]

Researchers eventually recognized that traits alone were not sufficient for identifying effective leaders since explanations based solely on traits ignored the interactions of leaders

---

EXHIBIT 11-1   Traits Associated with Leadership

1. *Drive*. Leaders exhibit a high effort level. They have a relatively high desire for achievement, they are ambitious, they have a lot of energy, they are tirelessly persistent in their activities, and they show initiative.

2. *Desire to lead*. Leaders have a strong desire to influence and lead others. They demonstrate the willingness to take responsibility.

3. *Honesty and integrity*. Leaders build trusting relationships with followers by being truthful or nondeceitful and by showing high consistency between word and deed.

4. *Self-confidence*. Followers look to leaders for an absence of self-doubt. Leaders, therefore, need to show self-confidence in order to convince followers of the rightness of their goals and decisions.

5. *Intelligence*. Leaders need to be intelligent enough to gather, synthesize, and interpret large amounts of information, and they need to be able to create visions, solve problems, and make correct decisions.

6. *Job-relevant knowledge*. Effective leaders have a high degree of knowledge about the company, industry, and technical matters. In-depth knowledge allows leaders to make well-informed decisions and to understand the implications of those decisions.

7. *Extraversion*. Leaders are energetic, lively people. They are sociable, assertive, and rarely silent or withdrawn.

Sources: Based on S. A. Kirkpatrick and E. A. Locke, "Leadership: Do Traits Really Matter?" *Academy of Management Executive* (May 1991), pp. 48–60; and T. A. Judge, J. E. Bono, R. Ilies, and M. W. Gerhardt, "Personality and Leadership: A Qualitative and Quantitative Review," *Journal of Applied Psychology* (August 2002), pp. 765–80.

---

and their group members as well as situational factors. Possessing the appropriate traits only made it more likely that an individual would be an effective leader. Therefore, leadership research from the late 1940s to the mid-1960s concentrated on the preferred behavioral styles that leaders demonstrated. Researchers wondered whether there was something unique in what effective leaders *did*—in other words, in their *behavior*.

What Behaviors Do Leaders Exhibit?

It was hoped that the **behavioral theories of leadership** approach would provide more definitive answers about the nature of leadership, and if successful, also have practical implications quite different from those of the trait approach. If trait research had been successful, it would have provided a basis for selecting the right people to assume formal leadership positions in organizations. In contrast, if behavioral studies were to turn up critical behavioral determinants of leadership, people could be trained to be leaders, which is precisely the premise behind management development programs.

A number of studies looked at behavioral styles. We'll briefly review three of the most popular: Kurt Lewin's studies at the University of Iowa, the Ohio State studies, and the University of Michigan studies. Then we'll see how the concepts developed in those studies were used in a grid created for appraising leadership styles.

WHAT DID THE UNIVERSITY OF IOWA STUDIES TELL US ABOUT LEADERSHIP BEHAVIOR?

One of the first studies of leadership behavior was done by Kurt Lewin and his associates at the University of Iowa.[4] In their studies, the researchers explored three leadership behaviors or styles: autocratic, democratic, and laissez-faire. An **autocratic style** is that of a leader who typically tends to centralize authority, dictate work methods, make unilateral decisions, and limit employee participation. A leader with a **democratic style** tends to involve employees

---

leader
Someone who can influence others and who has managerial authority.

leadership
The process of leading a group and influencing that group to achieve its goals.

trait theories of leadership
Theories that isolate characteristics (traits) that differentiate leaders from nonleaders.

behavioral theories of leadership
Theories that isolate behaviors that differentiate effective leaders from ineffective leaders.

autocratic style
A leader who centralizes authority, dictates work methods, makes unilateral decisions, and limits employee participation.

democratic style
A leader who involves employees in decision making, delegates authority, encourages participation in deciding work methods, and uses feedback to coach employees.

Democratic-participatory style describes the leadership of Francisco Gonzalez, chairman and CEO of BBVA, a global banking group based in Spain. Gonzalez involves employees in decision making and promotes teamwork as the key to generating customer value. With BBVA continuing its global expansion, the company needs to fill a growing number of management positions. It identifies managerial talent whose style is participatory by using a survey that allows employees to evaluate each other based on work habits, assuring that future leaders are democratic rather than autocratic.Gonzalez is shown here at a BBVA technology event during a presentation of the bank's strategic innovation and transformation plan.

in decision making, delegates authority, encourages participation in deciding work methods and goals, and uses feedback as an opportunity to coach employees. The democratic style can be further classified in two ways: consultative and participative. A *democratic-consultative leader* seeks input and hears the concerns and issues of employees but makes the final decision him- or herself. In this capacity, the democratic-consultative leader is using the input as an information-seeking exercise. A *democratic-participative leader* often allows employees to have a say in what's decided. Here, decisions are made by the group, with the leader providing one input to that group. Finally, the **laissez-faire style** generally gives his or her employees complete freedom to make decisions and to complete their work in whatever way they see fit. A laissez-faire leader might simply provide necessary materials and answer questions.

Lewin and his associates wondered which one of the three leadership styles was most effective. On the basis of their studies of leaders from boys' clubs, they concluded that the laissez-faire style was ineffective on every performance criterion when compared with both democratic and autocratic styles. Quantity of work done was equal in groups with democratic and autocratic leaders, but work quality and group satisfaction were higher in democratic groups. The results suggest that a democratic leadership style could contribute to both good quantity and high quality of work.

Later studies of autocratic and democratic styles of leadership showed mixed results. For example, democratic leadership styles sometimes produced higher performance levels than autocratic styles, but at other times they produced group performance that was lower than or equal to that of autocratic styles. Nonetheless, more consistent results were generated when a measure of employee satisfaction was used.

Group members' satisfaction levels were generally higher under a democratic leader than under an autocratic one.[5] Did this finding mean that managers should always exhibit a democratic style of leadership? Two researchers, Robert Tannenbaum and Warren Schmidt, attempted to provide that answer.[6]

Tannenbaum and Schmidt developed a continuum of leader behaviors (see Exhibit 11-2). The continuum illustrates that a range of leadership behaviors, all the way from boss centered (autocratic) on the left side of the model to employee centered (laissez-faire) on the right side of the model, is possible. In deciding which leader behavior from the continuum to use, Tannenbaum and Schmidt proposed that managers look at forces within themselves (such as comfort level with the chosen leadership style), forces within the employees (such as readiness to assume responsibility), and forces within the situation (such as time pressures). They suggested that managers should move toward more employee-centered styles in the long run because such behavior would increase employees' motivation, decision quality, teamwork, morale, and development.

This dual nature of leader behaviors—that is, focusing on the work to be done and focusing on the employees—is also a key characteristic of the Ohio State and University of Michigan studies.

WHAT DID THE OHIO STATE STUDIES SHOW? The most comprehensive and replicated of the behavioral theories resulted from research that began at Ohio State University in the late 1940s.[7] These studies sought to identify independent dimensions of leader behavior. Beginning with more than 1,000 dimensions, the researchers eventually narrowed the list down to two categories that accounted for most of the leadership behavior described by employees. They called these two dimensions initiating structure and consideration.

Initiating structure refers to the extent to which a leader is likely to define and structure his or her role and those of employees in the search for goal attainment. It includes behavior that attempts to organize work, work relationships, and goals. For example, the leader who is characterized as high in initiating structure assigns group members to particular tasks, expects workers to maintain definite standards of performance, and emphasizes meeting deadlines.

Consideration is defined as the extent to which a leader has job relationships characterized by mutual trust and respect for employees' ideas and feelings. A leader who is high

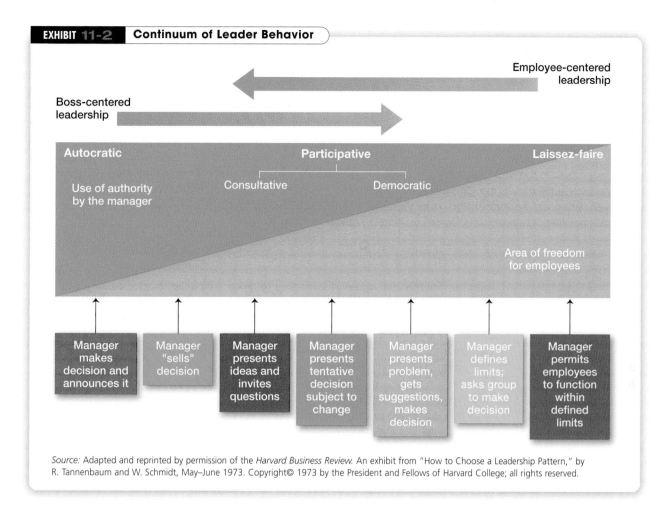

EXHIBIT 11-2 **Continuum of Leader Behavior**

Employee-centered leadership

Boss-centered leadership

Autocratic

Use of authority by the manager

Participative

Consultative

Democratic

Laissez-faire

Area of freedom for employees

| Manager makes decision and announces it | Manager "sells" decision | Manager presents ideas and invites questions | Manager presents tentative decision subject to change | Manager presents problem, gets suggestions, makes decision | Manager defines limits; asks group to make decision | Manager permits employees to function within defined limits |

Source: Adapted and reprinted by permission of the *Harvard Business Review.* An exhibit from "How to Choose a Leadership Pattern," by R. Tannenbaum and W. Schmidt, May–June 1973. Copyright© 1973 by the President and Fellows of Harvard College; all rights reserved.

in consideration helps employees with personal problems, is friendly and approachable, and treats all employees as equals. He or she shows concern for his or her followers' comfort, well-being, status, and satisfaction.

Extensive research based on these definitions found that a leader who is high in initiating structure and consideration (a high-high leader) achieved high employee performance and satisfaction more frequently than one who rated low on either consideration, initiating structure, or both. However, the high-high style did not always yield positive results. For example, leader behavior characterized as high on initiating structure led to greater rates of grievances, absenteeism, and turnover, and lower levels of job satisfaction for workers performing routine tasks. Other studies found that high consideration was negatively related to performance ratings of the leader by his or her manager. In conclusion, the Ohio State studies suggested that the high-high style generally produced positive outcomes, but enough exceptions were found to indicate that situational factors needed to be integrated into the theory.

HOW DID THE UNIVERSITY OF MICHIGAN STUDIES DIFFER? Leadership studies undertaken at the University of Michigan's Survey Research Center, at about the same time as those being done at Ohio State, had similar research objectives: to locate the behavioral characteristics of leaders that were related to performance effectiveness. The Michigan group also

laissez-faire style
A leader who generally gives employees complete freedom to make decisions and to complete their work however they see fit.

initiating structure
The extent to which a leader defines and structures his or her role and the roles of employees to attain goals.

consideration
The extent to which a leader has job relationships characterized by mutual trust, respect for employees' ideas, and regard for their feelings.

Both the Ohio State and Michigan studies have added a lot to our understanding of effective leadership.[8] Prior to the completion of these studies, it was widely thought by researchers and practicing managers that one style of leadership was good and another bad. However, as the research showed, both leader behavior dimensions—job-centered and employee-centered in the Michigan studies, and initiating structure and consideration in the Ohio State studies—are necessary for effective leadership. That dual focus of "what" a leader does still holds today. Leaders are expected to focus on both the task and on the people he or she is leading. Even the later contingency leadership theories used the people/task distinction to define a leader's style. Finally, these early behavioral studies were important for the "systematic methodology they introduced and the increased awareness they generated concerning the importance of leader behavior." Although the behavioral theories may not have been the final chapter in the book on leadership, they "served as a springboard for the leadership research that followed."

o

came up with two dimensions of leadership behavior, which they labeled employee oriented and production oriented.[9] Leaders who were **employee oriented** emphasized interpersonal relations; they took a personal interest in the needs of their employees and accepted individual differences among members. Leaders who were **production oriented**, in contrast, tended to emphasize the technical or task aspects of the job, were concerned mainly with accomplishing their group's tasks, and regarded group members as a means to that end.

The conclusions of the Michigan researchers strongly favored leaders who were employee oriented. Employee-oriented leaders were associated with higher group productivity and higher job satisfaction. Production-oriented leaders were associated with lower group productivity and lower worker satisfaction.

WHAT IS THE MANAGERIAL GRID? The behavioral dimensions from these early leadership studies provided the basis for the development of a two-dimensional grid for appraising leadership styles. This **managerial grid** used the behavioral dimensions "concern for people" and "concern for production" and evaluated a leader's use of these behaviors, ranking them on a scale from 1 (low) to 9 (high).[10] Although the grid (shown in Exhibit 11-3) had 81 potential categories into which a leader's behavioral style might fall, only five styles were named: impoverished management (1,1), task management (9,1), middle-of-the-road management (5,5), country club management (1,9), and team management (9,9). Of these five styles, the researchers concluded that managers performed best when using a 9,9 style. Unfortunately, the grid offered no answers to the question of what made a manager an effective leader; it only provided a framework for conceptualizing leadership style. In fact, there's little substantive evidence to support the conclusion that a 9,9 style is most effective in all situations.[11]

Leadership researchers were discovering that predicting leadership success involved something more complex than isolating a few leader traits or preferable behaviors. They began looking at situational influences. Specifically, which leadership styles might be suitable in different situations and what were these different situations?

11.3 Describe the four major contingency leadership theories.

What Do the Contingency Theories of Leadership Tell Us?

"The corporate world is filled with stories of leaders who failed to achieve greatness because they failed to understand the context they were working in . . ."[12] In this section we examine four contingency theories—Fiedler, Hersey-Blanchard, leader-participation, and path-goal. Each looks at defining leadership style and the situation, and attempts to answer the *if-then* contingencies (that is, *if* this is the context or situation, *then* this is the best leadership style to use).

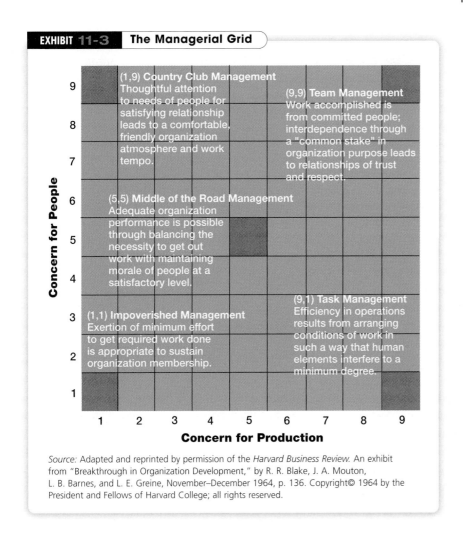

EXHIBIT 11-3 | **The Managerial Grid**

(1,9) **Country Club Management** Thoughtful attention to needs of people for satisfying relationship leads to a comfortable, friendly organization atmosphere and work tempo.

(9,9) **Team Management** Work accomplished is from committed people; interdependence through a "common stake" in organization purpose leads to relationships of trust and respect.

(5,5) **Middle of the Road Management** Adequate organization performance is possible through balancing the necessity to get out work with maintaining morale of people at a satisfactory level.

(1,1) **Impoverished Management** Exertion of minimum effort to get required work done is appropriate to sustain organization membership.

(9,1) **Task Management** Efficiency in operations results from arranging conditions of work in such a way that human elements interfere to a minimum degree.

Concern for People (vertical axis) / **Concern for Production** (horizontal axis)

Source: Adapted and reprinted by permission of the *Harvard Business Review.* An exhibit from "Breakthrough in Organization Development," by R. R. Blake, J. A. Mouton, L. B. Barnes, and L. E. Greine, November–December 1964, p. 136. Copyright© 1964 by the President and Fellows of Harvard College; all rights reserved.

What Was the First Comprehensive Contingency Model?

The first comprehensive contingency model for leadership was developed by Fred Fiedler.[13] The **Fiedler contingency model** proposed that effective group performance depended upon properly matching the leader's style and the amount of control and influence in the situation. The model was based on the premise that a certain leadership style would be most effective in different types of situations. The keys were (1) define those leadership styles and the different types of situations and then (2) identify the appropriate combinations of style and situation.

Fiedler proposed that a key factor in leadership success was an individual's basic leadership style, either task oriented or relationship oriented. To measure a leader's style, Fiedler developed the **least-preferred co-worker (LPC) questionnaire**. This questionnaire contained 18 pairs of contrasting adjectives—for example, pleasant–unpleasant, cold–warm, boring–interesting, or friendly–unfriendly. Respondents were asked to think of all the coworkers they had ever had and to describe that one person they *least enjoyed* working with by rating him or her on a scale of 1 to 8 for each of the sets of adjectives (the 8 always described the positive adjective out of the pair and the 1 always described the negative adjective out of the pair).

If the leader described the least preferred coworker in relatively positive terms (in other words, a "high" LPC score—a score of 64 or above), then the respondent was primarily interested in good personal relations with coworkers and the style would be described as *relationship oriented*. In contrast, if you saw the least preferred coworker in relatively unfavorable terms (a low LPC score—a score of 57 or below), you were primarily interested in productivity and getting the job done; thus, your style would be labeled as *task oriented*. Fiedler did acknowledge that a small number of people might fall in between these two extremes and not have a cut-and-dried leadership style. One other important point is that Fiedler assumed a person's leadership style was fixed regardless of the situation. In other words, if you were a relationship-oriented leader, you'd always be one, and the same for task-oriented.

After an individual's leadership style had been assessed through the LPC, it was time to evaluate the situation in order to be able to match the leader with the situation. Fiedler's research uncovered three contingency dimensions that defined the key situational factors in leader effectiveness. These were:

▶ *Leader-member relations:* the degree of confidence, trust, and respect employees had for their leader; rated as either good or poor.
▶ *Task structure:* the degree to which job assignments were formalized and structured; rated as either high or low.
▶ *Position power:* the degree of influence a leader had over activities such as hiring, firing, discipline, promotions, and salary increases; rated as either strong or weak.

Each leadership situation was evaluated in terms of these three contingency variables, which when combined produced eight possible situations that were either favorable or unfavorable for the leader. (See the bottom of the chart in Exhibit 11-4). Situations I, II, and III were classified as highly favorable for the leader. Situations IV, V, and VI were moderately favorable for the leader. And situations VII and VIII were described as highly unfavorable for the leader.

Once Fiedler had described the leader variables and the situational variables, he had everything he needed to define the specific contingencies for leadership effectiveness. To do so, he studied 1,200 groups where he compared relationship-oriented versus task-oriented leadership styles in each of the eight situational categories. He concluded that task-oriented leaders

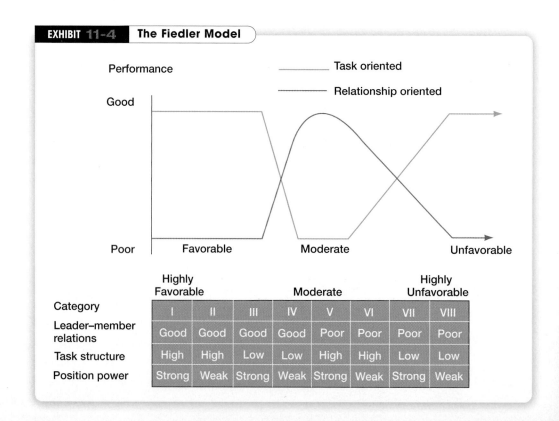

EXHIBIT 11-4 **The Fiedler Model**

Category	Highly Favorable			Moderate			Highly Unfavorable	
	I	II	III	IV	V	VI	VII	VIII
Leader–member relations	Good	Good	Good	Good	Poor	Poor	Poor	Poor
Task structure	High	High	Low	Low	High	High	Low	Low
Position power	Strong	Weak	Strong	Weak	Strong	Weak	Strong	Weak

performed better in very favorable situations and in very unfavorable situations. (See the top of Exhibit 11-4 where performance is shown on the vertical axis and situation favorableness is shown on the horizontal axis.) On the other hand, relationship-oriented leaders performed better in moderately favorable situations.

Because Fiedler treated an individual's leadership style as fixed, there were only two ways to improve leader effectiveness. First, you could bring in a new leader whose style better fit the situation. For instance, if the group situation was highly unfavorable but was led by a relationship-oriented leader, the group's performance could be improved by replacing that person with a task-oriented leader. The second alternative was to change the situation to fit the leader. This could be done by restructuring tasks; by increasing or decreasing the power that the leader had over factors such as salary increases, promotions, and disciplinary actions; or by improving the leader-member relations.

Once successful as a general interest magazine, *Reader's Digest* has steadily lost readers, advertising revenues, and profits since the 1990s. The three women shown here were hired by the magazine's publishers to lead a change in the magazine's direction from a general-interest format aimed at a broad audience to a narrower reader base that holds conservative social values. Leading the change are, from left, Eva Dillon, president of the magazine, related books, and Web sites division; Peggy Northrop, U.S. editor-in-chief; and Mary Berner, president and chief executive of *Reader's Digest* Association. According to Fiedler's contingency model, the success of these leaders depends on the match between their leadership style and the influences of their situation.

Research testing the overall validity of Fiedler's model has shown considerable evidence to support the model.[14] However, his theory wasn't without criticisms. The major one is that it's probably unrealistic to assume that a person can't change his or her leadership style to fit the situation. Effective leaders can, and do, change their styles. Another is that the LPC wasn't very practical. Finally, the situation variables were difficult to assess.[15] Despite its shortcomings, the Fiedler model showed that effective leadership style needed to reflect situational factors.

How Do Followers' Willingness and Ability Influence Leaders?

Paul Hersey and Ken Blanchard developed a leadership theory that has gained a strong following among management development specialists.[16] This model, called **situational leadership theory (SLT)**, is a contingency theory that focuses on followers' readiness. Before we proceed, there are two points we need to clarify: Why a leadership theory focuses on the followers, and what is meant by the term *readiness*.

The emphasis on the followers in leadership effectiveness reflects the reality that it *is* the followers who accept or reject the leader. Regardless of what the leader does, the group's effectiveness depends on the actions of the followers. This is an important dimension that has been overlooked or underemphasized in most leadership theories. And **readiness**, as defined by Hersey and Blanchard, refers to the extent to which people have the ability and willingness to accomplish a specific task.

SLT uses the same two leadership dimensions that Fiedler identified: task and relationship behaviors. However, Hersey and Blanchard go a step further by considering each as either high or low and then combining them into four specific leadership styles described as follows:

▶ *Telling* (high task–low relationship): The leader defines roles and tells people what, how, when, and where to do various tasks.

▶ *Selling* (high task–high relationship): The leader provides both directive and supportive behavior.

▶ *Participating* (low task–high relationship): The leader and followers share in decision making; the main role of the leader is facilitating and communicating.

▶ *Delegating* (low task–low relationship): The leader provides little direction or support.

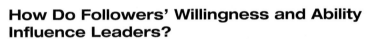

situational leadership theory (SLT)
A leadership contingency theory that focuses on followers' readiness.

readiness
The extent to which people have the ability and willingness to accomplish a specific task.

The final component in the model is the four stages of follower readiness:

▶ *R1:* People are both *unable and unwilling* to take responsibility for doing something. Followers aren't competent or confident.

▶ *R2:* People are *unable but willing* to do the necessary job tasks. Followers are motivated but lack the appropriate skills.

▶ *R3:* People are *able but unwilling* to do what the leader wants. Followers are competent, but don't want to do something.

▶ *R4:* People are both *able and willing* to do what is asked of them.

SLT essentially views the leader-follower relationship as like that of a parent and a child. Just as a parent needs to relinquish control when a child becomes more mature and responsible, so, too, should leaders. As followers reach higher levels of readiness, the leader responds not only by decreasing control over their activities but also decreasing relationship behaviors. The SLT says if followers are at R1 (*unable* and *unwilling* to do a task), the leader needs to use the telling style and give clear and specific directions; if followers are at R2 (*unable* and *willing*), the leader needs to use the selling style and display high task orientation to compensate for the followers' lack of ability and high relationship orientation to get followers to "buy into" the leader's desires; if followers are at R3 (*able* and *unwilling*), the leader needs to use the participating style to gain their support; and if employees are at R4 (both *able* and *willing*), the leader doesn't need to do much and should use the delegating style.

SLT has intuitive appeal. It acknowledges the importance of followers and builds on the logic that leaders can compensate for ability and motivational limitations in their followers. However, research efforts to test and support the theory generally have been disappointing.[18] Possible explanations include internal inconsistencies in the model as well as problems with research methodology. Despite its appeal and wide popularity, we have to be cautious about any enthusiastic endorsement of SLT.

How Participative Should a Leader Be?

Back in 1973, Victor Vroom and Phillip Yetton developed a **leader-participation model** that related leadership behavior and participation to decision making.[19] Recognizing that task structures have varying demands for routine and nonroutine activities, these researchers argued that leader behavior must adjust to reflect the task structure. Vroom and Yetton's model was normative. That is, it provided a sequential set of rules to be followed in determining the form and amount of participation in decision making in different types of situations. The model was a decision tree incorporating seven contingencies (whose relevance could be identified by making yes or no choices) and five alternative leadership styles.

More recent work by Vroom and Arthur Jago has revised that model.[20] The new model retains the same five alternative leadership styles but expands the contingency variables to twelve—from the leader's making the decision completely by himself or herself to sharing the problem with the group and developing a consensus decision. These variables are listed in Exhibit 11-5.

EXHIBIT 11-5 **Contingency Variables in the Revised Leader-Participation Model**

1. Importance of the decision
2. Importance of obtaining follower commitment to the decision
3. Whether the leader has sufficient information to make a good decision
4. How well structured the problem is
5. Whether an autocratic decision would receive follower commitment
6. Whether followers "buy into" the organization's goals
7. Whether there is likely to be conflict among followers over solution alternatives
8. Whether followers have the necessary information to make a good decision
9. Time constraints on the leader that may limit follower involvement
10. Whether costs to bring geographically dispersed members together are justified
11. Importance to the leader of minimizing the time it takes to make the decision
12. Importance of using participation as a tool for developing follower decision skills

Source: S. P. Robbins and T. A. Judge, *Organizational Behavior* 13th ed. (Upper Saddle River, NJ: Prentice Hall, 2009), p. 400.

Research on the original leader-participation model was encouraging.[21] But, unfortunately, the model is far too complex for the typical manager to use regularly. In fact, Vroom and Jago have developed a computer program to guide managers through all the decision branches in the revised model. Although we obviously can't do justice to this model's sophistication in this discussion, it has provided us with some solid, empirically supported insights into key contingency variables related to leadership effectiveness. Moreover, the leader-participation model confirms that leadership research should be directed at the situation rather than at the person. That is, it probably makes more sense to talk about autocratic and participative situations than autocratic and participative leaders. As House does in his path-goal theory (discussed next), Vroom, Yetton, and Jago argue against the notion that leader behavior is inflexible. The leader-participation model assumes that the leader can adapt his or her style to different situations.[22]

How Do Leaders Help Followers?

Currently, one of the most respected approaches to understanding leadership is **path-goal theory**, which states that the leader's job is to assist followers in attaining their goals and to provide direction or support needed to ensure that their goals are compatible with the goals of the group or organization. Developed by Robert House, path-goal theory takes key elements from the expectancy theory of motivation (see Chapter 10).[23] The term *path-goal* is derived from the belief that effective leaders clarify the path to help their followers get from where they are to the achievement of their work goals and make the journey along the path easier by reducing roadblocks and pitfalls.

House identified four leadership behaviors:

- *Directive leader:* Lets subordinates know what's expected of them, schedules work to be done, and gives specific guidance on how to accomplish tasks.
- *Supportive leader:* Shows concern for the needs of followers and is friendly.
- *Participative leader:* Consults with group members and uses their suggestions before making a decision.
- *Achievement oriented leader:* Sets challenging goals and expects followers to perform at their highest level.

In contrast to Fiedler's view that a leader couldn't change his or her behavior, House assumed that leaders are flexible and can display any or all of these leadership styles depending on the situation.

As Exhibit 11-6 illustrates, path-goal theory proposes two situational or contingency variables that moderate the leadership behavior-outcome relationship: those in the *environment* that are outside the control of the follower (factors including task structure, formal authority system, and the work group) and those that are part of the personal characteristics of the *follower* (including locus of control, experience, and perceived ability). Environmental factors determine the type of leader behavior required if subordinate outcomes are to be maximized; personal

Shelley Roberts, managing director of Tiger Airways, is an achievement-oriented leader. She accepted the challenging goal of guiding the Singapore-based budget airline through an expansion in Australia, a market dominated by the established Qantas Airlines. Roberts earned a reputation as a high achiever through successful senior leadership positions in both airline and airport management. She was a senior executive at Britain's low-budget EasyJet airline when it entered the European market and successfully competed against carriers like British Airways. In this photo, Roberts and the West Tigers' rugby club members pull a plane out of its hanger during the launch of the Tiger Airways new route between Melbourne and Sydney.

leader-participation model
A leadership contingency theory that's based on a sequential set of rules for determining how much participation a leader uses in decision making according to different types of situations.

path-goal theory
A leadership theory that says the leader's job is to assist followers in attaining their goals and to provide direction or support needed to ensure that their goals are compatible with the organization's or group's goals.

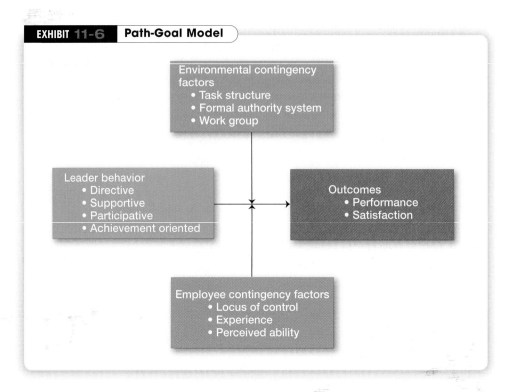

EXHIBIT 11-6 Path-Goal Model

characteristics of the follower determine how the environment and leader behavior are interpreted. The theory proposes that a leader's behavior won't be effective if it's redundant with what the environmental structure is providing or is incongruent with follower characteristics. For example, some predictions from path-goal theory are:

▶ Directive leadership leads to greater satisfaction when tasks are ambiguous or stressful than when they are highly structured and well laid out. The followers aren't sure what to do, so the leader needs to give them some direction.

▶ Supportive leadership results in high employee performance and satisfaction when subordinates are performing structured tasks. In this situation, the leader only needs to support followers, not tell them what to do.

▶ Directive leadership is likely to be perceived as redundant among subordinates with high perceived ability or with considerable experience. These followers are quite capable so they don't need a leader to tell them what to do.

▶ The clearer and more bureaucratic the formal authority relationships, the more leaders should exhibit supportive behavior and deemphasize directive behavior. The organizational situation has provided the structure as far as what is expected of followers, so the leader's role is simply to support.

▶ Directive leadership will lead to higher employee satisfaction when there is substantive conflict within a work group. In this situation, the followers need a leader who will take charge.

▶ Subordinates with an internal locus of control will be more satisfied with a participative style. Because these followers believe that they control what happens to them, they prefer to participate in decisions.

▶ Subordinates with an external locus of control will be more satisfied with a directive style. These followers believe that what happens to them is a result of the external environment so they would prefer a leader who tells them what to do.

▶ Achievement-oriented leadership will increase subordinates' expectancies that effort will lead to high performance when tasks are ambiguously structured. By setting challenging goals, followers know what the expectations are.

Research on the path-goal model is generally encouraging. Although not every study has found support, the majority of the evidence supports the logic underlying the theory.[24] In summary, an employee's performance and satisfaction are likely to be positively influenced when the leader chooses a leadership style that compensates for shortcomings in either the employee or the work setting. However, if the leader spends time explaining tasks that are already clear or when the employee has the ability and experience to handle them without interference, the employee is likely to see such directive behavior as redundant or even insulting.

What Is Leadership Like Today?

What are the latest views of leadership and what issues do today's leaders have to deal with? In this section, we're going to look at three contemporary views of leadership: transformational-transactional leadership, charismatic-visionary leadership, and team leadership. In addition, we'll discuss some issues that leaders have to face in leading effectively in today's environment.

Describe modern views of leadership and the issues facing today's leaders.

11.4

What Do the Three Contemporary Views of Leadership Tell Us?

Remember our discussion at the beginning of this chapter where we said that leadership studies have long had the goal of describing what it takes to be an effective leader. That goal hasn't changed! Even the contemporary views of leadership are interested in answering that question. These views of leadership have a common theme: leaders who inspire and support followers.

HOW DO TRANSACTIONAL LEADERS DIFFER FROM TRANSFORMATIONAL LEADERS? Many early leadership theories viewed leaders as **transactional leaders**; that is, leaders who lead primarily by using social exchanges (or transactions). Transactional leaders guide or motivate followers to work toward established goals by exchanging rewards for their productivity.[25] But there's another type of leader—a **transformational leader**—who stimulates and inspires (transforms) followers to achieve extraordinary outcomes. Examples include Jim Goodnight of SAS Institute and Andrea Jung of Avon. They pay attention to the concerns and developmental needs of individual followers; they change followers' awareness of issues by helping those followers look at old problems in new ways; and they are able to excite, arouse, and inspire followers to exert extra effort to achieve group goals.

Transactional and transformational leadership shouldn't be viewed as opposing approaches to getting things done.[26] Transformational leadership develops from transactional leadership. It produces levels of employee effort and performance that go beyond what would occur with a transactional approach alone. Moreover, transformational leadership is more than charisma since the transformational leader attempts to instill in followers the ability to question not only established views but those views held by the leader.[27]

The evidence supporting the superiority of transformational leadership over transactional leadership is overwhelmingly impressive. For instance, studies that looked at managers in different settings, including the military and business, found that transformational leaders were evaluated as more effective, higher performers, more promotable than their transactional counterparts, and more interpersonally sensitive.[28] In addition, evidence indicates that transformational leadership is strongly correlated with lower turnover rates and higher levels of productivity, employee satisfaction, creativity, goal attainment, and follower well-being.[29]

transactional leaders
Leaders who lead primarily by using social exchanges (or transactions).

transformational leaders
Leaders who stimulate and inspire (transform) followers to achieve extraordinary outcomes.

Amazon.com founder and CEO Jeff Bezos is a charismatic leader who has the energy, optimism, enthusiasm, confidence, and drive to set and pursue goals for risky new ventures and to inspire his employees to work hard to achieve them. Starting his company in 1994 with the vision of providing consumers with the service of an online bookstore, Bezos has built Amazon into the largest retailer on the Web. He reinvented the company by introducing a product innovation, the Kindle electronic reader, that began with his long-term vision of "every book, ever printed, in any language, all available in less than 60 seconds."

HOW DO CHARISMATIC LEADERSHIP AND VISIONARY LEADERSHIP DIFFER?

Jeff Bezos, founder and CEO of Amazon.com, is a person who exudes energy, enthusiasm, and drive.[30] He's fun-loving (his legendary laugh has been described as a flock of Canadian geese on nitrous oxide), but has pursued his vision for Amazon.com with serious intensity and has demonstrated an ability to inspire his employees through the ups and downs of a rapidly growing company. Bezos is what we call a **charismatic leader**—that is, an enthusiastic, self-confident leader whose personality and actions influence people to behave in certain ways.

Several authors have attempted to identify personal characteristics of the charismatic leader.[31] The most comprehensive analysis identified five such characteristics: they have a vision, the ability to articulate that vision, willingness to take risks to achieve that vision, sensitivity to both environmental constraints and follower needs, and behaviors that are out of the ordinary.[32]

There's an increasing body of evidence that shows impressive correlations between charismatic leadership and high performance and satisfaction among followers.[33] Although one study found that charismatic CEOs had no impact on subsequent organizational performance, charisma is still believed to be a desirable leadership quality.[34]

If charisma is desirable, can people learn to be charismatic leaders? Or are charismatic leaders born with their qualities? Although a small number of experts still think that charisma can't be learned, most believe that individuals can be trained to exhibit charismatic behaviors.[35] For example, researchers have succeeded in teaching undergraduate students to "be" charismatic. How? They were taught to articulate a far-reaching goal, communicate high performance expectations, exhibit confidence in the ability of subordinates to meet those expectations, and empathize with the needs of their subordinates; they learned to project a powerful, confident, and dynamic presence; and they practiced using a captivating and engaging voice tone. The researchers also trained the student leaders to use charismatic nonverbal behaviors including leaning toward the follower when communicating, maintaining direct eye contact, and having a relaxed posture and animated facial expressions. In groups with these "trained" charismatic leaders, members had higher task performance, higher task adjustment, and better adjustment to the leader and to the group than did group members who worked in groups led by non-charismatic leaders.

One last thing we should say about charismatic leadership is that it may not always be necessary to achieve high levels of employee performance. It may be most appropriate when the follower's task has an ideological purpose or when the environment involves a high degree of stress and uncertainty.[36] This may explain why, when charismatic leaders surface, it's more likely to be in politics, religion, or wartime; or when a business firm is starting up or facing a survival crisis. For example, Martin Luther King Jr. used his charisma to bring about social equality through nonviolent means; and Steve Jobs achieved unwavering loyalty and commitment from Apple's technical staff in the early 1980s by articulating a vision of personal computers that would dramatically change the way people lived.

Although the term *vision* is often linked with charismatic leadership, **visionary leadership** is different since it's the ability to create and articulate a realistic, credible, and attractive vision of the future that improves upon the present situation.[37] This vision, if properly selected and implemented, is so energizing that it "in effect jump-starts the future by calling forth the skills, talents, and resources to make it happen."[38]

An organization's vision should offer clear and compelling imagery that taps into people's emotions and inspires enthusiasm to pursue the organization's goals. It should be able to generate possibilities that are inspirational and unique and offer new ways of doing things that are clearly better for the organization and its members. Visions that are clearly articulated and have powerful imagery are easily grasped and accepted. For instance, Michael Dell created a vision of a business that sells and delivers customized PCs directly to customers in less than a week. The late Mary Kay Ash's vision of women as entrepreneurs selling products that improved their self-image gave impetus to her cosmetics company, Mary Kay Cosmetics.

WHAT ABOUT LEADERS AND TEAMS? Because leadership is increasingly taking place within a team context and more organizations are using work teams, the role of the leader in guiding team members has become increasingly important. The role of team leader *is* different from the traditional leadership role, as J. D. Bryant, a supervisor at Texas Instruments' Forest Lane plant in Dallas, discovered.[39] One day he was contentedly overseeing a staff of 15 circuit board assemblers. The next day he was told that the company was going to use employee teams and he was to become a "facilitator." He said, "I'm supposed to teach the teams everything I know and then let them make their own decisions." Confused about his new role, he admitted, "There was no clear plan on what I was supposed to do." What *is* involved in being a team leader?

Many leaders are not equipped to handle the change to employee teams. As one consultant noted, "Even the most capable managers have trouble making the transition because all the command-and-control type things they were encouraged to do before are no longer appropriate. There's no reason to have any skill or sense of this."[40] This same consultant estimated that "probably 15 percent of managers are natural team leaders; another 15 percent could never lead a team because it runs counter to their personality—that is, they're unable to sublimate their dominating style for the good of the team. Then there's that huge group in the middle: Team leadership doesn't come naturally to them, but they can learn it."[41]

The challenge for many managers is learning how to become an effective team leader. They have to learn skills such as patiently sharing information, being able to trust others and to give up authority, and understanding when to intervene. And effective team leaders have mastered the difficult balancing act of knowing when to leave their teams alone and when to get involved. New team leaders may try to retain too much control at a time when team members need more autonomy, or they may abandon their teams at times when the teams need support and help.[42]

One study looking at organizations that had reorganized themselves around employee teams found certain common responsibilities of all leaders. These included coaching, facilitating, handling disciplinary problems, reviewing team and individual performance, training, and communication.[43] However, a more meaningful way to describe the team leader's job is to focus on two priorities: (1) managing the team's external boundary and (2) facilitating the team process.[44] These priorities entail four specific leadership roles as shown in Exhibit 11-7.

Right or Wrong?

The definition of "friend" on social networking sites such as Facebook and MySpace is so broad that even strangers may tag you. But it doesn't feel weird because nothing really changes when a stranger does this. However, what if your boss, who isn't much older than you are, asks you to be a friend on these sites? What then? What are the implications if you refuse the offer? What are the implications if you accept? What ethical issues might arise because of this? What would you do?

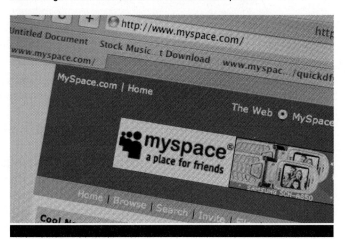

What Issues Do Today's Leaders Face?

It's not easy being a chief information officer (CIO) today. As the person responsible for managing a company's information technology activities, there are a lot of external and internal pressures. Technology continues to change rapidly—almost daily, it sometimes seems. Business costs continue to rise. Rob Carter, CIO of FedEx, is on the hot seat facing such challenges.[45] He's responsible for all the computer and communication systems that provide around-the-clock and around-the-globe support for FedEx's products and services. If anything goes wrong, you know who takes the heat. However, Carter has been an effective leader in this seemingly chaotic environment.

charismatic leaders
Enthusiastic, self-confident leaders whose personalities and actions influence people to behave in certain ways.

visionary leadership
The ability to create and articulate a realistic, credible, and attractive vision of the future that improves on the present situation.

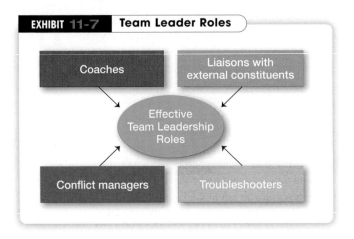

EXHIBIT 11-7 Team Leader Roles

Coaches

Liaisons with external constituents

Effective Team Leadership Roles

Conflict managers

Troubleshooters

Leading effectively in today's environment is unlikely to involve such challenges for most leaders. However, twenty-first-century leaders do face some important leadership issues. In this section, we look at these issues including empowering employees, cross-cultural leadership, and emotional intelligence and leadership. We'll also look at gender differences in leadership in the "Managing Diversity" box.

WHY DO LEADERS NEED TO EMPOWER EMPLOYEES? As we've described in different places throughout the text, managers are increasingly leading by not leading; that is, by empowering their employees. **Empowerment** involves increasing the decision-making discretion of workers. Millions of individual employees and employee teams are making the key operating decisions that directly affect their work. They're developing budgets, scheduling workloads, controlling inventories, solving quality problems, and engaging in similar activities that until very recently were viewed exclusively as part of the manager's job.[46] For instance, at The Container Store, any employee who gets a customer request has permission to take care of it. The company's cochairman Garret Boone says, "Everybody we hire, we hire as a leader. Anybody in our store can take an action that you might think of typically being a manager's action."[47]

One reason more companies are empowering employees is the need for quick decisions by those people who are most knowledgeable about the issues—often those at lower organizational levels. If organizations want to successfully compete in a dynamic global economy, employees have to be able to make decisions and implement changes quickly. Another reason is that organizational downsizings left many managers with larger spans of control. In order to cope with the increased work demands, managers had to empower their people. Although empowerment is not a universal answer, it can be beneficial when employees have the knowledge, skills, and experience to do their jobs competently.

Technology also has contributed to the increases in employee empowerment. Managers face unique challenges in leading empowered employees who aren't physically present in the workplace as the "Technology and the Manager's Job" box discusses.

DOES NATIONAL CULTURE AFFECT LEADERSHIP? One general conclusion that surfaces from leadership research is that effective leaders do not use a single style. They adjust their style to the situation. Although not mentioned explicitly, national culture is certainly an important situational variable in determining which leadership style will be most effective. What works in China isn't likely to be effective in France or Canada. For instance, one study of Asian leadership styles revealed that Asian managers preferred leaders who were competent decision makers, effective communicators, and supportive of employees.[48]

National culture affects leadership style because it influences how followers will respond. Leaders can't (and shouldn't) just choose their styles randomly. They're constrained by the cultural conditions their followers have come to expect. Exhibit 11-8 provides some findings from selected examples of cross-cultural leadership studies.

TECHNOLOGY AND THE MANAGER'S JOB

VIRTUAL LEADERSHIP

How do you lead people who are physically separated from you and with whom your interactions are primarily written digital communications?[49] That's the challenge of being a virtual leader. And unfortunately, leadership research has been directed mostly at face-to-face and verbal situations. But we can't ignore the reality that today's managers and their employees are increasingly being linked by technology rather than by geographic proximity. So what guidance can be provided to leaders who must inspire and motivate dispersed employees?

It's easy to soften harsh words in face-to-face communication with nonverbal action. A smile or a comforting gesture can go a long way in lessening the blow behind strong words like *disappointed*, *unsatisfactory*, *inadequate*, or *below expectations*. That nonverbal component doesn't exist in online interactions. The *structure* of words in a digital communication also has the power to motivate or demotivate the receiver. A manager who inadvertently sends a message in short phrases or in ALL CAPS may get a very different response than if the message had been sent in full sentences using appropriate punctuation.

To be an effective virtual leader, managers must recognize that they have choices in the words and structure of their digital communications. They also need to develop the skill of "reading between the lines" in the messages they receive. It's important to try and decipher the emotional content of a message as well as the written content. Also, virtual leaders need to think carefully about what actions they want their digital messages to initiate. Be clear about what's expected and follow up on messages.

For an increasing number of managers, good interpersonal skills may include the abilities to communicate support and leadership through digital communication and to read emotions in others' messages. In this "new world" of communication, writing skills are likely to become an extension of interpersonal skills.

Because most leadership theories were developed in the United States, they have an American bias. They emphasize follower responsibilities rather than rights; assume self-gratification rather than commitment to duty or altruistic motivation; assume centrality of work and democratic value orientation; and stress rationality rather than spirituality, religion, or superstition.[50] However, the GLOBE research program, which we first

EXHIBIT 11-8   Cross-Cultural Leadership

▶ Korean leaders are expected to be paternalistic toward employees.
▶ Arab leaders who show kindness or generosity without being asked to do so are seen by other Arabs as weak.
▶ Japanese leaders are expected to be humble and speak frequently.
▶ Scandinavian and Dutch leaders who single out individuals with public praise are likely to embarrass, not energize, those individuals.
▶ Effective leaders in Malaysia are expected to show compassion while using more of an autocratic than a participative style.
▶ Effective German leaders are characterized by high performance orientation, low compassion, low self-protection, low team orientation, high autonomy, and high participation.

Sources: Based on J. C. Kennedy, "Leadership in Malaysia: Traditional Values, International Outlook," *Academy of Management Executive* (August 2002), pp. 15–17; F. C. Brodbeck, M. Frese, and M. Javidan, "Leadership Made in Germany: Low on Compassion, High on Performance," *Academy of Management Executive* (February 2002), pp. 16–29; M. F. Peterson and J. G. Hunt, "International Perspectives on International Leadership," *Leadership Quarterly* (Fall 1997), pp. 203–31; R. J. House and R. N. Aditya, "The Social Scientific Study of Leadership: Quo Vadis?" *Journal of Management* 23, no. 3 (1997), p. 463; and R. J. House, "Leadership in the Twenty-First Century," in A. Howard (ed.), *The Changing Nature of Work* (San Francisco: Jossey-Bass, 1995), p. 442.

empowerment
The act of increasing the decision-making discretion of workers.

introduced in Chapter 2, is the most extensive and comprehensive cross-cultural study of leadership ever undertaken. The GLOBE study has found that there are some universal aspects to leadership. Specifically, a number of elements of transformational leadership appear to be associated with effective leadership regardless of what country the leader is in.[51] These include vision, foresight, providing encouragement, trustworthiness, dynamism, positiveness, and proactiveness. The results led two members of the GLOBE team to conclude that "effective business leaders in any country are expected by their subordinates to provide a powerful and proactive vision to guide the company into the future, strong motivational skills to stimulate all employees to fulfill the vision, and excellent planning skills to assist in implementing the vision."[52] Some people suggest that the universal appeal of these transformational leader characteristics is due to the pressures toward common technologies and management practices, as a result of global competitiveness and multinational influences.

HOW DOES EMOTIONAL INTELLIGENCE AFFECT LEADERSHIP? We introduced emotional intelligence (EI) in our discussion of emotions in Chapter 8. We revisit the topic here because of recent studies indicating that EI—more than IQ, expertise, or any other single factor—is the best predictor of who will emerge as a leader.[53]

As we said in our earlier discussion of trait research, leaders need basic intelligence and job-relevant knowledge. But IQ and technical skills are "threshold capabilities." They're necessary but not sufficient requirements for leadership. It's the possession of the five components of emotional intelligence—self-awareness, self-management, self-motivation, empathy, and social skills—that allows an individual to become a star performer. Without EI, a person can have outstanding training, a highly analytical mind, a long-term vision, and an endless supply of terrific ideas but still not make a great leader, especially as individuals move up in an organization. The evidence indicates that the higher the rank of a person considered to be a star performer, the more that EI capabilities surface as the reason for his or her effectiveness. Specifically, when star performers were compared with average ones in senior management positions, nearly 90 percent of the difference in their effectiveness was attributable to EI factors rather than basic intelligence.

Interestingly, it's been pointed out that the maturing of Rudolph Giuliani's leadership effectiveness closely followed the development of his emotional intelligence. For the better part of the eight years he was mayor of New York, Giuliani ruled with an iron fist. He talked tough, picked fights, and demanded results. The result was a city that was cleaner, safer, and better governed—but also more polarized. Critics called Giuliani a tin-eared tyrant. In the eyes of many, something important was missing from his leadership. That something, his critics acknowledged, emerged as the World Trade Center collapsed. It was a newfound

Ken Chenault, CEO of American Express, is a leader with high emotional intelligence. Since joining the company in 1981, he has emerged as a star performer in a job that demands interacting with employees, customers, and political leaders throughout the world. Chenault is described as achievement oriented, open to discussion, respectful, ethical, and trustworthy. Mentally tough, he welcomes constructive confrontation but is humble and conducts himself in a respectful and quietly assured manner. In this photo Chenault visits with Ruth Simmons, president of Brown University, during an event that honored both of them as two of America's best leaders.

MANAGING DIVERSITY | Do Men and Women Lead Differently?

Are there gender differences in leadership styles? Are men more effective leaders, or does that honor belong to women? Even asking those questions is certain to evoke reactions on both sides of the debate.[54]

The evidence indicates that the two sexes are more alike than different in the ways they lead. Much of this similarity is based on the fact that leaders, regardless of gender, perform similar activities in influencing others. That's their job, and the two sexes do it equally well. The same holds true in other professions. For instance, although the stereotypical nurse is a woman, men are equally effective and successful in this career.

Saying the sexes are more alike than different still means the two are not exactly the same. The most common difference lies in leadership styles. Women tend to use a more democratic style. They encourage participation of their followers and are willing to share their positional power with others. In addition, women tend to influence others best through their ability to be charmingly influential. Men, on the other hand, tend to typically use a task-centered leadership style. This approach includes directing activities of others and relying on their positional power to control the organization's activities. But surprisingly, even this difference is blurred. All things considered, when a woman is a leader in a traditionally male-dominated job (such as that of a police officer), she tends to lead in a manner that is more task centered.

Further compounding this issue are the changing roles of leaders in today's organizations. With an increased emphasis on teams, employee involvement, and interpersonal skills, democratic leadership styles are more in demand. Leaders need to be more sensitive to their followers' needs and more open in their communications; they need to build more trusting relationships. And many of these factors are behaviors that women have typically grown up developing.

So what do you think? Is there a difference between the sexes in terms of leadership styles? Do men or women make better leaders? Would you prefer to work for a man or a woman? What's your opinion?

---

compassion to complement his command: a mix of resolve, empathy, and inspiration that brought comfort to millions.[55] It's likely that Giuliani's emotional capacities and compassion for others were stimulated by a series of personal hardships—including prostate cancer and the highly visible breakup of his marriage—both of which had taken place less than a year before the terrorist attacks on the World Trade Center.[56]

EI has been shown to be positively related to job performance at all levels. But it appears to be especially relevant in jobs that demand a high degree of social interaction. And of course, that's what leadership is all about. Great leaders demonstrate their EI by exhibiting all five of its key components—self-awareness, self-management, self-motivation, empathy, and social skills (see p. 222).

The recent evidence makes a strong case for concluding that EI is an essential element in leadership effectiveness.[57] As such, it could be added to the list of traits associated with leadership that we described earlier in the chapter. EI may be something that comes easier for women leaders particularly. The "Managing Diversity" box looks more closely at the role of gender and leadership.

Why Is Trust the Essence of Leadership?

Trust, or lack of trust, is an increasingly important issue in today's organizations.[58] In today's uncertain environment, leaders need to build, or even rebuild, trust and credibility. Before we can discuss ways leaders can do that, we have to know what trust and credibility are and why they're so important.

Discuss trust as the essence of leadership.

11.5

The main component of credibility is honesty. Surveys show that honesty is consistently singled out as the number one characteristic of admired leaders. "Honesty is absolutely essential to leadership. If people are going to follow someone willingly, whether it be into battle or into the boardroom, they first want to assure themselves that the person is worthy of their trust."[59] In addition to being honest, credible leaders are competent and inspiring. They are personally able to effectively communicate their confidence and enthusiasm. Thus, followers judge a leader's **credibility** in terms of his or her honesty, competence, and ability to inspire.

credibility
The degree to which followers perceive someone as honest, competent, and able to inspire.

Trust is closely entwined with the concept of credibility, and, in fact, the terms are often used interchangeably. **Trust** is defined as the belief in the integrity, character, and ability of a leader. Followers who trust a leader are willing to be vulnerable to the leader's actions because they are confident that their rights and interests will not be abused.[60] Research has identified five dimensions that make up the concept of trust:[61]

▶ *Integrity:* honesty and truthfulness
▶ *Competence:* technical and interpersonal knowledge and skills
▶ *Consistency:* reliability, predictability, and good judgment in handling situations
▶ *Loyalty:* willingness to protect a person, physically and emotionally
▶ *Openness:* willingness to share ideas and information freely

Of these five dimensions, integrity seems to be the most critical when someone assesses another's trustworthiness.[62] Both integrity and competence were seen in our earlier discussion of leadership traits found to be consistently associated with leadership.

Workplace changes have reinforced why such leadership qualities are important. For instance, trends of employee empowerment and self-managed work teams have reduced many of the traditional control mechanisms used to monitor employees. If a work team is free to schedule its own work, evaluate its own performance, and even make its own hiring decisions, trust becomes critical. Employees have to trust managers to treat them fairly, and managers have to trust employees to conscientiously fulfill their responsibilities.

Also, leaders have to increasingly lead others who may not be in their immediate work group or even may be physically separated—members of cross-functional or virtual teams, individuals who work for suppliers or customers, and perhaps even people who represent other organizations through strategic alliances. These situations don't allow leaders the luxury of falling back on their formal positions for influence. Many of these relationships, in fact, are fluid and fleeting. So the ability to quickly develop trust and sustain that trust is crucial to the success of the relationship.

Why is it important that followers trust their leaders? Research has shown that trust in leadership is significantly related to positive job outcomes including job performance, organizational citizenship behavior, job satisfaction, and organizational commitment.[63] Given the importance of trust to effective leadership, how can leaders build trust? The "Developing Your Trust-Building Skill" box looks at ways to develop trust-building skills.

Now, more than ever, managerial and leadership effectiveness depends on the ability to gain the trust of followers.[64] Downsizing, corporate financial misrepresentations, and the increased use of temporary employees have undermined employees' trust in their leaders and shaken the confidence of investors, suppliers, and customers. A survey found that only 39 percent of U.S. employees and 51 percent of Canadian employees trusted their executive leaders.[65] Today's leaders are faced with the challenge of rebuilding and restoring trust with employees and with other important organizational stakeholders.

As a vital component of effective leadership, trust includes the five key dimensions of integrity, competence, consistency, loyalty, and openness. Indra Nooyi, CEO and chair of PepsiCo, scores high on all these dimensions, which have contributed to her high job performance and career success. Since joining the company in 1994 as a senior vice president of strategy and development, Nooyi has earned the trust of top managers as she helped them make tough decisions that moved the company away from fast food to focusing on beverages and packaged food. Nooyi is shown here leading a meeting with other top executives at company headquarters in Purchase, New York.

A Final Thought Regarding Leadership

Despite the belief that some leadership style will always be effective regardless of the situation, leadership may not always be important! Research indicates that, in some situations, any behaviors a leader exhibits are irrelevant. In other words, certain individual, job, and organizational variables can act as "substitutes for leadership," negating the influence of the leader.[66]

For instance, follower characteristics such as experience, training, professional orientation, or need for independence can neutralize the effect of leadership. These characteristics can replace the employee's need for a

Developing Your *Trust-Building* Skill

About the Skill

Given the importance trust plays in the leadership equation, today's leaders should actively seek to build trust with their followers. Here are some suggestions for achieving that goal.[67]

Steps in Practicing the Skill

1 **Practice openness.** Mistrust comes as much from what people don't know as from what they do know. Openness leads to confidence and trust. So keep people informed; make clear the criteria on how decisions are made; explain the rationale for your decisions; be candid about problems; and fully disclose relevant information.

2 **Be fair.** Before making decisions or taking actions, consider how others will perceive them in terms of objectivity and fairness. Give credit where credit is due; be objective and impartial in performance appraisals; and pay attention to equity perceptions in reward distributions.

3 **Speak your feelings.** Leaders who convey only hard facts come across as cold and distant. When you share your feelings, others will see you as real and human. They will know who you are and their respect for you will increase.

4 **Tell the truth.** If honesty is critical to credibility, you must be perceived as someone who tells the truth. Followers are more tolerant of being told something they "don't want to hear" than of finding out that their leader lied to them.

5 **Be consistent.** People want predictability. Mistrust comes from not knowing what to expect. Take the time to think about your values and beliefs. Then let them consistently guide your decisions. When you know your central purpose, your actions will follow accordingly, and you will project a consistency that earns trust.

6 **Fulfill your promises.** Trust requires that people believe that you're dependable. So you need to keep your word. Promises made must be promises kept.

7 **Maintain confidences.** You trust those whom you believe to be discrete and whom you can rely on. If people make themselves vulnerable by telling you something in confidence, they need to feel assured that you won't discuss it with others or betray that confidence. If people perceive you as someone who leaks personal confidences or someone who can't be depended on, you won't be perceived as trustworthy.

8 **Demonstrate confidence.** Develop the admiration and respect of others by demonstrating technical and professional ability. Pay particular attention to developing and displaying your communication, negotiating, and other interpersonal skills.

Practicing the Skill

You're a new manager. Your predecessor, who was popular and who is still with your firm, concealed from your team how far behind they are on their goals this quarter. As a result, your team members are looking forward to a promised day off that they're not entitled to and will not be getting.

It's your job to tell them the bad news. How will you do it?

---

leader's support or ability to create structure and reduce task ambiguity. Similarly, jobs that are inherently unambiguous and routine or that are intrinsically satisfying may place fewer demands on the leadership variable. Finally, such organizational characteristics as explicit formalized goals, rigid rules and procedures, or cohesive work groups can substitute for formal leadership.

trust
The belief in the integrity, character, and ability of a leader.

Review and 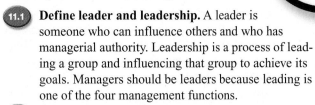 Applications

Chapter Summary

11.1 **Define leader and leadership.** A leader is someone who can influence others and who has managerial authority. Leadership is a process of leading a group and influencing that group to achieve its goals. Managers should be leaders because leading is one of the four management functions.

11.2 **Compare and contrast early leadership theories.** Early attempts to define leader traits were unsuccessful although later attempts found seven traits associated with leadership.

The University of Iowa studies explored three leadership styles. The only conclusion was that group members were more satisfied under a democratic leader than under an autocratic one. The Ohio State studies identified two dimensions of leader behavior—initiating structure and consideration. A leader high in both those dimensions at times achieved high group task performance and high group member satisfaction, but not always. The University of Michigan studies looked at employee-oriented leaders and production-oriented leaders. They concluded that leaders who were employee oriented could get high group productivity and high group member satisfaction. The managerial grid looked at leaders' concern for production and concern for people and identified five leader styles. Although it suggested that a leader who was high in concern for production and high in concern for people was the best, there was no substantive evidence for that conclusion.

As the behavioral studies showed, a leader's behavior has a dual nature: a focus on the task and a focus on the people.

11.3 **Describe the four major contingency leadership theories.** Fiedler's model attempted to define the best style to use in particular situations. He measured leader style—relationship oriented or task oriented—using the least-preferred co-worker questionnaire. Fiedler also assumed a leader's style was fixed. He measured three contingency dimensions: leader-member relations, task structure, and position power. The model suggests that task-oriented leaders performed best in very favorable and very unfavorable situations, and relationship-oriented leaders performed best in moderately favorable situations.

Hersey and Blanchard's situational leadership theory focused on followers' readiness. They identified four leadership styles: telling (high task–low relationship), selling (high task–high relationship), participating (low task–high relationship), and delegating (low task–low relationship). They also identified four stages of readiness: unable and unwilling (use telling style); unable but willing (use selling style); able but unwilling (use participative style); and able and willing (use delegating style).

The leader-participation model relates leadership behavior and participation to decision making. It uses a decision tree format with seven contingencies and five alternative leadership styles.

The path-goal model developed by Robert House identified four leadership behaviors: directive, supportive, participative, and achievement-oriented. He assumes that a leader can and should be able to use any of these styles. The two situational contingency variables were found in the environment and in the follower. Essentially the path-goal model says that a leader should provide direction and support as needed; that is, structure the path so the followers can achieve goals.

11.4 **Describe modern views of leadership and the issues facing today's leaders.** A transactional leader exchanges rewards for productivity where a transformational leader stimulates and inspires followers to achieve goals.

A charismatic leader is an enthusiastic and self-confident leader whose personality and actions influence people to behave in certain ways. People can learn to be charismatic. A visionary leader is able to create and articulate a realistic, credible, and attractive vision of the future.

A team leader has two priorities: manage the team's external boundary and facilitate the team process. Four leader roles are involved: liaison with external constituencies, troubleshooter, conflict manager, and coach.

The issues facing leaders today include employee empowerment, national culture, and emotional intelligence. As employees are empowered, the leader's role tends to be one of not leading. As leaders adjust their style to the situation, one of the most important situational characteristics is national culture. Finally, EI is proving to be an essential element in leadership effectiveness.

11.5 **Discuss trust as the essence of leadership.** The five dimensions of trust include integrity, competence, consistency, loyalty, and truthfulness. Integrity refers to one's honesty and truthfulness. Competence involves an individual's technical and interpersonal knowledge and skills. Consistency relates to an individual's reliability, predictability, and good judgment in handling situations. Loyalty is an individual's willingness to protect and save face for another person. Openness means that you can rely on the individual to give you the whole truth.

 To check your understanding of learning outcomes **11.1** – **11.5**, go to **mymanagementlab.com** and try the chapter questions.

Understanding the Chapter

1. Discuss the strengths and weaknesses of the trait theory.
2. What would a manager need to know to use Fiedler's contingency model? Be specific.
3. Do you think that most managers in real life use a contingency approach to increase their leadership effectiveness? Discuss.
4. "All managers should be leaders, but not all leaders should be managers." Do you agree or disagree with this statement? Support your position.
5. Do you think trust evolves out of an individual's personal characteristics or out of specific situations? Explain.
6. Do followers make a difference in whether a leader is effective? Discuss.
7. Research how organizations can develop effective leaders and write a short report explaining your findings.
8. When might leaders be irrelevant?

Understanding Yourself

Do Others See Me as Trustworthy?

Effective leaders have built a trusting relationship between themselves and those they seek to lead. This instrument provides you with insights into how trustworthy others are likely to perceive you.

INSTRUMENT   For each of the nine statements, respond using one of these answers:

1 = Strongly disagree
2 = Disagree
3 = Slightly disagree
4 = Neither agree nor disagree
5 = Slightly agree
6 = Agree
7 = Strongly agree

I am seen as someone who:

1.	Is reliable.	1	2	3	4	5	6	7
2.	Is always honest.	1	2	3	4	5	6	7
3.	Succeeds by stepping on other people.	1	2	3	4	5	6	7
4.	Tries to get the upper hand.	1	2	3	4	5	6	7
5.	Takes advantage of others' problems.	1	2	3	4	5	6	7
6.	Keeps my word.	1	2	3	4	5	6	7
7.	Doesn't mislead others.	1	2	3	4	5	6	7
8.	Tries to get out of my commitments.	1	2	3	4	5	6	7
9.	Takes advantage of people who are vulnerable.	1	2	3	4	5	6	7

SCORING KEY   To calculate your trustworthiness score, add up responses to items 1, 2, 6, and 7. For the other five items, reverse the score (7 becomes 1, 6 becomes 2, etc.). Add up the total.

ANALYSIS AND INTERPRETATION   Your total trustworthiness score will range between 9 and 63. The higher your score, the more you're perceived as a person who can be trusted. Scores of 45 or higher suggest others are likely to perceive you as trustworthy; while scores below 27 suggest that people will not see you as someone who can be trusted.

If you want to build trust with others, look at the behaviors this instrument measures. Then think about what you can do to improve your score on each. Examples might include being more open, speaking your feelings, giving generous credit to others, telling the truth, showing fairness and consistency, following through on promises and commitments, and maintaining confidences.

Source: Based on P. Bromiley and L. Cummings, "The Organizational Trust Inventory," in R. M. Kramer and T. R. Tyler (eds.), *Trust in Organizations* (Thousand Oaks, CA: Sage, 1996), pp. 328–29.

FYIA (For Your Immediate Action)

Preferred Bank Card, Inc.

Reply   Reply All   Forward

To: Pat Muenks, VP Employee Relations
From: Jan Plemmons, Customer Service Director
Subject: **Leadership Training**

I agree completely with your recommendation that we need a leadership training program for our customer service team leaders. These leaders struggle with keeping our customer service reps focused on our goal of providing timely, accurate, and friendly service to our bank card holders who call in with questions or complaints.

Can you put together a one-page proposal that describes the leadership topics you think should be covered? Also, give me some suggestions for how we might present the information in a way that would be interesting. We need to get started on this immediately, so please get this report to me by early next week.

This fictionalized company and message were created for educational purposes only. It is not meant to reflect positively or negatively on management practices by any company that may share this name.

GROWING LEADERS

How important are excellent leaders to organizations? If you were to ask 3M CEO George Buckley, he'd say extremely important. But he'd also say that excellent leaders don't just pop up out of nowhere. A company has to cultivate leaders who have the skills and abilities to help it survive and thrive. And like a successful baseball team with strong performance statistics that has a player development plan in place, 3M has its own farm system. Except its farm system is designed to develop company leaders.

3M's leadership development program is so effective that in 2009 *Chief Executive* magazine and Hay Consulting Group named the company the best at developing future leaders. What is 3M's leadership program all about? About eight years ago, the company's former CEO (Jim McNerney, who is now Boeing's CEO) and his top team spent 18 months developing a new leadership model for the company. After numerous brainstorming sessions and much heated debate, the group finally agreed on six "leadership attributes" that they believed were essential for the company to become skilled at executing strategy and being accountable. Those six attributes included the ability to "chart the course; energize and inspire others; demonstrate ethics, integrity, and compliance; deliver results; raise the bar; and innovate resourcefully." And now under Buckley's guidance, the company is continuing and reinforcing its pursuit of leadership excellence with these six attributes.

When asked about his views on leadership, Buckley said that he believes there is a difference between leaders and managers. "A leader is as much about inspiration as anything else. A manager is more about process." He believes that the key to developing leaders is to focus on those things that can be developed—like strategic thinking. Buckley also believes that leaders should not be promoted up and through the organization too quickly. They need time to experience failures and what it takes to rebuild.

Finally, when asked about his own leadership style. Buckley responded that, "The absolutely best way for me to be successful is to have people working for me who are better. Having that kind of emotional self-confidence is vital to leaders. You build respect in those people because you admire what they do. Having built respect, you build trust. However hokey it sounds, it works." And it must be working as the company was named the number one most admired company in the medical and other precision equipment division of *Fortune's* most admired ranking for 2009.

Discussion Questions

1. What do you think about Buckley's statement that leaders and managers differ? Do you agree? Why or why not?
2. What leadership models/theories/issues do you see in this case? List and describe.
3. Take each of the six leadership attributes that the company feels is important. Explain what you think each one involves. Then discuss how those attributes might be developed and measured.
4. What did this case teach you about leadership?

Sources: J. Kerr and R. Albright, "Finding and Cultivating Finishers," *Leadership Excellence* (July 2009), p. 20; D. Jones, "3M CEO Emphasizes Importance of Leaders," *USA Today,* May 18, 2009, p. 4B; G. Colvin, "World's Most Admired Companies 2009," *Fortune,* March 16, 2009, pp. 75+; and M. C. Mankins and R. Steele, "Turning Great Strategy into Great Performance," *Harvard Business Review* (July/August 2005), pp. 64–72.

12

Communication and Interpersonal Skills

Gossip Girls

Sixty percent. That's the percentage of respondents in a recent employee survey who said that gossip was their biggest pet peeve about their jobs. Most gossip centers around the workplace and the personal lives of coworkers. How often have you gossiped at work . . . either as a sender or a receiver? Although you may think workplace gossip is harmless, it can have some pretty serious consequences. First, spreading rumors can damage morale and increase anxiety. Secondly, it can hamper productivity and impact performance. And it can lead to something you might not even have considered, as it did for four former employees of the town of Hooksett, New Hampshire. Fired by the city council for gossiping about their boss, they learned the hard way that gossip can cost you your job.[1]

The longtime employees were fired because one of the women had used derogatory terms to describe the town administrator and because all of them had discussed a rumor that he was having an affair with a female subordinate. All four of the women acknowledged feeling resentment toward the woman, who worked in a specially created position and was paid more than two of the employees, despite having less experience and seniority.

Despite an appeal of their dismissal by the four employees, the Hooksett council didn't budge and stated, "These employees do not represent the best interests of the town of Hooksett and the false rumors, gossip and derogatory statements have contributed to a negative working environment and malcontent among their fellow employees." Despite national media attention and a petition signed by 419 residents asking for the women to be reinstated, the city council didn't waver on its decision. An attorney for the four women said that his clients were, "legitimately questioning the conduct of their supervisor, and whether the female subordinate was getting preferential treatment. It almost cheapens it to call it gossip. It might have been idle, not particularly thoughtful, talk. But there was no harm intended."

Although the four women represented nearly 50 years of combined service to the city and all had positive performance reviews, the town council believed that the women's actions were "insubordinate" and "dishonest." All four received a settlement for being fired, which cost the town a total of $330,000. The settlement agreement also stipulated, however, that two of the women can never apply for a job with the town again.

Communication takes place every day in every organization. In all areas. By all organizational members. Most of that communication tends to be work-related, but as this story shows, sometimes that communication doesn't lead to positive outcomes. In this chapter, we're going to look at basic concepts of interpersonal communication. We'll explain the communication process, methods of communicating, barriers to effective communication, and ways to overcome those barriers. In addition, we'll review several communication-based interpersonal skills including active listening, providing feedback, delegating, managing conflict, and negotiating. Managers must be proficient at these skills to be able to manage effectively in today's organizations.

How Do Managers Communicate Effectively?

Describe what managers need to know about communicating effectively.

12.1

The importance of effective communication for managers cannot be overemphasized for one specific reason: Everything a manager does involves communicating. Not *some* things but *everything*! A manager can't formulate strategy or make a decision without information. That information has to be communicated. Once a decision is made, communication must again take place. Otherwise, no one will know that a decision has been made.

The best idea, the most creative suggestion, or the finest plan cannot take form without communication. Managers, therefore, need effective communication skills. We're not suggesting, of course, that good communication skills alone make a successful manager. We can say, however, that ineffective communication skills can lead to a continuous stream of problems for a manager.

How Does the Communication Process Work?

Communication can be thought of as a process or flow. Communication problems occur when deviations or blockages disrupt that flow. Before communication can take place, a purpose, expressed as a message to be conveyed, is needed. It passes between a source (the sender) and a receiver. The message is encoded (converted to symbolic form) and is passed by way of some medium (channel) to the receiver, who retranslates (decodes) the message initiated by the sender. The result is **communication**, which is a transfer of understanding and meaning from one person to another.[2]

Exhibit 12-1 depicts the **communication process**. This model has seven parts: (1) the communication source or sender, (2) encoding, (3) the message, (4) the channel, (5) decoding, (6) the receiver, and (7) feedback.

The source initiates a message by **encoding** a thought. Four conditions affect the encoded message: skill, attitudes, knowledge, and the social cultural system. Our message in our communication to you in this book depends on our writing *skills*; if we don't have the requisite writing skills, our message will not reach you in the form desired. Keep in mind that a person's total communicative success includes speaking, reading, listening, and reasoning skills as well. As we discussed in Chapter 8, our attitudes influence our behavior. We hold predisposed ideas on numerous topics, and our communications are affected by these *attitudes*. Furthermore, we're restricted in our communicative activity by the extent of our *knowledge* of the particular topic. We can't communicate what we don't know, and should our knowledge be too extensive, it's possible that our receiver will not understand our message. Clearly, the amount of knowledge the source holds about his or her subject will affect the message he or she seeks to transfer. And, finally, just as attitudes influence our behavior, so does our *position in the social cultural system* in which we exist. Your beliefs and values, all part of your culture, act to influence you as a communicative source.

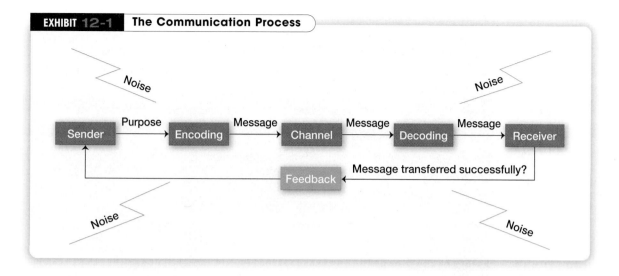

EXHIBIT 12-1 | **The Communication Process**

The **message** is the actual physical product from the source that conveys some purpose. When we speak, the words spoken are the message. When we write, the writing is the message. When we paint, the picture is the message. When we gesture, the movements of our arms, the expressions on our faces are the message.[3] Our message is affected by the code or group of symbols we use to transfer meaning, the content of the message itself, and the decisions that we make in selecting and arranging both codes and content.[4]

The **channel** is the medium through which the message travels. It's selected by the source, who must determine which channel is formal and which one is informal. Formal channels are established by the organization and transmit messages that pertain to the job-related activities of members. They traditionally follow the authority network within the organization. Other forms of messages, such as personal or social, follow the informal channels in the organization.

The receiver is the person to whom the message is directed. However, before the message can be received, the symbols in it must be translated into a form that can be understood by the receiver—the **decoding** of the message. Just as the encoder was limited by his or her skills, attitudes, knowledge, and social cultural system, the receiver is equally restricted. Accordingly, the source must be skillful in writing or speaking; the receiver must be skillful in reading or listening, and both must be able to reason. A person's knowledge, attitudes, and cultural background influence his or her ability to receive, just as they do the ability to send.

The final link in the communication process is a feedback loop. "If a communication source decodes the message that he encodes, if the message is put back into his system, we have feedback."[5] **Feedback** is the check on how successful we have been in transferring our messages as originally intended. It determines whether understanding has been achieved. Given the cultural diversity that exists in our workforce today, the importance of effective feedback to ensure proper communications cannot be overstated.[6]

communication
A transfer of understanding and meaning from one person to another.

communication process
The seven-step process in which understanding and meaning is transferred from one person to another.

encoding
Converting a message into symbolic form.

message
A purpose for communicating that's to be conveyed.

channel
The medium by which a message travels.

decoding
Translating a received message.

feedback
Checking to see how successfully a message has been transferred.

Kicking off the grand opening celebration of a new Cabela's outdoor-supply store, the company's sales manager and store manager high-five each other before delivering an employee pep talk. For this type of message, oral communication is much more effective than written communication because it gives the senders and the receivers of the message the opportunity to respond rapidly to what they hear. Before opening the doors of the store to customers, the managers take this opportunity to give employees last-minute details about their work and to motivate them in giving customers a special welcome to the store.

Are Written Communications More Effective Than Verbal Ones?

Written communications include memos, letters, e-mail, organizational periodicals, bulletin boards, or any other device that transmits written words or symbols. Why would a sender choose to use written communications? Because they're tangible, verifiable, and more permanent than the oral variety. Typically, both sender and receiver have a record of the communication. The message can be stored for an indefinite period of time. If questions arise about the content of the message, it's physically available for later reference. This feature is particularly important for complex or lengthy communications. For example, the marketing plan for a new product is likely to contain a number of tasks spread out over several months. By putting it in writing, those who have to carry out the plan can readily refer to the document over the life of the plan. A final benefit of written communication comes from the process itself. Except in rare instances, such as when presenting a formal speech, more care is taken with the written word than with the spoken word. Having to put something in writing forces a person to think more carefully about what he or she wants to convey. Therefore, written communications are more likely to be well thought out, logical, and clear.

Of course, written messages have their drawbacks. Writing may be more precise, but it also consumes a great deal of time. You could convey far more information to your college instructor in a one-hour oral exam than in a one-hour written exam. In fact, you could probably say in 10 to 15 minutes what it takes you an hour to write. The other major disadvantage is feedback or, rather, lack of it. Oral communications allow receivers to respond rapidly to what they think they hear. However, written communications don't have a built-in feedback mechanism. Sending a memo is no assurance that it will be received and, if it is received, no guarantee that the recipient will interpret it as the sender meant. The latter point is also relevant in oral communication, but it's easier in such cases merely to ask the receiver to summarize what you have said. An accurate summary presents feedback evidence that the message has been received and understood.

Is the Grapevine an Effective Way to Communicate?

The **grapevine** is the unofficial way that communications take place in an organization. It's neither authorized nor supported by the organization. Rather, information is spread by word of mouth—and even through electronic means. Ironically, good information passes among us rapidly, but bad information travels even faster.[7] The grapevine gets information out to organizational members as quickly as possible.

─────● **From the Past to the Present** ●─────

One of the most famous studies of the grapevine was conducted by management researcher Keith Davis who investigated the communication patterns among 67 managerial personnel.[8] The approach he used was to learn from each communication recipient how he or she first received a given piece of information and then trace it back to its source. It was found that, while the grapevine was an important source of information, only 10 percent of the executives acted as liaison individuals (that is, passed the information on to more than one other person). For example, when one executive decided to resign to enter the insurance business, 81 percent of the executives knew about it, but only 11 percent transmitted this information to others. At the time, this study was interesting both because of what it found, but more importantly because of what it showed about how the communication network worked.

Recent research by IBM and Massachusetts Institute of Technology using a similar type of analysis focused more on people's social networks of contacts at work rather than on how information flowed through the organizational grapevine. However, what was noticeably interesting about this study was that it found that employees who have strong communication ties with their managers tend to bring in more money than those who steer clear of the boss.

What managers can learn from both these studies is that it's important to understand the social and communication networks that employees use as they do their work. Know who the key contact points are so that if you ever need to find out or relay information, you know who to go to.

──────────────────● ──────────────────

The biggest question raised about grapevines, however, focuses on the accuracy of the rumors. Research on this topic has found somewhat mixed results. In an organization characterized by openness, the grapevine may be extremely accurate. In an authoritative culture, the rumor mill may not be accurate. But even then, although the information flowing is inaccurate, it still contains some element of truth. Rumors about major layoffs, plant closings, and the like may be filled with inaccurate information regarding who will be affected or when it may occur. Nonetheless, the reports that something is about to happen are probably on target.

How Do Nonverbal Cues Affect Communication?

Some of the most meaningful communications are neither spoken nor written. These are nonverbal communications. A loud siren or a red light at an intersection tells you something without words. A college instructor doesn't need words to know that students are bored; their eyes get glassy or they begin to read the school newspaper during class. Similarly, when papers start to rustle and notebooks begin to close, the message is clear: Class time is about over. The size of a person's office and desk or the clothes he or she wears also convey messages to others. However, the best-known areas of nonverbal communication are body language and verbal intonation.

Body language refers to gestures, facial expressions, and other body movements.[9] A snarl, for example, says something different from a smile. Hand motions, facial expressions, and other gestures can communicate emotions or temperaments such as aggression, fear, shyness, arrogance, joy, and anger.[10]

Verbal intonation refers to the emphasis someone gives to words or phrases. To illustrate how intonations can change the meaning of a message, consider the student who asks the instructor a question. The instructor replies, "What do you mean by that?" The student's reaction will vary, depending on the tone of the instructor's response. A soft, smooth tone creates a different meaning from one that is abrasive with a strong emphasis on the last word. Most of us would view the first intonation as coming from someone who sincerely sought clarification, whereas the second suggests that the person is aggressive or defensive. The adage, "It's not what you say but how you say it," is something managers should remember as they communicate.

---

grapevine
An unofficial channel of communication.

body language
Nonverbal communication cues such as facial expressions, gestures, and other body movements.

verbal intonation
An emphasis given to words or phrases that conveys meaning.

The fact that every oral communication also has a nonverbal message cannot be overemphasized.[11] Why? Because the nonverbal component is likely to carry the greatest impact. Research indicates that from 65 to 90 percent of the message of every face-to-face conversation is interpreted through body language. Without complete agreement between the spoken words and the body language that accompanies it, receivers are more likely to react to body language as the "true meaning."[12]

What Barriers Keep Communication from Being Effective?

A number of interpersonal and intrapersonal barriers help to explain why the message decoded by a receiver is often different from that which the sender intended. We summarize the more prominent barriers to effective communication in Exhibit 12-2 and briefly describe them here.

HOW DOES FILTERING AFFECT COMMUNICATION? Filtering refers to the way that a sender manipulates information so that it will be seen more favorably by the receiver. For example, when a manager tells his boss what he feels that boss wants to hear, he is filtering information. Does filtering happen much in organizations? Sure it does. As information is passed up to senior executives, it has to be condensed and synthesized by subordinates so upper management doesn't become overloaded with information. Those doing the condensing filter communications through their own personal interests and perceptions of what's important.

The extent of filtering tends to be the function of the organization's culture and number of vertical levels in the organization. More vertical levels in an organization mean more opportunities for filtering. As organizations become less dependent on strict hierarchical arrangements and instead use more collaborative, cooperative work arrangements, information filtering may become less of a problem. In addition, the ever-increasing use of e-mail to communicate in organizations reduces filtering because communication is more direct as intermediaries are bypassed. Finally, the organizational culture encourages or discourages filtering by the type of behavior it rewards. The more that organizational rewards emphasize style and appearance, the more managers will be motivated to filter communications in their favor.

HOW DOES SELECTIVE PERCEPTION AFFECT COMMUNICATION? The second barrier is selective perception. We've mentioned selective perception before in this book. We discuss it again here because the receivers in the communication process selectively see

EXHIBIT 12-2	**Barriers to Effective Communication**

BARRIER	DESCRIPTION
Filtering	The deliberate manipulation of information to make it appear more favorable to the receiver.
Selective Perception	Receiving communications on the basis of what one selectively sees and hears depending on his or her needs, motivation, experience, background, and other personal characteristics.
Information Overload	When the amount of information one has to work with exceeds one's processing capacity.
Emotions	How the receiver feels when a message is received.
Language	Words have different meanings to different people. Receivers will use their definition of words being communicated.
Gender	How males and females react to communication may be different, and they each have a different communication style.
National Culture	Communication differences arising from the different languages that individuals use to communicate and the national culture of which they are a part.

and hear based on their needs, motivations, experience, background, and other personal characteristics. Receivers also project their interests and expectations into communications as they decode them. The employment interviewer who expects a female job applicant to put her family ahead of her career is likely to see that tendency in female applicants, regardless of whether the applicants would do so or not. As we said in Chapter 8, we don't see reality; rather, we interpret what we see and call it reality.

HOW DOES INFORMATION OVERLOAD AFFECT COMMUNICATION? Individuals have a finite capacity for processing data. For instance, consider the international sales representative who returns home to find that she has more than 600 e-mails waiting for her. It's not possible to fully read and respond to each one of those messages without facing **information overload**.

Today's typical executive frequently complains of information overload.[13] The demands of keeping up with e-mail, phone calls, faxes, meetings, and professional reading create an onslaught of data that is nearly impossible to process and assimilate. What happens when you have more information than you can sort out and use? You're likely to select out, ignore, pass over, or forget information. Or you may put off further processing until the overload situation is over. In any case, the result is lost information and less effective communication.

HOW DO EMOTIONS AFFECT COMMUNICATION? How a receiver feels when a message is received influences how he or she interprets it. You'll often interpret the same message differently, depending on whether you're happy or distressed. Extreme emotions are most likely to hinder effective communications. In such instances, we often disregard our rational and objective thinking processes and substitute emotional judgments. It's best to avoid reacting to a message when you're upset because you're not likely to be thinking clearly.

HOW DOES LANGUAGE AFFECT COMMUNICATION? Words mean different things to different people. "The meanings of words are not in the words; they are in us."[14] Age, education, and cultural background are three of the more obvious variables that influence the language a person uses and the definitions he or she applies to words. Columnist George F. Will and rap artist Nelly both speak English. But the language one uses is vastly different from how the other speaks.

In an organization, employees usually come from diverse backgrounds and, therefore, have different patterns of speech. Additionally, the grouping of employees into departments creates specialists who develop their own **jargon** or technical language.[15] In large organizations, members are also frequently widely dispersed geographically—even operating in different countries—and individuals in each locale will use terms and phrases that are unique to their area.[16] And the existence of vertical levels can also cause language problems. The language of senior executives, for instance, can be mystifying to regular employees not familiar with management jargon. Keep in mind that while we may speak the same language, our use of that language is far from uniform. Senders tend to assume that the words and phrases they use mean the same to the receiver as they do to them. This assumption, of

One of the barriers to effective communication is information overload. Because people have a limit to how much information they can process, too much information can affect the communication process. When it becomes almost impossible to process and assimilate too much data, people are prone to ignore, pass over, or forget information. This often results in lost information or less effective communication. Efforts to remove the barrier of information overload include an experiment by Intel Corporation's chip design group. They tried establishing periods of quiet time for employees and limiting e-mail messages, but employees said they found the experiment too restrictive. The end-of-chapter Case Application describes another organization that tried something similar . . . with similar results.

---

filtering
Deliberately manipulating information to make it appear more favorable to the receiver.

selective perception
Selectively perceiving or hearing a communication based on your own needs, motivations, experiences, or other personal characteristics.

information overload
What results when information exceeds processing capacity.

jargon
Technical language.

course, is incorrect and creates communication barriers. Knowing how each of us modifies the language would help minimize those barriers.

HOW DOES GENDER AFFECT COMMUNICATION? Effective communication between the sexes is important in all organizations if they are to meet organizational goals. But how can we manage the various differences in communication styles? To keep gender differences from becoming persistent barriers to effective communication requires acceptance, understanding, and a commitment to communicate adaptively with each other. Both men and women need to acknowledge that there are differences in communication styles, that one style isn't better than the other, and that it takes real effort to talk with each other successfully. See the "Managing Diversity" box for more information on how men and women communicate.

HOW DOES NATIONAL CULTURE AFFECT COMMUNICATION? Finally, communication differences can also arise from the different languages that individuals use to communicate and the national culture of which they're a part.[17] For example, let's compare countries that place a high value on individualism (such as the United States) with countries where the emphasis is on collectivism (such as Japan).[18]

In the United States, communication patterns tend to be oriented to the individual and clearly spelled out. Managers in the United States rely heavily on memoranda, announcements, position papers, and other formal forms of communication to state their positions on issues. Supervisors here may hoard information in an attempt to make themselves look good (filtering) and as a way of persuading their employees to accept decisions and plans. And for their own protection, lower-level employees also engage in this practice.

MANAGING DIVERSITY | The Communication Styles of Men and Women

"You don't understand what I'm saying, and you never listen!" "You're making a big deal out of nothing." Have you said statements like these to friends of the opposite sex? Most of us probably have! Research shows, as does personal experience, that men and women communicate differently.[19]

Deborah Tannen has studied the ways that men and women communicate and reports some interesting differences. The essence of her research is that men use talk to emphasize status, while women use it to create connection. She states that communication between the sexes can be a continual balancing act of juggling our conflicting needs for intimacy, which suggests closeness and commonality, and independence, which emphasizes separateness and differences. It's no wonder, then, that communication problems arise! Women speak and hear a language of connection and intimacy. Men hear and speak a language of status and independence. For many men, conversations are merely a way to preserve independence and maintain status in a hierarchical social order. Yet for many women, conversations are negotiations for closeness and seeking out support and confirmation. Let's look at a few examples of what Tannen has described.

Men frequently complain that women talk on and on about their problems. Women, however, criticize men for not listening. What's happening is that when a man hears a woman talking about a problem, he frequently asserts his desire for independence and control by offering solutions. Many women, in contrast, view conversing about a problem as a way to promote closeness. The woman talks about a problem to gain support and connection, not to get the male's advice.

Here's another example: Men are often more direct than women in conversation. A man might say, "I think you're wrong on that point." A woman might say, "Have you looked at the marketing department's research report on that issue?" The implication in the woman's comment is that the report will point out the error. Men frequently misread women's indirectness as "covert" or "sneaky," but women aren't as concerned as men with the status and one-upmanship that directness often creates.

Finally, men often criticize women for seeming to apologize all the time. Men tend to see the phrase "I'm sorry" as a sign of weakness because they interpret the phrase to mean the woman is accepting blame, when he may know she's not to blame. The woman also knows she's not at fault. Yet she's typically using "I'm sorry" to express regret: "I know you must feel bad about this and I do, too."

How can these differences in communication styles be managed? Keeping gender differences from becoming persistent barriers to effective communication requires acceptance, understanding, and a commitment to communicate adaptively with each other. Both men and women need to acknowledge that there are differences in communication styles, that one style isn't better than the other, and that it takes real effort to "talk" with each other successfully.

In collectivist countries, such as Japan, there's more interaction for its own sake and a more informal manner of interpersonal contact. The Japanese manager, in contrast to the U.S. manager, engages in extensive verbal consultation with employees over an issue first and draws up a formal document later to outline the agreement that was made. The Japanese value decisions by consensus, and open communication is an inherent part of the work setting. Also, face-to-face communication is encouraged.[20]

Cultural differences can affect the way a manager chooses to communicate.[21] And these differences undoubtedly can be a barrier to effective communication if not recognized and taken into consideration.

How Can Managers Overcome Communication Barriers?

Given these barriers to communication, what can managers do to overcome them? The following suggestions should help make communication more effective (see also Exhibit 12-3).

WHY USE FEEDBACK? Many communication problems are directly attributed to misunderstanding and inaccuracies. These problems are less likely to occur if the manager gets feedback, both verbal and nonverbal.

A manager can ask questions about a message to determine whether it was received and understood as intended. Or the manager can ask the receiver to restate the message in his or her own words. If the manager hears what was intended, understanding and accuracy should improve. Feedback can also be more subtle as general comments can give a manager a sense of the receiver's reaction to a message.

Feedback doesn't have to be verbal. If a sales manager e-mails information about a new monthly sales report that all sales representatives will need to complete and some of them don't turn it in, the sales manager has received feedback. This feedback suggests that the sales manager needs to clarify the initial communication. Similarly, managers can look for nonverbal cues to tell whether someone's getting the message.

WHY SHOULD SIMPLIFIED LANGUAGE BE USED? Because language can be a barrier, managers should consider the audience to whom the message is directed and tailor the language to them. Remember, effective communication is achieved when a message is both received and *understood*. This means, for example, that a hospital administrator should always try to communicate in clear, easily understood terms and to use language tailored to different employee groups. Messages to the surgical staff should be purposefully different from that used with office employees. Jargon can facilitate understanding if it's used within a group that knows what it means, but can cause problems when used outside that group.

EXHIBIT 12-3	Overcoming Barriers to Effective Communication
Use Feedback	Check the accuracy of what has been communicated—or what you think you heard.
Simplify Language	Use words that the intended audience understands.
Listen Actively	Listen for the full meaning of the message without making premature judgment or interpretation—or thinking about what you are going to say in response.
Constrain Emotions	Recognize when your emotions are running high. When they are, don't communicate until you have calmed down.
Watch Nonverbal Cues	Be aware that your actions speak louder than your words. Keep the two consistent.

WHY MUST WE LISTEN ACTIVELY? When someone talks, we hear. But too often we don't listen. Listening is an active search for meaning, whereas hearing is passive. In listening, the receiver is also putting effort into the communication.

Many of us are poor listeners. Why? Because it's difficult, and most of us would rather do the talking. Listening, in fact, is often more tiring than talking. Unlike hearing, **active listening**, which is listening for full meaning without making premature judgments or interpretations, demands total concentration. The average person normally speaks at a rate of about 125 to 200 words per minute. However, the average listener can comprehend up to 400 words per minute.[22] The difference leaves lots of idle brain time and opportunities for the mind to wander.

Active listening is enhanced by developing empathy with the sender—that is, by putting yourself in the sender's position. Because senders differ in attitudes, interests, needs, and expectations, empathy makes it easier to understand the actual content of a message. An empathetic listener reserves judgment on the message's content and carefully listens to what is being said. The goal is to improve one's ability to get the full meaning of a communication without distorting it by premature judgments or interpretations. Other specific behaviors that active listeners demonstrate are discussed in the "Developing Your Active-Listening Skill" box.

Developing Your *Active-Listening* Skill

About the Skill

Active listening requires you to concentrate on what is being said. It's more than just hearing the words. It involves a concerted effort to understand and interpret the speaker's message.

Steps in Practicing the Skill

1 **Make eye contact.** How do you feel when somebody doesn't look at you when you're speaking? If you're like most people, you're likely to interpret this behavior as aloofness or disinterest. Making eye contact with the speaker focuses your attention, reduces the likelihood that you will become distracted, and encourages the speaker.

2 **Exhibit affirmative nods and appropriate facial expressions.** The effective listener shows interest in what is being said through nonverbal signals. Affirmative nods and appropriate facial expressions, when added to good eye contact, convey to the speaker that you're listening.

3 **Avoid distracting actions or gestures that suggest boredom.** In addition to showing interest, you must avoid actions that suggest that your mind is somewhere else. When listening, don't look at your watch, shuffle papers, play with your pencil, or engage in similar distractions. They make the speaker feel that you're bored or disinterested, or indicate that you aren't fully attentive.

4 **Ask questions.** The critical listener analyzes what he or she hears and asks questions. This behavior provides clarification, ensures understanding, and assures the speaker that you're listening.

5 **Paraphrase using your own words.** The effective listener uses phrases such as "What I hear you saying is . . ." or "Do you mean . . .?" Paraphrasing is an excellent control device to check on whether you're listening carefully and to verify that what you heard is accurate.

6 **Avoid interrupting the speaker.** Let the speaker complete his or her thought before you try to respond. Don't try to second-guess where the speaker's thoughts are going. When the speaker is finished, you'll know it.

7 **Don't overtalk.** Most of us would rather express our own ideas than listen to what someone else says. Talking might be more fun and silence might be uncomfortable, but you can't talk and listen at the same time. The good listener recognizes this fact and doesn't overtalk.

8 **Make smooth transitions between the roles of speaker and listener.** The effective listener makes transitions smoothly from speaker to listener and back to speaker. From a listening perspective, this means concentrating on what a speaker has to say and practicing not thinking about what you're going to say as soon as you get your chance.

Practicing the Skill

Ask a friend to tell you about his or her day and listen without interrupting. When your friend has finished speaking, ask two or three questions, if needed, to obtain more clarity and detail. Listen carefully to the answers. Now summarize your friend's day in no more than five sentences.

How well did you do? Let your friend rate the accuracy of your paraphrase (and try not to interrupt).

WHY MUST WE CONSTRAIN EMOTIONS? It would be naïve to assume that managers always communicate in a rational manner. We know that emotions can cloud and distort communication. A manager who's upset over an issue is more likely to misconstrue incoming messages and fail to communicate his or her outgoing messages clearly and accurately. What to do? The simplest answer is to calm down and get emotions under control before communicating. The following is a good example of why it's important to be aware of your emotions before communicating.

Neal L. Patterson, CEO of Cerner Corporation, a health care software development company based in Kansas City, was upset with the fact that employees didn't seem to be putting in enough hours. So he sent an angry and emotional e-mail to about 400 company managers that said, in part:

> We are getting less than 40 hours of work from a large number of our K.C.-based EMPLOYEES. The parking lot is sparsely used at 8 a.m.; likewise at 5 p.m. As managers, you either do not know what your EMPLOYEES are doing, or you do not CARE. You have created expectations on the work effort which allowed this to happen inside Cerner, creating a very unhealthy environment. In either case, you have a problem and you will fix it or I will replace you . . . I will hold you accountable. You have allowed things to get to this state. You have two weeks. Tick, tock."[23]

Although the e-mail was meant only for the company's managers, it was leaked and posted on an Internet discussion site. The tone of the e-mail surprised industry analysts, investors, and of course, Cerner's managers and employees. The company's stock price dropped 22 percent over the next three days. Patterson apologized to his employees and acknowledged, "I lit a match and started a firestorm."

Roman Garza, manager of a Target store, concentrates intensely while listening to an employee who approached him about a work scheduling concern. Garza's active listening skill requires intense concentration so he can focus on the speaker and tune out the many customary noises and distractions in a retail store environment. Effective listening also requires that Garza empathizes with the employee by trying to understand what she is saying, by listening objectively without judging the content of what she is saying, and by taking responsibility for doing whatever is needed to get the full meaning of what she intends to communicate.

WHY THE EMPHASIS ON NONVERBAL CUES? If actions speak louder than words, then it's important to make sure your actions align with and reinforce the words that go along with them. An effective communicator watches his or her nonverbal cues to ensure that they convey the desired message.

How Is Technology Affecting Managerial Communication?

Explain how technology affects managerial communication. **12.2**

Information technology has radically changed the way organizational members communicate. For example, it has significantly improved a manager's ability to monitor individual and team performance, it has allowed employees to have more complete information to make faster decisions, and it has provided employees more opportunities to collaborate and share information. In addition, information technology has made it possible for people in organizations to be fully accessible 24 hours a day, 7 days a week, regardless of where they are. Employees don't have to be at their desks with their computers turned on in order to communicate with others in the organization. Three developments in information technology appear to have had a significant effect on current managerial communication: networked computer systems, wireless capabilities, and knowledge management systems.

active listening
Listening for full meaning without making premature judgments or interpretations.

What Are Networked Communication Capabilities?

In a networked computer system, an organization links its computers together through compatible hardware and software, creating an integrated organizational network. Organization members can then communicate with each other and tap into information whether they're down the hall, across town, or anywhere on the globe. Although the mechanics of how network systems work are beyond the scope of this book, we'll address some of the communication applications.

E-mail is the instantaneous transmission of messages on computers that are linked together. Messages wait at a receiver's computer and are read at the receiver's convenience. E-mail is fast and cheap and can be used to send the same message to many people at the same time. It's a quick and convenient way for organization members to share information and communicate. Files can also be attached to e-mail messages, which enables the receiver to have a hard copy of a document.

Some organization members who find e-mail slow and cumbersome are using *instant messaging (IM)*. This interactive, real-time communication takes place among computer users who are logged on to the computer network at the same time. Instant messaging was first popular among teens and preteens who wanted to communicate with their friends online. Now it's moved to the workplace. With IM, information that needs to be communicated can be done so instantaneously without waiting for colleagues to read e-mail messages. However, instant messaging is not without its drawbacks. It requires users to be logged on to the organization's computer network at the same time, which potentially leaves the network open to security breaches.

A *voice mail* system digitizes a spoken message, transmits it over the network, and stores the message on a disk for the receiver to retrieve later.[25] This capability allows information to be transmitted even though a receiver may not be physically present to take the information. Receivers can choose to save the message for future use, delete it, or route it to other parties.

Fax machines can transmit documents containing both text and graphics over ordinary telephone lines. A sending fax machine scans and digitizes the document, and a receiving fax machine reads the scanned information and reproduces it in hard-copy form. Information that's best viewed in printed form can be easily and quickly shared by organization members.

Electronic data interchange (EDI) is a way for organizations to exchange business transaction documents such as invoices or purchase orders, using direct, computer-to-computer networks. Organizations often use EDI with vendors, suppliers, and customers because it saves time and money. How? Information on transactions is transmitted from one organization's computer system to another through an interorganizational telecommunications network. The printing and handling of paper documents at one organization are eliminated as is the inputting of data at the other organization.

Meetings—one-on-one, team, divisional, or organization-wide—have always been one way to share information. The limitations of technology used to dictate that meetings take place among people in the same physical location. But that's no longer the case. *Teleconferencing* allows a group of people to confer simultaneously using telephone or e-mail group communications software. If meeting participants can see each other over video screens, the simultaneous conference is called *videoconferencing*. Work groups, large and small, which might be in different locations, can use these communication network tools to collaborate and share information. Doing so is often much less expensive than incurring travel costs for bringing members together from several locations.

Networked computer systems allow for organizational *intranets and extranets*. An intranet is an organizational communication network that uses Internet technology but is accessible only to organizational employees. Many organizations are using intranets as ways for employees to share information and collaborate on documents and projects—as well as access company policy manuals and employee-specific materials, such as employee benefits—from different locations.[26] An extranet is an organizational communication network that uses Internet technology and allows authorized users inside the organization

TECHNOLOGY AND THE MANAGER'S JOB

FYEO—DECODING COMMUNICATION JARGON

Okay . . . how well do you know the net lingo?[27] If you received an e-mail or text message with GFTD written in it, would you know what that meant? What about NSFW or BIL? When an employee received an e-mail at work from a friend with an attached slideshow entitled "Awkward Family Photos," she clicked through it and saw some pretty unusual—yes, awkward—photos. Looking back at the e-mail, that's when she also saw the abbreviation "NSFW" written at the bottom. Not knowing what that was, she looked the abbreviation up on netlingo.com (one of several Web sites that translate Internet and texting abbreviations). Come to find out, she should have paid more attention to the abbreviation since NSFW stands for "not safe for work."

"As text-messaging shorthand becomes increasingly widespread in e-mails, text messages, and Tweets," people need to be aware of what it means. At many workplaces, a working knowledge of Net lingo is becoming necessary. As employees use social media sites like Twitter and Facebook and even text messaging to communicate with colleagues and customers, the shorthand abbreviations are often necessary to stay within message length limits. However, as the NSFW example showed, not knowing or even misunderstanding the lingo can lead to surprises, inappropriate responses, or miscommunications.

(BTW—which is net lingo for "by the way"—FYEO means "for your eyes only," GFTD stands for "gone for the day," and BIL is "boss is listening.")

to communicate with certain outsiders such as customers or vendors. Most of the large auto manufacturers, for example, have extranets that allow faster and more convenient communication with dealers.

Finally, organizations are using *Internet-based voice communication*. Popular Web sites such as Skype, Vonage, and Yahoo!, among others, let users chat with each other. And a number of companies are using these services for employees to use in conference calls or for instant messaging.

How Have Wireless Capabilities Affected Communication?

At Seattle-based Starbucks Corporation, district managers use mobile technology, giving them more time to spend in the company's stores. A company executive says, "These are the most important people in the company. Each has between 8 to 10 stores that he or she services. And while their primary job is outside of the office—and in those stores—they still need to be connected."[28] As this example shows, wireless communication technology has the ability to improve work for managers and employees.

While networked computer systems require organizations and organizational members to be connected by wires, wireless communication doesn't. Smartphones, netbook computers, notebook computers, and other pocket communication devices have spawned a whole new way for managers to "keep in touch." Globally, millions of users use wireless technology to send and receive information from anywhere. One result: Employees no longer have to be at their desks with their computers plugged in and turned on in order to communicate with others in the organization. As technology continues to advance in this area, we'll see more and more organization members using wireless communication as a way to collaborate and share information.[29]

How Does Knowledge Management Affect Communication?

Part of a manager's responsibility in fostering an environment conducive to learning and effective communications is to create learning capabilities throughout the organization. These opportunities should extend from the lowest to the highest levels in all areas. How

Right or Wrong?

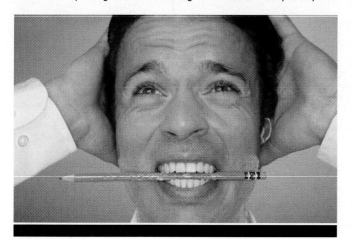

How honest should managers be with employees about a company's worsening financial condition?[24] When one business owner who owns a legal services firm mentioned to his employees that the business was not doing well, it ended up scaring them. "People started crying. One person gave notice and left for a job at another company." What do you think? What would be achieved by telling them? Is not telling them unethical? Why or why not?

can managers create such an environment? An important step is recognizing the value of knowledge as a major resource, just like cash, raw materials, or office equipment. To illustrate the value of knowledge, think about how you register for your college classes. Do you talk to others who have had a certain professor? Do you listen to their experiences with this individual and make your decision based on what they have to say (their knowledge about the situation)? If you do, you're tapping into the value of knowledge. But in an organization, just recognizing the value of accumulated knowledge or wisdom isn't enough. Managers must deliberately manage that base of knowledge. **Knowledge management** involves cultivating a learning culture in which organizational members systematically gather knowledge and share it with others in the organization so as to achieve better performance.[30] For instance, accountants and consultants at Ernst and Young document best practices that they've developed, unusual problems they've dealt with, and other work information. This "knowledge" is then shared with all employees through computer-based applications and through community of interest teams that meet regularly throughout the company. Many other organizations—General Electric, Toyota, Hewlett-Packard—have recognized the importance of knowledge management within a learning organization (see Chapter 5). Today's technologies are helping improve knowledge management and facilitating organizational communications and decision making.

What Interpersonal Skills Do Managers Need?

> 12.3 Discuss the interpersonal skills that every manager needs.

Would it surprise you to know that more managers are probably fired because of poor interpersonal skills than for a lack of technical ability?[31] Moreover, a survey of top executives at *Fortune* 500 companies found that interpersonal skills were the most important consideration in hiring senior-level employees.[32] Because managers ultimately get things done through others, competencies in leadership, communication, and other interpersonal skills are prerequisites to managerial effectiveness.[33] Therefore, the rest of this chapter focuses on key interpersonal skills that every manager needs.[34]

Why Are Active Listening Skills Important?

Previously, we discussed the importance of active listening. It's one of the most important interpersonal skills that managers can develop. But active listening is hard work. You have to concentrate, and you have to want to fully understand what a speaker is saying. Students who use active listening techniques for an entire 75-minute lecture are as tired as their instructor when the lecture is over because they've put as much energy into listening as the instructor put into speaking.

Active listening requires four essential elements: (1) intensity, (2) empathy, (3) acceptance, and (4) a willingness to take responsibility for completeness.[35] As noted, the human brain is capable of handling a speaking rate that's faster than that of the average speaker, leaving a lot of time for daydreaming. The active listener *concentrates intensely* on what the speaker is saying and tunes out the thousands of miscellaneous thoughts (about money, sex, vacation, parties, exams, and so on) that create distractions. What do active listeners do with their idle brain time? They summarize and integrate what has been said. They put each new bit of information into the context of what preceded it.

Empathy requires you to put yourself into the speaker's shoes. You try to understand what the speaker wants to communicate rather than what you want to hear. Notice that empathy demands both knowledge of the speaker and flexibility on your part. You need to suspend your own thoughts and feelings and adjust what you see and feel to your speaker's world. In that way, you increase the likelihood that you'll interpret the message in the way the speaker intended.

An active listener demonstrates *acceptance*. He or she listens objectively without judging content, which is not an easy task. It's natural to be distracted by what a speaker says, especially when we disagree with it. When we hear something we disagree with, we have a tendency to begin formulating our mental arguments to counter what is being said. Of course, in doing so, we miss the rest of the message. The challenge for the active listener is to absorb what's being said and withhold judgment on content until the speaker is finished.

The final ingredient of active listening is taking *responsibility for completeness*. That is, the listener does whatever is necessary to get the full intended meaning from the speaker's communication. Two widely used active listening techniques are listening for feeling as well as for content and asking questions to ensure understanding. (Look back at the "Developing Your Active-Listening Skill" box on p. 328 for additional information.)

Why Are Feedback Skills Important?

Ask a manager about the performance feedback he or she gives employees, and you're likely to get a qualified answer. If the feedback is positive, it's likely to be given promptly and enthusiastically. Negative feedback is often treated differently.[37] Like most of us, managers don't particularly enjoy communicating bad news. They fear offending the receiver or having to deal with his or her emotions. The result is that negative feedback is often avoided, delayed, or substantially distorted. In this section, we want to show you the importance of providing both positive and negative feedback and to identify specific techniques to help make your feedback more effective.

HOW ARE POSITIVE AND NEGATIVE FEEDBACK DIFFERENT? We know that managers treat positive and negative feedback differently. So do receivers. You need to understand this fact and adjust your feedback style accordingly.

Positive feedback is more readily and accurately perceived than negative feedback. Furthermore, whereas positive feedback is almost always accepted, negative feedback often meets resistance.[38] Why? The logical answer appears to be that people want to hear good news and block out the rest. Positive feedback fits what most people wish to hear and already believe about themselves. Does this mean, then, that you should avoid giving negative feedback? No! What it means is that you need to be aware of potential resistance and learn to use negative feedback in situations in which it's most likely to be accepted.[39] What are those situations? Research indicates that negative feedback is most likely to be accepted when it comes from a credible source or if it's objective. Subjective impressions carry weight only when they come from a person with high status and credibility.[40] In other words, negative feedback that's supported by hard data—numbers, specific examples, and the like—is more likely to be accepted. Negative feedback that's subjective can be a meaningful tool for experienced managers, particularly those in upper levels of the organization who have built the trust and earned the respect of their employees. From less experienced managers, those in the lower ranks of the organization, and those whose reputations have not yet been established, negative feedback that's subjective in nature is not likely to be well received.

HOW DO YOU GIVE EFFECTIVE FEEDBACK? Six specific suggestions can help you become more effective in providing feedback.[41] These are as follows:

▶ *Focus on specific behaviors.* Feedback should be specific rather than general. Avoid statements such as "You have a bad attitude" or "I'm really impressed with the good job

and the survey says...[36]

44 percent of men said they have heard a sexually inappropriate comment at work.

22 percent of women said the same.

64 seconds is how long it takes to retrieve your train of thought after an e-mail interruption.

84 percent of workers think it's very common for employees to engage in office gossip.

63 percent of those workers think gossip has a negative effect on the workplace.

16 thousand is the average number of words spoken in a day by women *and* men.

28 percent of a day is how much the average U.S. worker loses to interruptions.

4 percent of large organizations have a formal process in place to capture knowledge.

knowledge management
Cultivating a learning culture in which organizational members systematically gather knowledge and share it with others.

you did." They are vague, and, although they provide information, they don't tell the receiver enough so that he or she can correct the "bad attitude," or on what basis you concluded that a good job has been done so the person knows what behaviors to repeat.

▶ *Keep feedback impersonal.* Feedback, particularly the negative kind, should be descriptive rather than judgmental or evaluative. No matter how upset you are, keep the feedback focused on job-related behaviors and never criticize someone personally because of an inappropriate action. Telling people they're incompetent, lazy, or the like is almost always counterproductive. It provokes such an emotional reaction that the performance deviation itself is apt to be overlooked. When you're criticizing, remember that you're censuring job-related behavior, not the person. You might be tempted to tell someone he or she is rude and insensitive (which just might be true); however, that's hardly impersonal. It's better to say something more specific, such as "You've interrupted me three times with questions that weren't urgent when you knew I was talking long distance to a customer in Brazil."

▶ *Keep feedback goal oriented.* Feedback should not be given primarily to "dump" or "unload" on another person. If you have to say something negative, make sure it's directed toward the receiver's goals. Ask yourself whom the feedback is supposed to help. If the answer is essentially you ("I've got something I just want to get off my chest"), bite your tongue and hold the comment. Such feedback undermines your credibility and lessens the meaning and influence of future feedback sessions.

▶ *Make feedback well timed.* Feedback is most meaningful to a receiver when only a short interval elapses between his or her behavior and the receipt of feedback about that behavior. For example, a new employee who makes a mistake is more likely to respond to his or her manager's suggestions for improving right after the mistake or at the end of the workday rather than during a performance review session six months from now. If you have to spend time recreating a situation and refreshing someone's memory of it, the feedback you are providing is likely to be ineffective. Moreover, if you're particularly concerned with changing behavior, delays in providing timely feedback on the undesirable actions lessen the likelihood that the feedback will bring about the desired change. Of course, making feedback prompt merely for promptness sake can backfire if you have insufficient information or if you're upset. In such instances, well timed could mean somewhat delayed.

▶ *Ensure understanding.* Is your feedback concise and complete enough that the receiver clearly and fully understands your communication? Remember that every successful communication requires both transference and understanding of meaning. If feedback is to be effective, you need to ensure that the receiver understands it. As suggested in our discussion of listening techniques, ask the receiver to rephrase the message to find out whether he or she fully captured the meaning you intended.

▶ *Direct negative feedback toward behavior that the receiver can control.* Little value comes from reminding a person of some shortcoming over which he or she has no control. Negative feedback should be directed toward behavior that the receiver can do something about. For instance, criticizing an employee who's late for work because she forgot to set her alarm clock is valid. Criticizing her for being late for work when the subway she takes to work every day had a power failure, stranding her for 90 minutes, is pointless. She was powerless to do anything to correct what happened—short of finding a different means of traveling to work, which may be unrealistic. In addition, when negative feedback is given concerning something that the receiver can control, it might be a good idea to indicate specifically what can be done to improve the situation. Such suggestions take some of the sting out of the criticism and offer guidance to receivers who understand the problem but don't know how to resolve it.

What Are Empowerment Skills?

As we've described in various places throughout this text, more and more managers are leading by empowering their employees. Millions of employees and teams

Guest services employees at Winchester Hospital meet every morning and later in the day to share news and receive up-to-date information that helps them make informed decisions about their work. Winchester empowers its staff to provide service excellence, from guest services employees shown here to medical professionals. Chefs, for example, are encouraged to create their own special dish for patients once a week, and medical staff is empowered to develop new patient programs. One group of nurses worked with the hospital's child life specialist to devise a program of bringing dogs to the hospital to visit patients. Empowerment contributes to the hospital's reputation as an employer that cares as deeply for its employees as for its patients.

of employees are making key operating decisions that directly affect their work. They're developing budgets, scheduling workloads, controlling inventories, solving quality problems, and engaging in activities that until recently were viewed exclusively as part of the manager's job.[42]

The increased use of empowerment is being driven by two forces. First is the need for quick decisions by those who are most knowledgeable about the issue, which requires moving decisions to lower levels. If organizations are to successfully compete in a dynamic global economy, they have to be able to make decisions and implement changes quickly. Second is the reality that the downsizing of organizations during the past two decades has left many managers with considerably larger spans of control than they had previously. In order to cope with the demands of an increased load, managers had to empower their employees. Two aspects of empowerment are understanding the value of delegating and knowing how to do it.

Delegation is the assignment of authority to another person to carry out specific activities. It allows an employee to make decisions—that is, it is a shift of decision-making authority from one organizational level to another lower one (see Exhibit 12-4). Delegation, however, should not be confused with participation. In participative decision making, authority is shared. With delegation, employees make decisions on their own. That's why delegation is such a vital component of worker empowerment!

DON'T MANAGERS ABDICATE THEIR RESPONSIBILITY WHEN THEY DELEGATE? When done properly, delegation is not abdication. The key word here is *properly*. If you, as a manager, dump tasks on an employee without clarifying the exact job to be done, the range of the employee's discretion, the expected level of performance, the time frame in which the tasks are to be completed, and similar concerns, you are abdicating responsibility and inviting trouble.[43] Don't fall into the trap, however, of assuming that, to avoid the appearance of abdicating, you should minimize delegation. Unfortunately, that's how many new and inexperienced

EXHIBIT 12-4   Effective Delegation

Authority

Top managers

Middle managers

First-line managers

Non-managerial employees

Effective delegation pushes authority down vertically through the ranks of an organization.

delegation
Assigning authority to another person to carry out specific activities.

managers interpret the situation. Lacking confidence in their employees or fearful that they'll be criticized for their employees' mistakes, these managers try to do everything themselves.

It might be true that you're capable of doing tasks better, faster, or with fewer mistakes. The catch is that your time and energy are scarce resources. It's not possible for you to do everything yourself. As a manager, you'll need to delegate to be effective in your job. This fact suggests two important points. First, you should expect and accept some mistakes by your employees. Mistakes are part of delegation. They're often good learning experiences for employees as long as their costs are not excessive. Second, to ensure that the costs of mistakes don't exceed the value of the learning, you need to put adequate controls in place. As we'll discuss shortly, delegation without feedback controls that let you know about potentially serious problems is a form of abdication.

How much authority should a manager delegate? Should he or she keep authority centralized, delegating only the minimal amount to complete the delegated duties? What contingency factors should be considered in determining the degree to which authority is delegated? Exhibit 12-5 presents the most widely cited contingency factors to provide some guidance in making those determinations.

HOW DO YOU DELEGATE EFFECTIVELY? Assuming that delegation is in order, how do you delegate? A number of methods have been suggested for differentiating the effective delegator from the ineffective one.[44]

▶ *Clarify the assignment.* First determine what is to be delegated and to whom. Identify the person who's most capable of doing the task and then determine whether he or she has the time and motivation to do the job. Assuming that you have a willing employee, it's your responsibility to provide clear information on what's being delegated, the results you expect, and any time or performance expectations you hold. Unless the project entails an overriding need to adhere to specific methods, you should ask an employee only to provide the desired results. That is, get agreement on what is to be done and the results expected, but let the employee decide by which means the work is to be completed. By focusing on goals and allowing the employee the freedom to use his or her own judgment as to how those goals are to be achieved, you increase trust between you and the employee, improve the employee's motivation, and enhance accountability for results.

| **EXHIBIT 12-5** | **Contingency Factors in Delegation** |

- **The size of the organization.** The larger the organization, the greater the number of decisions that have to be made. Because top managers in an organization have only so much time and can obtain only so much information, in larger organizations they become increasingly dependent on the decision making of lower-level managers. Therefore, managers in large organizations resort to increased delegation.

- **The importance of the duty or decision.** The more important a duty or decision (as expressed in terms of cost and impact on the future of an organization), the less likely it is to be delegated. For instance, a department head may be delegated authority to make expenditures up to $7,500, and division heads and vice presidents up to $50,000 and $125,000, respectively.

- **Task complexity.** The more complex the task, the more difficult it is for top management to possess current and sufficient technical information to make effective decisions. Complex tasks require greater expertise, and decisions about them should be delegated to the people who have the necessary technical knowledge.

- **Organizational culture.** If management has confidence and trust in employees, the culture will support a greater degree of delegation. However, if top management does not have confidence in the abilities of lower-level managers, it will delegate authority only when absolutely necessary. In such instances, as little authority as possible is delegated.

- **Qualities of employees.** A final contingency consideration is the qualities of employees. Delegation requires employees with the skills, abilities, and motivation to accept authority and act on it. If these are lacking, top management will be reluctant to relinquish authority.

▶ *Specify employees' range of discretion.* Every act of delegation comes with constraints. You're delegating authority to act but not unlimited authority. You're delegating the authority to act on certain issues within certain parameters. You need to specify what those parameters are so that employees know, in no uncertain terms, the range of their discretion. When those parameters have been successfully communicated, both you and employees will have the same idea of the limits to the authority and how far they can go without further approval.

▶ *Allow employees to participate.* One of the best ways to decide how much authority will be necessary is to allow employees who will be held accountable for the tasks to participate in that decision. Be aware, however, that participation can present its own set of potential problems as a result of employees' self-interest and biases in evaluating their own abilities. Some employees might be personally motivated to expand their authority beyond what they need and beyond what they are capable of handling. Allowing such people too much participation in deciding what tasks they should take on and how much authority they must have to complete those tasks can undermine the effectiveness of the delegation process.

▶ *Inform others that delegation has occurred.* Delegation should not take place in a vacuum. Not only do you and your employees need to know specifically what has been delegated and how much authority has been granted; anyone else who's likely to be affected by the delegation act needs to be informed, including people outside the organization as well as inside it. Essentially, you need to convey what has been delegated (the task and amount of authority) and to whom. Failure to inform others makes conflict likely and decreases the chances that your employees will be able to accomplish the delegated act efficiently.

▶ *Establish feedback controls.* To delegate without instituting feedback controls is inviting problems. It is always possible that employees will misuse the discretion they have been given. Controls to monitor employees' progress increase the likelihood that important problems will be identified early and that the task will be completed on time and to the desired specification. Ideally, these controls should be determined at the time of initial assignment. Agree on a specific time for completion of the task, and then set progress dates by which the employees will report on how well they are doing and on any major problems that have surfaced. These controls can be supplemented with periodic spot checks to ensure that authority guidelines are not being abused, organization policies are being followed, proper procedures are being met, and the like. Too much of a good thing can be dysfunctional. If the controls are too constraining, employees will be deprived of the opportunity to build self-confidence. As a result, much of the motivational aspect of delegation may be lost. A well-designed control system, which we will elaborate on in more detail in the next chapter, permits your employees to make small mistakes but quickly alerts you when big mistakes are imminent.

How Do You Manage Conflict?

The ability to manage conflict is undoubtedly one of the most important skills a manager needs to possess.[45] A study of middle- and top-level executives by the American Management Association revealed that the average manager spends approximately 20 percent of his or her time dealing with conflict.[46] The importance of conflict management is reinforced by a survey of the topics managers consider most important in management development programs; conflict management was rated as more important than decision making, leadership, or communication skills.[47]

WHAT IS CONFLICT MANAGEMENT? Conflict is *perceived* incompatible differences resulting in some form of interference or opposition. Whether the differences are real is irrelevant. If people perceive that differences exist, then there is conflict.

conflict
Perceived differences resulting in interference or opposition.

Three different views have evolved regarding conflict.[48] The **traditional view of conflict** argues that conflict must be avoided—that it indicates a problem within the group. Another view, the **human relations view of conflict**, argues that conflict is a natural and inevitable outcome in any group and need not be negative, but has potential to be a positive force in contributing to a group's performance. The third and most recent view, the **interactionist view of conflict**, proposes that not only can conflict be a positive force in a group but that some conflict is *absolutely necessary* for a group to perform effectively.

The interactionist view doesn't suggest that all conflicts are good. Some conflicts— **functional conflicts**—are constructive and support an organization's goals and improve performance. Other conflicts—**dysfunctional conflicts**—are destructive and prevent organizations from achieving goals. Exhibit 12-6 illustrates the challenge facing managers.

When is conflict functional and when is it dysfunctional? Research indicates that you need to look at the *type* of conflict.[49] **Task conflict** relates to the content and goals of the work. **Relationship conflict** focuses on interpersonal relationships. **Process conflict** refers to how the work gets done. Research shows that *relationship* conflicts are almost always dysfunctional because the interpersonal hostilities increase personality clashes and decrease mutual understanding and the tasks don't get done. On the other hand, low levels of process conflict and low-to-moderate levels of task conflict are functional. For *process* conflict to be productive, it must be minimal. Otherwise, intense arguments over who should do what may become dysfunctional since they can lead to uncertainty about task assignments, increase the time to complete tasks, and lead to members working at cross-purposes. However, a low-to-moderate level of *task* conflict consistently has a positive effect on group performance because it stimulates discussion of ideas that help groups be more innovative.[50] Because we

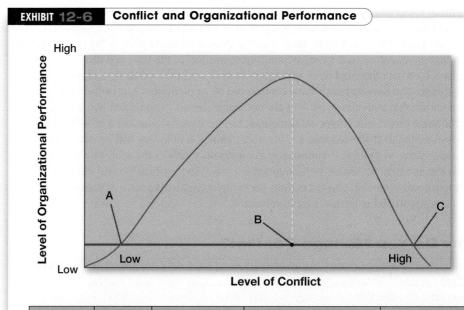

EXHIBIT 12-6 **Conflict and Organizational Performance**

Situation	Level of Conflict	Type of Conflict	Organization's Internal Characteristics	Level of Organizational Performance
A	Low or none	Dysfunctional	Apathetic Stagnant Unresponsive to change Lack of new ideas	Low
B	Optimal	Functional	Viable Self-critical Innovative	High
C	High	Dysfunctional	Disruptive Chaotic Uncooperative	Low

don't yet have a sophisticated measuring instrument for assessing whether conflict levels are optimal, too high, or too low, the manager must try to judge that intelligently.

WHICH CONFLICTS DO YOU HANDLE? When group conflict levels are too high, managers can select from five conflict management options: avoidance, accommodation, forcing, compromise, and collaboration.[51] (See Exhibit 12-7 for a description of these techniques.) Keep in mind that no one option is ideal for every situation. Which approach to use depends on the circumstances.

Regardless of our desires, reality tells us that some conflicts are unmanageable.[52] When antagonisms are deeply rooted, when one or both parties wish to prolong a conflict, or when emotions run so high that constructive interaction is impossible, your efforts to manage the conflict are unlikely to meet with much success. Don't be lured into the naïve belief that a good manager can resolve every conflict effectively. Some aren't worth the effort; some are outside your realm of influence. Still others may be functional and, as such, are best left alone.

HOW DOES A MANAGER STIMULATE CONFLICT? What about the other side of conflict management—situations that require managers to stimulate conflict? The notion of stimulating conflict is often difficult to accept. For almost all of us the term *conflict* has a negative connotation, and the idea of purposely creating conflict seems to be the antithesis of good management. Few of us enjoy being in conflict situations, yet evidence demonstrates that in some situations an increase in conflict is constructive.[53] Although no clear demarcation separates functional from dysfunctional conflict, and no definitive method is available for assessing the need for more conflict, an affirmative answer to one or more of the following questions may suggest a need for conflict stimulation.[54]

▶ Are you surrounded by "yes" people?
▶ Are employees afraid to admit ignorance and uncertainties to you?

EXHIBIT 12-7	**Conflict Management: What Works Best and When**

STRATEGY	BEST USED WHEN
Avoidance	Conflict is trivial, when emotions are running high and time is needed to cool them down, or when the potential disruption from an assertive action outweighs the benefits of resolution
Accommodation	The issue under dispute isn't that important to you or when you want to build up credits for later issues
Forcing	You need a quick resolution on important issues that require unpopular actions to be taken and when commitment by others to your solution is not critical
Compromise	Conflicting parties are about equal in power, when it is desirable to achieve a temporary solution to a complex issue, or when time pressures demand an expedient solution
Collaboration	Time pressures are minimal, when all parties seriously want a win-win solution, and when the issue is too important to be compromised

traditional view of conflict
The view that all conflict is bad and must be avoided.

human relations view of conflict
The view that conflict is natural and inevitable and has the potential to be a positive force.

interactionist view of conflict
The view that some conflict is necessary for an organization to perform effectively.

functional conflicts
Conflict that's constructive and supports an organization's goals.

dysfunctional conflicts
Conflict that's destructive and prevents an organization from achieving its goals.

task conflict
Conflict that relates to the content and goals of work.

relationship conflict
Conflict that focuses on interpersonal relationships.

process conflict
Conflict that refers to how the work gets done.

▶ Are decision makers so focused on reaching a compromise that they lose sight of values, long-term objectives, or the organization's welfare?

▶ Do managers believe that it's in their best interest to maintain the impression of peace and cooperation in their unit, regardless of the price?

▶ Are decision makers excessively concerned about hurting the feelings of others?

▶ Do managers believe that popularity is more important for obtaining organizational rewards than competence and high performance?

▶ Do managers put undue emphasis on obtaining consensus for their decisions?

▶ Do employees show unusually high resistance to change?

▶ Is there a lack of new ideas?

We know a lot more about resolving conflict than about stimulating it. That's only natural, because human beings have been concerned with the subject of conflict reduction for hundreds, maybe thousands, of years. The dearth of ideas on conflict stimulation techniques reflects the recent interest in the subject. The following are some preliminary suggestions that managers might want to use.[55]

The initial step in stimulating functional conflict is for managers to convey to employees the message, supported by actions, that conflict has its legitimate place. This step may require changing the culture of the organization. Individuals who challenge the status quo, suggest innovative ideas, offer divergent opinions, and demonstrate original thinking need to be rewarded visibly with promotions, salary, and other positive reinforcers.

As far back as Franklin D. Roosevelt's administration, and probably before, the White House consistently has used communication to stimulate conflict. Senior officials plant possible decisions with the media through the infamous "reliable source" route. For example, the name of a prominent judge is leaked as a possible Supreme Court appointment. If the candidate survives the public scrutiny, his or her appointment will be announced by the president. However, if the candidate is found lacking by the media and the public, the president's press secretary or other high-level official may make a formal statement such as, "At no time was this candidate under consideration." Regardless of party affiliation, occupants of the White House have regularly used the *reliable source method* as a conflict stimulation technique. It is all the more popular because of its handy escape mechanism. If the conflict level gets too high, the source can be denied and eliminated.

Ambiguous or threatening messages also encourage conflict. Information that a plant might close, that a department is likely to be eliminated, or that a layoff is imminent can reduce apathy, stimulate new ideas, and force reevaluation—all positive outcomes of increased conflict. Another widely used method for shaking up a stagnant unit or organization is to bring in outsiders either from outside or by internal transfer with backgrounds, values, attitudes, or managerial styles that differ from those of present members. Many large corporations have used this technique during the past decade to fill vacancies on their boards of directors. Women, minority group members, consumer activists, and others whose backgrounds and interests differ significantly from those of the rest of the board have been selected to add a fresh perspective.

We also know that *structural variables* are a source of conflict. It is, therefore, only logical that managers look to structure as a conflict stimulation device. Centralizing decisions, realigning work groups, increasing formalization, and increasing interdependencies between units are all structural devices that disrupt the status quo and increase conflict levels.

Finally, one can appoint a **devil's advocate**, a person who purposely presents arguments that run

As a necessary part of the creative process, functional conflict has a legitimate place in innovative organizations. John Chambers, CEO of Cisco Systems, is respected worldwide as a leader of innovation who has the ability to drive an entrepreneurial culture. At Cisco, he has created a culture of trust, open communication, teamwork, and collaboration that generates a steady flow of new ideas. He has formed cross-functional teams that work through problems by exploring alternative viewpoints of employees from different disciplines. Functional conflict helps Cisco adapt to new and shifting technologies and rapidly changing business environments. Chambers is shown here communicating with students of the Mediterranean Youth Technology Club in Israel.

counter to those proposed by the majority or against current practices. He or she plays the role of the critic, even to the point of arguing against positions with which he or she actually agrees. A devil's advocate acts as a check against groupthink and practices that have no better justification than "that's the way we've always done it around here." When thoughtfully listened to, the advocate can improve the quality of group decision making. On the other hand, others in the group often view advocates as time wasters, and their appointment is almost certain to delay any decision process.

What Are Negotiation Skills?

We know that lawyers and auto salespeople spend a significant amount of time on their jobs negotiating. But so, too, do managers. They have to negotiate salaries for incoming employees, cut deals with their bosses, work out differences with their peers, and resolve conflicts with employees. Others have to negotiate labor contracts and other agreements with people outside their organizations. For our purposes, we will define **negotiation** as a process in which two or more parties who have different preferences must make a joint decision and come to an agreement. To achieve this goal, both parties typically use a bargaining strategy.

HOW DO BARGAINING STRATEGIES DIFFER? Two general approaches to negotiation are distributive bargaining and integrative bargaining.[56] Let's see what's involved in each.

You see a used car advertised for sale in the newspaper. It appears to be just what you've been looking for. You go out to see the car. It's great, and you want it. The owner tells you the asking price. You don't want to pay that much. The two of you then negotiate over the price. The negotiating process you are engaging in is called **distributive bargaining**. Its most identifying feature is that it operates under zero-sum conditions.[57] That is, any gain you make is at the expense of the other person, and vice versa. Every dollar you can get the seller to cut from the price of the used car is a dollar you save. Conversely, every dollar more he or she can get from you comes at your expense. Thus, the essence of distributive bargaining is negotiating over who gets what share of a fixed pie. Probably the most widely cited examples of distributive bargaining are traditional labor-management negotiations over wages and benefits. Typically, labor's representatives come to the bargaining table determined to get as much as they can from management. Because every cent more that labor negotiates increases management's costs, each party bargains aggressively and often treats the other as an opponent who must be defeated. In distributive bargaining, each party has a target point that defines what he or she would like to achieve. Each also has a resistance point that marks the lowest acceptable outcome (see Exhibit 12-8). The area between

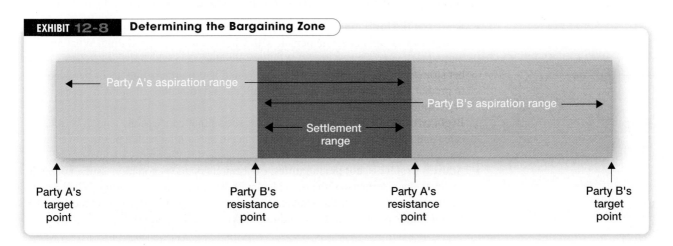

EXHIBIT 12-8 **Determining the Bargaining Zone**

Party A's aspiration range

Party B's aspiration range

Settlement range

Party A's target point

Party B's resistance point

Party A's resistance point

Party B's target point

devil's advocate
A person who purposely presents arguments that run counter to those proposed by the majority or against current practices.

negotiation
A process in which two or more parties who have different preferences must make a joint decision and come to an agreement.

distributive bargaining
Negotiation under zero-sum conditions, in which any gain by one party involves a loss to the other party.

their resistance points is the settlement range. As long as these ranges of aspiration overlap each other to some extent, there exists a settlement area in which each one's aspirations can be met.

When engaged in distributive bargaining, you should try to get your opponent to agree to your specific target point or to get as close to it as possible. Examples of such tactics are persuading your opponent of the impossibility of getting to his or her target point and the advisability of accepting a settlement near yours; arguing that your target is fair, but your opponent's isn't; and attempting to get your opponent to feel emotionally generous toward you and thus accept an outcome close to your target point.

A sales representative for a women's sportswear manufacturer has just closed a $25,000 order from an independent clothing retailer. The sales rep calls in the order to her firm's credit department. She is told that the firm can't approve credit to this customer because of a past slow pay record. The next day, the sales rep and the firm's credit manager meet to discuss the problem. The sales rep doesn't want to lose the business. Neither does the credit manager, but he also doesn't want to get stuck with an uncollectible debt. The two openly review their options. After considerable discussion, they agree on a solution that meets both their needs. The credit manager will approve the sale, but the clothing store's owner will provide a bank guarantee that will assure payment if the bill isn't paid within 60 days.

The sales-credit negotiation is an example of **integrative bargaining**. In contrast to distributive bargaining, integrative problem solving operates under the assumption that at least one settlement can create a win-win solution. In general, integrative bargaining is preferable to distributive bargaining. Why? Because the former builds long-term relationships and facilitates working together in the future. It bonds negotiators and allows each to leave the bargaining table feeling that he or she has achieved a victory. Distributive bargaining, on the other hand, leaves one party a loser. It tends to build animosities and deepen divisions between people who have to work together on an ongoing basis.

Why, then, don't we see more integrative bargaining in organizations? The answer lies in the conditions necessary for this type of negotiation to succeed. These conditions include openness with information and frankness between parties, a sensitivity by each party to the other's needs, the ability to trust one another, and a willingness by both parties to maintain flexibility.[58] Because many organizational cultures and intraorganizational relationships are not characterized by openness, trust, and flexibility, it isn't surprising that negotiations often take on a win-at-any-cost dynamic. With that in mind, let's look at some suggestions for negotiating successfully.

HOW DO YOU DEVELOP EFFECTIVE NEGOTIATION SKILLS? The essence of effective negotiation can be summarized in the following seven recommendations.[59]

▶ **Research the individual with whom you'll be negotiating.** Acquire as much information as you can about the person with whom you'll be negotiating. What are that individual's interests and goals? What people must he or she appease? What is his or her strategy? This information will help you to better understand his or her behavior, to predict his or her responses to your offers, and to frame solutions in terms of his or her interests.

▶ **Begin with a positive overture.** Research shows that concessions tend to be reciprocated and lead to agreements. As a result, begin bargaining with a positive overture—perhaps a small concession—and then reciprocate the other party's concessions.

▶ **Address problems, not personalities.** Concentrate on the negotiation issues, not on the personal characteristics of the individual with whom you're negotiating. When negotiations get tough, avoid the tendency to attack the other party. Remember it's that person's ideas or position that you disagree with, not with him or her personally.

integrative bargaining
Negotiation in which there is at least one settlement that involves no loss to either party.

▸ **Pay little attention to initial offers.** Treat an initial offer as merely a point of departure. Everyone has to have an initial position, and initial positions tend to be extreme and idealistic. Treat them as such.

▸ **Emphasize win-win solutions.** If conditions are supportive, look for an integrative solution. Frame options in terms of the other party's interests and look for solutions that can allow this individual, as well as yourself, to declare a victory.

▸ **Create an open and trusting climate.** Skilled negotiators are better listeners, ask more questions, focus on their arguments more directly, are less defensive, and have learned to avoid words or phrases that can irritate the person with whom they're negotiating (such as a "generous offer," "fair price," or "reasonable arrangement"). In other words, they're better at creating an open and trusting climate that is necessary for reaching a win-win settlement.

▸ **If needed, be open to accepting third-party assistance.** When stalemates are reached, consider the use of a neutral third party—a mediator, an arbitrator, or a conciliator. Mediators can help parties come to an agreement, but they don't impose a settlement. Arbitrators hear both sides of the dispute, then impose a solution. Conciliators are more informal and act as a communication conduit, passing information between the parties, interpreting messages, and clarifying misunderstandings.

Review and Applications

Chapter Summary

 Describe what managers need to know about communicating effectively. Communication is the transfer and understanding of meaning. There are seven elements in the communication process. First there is a *sender* or source who has a message. A *message* is a purpose to be conveyed. *Encoding* is converting a message into symbols. A *channel* is the medium a message travels along. *Decoding* is when the *receiver* retranslates a sender's message. Finally, there is *feedback*. The barriers to effective communication include filtering, emotions, information overload, defensiveness, language, and national culture. Managers can overcome these barriers by using feedback, simplifying language, listening actively, constraining emotions, and watching for nonverbal clues.

 Explain how technology affects managerial communication. Technology has radically changed the way organizational members communicate. It improves a manager's ability to monitor performance; it gives employees more complete information to make faster decisions; it has provided employees more opportunities to collaborate and share information; and it has made it possible for people to be fully accessible, anytime anywhere. IT has affected managerial communication through the use of networked computer systems, wireless capabilities, and knowledge management systems.

12.3 **Discuss the interpersonal skills that every manager needs.** Behaviors related to effective *active listening* are making eye contact, exhibiting affirmative nods and appropriate facial expressions, avoiding distracting actions or gestures, asking questions, paraphrasing, avoiding interruption of the speaker, not overtalking, and making smooth transitions between the roles of speaker and listener. In order to

provide effective feedback, you must focus on specific behaviors; keep feedback impersonal, goal oriented, and well timed; ensure understanding; and direct negative feedback toward behavior that the recipient can control. Contingency factors guide managers in determining the degree to which authority should be *delegated*. These factors include the size of the organization (larger organizations are associated with increased delegation); the importance of the duty or decision (the more important a duty or decision is, the less likely it is to be delegated); task complexity (the more complex the task is, the more likely it is that decisions about the task will be delegated); organizational culture (confidence and trust in subordinates are associated with delegation); and qualities of subordinates (delegation requires subordinates with the skills, abilities, and motivation to accept authority and act on it). Behaviors related to *effective delegating* are clarifying the assignment, specifying the employee's range of discretion, allowing the employee to participate, informing others that delegation has occurred, and establishing feedback controls. The steps to be followed in *analyzing and resolving conflict* situations begin by identifying your underlying conflict-handling style. Second, select only conflicts that are worth the effort and that can be managed. Third, evaluate the conflict players. Fourth, assess the source of the conflict. Finally, choose the conflict resolution option that best reflects your style and the situation. Effective *negotiation* skills require researching the individual with whom you'll be negotiating; beginning with a positive overture; addressing problems, not personalities; paying little attention to the first offer; emphasizing win-win solutions; creating an open and trusting climate; and being open to third-party assistance, if needed.

 To check your understanding of learning outcomes **12.1** – **12.3**, go to **mymanagementlab.com** and try the chapter questions.

Understanding the Chapter

1. Which type of communication do you think is most effective in a work setting? Why?

2. Why isn't effective communication synonymous with *agreement?*

3. Which do you think is more important for a manager: speaking accurately or listening actively? Why?

4. "Ineffective communication is the fault of the sender." Do you agree or disagree with this statement? Discuss.

5. Is information technology helping managers be more efficient and effective? Explain your answer.

6. Why are effective interpersonal skills so important to a manager's success?

7. How might a manager use the grapevine to his or her advantage? Support your response.

8. Research the characteristics of a good communicator. Write up your findings in a bulleted list report. Be sure to cite your sources.

Understanding Yourself

How Good Are My Listening Skills?

Effective communicators have developed good listening skills. This instrument is designed to provide you with some insights into your listening skills.

INSTRUMENT   Respond to each of the 15 statements using the following scale:

> **1** = Strongly agree
> **2** = Agree
> **3** = Neither agree or disagree
> **4** = Disagree
> **5** = Strongly disagree

1.	I frequently attempt to listen to several conversations at the same time.	1	2	3	4	5
2.	I like people to give me only the facts and then let me make my own interpretation.	1	2	3	4	5
3.	I sometimes pretend to pay attention to people.	1	2	3	4	5
4.	I consider myself a good judge of nonverbal communications.	1	2	3	4	5
5.	I usually know what another person is going to say before he or she says it.	1	2	3	4	5
6.	I usually end conversations that don't interest me by diverting my attention from the speaker.	1	2	3	4	5
7.	I frequently nod, frown, or provide other nonverbal cues to let the speaker know how I feel about what he or she is saying.	1	2	3	4	5
8.	I usually respond immediately when someone has finished talking.	1	2	3	4	5
9.	I evaluate what is being said while it is being said.	1	2	3	4	5
10.	I usually formulate a response while the other person is still talking.	1	2	3	4	5
11.	The speaker's "delivery" style frequently keeps me from listening to content.	1	2	3	4	5
12.	I usually ask people to clarify what they have said rather than guess at the meaning.	1	2	3	4	5
13.	I make a concerted effort to understand other people's points of view.	1	2	3	4	5
14.	I frequently hear what I expect to hear rather than what is said.	1	2	3	4	5
15.	Most people feel that I have understood their point of view when we disagree.	1	2	3	4	5

SCORING KEY   You score this instrument by adding up your responses for all items; however, you need to reverse your scores (5 becomes 1, 4 becomes 2, etc.) for statements 4, 12, 13, and 15.

ANALYSIS AND INTERPRETATION   Scores range from 15 to 75. The higher your score, the better listener you are. While any cutoffs are essentially arbitrary, if you score 60 or above, your listening skills are fairly good. Scores of 40 or less indicate you need to make a serious effort at improving your listening skills. You might want to start by looking at the "**Developing Your Active-Listening Skill**" box included in this chapter.

Source: Adapted from E. C. Glenn and E. A. Pood, "Listening Self-Inventory," *Supervisory Management* (January 1989), pp. 12–15. Used with permission of publisher; © 1989 American Management Association, New York.

Stone, Hartwick, and Mueller Talent Management Associates

Reply   Reply All   Forward

To: Chris Richards
From: Dana Gibson
Subject: **Office Gossip**

I need some advice, Chris. As you know, my department and all its employees are being transferred from Los Angeles to Dallas. We've had to keep the information "under wraps" for competitive reasons. However, one of my employees asked me point blank yesterday about a rumor she's heard that this move is in the works. I didn't answer her question directly. But I'm afraid that the office grapevine is going to start spreading inaccurate information and then affect morale and productivity. What should I do now? Send me your written response soon (confidential, please!) about what you would do.

This fictionalized company and message were created for educational purposes only. It is not meant to reflect positively or negatively on management practices by any company that may share this name.

CASE APPLICATION
OUT WITH E-MAIL

It's estimated that during 2008, each corporate user of e-mail sent or received over 150 messages per day. By 2011, that number is estimated to be well over 225. Another study found that one-third of e-mail users feel stressed by heavy e-mail volume. Once imagined to be a time-saver, has the inbox become a burden?

U.S. Cellular's Chief Operating Officer Jay Ellison thought so and did something about it. He imposed a "no e-mail Friday" rule, a move that a growing number of companies are taking. Although most bans typically allow e-mailing clients and customers or responding to urgent matters, the intent is to slow down the routine internal e-mails that take up time and clog the organization's computer network. The limits also aim at encouraging more face-to-face and phone contact with coworkers and customers. Ellison also hoped that it would give his employees a small respite from the e-mail onslaught. What he got, however, was a rebellion. One employee confronted him saying that Ellison didn't understand how much work had to get done and how much easier it was when using e-mail.

Discussion Questions

1. What advantages and disadvantages are there to e-mail as a form of communication? In addition to your own personal experience with e-mail, do some research before answering this question.

2. Why do you think the employees rebelled?

3. What's your opinion about Ellison's actions? Was he right or wrong? Be sure to look at this from the perspective of both the organization and the employees.

4. What other approaches might Ellison have taken to address this issue of out-of-control e-mail?

Sources: S. Shellenbarger, "A Day Without Email Is Like . . ."*Wall Street Journal,* October 11, 2007, pp. D1+; M. Kessler, "Fridays Go from Casual to E-Mail-Free," *USA Today,* October 5, 2007, p. 1A; D. Beizer, "Email Is Dead," *Fast Company,* July/August 2007, p. 46; O. Malik, "Why Email Is Bankrupt," *Business 2.0,* July 2007, p. 46; and D. Brady, "*!#?@ the E-Mail. Can We Talk?" *BusinessWeek,* December 4, 2006, p. 109.

CHAPTER

13

Foundations
of
Control

learning outcomes

13.1 **Explain** the nature and importance of control. p.350

13.2 **Describe** the three steps in the control process. p.352

13.3 **Discuss** the types of controls organizations and managers use. p.357

13.4 **Discuss** contemporary issues in control. p.362

Baggage Blunders

Terminal 5 (T5), built by British Airways for $8.6 billion, is London Heathrow Airport's newest state-of-the-art facility.[1] Made of glass, concrete, and steel, it's the largest free-standing building in the United Kingdom and has over 10 miles of belts for moving luggage. At the terminal's unveiling in March 2008, Queen Elizabeth II called it a "twenty-first-century gateway to Britain." Alas . . . the accolades didn't last long! After two decades in planning and 100 million hours in manpower, opening day didn't work out as planned. Endless lines and major baggage handling delays led to numerous flight cancellations stranding many irate passengers. Airport operators said the problems were triggered by glitches in the terminal's high-tech baggage-handling system.

With its massive automation features, T5 was planned to ease congestion at Heathrow and improve the flying experience for the 30 million passengers expected to pass through it annually. With 96 self-service check-in kiosks, over 90 fast check-in bag drops, 54 standard check-in desks, and over 10 miles in suitcase moving belts that were supposed to be able to process 12,000 bags per hour, the facility's design seemed to support those goals.

However, within the first few hours of the terminal's opening, problems developed. Presumably understaffed, baggage workers were unable to clear incoming luggage fast enough. Arriving passengers waited more than an hour for their bags. Departing passengers tried in vain to check in for flights. Flights left with empty cargo holds. Sometime on day one, the airline checked in only those passengers with no luggage. And it didn't help that the moving belt system jammed at one point. Lesser problems also became apparent: a few broken escalators, some hand dryers that didn't work, a gate that wouldn't function at the new Underground station, and inexperienced ticket sellers who didn't know the fares between Heathrow and various stations on the Piccadilly line. By the end of the first full day of operation, Britain's Department of Transportation released a statement calling for British Airways and the airport operator BAA to "work hard to resolve these issues and limit disruptions to passengers."

You might be tempted to think that all of this could have been prevented if British Airways had only tested the system. But thorough runs of all systems "from toilets to check in and seating" took place six months before opening, including four full-scale test runs using 16,000 volunteers.

Although T5's debut was far from perfect, things have certainly changed. A recent customer satisfaction survey showed that 80 percent of passengers waited less than five minutes to check in. And those passengers are extremely satisfied with the terminal's lounges, catering, facilities, and ambience. It's a nice ending to the chaotic beginning.

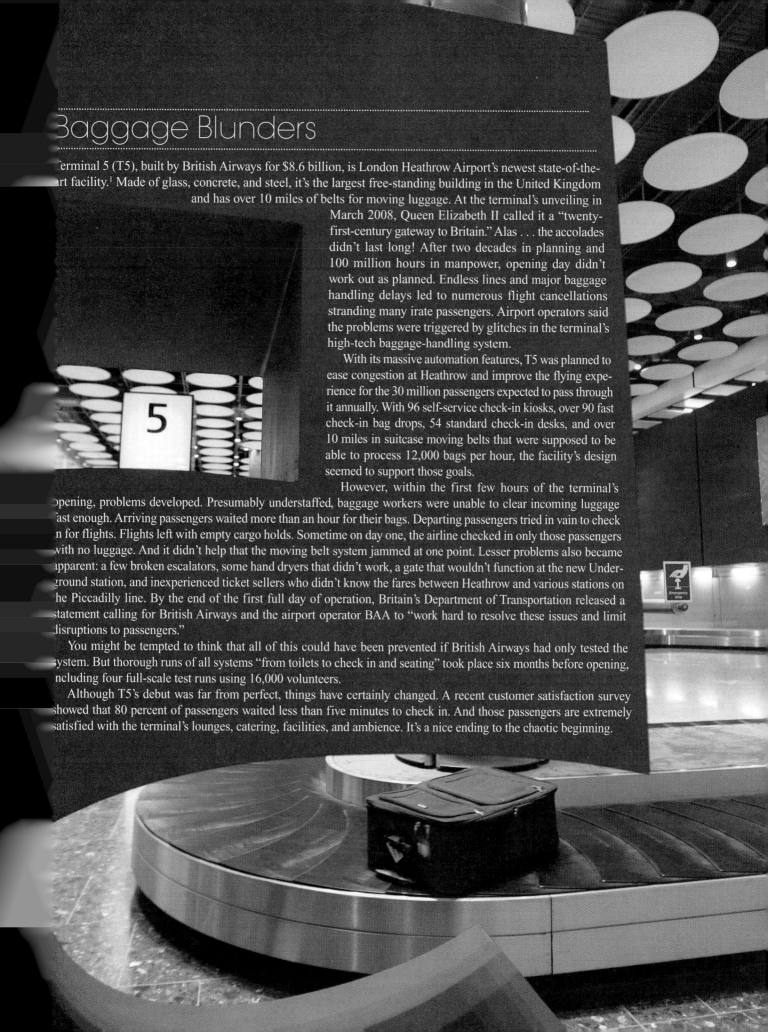

Controlling is the final step in the management process. Managers must monitor whether goals that were established as part of the planning process are being accomplished efficiently and effectively. That's what they do when they control. Appropriate controls can help managers look for specific performance gaps and areas for improvement. As the T5 story shows, things don't always go as planned. But that's why controlling is so important! In this chapter, we'll look at the fundamental elements of controlling including the control process, the types of controls that managers can use, and contemporary issues in control.

What Is Control and Why Is It Important?

Explain the nature and importance of control.

13.1

"Bailout" was the magic word that cost Domino's Pizza 11,000 free pizzas. The company had prepared an Internet coupon for an ad campaign that was considered but not approved. However, when someone apparently typed "bailout" into a Domino's promotional code window and found it was good for a free medium pizza, the word spread like wildfire on the Web. Somewhere, somehow, a lack of control cost the company big time.[2]

What Is Control?

Control is the management function that involves monitoring activities to ensure that they're being accomplished as planned and correcting any significant deviations. Managers can't really know whether their units are performing properly until they've evaluated what activities have been done and have compared the actual performance with the desired standard. An effective control system ensures that activities are completed in ways that lead to the attainment of the organization's goals. The effectiveness of a control system is determined by how well it facilitates goal achievement. The more a control system helps managers achieve their organization's goals, the better it is.

Why Is Control Important?

A press operator at the Denver Mint noticed a flaw—an extra up leaf or an extra down leaf—on Wisconsin state quarters being pressed at one of his five press machines. He stopped the machine and left for a meal break. When he returned, he saw the machine running and assumed that someone had changed the die in the machine. However, after a routine inspection, the machine operator realized the die had not been changed. The faulty press had likely been running for over an hour and thousands of the flawed coins were now "commingled" with unblemished quarters. As many as 50,000 of the faulty coins entered circulation, setting off a coin collector buying frenzy.[3]

Can you see now why controlling is such an important managerial function? Planning can be done, an organizational structure created to facilitate efficient achievement of goals, and employees motivated through effective leadership. But there's no assurance that activities are going as planned and that the goals employees and managers are working toward are, in fact, being attained. Control is important, therefore, because it's the only way that managers know whether organizational goals are being met and if not, the reasons why. The value of the control function can be seen in three specific areas: planning, empowering employees, and protecting the workplace.

In Chapter 4, we described goals, which provide specific direction to employees and managers, as the foundation of planning. However, just stating goals or having employees accept goals doesn't guarantee that the necessary actions to accomplish those goals have been taken. As the old saying goes, "The best-laid plans often go awry." The effective manager follows up to ensure that what employees are supposed to do is, in fact, being done and goals are being achieved. As the final step in the management process, controlling provides the critical link back to planning. (See Exhibit 13-1.) If managers didn't control, they'd have no way of knowing whether their goals and plans were being achieved and what future actions to take.

The second reason controlling is important is because of employee empowerment. Many managers are reluctant to empower their employees because they fear something will go wrong for which they would be held responsible. But an effective control system can provide information and feedback on employee performance and minimize the chance of potential problems.

The final reason that managers control is to protect the organization and its assets.[4] Organizations face threats from natural disasters, financial pressures and scandals, workplace violence, supply chain disruptions, security breaches, and even possible terrorist attacks. Managers must protect organizational assets in the event that any of these should happen. Comprehensive controls and backup plans will assure minimal work disruptions.

Right or Wrong?

The practice is called "sweethearting."[5] It's when cashiers use subtle tricks to pass free goods to friends, doing things such as concealing the bar code, slipping an item behind the scanner, passing two items at a time but only charging for one. It's impossible for even the most watchful human eyes to keep it from happening. So retailers are using technology to block it. Surveillance cameras are used to record and study cashiers staffing checkout lines. What do you think? Is surveillance less invasive when it's a computer watching instead of a human? How could an organization make sure it's doing things ethically?

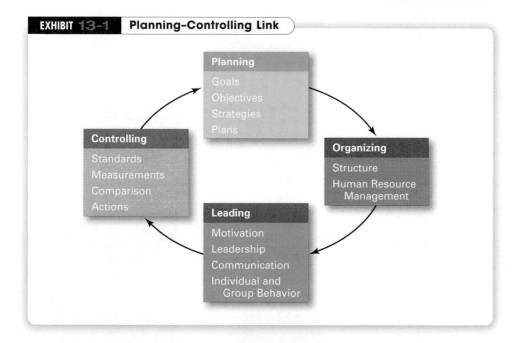

EXHIBIT 13-1 **Planning-Controlling Link**

Planning
Goals
Objectives
Strategies
Plans

Organizing
Structure
Human Resource Management

Leading
Motivation
Leadership
Communication
Individual and Group Behavior

Controlling
Standards
Measurements
Comparison
Actions

control
The management function that involves monitoring activities to ensure that they're being accomplished as planned and correcting any significant deviations.

What Takes Place as Managers Control?

13.2 Describe the three steps in the control process.

When Maggine Fuentes joined Core Systems in Painesville, Ohio, as HR manager, she knew that her top priority was reducing employee injuries. The number of injuries was "through the roof; above the industry average." The high frequency and severity of the company's injury rates not only affected employee morale but also resulted in lost workdays and affected the bottom line.[6] Maggine relied on the control process to turn this situation around.

The **control process** is a three-step process of measuring actual performance, comparing actual performance against a standard, and taking managerial action to correct deviations or to address inadequate standards. (See Exhibit 13-2.) The control process assumes that performance standards already exist, and they do. They're the specific goals created during the planning process.

What Is Measuring?

To determine actual performance, a manager must first get information about it. Thus, the first step in control is measuring.

HOW DO MANAGERS MEASURE? Four common sources of information frequently used to measure actual performance are personal observation, statistical reports, oral reports, and written reports. Each has particular strengths and weaknesses; however, use of a combination of them increases both the number of input sources and the probability of receiving reliable information.

EXHIBIT 13-2 | **The Control Process**

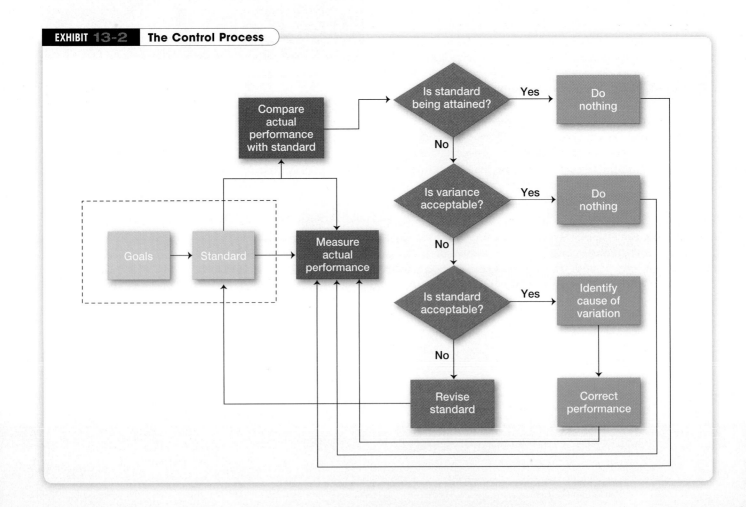

Personal observation provides firsthand, intimate knowledge of the actual activity—information that is not filtered through others. It permits intensive coverage because minor as well as major performance activities can be observed, and it provides opportunities for the manager to read between the lines. **Management by walking around (MBWA)** is a phrase that is used to describe when a manager is out in the work area, interacting directly with employees, and exchanging information about what's going on. Management by walking around can pick up factual omissions, facial expressions, and tones of voice that may be missed by other sources. Unfortunately, in a time when quantitative information suggests objectivity, personal observation is often considered an inferior information source. It is subject to perceptual biases; what one manager sees, another might not. Personal observation also consumes a good deal of time. Finally, this method suffers from obtrusiveness. Employees might interpret a manager's overt observation as a lack of confidence or a sign of mistrust.

The widespread use of computers has led managers to rely increasingly on *statistical reports* for measuring actual performance. This measuring device, however, isn't limited to computer outputs. It also includes graphs, bar charts, and numerical displays of any form that managers can use for assessing performance. Although statistical information is easy to visualize and effective for showing relationships, it provides limited information about an activity. Statistics report on only a few key areas and may often ignore other important, often subjective, factors.

Information can also be acquired through *oral reports*—that is, through conferences, meetings, one-to-one conversations, or telephone calls. In organizations in which employees work in a cultural environment, this approach may be the best way to keep tabs on work performance. For instance, at the Ken Blanchard Companies in Escondido, California, managers are expected to hold one-on-one meetings with each of their employees at least once every two weeks.[7] The advantages and disadvantages of this method of measuring performance are similar to those of personal observation. Although the information is filtered, it is fast, allows for feedback, and permits expression and tone of voice as well as words themselves to convey meaning. Historically, one of the major drawbacks of oral reports has been the problem of documenting information for later reference. However, our technological capabilities have progressed in the past couple of decades to the point where oral reports can be efficiently taped and become as permanent as if they were written.

Actual performance may also be measured by *written reports*. Like statistical reports, they are slower yet more formal than firsthand or secondhand oral measures. This formality also often gives them greater comprehensiveness and conciseness than found in oral reports. In addition, written reports are usually easy to catalog and reference.

Given the varied advantages and disadvantages of each of these four measurement techniques, managers should use all four for comprehensive control efforts.

WHAT DO MANAGERS MEASURE? *What* managers measure is probably more critical to the control process than how they measure. Why? The selection of the wrong criteria can result in serious dysfunctional consequences. Besides, what we measure determines, to a great extent, what people in the organization will attempt to excel at.[8] For example, assume that your instructor has required a total of 10 writing assignments from the exercises at the end of each textbook chapter. But, in the grade computation section of the syllabus, you notice that these assignments are not scored. In fact, when you ask your professor about this, she replies that these writing assignments are for your own enlightenment and do not affect your grade for the course; grades are solely a function of how well you perform on the three exams. We predict that you would, not surprisingly, exert most, if not all, of your effort toward doing well on the three exams.

---

control process
A three-step process of measuring actual performance, comparing actual performance against a standard, and taking managerial action to correct deviations or to address inadequate standards.

management by walking around (MBWA)
When a manager is out in the work area interacting with employees.

Believing that personal observation is an excellent source of information for measuring performance, General Electric's CEO Jeffrey Immelt is a practitioner of management by walking around. He uses his communication and leadership skills by spending more than half of his work time traveling the world and personally interacting with employees, customers, and suppliers. MBWA gives Immelt and other managers the opportunity to learn about problems and concerns first hand and to respond to them in a face-to-face interchange. In this photo, Immelt (right) listens to an employee while he tours a GE engine factory in Lynn, Massachusetts.

Some control criteria are applicable to any management situation. For instance, because all managers, by definition, direct the activities of others, criteria such as employee satisfaction or turnover and absenteeism rates can be measured. Most managers have budgets for their area of responsibility set in monetary units (dollars, pounds, francs, lire, and so on). Keeping costs within budget is, therefore, a fairly common control measure. However, any comprehensive control system needs to recognize the diversity of activities among managers. For example, a production manager in a paper tablet manufacturing plant might use measures of the quantity of tablets produced per day, tablets produced per labor hour, scrap tablet rate, or percentage of rejects returned by customers. On the other hand, the manager of an administrative unit in a government agency might use number of document pages produced per day, number of orders processed per hour, or average time required to process service calls. Marketing managers often use measures such as percent of market held, number of customer visits per salesperson, or number of customer impressions per advertising medium.

As you might imagine, some activities are more difficult to measure in quantifiable terms. It is more difficult, for instance, for a manager to measure the performance of a medical researcher or a middle school counselor than of a person who sells life insurance. But most activities can be broken down into objective segments that allow for measurement. The manager needs to determine what value a person, department, or unit contributes to the organization and then convert the contribution into standards.

Most jobs and activities can be expressed in tangible and measurable terms. When a performance indicator cannot be stated in quantifiable terms, managers should look for and use subjective measures. Certainly, subjective measures have significant limitations. Still, they are better than having no standards at all and ignoring the control function. If an activity is important, the excuse that it's difficult to measure is inadequate. In such cases, managers should use subjective performance criteria. Of course, any analysis or decisions made on the basis of subjective criteria should recognize the limitations of the data.

How Do Managers Compare Actual Performance to Planned Goals?

The comparing step determines the variation between actual performance and the standard. Although some variation in performance can be expected in all activities, it's critical to determine an acceptable **range of variation** (see Exhibit 13-3). Deviations outside this range need attention. Let's work through an example.

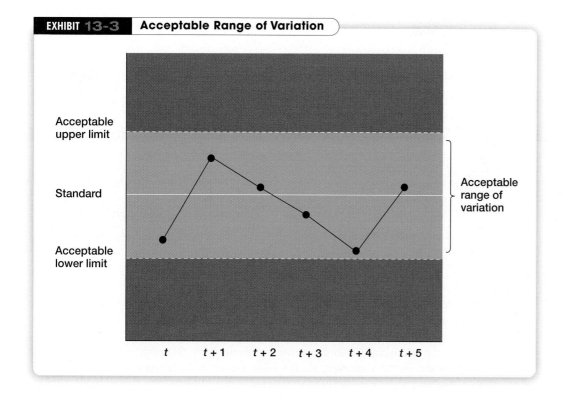

EXHIBIT 13-3 **Acceptable Range of Variation**

Acceptable upper limit

Standard

Acceptable lower limit

Acceptable range of variation

| t | t + 1 | t + 2 | t + 3 | t + 4 | t + 5 |

Chris Tanner is a sales manager for Green Earth Gardening Supply, a distributor of specialty plants and seeds in the Pacific Northwest. Chris prepares a report during the first week of each month that describes sales for the previous month, classified by product line. Exhibit 13-4 displays both the sales goals (standard) and actual sales figures for the month

From the Past to the Present

We introduced benchmarking in the planning chapter (Chapter 4) as a way for organizations to promote quality.[9] Not surprisingly, since planning and controlling are so closely linked, it also has implications for control. Benchmarking has been a highly utilized management tool. Although Xerox is often credited with the first widespread benchmarking effort in the United States, the practice can actually be traced back much further than that.

The benefits of benchmarking have long been recognized in the manufacturing industry. At the Midvale Steel Company plant where he was employed, Frederick W. Taylor (of scientific management fame) used concepts of benchmarking to find the "one best way" to perform a job and to find the best worker to perform the job. Even Henry Ford recognized the benefits. During a tour of a Chicago slaughterhouse in 1912, Ford watched as carcasses were hung from hooks mounted on a monorail. As each man performed his job, he pushed the carcass to the next work station. Some six months later, Ford's assembly line based on the same concept started producing cars. "The idea that revolutionized manufacturing was imported from another industry."

Today, managers in diverse industries such as health care, education, and financial services are discovering what manufacturers have long recognized—the benefits of benchmarking. For instance, the American Medical Association developed more than 100 standard measures of performance to improve medical care. Carlos Ghosn, CEO of Nissan, benchmarked Wal-Mart's operations in purchasing, transportation, and logistics. At its most basic, benchmarking means learning from others. However, as a tool for monitoring and measuring organizational and work performance, benchmarking can be used to identify specific performance gaps and potential areas of improvement.

range of variation
The acceptable parameters of variance between actual performance and a standard.

EXHIBIT 13-4	Example of Determining Significant Variation

Green Earth Gardening Supply—June Sales

PRODUCT	STANDARD	ACTUAL	OVER (UNDER)
Vegetable plants	1,075	913	(612)
Perennial flowers	630	634	4
Annual flowers	800	912	112
Herbs	160	140	(20)
Flowering bulbs	170	286	116
Flowering bushes	225	220	(5)
Heirloom seeds	540	672	132
Total	3,600	3,777	177

of June. After looking at the numbers, should Chris be concerned? Sales were a bit higher than originally targeted, but does that mean there were no significant deviations? That depends on what Chris thinks is *significant*; that is, outside the acceptable range of variation. Even though overall performance was generally quite favorable, some product lines need closer scrutiny. For instance, if sales of heirloom seeds, flowering bulbs, and annual flowers continue to be over what was expected, Chris might need to order more product from nurseries to meet customer demand. Because sales of vegetable plants were 15 percent below goal, Chris may need to run a special on them. As this example shows, both overvariance and undervariance may require managerial attention, which is the third step in the control process.

What Managerial Action Can Be Taken?

Managers can choose among three possible courses of action: do nothing, correct the actual performance, or revise the standards. Because "do nothing" is self-explanatory, let's look at the other two.

HOW DO YOU CORRECT ACTUAL PERFORMANCE? Depending on what the problem is, a manager could take different corrective actions. For instance, if unsatisfactory work is the reason for performance variations, the manager could correct it by things such as training programs, disciplinary action, changes in compensation practices, and so forth. One decision that a manager must make is whether to take **immediate corrective action**, which corrects problems at once to get performance back on track, or to use **basic corrective action**, which looks at how and why performance deviated before correcting the source of deviation. It's not unusual for managers to rationalize that they don't have time to find the source of a problem (basic corrective action) and continue to perpetually "put out fires" with immediate corrective action. Effective managers analyze deviations and if the benefits justify it, take the time to pinpoint and correct the causes of variance.

HOW DO YOU REVISE THE STANDARD? It's possible that the variance was a result of an unrealistic standard—too low or too high a goal. That means it's the standard that needs corrective action, not the performance. If performance consistently exceeds the goal, then a manager should look at whether the goal is too easy and needs to be raised. On the other hand, managers must be cautious about revising a standard downward. It's natural to blame the goal when an employee or a team falls short. For instance, students who get a low score on a test often attack the grade cutoff standards as too high. Rather than accept the fact that their performance was inadequate, they will argue that the standards are unreasonable. Likewise, salespeople who don't meet their monthly quota often want to blame what they think is an unrealistic quota. The point is that when performance isn't up to par, don't immediately blame the goal or standard. If you believe the standard is realistic, fair, and achievable, tell employees that you expect future work to improve, and then take the necessary corrective action to help make that happen.

What Should Managers Control?

Cost efficiency. The length of time customers are kept on hold. Customers being satisfied with the service provided. These are just a few of the important performance indicators that executives in the intensely competitive call-center service industry measure. To make good decisions, managers in this industry want and need this type of information so they can control work performance.

> **Discuss** the types of controls organizations and managers use.
> **13.3**

How do managers know what to control? In this section, we're first going to look at the decision of *what* to control in terms of when control takes place. Then, we're going to discuss some different areas in which managers might choose to establish controls.

When Does Control Take Place?

Management can implement controls before an activity commences, while the activity is going on, or after the activity has been completed. The first type is called feedforward control, the second is concurrent control, and the last is feedback control (see Exhibit 13-5).

WHAT IS FEEDFORWARD CONTROL? The most desirable type of control—**feedforward control**—prevents problems since it takes place before the actual activity.[11] For instance, when McDonald's opened its first restaurant in Moscow, it sent company quality control experts to help Russian farmers learn techniques for growing high-quality potatoes and to help bakers learn processes for baking high-quality breads. Why? McDonald's demands consistent product quality no matter the geographical location. They want a cheeseburger in Moscow to taste like one in Omaha. Still another example of feedforward control is the scheduled preventive maintenance programs on aircraft done by the major airlines. These are designed to detect and hopefully to prevent structural damage that might lead to an accident.

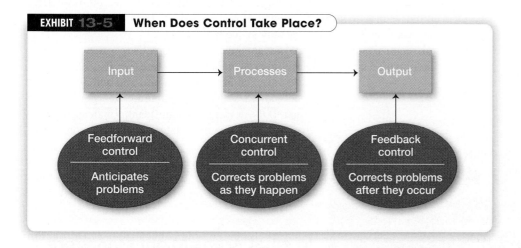

EXHIBIT 13-5   When Does Control Take Place?

immediate corrective action
Corrective action that addresses problems at once to get performance back on track.

basic corrective action
Corrective action that looks at how and why performance deviated before correcting the source of deviation.

feedforward control
Control that takes place before a work activity is done.

The key to feedforward controls is taking managerial action *before* a problem occurs. That way, problems can be prevented rather than having to correct them after any damage—poor quality products, lost customers, lost revenue, etc.—has already been done. However, these controls require timely and accurate information that isn't always easy to get. Thus, managers frequently end up using the other two types of control.

WHEN IS CONCURRENT CONTROL USED? Concurrent control, as its name implies, takes place while a work activity is in progress. For instance, the director of business product management at Google and his team keep a watchful eye on one of Google's most profitable businesses—online ads. They watch "the number of searches and clicks, the rate at which users click on ads, the revenue this generates—everything is tracked hour by hour, compared with the data from a week earlier and charted."[12] If they see something that's not working particularly well, they fine-tune it.

Technical equipment (such as computers and computerized machine controls) can be designed to include concurrent controls. For example, you've probably experienced this with word processing software that alerts you to a misspelled word or incorrect grammatical usage. Also, many organizational quality programs rely on concurrent controls to inform workers whether their work output is of sufficient quality to meet standards.

The best-known form of concurrent control, however, is direct supervision. For example, NVIDIA's CEO Jen-Hsun Huang had his office cubicle torn down and replaced with a conference table so he's now available to employees at all times to discuss what's going on.[13] Even GE's CEO Jeff Immelt spends 60 percent of his workweek on the road talking to employees and visiting the company's numerous locations.[14] All managers can benefit from using concurrent control because they can correct problems before they become too costly. MBWA, which we described earlier in this chapter, is a great way for managers to do this.

WHY IS FEEDBACK CONTROL SO POPULAR? The most popular type of control relies on feedback. In feedback control, the control takes place *after* the activity is done. For instance, remember our earlier Denver Mint example. The flawed Wisconsin quarters were discovered with feedback control. The damage had already occurred even though the organization corrected the problem once it was discovered. And that's the major problem with this type of control. By the time a manager has the information, the problems have already occurred, leading to waste or damage. However, in many work areas, the financial area being one example, feedback is the only viable type of control.

Feedback controls do have two advantages.[15] First, feedback gives managers meaningful information on how effective their planning efforts were. Feedback that shows little variance between standard and actual performance indicates that the planning was generally on target. If the deviation is significant, a manager can use that information to formulate new plans. Second, feedback can enhance motivation. People want to know how well they're doing, and feedback provides that information. (See the "Developing Your Performance Feedback Skill" box on performance feedback.)

To maintain high product quality, Toyota Motor Corporation initially developed and produced cars only in Japan and exported them to markets abroad. When Toyota decided to produce vehicles outside of Japan, the company used feedforward control for quality assurance by establishing a Global Production Center in Japan. At the GPC, managers and employees of overseas plants learn the production skills needed to ensure that quality is built into the vehicles. Shown here is an experienced production master (left) teaching a spray-painting technique at the GPC in Japan. Toyota has also built GPCs in the United States, the United Kingdom, and Thailand as it continues its global production expansion.

In What Areas Might Managers Need Controls?

Most organizations consist of countless activities taking place in different locations and functional areas of the organization. So *what* gets controlled? We need to look at some of the specific areas and control tools that managers can use.

Developing Your *Performance Feedback* Skill

About the Skill

One of the more critical feedback sessions will occur when you, as a manager, are using feedback control to address performance issues.

Steps in Practicing the Skill

1 **Schedule the feedback session in advance and be prepared.** One of the biggest mistakes you can make is to treat feedback control lightly. Simply calling in an employee and giving feedback that's not well organized serves little purpose for you and your employee. For feedback to be effective, you must plan ahead. Identify the issues you wish to address and cite specific examples to reinforce what you are saying. Furthermore, set aside the time for the meeting with the employee. Make sure that what you do is done in private and can be completed without interruptions. That may mean closing your office door (if you have one), not taking phone calls, and the like.

2 **Put the employee at ease.** Regardless of how you feel about the feedback, you must create a supportive climate for the employee. Recognize that giving and getting this feedback can be an emotional event even when the feedback is positive. By putting your employee at ease, you begin to establish a supportive environment in which understanding can take place.

3 **Make sure the employee knows the purpose of this feedback session.** What is the purpose of the meeting? That's something any employee will be wondering. Clarifying what you are going to do sets the appropriate stage for what is to come.

4 **Focus on specific rather than general work behaviors.** Feedback should be specific rather than general. General statements are vague and provide little useful information—especially if you are attempting to correct a problem.

5 **Keep comments impersonal and job related.** Feedback should be descriptive rather than judgmental or evaluative, especially when you are giving negative feedback. No matter how upset you are, keep the feedback job related and never criticize someone personally because of an inappropriate action. You're correcting job-related behavior, not the person.

6 **Support feedback with hard data.** Tell your employee how you came to your conclusion on his or her performance. Hard data help your employees to identify with specific behaviors. Identify the "things" that were done correctly and provide a detailed critique. And, if you need to criticize, state the basis of your conclusion that a good job was not completed.

7 **Direct the negative feedback toward work-related behavior that the employee controls.** Negative feedback should be directed toward work-related behavior that the employee can do something about. Indicate what he or she can do to improve the situation. This practice helps take the sting out of the criticism and offers guidance to an individual who understands the problem but doesn't know how to resolve it.

8 **Let the employee speak.** Get the employee's perceptions of what you are saying, especially if you are addressing a problem. Of course, you're not looking for excuses, but you need to be empathetic to the employee. Get his or her side. Maybe there's something that has contributed to the issue. Letting the employee speak involves your employee and just might provide information you were unaware of.

9 **Ensure that the employee has a clear and full understanding of the feedback.** Feedback must be concise and complete enough so that your employee clearly and fully understands what you have said. Consistent with active listening techniques, have your employee rephrase the content of your feedback to check whether it fully captures your meaning.

10 **Detail a future plan of action.** Performing doesn't stop simply because feedback occurred. Good performance must be reinforced, and new performance goals set. However, when performance deficiencies are the issue, time must be devoted to helping your employee develop a detailed, step-by-step plan to correct the situation. This plan includes what has to be done, when, and how you will monitor the activities. Offer whatever assistance you can to help the employee, but make it clear that it is the employee, not you, who has to make the corrections.

Practicing the Skill

Think of a skill you would like to acquire or improve, or a habit you would like to break. Perhaps you would like to learn a foreign language, start exercising, quit smoking, ski better, or spend less. For the purpose of this exercise, assume you have three months to make a start on your project and all the necessary funds. Draft a plan of action that outlines what you need to do, when you need to do it, and how you will know that you have successfully completed each step of your plan. Be realistic, but don't set your sights too low either.

Review your plan. What outside help or resources will you require? How will you get them? Add these to your plan. Could someone else follow the steps you've outlined to achieve the goal you set? What modifications would you have to make, if any?

concurrent control
Control that takes place while a work activity is in progress.

feedback control
Control that takes place after a work activity is done.

359

HOW DO MANAGERS KEEP TRACK OF FINANCES? Every business wants to earn a profit. To achieve this goal, managers need financial controls. For instance, they might analyze quarterly income statements for excessive expenses. They might calculate financial ratios to ensure that sufficient cash is available to pay ongoing expenses, that debt levels haven't become too high, or that assets are being used productively.

Traditional financial measures managers might use include ratio analysis and budget analysis. Exhibit 13-6 summarizes some of the most popular financial ratios that managers will analyze. Liquidity ratios measure an organization's ability to meet its current debt obligations. Leverage ratios examine the organization's use of debt to finance its assets and whether it's able to meet the interest payments on the debt. Activity ratios assess how efficiently a company is using its assets. Finally, profitability ratios measure how efficiently and effectively the company is using its assets to generate profits. These are calculated using selected information from the organization's two primary financial statements (the balance sheet and the income statement), which are then expressed as a percentage or ratio. Because you've probably studied these ratios in other accounting or finance courses, or will in the near future, we won't elaborate on how they're calculated. We mention them here to remind you that managers use such ratios as internal control tools.

Budgets are another type of financial control tool that are used for planning and controlling. When a budget is formulated, it's a planning tool because it indicates which work activities are important and what and how much resources should be allocated to those activities. But budgets are also used for controlling since they provide managers with quantitative standards against which to measure and compare resource consumption. If deviations are significant enough to require action, the manager examines what has happened and tries to uncover why. With this information, necessary action can be taken. For example, if you use a personal budget for monitoring and controlling your monthly expenses, you might find that one month your miscellaneous expenses were higher than you had budgeted for. At that point, you might cut back spending in another area or work extra hours to get more income.

EXHIBIT 13-6   Popular Financial Ratios

OBJECTIVE	RATIO	CALCULATION	MEANING
Liquidity	Current ratio	$\dfrac{\text{Current assets}}{\text{Current liabilities}}$	Tests the organization's ability to meet short-term obligations
	Acid test	$\dfrac{\text{Current assets} - \text{inventories}}{\text{Current liabilities}}$	Tests liquidity more accurately when inventories turn over slowly or are difficult to sell
Leverage	Debt to assets	$\dfrac{\text{Total debt}}{\text{Total assets}}$	The higher the ratio, the more leveraged the organization
	Times interest earned	$\dfrac{\text{Profits before interest and taxes}}{\text{Total interest charges}}$	Measures how many times the organization is able to cover its interest expenses
Activity	Inventory turnover	$\dfrac{\text{Sales}}{\text{Inventory}}$	The higher the ratio, the more efficiently inventory assets are being used
	Total asset turnover	$\dfrac{\text{Sales}}{\text{Total assets}}$	The fewer assets used to achieve a given level of sales, the more efficiently management is using the organization's total assets
Profitability	Profit margin on sales	$\dfrac{\text{Net profit after taxes}}{\text{Total sales}}$	Identifies the profits that are being generated
	Return on investment	$\dfrac{\text{Net profit after taxes}}{\text{Total assets}}$	Measures the efficiency of assets to generate profits

HOW IS AN ORGANIZATION'S INFORMATION CONTROLLED? A computer with personal information (Social Security numbers, birth dates, etc.) on some 26.5 million military veterans stored on it was stolen from the residence of a Department of Veteran Affairs employee who had taken the computer home without authorization. Although the computer was eventually recovered with no loss of personal information, the situation could have been damaging to a large number of people.[16] Talk about the need for information controls! Managers deal with information controls in two ways: (1) as a tool to help them control other organizational activities and (2) as an organizational area they need to control.

Managers need the right information at the right time and in the right amount to help them *monitor and measure organizational activities*. In measuring actual performance, managers need information about what is happening within their area of responsibility and about the standards in order to be able to compare actual performance with the standard. They also rely on information to help them determine if deviations are acceptable. Finally, they rely on information to help them develop appropriate courses of action. Information *is* important! Most of the information tools that managers use come from the organization's management information system.

A **management information system (MIS)** is a system used to provide managers with needed information on a regular basis. In theory, this system can be manual or computer-based, although most organizations have moved to computer-supported applications. The term *system* in MIS implies order, arrangement, and purpose. Further, an MIS focuses specifically on providing managers with *information* (processed and analyzed data), not merely *data* (raw, unanalyzed facts). A library provides a good analogy. Although it can contain millions of volumes, a library doesn't do you any good if you can't find what you want quickly. That's why librarians spend a great deal of time cataloging a library's collections and ensuring that materials are returned to their proper locations. Organizations today are like well-stocked libraries. There's no lack of data. There is, however, an inability to process that data so that the right information is available to the right person when he or she needs it. An MIS collects data and turns them into relevant information for managers to use.

It seems that every week, there's another news story about information security breaches. A recent survey found that 85 percent of privacy and security professionals acknowledged a reportable data breach occurred within their organizations within the last year alone.[17] Because information is critically important to everything an organization does, managers must have comprehensive and secure controls in place to *protect that information*. Such controls can range from data encryption to system firewalls to data backups, and other techniques as well.[18] Problems can lurk in places that an organization might not even have considered, like search engines. Sensitive, defamatory, confidential, or embarrassing organizational information has found its way into search engine results. For instance, detailed monthly expenses and employee salaries on the National Speleological Society's Web site turned up in a Google search.[19] Equipment such as laptop computers and even RFID (radio-frequency identification) tags are vulnerable to viruses and hacking. Needless to say, information controls should be monitored regularly to ensure that all possible precautions are in place to protect important information.

Delta Airlines uses a balanced scorecard approach to evaluate its organizational performance. In addition to measuring performance in the financial, customer, and internal processes areas, Delta developed a scorecard to address its commitment to environmental sustainability. The airline's new environmental management information system tracks and verifies compliance of hazardous chemical usage in maintaining and rebuilding its airplanes at the company's Technical Operations Center in Atlanta. The EMIS also tracks hazardous chemicals and wastes and verifies environmental compliance at 100 airports in the United States where Delta operates.

WHAT IS THE BALANCED SCORECARD APPROACH TO CONTROL? The **balanced scorecard** approach is a way to evaluate organizational performance from more than just the financial perspective.[20] A balanced scorecard typically looks at four areas that contribute to a company's performance: financial, customer, internal processes, and people/innovation/growth assets. According to this approach, managers should develop goals in each of the four areas and then measure whether the goals are being met.

Although a balanced scorecard makes sense, managers will tend to focus on areas that drive their organization's success and use scorecards that reflect those strategies.[21] For example, if strategies are customer-centered, then the customer area is likely to get more attention than the other three areas. Yet, you can't focus on measuring only one performance area because others are affected as well. For instance, at IBM Global Services in Houston, managers developed a scorecard around an overriding strategy of customer satisfaction. However, the other areas (financial, internal processes, and people/innovation/growth) support that central strategy. The division manager described it as follows, "The internal processes part of our business is directly related to responding to our customers in a timely manner, and the learning and innovation aspect is critical for us since what we're selling our customers above all is our expertise. Of course, how successful we are with those things will affect our financial component."[22]

What Contemporary Control Issues Do Managers Confront?

13.4 Discuss contemporary issues in control.

The employees of Integrated Information Systems Inc. didn't think twice about exchanging digital music over a dedicated office server they had set up. Like office betting on college and pro sports, it was technically illegal, but harmless, or so they thought. But after the company had to pay a $1 million settlement to the Recording Industry Association of America, managers wished they had controlled the situation better.[23] Control is an important managerial function. We're going to look at two control issues that managers face today: cross-cultural differences and workplace concerns.

Do Controls Need To Be Adjusted for Cultural Differences?

The concepts of control that we've discussed are appropriate for organizational units that aren't geographically distant or culturally distinct. But what about global organizations? Would control systems be different, and what should managers know about adjusting controls for national differences?

Methods of controlling employee behavior and operations can be quite different in different countries. In fact, the differences in organizational control systems of global organizations are primarily in the measurement and corrective action steps of the control process. In a global corporation, for instance, managers of foreign operations tend not to be closely controlled by the home office if for no other reason than that distance keeps managers from being able to observe work directly. Because distance creates a tendency for formalized controls, the home office of a global company often relies on extensive, formal reports for control. The global company may also use information technology to control work activities. For instance, IYG Holding Company (a wholly owned subsidiary of Ito-Yokado Co., Ltd., and Seven-Eleven Japan Co., Ltd, that own the 7-Eleven convenience store chain) uses automated cash registers not only to record sales and monitor inventory but also to schedule tasks for store managers and to track their use of the built-in analytical graphs and forecasts. If managers don't use them enough, they're told to increase their activities.[24]

Technology's impact on control is most evident in comparisons of technologically advanced nations with more primitive countries. Organizations in technologically advanced nations such as the United States, Japan, Canada, Great Britain, Germany, and Australia use indirect control devices—particularly computer-related reports and analyses—in addition to standardized rules and direct supervision to ensure that activities are going as planned. In less technologically advanced countries, direct supervision and highly centralized decision making are the basic means of control.

Also, constraints on what corrective action managers can take may affect managers in foreign countries because laws in some countries do not allow managers the option of closing facilities, laying off employees, or bringing in a new management team from outside the country. Finally, another challenge for global companies in collecting data is comparability. For instance, a company's manufacturing facility in Mexico might produce the same products as a facility in Scotland. However, the Mexican facility might be much more labor intensive than its Scottish counterparts (to take advantage of lower labor costs in Mexico). If top-level executives were to control costs by, for example, calculating labor costs per unit or output per worker, the figures would not be comparable. Managers in global companies must address these types of global control challenges.

TECHNOLOGY AND THE MANAGER'S JOB

MONITORING EMPLOYEES

Technological advances have made the process of managing an organization much easier.[25] But technological advancements have also provided employers a means of sophisticated employee monitoring. Although most of this monitoring is designed to enhance worker productivity, it could, and has been, a source of concern over worker privacy. These advantages have also brought with them difficult questions regarding what managers have the right to know about employees and how far they can go in controlling employee behavior, both on and off the job. Consider the following:

- The mayor of Colorado Springs, Colorado, reads the e-mail messages that city council members send to each other from their homes. He defended his actions by saying he was making sure that e-mails to each other were not being used to circumvent the state's "open meeting" law that requires most council business to be conducted publicly.
- The U.S. Internal Revenue Service's internal audit group monitors a computer log that shows employee access to taxpayers' accounts. This monitoring activity allows management to check and see what employees are doing on their computers.
- American Express has an elaborate system for monitoring telephone calls. Daily reports are provided to supervisors that detail the frequency and length of calls made by employees, as well as how quickly incoming calls are answered.
- Employers in several organizations require employees to wear badges at all times while on company premises. These badges contain a variety of data that allow employees to enter certain locations in the organization. Smart badges, too, can transmit where the employee is at all times!

Then, there's the issue of just how much control a company should have over the private lives of its employees. Where should an employer's rules and controls end? Does the boss have the right to dictate what you do on your free time and in your own home? Could your boss keep you from engaging in riding a motorcycle, skydiving, smoking, drinking alcohol, or eating junk food? Again, the answers may surprise you. Today many organizations, in their quest to control safety and health insurance costs, are delving into their employees' private lives.

Although controlling employees' behaviors on and off the job may appear unjust or unfair, nothing in our legal system prevents employers from engaging in these practices. Rather, the law is based on the premise that if employees don't like the rules, they have the option of quitting. Managers, too, typically defend their actions in terms of ensuring quality, productivity, and proper employee behavior. For instance, an IRS audit of its southeastern regional offices found that 166 employees took unauthorized looks at the tax returns of friends, neighbors, and celebrities.

When does management's need for information about employee performance cross over the line and interfere with a worker's right to privacy? Is technology being misused? Is any action by management acceptable as long as employees are notified ahead of time that they will be monitored? What's your opinion?

balanced scorecard
A performance measurement tool that looks at more than just the financial perspective.

What Challenges Do Managers Face in Controlling the Workplace?

Today's workplaces present considerable control challenges for managers. From monitoring employees' computer usage at work to protecting the workplace against disgruntled employees intent on doing harm, managers need controls to ensure that work can be done efficiently and effectively as planned.

IS MY WORK COMPUTER REALLY MINE? If you work, do you think you have a right to privacy at your job? What can your employer find out about you and your work? You might be surprised at the answers! Employers can (and do), among other things, read your e-mail (even those marked "personal or confidential"), tap your telephone, monitor your work by computer, store and review computer files, monitor you in an employee bathroom or dressing room, and track your whereabouts in a company vehicle. And these actions aren't that uncommon. In fact, some 26 percent of companies have fired workers for misusing the Internet, another 25 percent have terminated workers for e-mail misuse, and 6 percent have fired employees for misusing office phones.[26]

Why do managers feel they need to monitor what employees are doing? A big reason is that employees are hired to work, not to surf the Web checking stock prices, watching online videos, playing fantasy baseball, or shopping for presents for family or friends. Recreational on-the-job Web surfing is thought to cost billions of dollars in lost work productivity annually. In fact, a survey of U.S. employers said that 87 percent of employees look at nonwork-related Web sites while at work and more than half engage in personal Web site surfing every day.[27] Watching online video has become an increasingly serious problem not only because of the time being wasted by employees but because it clogs already strained corporate computer networks.[28] If you had to guess the video site most being viewed at work, what would you guess? If you said YouTube, you'd be absolutely correct![29] However, as innocent as it may seem (after all, it may be just a 30-second video), all this nonwork adds up to significant costs to businesses.

Another reason that managers monitor employee e-mail and computer usage is that they don't want to risk being sued for creating a hostile workplace environment because of offensive messages or an inappropriate image displayed on a coworker's computer screen. Concerns about racial or sexual harassment are one reason companies might want to monitor or keep backup copies of all e-mail. Electronic records can help establish what actually happened so managers can react quickly.[30]

Finally, managers want to ensure that company secrets aren't being leaked.[31] In addition to typical e-mail and computer usage, companies are monitoring instant messaging, blogs, and other social media outlets, and banning phone cameras in the office. Managers need to be certain that employees are not, even inadvertently, passing information on to others who could use that information to harm the company.

Because of the potentially serious costs and given the fact that many jobs now entail computers, many companies have workplace monitoring policies. Such policies should control employee behavior in a nondemeaning way, and employees should be informed about those policies.

Daniel Lorello is one of a growing number of employee thieves who try to sell their stolen property on auction Web sites like eBay. Lorello, an archivist for the New York State Department of Education, had unrestricted access to the archives at the state library from which he stole hundreds of historic documents, sold them on eBay, and used the profits to pay for home renovations, tuition, and his daughter's $10,000 credit card debt. After a history enthusiast alerted authorities to the posting on eBay of an 1823 letter by John C. Calhoun, Lorello was arrested, pleaded guilty to theft, and was sentenced to state prison. Lorello's mug shots are shown here taped to a photograph of Calhoun's letter.

IS EMPLOYEE THEFT ON THE RISE? Would you be surprised to find that up to 85 percent of all organizational theft and fraud is committed by employees, not outsiders?[32] And, it's a costly problem—estimated to be around $4,500 per worker per year.[33] In a recent survey of U.S. companies, 20 percent said that workplace theft has become a moderate to very big problem.[34]

Employee theft is defined as any unauthorized taking of company property by employees for their personal use.[35] It can range from embezzlement to fraudulent filing of expense reports to removing equipment, parts, software, or office supplies from company premises. Although retail businesses have long faced serious potential losses from employee theft, loose financial controls at start-ups and small companies and the ready availability of information technology have made employee stealing an escalating problem in all kinds and sizes of organizations. It's a control issue that managers need to educate themselves about and be prepared to deal with it.[36]

Why do employees steal? The answer depends on whom you ask.[37] Experts in various fields—industrial security, criminology, clinical psychology—have different perspectives. The industrial security people propose that people steal because the opportunity presents itself through lax controls and favorable circumstances. Criminologists say that it's because people have financial-based pressures (such as personal financial problems) or vice-based pressures (such as gambling debts). And the clinical psychologists suggest that people steal because they can rationalize whatever they're doing as being correct and appropriate behavior ("everyone does it," "they had it coming," "this company makes enough money and they'll never miss anything this small," "I deserve this for all that I put up with," and so forth).[38] Although each approach provides compelling insights into employee theft and has been instrumental in attempts to deter it, unfortunately, employees continue to steal. What can managers do?

The concept of feedforward, concurrent, and feedback control is useful for identifying measures to deter or reduce employee theft.[39] Exhibit 13-7 summarizes several possible managerial actions.

EXHIBIT 13-7 | **Controlling Employee Theft**

FEEDFORWARD	CONCURRENT	FEEDBACK
Engage in careful prehiring screening.	Treat employees with respect and dignity.	Make sure employees know when theft or fraud has occurred—not naming names but letting people know that these incidents are not acceptable.
Establish specific policies defining theft and fraud and discipline procedures.	Openly communicate the costs of stealing.	
	Let employees know on a regular basis about their successes in preventing theft and fraud.	Use the services of professional investigators.
Involve employees in writing policies.		Redesign control measures.
Educate and train employees about the policies.	Use video surveillance equipment if conditions warrant.	Evaluate your organization's culture and the relationships of managers and employees.
Have professionals review your internal security controls.	Install "lock-out" options on computers, telephones, and e-mail.	
	Use corporate hotlines for reporting incidences.	
	Set a good example.	

Sources: Based on A. H. Bell and D. M. Smith, "Protecting the Company Against Theft and Fraud," *Workforce Online,* http://www.workforce.com (December 3, 2000); J. D. Hansen, "To Catch a Thief," *Journal of Accountancy* (March 2000), pp. 43–46; and J. Greenberg, "The Cognitive Geometry of Employee Theft," in *Dysfunctional Behavior in Organizations: Nonviolent and Deviant Behavior* (Stamford, CT: JAI Press, 1998), pp. 147–193.

employee theft
Any unauthorized taking of company property by employees for their personal use.

Stress caused by job loss is a major contributor to workplace violence during times of economic uncertainty. Threatened by layoffs and plant closings, the employees shown here at a French factory owned by Germany's Continental AG tire company displayed strong emotions of anger and rage and resorted to violence by burning tires made at the factory. Continental announced that its plans to eliminate 1,900 jobs and close plants with the highest production costs were necessary because the demand for tires has declined substantially worldwide. Employee protests at other Continental factories in France included workers who stormed into a management meeting and shouted at the managers while pelting them with eggs and shoes.

WHAT CAN MANAGERS DO ABOUT WORKPLACE VIOLENCE? On June 25, 2008, in Henderson, Kentucky, an employee at a plastics plant returned hours after arguing with his supervisor over his not wearing safety goggles and for using his cell phone while working on the assembly line. He shot and killed the supervisor, four other coworkers, and himself. In April 2007, the same month in which the Virginia Tech shootings occurred, a gunman at his former workplace in Troy, Michigan, and one at NASA in Houston shot and killed a person. On January 30, 2006, a former employee who was once removed from a Santa Barbara, California, postal facility because of "strange behavior" came back and shot five workers to death, critically wounded another, and killed herself. On January 26, 2005, an autoworker at a Jeep plant in Toledo, Ohio, who had met the day before with plant managers about a problem with his work, came in and killed a supervisor and wounded two other employees before killing himself. In April 2003, a manager of a Boston Market restaurant in Indianapolis was killed by a fellow employee after the restaurant closed because the manager had refused the employee's sexual advances. In July 2003, an employee at an aircraft assembly plant in Meridian, Mississippi, walked out of a mandatory class on ethics and respect in the workplace, returned with firearms and ammunition, shot 14 of his coworkers, killing 5 and himself.[40] Is workplace violence really an issue for managers? Yes. The latest data available (2007) showed an increase in workplace homicides (610). However, despite this increase, workplace homicides have declined 44 percent from the high of 1,080 reported in 1994.[41] But workplace violence doesn't just include homicides. The U.S. National Institute of Occupational Safety and Health says that each year, some 2 million American workers are victims of some form of workplace violence such as verbal abuse, yelling at coworkers, purposeful damage of machines or furniture, or assaulting coworkers. In an average week, 1 employee is killed and at least 25 are seriously injured in violent assaults by current or former coworkers. And according to a Department of Labor survey, 58 percent of firms reported that managers received verbal threats from workers.[42] Anger, rage, and violence in the workplace are intimidating to coworkers and adversely affect their productivity. The annual cost to U.S. businesses is estimated to be between $20 billion and $35 billion.[43] And office rage isn't a uniquely American problem. A survey of aggressive behaviors in Britain's workplaces found that 18 percent of managers say they have personally experienced harassment or verbal bullying, and 9 percent claim to have experienced physical attacks.[44]

What factors are believed to contribute to workplace violence? Undoubtedly, employee stress caused by job uncertainties, declining value of retirement accounts, long hours, information overload, other daily interruptions, unrealistic deadlines, and uncaring managers play a role. Even office layout designs with small cubicles where employees work amidst the noise and commotion from those around them have been cited as contributing to the problem.[45] Other experts have described dangerously dysfunctional work environments characterized by the following as primary contributors to the problem:[46]

▶ Employee work driven by TNC (time, numbers, and crises).
▶ Rapid and unpredictable change where instability and uncertainty plague employees.
▶ Destructive communication style where managers communicate in excessively aggressive, condescending, explosive, or passive-aggressive styles; excessive workplace teasing or scapegoating.
▶ Authoritarian leadership with a rigid, militaristic mind-set of managers versus employees; employees aren't allowed to challenge ideas, participate in decision making, or engage in team-building efforts.
▶ Defensive attitude where little or no performance feedback is given; only numbers count; and yelling, intimidation, or avoidance are the preferred ways of handling conflict.
▶ Double standards in terms of policies, procedures, and training opportunities for managers and employees.

▶ Unresolved grievances because there are no mechanisms or only adversarial ones in place for resolving them; dysfunctional individuals may be protected or ignored because of long-standing rules, union contract provisions, or reluctance to take care of problems.

▶ Emotionally troubled employees and no attempt by managers to get help for these people.

▶ Repetitive, boring work where there's no chance for doing something else or for new people coming in.

▶ Faulty or unsafe equipment or deficient training, which keeps employees from being able to work efficiently or effectively.

▶ Hazardous work environment in terms of temperature, air quality, repetitive motions, overcrowded spaces, noise levels, excessive overtime, and so forth. To minimize costs, no additional employees are hired when workload becomes excessive leading to potentially dangerous work expectations and conditions.

▶ Culture of violence where there's a history of individual violence or abuse; violent or explosive role models; or tolerance of on-the-job alcohol or drug abuse.

Reading through this list, you surely hope that workplaces where you'll spend your professional life won't be like this. However, the competitive demands of succeeding in a 24/7 global economy put pressure on organizations and employees in many ways.

What can managers do to deter or reduce possible workplace violence? Once again, the concept of feedforward, concurrent, and feedback control can help identify actions that managers can take.[47] Exhibit 13-8 summarizes several suggestions.

EXHIBIT 13-8   **Controlling Workplace Violence**

FEEDFORWARD	CONCURRENT	FEEDBACK
Ensure management's commitment to functional, not dysfunctional, work environments.	MBWA (managing by walking around) to identify potential problems; observe how employees treat and interact with each other.	Communicate openly about incidences and what's being done.
Provide employee assistance programs (EAPs) to help employees with behavioral problems.	Allow employees or work groups to "grieve" during periods of major organizational change.	Investigate incidences and take appropriate action.
Enforce organizational policy that any workplace rage, aggression, or violence will not be tolerated.	Be a good role model in how you treat others.	Review company policies and change, if necessary.
Use careful prehiring screening.	Use corporate hotlines or some other mechanism for reporting and investigating incidences.	
Never ignore threats.	Use quick and decisive intervention.	
Train employees about how to avoid danger if situation arises.	Get expert professional assistance if violence erupts.	
Clearly communicate policies to employees.	Provide necessary equipment or procedures for dealing with violent situations (cell phones, alarm system, code names or phrases, and so forth).	

Sources: Based on M. Gorkin, "Five Strategies and Structures for Reducing Workplace Violence," *Workforce Management Online*, December 3, 2000; "Investigating Workplace Violence: Where Do You Start?" *Workforce Management Online*, December 3, 2000; "Ten Tips on Recognizing and Minimizing Violence," *Workforce Management Online*, December 3, 2000; and "Points to Cover in a Workplace Violence Policy," *Workforce Management Online*, December 3, 2000.

Review and  Applications

Chapter Summary

 Explain the nature and importance of control. Control is the management function that involves monitoring activities to ensure that they're being accomplished as planned and correcting any significant deviations.

As the final step in the management process, controlling provides the link back to planning. If managers didn't control, they'd have no way of knowing whether goals were being met.

Control is important because (1) it's the only way to know if goals are being met and if not, why; (2) it provides information and feedback so managers feel comfortable empowering employees; and (3) it helps protect an organization and its assets.

 Describe the three steps in the control process. The three steps in the control process are measuring, comparing, and taking action. Measuring involves deciding how to measure actual performance and what to measure. Comparing involves looking at the variation between actual performance and the standard (goal). Deviations outside an acceptable range of variation need attention.

Taking action can involve the following: do nothing, correct the actual performance, or revise the standards. Doing nothing is self-explanatory. Correcting the actual performance can involve different corrective actions, which can either be immediate or basic. Standards can be revised by either raising or lowering them.

 Discuss the types of controls organizations and managers use. Feedforward controls take place before a work activity is done. Concurrent controls take place while a work activity is being done. Feedback controls take place after a work activity is done.

Financial controls that managers can use include financial ratios (liquidity, leverage, activity, and profitability) and budgets. One information control managers can use is an MIS, which provides managers with needed information on a regular basis. Others include comprehensive and secure controls such as data encryption, system firewalls, data backups, and so forth that protect the organization's information. Also, balanced scorecards provide a way to evaluate an organization's performance in four different areas rather than just from the financial perspective.

 Discuss contemporary issues in control. Adjusting controls for cross-cultural differences may be needed primarily in the areas of measuring and taking corrective actions.

Workplace concerns include workplace privacy, employee theft, and workplace violence. For each of these, managers need to have policies in place to control inappropriate actions and ensure that work is getting done efficiently and effectively.

 To check your understanding of learning outcomes – , go to **mymanagementlab.com** and try the chapter questions.

Understanding the Chapter

1. What is the role of control in management?
2. Describe four methods managers can use to acquire information about actual work performance.
3. How are planning and control linked? Is the control function linked to the organizing and leading functions of management? Explain.
4. In Chapter 7 we discussed the "white-water rapids" view of change. Do you think it's possible to establish and maintain effective standards and controls in this type of environment? Discuss.
5. Why is it that *what* is measured is more critical to the control process than *how* it is measured?
6. Why do you think feedback control is the most popular type of control? Justify your response.
7. "Every individual employee in an organization plays a role in controlling work activities." Do you agree with this statement, or do you think control is something that only managers are responsible for? Explain.
8. How could you use the concept of control in your personal life? Be specific. (Think in terms of feedforward, concurrent, and feedback controls as well as specific controls for the different aspects of your life—school, work, family relationships, friends, hobbies, etc.)

Understanding Yourself

How Good Am I at Disciplining Others?

Disciplining employees is probably one of the most difficult things a manager does. However, it's an important managerial tool. This instrument is based on the literature defining preferred discipline techniques. It's not a precise tool, but it will give you some insights into how effective you might be in using discipline in the workplace.

INSTRUMENT   This test contains eight disciplining practices. For each statement, select the answer that best describes you. Remember to respond as you have behaved or would behave, not as you think you should behave. If you have no managerial experience, answer the statements assuming you are a manager. Use the following scale to express your response:

1 = Usually

2 = Sometimes

3 = Seldom

When disciplining an employee:

1.	I provide ample warning before taking formal action.	1	2	3
2.	I wait for a pattern of infractions before calling it to the employee's attention.	1	2	3
3.	Even after repeated offenses, I prefer informal discussion about correcting the problem rather than formal disciplinary action.	1	2	3
4.	I delay confronting the employee about an infraction until his or her performance-appraisal review.	1	2	3
5.	In discussing an infraction with the employee, my style and tone are serious.	1	2	3
6.	I explicitly seek to allow the employee to explain his or her position.	1	2	3
7.	I remain impartial in allocating punishment.	1	2	3
8.	I allocate stronger penalties for repeated offenses.	1	2	3

SCORING KEY   Add up the points for questions 2, 3, and 4. For the other 5 questions (1, 5, 6, 7, and 8), reverse score them by giving a "1" response 3 points and a "3" response 1 point.

ANALYSIS AND INTERPRETATION   Your score on this test will range from 8 to 24. A score of 22 or higher indicates excellent skills at disciplining. You understand that effective discipline involves providing ample warning, acting in a timely fashion, using a calm and serious tone, being specific about the problem, keeping the process impersonal, and that disciplinary action should be progressive and consider mitigating circumstances. A score in the 19 to 21 range suggests some deficiencies. A score below 19 indicates considerable room for improvement.

Source: S. P. Robbins, *Training in Interpersonal Skills: TIPS for Managing People at Work* (Upper Saddle River, NJ: Prentice Hall, 1989), pp. 104–105.

FYIA (For Your Immediate Action)

Collins State College—School of Accountancy

Reply   Reply All   Forward

To: Matt Wrobeck, Ethics Committee Chair
From: Dr. Rebecca Rodriguez, Director
Subject: **Minimizing Student Cheating**

Matt, you've probably heard that several of our faculty members want to develop some specific controls to minimize opportunities for our students to cheat on homework assignments and exams. As the ethics committee chair, I'd like you to work with them on developing some suggestions. As you look at this topic, please think in terms of ways to control cheating (1) before it happens, (2) while in-class exams or assignments are being completed, and (3) after it has happened.

Keep your list brief (around a page) and send it to me by the end of the week. I'd like to get this out to our entire faculty at our next scheduled monthly meeting.

This fictionalized company and message were created for educational purposes only. It is not meant to reflect positively or negatively on management practices by any company that may share this name.

OFF COURSE

Just after midnight on March 22, 2006, the *Queen of the North* ferry, part of the BC Ferries system, hit rocks off Gil Island, south of Prince Rupert. It was immediately clear that the ferry was in trouble, and within 15 minutes, *all* the passengers and crew were off the ship and in the ferry's lifeboats. As local townspeople and the Coast Guard rescued the passengers from the lifeboats, the ferry sank, a little more than an hour after first striking the rocks. Initial media reports celebrated the fact that all 99 passengers and crew had managed to get off the ferry safely. The crew was widely praised for conducting an orderly evacuation, something employees practice and train for at regular intervals.

On day two, passengers were reported missing. While international maritime regulations require that ferries record identifying information about all passengers (name, gender, and whether they are adults, children, or infants), the Canadian government doesn't require BC's ferry fleet to meet international standards. Passenger names aren't collected and ferry staff don't even take a head count after loading. The number of passengers is only roughly determined by the number of tickets sold. Thus, the initial reports from BC Ferries that all passengers and crew survived were based on the simple belief that everyone had been evacuated. Demands for explanations of what had gone wrong arose.

The regional director of communications for Transport Canada (a governmental agency) reported the *Queen of the North* passed an annual safety inspection less than 3 weeks earlier, including a lifeboat drill that required passengers be evacuated in less than 30 minutes. "They did very well at it and they obviously did very well when it happened for real," he said.

The internal investigation BC Ferries conducted after the incident concluded that "human factors were the primary cause" of what happened. During the investigation, crew members responsible for navigating the ship that night claimed that they were unfamiliar with newly installed steering equipment. In addition, they had turned off a monitor displaying their course, because they could not turn on the night settings. The bridge crew used the equipment "in a way different than as instructed," the report noted, although this was not cited as a cause of running the boat aground. The report also concluded that the crew maintained a "casual watch-standing behavior," had "lost situational awareness," and "failed to appreciate the vessel's impending peril." Transcripts of radio calls that evening noted that music was heard playing on the bridge.

Regarding the evacuation, though the crew was praised for acting quickly, several things made the evacuation more difficult than need be. There was no master key to the sleeping cabins; rather multiple keys had to be tried. A chalk X is supposed to be drawn on searched cabin doors, but no one had chalk. As well, only 53 of the 55 cabins were confirmed to have been searched.

Discussion Questions

1. Describe the type(s) of control that could be used to improve the BC Ferries service to prevent an accident such as this occurring again. Be specific.

2. Assume that you are the president of BC Ferries. You have read the report of the investigation and noted some of the problems found. What would you do? Explain your reasoning.

3. Would some types of controls be more important than others in this situation? Discuss.

Sources: Based on "Union Will Defend Fired Ferry Workers," *Kamloops Daily News*, May 7, 2007, p. A5; C. Montgomery and I. Austin, "Human Error Is Faulted for Ship Sinking," *Province* (Vancouver), March 27, 2007, p. A6; C. E. Harnett, "Human Error Sank B.C. Ferry," *Calgary Herald*, March 27, 2007, p. A5; C. E. Harnett, "Ferry Brass," *Times Colonist* (Victoria), June 6, 2006, p. A3; C. Montgomery, "Loose Manifest Rules Led to Miscount," *Province* (Vancouver), March 28, 2006, p. A4; E. Baron and E. O'Connor, "Why So Far Off Course?" *Province* (Vancouver), March 23, 2006, p. A3; and W. Boei, M. Bridge, and L. Pynn, "99 Escape After Ship Runs Aground, Slides into Depths," *Vancouver Sun*, March 23, 2006, p. A1.

14

Operations Management

learning outcomes

14.1 Define operations management and explain its role. p.374

14.4 Discuss contemporary issues in managing operations. p.385

14.3 Describe how value chain management is done. p.380

14.2 Define the nature and purpose of value chain management. p.377

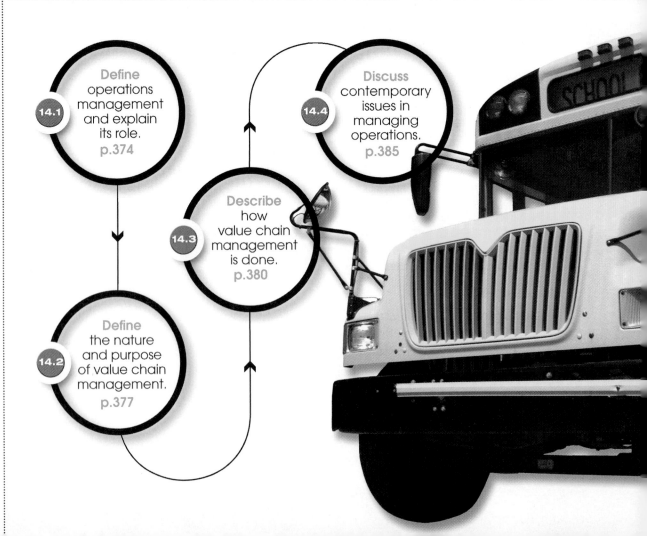

Smooth Ride

Big yellow school buses. They're a common sight at the beginning and ending of the school day in many communities. One company that manufactures those school buses is Blue Bird North Georgia.[1] School buses are a product where quality is paramount. After all, that product is carrying precious cargo! However, achieving an organizational culture that's dedicated to quality and to efficient manufacturing isn't an easy thing to do.

Blue Bird's plant in Lafayette, Georgia, started on its "lean" journey—that is, having a lean, efficient operations system—in 2003. The manager of engineering said at that time, "Quality was at an all-time low. The plant was lacking in strategic systems and procedures to control quality, materials, production, finance and human resources." That year under new management, Blue Bird got serious about tackling its quality issues and implemented specific programs including a material review board that evaluates and monitors materials usage; a quality control lab equipped with a computerized maintenance management system; an employee suggestion system; weekly management roundtable meetings; and a safety incentive program. One key contributor to the company's success is measurement. They're determined to measure everything. The facility's production manager said, "If you don't measure something, you don't know how well you're doing."

Just how effective have these programs been? Pretty effective! The customer reject rate is basically zero, with on-time delivery at 100 percent. The director of quality and risk management said, "Doing it right the first time takes a lot less time." Safety has also improved. The company's recordable injury rate was down 65 percent, and time lost due to injuries was down by 87 percent. After four years of hard work, the company achieved initial ISO 9001-2000 certification in March 2007. In addition, the facility was named one of *Industry Week's* Best Plants for three years running.

Every organization produces something, whether it's a good or a service. Technology has completely changed how this is done. This chapter focuses on how organizations do that through a process called *operations management*. We also look at the important role that managers play in managing those operations.

Why Is Operations Management Important to Organizations?

14.1 Define operations management and explain its role.

You've probably never given much thought to how organizations "produce" the goods and services that you buy or use. But it's an important process. Without it, you wouldn't have a car to drive or McDonald's fries to snack on, or even a hiking trail in a local park to enjoy. Organizations need to have well-thought-out and well-designed operating systems, organizational control systems, and quality programs to survive in today's increasingly competitive global environment. And it's the manager's job to manage those things.

What Is Operations Management?

The term **operations management** refers to the design, operation, and control of the transformation process that converts such resources as labor and raw materials into goods and services that are sold to customers. Exhibit 14-1 portrays a simplified overview of the transformation process of creating value by converting inputs into outputs. The system takes inputs—people, technology, equipment, materials, and information—and transforms them through various processes, procedures, and work activities into finished goods and services. These processes, procedures, and work activities are found throughout the organization. For example, department members in marketing, finance, research and development, human resources, and accounting convert inputs into outputs such as sales, increased market share, high rates of return on investments, new and innovative products, motivated and committed employees, and accounting reports. As a manager, you'll need to be familiar with operations management concepts, regardless of the area in which you're managing, in order to achieve your goals more effectively and efficiently.

Why is operations management so important to organizations and managers? First, it encompasses processes in all organizations—services as well as manufacturing. Second, it's important in effectively and efficiently managing productivity. And third, it plays a strategic role in an organization's competitive success. Let's look more closely at each of these.

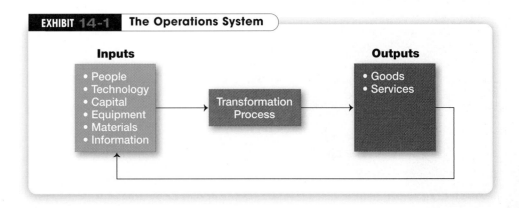

EXHIBIT 14-1   The Operations System

Inputs
- People
- Technology
- Capital
- Equipment
- Materials
- Information

Transformation Process

Outputs
- Goods
- Services

How Do Service and Manufacturing Firms Differ?

With a menu that offers over 200 items, The Cheesecake Factory restaurants rely on a finely tuned production system. One food-service consultant says, "They've evolved with this highly complex menu combined with a highly efficient kitchen."[2]

All organizations produce goods or services through the **transformation process**. Simply stated, every organization has an operations system that creates value by transforming inputs into finished goods and services outputs. For manufacturers, the products are obvious: cars, cell phones, or food products. After all, **manufacturing organizations** produce physical goods. It's easy to see the operations management (transformation) process at work in these types of organizations because raw materials are turned into recognizable physical products. But that transformation process isn't as readily evident in **service organizations** because they produce nonphysical outputs in the form of services. For instance, hospitals provide medical and health care services that help people manage their personal health; taxi companies provide transportation services that move people from one location to another; cruise lines provide vacation and entertainment services; and residential plumbers and electricians ensure that we have electricity and running water where we live. All of these service organizations transform inputs into outputs. For example, look at your college. College administrators bring together inputs—instructors, books, academic journals, multimedia classrooms, and similar resources—to transform "unenlightened" students into educated and skilled individuals.

The reason we're making this point is that the U.S. economy, and to a large extent the global economy, is dominated by the creation and sale of services. Most of the world's developed countries are predominantly service economies. In the United States, for instance, over 79 percent of all economic activity is services, and in the European Union, it's over 71 percent.[3] In lesser-developed countries, the services sector is less important. For instance, in Nigeria, it accounts for only 31 percent of economic activity; in Laos, only 26.6 percent; and in Vietnam, 38.4 percent.[4]

How Do Businesses Improve Productivity?

One jetliner has some 4 million parts. Efficiently assembling such a finely engineered product requires intense focus. Boeing and Airbus, the two major global manufacturers, have copied techniques from Toyota. However, not every technique can be copied because airlines demand more customization than do car buyers, and there are significantly more rigid safety regulations for jetliners than for cars.[5] At the Evans Findings Company in East Providence, Rhode Island, which makes the tiny cutting devices on dental-floss containers, one production shift each day is run without people.[6] The company's goal is to do as much as possible with no labor. And it's not because they don't care about their employees. Instead, like many U.S. manufacturers, Evans needed to improve productivity in order to survive, especially against low-cost competitors. So they turned to "lights-out" manufacturing where machines are designed to be so reliable that they make flawless parts on their own, without people operating them.

Although most organizations don't make products that have 4 million parts and most organizations can't function without people, improving productivity has become a major goal in virtually every organization. For countries, high productivity can lead to economic growth and development. Employees can receive higher wages and company profits

At Mutual of Omaha, employees spend part of their workday walking on a treadmill desk while answering customer calls. Installing treadmills in the workplace is a corporate wellness initiative that improves employees' fitness, increases their energy, and relieves stress. For employers, giving workers the opportunity to exercise during work hours results in increased employee productivity, lower employee absenteeism, and reduced health care costs. An obese employee can cost a company 20 to 40 percent more than an average-weight person, adding on average $9,000 each year for obesity-related employee health care. Walking while working can significantly help in reducing these costs.

operations management
The study and application of the transformation process.

transformation process
The process that converts resources into finished goods and services.

manufacturing organizations
Organizations that produce physical goods.

service organizations
Organizations that produce nonphysical products in the form of services.

can increase without causing inflation. For individual organizations, increased productivity gives them a more competitive cost structure and the ability to offer more competitive prices.

Over the past decade, U.S. businesses have made dramatic improvements to increase their efficiency. For example, at Latex Foam International's state-of-the-art digital facility in Shelton, Connecticut, engineers monitor all the factory's operations. The facility boosted capacity by 50 percent in a smaller space and achieved a 30 percent efficiency gain.[7] And it's not just in manufacturing that companies are pursuing productivity gains. Pella Corporation's purchasing office improved productivity by reducing purchase order entry times anywhere from 50 percent to 86 percent, decreasing voucher processing by 27 percent, and eliminating 14 financial systems. Its information technology department slashed e-mail traffic in half and implemented work design improvements for heavy PC users such as call center users. The human resources department cut the time to process benefit enrollment by 156.5 days. And the finance department now takes 2 days, instead of 6, to do its end-of-month closeout.[8]

Organizations that hope to succeed globally are looking for ways to improve productivity. For example, McDonald's Corporation drastically reduced the time it takes to cook its french fries—65 seconds as compared to the 210 seconds it once took, saving time and other resources.[9] The Canadian Imperial Bank of Commerce, based in Toronto, automated its purchasing function, saving several million dollars annually.[10] And Skoda, the Czech car company owned by Germany's Volkswagen AG, improved its productivity through an intensive restructuring of its manufacturing process.[11]

Productivity is a composite of people and operations variables. To improve productivity, managers must focus on both. The late W. Edwards Deming, a renowned quality expert, believed that managers, not workers, were the primary source of increased productivity. He outlined 14 points for improving management's productivity (see the "From the Past to the Present" box for more information). A close look at these suggestions reveals Deming's understanding of the interplay between people and operations. High productivity can't come solely from good "people management." The truly effective organization will maximize

From the Past to the Present

William Edwards Deming was an American statistician, professor, author, lecturer, and consultant.[12] He is widely credited with improving production in the United States during World War II, although he's probably best known for his work in Japan. From 1950 onward, he taught Japanese top managers how to improve product design, product quality, testing, and sales, primarily through applying statistical methods. His philosophy has been summarized as follows: "Dr. W. Edwards Deming taught that by adopting appropriate principles of management, organizations can increase quality and simultaneously reduce costs (by reducing waste, rework, staff attrition and litigation while increasing customer loyalty). The key is to practice continual improvement and think of manufacturing as a system, not as bits and pieces."

Putting that philosophy into practice required following Deming's 14 points for improving management's productivity. These suggestions are as follows:

▶ Plan for the long-term future.
▶ Never be complacent concerning the quality of your product.

▶ Establish statistical control over your production processes and require your suppliers to do so as well.
▶ Deal with the best and fewest number of suppliers.
▶ Find out whether your problems are confined to particular parts of the production process or stem from the overall process itself.
▶ Train workers for the job that you are asking them to perform.
▶ Raise the quality of your line supervisors.
▶ Drive out fear.
▶ Encourage departments to work closely together rather than to concentrate on departmental or divisional distinctions.
▶ Do not adopt strictly numerical goals.
▶ Require your workers to do quality work.
▶ Train your employees to understand statistical methods.
▶ Train your employees in new skills as the need arises.
▶ Make top managers responsible for implementing these principles.

These principles have withstood the test of time and are still applicable for managers looking to improve productivity.

productivity by successfully integrating people into the overall operations system. For instance, at Simplex Nails Manufacturing in Americus, Georgia, employees were an integral part of the company's much-needed turnaround effort.[13] Some production workers were redeployed on a plant-wide clean-up and organization effort, which freed up floor space. The company's sales force was retrained and refocused to sell what customers wanted rather than what was in inventory. The results were dramatic. Inventory was reduced by more than 50 percent, the plant had 20 percent more floor space, orders were more consistent, and employee morale improved. Here's a company that understood the important interplay between people and the operations system.

What Role Does Operations Management Play in a Company's Strategy?

Modern manufacturing originated over 100 years ago in the United States, primarily in Detroit's automobile factories. The success that U.S. manufacturers experienced during World War II led manufacturing executives to believe that troublesome production problems had been conquered. Instead, these executives focused on improving other functional areas such as finance and marketing, and paid little attention to manufacturing.

However, as U.S. executives neglected production, managers in Japan, Germany, and other countries took the opportunity to develop modern, technologically advanced facilities that fully integrated manufacturing operations into strategic planning decisions. The competition's success realigned world manufacturing leadership. U.S. manufacturers soon discovered that foreign goods were being made not only less expensively but also with better quality. Finally, by the late 1970s, U.S. executives recognized that they were facing a true crisis and responded. They invested heavily in improving manufacturing technology, increased the corporate authority and visibility of manufacturing executives, and began incorporating existing and future production requirements into the organization's overall strategic plan. Today, successful organizations recognize the crucial role that operations management plays as part of the overall organizational strategy to establish and maintain global leadership.[14]

The strategic role that operations management plays in successful organizational performance can be seen clearly as more organizations move toward managing their operations from a value chain perspective, which we're going to discuss next.

What Is Value Chain Management and Why Is It Important?

Define the nature and purpose of value chain management. **14.2**

It's 11 P.M., and you're reading a text message from your parents saying they want to buy you a laptop for your birthday this year and to order it. You log on to Dell's Web site and configure your dream machine. You hit the order button and within three or four days, your dream computer is delivered to your front door, built to your exact specifications, ready to set up and use immediately to type that management assignment due tomorrow. Or consider Siemens AG's Computed Tomography manufacturing plant in Forcheim, Germany, which has established partnerships with about 30 suppliers. These suppliers are partners in the truest sense as they share responsibility with the plant for overall process performance. This arrangement has allowed Siemens to eliminate all inventory warehousing and streamlined the number of times paper changes hands to order parts from 18 to 1. At the Timken's plant in Canton, Ohio, electronic purchase orders are sent across the street to an adjacent "Supplier City" where many of its key suppliers have set up shop. The process takes milliseconds and costs less than 50 cents per purchase order. And when Black & Decker extended its line of handheld tools to include a glue gun, it totally outsourced the entire design and production to the leading glue gun manufacturer. Why? Because they understood that glue guns don't require motors, which was what Black & Decker did best.[15]

As these examples show, closely integrated work activities among many different players are possible. How? The answer lies in value chain management. The concepts of value chain management have transformed operations management strategies and turned organizations around the world into finely tuned models of efficiency and effectiveness strategically positioned to exploit competitive opportunities.

What Is Value Chain Management?

Every organization needs customers if it's going to survive and prosper. Even a not-for-profit organization must have "customers" who use its services or purchase its products. Customers want some type of value from the goods and services they purchase or use, and these customers decide what has value. Organizations must provide that value to attract and keep customers. **Value** is defined as the performance characteristics, features and attributes, and any other aspects of goods and services for which customers are willing to give up resources (usually money). For example, when you purchase Rihanna's new CD at Best Buy, a new pair of Australian sheepskin Ugg boots online at the company's Web site, a Wendy's bacon cheeseburger at the drive-through location on campus, or a haircut from your local hair salon, you're exchanging (giving up) money in return for the value you need or desire from these products—providing music during your evening study time, keeping your feet warm *and* fashionable during winter's cold weather, alleviating the lunchtime hunger pangs quickly since your next class starts in 15 minutes, or looking professionally groomed for the job interview you've got next week.

How *is* value provided to customers? Through transforming raw materials and other resources into some product or service that end users need or desire when, where, and how they want it. However, that seemingly simple act of turning varied resources into something that customers value and are willing to pay for involves a vast array of interrelated work activities performed by different participants (suppliers, manufacturers, and even customers)—that is, it involves the value chain. The **value chain** is the entire series of organizational work activities that add value at each step from raw materials to finished product. In its entirety, the value chain can encompass the supplier's suppliers to the customer's customer.[16]

Value chain management is the process of managing the sequence of activities and information along the entire value chain. In contrast to supply chain management, which is *internally* oriented and focuses on efficient flow of incoming materials (resources) to the organization, value chain management is *externally* oriented and focuses on both incoming materials and outgoing products and services. Although supply chain management is

Jibun Bank in Japan provides value to customers through a service that they desire when, where, and how they want it. Jibun, which means "personal" in Japanese, is the first bank in the world to use the mobile phone as a primary access channel. It offers customers the entire lifecycle of banking services, from account opening to account closure. Services include standard transactions such as deposits and funds transfers and more complex bank offerings such as foreign currency deposits, loans, and e-shopping payments. In this photo a customer is learning about Jibun's customized approach to her individual banking needs and how the bank's services are accessible to her anywhere and anytime.

efficiency oriented (its goal is to reduce costs and make the organization more productive), value chain management is effectiveness oriented and aims to create the highest value for customers.[17]

What Are the Goals of Value Chain Management?

Who has the power in the value chain? Is it the supplier providing needed resources and materials? After all, suppliers have the ability to dictate prices and quality. Is it the manufacturer that assembles those resources into a valuable product or service? A manufacturer's contribution in creating a product or service is quite obvious. Is it the distributor that makes sure the product or service is available where and when the customer needs it? Actually, it's none of these. In value chain management, ultimately customers are the ones with the power.[18] They're the ones who define what value is and how it's created and provided. Using value chain management, managers seek to find that unique combination in which customers are offered solutions that truly meet their needs and at a price that can't be matched by competitors.[19] For example, in an effort to better anticipate customer demand and replenish customer stocks, Shell Chemical Company developed a supplier inventory management order network. The software used in this network allows managers to track shipment status, calculate safety stock levels, and prepare resupply schedules.[20] With this capability Shell Chemical enables its customers to purchase goods when desired and to receive them immediately.

A good value chain is one in which a sequence of participants works together as a team, each adding some component of value—such as faster assembly, more accurate information, or better customer response and service—to the overall process.[21] The better the collaboration among the various chain participants, the better the customer solutions. When value is created for customers and their needs and desires are satisfied, everyone along the chain benefits. For example, at Iomega Corporation, a manufacturer of personal computer storage devices, managing the value chain started first with improved relationships with internal suppliers, then expanded out to external suppliers and customers. As the company's experience with value chain management intensified and improved, so did its connection to customers, which ultimately paid off for all its value chain partners.[22]

How Does Value Chain Management Benefit Businesses?

Collaborating with external and internal partners in creating and managing a successful value chain strategy requires significant investments in time, energy, and other resources, and a serious commitment by all chain partners. Given this, why would managers ever choose to implement value chain management? A survey of manufacturers noted four primary benefits of value chain management: improved procurement, improved logistics, improved product development, and enhanced customer order management.[23]

Right or Wrong?

What happens when one partner in a value chain wields its power and makes significant demands?[24] For example, Wal-Mart required all its major suppliers to have RFID (radio frequency identification) tags installed on all their products. In doing so, Wal-Mart hoped to save more than $8 billion annually by reducing theft and stocking out of items. But it's costing each supplier up to $23 million to meet this demand. What do you think? Is this ethical? Why or why not?

---

value
The performance characteristics, features, attributes, and other aspects of goods and services, for which customers are willing to give up resources.

value chain
The entire series of work activities that add value at each step from raw materials to finished product.

value chain management
The process of managing the sequence of activities and information along the entire value chain.

How Is Value Chain Management Done?

14.3 Describe how value chain management is done.

The dynamic, competitive environment facing contemporary global organizations demands new solutions.[25] Understanding how and why value is determined by the marketplace has led some organizations to experiment with a new **business model**—that is, a strategic design for how a company intends to profit from its broad array of strategies, processes, and activities. For example, IKEA, the home furnishings manufacturer, transformed itself from a small, Swedish mail-order furniture operation into the world's largest retailer of home furnishings by reinventing the value chain in the home furnishings industry. The company offers customers well-designed products at substantially lower prices in return for the customers' willingness to take on certain key tasks traditionally done by manufacturers and retailers—such as getting the furniture home and assembling it.[26] The company's adoption of a unique business model and willingness to abandon old methods and processes have worked well. And, it also helped that IKEA recognized the importance of managing its value chain.

What Are the Requirements for Successful Value Chain Management?

So what does successful value chain management require? Exhibit 14-2 summarizes the six main requirements: coordination and collaboration, technology investment, organizational processes, leadership, employees/human resources, and organizational culture and attitudes. Let's look at each of these elements more closely.

COORDINATION AND COLLABORATION. For the value chain to achieve its goal of meeting and exceeding customers' needs and desires, comprehensive and seamless integration among all members of the chain is absolutely necessary. All partners in the value chain must identify things that they may not value but that customers do. Sharing information and being flexible as far as who in the value chain does what are important steps in building coordination and collaboration (see the "Developing Your Collaboration Skill" box). This sharing of information and analysis requires open communication among the various value chain partners. For example, Furon Company, a manufacturer of specialty polymer products, believes that better communication with customers and

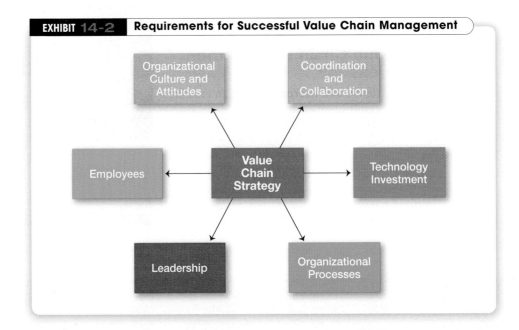

EXHIBIT 14-2 **Requirements for Successful Value Chain Management**

Developing Your *Collaboration* Skill

About the Skill

Collaboration is the teamwork, synergy, and cooperation used by individuals when they seek a common goal. Given that value chain management is contingent on all partners working together, collaboration is critically important to the process.

Steps in Practicing the Skill

1 **Look for common points of interest.** The best way to start working together in a collaborative fashion is to seek commonalities that exist among the parties. Common points of interest enable communications to be more effective.

2 **Listen to others.** Collaboration is a team effort. Everyone has valid points to offer, and each individual should have an opportunity to express his or her ideas.

3 **Check for understanding.** Make sure you understand what the other person is saying. Use feedback when necessary.

4 **Accept diversity.** Not everything in a collaborative effort will "go your way." Be willing to accept different ideas and different ways of doing things. Be open to these ideas and the creativity that surrounds them.

5 **Seek additional information.** Ask individuals to provide additional information. Encourage others to talk and more fully explain suggestions. This brainstorming opportunity can assist in finding creative solutions.

6 **Don't become defensive.** Collaboration requires open communications. Discussions may focus on things you and others may not be doing or need to do better. Don't take the constructive feedback as personal criticism. Focus on the topic being discussed, not on the person delivering the message. Recognize that you cannot always be right!

Practicing the Skill

Interview managers from three different organizations about how they collaborate with others. What specific tips have they discovered for effectively collaborating with others? What problems have they encountered when collaborating? How have they dealt with these problems?

---

with suppliers has facilitated timely delivery of goods and services and opened up additional business opportunities for all its value chain partners.[27]

TECHNOLOGY INVESTMENT. Successful value chain management isn't possible without a significant investment in information technology. The payoff from this investment is that information technology can be used to restructure the value chain to better serve end users.[28] For example, Rollerblade, Inc., invested significant amounts of dollars in developing a Web site and used it to educate customers about its products. Although the company has chosen not to sell its products over the Web for fear of antagonizing its dealer network, managers remain flexible about the issue and would reconsider if they felt that value could be better delivered to customers by doing so.[29]

What types of technology are important? According to experts, the key tools include a supporting enterprise resource planning (ERP) software system that links all of an organization's activities, sophisticated work planning and scheduling software, customer relationship management systems, business intelligence capabilities, and e-business connections with trading network partners.[30] For instance, Dell Inc. manages its supplier relationships almost exclusively online. The company has one Web site for customers and one for suppliers. The supplier Web site is the primary mode of communication between Dell and its largest suppliers. The company's investment in this type of information technology allows it to meet customers' needs in a way that competitors haven't been able to match.[31]

business model
A strategic design for how a company intends to profit from its broad array of strategies, processes, and activities.

ORGANIZATIONAL PROCESSES. Value chain management radically changes **organizational processes**—that is, the way organizational work is done.[32] Managers must critically evaluate all organizational processes from beginning to end by looking at core competencies—the organization's unique skills, capabilities, and resources—to determine where value is being added. Nonvalue-adding activities are eliminated. Questions such as "Where can internal knowledge be leveraged to improve flow of material and information?" "How can we better configure our product to satisfy both customers and suppliers?" "How can the flow of material and information be improved?" and "How can we improve customer service?" should be asked for each process. For example, when managers at Deere & Company implemented value chain management in its Worldwide Commercial and Consumer Equipment Division, a thorough process evaluation revealed that work activities needed to be better synchronized and interrelationships between multiple links in the value chain better managed. They changed numerous work processes division-wide in order to improve these relationships.[33]

Three important conclusions can be made about how organizational processes must change. First, better demand forecasting is necessary and possible because of closer ties with customers and suppliers. For example, in an effort to make sure that Listerine was on the store shelves when customers wanted it, Wal-Mart collaborated with product manufacturer Pfizer Consumer Healthcare on improving product demand forecast information. Through their mutual efforts, the partners boosted Wal-Mart's sales of Listerine by $6.5 million. Customers also benefited because they were able to purchase the product when and where they wanted it.

Second, selected functions may need to be done collaboratively with other partners in the value chain. This collaboration may even extend to sharing employees. For instance, Saint-Gobain Performance Plastics, headquartered in Northboro, Massachusetts, places its own employees in customer sites and brings employees of suppliers and customers to work on its premises. Saint-Gobain's CEO says this type of collaboration is essential if an organization wants to "go from being a mere component supplier to being a solutions provider."[34]

Finally, new measures are needed for evaluating the performance of various activities along the value chain. Because the goal in value chain management is meeting and exceeding customers' needs and desires, managers need a better picture of how well value is being created and delivered to customers. For instance, when Nestlé USA implemented a value chain management approach, it redesigned its measurement system to focus on one consistent set of factors, including accuracy of demand forecasts and production plans, on-time delivery, and customer service levels. This redesign allowed management to more quickly identify problems and take actions to resolve them.[36]

LEADERSHIP. The importance of leadership to value chain management is plain and simple—successful value chain management isn't possible without strong and committed leadership.[37] From top organizational levels to lower levels, managers must support, facilitate, and promote the implementation and ongoing practice of value chain management. J. Michael Hagan, CEO of Furon Company, describes his role as follows: "Value is a mind-set that not only has to be driven from the top down, but also from the bottom up. Everyone has to be asking whether a given task adds value, and if it doesn't why do it."[38] Managers must make a serious commitment to identifying what value is, how that value can best be provided, and how successful those efforts have been. That type of organizational atmosphere or culture in which all efforts are focused on delivering superb customer value isn't possible without a serious commitment on the part of the organization's leaders.

Also, it's important that leaders outline expectations for what's involved in the organization's pursuit of value chain management. Ideally, articulating expectations should start with a vision or mission statement that expresses the organization's commitment to identifying, capturing, and providing the highest possible value to customers. For example, when American Standard Companies began its pursuit of value chain management, the CEO attended dozens of meetings across the country explaining the changing competitive environment and why the company needed to create better working relationships with its value chain partners.[39] Throughout the organization, then, managers should clarify expectations regarding each employee's role in the value chain. Being clear about expectations also extends to partners. For example, managers at American Standard identified clear requirements for suppliers and were prepared to drop any that couldn't meet them. The company was so serious about its expectations that it did cut hundreds of suppliers from air conditioning, bath and kitchen, and vehicle control systems businesses. The upside, though, was that those suppliers that met the expectations benefited from more business and American Standard had partners that could deliver better value to customers.

EMPLOYEES/HUMAN RESOURCES. We know from our discussions of management theories and approaches throughout this textbook that employees are the organization's most important resource. So, not surprisingly, employees play an important part in value chain management. Three main human resources requirements for value chain management are flexible approaches to job design, an effective hiring process, and ongoing training.

Flexibility is the key description of job design in a value chain management organization. Traditional functional job roles—such as marketing, sales, accounts payable, customer service, and so forth—are inadequate in a value chain management environment. Instead, jobs need to be designed around work processes that link all functions involved in creating and providing value to customers. This type of flexible job design supports the company's commitment to providing superb customer value.[40] In designing jobs for a value chain approach, the focus needs to be on how each activity performed by an employee can best contribute to the creation and delivery of customer value, which requires flexibility in what employees do and how they do it.

The fact that jobs in a value chain management organization must be flexible contributes to the second requirement: Flexible jobs require employees who are flexible. In a value chain organization, employees may be assigned to work teams that tackle a given process and are often asked to do different things on different days, depending on need. In an environment focusing on collaborative relationships that may change as customer

Employees play an important part in Apple's value chain that focuses on satisfying customer needs. Apple retail stores hire people who are flexible, can quickly learn and adapt, and are passionate about the iPods, iPhones, computers, and other products they sell. Training programs focus on teaching employees how to work together in a collaborative environment that makes customers feel comfortable. Employees are also trained in Apple's approach to selling, which requires that they are sharers of information rather than just sellers of products so customers' shopping experience is one of learning as well as buying. Ongoing training keeps employees up to date on the latest Apple and third-party products so they can give customers expert technical advice.

organizational processes
The way organizational work is done.

needs change, employees' ability to be flexible is critical. Accordingly, the organization's hiring process must be designed to identify those employees who have the ability to quickly learn and adapt.

Finally, the need for flexibility also requires a significant investment in ongoing employee training. Whether the training involves learning how to use information technology software, how to improve the flow of materials throughout the chain, how to identify activities that add value, how to make better decisions faster, or how to improve any number of other potential work activities, managers must see to it that employees have the knowledge and tools they need to do their jobs. For example, at defense and electronics contractor Alenia Marconi Systems, based in Portsmouth, England, ongoing training is part of the company's commitment to efficiently and effectively meet the needs of customers. Employees continually receive technical training as well as training in strategic issues including the importance of emphasizing people and customers, not just sales and profits.[41]

ORGANIZATIONAL CULTURE AND ATTITUDES. The last requirement for value chain management is having a supportive organizational culture and attitudes. Those cultural attitudes include sharing, collaborating, openness, flexibility, mutual respect, and trust. And these attitudes encompass not only the internal partners in the value chain but external partners as well. For instance, American Standard has chosen to practice these attitudes the old-fashioned way—with lots of face time and telephone calls. One of the company's suppliers, St. Louis–based White Rogers, described their relationship as follows: "Their goals are our goals, because both companies focus on growth. The keys to the relationship are mutual respect and open communications at all levels. No one has to go through a liaison. If our engineers need to talk to theirs, we just go right to the source."[42] However, as we mentioned earlier, Dell has taken a completely different approach, as it works with its value chain partners almost exclusively through cyberspace.[43] Both approaches, however, reflect each company's commitment to developing long-lasting, mutually beneficial, and trusting relationships that best meet customers' needs.

What Are the Obstacles to Value Chain Management?

As desirable as value chain management may be, managers must tackle several obstacles in managing the value chain including organizational barriers, cultural attitudes, required capabilities, and people (see Exhibit 14-3).

ORGANIZATIONAL BARRIERS. Organizational barriers are among the most difficult obstacles to handle. These barriers include refusal or reluctance to share information,

EXHIBIT 14-3   Obstacles to Successful Value Chain Management

Organizational Barriers

Cultural Attitudes

Obstacles to Value Chain Management

People

Required Capabilities

reluctance to shake up the status quo, and security issues. Without shared information, close coordination and collaboration is impossible. And the reluctance or refusal of employees to shake up the status quo can impede efforts toward value chain management and prevent its successful implementation. Finally, because value chain management relies heavily on a substantial information technology infrastructure, system security and Internet security breaches are issues that need to be addressed.

CULTURAL ATTITUDES. Unsupportive cultural attitudes—especially trust and control—also can be obstacles to value chain management. The trust issue is a critical one, both lack of trust and too much trust. To be effective, partners in a value chain must trust each other. There must be a mutual respect for, and honesty about, each partner's activities all along the chain. When that trust doesn't exist, the partners will be reluctant to share information, capabilities, and processes. But too much trust also can be a problem. Just about any organization is vulnerable to theft of intellectual property—that is, proprietary information that's critical to an organization's efficient and effective functioning and competitiveness. You need to be able to trust your value chain partners so your organization's valuable assets aren't compromised.[44] Another cultural attitude that can be an obstacle is the belief that when an organization collaborates with external and internal partners, it no longer controls its own destiny. However, this just isn't the case. Even with the intense collaboration that's important to value chain management, organizations still control critical decisions such as what customers value, how much value they desire, and what distribution channels are important.[45]

REQUIRED CAPABILITIES. We know from our earlier discussion of requirements for the successful implementation of value chain management that there are numerous capabilities value chain partners need. Several of these—coordination and collaboration, the ability to configure products to satisfy customers and suppliers, and the ability to educate internal and external partners—aren't easy. But they're essential to capturing and exploiting the value chain. Many of the companies we've described throughout this section endured critical, and oftentimes difficult, self-evaluations of their capabilities and processes in order to become more effective and efficient at managing their value chains.

PEOPLE. The final obstacles to successful value chain management can be an organization's people. Without their unwavering commitment to do whatever it takes, value chain management won't be successful. If employees refuse to be flexible in their work—how and with whom they work—collaboration and cooperation throughout the value chain will be hard to achieve. In addition, value chain management takes an incredible amount of time and energy on the part of an organization's employees. Managers must motivate those high levels of effort from employees, which isn't an easy thing to do.

What Contemporary Issues Do Managers Face in Managing Operations?

Redesigned milk jugs that have been adopted by Wal-Mart and Costco are cheaper to ship, better for the environment, cost less, and keep the milk fresher. Experts say this type of redesign is "an example of the changes likely to play out in the American economy over the next two decades. In an era of soaring global demand and higher costs for energy and materials, virtually every aspect of the economy needs to be re-examined and many products must be redesigned for greater efficiency."[46]

Discuss contemporary issues in managing operations. **14.4**

   If you somehow thought that managing operations didn't really matter in today's online 24/7 global economy, think again. It does matter . . . a lot. We're going to look at three contemporary issues that managers face in managing operations: technology's role in operations management, quality initiatives, and project management.

Implementing its strategy of becoming a market leader in environmental responsibility and energy management, McDonald's is using new technology for networking its restaurant kitchen equipment to lower energy consumption and to increase operational efficiency. The technology provides communication and data exchange between various pieces of kitchen equipment to allow for the development of process improvement applications, to manage energy use, and to reduce maintenance costs. It also enables McDonald's franchisees to create restaurants that are easier to operate, save energy, and offer new services.

What Role Does Technology Play in Operations Management?

As we know from our previous discussion of value chain management, today's competitive marketplace has put tremendous pressure on organizations to deliver products and services that customers value in a timely manner. Smart companies are looking at ways to harness technology to improve operations management. Many fast-food companies are competing to see who can provide faster and better service to drive-through customers. With drive-through now representing a huge portion of sales, faster and better delivery can be a significant competitive edge. For instance, Wendy's added awnings to some of its menu boards and replaced some of the text with pictures. Others use confirmation screens, a technology that helped McDonald's boost accuracy by more than 11 percent. And technology used by two national chains tells managers how much food they need to prepare by counting vehicles in the drive-through line and factoring in demand for current promotional and popular staple items.[47]

Although an organization's production activities are driven by the recognition that the customer is king, managers still need to be more responsive. For instance, operations managers need systems that can reveal available capacity, status of orders, and product quality while products are in the process of being manufactured, not just after the fact. To connect more closely with customers, production must be synchronized across the enterprise. To avoid bottlenecks and slowdowns, the production function must be a full partner in the entire business system.

What's making such extensive collaboration possible is technology. Technology is also allowing organizations to control costs particularly in the areas of predictive maintenance, remote diagnostics, and utility cost savings. For instance, Internet-compatible equipment contains embedded Web servers that can communicate proactively—that is, if a piece of equipment breaks or reaches certain preset parameters indicating that it's about to break, it asks for help. But technology can do more than sound an alarm or light up an indicator button. For instance, some devices have the ability to initiate e-mail or signal a pager at a supplier, the maintenance department, or contractor describing the specific problem and requesting parts and service. How much is such e-enabled maintenance control worth? It can be worth quite a lot if it prevents equipment breakdowns and subsequent production downtime.

Managers who understand the power of technology to contribute to more effective and efficient performance know that managing operations is more than the traditional view of simply producing the product. Instead, the emphasis is on working together with all the organization's business functions to find solutions to customers' business problems. (See the "Technology and the Manager's Job" box for more information on technology's role in the factory of the future.)

How Do Managers Control Quality?

Quality problems are expensive. For example, even though Apple has had phenomenal success with its iPod, the batteries in the first three versions died after 4 hours instead of lasting up to 12 hours, as buyers expected. Apple's settlement with consumers cost close to $100 million. At Schering-Plough, problems with inhalers and other pharmaceuticals were traced to chronic quality control shortcomings, for which the company eventually paid a $500 million fine. And the auto industry paid $14.5 billion to cover the cost of warranty and repair work in one year.[48]

Many experts believe that organizations unable to produce high-quality products won't be able to compete successfully in the global marketplace. What is quality? When you consider a product or service to have quality, what does that mean? Does it mean that the

WELCOME TO THE FACTORY OF THE FUTURE!

What would the ideal factory of the future look like?[49] Experts at Georgia Tech's Manufacturing Research Center say that three important trends are driving what tomorrow's factories will look like. One trend is *globalization of the supply chain.* In the factories of the future, design and business processes will be performed where it's most efficient and effective to do so. For example, parts for Boeing's 787 Dreamliner are produced around the world and then come together in Boeing's U.S. facilities. The second trend is *technology that simultaneously dematerializes the product while vastly increasing complexity.* The challenge for managing operations is that despite simplicity in products, the production process is becoming more complex. The third trend is *demographics and the impact on demand patterns.* Products will have shorter life cycles and more variety and choices. "The challenge is for the future factory to be both adaptable over many different product lifecycles and flexible with regard to the number of different products being produced in the same time frame."

Given these trends, it's clear that technology will continue to play a key role in transformation processes that need to be collaborative, adaptive, flexible, and responsive. But keep in mind that technology is simply a tool. Future factories will also require a talented and skilled workforce and a clear understanding of managing operations processes. Those are the challenges facing managers who want their organizations to survive and thrive.

product doesn't break or quit working—that is, that it's reliable? Does it mean that the service is delivered in a way that you intended? Does it mean that the product does what it's supposed to do? Or does quality mean something else? Exhibit 14-4 provides a description of several quality dimensions. We're going to define quality as the ability of a product or service to reliably do what it's supposed to do and to satisfy customer expectations.

HOW IS QUALITY ACHIEVED? How quality is achieved is an issue managers must address. A good way to look at quality initiatives is with the management functions—planning, organizing and leading, and controlling—that need to take place.

EXHIBIT 14-4 **What Is Quality?**

Product Quality Dimensions

1. Performance—Operating characteristics
2. Features—Important special characteristics
3. Flexibility—Meeting operating specifications over some period of time
4. Durability—Amount of use before performance deteriorates
5. Conformance—Match with preestablished standards
6. Serviceability—Ease and speed of repair or normal service
7. Aesthetics—How a product looks and feels
8. Perceived quality—Subjective assessment of characteristics (product image)

Service Quality Dimensions

1. Timeliness—Performed in promised period of time
2. Courtesy—Performed cheerfully
3. Consistency—Giving all customers similar experiences each time
4. Convenience—Accessibility to customers
5. Completeness—Full service, as required
6. Accuracy—Performed correctly each time

Sources: Based on J. W. Dean and J. R. Evans, *Total Quality: Management, Organization and Society* (St. Paul, MN: West Publishing Company, 1994); H. V. Roberts and B. F. Sergesketter, *Quality Is Personal* (New York: The Free Press, 1993); D. Garvin, *Managed Quality: The Strategic and Competitive Edge* (New York: The Free Press, 1988); and M. A. Hitt, R. D. Ireland, and R. E. Hoskisson, *Strategic Management,* 4th ed. (Cincinnati: South-Western Publishing, 2001), p. 121.

When *planning for quality,* managers must have quality improvement goals and strategies and plans to achieve those goals. Goals can help focus everyone's attention toward some objective quality standard. For instance, Caterpillar's goal is to apply quality improvement techniques to help cut costs.[50] Although this goal is specific and challenging, managers and employees are partnering together to pursue well-designed strategies to achieve the goals, and are confident they can do so.

When *organizing and leading for quality,* it's important for managers to look to their employees. For instance, at the Moosejaw, Saskatchewan, plant of General Cable Corporation, every employee participates in continual quality assurance training. In addition, the plant manager believes wholeheartedly in giving employees the information they need to do their jobs better. He says, "Giving people who are running the machines the information is just paramount. You can set up your cellular structure, you can cross-train your people, you can use lean tools, but if you don't give people information to drive improvement, there's no enthusiasm." Needless to say, this company shares production data and financial performance measures with all employees.[51]

Organizations with extensive and successful quality improvement programs tend to rely on two important people approaches: cross-functional work teams and self-directed or empowered work teams. Because achieving product quality is something that all employees from upper to lower levels must participate in, it's not surprising that quality-driven organizations rely on well-trained, flexible, and empowered employees.

Finally, managers must recognize when *controlling for quality* that quality improvement initiatives aren't possible without having some way to monitor and evaluate their progress. Whether it involves standards for inventory control, defect rate, raw materials procurement, or other operations management areas, controlling for quality is important. For instance, at the Northrup Grumman Corporation plant in Rolling Meadows, Illinois, several quality controls have been implemented, such as automated testing and IT that integrates product design and manufacturing and tracks process quality improvements. Also, employees are empowered to make accept/reject decisions about products throughout the manufacturing process. The plant manager explains, "This approach helps build quality into the product rather than trying to inspect quality into the product." But one of the most important things they do is "go to war" with their customers—soldiers preparing for war or live combat situations. Again, the plant manager says, "What discriminates us is that we believe if we can understand our customer's mission as well as they do, we can help them be more effective. We don't wait for our customer to ask us to do something. We find out what our customer is trying to do and then we develop solutions."[52]

Quality improvement success stories can be found globally. For example, at a Delphi assembly plant in Matamoros, Mexico, employees worked hard to improve quality and made significant strides. For instance, the customer reject rate on shipped products is now 10 ppm (parts per million), down from 3,000 ppm—an improvement of almost 300 percent.[53] Quality initiatives at several Australian companies including Alcoa of Australia, Wormald Security, and Carlton and United Breweries have led to significant quality improvements.[54] At Valeo Klimasystemme GmbH of Bad Rodach, Germany, assembly teams build different climate-control systems for high-end German cars including Mercedes and BMW. Quality initiatives by those teams have led to significant improvements.[55]

WHAT QUALITY GOALS MIGHT ORGANIZATIONS PURSUE? To publicly demonstrate their commitment to quality, many organizations worldwide have pursued challenging quality goals. The two best-known are ISO 9000 and Six Sigma.

ISO 9000 is a series of international quality management standards established by the International Organization for Standardization (www.iso.org), which sets uniform guidelines for processes to ensure that products conform to customer requirements. These standards cover everything from contract review to product design to product delivery. The ISO 9000 standards have become the internationally recognized standard for evaluating and comparing companies in the global marketplace. In fact, this type of certification can be a prerequisite for doing business globally. Achieving ISO 9000 certification provides proof that a quality operations system is in place. The latest survey of ISO 9000 certificates—awarded in 175 countries—showed that the number of registered sites worldwide were over 900,000.[56]

Johnson Controls embraced Six Sigma in 2000 as a step toward fulfilling its mission of "exceeding customers' increasing expectations," and today it's an integral part of Johnson's culture of continuous quality improvement. The company deployed Six Sigma at its worldwide locations, including at the car-seat assembly plant in Beijing, China, shown here, and trained more than 2,000 employees in its techniques. Six Sigma gave Johnson Controls the methods and analytical tools to drive waste and costs out of its operating processes, generating more than $1 billion in savings as well as improving customer satisfaction and inventory management.

More than 30 years ago, Motorola popularized the use of stringent quality standards more through a trademarked quality improvement program called **Six Sigma**.[57] Very simply, Six Sigma is a quality standard that establishes a goal of no more than 3.4 defects per million units or procedures. What does the name mean? *Sigma* is the Greek letter that statisticians use to define a standard deviation from a bell curve. The higher the sigma, the fewer the deviations from the norm—that is, the fewer the defects. At One Sigma, two-thirds of whatever is being measured falls within the curve. Two Sigma covers about 95 percent. At Six Sigma, you're about as close to defect-free as you can get.[58] It's an ambitious quality goal! Although it's an extremely high standard to achieve, many quality-driven businesses are using it and benefiting from it. For instance, General Electric estimates that it has saved billions since 1995, according to company executives.[59] Other examples of companies pursuing Six Sigma include ITT Industries, Dow Chemical, 3M Company, American Express, Sony Corporation, Nokia Corporation, and Johnson & Johnson. Although manufacturers seem to make up the bulk of Six Sigma users, service companies such as financial institutions, retailers, and health care organizations are beginning to apply it. What impact can Six Sigma have? Let's look at an example.

It used to take Wellmark Blue Cross & Blue Shield, a managed-care health care company, 65 days or more to add a new doctor to its medical plans. Now, thanks to Six Sigma, the company discovered that half the processes they used were redundant. With those unnecessary steps gone, the job now gets done in 30 days or less and with reduced staff. The company also has been able to reduce its administrative expenses by $3 million per year, an amount passed on to consumers through lower health premiums.[60]

Although it's important for managers to recognize that many positive benefits come from obtaining ISO 9000 certification or Six Sigma, the key benefit comes from the quality improvement journey itself. In other words, the goal of quality certification should be having work processes and an operations system in place that enable organizations to meet customers' needs and employees to perform their jobs in a consistent high-quality way.

How Are Projects Managed?

As we discussed in Chapter 5, many organizations are structured around projects. A **project** is a one-time-only set of activities with a definite beginning and ending point.[61] Projects vary

ISO 9000
A series of international quality standards that set uniform guidelines for processes to ensure that products conform to customer requirements.

Six Sigma
A quality standard that establishes a goal of no more than 3.4 defects per million units or procedures.

project
A one-time-only set of activities with a definite beginning and ending point.

in size and scope, from a NASA space shuttle launch to a wedding. **Project management** is the task of getting the activities done on time, within budget, and according to specifications.

Project management has actually been around for a long time in industries such as construction and movie making, but now it has expanded into almost every type of business. What explains the growing popularity of project management? It fits well with a dynamic environment and the need for flexibility and rapid response. Organizations are increasingly undertaking projects that are somewhat unusual or unique, have specific deadlines, contain complex interrelated tasks requiring specialized skills, and are temporary in nature. These types of projects don't lend themselves well to the standardized operating procedures that guide routine and continuous organizational activities.[62]

In the typical project, team members are temporarily assigned to and report to a project manager, who coordinates the project's activities with other departments and reports directly to a senior executive. The project is temporary: It exists only long enough to complete its specific objectives. Then it's wound down and closed up; members move on to other projects, return to their permanent departments, or leave the organization.

WHAT ARE SOME POPULAR PROJECT SCHEDULING TOOLS? If you were to observe a group of supervisors or department managers for a few days, you would see them regularly detailing what activities have to be done, the order in which they are to be done, who is to do each, and when they are to be completed. The managers are doing what we call scheduling. The following discussion reviews some useful scheduling devices.

How do you use a Gantt chart? The **Gantt chart** is a planning tool developed around the turn of the century by Henry Gantt. The idea behind the Gantt chart is relatively simple. It's essentially a bar graph, with time on the horizontal axis and the activities to be scheduled on the vertical axis. The bars show output, both planned and actual, over a period of time. The Gantt chart visually shows when tasks are supposed to be done and compares the assigned date with the actual progress on each. This simple but important device allows managers to detail easily what has yet to be done to complete a job or project and to assess whether it's ahead of, behind, or on schedule.

Exhibit 14-5 shows a Gantt chart that was developed for book production by a manager in a publishing firm. Time is expressed in months across the top of the chart. Major activities are listed down the left side. The planning comes in deciding what activities need to be done to get the book finished, the order in which those activities need to be done, and the time that should be allocated to each activity. The green shading represents actual progress made in completing each activity.

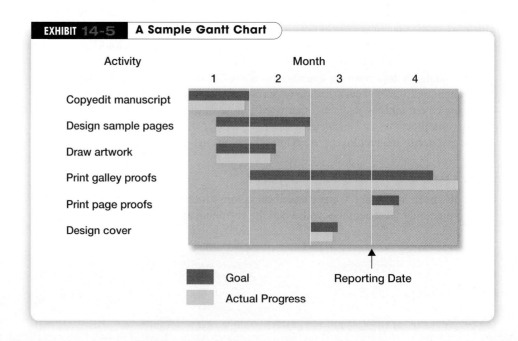

EXHIBIT 14-5   A Sample Gantt Chart

Activity	Month

Activities: Copyedit manuscript, Design sample pages, Draw artwork, Print galley proofs, Print page proofs, Design cover

Legend: ■ Goal   ■ Actual Progress   ↑ Reporting Date

A Gantt chart, then, actually becomes a managerial control device as the manager looks for deviations from the plan. In this case, most activities were completed on time. However, if you look at the "print galley proofs" activity, you will notice that it actually took two weeks longer than planned to do this. Given this information, the manager might want to take some corrective action—either to make up the lost two weeks or to ensure that no further delays will occur. At this point, the manager can expect that the book will be published at least two weeks late if no corrective action is taken.

A modified version of the Gantt chart is a **load chart**. Instead of listing activities on the vertical axis, load charts list either whole departments or specific resources. This information allows managers to plan and control for capacity utilization. In other words, load charts schedule capacity by workstations. For example, Exhibit 14-6 shows a load chart for six production editors at the same publishing firm. Each editor supervises the design and production of several books. By reviewing the load chart, the executive editor who supervises the six production editors can see who is free to take on a new book. If everyone is fully scheduled, the executive editor might decide not to accept any new projects, to accept some new projects and delay others, to ask the editors to work overtime, or to employ more production editors.

What is a PERT network analysis? Gantt and load charts are helpful as long as the activities or projects being scheduled are few and independent of each other. But what if a manager had to plan a large project—such as a complex reorganization, the launching of a major cost-reduction campaign, or the development of a new product—that required coordinating inputs from marketing, production, and product design personnel? Such projects require coordinating hundreds or thousands of activities, some of which must be done simultaneously and some of which cannot begin until earlier activities have been completed. If you are constructing a shopping mall, you obviously cannot start erecting walls until the foundation has been laid. How, then, can you schedule such a complex project? You could use the program evaluation and review technique.

The program evaluation and review technique—usually just called PERT, or the **PERT network analysis**—was originally developed in the late 1950s for coordinating the more than

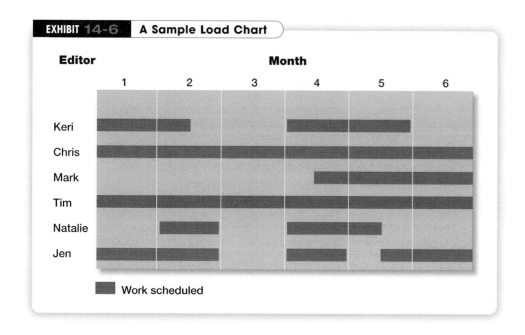

EXHIBIT 14-6 **A Sample Load Chart**

Work scheduled

3,000 contractors and agencies working on the Polaris submarine weapon system. This project was incredibly complicated, with hundreds of thousands of activities that had to be coordinated. PERT is reported to have cut two years off the completion date for the Polaris project.

A PERT network is a flowchart-like diagram that depicts the sequence of activities needed to complete a project and the time or costs associated with each activity. With a PERT network, a project manager must think through what has to be done, determine which events depend on one another, and identify potential trouble spots (see Exhibit 14-7). PERT also makes it easy to compare the effects alternative actions will have on scheduling and costs. PERT allows managers to monitor a project's progress, identify possible bottlenecks, and shift resources as necessary to keep the project on schedule.

To understand how to construct a PERT network, you need to know three terms: *events, activities*, and *critical path*. Let us define these terms, outline the steps in the PERT process, and then develop an example. **Events** are end points that represent the completion of major activities. Sometimes called milestones, events indicate that something significant has happened (such as receipt of purchased items) or an important component is finished. In PERT, events represent a point in time. **Activities**, on the other hand, are the actions that take place. Each activity consumes time, as determined on the basis of the time or resources required to progress from one event to another. The **critical path** is the longest or most time-consuming sequence of events and activities required to complete the project in the shortest amount of time.[63] Let's apply PERT to a construction manager's task of building a 6,500-square-foot custom home.

As a construction manager, you recognize that time really is money in your business. Delays can turn a profitable job into a money loser. Accordingly, you must determine how long it will take to complete the house. You have carefully dissected the entire project into activities and events. Exhibit 14-8 outlines the major events in the construction project and your estimate of the expected time required to complete each activity. Exhibit 14-9 depicts the PERT network based on the data in Exhibit 14-8.

How does PERT operate? Your PERT network tells you that if everything goes as planned, it will take just over 32 weeks to build the house. This time is calculated by tracing the network's critical path: A B C D E I J K L M N P Q. Any delay in completing the events along this path will delay the completion of the entire project. For example, if it took six weeks

---

EXHIBIT 14-7 **Developing PERT Charts**

Developing a PERT network requires the manager to identify all key activities needed to complete a project, rank them in order of dependence, and estimate each activity's completion time. This procedure can be translated into five specific steps:

1. Identify every significant activity that must be achieved for a project to be completed. The accomplishment of each activity results in a set of events or outcomes.

2. Ascertain the order in which these events must be completed.

3. Diagram the flow of activities from start to finish, identifying each activity and its relationship to all other activities. Use circles to indicate events and arrows to represent activities. The result is a flowchart diagram that we call the PERT network.

4. Compute a time estimate for completing each activity, using a weighted average that employs an optimistic time estimate (t_o) of how long the activity would take under ideal conditions, a most-likely estimate (t_m) of the time the activity normally should take, and a pessimistic estimate (t_p) that represents the time that an activity should take under the worst possible conditions. The formula for calculating the expected time (t_e) is then

$$t_e = \frac{t_o + 4t_m + t_p}{6}$$

5. Finally, using a network diagram that contains time estimates for each activity, the manager can determine a schedule for the start and finish dates of each activity and for the entire project. Any delays that occur along the critical path require the most attention because they delay the entire project. That is, the critical path has no slack in it; therefore, any delay along that path immediately translates into a delay in the final deadline for the completed project.

EXHIBIT 14-8 **Major Activities in Building a Custom Home**

EVENT	DESCRIPTION	TIME (WEEKS)	PRECEDING ACTIVITY
A	Approve design and get permits	3	None
B	Perform excavation/lot clearing	1	A
C	Pour footers	1	B
D	Erect foundation walls	2	C
E	Frame house	4	D
F	Install windows	0.5	E
G	Shingle roof	0.5	E
H	Install brick front and siding	4	F, G
I	Install electrical, plumbing, and heating and A/C rough-ins	6	E
J	Install insulation	0.25	I
K	Install Sheetrock	2	J
L	Finish and sand Sheetrock	7	K
M	Install interior trim	2	L
N	Paint house (interior and exterior)	2	H, M
O	Install all cabinets	0.5	N
P	Install flooring	1	N
Q	Final touch-up and turn over house to home owner	1	O, P

instead of four to frame the house (event E), the entire project would be delayed by two weeks (or the time beyond that expected). But a one-week delay for installing the brick (event H) would have little effect because that event is not on the critical path. By using PERT, the construction manager would know that no corrective action would be needed. Further delays in installing the brick, however, could present problems—for such delays may, in actuality, result in a new critical path. Now back to our original critical path dilemma.

Notice that the critical path passes through N, P, and Q. Our PERT chart (Exhibit 14-9) tells us that these three activities take four weeks. Wouldn't path N O Q be faster? Yes. The PERT network shows that it takes only 3.5 weeks to complete that path. So why isn't N O Q on the critical path? Because activity Q cannot begin until both activities O and P are completed. Although activity O takes half a week, activity P takes one full week. So, the earliest we can begin Q is after one week. What happens to the difference between the critical activity (activity P) time and the noncritical activity (activity O) time? The difference, in this case half a week, becomes slack time. **Slack time** is the time difference between the

EXHIBIT 14-9 **A PERT Network for Building a Custom Home**

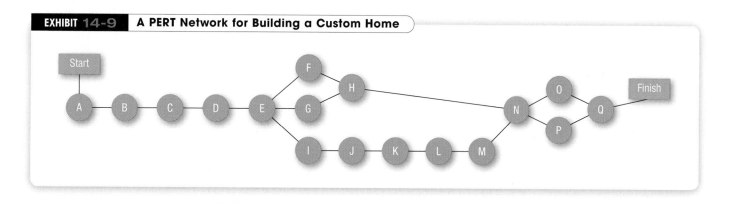

events
End points that represent the completion of major activities.

activities
Actions that take place.

critical path
The longest or most time-consuming sequence of events and activities required to complete a project in the shortest amount of time.

slack time
The time difference between the critical path and all other paths.

critical path and all other paths. What use is there for slack? If the project manager notices some slippage on a critical activity, perhaps slack time from a noncritical activity can be borrowed and temporarily assigned to work on the critical one.

Isn't PERT both a planning and a control tool? As you can see, PERT is both a planning and a control tool. Not only does PERT help us estimate the times associated with scheduling a project, but it also gives us clues about where our controls should be placed. Because any event on the critical path that is delayed will delay the overall project (making us not only late but also probably over budget), our attention needs to be focused on the critical activities at all times. For example, if activity F (installing windows) is delayed by a week because supplies have not arrived, that is not a major issue. It's not on the critical path. But if activity P (installing flooring) is delayed from one week to two weeks, the entire project will be delayed by one week. Consequently, anything that has the immediate potential for delaying a project (critical activities) must be monitored closely.

Review and  Applications

Chapter Summary

 Define operations management and explain its role. Operations management is the transformation process that converts resources into finished goods and services. Manufacturing organizations produce physical goods. Service organizations produce nonphysical outputs in the form of services. Productivity is a composite of people and operations variables. A manager should look for ways to successfully integrate people into the overall operations system. Organizations must recognize the crucial role that operations management plays as part of their overall strategy in achieving successful performance.

14.2 Define the nature and purpose of value chain management. The value chain is the sequence of organizational work activities that add value at each step from raw materials to finished product. Value chain management is the process of managing the sequence of activities and information along the entire product chain.

The goal of value chain management is to create a value chain strategy that meets and exceeds customers' needs and desires and allows for full and seamless integration among all members of the chain.

There are four benefits from value chain management: improved procurement, improved logistics, improved product development, and enhanced customer order management.

 Describe how value chain management is done. The six main requirements for successful value chain management include coordination and collaboration, investment in technology, organizational processes, leadership, employees or human resources, and organizational culture and attitudes.

The obstacles to value chain management include organizational barriers (refusal to share information, reluctance to shake up the status quo, or security issues), unsupportive cultural attitudes, lack of required capabilities, and employees unwilling or unable to do it.

 Discuss contemporary issues in managing operations. Companies are looking at ways to harness technology to improve their operations management using extensive collaboration and cost control.

ISO 9000 is a series of international quality management standards that set uniform guidelines for processes to ensure that products conform to customer requirements. Six Sigma is a quality standard that establishes a goal of no more than 3.4 defects per million units or procedures.

Project management involves getting a project's activities done on time, within budget, and accomplished to specifications. A project is a one-time-only set of activities that has a definite beginning and ending point in time. Popular project scheduling tools include Gantt charts, load charts, and PERT network analysis.

Understanding the Chapter

1. What is operations management and how is it used in both manufacturing and service organizations?

2. What strategic role does operations management play?

3. How might operations management apply to other managerial functions besides control?

4. What types of organizational benefits does value chain management provide?

5. Explain why managing productivity is important in operations management.

6. Who has the power in the value chain? Explain your response.

7. Choose two tasks that you do every week (for example, shop for groceries, host a poker party, clean your house/apartment, do laundry). For each one, identify how you could (a) be more productive in doing that task and (b) have higher-quality output from that task.

Understanding Yourself

What's My Negotiating Style?

INSTRUMENT Listed below are seven characteristics related to a person's negotiating style. Each characteristic demonstrates a range of variation. Indicate your own preference by selecting a point along the 1-to-5 continuum for each characteristic.

			1	2	3	4	5	
1.	Approach	Confrontational	1	2	3	4	5	Collaborative
2.	Personality	Emotional	1	2	3	4	5	Rational
3.	Formality	High	1	2	3	4	5	Low
4.	Communication	Indirect	1	2	3	4	5	Direct
5.	Candidness	Closed	1	2	3	4	5	Open
6.	Search for options	Limited	1	2	3	4	5	Many
7.	Willingness to use power	Low	1	2	3	4	5	High

SCORING KEY To calculate your score, add up the scores for the 7 items

ANALYSIS AND INTERPRETATION People differ in the way they handle negotiations. This instrument attempts to tap the key dimensions that differentiate preferences in negotiation style.

Your score on this test will range between 7 and 35. Research indicates that negotiation style is influenced by a number of factors—including the situation, your cultural background, and your work occupation. Nevertheless, experts in negotiation generally recommend individuals use a style that will result in a high score on this test. That is, they favor collaboration, rationality, a direct communication style, etc. We think it best to consider your total score in a situational context. For instance, while a high total score may generally be favorable, the use of an informal style may be a handicap for North Americans or Europeans when negotiating with Nigerians, who favor high formality. Similarly, Latin Americans tend to show their emotions in negotiation. So if you're negotiating with Brazilians or Costa Ricans, a more emotional approach on your part may be appropriate or even expected.

Sources: Based on R. Fisher and W. Ury, *Getting to Yes* (New York: Penguin, 1981); and J. W. Salacuse, "Ten Ways That Culture Affects Negotiating Style: Some Survey Results," *Negotiation Journal*, July 1998, pp. 221–39.

FYIA (For Your Immediate Action)

WestWood Travel Services

Reply   Reply All   Forward

To: Ebben Crawford, Director of Operations
From: Anne Mendales, President
Subject: **ISO 9001 Certification**

I've been doing a lot of reading on total quality management and I think we need to look at using TQM principles. Since our business has grown from one office to five offices with nearly 50 employees, I want to ensure that we're doing everything we can to meet our clients' needs, especially since we've lost some clients to competitors. Could you do an analysis describing how we might apply the concepts of customer focus, continuous process improvement, benchmarking, training, teamwork, and empowerment to our travel business to make us more competitive? Write up your analysis in a bulleted list format (no more than two pages please) and get it to me by the end of the week.

This fictionalized company and message were created for educational purposes only. It is not meant to reflect positively or negatively on management practices by any company that may share this name.

CASE APPLICATION

STIRRING THINGS UP

The steaming cup of coffee placed in a customer's hand at any Starbucks starts as coffee beans (berries) plucked from fields of coffee plants. From harvest to storage to roasting to retail to cup, Starbucks understands the important role each participant in its value chain plays.

Starbucks offers a selection of coffees from around the world, and its coffee buyers personally travel to the coffee-growing regions of Latin America, Africa/Arabia, and Asia/Pacific to select and purchase the highest-quality *arabica* beans. Once the beans arrive at any one of its five roasting facilities (in Washington, Pennsylvania, Nevada, South Carolina, or Amsterdam), Starbucks' master professional roasters do their "magic" in creating the company's rich signature roast coffees, a process that's the "cumulative result of expert roasters knowing coffee and bringing balance to all of its flavor attributes." There are many potential challenges in "transforming" the raw material into the quality product and experience that customers expect at Starbucks. Weather, shipping and logistics, technology, political instability, and so forth could potentially impact what Starbucks is in business to do. Although those are significant operations management challenges, the most challenging issue facing Starbucks today is balancing its vision of the uniquely Starbucks' coffee experience with the realities of selling a $4 latte.

Starbucks' products have become an unaffordable luxury for many. As revenues and profits have fallen during the economic downturn, CEO Howard Schultz realized that "the company needed to change almost everything about how it operates." Although it built its business as "the anti-fast-food joint," the recession and growing competition forced Starbucks to become more streamlined. Under one new initiative put into effect at its U.S. stores, employee time wasters such as bending over to scoop coffee from below the counter, idly standing by waiting for expired coffee to drain, or dawdling at the pastry case are discouraged. Instead, employees are to keep busy doing something, such as helping customers or cleaning. At one of the first stores to implement the "lean" techniques, the store manager looked for ways for her employees to be more efficient with simple things like keeping items in the same place, moving drink toppings closer to where drinks are handed to customers, and altering the order of assembly. After two months under the new methods, her store experienced a 10 percent increase in transactions.

Discussion Questions

1. Would you describe Starbucks' production/operations technology in its retail stores as unit, mass, or process? Explain your choice. (Hint: You'll probably need to review this material found in Chapter 5's "From the Past to the Present" box.) How does its production/operations technology approach affect the way products are produced?

2. What uncertainties does Starbucks face in its value chain? Can Starbucks manage those uncertainties? If so, how? If not, why not?

3. Go the company's Web site, www.starbucks.com, and find the information on the company's environmental activities from bean to cup. Select one of the steps in the chain (or your professor may assign one). Describe what environmental actions it's taking. How might these affect the way Starbucks "produces" its products?

4. Research the concept of *lean manufacturing*. What does it mean? What benefits does "lean" offer? How might a business like Starbucks further utilize the concepts of being lean?

Sources: S. Berfield, "Starbucks: Howard Schultz vs. Howard Schultz," *BusinessWeek Online,* August 6, 2009; J. Jargon, "Latest Starbucks Buzzword: 'Lean' Japanese Techniques," *Wall Street Journal,* August 4, 2009, p. A1; and "Starbucks Opens LEED Certified Coffee Roasting Plant," News Release, http://www.starbucks.com (February 19, 2009).

Endnotes

Chapter 1

1. Based on Life Is Good Web site, http://www.lifeisgood.com; J. Larson, "Life Is Good: Spreading Happiness to Troubled Kids," Video clip on *NBC Today,* July 29, 2008, http://www.msnbc.msn.com/id/21134540/vp/25902982; E. Wilson, "Everything's Fine! My T-Shirt Says So," *New York Times Online,* July 24, 2008; G. Rifkin, "Millions in Sales from 3 Simple Words," *New York Times Online,* November 22, 2007; and L. Buchanan, "Life Lessons," *Inc.,* October 2006, pp. 86–92.

2. The Walt Disney Company, Letter to Shareholders, *2008 Annual Report,* pp. 2–3.

3. "Right or Wrong?" box based on C. Tuna and K. J. Winstein, "Economy Promises to Fuel Résumé Fraud," *Wall Street Journal,* November 17, 2008, p. B4; K. J. Winstein and T. Audi, "MGM Mirage CEO Resigns Amid Questions About MBA," *Wall Street Journal,* November 14, 2008, pp. 1+; K. J. Winstein, "Inflated Credentials Surface in Executive Suite," *Wall Street Journal,* November 13, 2008, pp. B1+; "Redoing Your Resume? Leave Off the Lies," *Training* (December 2006), p. 9; J. O'Donnell, "CEO Left Radio Shack with His Whole Life in Turmoil," *USA Today,* February 27, 2006; and "Lies, Damn Lies, and Statistics," *Wired,* March 2004, p. 60.

4. "From the Past to the Present" box based on Dictionary.com Unabridged, based on the Random House Dictionary, © Random House, Inc. 2009, http://dictionary.reference.com/browse/manage; Online Etymology Dictionary, http://www.etymonline.com, June 5, 2009; P. F. Drucker, *Management: Revised Edition* (New York: HarperCollins Publishers, 2008); and F. W. Taylor, *Principles of Scientific Management* (New York: Harper, 1911), p. 44. For other information on Taylor, see S. Wagner-Tsukamoto, "An Institutional Economic Reconstruction of Scientific Management: On the Lost Theoretical Logic of Taylorism," *Academy of Management Review* (January 2007), pp. 105–117; R. Kanigel, *The One Best Way: Frederick Winslow Taylor and the Enigma of Efficiency* (New York: Viking, 1997); and M. Banta, *Taylored Lives: Narrative Productions in the Age of Taylor, Veblen, and Ford* (Chicago: University of Chicago Press, 1993).

5. H. Fayol, *Industrial and General Administration* (Paris: Dunod, 1916).

6. For a comprehensive review of this question, see C. P. Hales, "What Do Managers Do? A Critical Review of the Evidence," *Journal of Management* (January 1986), pp. 88–115.

7. H. Mintzberg, *The Nature of Managerial Work* (New York: Harper & Row, 1973).

8. S. J. Carroll and D. A. Gillen, "Are the Classical Management Functions Useful in Describing Managerial Work?" *Academy of Management Review* (January 1987), p. 48.

9. See, for example, J. G. Harris, D. W. DeLong, and A. Donnellon, "Do You Have What It Takes to Be an E-Manager?" *Strategy and Leadership* (August 2001), pp. 10–14; C. Fletcher and C. Baldry, "A Study of Individual Differences and Self-Awareness in the Context of Multi-Source Feedback," *Journal of Occupational and Organizational Psychology* (September 2000), pp. 303–319; and R. L. Katz, "Skills of an Effective Administrator," *Harvard Business Review* (September–October 1974), pp. 901–902.

10. "Developing Your Political Skill" box based on S. Y. Todd, K. J. Harris, R. B. Harris, and A. R. Wheeler, "Career Success Implications of Political Skill," *Journal of Social Psychology* (June 2009), pp. 179–204; G. R. Ferris, D. C. Treadway, P. L. Perrewé, R. L. Brouer, C. Douglas, and S. Lux, "Political Skill in Organizations," *Journal of Management* (June 2007), pp. 290–329; K. J. Harris, K. M. Kacmar, S. Zivnuska, and J. D. Shaw, "The Impact of Political Skill on Impression Management Effectiveness," *Journal of Applied Psychology* (January 2007), pp. 278–285; and G. R. Ferris, D. C. Treadway, R. W. Kolodinsky, W. A. Hochwarter, C. J. Kacmar, C. Douglas, and D. D. Frink, "Development and Validation of the Political Skill Inventory," *Journal of Management* (February 2005), pp. 126–152.

11. "Frequently Asked Questions," *U.S. Small Business Administration,* http://www.sba.gov/advo, September 2008; T. L. Hatten, *Small Business: Entrepreneurship and Beyond* (Upper Saddle River, NJ: Prentice Hall, 1997), p. 5; L. W. Busenitz, "Research on Entrepreneurial Alertness," *Journal of Small Business Management* (October 1996), pp. 35–44; and J. W. Carland, F. Hoy, W. R. Boulton, and J. C. Carland, "Differentiating Entrepreneurs from Small Business Owners: A Conceptualization," *Academy of Management Review* 9, no. 2 (1984), pp. 354–359.

12. "And the Survey Says . . ." box based on C. Kincaid, "On the Front Lines," *Training* (June 2009), pp. 48–49; "Recession Weather-Proofed," *Training* (March/April 2009), p. 8; "DiversityInc. Top50 Facts & Figures," *DiversityInc.,* March/April 2009, pp. 16–17; J. Yang and V. Salazar, "What Makes Good Employees Quit?" *USA Today,* February 10, 2009, p. 1B; J. MacIntyre, "Figuratively Speaking," *Springfield, Missouri, Business Journal* (December 15–21, 2008), p. 20; B. Levisohn, "It's All Yours, Boss," *BusinessWeek,* November 3, 2008, p. 30; J. Yang and S. Parker, "Characterizing Relationship with Boss," *USA Today,* October 16, 2008, p. 1B; R. I. Sutton, "Are You Being a Jerk? Again?" *BusinessWeek,* August 25–September 1, 2008, p. 52; J. MacIntyre, "Women in Management," *Springfield, Missouri, Business Journal* (August 2008), p. 14; and "Lonesome for the Boss," *Training* (July/August 2008), p. 9.

13. T. Shelton, "Best Buy's New ROLE," *Training* (June 2009), pp. 24–28; and T. J. Erickson, "Task, Not Time: Profile of a Gen Y Job," *Harvard Business Review* (February 2008), p. 19.

14. T. W. Martin, "May I Help You?" *Wall Street Journal,* April 23, 2009, p. R4.

15. W. Yardley and R. Perez-Peña, "Seattle Paper Shifts Entirely to the Web," *New York Times Online,* March 17, 2009.

16. F. F. Reichheld, "Lead for Loyalty," *Harvard Business Review* (July–August 2001), p. 76.

17. K. A. Eddleston, D. L. Kidder, and B. E. Litzky, "Who's the Boss? Contending with Competing Expectations from Customers and Management," *Academy of Management Executive* (November 2002), pp. 85–95.

18. See, for instance, B. A. Gutek, M. Groth, and B. Cherry, "Achieving Service Success Through Relationships and Enhanced Encounters," *Academy of Management Executive* (November 2002), pp. 132–44; Eddleston, Kidder, and Litzky, "Who's the Boss? Contending with Competing Expectations from Customers and Management"; S. D. Pugh, J. Dietz, J. W. Wiley, and S. M. Brooks, "Driving Service Effectiveness Through Employee-Customer Linkages," *Academy of Management Executive* (November 2002), pp. 73–84; S. D. Pugh, "Service with a Smile: Emotional Contagion in the Service Encounter," *Academy of Management Journal* (October 2001), pp. 1018–27; W. C. Tsai, "Determinants and Consequences of Employee Displayed Positive Emotions," *Journal of Management* 27, no. 4, (2001), pp. 497–512; Naumann and Jackson, Jr., "One More Time: How Do You Satisfy Customers?"; and M. D. Hartline and O. C. Ferrell, "The Management of Customer-Contact Service Employees: An Empirical Investigation," *Journal of Marketing* (October 1996), pp. 52–70.

19. R. A. Hattori and J. Wycoff, "Innovation DNA," *Training and Development* (January 2002), p. 24.

20. R. Wagner, "One Store, One Team at Best Buy," *Gallup Brain,* August 12, 2004, http://brain.gallup.com/content (November 28, 2005).

21. K. A. Tucker and V. Allman, "Don't Be a Cat-and-Mouse Manager," The Gallup Organization, http://www.brain.gallup.com (September 9, 2004).

22. "WorkUSA® 2004/2005: Effective Employees Drive Financial Results," Watson Wyatt Worldwide, Washington, DC.

Chapter 2

1. R. A. Clark, M. D. Hartline, and K. C. Jones, "The Effects of Leadership Style on Hotel Employees' Commitment to Service Quality," *Cornell Hospitality Quarterly* (May 2009), pp. 209–231; C. Crowell, "Staff Management Is Key for Smaller Budgets," *Hotel & Motel Management,* February 2009, pp. 4+; G. Withiam, "Scripts Can Ensure Quality but Must Be Used Carefully," *Hotel & Motel Management,* January 19, 2009, p. 20; B. De Lollis, "Most Hotels Likely to See Occupancy Rates Fall Next Year," *USA Today Online,* November 11, 2008; G. Kranz, "Hospitality's Sharpened Focus," *Workforce Management Online,* September 2008; A. Dombey, "How To: Excel in Service Delivery," *Caterer & Hotelkeeper,* June 12, 2008, p. 57: M. Nelson, "The Ten-Dollar Test Toward Customer Satisfaction," *Executive Housekeeping Today,* May 2008, pp. 5+; and H. Dolezalek, "We Train to Please," *Training* (March/April 2008), pp. 34–35.

2. J. Robison, "What Leaders Must Do Next," *The Gallup Management Journal Online,* http://gmj.com (June 11, 2009).

3. J. Revell, "How to Profit in the New Economy," *CNNMoney.com,* June 12, 2009.

4. Ibid.

5. M. Saltmarsh, "O.E.C.D. Improved Its Outlook for Economy," *New York Times Online,* June 24, 2009; and B. Knowlton, "Global Economy Called Worst Since 1945," *New York Times Online,* April 23, 2009.

6. A. Ignatius, "Trust Revisited," *Harvard Business Review* (June 2009), p. 8.

7. N. Gibbs, "25 People to Blame," *BusinessWeek,* February 23, 2009, p. 20.

8. Ibid.

9. F. Zakaria, "Greed Is Good (To a Point)," *Newsweek,* June 22, 2009, pp. 41–47.

10. Ibid.

11. B. Davis and J. Hilsenrath, "Federal Intervention Pits 'Gets' vs. 'Get-Nots,'" *Wall Street Journal,* June 15, 2009, pp. A1+.

12. "Technology and the Manager's Job " box based on R. M. Kesner, "Running Information Services as a Business: Managing IS Commitments Within the Enterprise," *Information Strategy* (Summer 2002), pp. 15–35.

13. R. M. Kidder, "Cleaning Up Damage of Economic Collapse Must be Rooted in Values, Argues Sociologist," *Ethics Newsline,* http://www.globalethics.org/newsline (June 15, 2009).

14. L. Meckler, "Public Wary of Deficit, Economic Intervention," *Wall Street Journal,* June 18, 2009, pp. A1+.

15. E. Beinhocker, I. Davis, and L. Mendonca, "The 10 Trends You Have to Watch," *Harvard Business Review* (July–August 2009), pp. 55–60.

16. P. F. Drucker, "The Global Economy and the Nation-State," *Foreign Affairs* (September–October 1997), pp. 159–171.

17. P. Dvorak, "Why Multiple Headquarters Multiply," *Wall Street Journal,* November 19, 2007, pp. B1+.

18. D. A. Aaker, *Developing Business Strategies,* 5th ed. (New York: John Wiley & Sons, 1998); and J. A. Byrne et al., "Borderless Management," *Business Week,* May 23, 1994, pp. 24–26.

19. B. Davis, "Migration of Skilled Jobs Abroad Unsettles Global-Economy Fans," *Wall Street Journal,* January 26, 2004, p. A1.

20. V. Couto, A. Divakaran, and M. Mani, "Is Backshoring the New Offshoring?" *Strategy & Business,* October 21, 2008, pp. 1–3.

21. J. Teresko, "United Plastics Picks China's Silicon Valley," *Industry Week,* January 2003, p. 58.

22. "Global Business: Getting the Frameworks Right," *Organization for Economic Cooperation and Development,* April 2000, p. 20.

23. "From the Past to the Present" box based on G. A. Gelade, P. Dobson, and K. Auer, "Individualism, Masculinity, and the Sources of Organizational Commitment," *Journal of Cross-Cultural Psychology* (September 2008), pp. 599–617; G. Hofstede, "The Cultural Relativity of Organizational Practices and Theories," *Journal of International Business Studies* (Fall 1983), pp. 75–89; and G. Hofstede, *Culture Consequences: International Differences in Work Related Values* (Beverly Hills, CA: Sage Publications, 1980), pp. 25–26. For an interesting discussion of collectivism and teams, see C. Gomez, B. L. Kirkman, and D. Shapiro,

"The Impact of Collectivism and In-Group Membership on the Evaluation Generosity of Team Members," *Academy of Management Journal* (December 2000), pp. 1097–1106. Hofstede's term for what we've called *quantity of life* and *quality of life* was actually *masculinity versus femininity*, but we've changed his terms because of their strong sexist connotation.

24. R. R. McRae, A. Terracciano, A. Realo, and J. Allik, "Interpreting GLOBE Societal Practices Scale," *Journal of Cross-Cultural Psychology* (November 2008), pp. 805–10; J. S. Chhokar, F. C. Brodbeck, and R. J. House, *Culture and Leadership Across the World: The GLOBE Book of In-Depth Studies of 25 Societies* (Philadelphia: Lawrence Erlbaum Associates, 2007); and R. J. House, P. J. Hanges, M. Javidan, P. W. Dorfman, and V. Gupta, *Culture, Leadership, and Organizations: The GLOBE Study of 62 Societies* (Thousand Oaks, CA: Sage Publications, 2004).

25. "Right or Wrong?" box based on Y. I. Kane and J. S. Lublin, "Apple Mum on Jobs's Treatment, Diagnosis," *Wall Street Journal,* June 30, 2009, pp. B1+; A. Hesseldahl, "Experts: Apple Disclosure 'Falls Short,'" *BusinessWeek Online,* June 23, 2009; Y. I. Kane and J. S. Lublin, "Jobs Had Liver Transplant," *Wall Street Journal,* June 20, 2009, pp. A1+; and R. M. Kidder, "Do Ailing CEOs of Publicly Traded Firms Have a Right to Medical Privacy?" *Ethics Newsline,* http://www.globalethics.org/newsline (January 19, 2009).

26. R. M. Kidder, "Must Capitalism Be Moral?" *Ethics Newsline,* http://www.globalethics.org/newsline (May 4, 2009).

27. P. Hohnen, founding director of the Global Reporting Initiative, quote found in *CFO,* July/August 2008, p. 18.

28. M. Conlin, "Sorry, I Composted Your Memorandum," *BusinessWeek,* February 18, 2008, p. 60; and CBS News Online, "Whole Foods Switching to Wind Power," http://www.cbsnews.com (January 12, 2006).

29. D. Dearlove and S. Crainer, "Enterprise Goes Social," *Chief Executive,* March 2002, p. 18; and "Bronze Winner: Ben & Jerry's Citizen Cool," *Brandweek,* March 18, 2002, p. R-24.

30. M. Friedman, *Capitalism and Freedom* (Chicago: University of Chicago Press, 1962); and M. Friedman, "The Social Responsibility of Business Is to Increase Profits," *New York Times Magazine,* September 13, 1970, p. 33.

31. "And the Survey Says . . . " box based on J. Yang and S. Ward, "What Items Have You Taken with You When Leaving a Job?" *USA Today,* April 20, 2008, p. 1B; J. Yang and K. Gelles, "Recession and Responsibility," *USA Today,* February 19, 2009, p. 1B; "Survey Finds That Companies Are Going Green," *Ethics Newsline,* http://www.globalethics.org/newsline (May 4, 2009); "One-Fourth of Teens Say Violent Behavior Is Acceptable: Poll," *Ethics Newsline,* http://www.globalethics.org/newsline (January 5, 2009); "CSR Staying Power," *Training* (March/April 2009), p. 10; "Majority of Investors Would Pull Funds from Unethical Company," *Ethics Newsline,* http://www.globalethics.org/newsline (September 24, 2007); C. Farrell, "Do-Gooders Doing Mischief," *BusinessWeek,* April 21, 2008, p. 18; K. Gelles, "Judging Right and Wrong," *USA Today,* June 24, 2008, p. 2D; J. Yang and K. Simmons, "Global Travel and Career," *USA Today,* November 26, 2008, p. 1B; and J. Yang and A. Gonzalez, "CEO Challenges," *USA Today,* December 23, 2008, p. 1B.

32. See, for instance, N. A. Ibrahim, J. P. Angelidis, and D. P. Howell, "The Corporate Social Responsiveness

Orientation of Hospital Directors: Does Occupational Background Make a Difference?" *Health Care Management Review* (Spring 2000), pp. 85–92.

33. See, for example, D. J. Wood, "Corporate Social Performance Revisited," *Academy of Management Review* (October 1991), pp. 703–708; and S. L. Wartick and P. L. Cochran, "The Evolution of the Corporate Social Performance Model," *Academy of Management Review* (October 1985), p. 763.

34. "$64B Diamond Industry Rocked by Fraud," *CNNMoney.com,* December 20, 2005; and E. B. Smith, "Wal-Mart Sets New Policy on Ethics," *USA Today,* January 28, 2005, p. 1B.

35. S. A. DiPiazza, "Ethics in Action," *Executive Excellence,* January 2002, pp. 15–16.

36. This example is based on J. F. Viega, T. D. Golden, and K. Dechant, "Why Managers Bend Company Rules," *Academy of Management Executive* (May 2004), pp. 84–90.

37. J. Liedtka, "Ethics and the New Economy," *Business and Society Review* (Spring 2002), p. 1.

38. D. H. Schepers, "Setting Global Standards: Guidelines for Creating Codes of Conduct in Multinational Corporations," *Business and Society* (December 2003), p. 496; and B. R. Gaummitz and J. C. Lere, "Contents of Codes of Ethics of Professional Business Organizations in the United States," *Journal of Business Ethics* (January 2002), pp. 35–49.

39. M. Weinstein, "Survey Says: Ethics Training Works," *Training* (November 2005), p. 15.

40. J. E. Fleming, "Codes of Ethics for Global Corporations," *Academy of Management News,* June 2005, p. 4.

41. T. F. Shea, "Employees' Report Card on Supervisors' Ethics: No Improvement," *HR Magazine* (April 2002), p. 29.

42. See also A. G. Peace, J. Weber, K. S. Hartzel, and J. Nightingale, "Ethical Issues in eBusiness: A Proposal for Creating the eBusiness Principles," *Business and Society Review* (Spring 2002), pp. 41–60.

43. "Managing Diversity" box based on C. Lindsay, "Paradoxes of Organizational Diversity: Living within the Paradoxes," in L. R. Jauch and J. L. Wall (eds.), *Proceedings of the 50th Academy of Management Conference,* San Francisco, 1990, pp. 374–78.

44. C. Rampell, "As Layoffs Surge, Women May Pass Men in Job Force," *New York Times Online,* February 6, 2009.

45. B. Tulgan, "Generation Y Defined: The New Young Workforce," *HR Tools Online,* http://www.hrtools.com/insights/bruce_tulgan (February 25, 2009).

46. See, for instance, P. Cappelli, J. Constantine, and C. Chadwick, "It Pays to Value Family: Work and Family Trade-Offs Reconsidered," *Industrial Relations* (April 2000), pp. 175–98; R. C. Barnett and D. T. Hall, "How to Use Reduced Hours to Win the War for Talent," *Organizational Dynamics* (March 2001), p. 42; and M. A. Verespej, "Balancing Act," *Industry Week,* May 15, 2000, pp. 81–85.

47. M. Conlin, "The New Debate over Working Moms," *BusinessWeek,* November 18, 2000, pp. 102–103.

48. M. Elias, "The Family-First Generation," *USA Today,* December 13, 2004, p. 5D.

49. J. Revell, C. Bigda, and D. Rosato, "The Rise of Freelance Nation," *CNNMoney.com,* June 12, 2009.

50. Ibid.

51. Ibid.

52. S. Armour, "Generation Y: They've Arrived at Work with a New Attitude," *USA Today,* November 6, 2005, pp. 1B+; B. Moses, "The Challenges of Managing Gen Y," *The Globe*

and Mail, March 11, 2005, p. C1; and C. A. Martin, *Managing Generation Y* (Amherst, MA: HRD Press, 2001).

53. Data from *The World Factbook 2009,* http://www.cia.gov/library/pulications/the-world-factbook/index.html (June 2009); and K. A. Eddleston, D. L. Kidder, and B. E. Litzky, "Who's the Boss? Contending with Competing Expectations from Customers and Management," *Academy of Management Executive* (November 2002), pp. 85–95.

54. A. J. Rucci, S. P. Kirn, and R. T. Quinn, "The Employee-Customer-Profit Chain at Sears," *Harvard Business Review* (January–February 1998), pp. 83–97.

55. S. Daley, "A Spy's Advice to French Retailers: Politeness Pays," *New York Times,* December 26, 2000, p. A4.

56. See, for instance, L. A. Bettencourt, K. P. Gwinner, and M. L. Meuter, "A Comparison of Attitude 'Personality' and Knowledge Predictors of Service-Oriented Organizational Citizenship Behaviors," *Journal of Applied Psychology* (February 2001), pp. 29–41; B. Schneider, D. E. Bowen, M. G. Ehrhart, and K. M. Holcombe, "The Climate for Service: Evolution of a Construct," in N. M. Ashkanasy, C. P. M. Wilderom, and M. F. Peterson (eds.), *Handbook of Organizational Culture and Climate* (Thousand Oaks, CA: Sage, 2000), pp. 21–36; and M. D. Hartline, J. G. Maxham III, and D. O. McKee, "Corridors of Influence in the Dissemination of Customer-Oriented Strategy to Customer Contact Service Employees," *Journal of Marketing* (April 2000), pp. 35–50.

57. A. Gabor, "He Made America Think About Quality," *Fortune,* October 30, 2000, pp. 292–93.

58. See, for example, J. McElroy, "Six Lessons for Ford," *Ward's Auto World*, December 2001, p. 17.

59. "Continuous Improvement: Ten Essential Criteria," *Measuring Business Excellence* (January 2002), p. 49.

60. "Winning with Kaizen," *IIE Solutions* (April 2002), p. 10.

61. J. A. M. Coyle-Shapiro, "Changing Employee Attitudes: The Independent Effects of TQM and Profit Sharing on Continuous Improvement Orientation," *Journal of Applied Behavioral Science* (March 2002), pp. 57–77.

62. M. Budman, "Jim Champy Puts His 'X' on Reengineering," *Across the Board* (March/April 2002), pp. 15–16.

Chapter 3

1. D. Reed, "Branson Takes New Approach to Airport," *USA Today,* May 5, 2009, pp. 1B+; C. Negroni, "In Missouri, Investors Seek a Profit in Branson Airport," *New York Times Online,* April 21, 2009; and P. Blais, "Branson Takes to the Air," *Planning,* November 2008, pp. 14–17.

2. See, for example, A. Nagurney, J. Dong, and P. L. Mokhtarian, "Multicriteria Network Equilibrium Modeling with Variable Weights for Decision-Making in the Information Age with Applications to the Telecommuting and Teleshopping," *Journal of Economic Dynamics and Control* (August 2002), pp. 1629–50.

3. J. Sawyer, "Problem-Solving Success Tips," *Business and Economic Review* (April/June 2002), pp. 23–24.

4. See J. Figueira and B. Roy, "Determining the Weights of Criteria in the Electre Type of Methods with a Revised Simons' Procedure," *European Journal of Operational Research* (June 1, 2002), pp. 317–26.

5. For instance, see M. Elliott, "Breakthrough Thinking," *IIE Solution,* October 2001, pp. 22–25; and B. Fazlollahi and R. Vahidov, "A Method for Generation of Alternatives by Decision Support Systems," *Journal of Management Information Systems* (Fall 2001), pp. 229–50.

6. D. Miller, Q. Hope, R. Eisenstat, N. Foote, and J. Galbraith, "The Problem of Solutions: Balancing Clients and Capabilities," *Business Horizons* (March/April 2002), pp. 3–12.

7. E. Teach, "Avoiding Decision Traps," *CFO,* June 2004, pp. 97–99; and D. Kahneman and A. Tversky, "Judgment Under Uncertainty: Heuristics and Biases," *Science* 185 (1974), pp. 1124–31.

8. Information for this section taken from S. P. Robbins, *Decide & Conquer* (Upper Saddle River, NJ: Financial Times/Prentice Hall, 2004).

9. T. A. Stewart, "Did You Ever Have to Make Up Your Mind?" *Harvard Business Review* (January 2006), p. 12; and E. Pooley, "Editor's Desk," *Fortune,* June 27, 2005, p. 16.

10. J. Pfeffer and R. I. Sutton, "Why Managing by Facts Works," *Strategy & Business* (Spring 2006), pp. 9–12.

11. See A. Langley, "In Search of Rationality: The Purposes Behind the Use of Formal Analysis in Organizations," *Administrative Science Quarterly* (December 1989), pp. 598–631; and H. A. Simon, "Rationality in Psychology and Economics," *Journal of Business* (October 1986), pp. 209–24.

12. "Technology and the Manager's Job" box based on H. W. K. Chia, C. L. Tan, and S. Y. Sung, "Enhancing Knowledge Discovery via Association-Based Evolution of Neural Logic Networks," *IEEE Transactions on Knowledge and Data Engineering* (July 2006), pp. 889–901; F. Harvey, "A Key Role in Detecting Fraud Patterns: Neural Networks," *Financial Times,* January 23, 2002, p. 3; D. Mitchell and R. Pavur, "Using Modular Neural Networks for Business Decisions," *Management Decision* (January/February 2002), pp. 58–64; B. L. Killingsworth, M. B. Hayden, and R. Schellenberger, "A Network Expert System Management System of Multiple Domains," *Journal of Information Science* (March–April 2001), p. 81; and S. Balakrishnan, N. Popplewell, and M. Thomlinson, "Intelligent Robotic Assembly," *Computers & Industrial Engineering* (December 2000), p. 467.

13. J. G. March, "Decision-Making Perspective: Decisions in Organizations and Theories of Choice," in A. H. Van de Ven and W. F. Joyce (eds.), *Perspectives on Organization Design and Behavior* (New York: Wiley-Interscience, 1981), pp. 232–33.

14. See D. R. A. Skidd, "Revisiting Bounded Rationality," *Journal of Management Inquiry* (December 1992), pp. 343–47; B. E. Kaufman, "A New Theory of Satisficing," *Journal of Behavioral Economics* (Spring 1990), pp. 35–51; and N. McK. Agnew and J. L. Brown, "Bounded Rationality: Fallible Decisions in Unbounded Decision Space," *Behavioral Science* (July 1986), pp. 148–61.

15. "From the Past to the Present" box based on D. A. Wren, *The Evolution of Management Thought,* 4th ed. (New York: John Wiley & Sons, Inc., 1994), p. 291; and H. A. Simon, *Administrative Behavior* (New York: Macmillan Company, 1945).

16. See, for example, G. McNamara, H. Moon, and P. Bromiley, "Banking on Commitment: Intended and Unintended Consequences of an Organization's Attempt to Attenuate Escalation of

Commitment," *Academy of Management Journal* (April 2002), pp. 443–52; V. S. Rao and A. Monk, "The Effects of Individual Differences and Anonymity on Commitment to Decisions," *Journal of Social Psychology* (August 1999), pp. 496–515; C. F. Camerer and R. A. Weber, "The Econometrics and Behavioral Economics of Escalation of Commitment: A Re-examination of Staw's Theory," *Journal of Economic Behavior and Organization* (May 1999), pp. 59–82; D. R. Bobocel and J. P. Meyer, "Escalating Commitment to a Failing Course of Action: Separating the Roles of Choice and Justification," *Journal of Applied Psychology* (June 1994), pp. 360–63; and B. M. Staw, "The Escalation of Commitment to a Course of Action," *Academy of Management Review* (October 1981), pp. 577–87.

17. W. Cole, "The Stapler Wars," *Time Inside Business,* April 2005, p. A5.

18. C. Flora, "When to Go with Your Gut," *Women's Health,* June 2009, pp. 68–70.

19. See E. Dane and M. G. Pratt, "Exploring Intuition and Its Role in Managerial Decision Making," *Academy of Management Review* (January 2007), pp. 33–54; M. H. Bazerman and D. Chugh, "Decisions Without Blinders," *Harvard Business Review* (January 2006), pp. 88–97; C. C. Miller and R. D. Ireland, "Intuition in Strategic Decision Making: Friend or Foe in the Fast-Paced 21st Century," *Academy of Management Executive* (February 2005), pp. 19–30; E. Sadler-Smith and E. Shefy, "The Intuitive Executive: Understanding and Applying 'Gut Feel' in Decision-Making," *Academy of Management Executive* (November 2004), pp. 76–91; and L. A. Burke and M. K. Miller, "Taking the Mystery Out of Intuitive Decision Making," *Academy of Management Executive* (October 1999), pp. 91–99.

20. C. C. Miller and R. D. Ireland, "Intuition in Strategic Decision Making: Friend or Foe," p. 20.

21. E. Sadler-Smith and E. Shefy, "Developing Intuitive Awareness in Management Education," *Academy of Management Learning & Education* (June 2007), pp. 186–205.

22. M. G. Seo and L. Feldman Barrett, "Being Emotional During Decision Making—Good or Bad? An Empirical Investigation," *Academy of Management Journal* (August 2007), pp. 923–40.

23. "And the Survey Says . . ." box based on B. Dumaine, "The Trouble with Teams," *Fortune,* September 5, 1994, pp. 86–92; A. S. Wellner, "A Perfect Brainstorm," *Inc.,* October 2003, pp. 31–35; "The Poll," *BusinessWeek,* August 21–28, 2006, p. 44; "Hurry Up and Decide," *BusinessWeek,* May 14, 2001, p. 16; J. MacIntyre, "Bosses and Bureaucracy," *Springfield, Missouri, Business Journal,* August 1–7, 2005, p. 29; J. Crick, "Hand Jive," *Fortune,* June 13, 2005, pp. 40–41; and "On the Road to Invention," *Fast Company,* February 2005, p. 16.

24. R. D. Hof and H. Green, "How Amazon Cleared That Hurdle," *BusinessWeek,* February 4, 2002, p. 59.

25. See, for instance, S. Schulz-Hardt, A. Mojzisch, F. C. Brodbeck, R. Kerschreiter, and D. Frey, "Group Decision Making in Hidden Profile Situations: Dissent as a Facilitator for Decision Quality," *Journal of Personality and Social Psychology* (December 2006), pp. 1080–83; and C. K. W. DeDreu and M. A. West, "Minority Dissent and Team Innovation: The Importance of Participation in Decision Making," *Journal of Applied Psychology* (December 2001), pp. 1191–1201.

26. S. Mohammed, "Toward an Understanding of Cognitive Consensus in a Group Decision-Making Context," *Journal of Applied Behavioral Science* (December 2001), p. 408.

27. M. J. Fambrough and S. A. Comerford, "The Changing Epistemological Assumptions of Group Theory," *Journal of Applied Behavioral Science* (September 2006), pp. 330–49.

28. "Managing Diversity" box based on N. J. Adler (ed.), *International Dimensions of Organizational Behavior,* 4th ed. (Cincinnati: South-Western College Publishing, 2001); B. C. McDonald and D. Hutcheson, "Dealing with Diversity Is Key to Tapping Talent," *Atlanta Business Chronicle,* December 18, 1998, pp. 45A+; and P. M. Elsass and L. M. Graves, "Demographic Diversity in Decision-Making Groups: The Experience of Women and People of Color," *Academy of Management Review* (October 1997), pp. 946–973.

29. R. A. Meyers, D. E. Brashers, and J. Hanner, "Majority-Minority Influence: Identifying Argumentative Patterns and Predicting Argument-Outcome Links," *Journal of Communication* (Autumn 2000), pp. 3–30.

30. I. L. Janis, *Groupthink* (Boston: Houghton Mifflin, 1982). See also J. Chapman, "Anxiety and Defective Decision Making: A Elaboration of the Groupthink Mode," *Management Decision* (October 2006), pp. 1391–1404.

31. See, for instance, T. Horton, "Groupthink in the Boardroom," *Directors and Boards* (Winter 2002), p. 9.

32. See, for example, T. W. Costello and S. S. Zalkind, eds., *Psychology in Administration: A Research Orientation* (Upper Saddle River, NJ: Prentice Hall, 1963), pp. 429–30; R. A. Cooke and J. A. Kernaghan, "Estimating the Difference Between Group Versus Individual Performance on Problem Solving Tasks," *Group and Organization Studies* (September 1987), pp. 319–42; and L. K. Michaelsen, W. E. Watson, and R. H. Black, "A Realistic Test of Individual Versus Group Consensus Decision Making," *Journal of Applied Psychology* (October 1989), pp. 834–39. See also J. Hollenbeck, D. R. Ilgen, J. A. Colquitt, and A. Ellis, "Gender Composition, Situational Strength, and Team Decision-Making Accuracy: A Criterion Decomposition Approach," *Organizational Behavior and Human Decision Processes* (May 2002), pp. 445–75.

33. See, for example, L. K. Michaelsen, W. E. Watson, and R. H. Black, "A Realistic Test of Individual Versus Group Consensus Decision Making," *Journal of Applied Psychology* (October 1989), pp. 834–39; and P. W. Pease, M. Beiser, and M. E. Tubbs, "Framing Effects and Choice Shifts in Group Decision Making," *Organizational Behavior and Human Decision Processes* (October 1993), pp. 149–65.

34. J. Wagstaff, "Brainstorming Requires Drinks," *Far Eastern Economic Review,* May 2, 2002, p. 34.

35. T. Kelley, "Six Ways to Kill a Brainstormer," *Across the Board* (March/April 2002), p. 12.

36. K. L. Dowling and R. D. St. Louis, "Asynchronous Implementation of the Nominal Group Technique: Is It Effective," *Decision Support Systems* (October 2000), pp. 229–48.

37. See also B. Andersen and T. Fagerhaug, "The Nominal Group Technique," *Quality Progress* (February 2000), p. 144.

38. J. Burdett, "Changing Channels: Using the Electronic Meeting System to Increase Equity in Decision Making," *Information Technology, Learning, and Performance Journal* (Fall 2000), pp. 3–12.

39. "Fear of Flying," *Business Europe,* October 3, 2001, p. 2.

40. "VC at Nestlé," *Business Europe,* October 3, 2001, p. 3.

41. M. Roberti, "Meet Me on the Web," *Fortune: Tech Supplement,* Winter 2002, p. 10.

42. See also, J. A. Hoxmeier and K. A. Kozar, "Electronic Meetings and Subsequent Meeting Behavior: Systems as Agents of Change," *Journal of Applied Management Studies* (December 2000), pp. 177–95.

43. See, for instance, P. Berthon, L. F. Pitt, and M. T. Ewing, "Corollaries of the Collective: The Influence of Organizational Culture and Memory Development on Perceived Decision-Making Context," *Academy of Marketing Science Journal* (Spring 2001), pp. 135–50.

44. J. de Haan, M. Yamamoto, and G. Lovink, "Production Planning in Japan: Rediscovering Lost Experiences or New Insights," *International Journal of Production Economics* (May 6, 2001), pp. 101–9.

45. "Right or Wrong?" box based on D. Ephron, "The Battle over the Battle of Fallujah," *Newsweek,* June 15, 2009, pp. 40–42; and K. Hall, "Konami Pulls Out of Fallujah Video Game," *BusinessWeek Online,* April 28, 2009.

46. "Developing Your Creative Skill" box based on S. P. Robbins, *Essentials of Organizational Behavior,* 8th ed. (Upper Saddle River, NJ: Prentice Hall, 2004); C. W. Wang and R. Y. Horng, "The Effects of Creative Problem Solving Training on Creativity, Cognitive Type, and R & D Performance," *R & D Management* (January 2002), pp. 35–46; S. Caudron, "Creativity 101," *Workforce* (March 2002), pp. 20, 24; and T. M. Amabile, "Motivating Creativity in Organizations," *California Management Review* (Fall 1997), pp. 42–52.

47. T. M. Amabile, "Motivating Creativity in Organizations," *California Management Review* (Fall 1997), pp. 39–58.

Chapter 4

1. The Associated Press, "Habitat for Humanity Gets $100 Million from Developer," *Wall Street Journal,* May 15, 2009, p. A5; G. Bluestein, The Associated Press, "Record Gift for Habitat for Humanity," *Springfield, Missouri, News-Leader,* May 15, 2009, p. 3B; The Associated Press, "Habitat for Humanity Gets $100 Million Gift," www.msnbc.msn.com (May 14, 2009); and "$100 Million Commitment Made to Habitat for Humanity by J. Ronald Terwilliger," www.habitat.org (May 14, 2009).

2. M. C. Mankins and R. Steele, "Stop Making Plans—Start Making Decisions," *Harvard Business Review* (January 2006), pp. 76–84; L. Bossidy and R. Charan, *Execution: The Discipline of Getting Things Done* (New York: Crown/Random House, 2002); P. Roberts, "The Art of Getting Things Done," *Fast Company,* June 2000, p. 162; H. Mintzberg, *The Rise and Fall of Strategic Planning* (New York: Free Press, 1994); G. Hamel and C. K. Prahalad, *Competing for the Future* (Boston: Harvard Business School Press, 1994); and D. Miller, "The Architecture of Simplicity," *Academy of Management Review* (January 1993), pp. 116–38.

3. See, for example, F. Delmar and S. Shane, "Does Business Planning Facilitate the Development of New Ventures?" *Strategic Management Journal* (December 2003), pp. 1165–1185; R. M. Grant, "Strategic Planning in a Turbulent Environment: Evidence from the Oil Majors," *Strategic Management Journal* (June 2003), pp. 491–517; P. J. Brews and M. R. Hunt, "Learning to Plan and Planning to Learn: Resolving the Planning School/Learning School Debate," *Strategic Management Journal* (December 1999), pp. 889–913; C. C. Miller and L. B. Cardinal, "Strategic Planning and Firm Performance: A Synthesis of More Than Two Decades of Research," *Academy of Management Journal* (March 1994), pp. 1649–85; N. Capon, J. U. Farley, and J. M. Hulbert, "Strategic Planning and Financial Performance: More Evidence," *Journal of Management Studies* (January 1994), pp. 22–38; D. K. Sinha, "The Contribution of Formal Planning to Decisions," *Strategic Management Journal* (October 1990), pp. 479–92; J. A. Pearce II, E. B. Freeman, and R. B. Robinson, Jr., "The Tenuous Link Between Formal Strategic Planning and Financial Performance," *Academy of Management Review* (October 1987), pp. 658–75; L. C. Rhyne, "Contrasting Planning Systems in High, Medium, and Low Performance Companies," *Journal of Management Studies* (July 1987), pp. 363–85; and J. A. Pearce II, K. K. Robbins, and R. B. Robinson, Jr., "The Impact of Grand Strategy and Planning Formality on Financial Performance," *Strategic Management Journal* (March–April 1987), pp. 125–34.

4. E. Bellman, "McDonald's Plans Expansion in India," *Wall Street Journal,* June 30, 2009, p. B4; Starbucks Advertisement, *USA Today,* June 30, 2009, p. 7A; and A. Chowdhury and S. Choudhury, "Tata Adds Jaguar, Land Rover to India's Luxury-Car Segment," *Wall Street Journal,* June 29, 2009, p. B3.

5. N. Casey, "Teen Idols: Aeropostale, Buckle Post Big Gains as Rivals Swoon," *Wall Street Journal,* May 22, 2009, p. B8; V. Dagher, "Hot Topic Goes Cold, Buckle Wears a Smile," *Wall Street Journal,* May 22, 2009, p C6; and J. B. Stewart, "A Retailer Bucks a Trend with Sales Success in Its Jeans," *Wall Street Journal,* May 13, 2009, p. D1.

6. H. J. Cho and V. Pucik, "Relationship Between Innovativeness, Quality, Growth, Profitability, and Market Value," *Strategic Management Journal* (June 2005), pp. 555–75; W. F. Joyce, "What Really Works," *Organizational Dynamics* (May 2005), pp. 118–129; M. A. Roberto, "Strategic Decision-Making Processes," *Group & Organization Management* (December 2004), pp. 625–658; A. Carmeli and A. Tischler, "The Relationships Between Intangible Organizational Elements and Organizational Performance," *Strategic Management Journal* (December 2004), pp. 1257–78; D. J. Ketchen, C. C. Snow, and V. L. Street, "Improving Firm Performance by Matching Strategic Decision-Making Processes to Competitive Dynamics," *Academy of Management Executive* (November 2004), pp. 29–43; E. H. Bowman and C. E. Helfat, "Does Corporate Strategy Matter?" *Strategic Management Journal,* 22 (2001), pp. 1–23; P. J. Brews and M. R. Hunt, "Learning to Plan and Planning to Learn: Resolving the Planning School-Learning School Debate," *Strategic Management Journal,* 20 (1999), pp. 889–913; D. J. Ketchen Jr., J. B. Thomas, and R. R. McDaniel Jr., "Process, Content and Context; Synergistic Effects on Performance," *Journal of Management,* 22,

no. 2 (1996), pp. 231–257; C. C. Miller and L. B. Cardinal, "Strategic Planning and Firm Performance: A Synthesis of More Than Two Decades of Research," *Academy of Management Journal* (December 1994), pp. 1649–65; and N. Capon, J. U. Farley, and J. M. Hulbert, "Strategic Planning and Financial Performance: More Evidence," *Journal of Management Studies* (January 1994), pp. 105–110.

7. C. K. Prahalad and G. Hamel, "The Core Competence of the Corporation," *Harvard Business Review* (May–June 1990), pp. 79–91.

8. "Right or Wrong" box based on S. Clifford, "Online Age Quiz Is a Window for Drug Makers," *New York Times Online*, March 26, 2009; S. McGuire, "Hearst Magazines Takes on Wellness with RealAge," *Medical Marketing & Media* (November 2007), p. 24; and L. A. Armour, "How Old Am I Really?" *Fortune*, April 19, 2004, pp. 134–35.

9. N. Argyres and A. M. McGahan, "Introduction: Michael Porter's Competitive Strategy," *Academy of Management Executive* (May 2002), pp. 41–42; and N. Argyres and A. M. McGahan, "An Interview with Michael Porter," *Academy of Management Executive* (May 2002), pp. 43–52.

10. N. A. Shepherd, "Competitive Advantage: Mapping Change and the Role of the Quality Manager of the Future," *Annual Quality Congress* (May 1998), pp. 53–60; T. C. Powell, "Total Quality Management as Competitive Advantage: A Review and Empirical Study," *Strategic Management Journal* (January 1995), pp. 15–37; and R. D. Spitzer, "TQM: The Only Source of Sustainable Competitive Advantage," *Quality Progress* (June 1993), pp. 59–64.

11. See R. J. Schonenberger, "Is Strategy Strategic? Impact of Total Quality Management on Strategy," *Academy of Management Executive* (August 1992), pp. 80–87; C. A. Barclay, "Quality Strategy and TQM Policies: Empirical Evidence," *Management International Review*, Special Issue (1993), pp. 87–98; R. Jacob, "TQM: More Than a Dying Fad?" *Fortune*, October 18, 1993, pp. 66–72; R. Krishnan, A. B. Shani, R. M. Grant, and R. Baer, "In Search of Quality Improvement Problems of Design and Implementation," *Academy of Management Executive* (November 1993), pp. 7–20; B. Voss, "Quality's Second Coming," *Journal of Business Strategy* (March–April 1994), pp. 42–46; and special issue of *Academy of Management Review* devoted to TQM, July 1994, pp. 390–584.

12. "Technology and the Manager's Job" box based on D. McGinn, "From Harvard to Las Vegas," *Newsweek*, April 18, 2005, pp. E8–E14; G. Lindsay, "Prada's High-Tech Misstep," *Business 2.0*, March 2004, pp. 72–75; G. Loveman, "Diamonds in the Data Mine," *Harvard Business Review* (May 2003), pp. 109–13; and L. Gary, "Simplify and Execute: Words to Live By in Times of Turbulence," *Harvard Management Update* (January 2003), p. 12.

13. R. Pear, "A.M.A. to Develop Measure of Quality of Medical Care," *New York Times Online*, February 21, 2006; and A. Taylor III, "Double Duty," *Fortune*, March 7, 2005, pp. 104–10.

14. *McDonald's Annual Report 2007*, http://www.mcdonalds.com (April 21, 2008).

15. S. Zesiger Callaway, "Mr. Ghosn Builds His Dream Car," *Fortune*, February 4, 2008, pp. 56–58.

16. "And the Survey Says . . ." box based on M. Weinstein, "Coming Up Short? Join the Club," *Training* (April 2006), p. 14; J. Yang and M. E. Mullins, "Employee's Concerns in

Mergers and Acquisitions," *USA Today*, June 6, 2007, p. 1B; J. Choi, D. Lovallo, and A. Tarasova, "Better Strategy for Business Units: A McKinsey Global Survey," *The McKinsey Quarterly Online*, http://www.mckinseyquarterly.com (July 2007); G. Kranz, "Workers Unprepared," *Workforce Management Online*, March 13, 2008; J. Yang, "Disaster Recovery Plan," *USA Today*, November 13, 2005, p. 1B; and American Management Association, "2003 Survey on Leadership Challenges," http://www.amanet.org.

17. See, for instance, J. Pfeffer, *Organizational Design* (Arlington Heights, IL: AHM Publishing, 1978), pp. 5–12; and C. K. Warriner, "The Problem of Organizational Purpose," *Sociological Quarterly* (Spring 1965), pp. 139–46.

18. D. Drickhamer, "Braced for the Future," *Industry Week*, October 2004, pp. 51–52.

19. P. N. Romani, "MBO by Any Other Name Is Still MBO," *Supervision* (December 1997), pp. 6–8; and A. W. Schrader and G. T. Seward, "MBO Makes Dollar Sense," *Personnel Journal* (July 1989), pp. 32–37.

20. "From the Past to the Present" box based on P. F. Drucker, *The Practice of Management* (New York: Harper & Row, 1954); J. F. Castellano and H. A. Roehm, "The Problem with Managing by Objectives and Results," *Quality Progress* (March 2001), pp. 39–46; J. Loehr and T. Schwartz, "The Making of a Corporate Athlete," *Harvard Business Review* (January 2001), pp. 120–28; A. J. Vogl, "Drucker, of Course," *Across the Board* (November/December 2000), p. 1. For information on goals and goal setting, see, for example, E. A. Locke, "Toward a Theory of Task Motivation and Incentives," *Organizational Behavior and Human Performance* (May 1968), pp. 157–89; E. A. Locke, K. N. Shaw, L. M. Saari, and G. P. Latham, "Goal Setting and Task Performance: 1969–1980," *Psychological Bulletin* (July 1981), pp. 12–52; E. A. Locke and G. P. Latham, *A Theory of Goal Setting and Task Performance* (Upper Saddle River, NJ: Prentice Hall, 1990); P. Ward and M. Carnes, "Effects of Posting Self-Set Goals on Collegiate Football Players' Skill Execution During Practice and Games," *Journal of Applied Behavioral Analysis* (Spring 2002), pp. 1–12; D. W. Ray, "Productivity and Profitability," *Executive Excellence* (October 2001), p. 14; D. Archer, "Evaluating Your Managed System," *CMA Management* (January 2000), pp. 12–14; and C. Antoni, "Management by Objectives: An Effective Tool for Teamwork," *International Journal of Human Resource Management* (February 2005), pp. 174–84. For information on participation in goal setting, see, for example, T. D. Ludwig and E. S. Geller, "Intervening to Improve the Safety of Delivery Drivers: A Systematic Behavioral Approach," *Journal of Organizational Behavior Management* (April 4, 2000), pp. 11–24; P. Latham and L. M. Saari, "The Effects of Holding Goal Difficulty Constant on Assigned and Participatively Set Goals," *Academy of Management Journal* (March 1979), pp. 163–68; M. Erez, P. C. Earley, and C. L. Hulin, "The Impact of Participation on Goal Acceptance and Performance: A Two Step Model," *Academy of Management Journal* (March 1985), pp. 50–66; and G. P. Latham, M. Erez, and E. A. Locke, "Resolving Scientific Disputes by the Joint Design of Crucial Experiments by the Antagonists: Application to the Erez Latham Dispute Regarding Participation in Goal Setting," *Journal of Applied Psychology* (November 1988), pp. 753–72. For information on effectiveness of MBO, see, for example, F. Dahlsten, A. Styhre, and M. Williander, "The Unintended

Consequences of Management by Objectives: The Volume Growth Target at Volvo Cars," *Leadership & Organization Development Journal* (July 2005), pp. 529–41; J. R. Crow, "Crashing with the Nose Up: Building a Cooperative Work Environment," *Journal for Quality and Participation* (Spring 2002), pp. 45–50; and E. C. Hollensbe and J. P. Guthrie, "Group Pay-for-Performance Plans: The Role of Spontaneous Goal Setting," *Academy of Management Review* (October 2000), pp. 864–72.

21. R. Rodgers and J. E. Hunter, "Impact of Management by Objectives on Organizational Productivity," *Journal of Applied Psychology* (April 1991), pp. 322–36.

22. G. P. Latham, "The Motivational Benefits of Goal-Setting," *Academy of Management Executive* (November 2004), pp. 126–29.

23. For additional information on goals, see, for instance, P. Drucker, *The Executive in Action* (New York: Harper-Collins Books, 1996), pp. 207–14; and E. A. Locke and G. P. Latham, *A Theory of Goal Setting and Task Performance* (Upper Saddle River, NJ: Prentice Hall, 1990).

24. J. L. Roberts, "Signed, Sealed, Delivered?" *Newsweek,* June 20, 2005, pp. 44–46.

25. Several of these factors were suggested by R. K. Bresser and R. C. Bishop, "Dysfunctional Effects of Formal Planning: Two Theoretical Explanations," *Academy of Management Review* (October 1983), pp. 588–99; and J. S. Armstrong, "The Value of Formal Planning for Strategic Decisions: Review of Empirical Research," *Strategic Management Journal* (July–September 1982), pp. 197–211.

26. K. Garber, "Powering the Information Age," *U.S. News & World Report,* April 2009, pp. 46–48; and S. Hamm, "It's Too Darn Hot," *BusinessWeek,* March 31, 2008, pp, 60–63.

27. "Developing Your Business Planning Skill" box—material for developing a business plan can be found at Small Business Administration, *The Business Plan Workbook* (Washington, DC, May 17, 2001); and on the Small Business Administration Web site, www.sba.gov. In addition, readers may also find useful such software as Business Plan Pro Software, available at www.businessplanpro.com.

28. A. Campbell, "Tailored, Not Benchmarked: A Fresh Look at Corporate Planning," *Harvard Business Review* (March–April 1999), pp. 41–50.

29. J. H. Sheridan, "Focused on Flow," *IW,* October 18, 1999, pp. 46–51.

30. Brews and Hunt, "Learning to Plan and Planning to Learn: Resolving the Planning School/Learning School Debate."

31. R. J. Newman, "Coming and Going," *U.S. News & World Report,* January 23, 2006, pp. 50–52; T. Atlas, "Bangalore's Big Dreams," *U.S. News & World Report,* May 2, 2005, pp. 50–52; and K. H. Hammonds," Smart, Determined, Ambitious, Cheap: The New Face of Global Competition," *Fast Company,* February 2003, pp. 90–97.

32. See, for example, P. Tarraf and R. Molz, "Competitive Intelligence," *SAM Advanced Management Journal* (Autumn 2006), pp. 24–34; W. M. Fitzpatrick, "Uncovering Trade Secrets: The Legal and Ethical Conundrum of Creative Competitive Intelligence," *S.A.M Advanced Management Journal* (Summer 2003), pp. 4–12; L. Lavelle, "The Case of the Corporate Spy," *BusinessWeek* (November 26, 2001), pp. 56–58; C. Britton, "Deconstructing Advertising: What Your Competitor's Advertising Can Tell You About Their Strategy," *Competitive Intelligence* (January/February 2002), pp. 15–19; and

L. Smith, "Business Intelligence Progress in Jeopardy," *Information Week* (March 4, 2002), p. 74.

33. S. Greenbard, "New Heights in Business Intelligence," *Business Finance* (March 2002), pp. 41–46; K. A. Zimmermann, "The Democratization of Business Intelligence," *KN World* (May 2002), pp. 20–21; and C. Britton, "Deconstructing Advertising: What Your Competitor's Advertising Can Tell You About Their Strategy," *Competitive Intelligence* (January/February 2002), pp. 15–19.

34. L. Weathersby, "Take This Job and ***** It," *Fortune,* January 7, 2002, p. 122.

35. "Starwood vs. Hilton," *Hotels' Investment Outlook* (June 2009), p. 14; R. Kidder, "Hotel Industry Roiled by Corporate Espionage Claim," *Ethics Newsline,* http://www.globalethicslorg/newsline; Reuters, "Hilton Hotels Is Subpoenaed in Espionage Case," *New York Times Online,* April 22, 2009; T. Audi, "U.S. Probes Hilton Over Theft Claims," *Wall Street Journal,* April 22, 2009, p. B1; and T. Audi, "Hilton Is Sued over Luxury Chain," *Wall Street Journal,* April 17, 2009, p. B1.

36. B. Rosner, "HR Should Get a Clue: Corporate Spying Is Real," *Workforce* (April 2001), pp. 72–75.

37. K. Western, "Ethical Spying," *Business Ethics* (September–October 1995), pp. 22–23.

Chapter 5

1. S. Perman, *In-N-Out Burger: A Behind-the-Counter Look at the Fast-Food Chain That Breaks All the Rules* (New York: Collins Business, 2009); J. L. Yang, "California's Cult Burger Chain Has Quite a Juicy Tale," *Fortune,* April 27, 2009, p. 14; "The Secret Sauce at In-N-Out Burger," *BusinessWeek,* April 20, 2009, pp. 68–69; J. Tayman, "Business Bookshelf: Fast Food, Family Feuds," *Wall Street Journal,* April 15, 2009, p. A13; and D. Arkst, "Burger Cult," *Fortune Small Business,* March 2009, p. 21.

2. M. Hiestand, "Making a Stamp on Football," *USA Today,* January 25, 2005, pp. 1C+.

3. S. E. Humphrey, J. D. Nahrgang, and F. P. Morgeson, "Integrating Motivational, Social, and Contextual Work Design Features: A Meta-Analytic Summary and Theoretical Expansion of the Work Design Literature," *Journal of Applied Psychology* (September 2007), pp. 1332–56.

4. E. Kelly, "Keys to Effective Virtual Global Teams," *The Academy of Management Executive* (May 2001), pp. 132–33; and D. Ancona, H. Bresman, and K. Kaeufer, "The Comparative Advantage of X-Team," *MIT Sloan Management Review* (Spring 2002), pp. 33–39.

5. R. S. Benchley, "Following Orders," *Chief Executive* (March 2002), p. 6.

6. R. Preston, "Inside Out," *Management Today* (September 2001), p. 37; and R. D. Clarke, "Over Their Heads," *Black Enterprise* (December 2000), p. 79.

7. See J. R. P. French and B. Raven, "The Bases of Social Power," in D. Cartwright and A. F. Zander, eds., *Group Dynamics: Research and Theory* (New York: Harper & Row, 1960), pp. 607–23.

8. "Developing Your Power Base Skill" box based on P. L. Hunsaker, *Training in Management Skills* (Upper Saddle River, NJ: Prentice Hall, 2001), Chapter 14.

9. L. Urwick, *The Elements of Administration* (New York: Harper & Row, 1944), pp. 52–53. See also, J. H. Gittel, "Supervisory Span, Relational Coordination, and Flight

Departure Performance: A Reassessment of Post-Bureaucracy Theory," *Organizational Science* (July/August 2001), pp. 468–83.

10. S. Harrison, "Is There a Right Span of Control? Simon Harrison Assesses the Relevance of the Concept of Span of Control to Modern Businesses," *Business Review* (February 2004), pp. 10–13.

11. P. C. Light, "From Pentagon to Pyramids: Whacking at Bloat," *Government Executive* (July 2001), p. 100.

12. See, for instance, D. Van Fleet, "Span of Management Research and Issues," *Academy of Management Journal* (September 1983), pp. 546–52; and S. H. Cady and P. M. Fandt, "Managing Impressions with Information: A Field Study of Organizational Realities," *Journal of Applied Behavioral Science* (June 2001), pp. 180–204.

13. Henri Fayol, *General and Industrial Management*, trans. C. Storrs (London: Pitman Publishing, 1949), pp. 19–42.

14. J. Zabojnik, "Centralized and Decentralized Decision Making in Organizations," *Journal of Labor Economics* (January 2002), pp. 1–22.

15. See P. Kenis and D. Knoke, "How Organizational Field Networks Shape Interorganizational Tie-Formation Rates," *Academy of Management Review* (April 2002), pp. 275–93.

16. E. W. Morrison, "Doing the Job Well: An Investigation of Pro-Social Rule Breaking," *Journal of Management* (February 2006), pp. 5–28.

17. Ibid.

18. T. Burns and G. M. Stalker, *The Management of Innovation* (London: Tavistock, 1961).

19. D. Dougherty, "Re-imagining the Differentiation and Integration of Work for Sustained Product Innovation," *Organization Science* (September/October 2001), pp. 612–31.

20. A. D. Chandler, Jr., *Strategy and Structure: Chapters in the History of the Industrial Enterprise* (Cambridge, MA: MIT Press, 1962).

21. See, for instance, L. L. Bryan and C. I. Joyce, "Better Strategy Through Organizational Design," *The McKinsey Quarterly,* no. 2 (2007), pp. 21–29; D. Jennings and S. Seaman, "High and Low Levels of Organizational Adaptation: An Empirical Analysis of Strategy, Structure, and Performance," *Strategic Management Journal* (July 1994), pp. 459–75; D. C. Galunic and K. M. Eisenhardt, "Renewing the Strategy-Structure-Performance Paradigm," in B. M. Staw and L. L. Cummings (eds.), *Research in Organizational Behavior*, vol. 16 (Greenwich, CT: JAI Press, 1994), pp. 215–55; R. Parthasarthy and S. P. Sethi, "Relating Strategy and Structure to Flexible Automation: A Test of Fit and Performance Implications," *Strategic Management Journal*, 14, no. 6 (1993), pp. 529–49; H. A. Simon, "Strategy and Organizational Evolution," *Strategic Management Journal* (January 1993), pp. 131–42; H. L. Boschken, "Strategy and Structure: Re-conceiving the Relationship," *Journal of Management* (March 1990), pp. 135–50; D. Miller, "The Structural and Environmental Correlates of Business Strategy," *Strategic Management Journal* (January–February 1987), pp. 55–76; and R. E. Miles and C. C. Snow, *Organizational Strategy, Structure, and Process* (New York: McGraw-Hill, 1978).

22. See, for instance, P. M. Blau and R. A. Schoenherr, *The Structure of Organizations* (New York: Basic Books, 1971); D. S. Pugh, "The Aston Program of Research: Retrospect and Prospect," in A. H. Van de Ven and W. F. Joyce (eds.),

Perspectives on Organization Design and Behavior (New York: John Wiley, 1981), pp. 135–66; and R. Z. Gooding and J. A. Wagner III, "A Meta-Analytic Review of the Relationship Between Size and Performance: The Productivity and Efficiency of Organizations and Their Subunits," *Administrative Science Quarterly* (December 1985), pp. 462–81.

23. J. Woodward, *Industrial Organization: Theory and Practice* (London: Oxford University Press, 1965).

24. See, for example, H. M. O'Neill, "Restructuring, Reengineering and Rightsizing: Do the Metaphors Make Sense?" *Academy of Management Executive* 8, no. 4 (1994), pp. 9–30; R. K. Reger, J. V. Mullane, L. T. Gustafson, and S. M. Demarie, "Creating Earthquakes to Change Organizational Mindsets," *Academy of Management Executive* 8, no. 4 (1994), pp. 31–41; and J. Tan, "Impact of Ownership Type on Environment–Strategy Linkage and Performance: Evidence from a Transitional Company," *Journal of Management Studies* (May 2002), pp. 333–54.

25. "From the Past to the Present" box based on J. Woodward, *Industrial Organization: Theory and Practice* (London: Oxford University Press, 1965). Also, see, for instance, C. Perrow, "A Framework for the Comparative Analysis of Organizations," *American Sociological Review* (April 1967), pp. 194–208; J. D. Thompson, *Organizations in Action* (New York: McGraw-Hill, 1967); J. Hage and M. Aiken, "Routine Technology, Social Structure, and Organizational Goals," *Administrative Science Quarterly* (September 1969), pp. 366–77; C. C. Miller, W. H. Glick, Y. D. Wang, and G. Huber, "Understanding Technology-Structure Relationships: Theory Development and Meta-Analytic Theory Testing," *Academy of Management Journal* (June 1991), pp. 370–99; M. Rousseau and R. A. Cooke, "Technology and Structure: The Concrete, Abstract, and Activity Systems of Organizations," *Journal of Management* (Fall–Winter 1984), pp. 345–61; and D. Gerwin, "Relationships Between Structure and Technology," in P. C. Nystrom and W. H. Starbuck (eds.), *Handbook of Organizational Design*, vol. 2 (New York: Oxford University Press, 1981), pp. 3–38.

26. J. C. Linder and S. Cantrell, "It's All in the Mind(set)," *Across the Board* (May/June 2002), pp. 38–42; and B. Holland, "Management's Sweet Spot," *New Zealand Management* (March 2002), pp. 60–61.

27. M. Song, "Samsung Electronics Net Rises 54%," *Wall Street Journal,* April 22, 2002, p. B4.

28. H. Mintzberg, *Structure in Fives: Designing Effective Organizations* (Upper Saddle River, NJ: Prentice Hall, 1983), p. 157.

29. R. J. Williams, J. J. Hoffman, and B. T. Lamont, "The Influence of Top Management Team Characteristics on M-Form Implementation Time," *Journal of Managerial Issues* (Winter 1995), pp. 466–80.

30. See, for example, G. J. Castrogiovanni, "Organization Task Environments: Have They Changed Fundamentally over Time?" *Journal of Management* 28, no. 2 (2002), pp. 129–50; D. F. Twomey, "Leadership, Organizational Design, and Competitiveness for the 21st Century," *Global Competitiveness* (Annual 2002), pp. S31–S40; M. Hammer, "Processed Change: Michael Hammer Sees Process as 'the Clark Kent of Business Ideas'—A Concept That Has the Power to Change a Company's Organizational Design," *Journal of Business Strategy* (November–December 2001), pp. 11–15; T. Clancy, "Radical Surgery: A View from the Operating Theater," *Academy of*

Management Executive (February 1994), pp. 73–78; I. I. Mitroff, R. O. Mason, and C. M. Pearson, "Radical Surgery: What Will Tomorrow's Organizations Look Like?" *Academy of Management Executive* (February 1994), pp. 11–21; and R. E. Hoskisson, C. W. L. Hill, and H. Kim, "The Multidivisional Structure: Organizational Fossil or Source of Value?" *Journal of Management* 19, no. 2 (1993) pp. 269–98.

31. Q. Hardy, "Google Thinks Small," *Forbes,* November 14, 2005, pp. 198–202.

32. See, for example, D. R. Denison, S. L. Hart, and J. A. Kahn, "From Chimneys to Cross-Functional Teams: Developing and Validating a Diagnostic Model," *Academy of Management Journal* (December 1996), pp. 1005–23; D. Ray and H. Bronstein, *Teaming Up: Making the Transition to a Self-Directed Team-Based Organization* (New York: McGraw-Hill, 1995); J. R. Katzenbach and D. K. Smith, *The Wisdom of Teams* (Boston: Harvard Business School Press, 1993); J. A. Byrne, "The Horizontal Corporation," *BusinessWeek,* December 20, 1993, pp. 76–81; B. Dumaine, "Payoff from the New Management," *Fortune,* December 13, 1993, pp. 103–110; and H. Rothman, "The Power of Empowerment," *Nation's Business,* June 1993, pp. 49–52.

33. C. Garvey, "Steer Teams with the Right Pay," *HR Magazine* (May 2002), pp. 70–78.

34. P. Kaihla, "Best-Kept Secrets of the World's Best Companies," *Business 2.0,* April 2006, p. 83; C. Taylor, "School of Bright Ideas," *Time Inside Business,* April 2005, pp. A8–A12; and B. Nussbaum, "The Power of Design," *BusinessWeek,* May 17, 2004, pp. 86–94.

35. See, for example, G. G. Dess, A. M. A. Rasheed, K. J. McLaughlin, and R. L. Priem, "The New Corporate Architecture," *Academy of Management Executive* (August 1995), pp. 7–20.

36. For additional readings on boundaryless organizations, see Rausch and Birkinshaw, June 2008; M. F. R. Kets de Vries, "Leadership Group Coaching in Action: The Zen of Creating High Performance Teams," *Academy of Management Executive* (February 2005), pp. 61–76; J. Child and R. G. McGrath, "Organizations Unfettered: Organizational Form in an Information-Intensive Economy," *Academy of Management Journal* (December 2001), pp. 1135–48; M. Hammer and S. Stanton, "How Process Enterprises Really Work," *Harvard Business Review* (November–December 1999), pp. 108–18; T. Zenger and W. Hesterly, "The Disaggregation of Corporations: Selective Intervention, High-Powered Incentives, and Modular Units," *Organization Science* 8 (1997), pp. 209–22; R. Ashkenas, D. Ulrich, T. Jick, and S. Kerr, *The Boundaryless Organization: Breaking the Chains of Organizational Structure* (San Francisco: Jossey-Bass, 1997); R. M. Hodgetts, "A Conversation with Steve Kerr," *Organizational Dynamics* (Spring 1996), pp. 68–79; and J. Gebhardt, "The Boundaryless Organization," *Sloan Management Review* (Winter 1996), pp. 117–19. For another view of boundaryless organizations, see B. Victor, "The Dark Side of the New Organizational Forms: An Editorial Essay," *Organization Science* (November 1994), pp. 479–82.

37. See, for instance, Y. Shin, "A Person-Environment Fit Model for Virtual Organizations," *Journal of Management* (December 2004), pp. 725–43; D. Lyons, "Smart and Smarter," *Forbes,* March 18, 2002, pp. 40–41; W. F. Cascio, "Managing a Virtual Workplace," *Academy of Management Executive* (August 2000), pp. 81–90; Dess, Rasheed,

McLaughlin, and Priem, "The New Corporate Architecture"; H. Chesbrough and D. Teece, "When Is Virtual Virtuous: Organizing for Innovation," *Harvard Business Review* (January–February 1996), pp. 65–73; and W. H. Davidow and M. S. Malone, *The Virtual Corporation* (New York: Harper Collins, 1992).

38. "Could Your Brand Pass the Tee Shirt Test?" *Fortune,* May 28, 2007, p. 122; M. Maddever, "The New School: An Inconvenient Truth," http://www.strategymag.com (April 2007); K. Hugh, "Goodson Forecasts Future Shock," http://www. adweek.com (March 5, 2007); J. Ewing, "Amsterdam's Red-Hot Ad Shops," *BusinessWeek,* December 18, 2006, p. 52; and T. Howard, "Strawberry Frog Hops to a Different Drummer," *USA Today,* October 10, 2005 p. 4B.

39. R. E. Miles, C. C. Snow, J. A. Matthews, G. Miles, and H. J. Coleman, Jr., "Organizing in the Knowledge Age: Anticipating the Cellular Form," *Academy of Management Executive* (November 1997), pp. 7–24; C. Jones, W. Hesterly, and S. Borgatti, "A General Theory of Network Governance: Exchange Conditions and Social Mechanisms," *Academy of Management Review* (October 1997), pp. 911–45; R. E. Miles and C. C. Snow, "The New Network Firm: A Spherical Structure Built on Human Investment Philosophy," *Organizational Dynamics* (Spring 1995), pp. 5–18; and R. E. Miles and C. C. Snow, "Causes of Failures in Network Organizations," *California Management Review* 34, no. 4 (1992), pp. 53–72.

40. G. Hoetker, "Do Modular Products Lead to Modular Organizations?" *Strategic Management Journal* (June 2006), pp. 501–18; C. H. Fine, "Are You Modular or Integral?" *Strategy & Business* (Summer 2005), pp. 44–51; D. A. Ketchen, Jr., and G. T. M. Hult, "To Be Modular or Not to Be? Some Answers to the Question," *Academy of Management Executive* (May 2002), pp. 166–67; M. A. Schilling, "The Use of Modular Organizational Forms: An Industry-Level Analysis," *Academy of Management Journal* (December 2001), pp. 1149–68; D. Lei, M. A. Hitt, and J. D. Goldhar, "Advanced Manufacturing Technology: Organizational Design and Strategic Flexibility," *Organization Studies* 17 (1996), pp. 501–23; R. Sanchez and J. Mahoney, "Modularity Flexibility and Knowledge Management in Product and Organization Design," *Strategic Management Journal* 17 (1996), pp. 63–76; and R. Sanchez, "Strategic Flexibility in Product Competition," *Strategic Management Journal* 16 (1995), pp. 135–59.

41. C. Hymowitz, "Have Advice, Will Travel," *Wall Street Journal,* June 5, 2006, pp. B1+.

42. S. Reed, A. Reinhardt, and A. Sains, "Saving Ericsson," *BusinessWeek,* November 11, 2002, pp. 64–68.

43. P. Engardio, "The Future of Outsourcing," *BusinessWeek,* January 30, 2006, pp. 50–58.

44. C. E. Connelly and D. G. Gallagher, "Emerging Trends in Contingent Work Research," *Journal of Management* (November 2004), pp. 959–83.

45. N. M. Adler, *International Dimensions of Organizational Behavior,* 5th ed. (Cincinnati, OH: South-Western, 2008), p. 62.

46. "Managers and Technology" box based on D. Darlin, "Software That Monitors Your Work, Wherever You Are," *New York Times Online,* http://www.nytimesonline.com (April 12, 2009); D. Pauleen and B. Harmer, "Away from the Desk . . . Always," *Wall Street Journal,* December 15, 2008, p. R8; J. Marquez, "Connecting a Virtual Workforce," *Workforce Management Online,* http://www.workforce.com (September 22, 2008); R. Yu, "Work Away from Work Gets Easier with Technology,"

USA Today, November 28, 2006, p. 8B; M. Weinstein, "Going Mobile," *Training* (September 2006), pp. 24–29; C. Cobbs, "Technology Helps Boost Multitasking," *Springfield, Missouri, News-Leader,* June 15, 2006, p. 5B; C. Edwards, "Wherever You Go, You're On the Job," *BusinessWeek,* June 20, 2005, pp. 87–90; and S. E. Ante, "The World Wide Work Space," *BusinessWeek,* June 6, 2005, pp. 106–108.

47. P. B. Smith and M. F. Peterson, "Demographic Effects on the Use of Vertical Sources of Guidance by Managers in Widely Differing Cultural Contexts," *International Journal of Cross Cultural Management* (April 2005), pp. 5–26.

48. P. Olson, "Tesco's Landing," *Forbes,* June 4, 2007, pp. 116–118; and P. M. Senge, *The Fifth Discipline: The Art and Practice of Learning Organizations* (New York: Doubleday, 1990).

49. "Right or Wrong" box based on M. W. Walsh, "A.I.G. Balks at Claims from Jet Ditching in Hudson," *New York Times Online,* June 12, 2009; and P. McGeehan, "Passengers, Here Are Your Bags," *New York Times Online,* May 18, 2009.

50. K. Shadur and M. A. Kienzle, "The Relationship Between Organizational Climate and Employee Perceptions of Involvement," *Group & Organization Management* (December 1999), pp. 479–503; M. J. Hatch, "The Dynamics of Organizational Culture," *Academy of Management Review* (October 1993), pp. 657–93; D. R. Denison, "What Is the Difference Between Organizational Culture and Organizational Climate? A Native's Point of View on a Decade of Paradigm Wars," paper presented at Academy of Management Annual Meeting, 1993, Atlanta, GA; and L. Smircich, "Concepts of Culture and Organizational Analysis," *Administrative Science Quarterly* (September 1983), p. 339.

51. J. A. Chatman and K. A. Jehn, "Assessing the Relationship Between Industry Characteristics and Organizational Culture: How Different Can You Be?" *Academy of Management Journal* (June 1994), pp. 522–53; and C. A. O'Reilly III, J. Chatman, and D. F. Caldwell, "People and Organizational Culture: A Profile Comparison Approach to Assessing Person-Organization Fit," *Academy of Management Journal* (September 1991), pp. 487–516.

52. P. Guber, "The Four Truths of the Storyteller," *Harvard Business Review* (December 2007), pp. 53–59; S. Denning, "Telling Tales," *Harvard Business Review* (May 2004), pp. 122–29; T. Terez, "The Business of Storytelling," *Workforce* (May 2002), pp. 22–24; J. Forman, "When Stories Create an Organization's Future," *Strategy & Business* (Second Quarter 1999), pp. 6–9; C. H. Deutsch, "The Parables of Corporate Culture," *New York Times,* October 13, 1991, p. F25; and D. M. Boje, "The Storytelling Organization: A Study of Story Performance in an Office-Supply Firm," *Administrative Science Quarterly* (March 1991), pp. 106–26.

53. E. Ransdell, "The Nike Story? Just Tell It!" *Fast Company,* January–February 2000, pp. 44–46.

54. J. Useem, "Jim McNerney Thinks He Can Turn 3M from a Good Company into a Great One—With a Little Help from His Former Employer, General Electric," *Fortune,* August 12, 2002, pp. 127–32.

55. Denning, "Telling Tales"; and A. M. Pettigrew, "On Studying Organizational Cultures," *Administrative Science Quarterly* (December 1979), p. 576.

56. D. Drickhamer, "Straight to the Heart," *Industry Week,* October 2003, pp. 36–38.

57. E. H. Schein, "Organizational Culture," *American Psychologist* (February 1990), pp. 109–19.

58. M. Zagorski, "Here's the Drill," *Fast Company,* February 2001, p. 58.

59. "Slogans That Work," *Forbes.com Special,* January 7, 2008, p. 99.

60. "And the Survey Says . . ." box based on J. Yang and A. Lewis, "Is Teleworking a Good Idea?" *USA Today,* October 28, 2008, p. 1B; A. R. Carey and S. Parker, "Workers Take Home Their Offices," *USA Today,* October 7, 2008, p. 1A; M. Weinstein, "It's a Balancing Act," *Training* (May 2009), p. 10; J. Yang and K. Gelles, "Working Remotely vs. in the Office," *USA Today,* April 24, 2008, p. 1B; "Drive Time: More Employees Get to Work Remotely," *Workforce Management Online,* http://www.workforce.com (September 23, 2008); and C. M. Pearson and C. L. Porath, "On the Nature, Consequences, and Remedies of Workplace Incivility: No Time for Nice? Think Again," *Academy of Management Executive* (February 2005), pp. 7–18.

61. E. H. Schein, *Organizational Culture and Leadership* (San Francisco: Jossey-Bass, 1985), pp. 314–15.

Chapter 6

1. C. Dougherty, "A Happy Family of 8,000, but for How Long?" *New York Times Online,* July 12, 2009; M. Luo, "For Small Employers, Shedding Workers and Tears," *New York Times Online,* May 7, 2009; M. Elias, "Those Doing Layoffs Can Feel the Pain," *USA Today,* April 23, 2009, p. 5D; and M. Cooper, "Handing Out the Pink Slips Can Hurt, Too," *New York Times Online,* February 1, 2009.

2. Material for this chapter is drawn from D. A. DeCenzo and S. P. Robbins, *Human Resources Management,* 9th ed. (New York: John Wiley & Sons, 2007).

3. "From the Past to the Present" box based on D. A. Wren and A. G. Bedeian, *The Evolution of Management Thought,* 6th ed. (New York: John Wiley & Sons, 2009), pp. 198–200; "Building Better Organizations: Industrial-Organizational Psychology in the Workplace," *Society for Industrial and Organizational Psychology,* http://www.siop.org (July 13, 2009); and M. Munsterberg, *Hugo Munsterberg: His Life and Work* (New York: Appleton-Century-Crofts, 1922).

4. C. Tuna, "Many Companies Hire as They Fire," *Wall Street Journal,* May 11, 2009, p. B6.

5. L. Greenhalgh, A. T. Lawrence, and R. I. Sutton, "Determinants of Work Force Reduction Strategies in Declining Organizations," *Academy of Management Review* (April 1988), pp. 241–54; "Even Non-Recruiting Companies Must Maintain Hiring Networks," *HR Focus* (November 2001), p. 8; M. N. Martinez, "The Headhunter Within," *HR Magazine* (August 2001), pp. 48–55; and L. G. Klaff, "New Internal Hiring Systems Reduce Cost and Boost Morale," *Workforce Management* (March 2004), pp. 76–79.

6. "Employee Referral Programs: Highly Qualified New Hires Who Stick Around," *Canadian HR Reporter* (June 4, 2001), p. 21; and C. Lachnit, "Employee Referral Saves Time, Saves Money, Delivers Quality," *Workforce* (June 2001), pp. 66–72.

7. "Managing Diversity" box based on D. C. Hannah, "Job Discrimination Hits Record High: Is the Economy to Blame?" *DiversityInc Online,* March 12, 2009; J. Levitz and P. Shishkin, "More Workers Cite Age Bias After Layoffs," *Wall Street Journal,* March 11, 2009, pp. D1+; and C. Ansberry, "Elderly Emerge as a New Class of Workers—And the Jobless," *Wall Street Journal,* February 23, 2009, pp. A1+.

8. J. Mooney, "Pre-Employment Testing on the Internet: Put Candidates a Click Away and Hire at Modem Speed," *Public Personnel Management* (Spring 2002), pp. 41–52.

9. See, for instance, R. D. Arvey and J. E. Campion, "The Employment Interview: A Summary and Review of Recent Research," *Personnel Psychology* (Summer 1982), pp. 281–322; and M. M. Harris, "Reconsidering the Employment Interview: A Review of Recent Literature and Suggestions for Future Research," *Personnel Psychology* (Winter 1989), pp. 691–726; J. H. Prager, "Nasty or Nice: 56-Question Quiz," *Wall Street Journal* (February 22, 2000), p. A4; and M. K. Zachary, "Labor Law for Supervisors," *Supervision* (March 2001), pp. 23–26.

10. See, for instance, G. Nicholsen, "Screen and Glean: Good Screening and Background Checks Help Make the Right Match for Every Open Position," *Workforce* (October 2000), p. 70.

11. R. A. Posthuma, F. P. Morgeson, and M. A. Campion, "Beyond Employment Interview Validity: A Comprehensive Narrative Review of Recent Research and Trends Over Time," *Personnel Psychology* (Spring 2002), pp. 1–81.

12. A. I. Huffcutt, J. M. Conway, P. L. Roth, and N. J. Stone, "Identification and Meta-Analysis Assessment of Psychological Constructs Measured in Employment Interviews," *Journal of Applied Psychology* (October 2001), pp. 897–913; and A. I. Huffcutt, J. A. Weekley, W. H. Wiesner, T. G. Degroot, and C. Jones, "Comparison of Situational and Behavioral Description Interview Questions for Higher-Level Positions," *Personnel Psychology* (Autumn 2001), pp. 619–44.

13. See E. Hermelin and I. T. Robertson, "A Critique and Standardization of Meta-Analytic Coefficients in Personnel Selection," *Journal of Occupational and Organizational Psychology* (September 2001), pp. 253–77; C. H. Middendorf and T. H. Macan, "Note-Taking in the Employment Interview: Effects on Recall and Judgments," *Journal of Applied Psychology* (April 2002), pp. 293–303; D. Butcher, "The Interview Rights and Wrongs," *Management Today* (April 2002), p. 4; and P. L. Roth, C. H. Can Iddekinge, A. I. Huffcutt, C. E. Eidson, and P. Bobko, "Corrections for Range Restriction in Structured Interview Ethnic Group Differences: The Value May Be Larger Than Researchers Thought," *Journal of Applied Psychology* (April 2002), pp. 369–76.

14. See P. J. Taylor and B. Small, "Asking Applicants What They Would Do Versus What They Did Do: A Meta-Analysis Comparison of Situation and Past Behavior Employment Interview Questions," *Journal of Occupational and Organizational Psychology* (September 2002), pp. 277–95; J. Merritt, "Improv at the Interview," *BusinessWeek* (February 3, 2003), p. 63; S. D. Mauer, "A Practitioner-Based Analysis of Interviewer Job Expertise and Scale Format as Contextual Factors in Situational Interviews," *Personnel Psychology* (Summer 2002), pp. 307–28; and J. M. Barclay, "Improving Selection Interviews with Structure: Organizations' Use of Behavioral Interviews," *Personnel Review* 30, no. 1 (2001), pp. 81–95.

15. Merrit, "Improv at the Interview," p. 63.

16. S. H. Applebaum and M. Donia, "The Realistic Downsizing Preview: A Management Intervention in the Prevention of Survivor Syndrome (Part II)," *Career Development International* (January 2001), pp. 5–19.

17. S. L. Premack and J. P. Wanous, "A Meta-Analysis of Realistic Job Preview Experiments," *Journal of Applied Psychology* (November 1985), pp. 706–20.

18. C. Garvey, "The Whirlwind of a New Job," *HR Magazine* (June 2001), pp. 110–118.

19. B. P. Sunoo, "Results-Oriented Customer Service Training," *Workforce* (May 2001), pp. 84–90.

20. See, for instance, E. G. Tripp, "Aging Aircraft and Coming Regulations: Political and Media Pressures Have Encouraged the FAA to Expand Its Pursuit of Real and Perceived Problems of Older Aircraft and Their Systems. Operators Will Pay," *Business and Commercial Aviation* (March 2001), pp. 68–75.

21. "Managers and Technology" box based on R. E. DeRouin, B. A. Fritzsche, and E. Salas, "E-Learning in Organizations," *Journal of Management* (December 2005), pp. 920–40; K. O'Leonard, *HP Case Study: Flexible Solutions for Multi-Cultural Learners* (Oakland, CA: Bersin & Associates, 2004); S. Greengard, "The Dawn of Digital HR," *Business Finance* (October 2003), pp. 55–59; and J. Hoekstra, "Three in One," *Online Learning* 5 (2001), pp. 28–32.

22. "A&S Interview: Sully's Tale," *Air & Space,* http://www.airspacemag.com (February 18, 2009); A. Altman, "Chesley B. Sullenberger III, *Time,* http://www.time.com (January 16, 2009); and K. Burke, Pete Donohue, and C. Siemaszko, "US Airways Airplane Crashes in Hudson River—Hero Pilot Chesley Sullenberger III Saves All Aboard," *New York Daily News,* http://www.nydailynews.com (January 16, 2009).

23. C. S. Duncan, J. D. Selby-Lucas, and W. Swart, "Linking Organizational Goals and Objectives to Employee Performance: A Quantitative Perspective," *Journal of American Academy of Business* (March 2002), pp. 314–18.

24. T. Galvin, "The 2002 Training Top 100," *Training* (March 2002), pp. 20–29.

25. R. Langlois, "Fairmont Hotels: Business Strategy Starts with People," *Canadian HR Reporter* (November 5, 2001), p. 19.

26. M. Dalahoussaye, "Show Me the Results," *Training* (March 2002), p. 28.

27. See, for example, R. E. Catalano and D. L. Kirkpatrick, "Evaluating Training Programs: The State of the Art," *Training and Development Journal* (May 1968), pp. 2–9.

28. A. Tziner, C. Joanis, and K. R. Murphy, "A Comparison of Three Methods of Performance Appraisal with Regard to Goal Properties, Goal Perception, and Rate Satisfaction," *Group and Organization Management* (June 2000), pp. 175–90; and T. W. Kent and T. J. Davis, "Using Retranslation to Develop Operational Anchored Scales to Assess the Motivational Context of Jobs," *International Journal of Management* (March 2002), pp. 10–16.

29. See also, C. A. Ramus and U. Steger, "The Roles of Supervisory Support Behaviors and Environmental Policy in Employee 'Ecoinitiatives' at Leading-Edge European Companies," *Academy of Management Journal* (August 2000), pp. 605–26.

30. See L. Atwater and J. Brett, "Feedback Format: Does It Influence Manager's Reaction to Feedback," *Journal of Occupational and Organizational Psychology* (December 2006), pp. 517–32.

31. See "Performance Appraisals," *Business Europe* (April 3, 2002), p. 3.

32. M. A. Peiperl, "Getting 360 Feedback Right," *Harvard Business Review* (January 2001), pp. 142–47.

33. T. J. Maurer, D. R. D. Mitchell, and F. G. Barbeite, "Predictors of Attitudes Toward a 360-Degree Feedback System and Involvement in Post-Feedback Management Development Activity," *Journal of Occupational and Organizational Psychology* (March 2002), pp. 87–107.

34. A. Evans, "From Every Angle," *Training* (September 2001), p. 22.

35. P. Kamen, "The Way That You Use It: Full Circle Can Build Better Organizations with the Right Approach," *CMA Management* (April 2003), pp. 10–13; M. Kennett, "First Class Coach," *Management Today* (December 2001), p. 84; and T. A. Beehr, L. Ivanitsjaya, C. P. Hansen, D. Erofeev, and D. M. Gudanowski, "Evaluation of 360 Degree Feedback Ratings: Relationships with Each Other and with Performance and Selection Predictors," *Journal of Organizational Behavior* (November 2001), pp. 775–788.

36. "And the Survey Says . . ." box based on T. McNicoll, "Leading Indicator," *Newsweek,* June 15, 2009, p. 18; J. Yang and K. Gelles, "Employers Look for Positive Attitude," *USA Today,* May 11, 2009, p. 1B; G. Kranz, "Layoffs Sour Survivors," *Workforce Management Online,* December 23, 2008; "Stymied by Diversity Hiring," *Training* (February 2009), p. 10; J. Yang and J. Snider, "How to Blow Your Interview," *USA Today,* March 10, 2009, p. 1B; "Benefits of e-Learning," *Training* (March/April 2009), p. 9; and J. MacIntyre, "Offensive Jargon," *Springfield, Missouri, Business Journal* (September 22–28, 2008), p. 22.

37. J. D. Glater, "Seasoning Compensation Stew," *New York Times,* March 7, 2001, pp. C1+.

38. This section based on R. I. Henderson, *Compensation Management in a Knowledge-Based World,* 9th ed. (Upper Saddle River, NJ: Prentice Hall, 2003).

39. M. P. Brown, M. C. Sturman, and M. J. Simmering, "Compensation Policy and Organizational Performance: The Efficiency, Operational and Financial Implications of Pay Levels and Pay Structure," *Academy of Management Journal* (December 2003), pp. 752–62; J. D. Shaw, N. P. Gupta, and J. E. Delery, "Pay Dispersion and Workforce Performance: Moderating Effects of Incentives and Interdependence," *Strategic Management Journal* (June 2002), pp. 491–512; E. Montemayor, "Congruence Between Pay Policy and Competitive Strategy in High-Performing Firms," *Journal of Management* 22, no. 6 (1996), pp. 889–908; and L. R. Gomez-Mejia, "Structure and Process of Diversification, Compensation Strategy, and Firm Performance," *Strategic Management Journal* 13 (1992), pp. 381–97.

40. J. D. Shaw, N. Gupta, A. Mitra, and G. E. Ledford, Jr., "Success and Survival of Skill-Based Pay Plans," *Journal of Management* (February 2005), pp. 28–49; C. Lee, K. S. Law, and P. Bobko, "The Importance of Justice Perceptions on Pay Effectiveness: A Two-Year Study of a Skill-Based Pay Plan," *Journal of Management* 26, no. 6 (1999), pp. 851–73; G. E. Ledford, "Paying for the Skills, Knowledge and Competencies of Knowledge Workers," *Compensation and Benefits Review* (July–August 1995), pp. 55–62; and E. E. Lawler III, G. E. Ledford Jr., and L. Chang, "Who Uses Skill-Based Pay and Why," *Compensation and Benefits Review* (March–April 1993), p. 22.

41. Shaw, Gupta, Mitra, and Ledford Jr., "Success and Survival of Skill-Based Pay Plans."

42. Information from Hewitt Associates Studies: "As Fixed Costs Increase, Employers Turn to Variable Pay Programs as Preferred Way to Reward Employees," August 21, 2007; "Hewitt Study Shows Pay-for-Performance Plans Replacing Holiday Bonuses," December 6, 2005; "Salaries Continue to Rise in Asia Pacific, Hewitt Annual Study Reports," November 23, 2005; and "Hewitt Study Shows Base Pay Increases Flat for 2006 with Variable Pay Plans Picking Up the Slack," Hewitt Associates, LLC, August 31, 2005, http://www.hewittassociates.com.

43. "Mandated Benefits: 2002 Compliance Guide," *Employee Benefits Journal* (June 2002), p. 64; and J. J. Kim, "Smaller Firms Augment Benefits, Survey Shows," *Wall Street Journal* (June 6, 2002), p. D2.

44. P. P. Shah, "Network Destruction: The Structural Implications of Downsizing," *Academy of Management Journal* (February 2000), pp. 101–12.

45. See, for example, K. A. Mollica and B. Gray, "When Layoff Survivors Become Layoff Victims: Propensity to Litigate," *Human Resource Planning* (January 2001), pp. 22–32.

46. S. Koudsi, "You're Stuck," *Fortune* (December 10, 2001), pp. 271–74.

47. S. Berfield, "After the Layoff, the Redesign," *BusinessWeek,* April 14, 2008, pp. 54–56; L. Uchitelle, "Retraining Laid-Off Workers, But for What?" *New York Times Online,* March 26, 2006; D. Tourish, N. Paulsen, E. Hobman, and P. Bordia, "The Downsides of Downsizing: Communication Processes and Information Needs in the Aftermath of a Workforce Reduction Strategy," *Management Communication Quarterly* (May 2004), pp. 485–516; J. Brockner, G. Spreitzer, A. Mishra, W. Hochwarter, L. Pepper, and J. Weinberg, "Perceived Control as an Antidote to the Negative Effects of Layoffs on Survivors' Organizational Commitment and Job Performance," *Administrative Science Quarterly* 49 (2004), pp. 76–100; and E. Krell, "Defusing Downsizing," *Business Finance* (December 2002), pp. 55–57.

48. A. Joshi, "Managing the Organizational Melting Pot: Dilemmas of Workplace Diversity," *Administrative Science Quarterly* (December 2001), pp. 783–84.

49. "Right or Wrong?" box based on S. Asci, "Many 'No-Pay' CEOs Actually Were Richly Compensated, Study Finds," *Workforce Management Online,* April 22, 2009; and News Release, "CEOs' One Dollar Salaries Often Purely Symbolic," *The Corporate Library,* http://www.thecorporatelibrary.com (April 16, 2009).

50. Diversity 50, *DiversityInc,* http://www.diversityinc.com (July 13, 2009).

51. See, for instance, K. Iverson, "Managing for Effective Workforce Diversity," *Cornell Hotel and Restaurant Administration Quarterly* (April 2000), pp. 31–38.

52. U.S. Equal Employment Opportunity Commission, "Sexual Harassment Charges EEOC and FEPAs Combined: FY 1997–FY 2006," *EEOC* (January 31, 2007). Available online at http://eeoc.gov/stats/harass.html.

53. Ibid.

54. N. F. Foy, "Sexual Harassment Can Threaten Your Bottom Line," *Strategic Finance* (August 2000), pp. 56–57.

55. "Federal Monitors Find Illinois Mitsubishi Unit Eradicating Harassment," *Wall Street Journal,* September 7, 2000, p. A8.

56. L. J. Munson, C. Hulin, and F. Drasgow, "Longitudinal Analysis of Dispositional Influences and Sexual Harassment: Effects on Job and Psychological Outcomes," *Personnel Psychology* (Spring 2000), p. 21.

57. See, for instance, G. L. Maatman Jr., "A Global View of Sexual Harassment," *HR Magazine* (July 2000), pp. 151–58.

58. "*Nichols v. Azteca Restaurant Enterprises*," *Harvard Law Review* (May 2002), p. 2074; A. J. Morrell, "Non-Employee Harassment," *Legal Report* (January/February 2000), p. 1. See also S. Lim and L. M. Cortina, "Interpersonal Mistreatment in

the Workplace: The Interface and Impact of General Incivility and Sexual Harassment," *Journal of Applied Psychology* (May 2005), pp. 483–496.

59. Although the male gender is referred to here, it is important to note that sexual harassment may involve people of either sex or the same sex. (See, for instance, *Oncale v. Sundowner Offshore Service, Inc.*, 118 S. Ct. 998.)

60. See also A. M. O'Leary-Kelly, L. Bowes-Sperry, C. A. Bates, and E. R. Lean, "Sexual Harassment at Work: A Decade (Plus) of Progress," *Journal of Management* (June 2009), pp. 503–36; M. Rotundo, D. H. Nguyen, and P. R. Sackett, "A Meta-Analytic Review of Gender Differences in Perceptions of Sexual Harassment," *Journal of Applied Psychology* (October 2001), pp. 914–922.

61. R. L. Wiener and L. E. Hurt, "How Do People Evaluate Social Sexual Conduct at Work? A Psychological Model," *Journal of Applied Psychology* (February 2000), p. 75.

62. *Meritor Savings Bank v. Vinson*, 477 U.S. 57 (1986).

63. R. D. Lee and P. S. Greenlaw, "Employer Liability for Employee Sexual Harassment: A Judicial Policy-Making Study," *Public Administration Review* (March/April 2000), p. 127.

64. Ibid.

65. "You and DuPont: Diversity," DuPont Company Documents (1999–2000). Available online at http://www.dupont.com/careers/you/diverse.html; and "DuPont Announces 2000 Dr. Martin Luther King, Days of Celebration," DuPont Company Documents (January 11, 2000). Accessed online at http://www.dupont.com/corp/whats-news/releases/00/001111.html.

66. It should be noted here that under the Title VII and the Civil Rights Act of 1991, the maximum award that can be given, under the Federal Act, is $300,000. However, many cases are tried under state laws, which permit unlimited punitive damages.

67. J. W. Janove, "Sexual Harassment and the Big Three Surprises," *HR Magazine* (November 2001), pp. 123–30; and L. A. Baar, and J. Baar, "Harassment Case Proceeds Despite Failure to Report," *HR Magazine* (June 2005), p. 159.

68. W. L. Kosanovich, J. L. Rosenberg, and L. Swanson, "Preventing and Correcting Sexual Harassment: A Guide to the Ellerth/Faragher Affirmative Defense," *Employee Relations Law Journal* (Summer 2002), pp. 79–99; M. Zall, "Workplace Harassment and Employer Liability," *Fleet Equipment* (January 2000), p. B1. See also, "Ruling Allows Defense in Harassment Cases," *HR Magazine* (August 2004), p. 30.

69. See, for instance, P. W. Dorfman, A. T. Cobb, and R. Cox, "Investigations of Sexual Harassment Allegations: Legal Means Fair—Or Does It?" *Human Resources Management* (Spring 2000), pp. 33–39.

70. C. Cash and G. R. Gray, "A Framework for Accommodating Religion and Spirituality in the Workplace," *Academy of Management Executive* 14, no. 3 (August 2000), p. 124.

71. D. P. Ashmos and D. Duchon, "Spirituality at Work: A Conceptualization and Measure," *Journal of Management Inquiry* (June 2000), p. 139.

72. A. A. Mohamed, J. Wisnieski, M. Askar, and I. Syed, "Toward a Theory of Spirituality in the Workplace," *Competitiveness Review* 14, no. 1 (Winter/Fall 2004), pp. 102–107.

73. See I. A. Mitroff and E. A. Denton, *A Spiritual Audit of Corporate America: A Hard Look at Spirituality, Religion, and Values in the Workplace* (San Francisco, CA: Jossey-Bass,

1999); J. Milliman, J. Ferguson, D. Trickett, and B. Condemi, "Spirit and Community at Southwest Airlines: An Investigation of a Spiritual Values-Based Model," *Journal of Organizational Change Management* 12, no. 3 (1999), pp. 221–33; E. H. Burack, "Spirituality in the Workplace," *Journal of Organizational Change Management* 12, no. 3 (1999), pp. 280–91; and F. Wagner-Marsh and J. Conley, "The Fourth Wave: The Spirituality-Based Firm," *Journal of Organizational Change Management* 12, no. 3 (1999); pp. 292–302.

74. M. Conlin, "Religion in the Workplace: The Growing Presence of Spirituality in Corporate America," *BusinessWeek*, November 1, 1999, pp. 151–158; and P. Paul, "A Holier Holiday Season," *American Demographics* (December 2001), pp. 41–45.

75. For a thorough review of the benefits of workplace spirituality, see J. Marques, S. Dhiman, and R. King, "Spirituality in the Workplace: Developing an Integral Model and a Comprehensive Definition," *Journal of American Academy of Business* (September 2005), pp. 81–92. See also M. Conlin, "Religion in the Workplace," p. 153; C. P. Neck and J. F. Milliman, "Thought Leadership: Finding Spiritual Fulfillment in Organizational Life," *Journal of Managerial Psychology* 9, no. 8 (1984), p. 9; D. W. McCormick, "Spirituality and Management," *Journal of Managerial Psychology* 9, no. 6 (1994), p. 5; E. Brandt, "Corporate Pioneers Explore Spirituality Peace," *HR Magazine* (April 1996), p. 82; P. Leigh, "The New Spirit at Work," *Training and Development* (February 1997), p. 193; and J. Milliman, A. Czaplewski, and J. Ferguson, "An Exploratory Empirical Assessment of the Relationship Between Spirituality and Employee Work Attitudes," paper presented at the national Academy of Management meeting, Washington, D.C. (August 2001).

76. See, for example, J. Marques, "HR's Crucial Role in the Establishment of Spirituality in the Workplace," *Journal of Academy of Business* (September 2005), pp. 27–31.

77. These examples taken from A. Zimmerman, R. G. Matthews, and K. Hudson, "Can Employers Alter Hiring Policies to Cut Health Costs?" *Wall Street Journal*, October 27, 2005, p. B1+; A. Fisher, "Helping Employees Stay Healthy," *Fortune*, August 8, 2005, p. 114; S. Armour, "Trend: You Smoke? You're Fired!" *USA Today*, May 12, 2005, p. 1A; and I. Mochari, "Belt-Tightening," *CFO Human Capital* (2005), pp. 10–12.

78. L. Cornwell, "More Companies Penalize Workers with Health Risks," *Springfield, Missouri, News-Leader*, September 10, 2007, p. 10A; and Zimmerman, Matthews, and Hudson, "Can Employers Alter Hiring Policies to Cut Health Costs?"

79. B. Pyenson and K. Fitch, "Smoking May Be Hazardous to Your Bottom Line," *Workforce Online*, http://www.workforce.com (December 2007); and L. Cornwell, The Associated Press, "Companies Tack on Fees on Insurance for Smokers," *Springfield, Missouri, News-Leader*, February 17, 2006, p. 5B.

80. M. Scott, "Obesity More Costly to U.S. Companies Than Smoking, Alcoholism," *Workforce Management*, http://www.workforce.com (April 9, 2008).

81. "Obesity Weighs Down Production," *Industry Week*, March 2008, pp. 22–23.

82. J. Appleby, "Companies Step Up Wellness Efforts," *USA Today*, August 1, 2005, pp. 1A+.

83. G. Kranz, "Prognosis Positive: Companies Aim to Get Workers Healthy," *Workforce Management*, http://www.workforce.com (April 15, 2008).

84. M. Conlin, "Hide the Doritos! Here Comes HR," *BusinessWeek,* April 28, 2008, pp. 94–96.

85. J. Fox, "Good Riddance to Pensions," *CNN Money,* January 12, 2006.

86. M. Adams, "Broken Pension System in Crying Need of a Fix," *USA Today,* November 15, 2005, p. 1B+.

87. D. Kansas, "Has the 401(k) Failed?" *Fortune,* June 22, 2009, pp. 94–98; S. Block, "Company Pensions Are Out on a Limb," *USA Today,* May 22, 2009, pp. 1B+; A. Feldman, "Retiring the 401(k) Contribution," *BusinessWeek,* November 24, 2008, p. 32; J. Appleby, "Traditional Pensions Are Almost Gone. Is Employer-Provided Health Insurance Next?" *USA Today,* November 13, 2007, pp. 1A+; S. Kelly, "FedEx, Goodyear Make Big Pension Plan Changes," *Workforce Management,* http://www.workforce.com (March 1, 2007); G. Colvin, "The End of a Dream," *Fortune,* http://www.cnnmoney.com (June 22, 2006); E. Porter and M. Williams Nash, "Benefits Go the Way of Pensions," *New York Times Online,* February 9, 2006; and Fox, "Good Riddance to Pensions."

Chapter 7

1. M. Andrews, "The Hospital of the Future," *U.S. News & World Report,* August 2009, pp. 68–74; C. Salter, "The Doctor of the Future," *Fast Company,* May 2009, pp. 64–70; L. Landro, "An Affordable Fix for Modernizing Medical Records," *Wall Street Journal,* April 30, 2009, p. A11; and J. Ioffe, "Tech Rx for Health Care," *Fortune,* March 16, 2009.

2. D. Rocks, "Reinventing Herman Miller," *BusinessWeek E.Biz,* April 3, 2000, p. EB96.

3. K. Grzbowska, "The Social Aspect of Introducing Changes into the Organization," *International Journals of Human Resources Development and Management* (February 2, 2007), p. 67; and I. M. Jawahar and G. L. McLaughlin, "Toward a Descriptive Stakeholder Theory: An Organizational Life Cycle Approach," *Academy of Management Review* (July 2001), pp. 397–415.

4. E. Shannon, "Agent of Change," *Time* (March 4, 2002), p. 17; B. Kenney, "SLA Head Shaffer Resigns Abruptly: Did 'Change Agent' Move Too Fast in Aggressive Restructuring," *Library Journal* (March 15, 2002), pp. 17–19; and T. Mudd, "Rescue Mission," *Industry Week* (May 1, 2000), pp. 30–37.

5. "Developing Your Change Management Skill" box based on J. P. Kotter and L. A. Schlesinger, "Choosing Strategies for Change," *Harvard Business Review* (March–April 1979), pp. 106–114; and T. A. Stewart, "Rate Your Readiness to Change," *Fortune,* February 7, 1994, pp. 106–110.

6. The idea for these metaphors came from P. Vaill, *Managing as a Performing Art: New Ideas for a World of Chaotic Change* (San Francisco: Jossey Bass, 1989).

7. K. Lewin, *Field Theory in Social Science* (New York: Harper & Row, 1951).

8. R. E. Levasseur, "People Skills: Change Management Tools—Lewin's Change Model," *Interfaces* (August 2001), pp. 71–74.

9. "From the Past to the Present" box based on D. A. Wren and A. G. Bedeian, *The Evolution of Management Thought,* 6th ed. (New York: John Wiley & Sons, Inc., 2009); "Biography and Quotes of Kurt Lewin," *About.com,* http://psychology.about.com (July 15, 2009); and K. T. Lewin, "The Dynamics of Group Action," *Educational Leadership,* January 1944, pp. 195–200.

10. D. Lieberman, "Nielsen Media Has Cool Head at the Top," *USA Today,* March 27, 2006, p. 3B.

11. L. S. Lüscher and M. W. Lewis, "Organizational Change and Managerial Sensemaking: Working Through Paradox," *Academy of Management Journal* (April 2008), pp. 221–40; F. Buckley and K. Monks, "Responding to Managers' Learning Needs in an Edge-of-Chaos Environment: Insights from Ireland," *Journal of Management* (April 2008), pp. 146–163; and G. Hamel, "Take It Higher," *Fortune,* February 5, 2001, pp. 169–170.

12. S. Hicks, "What Is Organization Development?" *Training and Development* (August 2000), p. 65; and H. Hornstein, "Organizational Development and Change Management: Don't Throw the Baby Out with the Bath Water," *Journal of Applied Behavioral Science* (June 2001), pp. 223–27.

13. J. Wolfram and S. Minahan, "A New Metaphor for Organization Development," *Journal of Applied Behavioral Science* (June 2006), pp. 227–43.

14. See, for instance, H. B. Jones, "Magic, Meaning, and Leadership: Weber's Model and the Empirical Literature," *Human Relations* (June 2001), p. 753.

15. G. Akin and I. Palmer, "Putting Metaphors to Work for a Change in Organizations," *Organizational Dynamics* (Winter 2000), pp. 67–79.

16. J. Grieves, "Skills, Values or Impression Management: Organizational Change and the Social Processes of Leadership, Change Agent Practice, and Process Consultation," *Journal of Management Development* (May 2000), p. 407.

17. M. McMaster, "Team Building Tips," *Sales & Marketing Management* (January 2002), p. 140; and "How To: Executive Team Building," *Training and Development* (January 2002), p. 16.

18. See, for example, J. D. Ford, L. W. Ford, and A. D'Amelio, "Resistance to Change: The Rest of the Story," *Academy of Management Review* (April 2008), pp. 362–77; A. Deutschman, "Making Change: Why Is It So Hard to Change Our Ways?" *Fast Company,* May 2005, pp. 52–62; S. B. Silverman, C. E. Pogson, and A. B. Cober, "When Employees at Work Don't Get It: A Model for Enhancing Individual Employee Change in Response to Performance Feedback," *Academy of Management Executive* (May 2005), pp. 135–47; C. E. Cunningham, C. A. Woodward, H. S. Shannon, J. MacIntosh, B. Lendrum, D. Rosenbloom, and J. Brown, "Readiness for Organizational Change: A Longitudinal Study of Workplace, Psychological and Behavioral Correlates," *Journal of Occupational and Organizational Psychology* (December 2002), pp. 377–92; M. A. Korsgaard, H. J. Sapienza, and D. M. Schweiger, "Beaten Before Begun: The Role of Procedural Justice in Planning Change," *Journal of Management* 28, no. 4 (2002), pp. 497–516; R. Kegan and L. L. Lahey, "The Real Reason People Won't Change," *Harvard Business Review* (November 2001), pp. 85–92; S. K. Piderit, "Rethinking Resistance and Recognizing Ambivalence: A Multidimensional View of Attitudes Toward an Organizational Change," *Academy of Management Review* (October 2000), pp. 783–94; C. R. Wanberg and J. T. Banas, "Predictors and Outcomes of Openness to Changes in a Reorganizing Workplace," *Journal of Applied Psychology* (February 2000), pp. 132–42; A. A. Armenakis and A. G. Bedeian, "Organizational Change: A Review of Theory and Research in the 1990s," *Journal of Management* 25, no. 3 (1999), pp. 293–315; and B. M. Staw, "Counterforces to Change," in P. S. Goodman and Associates (eds.), *Change in Organizations* (San Francisco: Jossey-Bass, 1982), pp. 87–121.

19. A. Reichers, J. P. Wanous, and J. T. Austin, "Understanding and Managing Cynicism About Organizational Change," *Academy of Management Executive* (February 1997), pp. 48–57; P. Strebel, "Why Do Employees Resist Change?" *Harvard Business Review* (May–June 1996), pp. 86–92; and J. P. Kotter and L.A. Schlesinger, "Choosing Strategies for Change," *Harvard Business Review* (March–April 1979), pp. 107–109.

20. "And the Survey Says . . ." box based on G. Kranz, "Fun in the Sun, Not the Office," *Workforce Management Online,* June 10, 2008; J. Yang and S. Ward, "An Innovation Gap?" *USA Today,* May 20, 2009, p. 1B; "Measured Success," *Industry Week,* October 2008, p. 62; J. Yang and K. Gelles, "Family Life vs. Career," *USA Today,* June 19, 2008, p. 1B; "Creating Organizational Transformations: McKinsey Global Survey Results," *The McKinsey Quarterly Online,* September 2, 2008; and "Male, Female Multitaskers Differ Little in Performance," *Wall Street Journal,* March 8, 2007, p. B6.

21. Adapted from the UK National Work-Stress Network, http://www.workstress.net.

22. R. S. Schuler, "Definition and Conceptualization of Stress in Organizations," *Organizational Behavior and Human Performance* (April 1980), p. 191.

23. The Associated Press, "Overwork Cited in Death of Japanese Worker," *New York Times Online,* July 10, 2008; "Jobs for Life," *The Economist,* http://www.economist.com (December 19, 2007); and B. L. de Mente, "Karoshi: Death from Overwork," Asia Pacific Management Forum, http://www.apmforum.com (May 2002).

24. See, for example, "Stressed Out: Extreme Job Stress: Survivors' Tales," *Wall Street Journal,* January 17, 2001, p. B1.

25. See, for instance, S. Bates, "Expert: Don't Overlook Employee Burnout," *HR Magazine* (August 2003), p. 14.

26. "Right or Wrong?" box based on D. Cole, "The Big Chill," *U.S. News & World Report,* December 6, 2004, pp. EE2-EE5.

27. H. Benson, "Are You Working Too Hard?" *Harvard Business Review* (November 2005), pp. 53–58; B. Cryer, R. McCraty, and D. Childre, "Pull the Plug on Stress," *Harvard Business Review* (July 2003), pp. 102–107; C. Daniels, "The Last Taboo"; C. L. Cooper and S. Cartwright, "Healthy Mind, Healthy Organization—A Proactive Approach to Occupational Stress," *Human Relations* (April 1994), pp. 455–71; C. A. Heaney et al., "Industrial Relations, Worksite Stress Reduction and Employee Well-Being: A Participatory Action Research Investigation," *Journal of Organizational Behavior* (September 1993), pp. 495–510; C. D. Fisher, "Boredom at Work: A Neglected Concept," *Human Relations* (March 1993), pp. 395–417; and S. E. Jackson, "Participation in Decision Making as a Strategy for Reducing Job-Related Strain," *Journal of Applied Psychology* (February 1983), pp. 3–19.

28. C. Mamberto, "Companies Aim to Combat Job-Related Stress," *Wall Street Journal,* August 13, 2007, p. B6.

29. "Employee Assistance Programs," *HR Magazine* (May 2003), p. 143.

30. "EAPs with the Most," *Managing Benefits Plans* (March 2003), p. 8; and K. Tyler, "Helping Employees Cope with Grief," *HR Magazine* (September 2003), pp. 55–58.

31. F. Hansen, "Employee Assistance Programs (EAPs) Grow and Expand Their Reach," *Compensation and Benefits Review* (March/April 2000), p. 13.

32. F. Phillips, "Employee Assistance Programs: A New Way to Control Health Care Costs," *Employee Benefit Plan Review* (August 2003), pp. 22–24.

33. K. Lee, "EAP Diversity Detracts from Original Focus, Some Say," *Employee Benefits News* (July 1, 2003), p. 1.

34. See, for instance, P. Petesch, "Workplace Fitness or Workplace Fits?" *HR Magazine* (July 2001), pp. 137–40.

35. C. Petersen, "Value of Complementary Care Rises, But Poses Challenges," *Managed HealthCare* (November 2000), pp. 47–48.

36. J. McGregor, "The World's Most Innovative Companies," *BusinessWeek,* April 24, 2006, p. 64.

37. J. E. Perry-Smith and C. E. Shalley, "The Social Side of Creativity: A Static and Dynamic Social Network Perspective," *Academy of Management Review* (January 2003), pp. 89–106; and P. K. Jagersma, "Innovate or Die: It's Not Easy, But It Is Possible to Enhance Your Organization's Ability to Innovate," *Journal of Business Strategy* (January–February 2003), pp. 25–28.

38. These definitions are based on T. M. Amabile, *Creativity in Context* (Boulder, CO: Westview Press, 1996).

39. C. Salter, "Mattel Learns to 'Throw the Bunny,'" *Fast Company,* November 2002, p. 22; and L. Bannon, "Think Tank in Toyland," *Wall Street Journal,* June 6, 2002, pp. B1, B3.

40. C. Vogel and J. Cagan, *Creating Breakthrough Products: Innovation from Product Planning to Program Approval* (Upper Saddle River, NJ: Prentice Hall, 2002).

41. R. W. Woodman, J. E. Sawyer, and R. W. Griffin, "Toward a Theory of Organizational Creativity," *Academy of Management Review* (April 1993), pp. 293–321.

42. T. M. Egan, "Factors Influencing Individual Creativity in the Workplace: An Examination of Quantitative Empirical Research," *Advances in Developing Human Resources* (May 2005), pp. 160–81; N. Madjar, G. R. Oldham, and M. G. Pratt, "There's No Place Like Home? The Contributions of Work and Nonwork Creativity Support to Employees' Creative Performance," *Academy of Management Journal* (August 2002), pp. 757–767; T. M. Amabile, C. N. Hadley, and S. J. Kramer, "Creativity Under the Gun," *Harvard Business Review* (August 2002), pp. 52–61; J. B. Sorensen and T. E. Stuart, "Aging, Obsolescence, and Organizational Innovation," *Administrative Science Quarterly* (March 2000), pp. 81–112; G. R. Oldham and A. Cummings, "Employee Creativity: Personal and Contextual Factors at Work," *Academy of Management Journal* (June 1996), pp. 607–34; and F. Damanpour, "Organizational Innovation: A Meta Analysis of Effects of Determinants and Moderators," *Academy of Management Journal* (September 1991), pp. 555–590.

43. P. R. Monge, M. D. Cozzens, and N. S. Contractor, "Communication and Motivational Predictors of the Dynamics of Organizational Innovations," *Organization Science* (May 1992), pp. 250–74.

44. Amabile, Hadley, and Kramer, "Creativity Under the Gun."

45. Madjar, Oldham, and Pratt, "There's No Place Like Home?"

46. See, for instance, J. E. Perry-Smith, "Social Yet Creative: The Role of Social Relationships in Facilitating Individual Creativity," *Academy of Management Journal* (February 2006), pp. 85–101; C. E. Shalley, J. Zhou, and G. R. Oldham, "The Effects of Personal and Contextual Characteristics on Creativity: Where Should We Go from Here?" *Journal of Management* 30, no. 6 (2004), pp. 933–58; J. E. Perry-Smith and C. E. Shalley, "The Social Side of Creativity: A Static and Dynamic Social Network Perspective"; J. M. George and J. Zhou, "When Openness to Experience and Conscientiousness

Are Related to Creative Behavior: An Interactional Approach," *Journal of Applied Psychology* (June 2001), pp. 513–24; J. Zhou, "Feedback Valence, Feedback Style, Task Autonomy, and Achievement Orientation: Interactive Effects on Creative Behavior," *Journal of Applied Psychology* 83 (1998), p. 261–76; T. M. Amabile, R. Conti, H. Coon, J. Lazenby, and M. Herron, "Assessing the Work Environment for Creativity," *Academy of Management Journal* (October 1996), pp. 1154–84; S. G. Scott and R. A. Bruce, "Determinants of Innovative People: A Path Model of Individual Innovation in the Workplace," *Academy of Management Journal* (June 1994), pp. 580–607; R. Moss Kanter, "When a Thousand Flowers Bloom: Structural, Collective, and Social Conditions for Innovation in Organization," in B. M. Staw and L. L. Cummings (eds.), *Research in Organizational Behavior*, vol. 10 (Greenwich, CT: JAI Press, 1988), pp. 169–211; and Amabile, *Creativity in Context*.

47. J. McGregor, "The World's Most Innovative Companies," p. 70.
48. Ibid.
49. J. Ramos, "Producing Change That Lasts," *Across the Board* (March 1994), pp. 29–33; T. Stjernberg and A. Philips, "Organizational Innovations in a Long-Term Perspective: Legitimacy and Souls-of-Fire as Critical Factors of Change and Viability," *Human Relations* (October 1993), pp. 1193–2023; and J. M. Howell and C. A. Higgins, "Champions of Change," *Business Quarterly* (Spring 1990), pp. 31–32.

Chapter 8

1. M. Conlin, "Making the Case for Unequal Pay and Perks," *BusinessWeek Online,* March 12, 2009; "Good Job, Microsoft," *The Bing Blog,* http://stanleybing.blogs.fortune.cnn.com (February 24, 2009); M. Conlin and J. Greene, "How to Make a Microserf Smile," *BusinessWeek,* September 10, 2007, pp. 56–59; M. Conlin, "Online Extra: Microsoft's Meet-My-Mood Offices," *BusinessWeek Online,* September 10, 2007; and M. Conlin and J. Greene, "Online Extra: Reshaping Microsoft's HR Agenda," *BusinessWeek Online,* September 10, 2007.
2. K. M. Kroll, "Absence-Minded," *CFO Human Capital,* 2006, pp. 12–14.
3. D. W. Organ, *Organizational Citizenship Behavior: The Good Soldier Syndrome* (Lexington, MA: Lexington Books, 1988), p. 4. See also J. L. Lavell, D. E. Rupp, and J. Brockner, "Taking a Multifoci Approach to the Study of Justice, Social Exchange, and Citizenship Behavior: The Target Similarity Model," *Journal of Management* (December 2007), pp. 841–66; and J. A. LePine, A. Erez, and D. E. Johnson, "The Nature and Dimensionality of Organizational Citizenship Behavior: A Critical Review and Meta-Analysis," *Journal of Applied Psychology* (February 2002), pp. 52–65.
4. R. Ilies, B. A. Scott, and T. A. Judge, "The Interactive Effects of Personal Traits and Experienced States on Intraindividual Patterns of Citizenship Behavior," *Academy of Management Journal* (June 2006), pp. 561–75; P. Cardona, B. S. Lawrence, and P. M. Bentler, "The Influence of Social and Work Exchange Relationships on Organizational Citizenship Behavior," *Group & Organization Management* (April 2004), pp. 219–47; M. C. Bolino and W. H. Turnley, "Going the Extra Mile: Cultivating and Managing Employee Citizenship Behavior," *Academy of Management Executive* (August 2003), pp. 60–73; M. C. Bolino, W. H. Turnley, and

J. J. Bloodgood, "Citizenship Behavior and the Creation of Social Capital in Organizations," *Academy of Management Review* (October 2002), pp. 505–22; and P. M. Podsakoff, S. B. MacKenzie, J. B. Paine, and D. G. Bachrach, "Organizational Citizenship Behaviors: A Critical Review of the Theoretical and Empirical Literature and Suggestions for Future Research," *Journal of Management* 26, no. 3 (2000), pp. 543–48.

5. M. C. Bolino and W. H. Turnley, "The Personal Costs of Citizenship Behavior: The Relationship Between Individual Initiative and Role Overload, Job Stress, and Work-Family Conflict," *Journal of Applied Psychology* (July 2005), pp. 740–48.
6. This definition adapted from R. W. Griffin and Y. P. Lopez, "Bad Behavior in Organizations: A Review and Typology for Future Research," *Journal of Management* (December 2005), pp. 988–1005.
7. S. J. Becker, "Empirical Validation of Affect, Behavior, and Cognition as Distinct Components of Behavior," *Journal of Personality and Social Psychology* (May 1984), pp. 1191–1205.
8. "A Case of Cognitive Dissonance," *U.S. News and World Report,* November 26, 2001, p. 10.
9. S. P. Robbins, *Essentials of Organizational Behavior,* 8th ed. (Upper Saddle River, NJ: Prentice Hall, 2004), p. 19.
10. D. R. May, R. L. Gilson, and L. M. Harter, "The Psychological Conditions of Meaningfulness, Safety and Availability and the Engagement of the Human Spirit at Work," *Journal of Occupational and Organizational Psychology* (March 2004), pp. 11–37; R. T. Keller, "Job Involvement and Organizational Commitment as Longitudinal Predictors of Job Performance: A Study of Scientists and Engineers," *Journal of Applied Psychology* (August 1997), pp. 539–45; W. Kahn, "Psychological Conditions of Personal Engagement and Disengagement at Work," *Academy of Management Journal* (December 1990), pp. 692–794; and P. P. Brooke, Jr., D. W. Russell and J. L. Price, "Discriminant Validation of Measures of Job Satisfaction, Job Involvement, and Organizational Commitment," *Journal of Applied Psychology* (May 1988), pp. 139–45. Also, see, for example, J. Smythe, "Engaging Employees to Drive Performance," *Communication World* (May/June 2008), pp. 20–22; A. B. Bakker and W. B. Schaufeli, "Positive Organizational Behavior: Engaged Employees in Flourishing Organizations," *Journal of Organizational Behavior* (February 2008), pp. 147–54; U. Aggarwal, S. Datta, and S. Bhargava, "The Relationship Between Human Resource Practices, Psychological Contract, and Employee Engagement—Implications for Managing Talent," *IIMB Management Review* (September 2007), pp. 313–25; M. C. Christian and J. E. Slaughter, "Work Engagement: A Meta-Analytic Review and Directions for Research in an Emerging Area," *AOM Proceedings* (August 2007), pp. 1–6; C. H. Thomas, "A New Measurement Scale for Employee Engagement: Scale Development, Pilot Test, and Replication," *AOM Proceedings* (August 2007), pp. 1–6; A. M. Saks, "Antecedents and Consequences of Employee Engagement," *Journal of Managerial Psychology* 21, no. 7 (2006), pp. 600–19; and A. Parsley, "Road Map for Employee Engagement," *Management Services* (Spring 2006), pp. 10–11.
11. "Driving Employee Engagement in a Global Workforce," *Watson Wyatt Worldwide,* 2007/2008, p. 2.
12. A. J. Elliott and P. G. Devine, "On the Motivational Nature of Cognitive Dissonance: Dissonance as Psychological

Discomfort," *Journal of Personality and Social Psychology* (September 1994), pp. 382–94.

13. L. Festinger, *A Theory of Cognitive Dissonance* (Stanford, CA: Stanford University Press, 1957); and C. Crossen, "Cognitive Dissonance Became a Milestone in 1950s Psychology," *Wall Street Journal,* December 4, 2006, p. B1.

14. H. C. Koh and E. H. Y. Boo, "The Link Between Organizational Ethics and Job Satisfaction: A Study of Managers in Singapore," *Journal of Business Ethics* (February 15, 2001), p. 309.

15. "And the Survey Says . . ." box based on G. Kranz, "Companies Not Listening to Employees," *Workforce Management Online,* July 8, 2008; M. Larson, "Survey Reveals Alarming Lack of Generational Workplace Interaction," *Workforce Management Online,* July 2008; C. Porath and C. Pearson, "How Toxic Colleagues Corrode Performance," *Harvard Business Review* (April 2009), p. 24; L. Petrecca, "Many Satisfied with Job Despite Tough Times," *USA Today,* March 13, 2009; L. T. Cullen, "SATs for J-O-B-S," *Time,* April 30, 2006, p. 89; and F. Panchak, "Wanted: Inspired Leaders," *IndustryWeek,* May 2005, p. 7.

16. See, for example, J. Jermias, "Cognitive Dissonance and Resistance to Change: The Influence of Commitment Confirmation and Feedback on Judgment Usefulness of Accounting Systems," *Accounting, Organizations, and Society* (March 2001), p. 141.

17. T. A. Judge, C. J. Thoresen, J. E. Bono, and G. K. Patton, "The Job Satisfaction-Job Performance Relationship: A Qualitative and Quantitative Review," *Psychological Bulletin* (May 2001), pp. 376–407.

18. L. Saari and T. A. Judge, "Employee Attitudes and Job Satisfaction," *Human Resource Management* (Winter 2004), pp. 395–407; and T. A. Judge and A. H. Church, "Job Satisfaction: Research and Practice," in C. L. Cooper and E. A. Locke (eds.), *Industrial and Organizational Psychology: Linking Theory with Practice* (Oxford, UK: Blackwell, 2000).

19. D. A. Harrison, D. A. Newman, and P. L. Roth, "How Important Are Job Attitudes? Meta-Analytic Comparisons of Integrative Behavioral Outcomes and Time Sequences," *Academy of Management Journal* (April 2006), pp. 305–25.

20. C. Arnst, "Better Loving Through Chemistry," *BusinessWeek,* October 24, 2005, p. 48.

21. CPP, Inc., Myers-Briggs Type Indicator® (MBTI®), http://www.cpp.com/products/mbti/index.asp (2006).

22. See, for instance, K. Garrety, R. Badham, V. Morrigan, W. Rifkin, and M. Zanko, "The Use of Personality Typing in Organizational Change: Discourse, Emotions, and the Reflective Subject," *Human Relations* (February 2003), pp. 211–35.

23. P. Moran, "Personality Characteristics and Growth-Orientation of the Small Business Owner Manger," *Journal of Managerial Psychology* (July 2000), p. 651; and M. Higgs, "Is There a Relationship Between the Myers-Briggs Type Indicator and Emotional Intelligence?" *Journal of Managerial Psychology* (September/October 2001), pp. 488–513.

24. J. M. Digman, "Personality Structure: Emergence of the Five Factor Model," in M. R. Rosenweig and L. W. Porter (eds.), *Annual Review of Psychology* 41 (Palo Alto, CA: Annual Reviews, 1990), pp. 417–40; O. P. John, "The Big Five Factor Taxonomy: Dimensions of Personality in the Natural Language and in Questionnaires," in L. A. Pervin (ed.), *Handbook of Personality Theory and Research* (New York: Guilford Press, 1990), pp. 66–100; and M. K. Mount, M. R. Barrick, and J. P. Strauss, "Validity of Observer Ratings of the Big Five Personality Factors," *Journal of Applied Psychology* (April 1996), pp. 272–80.

25. See G. Vittorio, C. Barbaranelli, and G. Guido, "Brand Personality: How to Make the Metaphor Fit," *Journal of Economic Psychology* (June 2001), p. 377; G. M. Hurtz and J. J. Donovan, "Personality and Job Performance: The Big Five Revisited," *Journal of Applied Psychology* (December 2000), p. 869; and W. A. Hochwarter, L. A. Witt, and K. M. Kacmar, "Perceptions of Organizational Politics as a Moderator of the Relationship Between Conscientiousness and Job Performance," *Journal of Applied Psychology* (June 2000), p. 472.

26. Barrick and Mount, "Autonomy as a Moderator of the Relationship Between the Big Five Personality Dimensions and Job Performance."

27. See also I. T. Robertson, H. Baron, P. Gibbons, R. Maclver, and G. Nyfield, "Conscientiousness and Managerial Performance," *Journal of Occupational and Organizational Psychology* (June 2000), pp. 171–78.

28. R. Barrick, M. Piotrowski, and G. L. Stewart, "Personality and Job Performance: Test of the Mediating Effects of Motivation Among Sales Representatives," *Journal of Applied Psychology* (February 2002), pp. 43–52.

29. This section is based on R. Bar-On and J. D. A. Parker, *The Handbook of Emotional Intelligence: Theory, Development, Assessment, and Application at Home, School, and in the Work Place* (San Francisco, CA: Jossey-Bass, 2000); B. E. Ashforth, "The Handbook of Emotional Intelligence: Theory, Development, Assessment, and Application at Home, School, and in the Work Place: A Review," *Personnel Psychology* (Autumn 2001), pp. 721–24: and S. Fox, "Promoting Emotional Intelligence in Organizations: Make Training in Emotional Intelligence Effective," *Personnel Psychology* (Spring 2002), pp. 236–40.

30. See, for instance, C. S. P. Fernandez, "Emotional Intelligence in the Workplace," *Journal of Public Health Management and Practice* (February 2007), pp. 80–82.

31. For an interesting perspective on the application of emotional intelligence, see P. J. Jordan, N. M. Ashkanasy, and C. E. J. Hartel, "Emotional Intelligence as a Moderator of Emotional and Behavioral Reactions to Job Insecurity," *Academy of Management Review* (July 2002), pp. 361–72.

32. "Right or Wrong?" box based on M. Conlin, "Are People in Your Office Acting Oddly?" *BusinessWeek,* April 13, 2009, p. 54; and J. Hoffman, "Working Hard to Look Busy," *New York Times Online,* January 25, 2009.

33. C. Cherniss and R. D. Caplan, "A Case Study of Implementing Emotional Intelligence Programs in Organizations," *Journal of Organizational Excellence* (Winter 2001), pp. 763–86; and S. B. Vanessa-Urch and W. Deuskat, "Building the Emotional Intelligence of Groups," *Harvard Business Review* (March 2001), pp. 81–91.

34. "Can't We All Just Get Along," *BusinessWeek* (October 9, 2000), p. 18.

35. C. Moller and S. Powell, "Emotional Intelligence and the Challenges of Quality Management," *Leadership and Organizational Development Journal* (July/August 2001), pp. 341–45.

36. See L.A. Downey, V. Papageorgiou, and C. Stough, "Examining the Relationship Between Leadership, Emotional Intelligence, and Intuition in Female Managers," *Leadership & Organization Development Journal* (April 2006), pp. 250–64.

37. See, for instance, J. Silvester, F. M. Anderson-Gough, N. R. Anderson, and A. R. Mohamed, "Locus of Control, Attributions and Impression Management in the Selection Interview," *Journal of Occupational and Organizational Psychology* (March 2002), pp. 59–77; D. W. Organ and C. N. Greene, "Role Ambiguity, Locus of Control, and Work Satisfaction," *Journal of Applied Psychology* (February 1974), pp. 101–02; and T. R. Mitchell, C. M. Smyser and S. E. Weed, "Locus of Control: Supervision and Work Satisfaction," *Academy of Management Journal* (September 1975), pp. 623–631.

38. R. G. Vleeming, "Machiavellianism: A Preliminary Review," *Psychology Reports* (February 1979), pp. 295–310.

39. P. Van Kenhove, I. Vermeir, and S. Verniers, "An Empirical Investigation of the Relationship Between Ethical Beliefs, Ethical Ideology, Political Preference and Need for Closure," *Journal of Business Ethics* (August 15, 2001), p. 347.

40. Based on J. Brockner, *Self-Esteem at Work* (Lexington, MA: Lexington Books, 1988), chs. 1–4.

41. See, for instance, R. Vermunt, D. van Knippenberg, B. van Knippenberg, and E. Blaauw, "Self-Esteem and Outcome Fairness: Differential Importance of Procedural and Outcome Considerations," *Journal of Applied Psychology* (August 2001), p. 621; T. A. Judge and J. E. Bono, "Relationship of Core Self-Evaluation Traits—Self-Esteem, Generalized Self Efficacy, Locus of Control, and Emotional Stability—With Job Satisfaction and Job Performance," *Journal of Applied Psychology* (February 2001), p. 80; and D. B. Fedor, J. M. Maslyn, W. D. Davis, and K. Mathieson, "Performance Improvement Efforts in Response to Negative Feedback: The Roles of Source Power and Recipient Self-Esteem," *Journal of Management* (January/February 2001), pp. 79–97.

42. M. Snyder, *Public Appearances, Private Realities: The Psychology of Self-Monitoring* (New York: W. H. Freeman, 1987).

43. See, for example, P. M. Fandt, "Managing Impressions with Information: A Field Study of Organizational Realities," *Journal of Applied Behavioral Science* (June 2001), pp. 180–205.

44. Ibid.

45. R. N. Taylor and M. D. Dunnette, "Influence of Dogmatism, Risk Taking Propensity, and Intelligence on Decision Making Strategies for a Sample of Industrial Managers," *Journal of Applied Psychology* (August 1974), pp. 420–423.

46. I. L. Janis and L. Mann, *Decision Making: A Psychological Analysis of Conflict, Choice, and Commitment* (New York: Free Press, 1977).

47. N. Kogan and M. A. Wallach, "Group Risk Taking as a Function of Members' Anxiety and Defensiveness," *Journal of Personality* (March 1967), pp. 50–63.

48. K. Hyrshy, "Entrepreneurial Metaphors and Concepts: An Exploratory Study," *Journal of Managerial Psychology* (July 2000), p. 653; and B. McCarthy, "The Cult of Risk Taking and Social Learning: A Study of Irish Entrepreneurs," *Management Decision* (August 2000), pp. 563–75.

49. J. L. Holland, *Making Vocational Choices: A Theory of Vocational Personalities and Work Environments* (Odessa, FL: Psychological Assessment Resources, 1997).

50. S. Bates, "Personality Counts: Psychological Tests Can Help Peg the Job Applicants Best Suited for Certain Jobs," *HR Magazine* (February 2002), pp. 28–38; and K. J. Jansen and A. K. Brown, "Toward a Multi-Level Theory of Person Environment Fit," *Academy of Management Proceedings from the Fifty Eighth Annual Meeting of the Academy of Management,* San Diego, CA (August 7–12, 1998), pp. HR: FR1–FR8.

51. See, for instance, G. W. M. Ip and M. H. Bond, "Culture, Values, and the Spontaneous Self-Concept," *Asian Journal of Psychology* 1 (1995), pp. 30–36; J. E. Williams, J. L. Saiz, D. L. Formyduval, M. L. Munick, E. E. Fogle, A. Adom, A. Haque, F. Neto, and J. Yu, "Cross-Cultural Variation in the Importance of Psychological Characteristics: A Seven-Year Country Study," *International Journal of Psychology* (October 1995), pp. 529–50; V. Benet and N. G. Walker, "The Big Seven Factor Model of Personality Description: Evidence for Its Cross-Cultural Generalizability in a Spanish Sample," *Journal of Personality and Social Psychology* (October 1995), pp. 701–18; R. R. McCrae and P. To. Costa Jr., "Personality Trait Structure as a Human Universal," *American Psychologist* (1997), pp. 509–16; and M. J. Schmit, J. A. Kihm, and C. Robie, "Development of a Global Measure of Personality," *Personnel Psychology* (Spring 2000), pp. 153–93.

52. J. F. Salgado, "The Five Factor Model of Personality and Job Performance in the European Community," *Journal of Applied Psychology* (February 1997), pp. 30–43. *Note:* This study covered the 15-nation European community and did not include the 10 countries that joined in 2004.

53. G. Kranz, "Organizations Look to Get Personal in '07," *Workforce Management,* http://www.workforce.com (June 19, 2007).

54. H. H. Kelley, "Attribution in Social Interaction," in E. Jones et al. (eds.), *Behavior* (Morristown, NJ: General Learning Press, 1972).

55. G. Miller and T. Lawson, "The Effect of an Informational Option on the Fundamental Attribution Error," *Personality and Social Psychology Bulletin* (June 1989), pp. 194–204. See also G. Charness and E. Haruvy, "Self-Serving Bias: Evidence from a Simulated Labour Relationship," *Journal of Managerial Psychology* (July 2000), p. 655; and T. J. Elkins, J. S. Phillips, and R. Konopaske, "Gender-Related Biases in Evaluations of Sex Discrimination Allegations: Is Perceived Threat a Key?" *Journal of Applied Psychology* (April 2002), pp. 280–93.

56. "Managing Diversity" box based on S. T. Fiske, "Social Cognition and Social Perception," *Annual Review of Psychology* (1993), pp. 155–94; G. N. Powell and Y. Kido, "Managerial Stereotypes in a Global Economy: A Comparative Study of Japanese and American Business Students' Perspectives," *Psychological Reports* (February 1994), pp. 219–26; and J. L. Hilton and W. von Hippel, "Stereotypes," in J. T. Spence, J. M. Darley, and D. J. Foss (eds.), *Annual Review of Psychology,* vol. 47 (Palo Alto, CA: Annual Reviews Inc., 1996), pp. 237–71.

57. "From the Past to the Present" box based on B. F. Skinner, *Contingencies of Reinforcement;* and S. P. Robbins and T. A. Judge, *Organizational Behavior,* 13th ed. (Upper Saddle River, NJ: Pearson Prentice Hall, 2009).

58. B. F. Skinner, *Contingencies of Reinforcement* (East Norwalk, CT: Appleton-Century-Crofts, 1971).

59. A. Applebaum, "Linear Thinking," *Fast Company,* December 2004, p. 35.

60. A. Bandura, *Social Learning Theory* (Upper Saddle River, NJ: Prentice Hall, 1977).

61. For an interesting article on the subject, see D. Nitsch, M. Baetz, and J. C. Hughes, "Why Code of Conduct Violations Go Unreported: A Conceptual Framework to Guide Intervention and Future Research," *Journal of Business Ethics* (April 2005), pp. 327–41.

62. S. Armour, "Generation Y: They've Arrived at Work with a New Attitude," *USA Today,* November 6, 2005, pp. 1B+.

63. N. Ramachandran, "New Paths at Work," *U.S. News & World Report,* March 20, 2006, p. 47.

64. D. Sacks, "Scenes from the Culture Clash," *Fast Company,* January/February 2006, p. 75.

65. Armour, "Generation Y," p. 2B.

66. Armour, "Generation Y"; B. Moses, "The Challenges of Managing Gen Y," *The Globe and Mail,* March 11, 2005, p. C1; and C. A. Martin, *Managing Generation Y* (Amherst, MA: HRD Press, 2001).

67. C. M. Pearson and C. L. Porath, "On the Nature, Consequences, and Remedies of Workplace Incivility: No Time for Nice? Think Again," *Academy of Management Executive* (February 2005), pp. 7–18.

68. J. Robison, "Be Nice: It's Good for Business," *Gallup Brain,* brain.gallup.com (August 12, 2004).

69. Y. Vardi and E. Weitz, *Misbehavior in Organizations* (Mahwah, NJ: Lawrence Erlbaum Associates, 2004), pp. 246–47.

Chapter 9

1. "Ferrari London Store Opening Stops Traffic," *License Magazine Online,* June 2009; S. Oster, "Open a Bank Account and Test Drive a Ferrari," *Wall Street Journal,* June 1, 2007, p. B3; "Kudos: Ferrari Named 'Best Place to Work' in Europe," http://www.edmonds.com (May 4, 2007); and M. Moskowitz and R. Levering, "100 Best Companies to Work For," "10 Great Companies to Work For in Europe," "Ferrari: Good Food, Good People, Lots of Fun—Sound Like a European Holiday? No, It's a Great Job," *Fortune,* January 7, 2003.

2. B. Mezrich, *Bringing Down the House: The Inside Story of Six MIT Students Who Took Vegas for Millions* (New York: Free Press, 2002). The 2008 film *21* was a fictional work based loosely on the story.

3. B. W. Tuckman and M. C. Jensen, "Stages of Small-Group Development Revisited," *Group and Organizational Studies* (December 1977), pp. 419–27; and M. F. Maples, "Group Development: Extending Tuckman's Theory," *Journal for Specialists in Group Work* (Fall 1988), pp. 17–23.

4. "And the Survey Says . . ." box based on K. Merriman, "Low-Trust Teams Prefer Individualized Pay," *Harvard Business Review* (November 2008), p. 32; B. J. West, J. L. Patera, and M. K. Carsten, "Team Level Positivity: Investigating Positive Psychological Capacities and Team Level Outcomes," *Journal of Organizational Behavior* (February 2009), p. 249; T. Purdum, "Teaming, Take 2," *IndustryWeek,* May 2005, pp. 41–43; L. G. Boiney, "Gender Impacts Virtual Work Teams," *The Graziadio Business Report,* Fall 2001, Pepperdine University; J. Yang and K. Simmons, "Traits of Good Team Players," *USA Today,* November 21, 2007, p. 1B; J. Yang and M. E. Mullins, "Workers More Productive in Small Groups," *USA Today,* January 10, 2007, p. 1B; and M. Weinstein, "Coming Up Short? Join the Club," *Training* (April 2006), p. 14.

5. L. N. Jewell and H. J. Reitz, *Group Effectiveness in Organizations* (Glenview, IL: Scott, Foresman, 1981); and M. Kaeter, "Repotting Mature Work Teams," *Training* (April 1994), pp. 54–56.

6. "From the Past to the Present" box based on E. J. Thomas and C. F. Fink, "Effects of Group Size," *Psychological Bulletin* (July 1963), pp. 371–84; and M. E. Shaw, *Group Dynamics:* *The Psychology of Small Group Behavior* (New York: McGraw-Hill, 1975).

7. S. E. Asch, "Effects of Group Pressure upon the Modification and Distortion of Judgments," in H. Guetzkow (ed.), *Groups, Leadership, and Men* (Pittsburgh, PA: Carnegie Press, 1951), pp. 177–90.

8. Asch, "Effects of Group Pressure upon the Modification and Distortion of Judgments."

9. R. Albanese and D. D. Van Fleet, "Rational Behavior in Groups: The Free Riding Tendency," *Academy of Management Review* (April 1985), pp. 244–55.

10. L. Berkowitz, "Group Standards, Cohesiveness, and Productivity," *Human Relations* (November 1954), pp. 509–519.

11. See, for example, R. A. Henry, J. Kmet, and A. Landa, "Examining the Impact of Interpersonal Cohesiveness on Group Accuracy Interventions: The Importance of Matching Versus Buffering," *Organizational Behavior and Human Decision Processes* (January 2002), pp. 25–43.

12. Cited in T. Purdum, "Teaming, Take 2," *IndustryWeek,* May 2005, p. 43; and C. Joinson, "Teams at Work," *HR Magazine* (May 1999), p. 30.

13. See, for example, S. A. Mohrman, S. G. Cohen, and A. M. Mohrman, Jr., *Designing Team-Based Organizations* (San Francisco: Jossey-Bass, 1995); P. MacMillan, *The Performance Factor: Unlocking the Secrets of Teamwork* (Nashville, TN: Broadman & Holman, 2001); and E. Salas, C. A. Bowers, and E. Eden (eds.), *Improving Teamwork in Organizations: Applications of Resource Management Training* (Mahwah, NJ: Lawrence Erlbaum, 2002).

14. Information for this section is based on J. R. Katzenbach and D. K. Smith, *The Wisdom of Teams* (Boston: Harvard Business School Press, 1993), pp. 21, 45, 85; and D. C. Kinlaw, *Developing Superior Work Teams* (Lexington, MA: Lexington Books, 1991), pp. 3–21.

15. S. Adams and L. Kydoniefs, "Making Teams Work: Bureau of Labor Statistics Learns What Works and What Doesn't," *Quality Progress* (January 2000), pp. 43–49.

16. D. Hoffman, "At Wachovia, Fund Teams Work: Bank's Buddy System Improves Performance," *Investment News* (February 2001), p. 8.

17. T. Capozzoli, "How to Succeed with Self-Directed Work Teams," *Supervision* (February 2002), pp. 25–27.

18. See, for instance, E. Sunstrom, DeMeuse, and D. Futrell, "Work Teams: Applications and Effectiveness," *American Psychologist* (February 1990), pp. 120–33.

19. J. S. McClenahen, "Bearing Necessities," *IndustryWeek,* October 2004, pp. 63–65; P. J. Kiger, "Acxiom Rebuilds from Scratch," *Workforce* (December 2002), pp. 52–55; and T. Boles, "Viewpoint—Leadership Lessons from NASCAR," *IndustryWeek,* May 21, 2002, http://www.industryweek.com.

20. M. Cianni and D. Wanuck, "Individual Growth and Team Enhancement: Moving Toward a New Model of Career Development," *Academy of Management Executive* (February 1997), pp. 105–15.

21. "Teams," *Training* (October 1996), p. 69; and C. Joinson "Teams at Work," p. 30.

22. G. M. Spreitzer, S. G. Cohen, and G. E. Ledford, Jr., "Developing Effective Self-Managing Work Teams in Service Organizations," *Group & Organization Management* (September 1999), pp. 340–66.

23. "Meet the New Steel," *Fortune,* October 1, 2007, pp. 68–71.

24. J. Appleby and R. Davis, "Teamwork Used to Save Money; Now It Saves Lives," *USA Today,* http://www.usatoday.com (March 1, 2001).

25. "Technology and the Manager's Job" box based on P. Evans, "The Wiki Factor," *BizEd,* January–February 2006, pp. 28–32; and M. McCafferty, "A Human Inventory," *CFO,* April 2005, pp. 83–85.

26. A. Malhotra, A. Majchrzak, R. Carman, and V. Lott, "Radical Innovation Without Collocation: A Case Study at Boeing-Rocketdyne," *MIS Quarterly* (June 2001), pp. 229–49.

27. A. Stuart, "Virtual Agreement," *CFO,* November 2007, p. 24.

28. A. Malhotra, A. Majchrzak, and B. Rosen, "Leading Virtual Teams," *Academy of Management Perspectives* (February 2007), pp. 60–70; B. L. Kirkman and J. E. Mathieu, "The Dimensions and Antecedents of Team Virtuality," *Journal of Management* (October 2005), pp. 700–18; J. Gordon, "Do Your Virtual Teams Deliver Only Virtual Performance?" *Training* (June 2005), pp. 20–25; L. L. Martins, L. L. Gilson, and M. T. Maynard, "Virtual Teams: What Do We Know and Where Do We Go From Here?" *Journal of Management* (December 2004), pp. 805–35; S. A. Furst, M. Reeves, B. Rosen, and R. S. Blackburn, "Managing the Life Cycle of Virtual Teams," *Academy of Management Executive* (May 2004), pp. 6–20; B. L. Kirkman, B. Rosen, P. E. Tesluk, and C. B. Gibson, "The Impact of Team Empowerment on Virtual Team Performance: The Moderating Role of Face-to-Face Interaction," *Academy of Management Journal* (April 2004), pp. 175–92; F. Keenan and S. E. Ante, "The New Teamwork," *Business Week E.Biz,* February 18, 2002, pp. EB12–EB16; and G. Imperato, "Real Tools for Virtual Teams," *Fast Company*, July 2000, pp. 378–87.

29. See, for instance, J. R. Hackman, "The Design of Work Teams," in J. W. Lorsch (ed.), *Handbook of Organizational Behavior* (Upper Saddle River, NJ: Prentice Hall, 1987), pp. 315–42; and M. A. Campion, G. J. Medsker, and C. A. Higgs, "Relations Between Work Group Characteristics and Effectiveness: Implications for Designing Effective Work Groups," *Personnel Psychology* (Winter 1993), pp. 823–50.

30. This model is based on M. A. Campion, E. M. Papper, and G. J. Medsker, "Relations Between Work Team Characteristics and Effectiveness: A Replication and Extension," *Personnel Psychology* (Summer 1996), pp. 429–452; D. E. Hyatt and T. M. Ruddy, "An Examination of the Relationship Between Work Group Characteristics and Performance: Once More into the Breech," *Personnel Psychology* (Autumn 1997), pp. 553–85; S. G. Cohen and D. E. Bailey, "What Makes Teams Work: Group Effectiveness Research from the Shop Floor to the Executive Suite," *Journal of Management* (September 1997), pp. 239–90; L. Thompson, *Making the Team* (Upper Saddle River, NJ: Prentice Hall, 2000), pp. 18–33; and J. R. Hackman, *Leading Teams: Setting the Stage for Great Performance* (Boston: Harvard Business School Press, 2002).

31. See M. Mattson, T. V. Mumford, and G. S. Sintay, "Taking Teams to Task: A Normative Model for Designing or Recalibrating Work Teams," paper presented at the National Academy of Management Conference, Chicago, August 1999; and G. L. Stewart and M. R. Barrick, "Team Structure and Performance: Assessing the Mediating Role of Intrateam Process and the Moderating Role of Task Type," *Academy of Management Journal* (April 2000), pp. 135–48.

32. Hyatt and Ruddy, "An Examination of the Relationship Between Work Group Characteristics and Performance," p. 577.

33. K. T. Dirks, "Trust in Leadership and Team Performance: Evidence from NCAA Basketball," *Journal of Applied Psychology* (December 2000), pp. 1004–1012; and M. Williams, "In Whom We Trust: Group Membership as an Affective Context for Trust Development," *Academy of Management Review* (July 2001), pp. 377–96.

34. R. R. Hirschfeld, M. J. Jordan, H. S. Field, W. F. Giles, and A. A. Armenakis, "Becoming Team Players: Team Members' Mastery of Team Knowledge as a Predictor of Team Task Proficiency and Observed Teamwork Effectiveness," *Journal of Applied Psychology* 91, no. 2 (2006), pp. 467–74.

35. S. T. Bell, "Deep-Level Composition Variables as Predictors of Team Performance: A Meta-Analysis," *Journal of Applied Psychology* 92, no. 3 (2007), pp. 595–615; and M. R. Barrick, G. L. Stewart, M. J. Neubert, and M. K. Mount, "Relating Member Ability and Personality to Work-Team Processes and Team Effectiveness," *Journal of Applied Psychology* (June 1998), pp. 377–91.

36. C. Margerison and D. McCann, *Team Management: Practical New Approaches* (London: Mercury Books, 1990).

37. E. Mannix and M. A. Neale, "What Differences Make a Difference: The Promise and Reality of Diverse Teams in Organizations," *Psychological Science in the Public Interest* (October 2005), pp. 31–55.

38. A. Deutschman, "Inside the Mind of Jeff Bezos," *Fast Company,* August 2004, pp. 50–58.

39. "Managing Diversity" box based on and K. B. Dahlin, L. R. Weingart, and P. J. Hinds, "Team Diversity and Information Use," *Academy of Management Journal* (December 2005), pp. 1107–23; B. L. Kirkman, P. E. Tesluk, and B. Rosen, "The Impact of Demographic Heterogeneity and Team Leader-Team Member Demographic Fit on Team Empowerment and Effectiveness," *Group & Organization Management* (June 2004), pp. 334–68; K. Lovelace, D. L. Shapiro, and L. R. Weingart, "Maximizing Cross-Functional New Product Teams' Innovativeness and Constraint Adherence: A Conflict Communications Perspective," *Academy of Management Journal* (August 2002), pp. 779–93; J. Jusko, "Diversity Enhances Decision Making," *IndustryWeek,* April 2, 2001, p. 9; F. Rice, "How to Make Diversity Pay," *Fortune,* August 8, 1994, pp. 78–86; M. L. Maznevski, "Understanding Our Differences: Performance in Decision-Making Groups with Diverse Members," *Human Relations* (May 1994), pp. 531–52; L. Strach and L. Wicander, "Fitting In: Issues of Tokenism and Conformity for Minority Women," *SAM Advanced Management Journal* (Summer 1993), pp. 22–25; C. R. Bantz, "Cultural Diversity and Group Cross-Cultural Team Research," *Journal of Applied Communication Research* (February 1993), pp. 1–19; and L. Copeland, "Making the Most of Cultural Differences at the Workplace," *Personnel* (June 1988), pp. 52–60.

40. Hyatt and Ruddy, "An Examination of the Relationship Between Work Group Characteristics and Performance"; J. D. Shaw, M. K. Duffy, and E. M. Stark, "Interdependence and Preference for Group Work: Main and Congruence Effects on the Satisfaction and Performance of Group Members," *Journal of Management* (June 2000), pp. 259–79; and S. A. Kiffin-Peterson and J. L. Cordery, "Trust, Individualism, and Job Characteristics of Employee Preference for Teamwork," *International Journal of Human Resource Management* (February 2003), pp. 93–116.

41. R. Wageman, "Critical Success Factors for Creating Superb Self-Managing Teams," *Organizational Dynamics* (Summer 1997), p. 55.

42. Campion, Papper, and Medsker, "Relations Between Work Team Characteristics and Effectiveness," p. 430; B. L. Kirkman and B. Rosen, "Powering Up Teams," *Organizational Dynamics* (Winter 2000), pp. 48–66; and D. C. Man and S. S. K. Lam, "The Effects of Job Complexity and Autonomy on Cohesiveness in Collectivist and Individualist Work Groups: A Cross-Cultural Analysis," *Journal of Organizational Behavior* (December 2003), pp. 979–1001.

43. K. Hess, *Creating the High-Performance Team* (New York: Wiley, 1987); Katzenbach and Smith, *The Wisdom of Teams,* pp. 43–64; K. D. Scott and A. Townsend, "Teams: Why Some Succeed and Others Fail," *HR Magazine* (August 1994), pp. 62–67; and K. Blanchard, D. Carew, and E. Parisi-Carew, "How to Get Your Group to Perform Like a Team," *Training and Development* (September 1996), pp. 34–37.

44. K. Tasa, S. Taggar, and G. H. Seijts, "The Development of Collective Efficacy in Teams: A Multilevel and Longitudinal Perspective," *Journal of Applied Psychology* (January 2007), pp. 17–27; C. B. Gibson, "The Efficacy Advantage: Factors Related to the Formation of Group Efficacy," *Journal of Applied Social Psychology* (October 2003), pp. 2153–2186; and D. I. Jung and J. J. Sosik, "Group Potency and Collective Efficacy: Examining Their Predictive Validity, Level of Analysis, and Effects of Performance Feedback on Future Group Performance," *Group & Organization Management* (September 2003), pp. 366–91.

45. K. A. Jehn, "A Qualitative Analysis of Conflict Types and Dimensions in Organizational Groups," *Administrative Science Quarterly* (September 1997), pp. 530–57. See also R. S. Peterson and K. J. Behfar, "The Dynamic Relationship Between Performance Feedback, Trust, and Conflict in Groups: A Longitudinal Study," *Organizational Behavior and Human Decision Processes* (September–November 2003), pp. 102–12.

46. K. H. Price, D. A. Harrison, and J. H. Gavin, "Withholding Inputs in Team Contexts: Member Composition, Interaction Processes, Evaluation Structure, and Social Loafing," *Journal of Applied Psychology* (December 2006), pp. 1375–84.

47. N. H. Woodward, "Make the Most of Team Building," *HR Magazine* (September 2006), pp. 73–76.

48. R. M. Yandrick, "A Team Effort," *HR Magazine* (June 2001), pp. 136–41.

49. Ibid.

50. M. A. Marks, C. S. Burke, M. J. Sabella, and S. J. Zaccaro, "The Impact of Cross-Training on Team Effectiveness," *Journal of Applied Psychology* (February 2002), pp. 3–14; and M. A. Marks, S. J. Zaccaro, and J. E. Mathieu, "Performance Implications of Leader Briefings and Team Interaction for Team Adaptation to Novel Environments," *Journal of Applied Psychology* (December 2000), p. 971.

51. C. Garvey, "Steer Teams with the Right Pay: Team-Based Pay Is a Success When It Fits Corporate Goals and Culture, and Rewards the Right Behavior," *HR Magazine* (May 2002), pp. 71–77.

52. R. Bond and P. B. Smith, "Culture and Conformity: A Meta-Analysis of Studies Using Asch's [1952, 1956] Line Judgment Task," *Psychological Bulletin* (January 1996), pp. 111–37.

53. I. L. Janis, *Groupthink,* 2nd ed. (New York: Houghton Mifflin Company, 1982), p. 175.

54. See P. C. Earley, "Social Loafing and Collectivism: A Comparison of the United States and the People's Republic of China," *Administrative Science Quarterly* (December 1989), pp. 565–81; and P. C. Earley, "East Meets West Meets Mideast: Further Explorations of Collectivistic and Individualistic Work Groups," *Academy of Management Journal* (April 1993), pp. 319–48.

55. N. J. Adler, *International Dimensions of Organizational Behavior,* 4th ed. (Cincinnati, OH: Southwestern, 2002), p. 142.

56. Ibid., p. 144.

57. K. B. Dahlin, L. R. Weingart, and P. J. Hinds, "Team Diversity and Information Use," *Academy of Management Journal* (December 2005), pp. 1107–23.

58. Adler, *International Dimensions of Organizational Behavior,* p. 142.

59. S. Paul, I. M. Samarah, P. Seetharaman, and P. P. Mykytyn, "An Empirical Investigation of Collaborative Conflict Management Style in Group Support System-Based Global Virtual Teams," *Journal of Management Information Systems* (Winter 2005), pp. 185–222.

60. This section is based on S. P. Robbins and T. A. Judge, *Organizational Behavior,* 13th ed. (Upper Saddle River, NJ: Pearson Prentice Hall, 2009), p. 339.

61. C. E. Naquin and R. O. Tynan, "The Team Halo Effect: Why Teams Are Not Blamed for Their Failures," *Journal of Applied Psychology* (April 2003), pp. 332–40.

62. A. B. Drexler and R. Forrester, "Teamwork—Not Necessarily the Answer," *HR Magazine* (January 1998), pp. 55–58. See also R. Saavedra, P. C. Earley, and L. Van Dyne, "Complex Interdependence in Task-Performing Groups," *Journal of Applied Psychology* (February 1993), pp. 61–72; and K. A. Jehn, G. B. Northcraft, and M. A. Neale, "Why Differences Make a Difference: A Field Study of Diversity, Conflict, and Performance in Work Groups," *Administrative Science Quarterly* (December 1999), pp. 741–63.

Chapter 10

1. "New ROLE," *Training* (June 2009), p. 4; C. Ressler and J. Thompson, *Why Work Sucks and How to Fix It* (New York: Penguin Group, 2008); J. Marquez, "Changing a Company's Culture, Not Just Its Schedules Pays Off," *Workforce Management Online,* November 17, 2008; S. Brown, "Results Should Matter, Not Just Working Late," *USA Today,* June 16, 2008, p. 4B; and J. Thottam, "Reworking Work," *Time,* July 25, 2005, pp. 50–55.

2. P. Bronson, "What Should I Do with My Life Now?" *Fast Company,* April 2009, pp. 35–37.

3. R. M. Steers, R. T. Mowday, and D. L. Shapiro, "The Future of Work Motivation Theory," *Academy of Management Review* (July 2004), pp. 379–87.

4. N. Ellemers, D. De Gilder, and S. A. Haslam, "Motivating Individuals and Groups at Work: A Social Identity Perspective on Leadership and Group Performance," *Academy of Management Review* (July 2004), pp. 459–78.

5. J. Krueger and E. Killham, "At Work, Feeling Good Matters," *Gallup Management Journal,* December 8, 2005, http://gmj.gallup.com.

6. "And the Survey Says . . ." box based on D. Heath and C. Heath, "I Love You. Now What?" *Fast Company,* October 2008, pp. 95–96; J. Yang and A. Gonzalez, "Most Preferred Forms of Recognition at Workplace," *USA Today,* May 4,

2009, p. 1B; "Fast Fact," *Training* (July/August 2008), p. 9; J. Posner, "No More Revolving Door," *Training* (July/August 2008), p. 52; G. Kranz, "Young Workers Willing to Trade Pay for Development," *Workforce Management Online,* December 30, 2008; and J. MacIntyre, "Workplace Attitudes," *Springfield, Missouri, Business Journal,* August 2008, p. 14.

7. M. Meece, "Using the Human Touch to Solve Workplace Problems," *New York Times Online,* April 3, 2008.

8. A. Maslow, *Motivation and Personality* (New York: McGraw-Hill, 1954); A. Maslow, D. C. Stephens, and G. Heil, *Maslow on Management* (New York: John Wiley & Sons, 1998); M. L. Ambrose and C. T. Kulik, "Old Friends, New Faces: Motivation Research in the 1990s," *Journal of Management* 25, no. 3 (1999), pp. 231–92; and "Dialogue," *Academy of Management Review* (October 2000), pp. 696–701.

9. N. K. Austin, "The Power of the Pyramid: The Foundation of Human Psychology and, Thereby, of Motivation, Maslow's Hierarchy Is One Powerful Pyramid," *Incentive* (July 2002), p. 10.

10. See, for example, D. T. Hall and K. E. Nongaim, "An Examination of Maslow's Need Hierarchy in an Organizational Setting," *Organizational Behavior and Human Performance* (February 1968), pp. 12–35; E. E. Lawler III and J. L. Suttle, "A Causal Correlational Test of the Need Hierarchy Concept," *Organizational Behavior and Human Performance* (April 1972), pp. 265–87; R. M. Creech, "Employee Motivation," *Management Quarterly* (Summer 1995), pp. 33–39; J. Rowan, "Maslow Amended," *Journal of Humanistic Psychology* (Winter 1998), pp. 81–92; J. Rowan, "Ascent and Descent in Maslow's Theory," *Journal of Humanistic Psychology* (Summer 1999), pp. 125–33; and Ambrose and Kulik, "Old Friends, New Faces: Motivation Research in the 1990s."

11. S. Fitch, "Zero Tolerance," *Forbes,* January 28, 2008, p. 52.

12. D. McGregor, *The Human Side of Enterprise* (New York: McGraw-Hill, 1960). For an updated description of Theories X and Y, see an annotated edition with commentary of *The Human Side of Enterprise* (McGraw-Hill, 2006); and G. Heil, W. Bennis, and D. C. Stephens, *Douglas McGregor, Revisited: Managing the Human Side of Enterprise* (New York: Wiley, 2000).

13. J. M. O'Brien, "The Next Intel," *Wired,* July 2002, pp. 100–107.

14. F. Herzberg, B. Mausner, and B. Snyderman, *The Motivation to Work* (New York: John Wiley, 1959); F. Herzberg, *The Managerial Choice: To Be Effective or to Be Human,* rev. ed. (Salt Lake City, Olympus, 1982); R. M. Creech, "Employee Motivation"; and Ambrose and Kulik, "Old Friends, New Faces: Motivation Research in the 1990s."

15. "From the Past to the Present" box based on D. A. Wren and A. G. Bedeian, *The Evolution of Management Thought* (New York: John Wiley & Sons, Inc., 2009); and Herzberg, Mausner, and Snyderman, *The Motivation to Work.*

16. D. C. McClelland, *The Achieving Society* (New York: Van Nostrand Reinhold, 1961); J. W. Atkinson and J. O. Raynor, *Motivation and Achievement* (Washington, DC: Winston, 1974); D. C. McClelland, *Power: The Inner Experience* (New York: Irvington, 1975); and M. J. Stahl, *Managerial and Technical Motivation: Assessing Needs for Achievement, Power, and Affiliation* (New York: Praeger, 1986).

17. McClelland, *The Achieving Society.*

18. McClelland, *Power: The Inner Experience*; D. C. McClelland and D. H. Burnham, "Power Is the Great Motivator," *Harvard Business Review* (March–April 1976), pp. 100–110.

19. D. Miron and D. C. McClelland, "The Impact of Achievement Motivation Training on Small Businesses," *California Management Review* (Summer 1979), pp. 13–28.

20. "McClelland: An Advocate of Power," *International Management* (July 1975), pp. 27–29.

21. R. M. Steers, R. T. Mowday, and D. L. Shapiro, "The Future of Work Motivation Theory"; E. A. Locke and G. P. Latham, "What Should We Do About Motivation Theory? Six Recommendations for the Twenty-First Century," *Academy of Management Review* (July 2004), pp. 388–403; and Ambrose and Kulik, "Old Friends, New Faces: Motivation Research in the 1990s."

22. Ambrose and Kulik, "Old Friends, New Faces: Motivation Research in the 1990s."

23. J. C. Naylor and D. R. Ilgen, "Goal Setting: A Theoretical Analysis of a Motivational Technique," in B. M. Staw and L. L. Cummings (eds.), *Research in Organizational Behavior,* vol. 6 (Greenwich, CT: JAI Press, 1984), pp. 95–140; A. R. Pell, "Energize Your People," *Managers Magazine,* December 1992, pp. 28–29; E. A. Locke, "Facts and Fallacies About Goal Theory: Reply to Deci," *Psychological Science* (January 1993), pp. 63–64; M. E. Tubbs, "Commitment as a Moderator of the Goal-Performance Relation: A Case for Clearer Construct Definition," *Journal of Applied Psychology* (February 1993), pp. 86–97; M. P. Collingwood, "Why Don't You Use the Research?" *Management Decision* (May 1993), pp. 48–54; M. E. Tubbs, D. M. Boehne, and J. S. Dahl, "Expectancy, Valence, and Motivational Force Functions in Goal-Setting Research: An Empirical Test," *Journal of Applied Psychology* (June 1993), pp. 361–73; E. A. Locke, "Motivation Through Conscious Goal Setting," *Applied and Preventive Psychology* 5 (1996), pp. 117–24; Ambrose and Kulik, "Old Friends, New Faces: Motivation Research in the 1990s"; E. A. Locke and G. P. Latham, "Building a Practically Useful Theory of Goal Setting and Task Motivation: A 35-Year Odyssey," *American Psychologist* (September 2002), pp. 705–17; Y. Fried and L. H. Slowik, "Enriching Goal-Setting Theory with Time: An Integrated Approach," *Academy of Management Review* (July 2004), pp. 404–22; and G. P. Latham, "The Motivational Benefits of Goal-Setting," *Academy of Management Executive* (November 2004), pp. 126–29.

24. J. A. Wagner III, "Participation's Effects on Performance and Satisfaction: A Reconsideration of Research and Evidence," *Academy of Management Review* (April 1994), pp. 312–30; J. George-Falvey, "Effects of Task Complexity and Learning Stage on the Relationship Between Participation in Goal Setting and Task Performance," *Academy of Management Proceedings,* on disk, 1996; T. D. Ludwig and E. S. Geller, "Assigned Versus Participative Goal Setting and Response Generalization: Managing Injury Control Among Professional Pizza Deliverers," *Journal of Applied Psychology* (April 1997), pp. 253–61; and S. G. Harkins and M. D. Lowe, "The Effects of Self-Set Goals on Task Performance," *Journal of Applied Social Psychology* (January 2000), pp. 1–40.

25. J. M. Ivancevich and J. T. McMahon, "The Effects of Goal Setting, External Feedback, and Self-Generated Feedback on Outcome Variables: A Field Experiment," *Academy of Management Journal* (June 1982), pp. 359–72; and Locke, "Motivation Through Conscious Goal Setting."

26. J. R. Hollenbeck, C. R. Williams, and H. J. Klein, "An Empirical Examination of the Antecedents of Commitment to

Difficult Goals," *Journal of Applied Psychology* (February 1989), pp. 18–23; see also J. C. Wofford, V. L. Goodwin, and S. Premack, "Meta-Analysis of the Antecedents of Personal Goal Level and of the Antecedents and Consequences of Goal Commitment," *Journal of Management* (September 1992), pp. 595–615; Tubbs, "Commitment as a Moderator of the Goal-Performance Relation"; J. W. Smither, M. London, and R. R. Reilly, "Does Performance Improve Following Multisource Feedback? A Theoretical Model, Meta-Analysis, and Review of Empirical Findings," *Personnel Psychology* (Spring 2005), pp. 171–203.

27. M. E. Gist, "Self-Efficacy: Implications for Organizational Behavior and Human Resource Management," *Academy of Management Review* (July 1987), pp. 472–85; and A. Bandura, *Self-Efficacy: The Exercise of Control* (New York: Freeman, 1997).

28. E. A. Locke, E. Frederick, C. Lee, and P. Bobko, "Effect of Self-Efficacy, Goals, and Task Strategies on Task Performance," *Journal of Applied Psychology* (May 1984), pp. 241–51; M. E. Gist and T. R. Mitchell, "Self-Efficacy: A Theoretical Analysis of Its Determinants and Malleability," *Academy of Management Review* (April 1992), pp. 183–211; A. D. Stajkovic and F. Luthans, "Self-Efficacy and Work-Related Performance: A Meta-Analysis," *Psychological Bulletin* (September 1998), pp. 240–61; and A. Bandura, "Cultivate Self-Efficacy for Personal and Organizational Effectiveness," in E. Locke (ed.), *Handbook of Principles of Organizational Behavior* (Malden, MA: Blackwell, 2004), pp. 120–36.

29. A. Bandura and D. Cervone, "Differential Engagement in Self-Reactive Influences in Cognitively-Based Motivation," *Organizational Behavior and Human Decision Processes* (August 1986), pp. 92–113; and R. Ilies and T. A. Judge, "Goal Regulation Across Time: The Effects of Feedback and 423 Affect," *Journal of Applied Psychology* (May 2005), pp. 453–67.

30. See J. C. Anderson and C. A. O'Reilly, "Effects of an Organizational Control System on Managerial Satisfaction and Performance," *Human Relations* (June 1981), pp. 491–501; and J. P. Meyer, B. Schacht-Cole, and I. R. Gellatly, "An Examination of the Cognitive Mechanisms by Which Assigned Goals Affect Task Performance and Reactions to Performance," *Journal of Applied Social Psychology* 18, no. 5 (1988), pp. 390–408.

31. See, for example, R. W. Griffin, "Toward an Integrated Theory of Task Design," in L. L. Cummings and B. M. Staw (eds.), *Research in Organizational Behavior*, vol. 9 (Greenwich, CT: JAI Press, 1987), pp. 79–120; and M. Campion, "Interdisciplinary Approaches to Job Design: A Constructive Replication with Extensions," *Journal of Applied Psychology* (August 1988), pp. 467–81.

32. S. Caudron, "The De-Jobbing of America," *Industry Week*, September 5, 1994, pp. 31–36; W. Bridges, "The End of the Job," *Fortune*, September 19, 1994, pp. 62–74; and K. H. Hammonds, K. Kelly, and K. Thurston, "Rethinking Work," *BusinessWeek*, October 12, 1994, pp. 75–87.

33. See J. R. Hackman and G. R. Oldham, "Motivation Through the Design of Work: Test of a Theory," *Organizational Behavior and Human Performance* (August 1976), pp. 250–279; Y. Fried and G. R. Ferris, "The Validity of the Job Characteristics Model: A Review and Meta Analysis," *Personnel Psychology* (Summer 1987), pp. 287–322; S. J. Zaccaro and E. F. Stone,

"Incremental Validity of an Empirically Based Measure of Job Characteristics," *Journal of Applied Psychology* (May 1988), pp. 245–252; and R. W. Renn and R. J. Vandenberg, "The Critical Psychological States: An Underrepresented Component in Job Characteristics Model Research," *Journal of Management* (February 1995), pp. 279–303.

34. G. Van Der Vegt, B. Emans, and E. Van Der Vliert, "Motivating Effects of Task and Outcome Interdependence in Work Teams," *Journal of Managerial Psychology* (July 2000), p. 829; and B. Bemmels, "Local Union Leaders' Satisfaction with Grievance Procedures," *Journal of Labor Research* (Summer 2001), pp. 653–669.

35. J. S. Adams, "Inequity in Social Exchanges," in L. Berkowitz (ed.), *Advances in Experimental Social Psychology*, vol. 2 (New York: Academic Press, 1965), pp. 267–300; and Ambrose and Kulik, "Old Friends, New Faces: Motivation Research in the 1990s."

36. See, for example, P. S. Goodman and A. Friedman, "An Examination of Adams' Theory of Inequity," *Administrative Science Quarterly* (September 1971), pp. 271–288; M. R. Carrell, "A Longitudinal Field Assessment of Employee Perceptions of Equitable Treatment," *Organizational Behavior and Human Performance* (February 1978), pp. 108–118; E. Walster, G. W. Walster, and W. G. Scott, *Equity: Theory and Research* (Boston: Allyn & Bacon, 1978); R. G. Lord and J. A. Hohenfeld, "Longitudinal Field Assessment of Equity Effects on the Performance of Major League Baseball Players," *Journal of Applied Psychology* (February 1979), pp. 19–26; J. E. Dittrich and M. R. Carrell, "Organizational Equity Perceptions, Employee Job Satisfaction, and Departmental Absence and Turnover Rates," *Organizational Behavior and Human Performance* (August 1979), pp. 29–40; and J. Greenberg, "Cognitive Reevaluation of Outcomes in Response to Underpayment Inequity," *Academy of Management Journal* (March 1989), pp. 174–84.

37. P. S. Goodman, "An Examination of Referents Used in the Evaluation of Pay," *Organizational Behavior and Human Performance* (October 1974), pp. 170–95; S. Ronen, "Equity Perception in Multiple Comparisons: A Field Study," *Human Relations* (April 1986), pp. 333–346; R. W. Scholl, E. A. Cooper, and J. F. McKenna, "Referent Selection in Determining Equity Perception: Differential Effects on Behavioral and Attitudinal Outcomes," *Personnel Psychology* (Spring 1987), pp. 113–127; and C. T. Kulik and M. L. Ambrose, "Personal and Situational Determinants of Referent Choice," *Academy of Management Review* (April 1992), pp. 212–37.

38. See, for example, R. C. Dailey and D. J. Kirk, "Distributive and Procedural Justice as Antecedents of Job Dissatisfaction and Intent to Turnover," *Human Relations* (March 1992), pp. 305–16; D. B. McFarlin and P. D. Sweeney, "Distributive and Procedural Justice as Predictors of Satisfaction with Personal and Organizational Outcomes," *Academy of Management Journal* (August 1992), pp. 626–37; M. A. Konovsky, "Understanding Procedural Justice and Its Impact on Business Organizations," *Journal of Management* 26, no. 3 (2000), pp. 489–511; J. A. Colquitt, "Does the Justice of One Interact with the Justice of Many? Reactions to Procedural Justice in Teams," *Journal of Applied Psychology* (August 2004), pp. 633–46; J. Brockner, "Why It's So Hard to Be Fair," *Harvard Business Review* (March 2006), pp. 122–29; and B. M. Wiesenfeld, W. B. Swann, Jr., J. Brockner, and C. A. Bartel, "Is More Fairness Always Preferred: Self-Esteem Moderates

Reactions to Procedural Justice," *Academy of Management Journal* (October 2007), pp. 1235–53.

39. "Right or Wrong?" box based on "MOSERS Staff Bonuses Criticized," The Associated Press, *Springfield, Missouri, News-Leader,* April 11, 2009, p. 5A; "MOSERS Staffers Receive Hefty Bonuses," *St. Louis Post Dispatch, Springfield, Missouri, News-Leader,* April 6, 2009, p. 13A; and C. Tuna, "The Perks Keep Flowing Despite Outcry," *Wall Street Journal,* April 3, 2009, p. B1+.

40. V. H. Vroom, *Work and Motivation* (New York: John Wiley, 1964).

41. See, for example, H. G. Heneman III and D. P. Schwab, "Evaluation of Research on Expectancy Theory Prediction of Employee Performance," *Psychological Bulletin* (July 1972), pp. 1–9; and L. Reinharth and M. Wahba, "Expectancy Theory as a Predictor of Work Motivation, Effort Expenditure, and Job Performance," *Academy of Management Journal* (September 1975), pp. 502–37.

42. See, for example, V. H. Vroom, "Organizational Choice: A Study of Pre- and Postdecision Processes," *Organizational Behavior and Human Performance* (April 1966), pp. 212–25; L. W. Porter and E. E. Lawler III, *Managerial Attitudes and Performance* (Homewood, IL: Richard D. Irwin, 1968); W. Van Eerde and H. Thierry, "Vroom's Expectancy Models and Work-Related Criteria: A Meta-Analysis," *Journal of Applied Psychology* (October 1996), pp. 575–86; and Ambrose and Kulik, "Old Friends, New Faces: Motivation Research in the 1990s."

43. See, for instance, M. Siegall, "The Simplistic Five: An Integrative Framework for Teaching Motivation," *The Organizational Behavior Teaching Review* 12, no. 4 (1987–88), pp. 141–143.

44. N. J. Adler with A. Gundersen, *International Dimensions of Organizational Behavior*, 5th ed. (Cincinnati, OH: South-Western College Publishing, 2008).

45. G. Hofstede, "Motivation, Leadership and Organization: Do American Theories Apply Abroad?" *Organizational Dynamics* (Summer 1980), p. 55.

46. Ibid.

47. J. K. Giacobbe-Miller, D. J. Miller, and V. I. Victorov, "A Comparison of Russian and U.S. Pay Allocation Decisions, Distributive Justice Judgments and Productivity Under Different Payment Conditions," *Personnel Psychology* (Spring 1998), pp. 137–63.

48. S. L. Mueller and L. D. Clarke, "Political-Economic Context and Sensitivity to Equity: Differences Between the United States and the Transition Economies of Central and Eastern Europe," *Academy of Management Journal* (June 1998), pp. 319–29.

49. I. Harpaz, "The Importance of Work Goals: An International Perspective," *Journal of International Business Studies* (First Quarter 1990), pp. 75–93.

50. G. E. Popp, H. J. Davis, and T. T. Herbert, "An International Study of Intrinsic Motivation Composition," *Management International Review* (January 1986), pp. 28–35.

51. R. W. Brislin, B. MacNab, R. Worthley, F. Kabigting Jr., and B. Zukis, "Evolving Perceptions of Japanese Workplace Motivation: An Employee-Manager Comparison," *International Journal of Cross-Cultural Management* (April 2005), pp. 87–104.

52. J. R. Billings and D. L. Sharpe, "Factors Influencing Flextime Usage Among Employed Married Women," *Consumer Interests Annual,* 1999, pp. 89–94; and I. Harpaz, "The Importance of

Work Goals: An International Perspective," *Journal of International Business Studies* (First Quarter 1990), pp. 75–93.

53. N. Ramachandran, "New Paths at Work," *U.S. News & World Report,* March 20, 2006, p. 47; S. Armour, "Generation Y: They've Arrived at Work with a New Attitude," *USA Today,* November 6, 2005, pp. B1+; and R. Kanfer and P. L. Ackerman, "Aging, Adult Development, and Work Motivation," *Academy of Management Review* (July 2004), pp. 440–58.

54. J. Sahadi, "Flex-time, Time Off—Who's Getting These Perks?" *CNNMoney.com,* June 25, 2007.

55. M. Arndt, "The Family That Flips Together . . . ," *BusinessWeek,* April 17, 2006, p. 14.

56. M. Conlin, "The Easiest Commute of All," *BusinessWeek,* December 12, 2005, pp. 78–80.

57. Ibid.

58. "Managing Diversity" box based on D. Jones, "Ford, Fannie Mae Tops in Diversity," *USA Today,* May 7, 2003, http://www.usatoday.com; S. N. Mehta, "What Minority Employees Really Want," *Fortune,* July 10, 2000, pp. 180–86; K. H. Hammonds, "Difference Is Power," *Fast Company,* July 2000, pp. 258–66; "Building a Competitive Workforce: Diversity, the Bottom Line," *Forbes,* April 3, 2000, pp. 181–94; and "Diversity: Developing Tomorrow's Leadership Talent Today," *BusinessWeek,* December 20, 1999, pp. 85–100.

59. T. D. Golden and J. F. Veiga, "The Impact of Extent of Telecommuting on Job Satisfaction: Resolving Inconsistent Findings," *Journal of Management* (April 2005), pp. 301–18.

60. See, for instance, M. Alpert, "The Care and Feeding of Engineers," *Fortune,* September 21, 1992, pp. 86–95; G. Poole, "How to Manage Your Nerds," *Forbes ASAP,* December 1994, pp. 132–36; T. J. Allen and R. Katz, "Managing Technical Professionals and Organizations: Improving and Sustaining the Performance of Organizations, Project Teams, and Individual Contributors," *Sloan Management Review* (Summer 2002), pp. S4–S5; and S. R. Barley and G. Kunda, "Contracting: A New Form of Professional Practice," *Academy of Management Perspectives* (February 2006), pp. 45–66.

61. R. J. Bohner, Jr., and E. R. Salasko, "Beware the Legal Risks of Hiring Temps," *Workforce* (October 2002), pp. 50–57.

62. J. P. Broschak and A. Davis-Blake, "Mixing Standard Work and Nonstandard Deals: The Consequences of Heterogeneity in Employment Arrangements," *Academy of Management Journal* (April 2006), pp. 371–93; M. L. Kraimer, S. J. Wayne, R. C. Liden, and R. T. Sparrowe, "The Role of Job Security in Understanding the Relationship Between Employees' Perceptions of Temporary Workers and Employees' Performance," *Journal of Applied Psychology* (March 2005), pp. 389–98; and C. E. Connelly and D. G. Gallagher, "Emerging Trends in Contingent Work Research," *Journal of Management* (November 2004), pp. 959–83.

63. C. Haddad, "FedEx: Gaining on the Ground," *BusinessWeek,* December 16, 2002, pp. 126–28; and L. Landro, "To Get Doctors to Do Better, Health Plans Try Cash Bonuses," *Wall Street Journal,* September 17, 2004, pp. A1+.

64. K. E. Culp, "Playing Field Widens for Stack's Great Game," *Springfield, Missouri, News-Leader,* January 9, 2005, pp. 1A+.

65. J. Case, "The Open-Book Revolution," *Inc.,* June 1995, pp. 26–50; J. P. Schuster, J. Carpenter, and M. P. Kane, *The Power of Open-Book Management* (New York: John Wiley, 1996); J. Case, "Opening the Books," *Harvard Business*

Review (March–April 1997), pp. 118–27; and D. Drickhamer, "Open Books to Elevate Performance," *Industry Week,* November 2002, p. 16.

66. L. DeMars, "Glazed Over in a Good Way," *CFO,* July 2007, p. 80.

67. F. Luthans and A. D. Stajkovic, "Provide Recognition for Performance Improvement," in E. A. Locke (ed.), *Principles of Organizational Behavior* (Oxford, England: Blackwell, 2000), pp. 166–80.

68. C. Huff, "Recognition That Resonates," *Workforce Management Online,* April 1, 2008.

69. M. Littman, "Best Bosses Tell All," *Working Woman,* October 2000, p. 54; and Hoover's Online, http://www.hoovers.com (June 20, 2003).

70. E. White, "Praise from Peers Goes a Long Way," *Wall Street Journal,* December 19, 2005, p. B3.

71. Ibid.

72. K. J. Dunham, "Amid Sinking Workplace Morale, Employers Turn to Recognition," *Wall Street Journal,* November 19, 2002, p. B8.

73. Cited in S. Caudron, "The Top 20 Ways to Motivate Employees," *Industry Week,* April 3, 1995, pp. 15–16. See also B. Nelson, "Try Praise," *Inc.,* September 1996, p. 115; and J. Wiscombe, "Rewards Get Results," *Workforce* (April 2002), pp. 42–48.

74. V. M. Barret, "Fight the Jerks," *Forbes,* July 2, 2007, pp. 52–54.

75. E. White, "The Best vs. the Rest," *Wall Street Journal,* January 30, 2006, pp. B1+.

76. R. K. Abbott, "Performance-Based Flex: A Tool for Managing Total Compensation Costs," *Compensation and Benefits Review* (March–April 1993), pp. 18–21; J. R. Schuster and P. K. Zingheim, "The New Variable Pay: Key Design Issues," *Compensation and Benefits Review* (March–April 1993), pp. 27–34; C. R. Williams and L. P. Livingstone, "Another Look at the Relationship Between Performance and Voluntary Turnover," *Academy of Management Journal* (April 1994), pp. 269–98; A. M. Dickinson and K. L. Gillette, "A Comparison of the Effects of Two Individual Monetary Incentive Systems on Productivity: Piece Rate Pay Versus Base Pay Plus Incentives," *Journal of Organizational Behavior Management* (Spring 1994), pp. 3–82; and C. B. Cadsby, F. Song, and F. Tapon, "Sorting and Incentive Effects of Pay for Performance: An Experimental Investigation," *Academy of Management Journal* (April 2007), pp. 387–405.

77. E. White, "Employers Increasingly Favor Bonuses to Raises," *Wall Street Journal,* August 28, 2006, p. B3.

78. "More Than 20 Percent of Japanese Firms Use Pay Systems Based on Performance," *Manpower Argus,* May 1998, p. 7; and E. Beauchesne, "Pay Bonuses Improve Productivity, Study Shows," *Vancouver Sun,* September 13, 2002, p. D5.

79. H. Rheem, "Performance Management Programs," *Harvard Business Review* (September–October 1996), pp. 8–9; G. Sprinkle, "The Effect of Incentive Contracts on Learning and Performance," *Accounting Review* (July 2000), pp. 299–326; and "Do Incentive Awards Work?" *HRFocus* (October 2000), pp. 1–3.

80. R. D. Banker, S. Y. Lee, G. Potter, and D. Srinivasan, "Contextual Analysis of Performance Impacts on Outcome-Based Incentive Compensation," *Academy of Management Journal* (August 1996), pp. 920–48.

81. T. Reason, "Why Bonus Plans Fail," *CFO,* January 2003, p. 53; and "Has Pay for Performance Had Its Day?" *The McKinsey Quarterly,* no. 4 (2002), accessed on Forbes Web site, http://www.forbes.com.

82. E. Frauenheim, "Downturn Puts New Emphasis on Engagement," *Workforce Management Online,* http://workforcemanagementonline.com (July 21, 2009); S. D. Friedman, "Dial Down the Stress Level," *Harvard Business Review* (December 2008), pp. 28–29; and S. E. Needleman, "Allaying Workers' Fears During Uncertain Times," *Wall Street Journal,* October 6, 2008.

Chapter 11

1. S. Hamm, "HCL's Leveraged Leap to India's Top Tech Circle," *BusinessWeek Online,* December 16, 2008; E. Frauenheim, "HCL Technologies," *Workforce Management,* October 20, 2008, p. 25; "Management by Democracy," *USA Today,* December 17, 2007, p. 2B; J. McGregor, "The Employee Is Always Right," *BusinessWeek Online,* November 9, 2007; and V. Nayar, "I Took the Road Less Traveled," *SiliconIndia,* November 2007, pp. 8–10.

2. Most leadership research has focused on the actions and responsibilities of managers and extrapolated the results to leaders and leadership in general.

3. See T. A. Judge, J. E. Bono, R. Ilies, and M. W. Gerhardt, "Personality and Leadership: A Qualitative and Quantitative Review," *Journal of Applied Psychology* (August 2002), pp. 765–80; and S. A. Kirkpatrick and E. A. Locke, "Leadership: Do Traits Matter?" *Academy of Management Executive* (May 1991), pp. 48–60.

4. K. Lewin and R. Lippitt, "An Experimental Approach to the Study of Autocracy and Democracy: A Preliminary Note," *Sociometry* 1 (1938), pp. 292–300; K. Lewin, "Field Theory and Experiment in Social Psychology: Concepts and Methods," *American Journal of Sociology* 44 (1939), pp. 868–96; K. Lewin, R. Lippitt, and R. K. White, "Patterns of Aggressive Behavior in Experimentally Created Social Climates," *Journal of Social Psychology* 10 (1939), pp. 271–301; and R. Lippitt, "An Experimental Study of the Effect of Democratic and Authoritarian Group Atmospheres," *University of Iowa Studies in Child Welfare* 16 (1940), pp. 43–95.

5. B. M. Bass, *Stodgill's Handbook of Leadership* (New York: Free Press, 1981), pp. 298–99.

6. R. Tannenbaum and W. H. Schmidt, "How to Choose a Leadership Pattern," *Harvard Business Review* (May/June 1973), pp. 162–80.

7. R. M. Stodgill and A. E. Coons, eds., *Leader Behavior: Its Description and Measurement,* Research Monograph No. 88 (Columbus: Ohio State University, Bureau of Business Research, 1951). See also S. Kerr, C. A. Schriesheim, C. J. Murphy, and R. M. Stodgill, "Toward a Contingency Theory of Leadership Based upon the Consideration and Initiating Structure Literature," *Organizational Behavior and Human Performance* (August 1974), pp. 62–82; and B. M. Fisher, "Consideration and Initiating Structure and Their Relationships with Leader Effectiveness: A Meta Analysis," in F. Hoy, ed., *Proceedings of the 48th Annual Academy of Management Conference* (Anaheim, CA, 1988), pp. 201–05.

8. "From the Past to the Present" box based on D. A. Wren and A. G. Bedeian, *The Evolution of Management Thought,* 6th ed. (New York: John Wiley & Sons, 2009), pp. 345–46.

9. R. Kahn and D. Katz, "Leadership Practices in Relation to Productivity and Morale," in D. Cartwright and A. Zander, eds., *Group Dynamics: Research and Theory*, 2nd ed. (Elmsford, NY: Pow, Paterson, 1960).

10. R. R. Blake and J. S. Mouton, *The Managerial Grid III* (Houston: Gulf Publishing, 1984).

11. L. L. Larson, J. G. Hunt, and R. N. Osborn, "The Great Hi-Hi Leader Behavior Myth: A Lesson from Occam's Razor," *Academy of Management Journal* (December 1976), pp. 628–41; and P. C. Nystrom, "Managers and the Hi-Hi Leader Myth," *Academy of Management Journal* (June 1978), pp. 325–31.

12. W. G. Bennis, "The Seven Ages of the Leader," *Harvard Business Review* (January 2004), p. 52.

13. F. E. Fiedler, *A Theory of Leadership Effectiveness* (New York: McGraw-Hill, 1967).

14. R. Ayman, M. M. Chemers, and F. Fiedler, "The Contingency Model of Leadership Effectiveness: Its Levels of Analysis," *Leadership Quarterly* (Summer 1995), pp. 147–67; C. A. Schriesheim, B. J. Tepper, and L. A. Tetrault, "Lease Preferred Co-Worker Score, Situational Control, and Leadership Effectiveness: A Meta-Analysis of Contingency Model Performance Predictions," *Journal of Applied Psychology* (August 1994), pp. 561–73; and L. H. Peters, D. D. Hartke, and J. T. Pholmann, "Fiedler's Contingency Theory of Leadership: An Application of the Meta-Analysis Procedures of Schmidt and Hunter," *Psychological Bulletin* (March 1985), pp. 274–85.

15. See E. H. Schein, *Organizational Psychology*, 3rd ed. (Upper Saddle River, NJ: Prentice Hall, 1980), pp. 116–17; and B. Kabanoff, "A Critique of Leader Match and Its Implications for Leadership Research," *Personnel Psychology* (Winter 1981), pp. 749–64.

16. P. Hersey and K. Blanchard, "So You Want to Know Your Leadership Style?" *Training and Development Journal* (February 1974), pp. 1–15; and P. Hersey and K. H. Blanchard, *Management of Organizational Behavior: Leading Human Resources*, 8th ed. (Upper Saddle River, NJ: Prentice Hall, 2001).

17. "And the Survey Says . . ." box based on "Still Haven't Closed the Gap," *Training* (March/April 2009), p. 9; J. Emery, S. Sitkin, and S. Siang, "In Challenging Times, Leadership Skills and Leader Development Matter," *Workforce Management Online,* February 2009; G. Kranz, "High-Potential Programs Have Rewards, Risks," *Workforce Management Online,* July 24, 2007; J. M. Kouzes and B. Z. Posner, "To Lead, Create a Shared Vision," *Harvard Business Review* (January 2009), p. 20; S. Armour, "Do Women Compete in Unhealthy Ways at Work?" *USA Today,* December 30, 2005, pp. 1B+; and "Leadership Needs Development," *Training* (February 2006), p. 7.

18. See, for instance, E. G. Ralph, "Developing Managers' Effectiveness: A Model with Potential," *Journal of Management Inquiry* (June 2004), pp. 152–63; C. L. Graeff, "Evolution of Situational Leadership Theory: A Critical Review," *Leadership Quarterly* 8, no. 2 (1997), pp. 153–70; and C. F. Fernandez and R. P. Vecchio, "Situational Leadership Theory Revisited: A Test of an Across-Jobs Perspective," *Leadership Quarterly* 8, no. 1 (1997), pp. 67–84.

19. V. H. Vroom and P. W. Yetton, *Leadership and Decision Making* (Pittsburgh: University of Pittsburgh Press, 1973).

20. V. H. Vroom and A. G. Yago, *The New Leadership: Managing Participation in Organizations* (Upper Saddle River, NJ: Prentice Hall, 1988). See especially Chapter 8.

21. See, for example, R. H. G. Field, "A Test of the Vroom Yetton Normative Model of Leadership," *Journal of Applied Psychology* (October 1982), pp. 523–32; C. R. Leana, "Power Relinquishment Versus Power Sharing: Theoretical Clarification and Empirical Comparison of Delegation and Participation," *Journal of Applied Psychology* (May 1987), pp. 228–33; J. T. Ettling and A. G. Yago, "Participation Under Conditions of Conflict: More on the Validity of the Vroom Yetton Model," *Journal of Management Studies* (January 1988), pp. 73–83; and R. H. G. Field and R. J. House, "A Test of the Vroom Yetton Model Using Manager and Subordinate Reports," *Journal of Applied Psychology* (June 1990), pp. 362–66.

22. For additional information about the exchanges that occur between the leader and the follower, see A. S. Phillips and A. G. Bedeian, "Leader Follower Exchange Quality: The Role of Personal and Interpersonal Attributes," *Academy of Management Journal* 37, no. 4 (1994), pp. 990–1001; and T. A. Scandura and C. A. Schriesheim, "Leader Member Exchange and Supervisor Career Mentoring as Complementary Constructs in Leadership Research," *Academy of Management Journal* 37, no. 6 (1994), pp. 1588–1602.

23. R. J. House, "A Path-Goal Theory of Leader Effectiveness," *Administrative Science Quarterly* (September 1971), pp. 321–38; House and T. R. Mitchell, "Path-Goal Theory of Leadership," *Journal of Contemporary Business* (Autumn 1974), p. 86; and R. J. House, "Path-Goal Theory of Leadership: Lessons, Legacy, and a Reformulated Theory," *Leadership Quarterly* (Fall 1996), pp. 323–52.

24. J. C. Wofford and L. Z. Liska, "Path-Goal Theories of Leadership: A Meta-Analysis," *Journal of Management* (Winter 1993), pp. 857–76; and A. Sagie, and M. Koslowsky, "Organizational Attitudes and Behaviors as a Function of Participation in Strategic and Tactical Change Decisions: An Application of Path-Goal Theory," *Journal of Organizational Behavior* (January 1994), pp. 37–47.

25. B. M. Bass and R. E. Riggio, *Transformational Leadership,* 2nd ed. (Mahwah, NJ: Lawrence Erlbaum Associates, Inc., 2006), p. 3.

26. B. M. Bass, "Leadership: Good, Better, Best," *Organizational Dynamics* (Winter 1985), pp. 26–40; and J. Seltzer and B. M. Bass, "Transformational Leadership: Beyond Initiation and Consideration," *Journal of Management* (December 1990), pp. 693–703.

27. B. J. Avolio and B. M. Bass, "Transformational Leadership, Charisma, and Beyond." Working paper, School of Management, State University of New York, Binghamton, 1985, p. 14.

28. R. S. Rubin, D. C. Munz, and W. H. Bommer, "Leading from Within: The Effects of Emotion Recognition and Personality on Transformational Leadership Behavior," *Academy of Management Journal* (October 2005), pp. 845–58; T. A. Judge and J. E. Bono, "Five-Factor Model of Personality and Transformational Leadership," *Journal of Applied Psychology* (October 2000), pp. 751–65; B. M. Bass and B. J. Avolio, "Developing Transformational Leadership: 1992 and Beyond," *Journal of European Industrial Training* (January 1990), p. 23; and J. J. Hater and B. M. Bass, "Supervisors' Evaluation and Subordinates' Perceptions of Transformational and Transactional Leadership," *Journal of Applied Psychology* (November 1988), pp. 695–702.

29. A. E. Colbert, A. L. Kristof-Brown, B. H. Bradley, and M. R. Barrick, "CEO Transformational Leadership: The

Role of Goal Importance Congruence in Top Management Teams," *Academy of Management Journal* (February 2008), pp. 81–96; R. F. Piccolo and J. A. Colquitt, "Transformational Leadership and Job Behaviors: The Mediating Role of Core Job Characteristics," *Academy of Management Journal* (April 2006), pp. 327–40; O. Epitropaki and R. Martin, "From Ideal to Real: A Longitudinal Study of the Role of Implicit Leadership Theories on Leader-Member Exchanges and Employee Outcomes," *Journal of Applied Psychology* (July 2005), pp. 659–76; J. E. Bono and T. A. Judge, "Self-Concordance at Work: Toward Understanding the Motivational Effects of Transformational Leaders," *Academy of Management Journal* (October 2003), pp. 554–71; T. Dvir, D. Eden, B. J. Avolio, and B. Shamir, "Impact of Transformational Leadership on Follower Development and Performance: A Field Experiment," *Academy of Management Journal* (August 2002), pp. 735–44; N. Sivasubramaniam, W. D. Murry, B. J. Avolio, and D. I. Jung, "A Longitudinal Model of the Effects of Team Leadership and Group Potency on Group Performance," *Group and Organization Management* (March 2002), pp. 66–96; J. M. Howell and B. J. Avolio, "Transformational Leadership, Transactional Leadership, Locus of Control, and Support for Innovation: Key Predictors of Consolidated-Business-Unit Performance," *Journal of Applied Psychology* (December 1993), pp. 891–911; R. T. Keller, "Transformational Leadership and the Performance of Research and Development Project Groups," *Journal of Management* (September 1992), pp. 489–501; and Bass and Avolio, "Developing Transformational Leadership."

30. F. Vogelstein, "Mighty Amazon," *Fortune,* May 26, 2003, pp. 60–74.

31. J. M. Crant and T. S. Bateman, "Charismatic Leadership Viewed from Above: The Impact of Proactive Personality," *Journal of Organizational Behavior* (February 2000), pp. 63–75; G. Yukl and J. M. Howell, "Organizational and Contextual Influences on the Emergence and Effectiveness of Charismatic Leadership," *Leadership Quarterly* (Summer 1999), pp. 257–83; and J. A. Conger and R. N. Kanungo, "Behavioral Dimensions of Charismatic Leadership," in J. A. Conger, R. N. Kanungo and Associates (eds.), *Charismatic Leadership* (San Francisco: Jossey-Bass, 1988), pp. 78–97.

32. J. A. Conger and R. N. Kanungo, *Charismatic Leadership in Organizations* (Thousand Oaks, CA: Sage, 1998).

33. K. S. Groves, "Linking Leader Skills, Follower Attitudes, and Contextual Variables via an Integrated Model of Charismatic Leadership," *Journal of Management* (April 2005), pp. 255–77; J. J. Sosik, "The Role of Personal Values in the Charismatic Leadership of Corporate Managers: A Model and Preliminary Field Study," *Leadership Quarterly* (April 2005), pp. 221–44; A. H. B. deHoogh, D. N. den Hartog, P. L. Koopman, H. Thierry, P. T. van den Berg, J. G. van der Weide, and C. P. M. Wilderom, "Leader Motives, Charismatic Leadership, and Subordinates' Work Attitudes in the Profit and Voluntary Sector," *Leadership Quarterly* (February 2005), pp. 17–38; J. M. Howell and B. Shamir, "The Role of Followers in the Charismatic Leadership Process: Relationships and Their Consequences," *Academy of Management Review* (January 2005), pp. 96–112; J. Paul, D. L. Costley, J. P. Howell, P. W. Dorfman, and D. Trafimow, "The Effects of Charismatic Leadership on Followers' Self-Concept Accessibility," *Journal of Applied Social Psychology* (September 2001), pp. 1821–44; J. A. Conger, R. N. Kanungo, and S. T. Menon, "Charismatic Leadership and Follower Effects," *Journal of Organizational Behavior* 21 (2000), pp. 747–67; R. W. Rowden, "The Relationship Between Charismatic Leadership Behaviors and Organizational Commitment," *Leadership & Organization Development Journal* (January 2000), pp. 30–35; G. P. Shea and C. M. Howell, "Charismatic Leadership and Task Feedback: A Laboratory Study of Their Effects on Self-Efficacy," *Leadership Quarterly* (Fall 1999), pp. 375–96; S. A. Kirkpatrick and E. A. Locke, "Direct and Indirect Effects of Three Core Charismatic Leadership Components on Performance and Attitudes," *Journal of Applied Psychology* (February 1996), pp. 36–51; D. A. Waldman, B. M. Bass, and F. J. Yammarino, "Adding to Contingent-Reward Behavior: The Augmenting Effect of Charismatic Leadership," *Group & Organization Studies* (December 1990), pp. 381–94; and R. J. House, J. Woycke, and E. M. Fodor, "Charismatic and Noncharismatic Leaders: Differences in Behavior and Effectiveness," in Conger and Kanungo, *Charismatic Leadership*, pp. 103–04.

34. B. R. Agle, N. J. Nagarajan, J. A. Sonnenfeld, and D. Srinivasan, "Does CEO Charisma Matter? An Empirical Analysis of the Relationships Among Organizational Performance, Environmental Uncertainty, and Top Management Team Perceptions of CEO Charisma," *Academy of Management Journal* (February 2006), pp. 161–74.

35. R. Birchfield, "Creating Charismatic Leaders," *Management* (June 2000), pp. 30–31; S. Caudron, "Growing Charisma," *IndustryWeek*, May 4, 1998, pp. 54–55; and J. A. Conger and R. N. Kanungo, "Training Charismatic Leadership: A Risky and Critical Task," in Conger and Kanungo, *Charismatic Leadership*, pp. 309–23.

36. J. G. Hunt, K. B. Boal, and G. E. Dodge, "The Effects of Visionary and Crisis-Responsive Charisma on Followers: An Experimental Examination," *Leadership Quarterly* (Fall 1999), pp. 423–48; R. J. House and R. N. Aditya, "The Social Scientific Study of Leadership: Quo Vadis?" *Journal of Management* 23, no. 3 (1997), pp. 316–23; and House, "A 1976 Theory of Charismatic Leadership."

37. This definition is based on M. Sashkin, "The Visionary Leader," in Conger and Kanungo et al., *Charismatic Leadership*, pp. 124–25; B. Nanus, *Visionary Leadership* (New York: Free Press, 1992), p. 8; N. H. Snyder and M. Graves, "Leadership and Vision," *Business Horizons* (January–February 1994), p. 1; and J. R. Lucas, "Anatomy of a Vision Statement," *Management Review* (February 1998), pp. 22–26.

38. Nanus, *Visionary Leadership*, p. 8.

39. S. Caminiti, "What Team Leaders Need to Know," *Fortune,* February 20, 1995, pp. 93–100.

40. Ibid., p. 93.

41. Ibid., p. 100.

42. N. Steckler and N. Fondas, "Building Team Leader Effectiveness: A Diagnostic Tool," *Organizational Dynamics* (Winter 1995), p. 20.

43. R. S. Wellins, W. C. Byham, and G. R. Dixon, *Inside Teams* (San Francisco: Jossey-Bass, 1994), p. 318.

44. Steckler and Fondas, "Building Team Leader Effectiveness," p. 21.

45. G. Colvin, "The FedEx Edge," *Fortune,* April 3, 2006, pp. 77–84.

46. A. Srivastava, K. M. Bartol, and E. A. Locke, "Empowering Leadership in Management Teams: Effects on Knowledge Sharing, Efficacy, and Performance," *Academy of Management Journal* (December 2006), pp. 1239–51; P. K. Mills and G. R. Ungson, "Reassessing the Limits of Structural Empowerment: Organizational Constitution and Trust as Controls," *Academy of Management Review* (January 2003), pp. 143–53; W. A. Rudolph and M. Sashkin, "Can Organizational Empowerment Work in Multinational Settings?" *Academy of Management Executive* (February 2002), pp. 102–15; C. Gomez and B. Rosen, "The Leader-Member Link Between Managerial Trust and Employee Empowerment," *Group & Organization Management* (March 2001), pp. 53–69; C. Robert and T. M. Probst, "Empowerment and Continuous Improvement in the United States, Mexico, Poland, and India," *Journal of Applied Psychology* (October 2000), pp. 643–58; R. C. Herrenkohl, G. T. Judson, and J. A. Heffner, "Defining and Measuring Employee Empowerment," *Journal of Applied Behavioral Science* (September 1999), p. 373; R. C. Ford and M. D. Fottler, "Empowerment: A Matter of Degree," *Academy of Management Executive* (August 1995), pp. 21–31; and W. A. Rudolph, "Navigating the Journey to Empowerment," *Organizational Dynamics* (Spring 1995), pp. 19–32.

47. T. A. Stewart, "Just Think: No Permission Needed," *Fortune,* January 8, 2001, pp. 190–92.

48. F. W. Swierczek, "Leadership and Culture: Comparing Asian Managers," *Leadership & Organization Development Journal* (December 1991), pp. 3–10.

49. "Technology and the Manager's Job" box based on L. A. Hambley, T. A. O'Neill, and T. J. B. Kline, "Virtual Team Leadership: The Effects of Leadership Style and Communication Medium on Team Interaction Styles and Outcomes," *Organizational Behavior and Human Decision Processes* (May 2007), pp. 1–20; and B. J. Avolio and S. S. Kahai, "Adding the 'E' to E-Leadership: How It May Impact Your Leadership," *Organizational Dynamics* (January 2003), pp. 325–38.

50. House, "Leadership in the Twenty-First Century," p. 443; M. F. Peterson and J. G. Hunt, "International Perspectives on International Leadership," *Leadership Quarterly* (Fall 1997), pp. 203–31; and J. R. Schermerhorn and M. H. Bond, "Cross-Cultural Leadership in Collectivism and High Power Distance Settings," *Leadership & Organization Development Journal* 18, no. 4/5 (1997), pp. 187–93.

51. R. J. House, P. J. Hanges, S. A. Ruiz-Quintanilla, P. W. Dorfman, and Associates, "Culture Specific and Cross-Culturally Generalizable Implicit Leadership Theories: Are the Attributes of Charismatic/Transformational Leadership Universally Endorsed?" *Leadership Quarterly* (Summer 1999), pp. 219–56; and D. E. Carl and M. Javidan, "Universality of Charismatic Leadership: A Multi-Nation Study," paper presented at the National Academy of Management Conference, Washington, DC, August 2001.

52. Carl and Javidan, "Universality of Charismatic Leadership," p. 29.

53. This section is based on D. Goleman, *Working with Emotional Intelligence* (New York: Bantam, 1998); D. Coleman, "What Makes a Leader?" *Harvard Business Review* (November/ December 1998), pp. 93–102; J. M. George, "Emotions and Leadership: The Role of Emotional Intelligence," *Human Relations* (August 2000),

pp. 1027–55; D. R. Caruso, J. D. Mayer, and P. Salovey, "Emotional Intelligence and Emotional Leadership," in R. E. Riggio, S. E. Murphy, and F. J. Pirozzolo (eds.), *Multiple Intelligences and Leadership* (Mahwah, NJ: Lawrence Erlbaum, 2002), pp. 55–74; and D. Coleman, R. E. Boyatzis, and A. McKee, *Primal Leadership: Realizing the Power of Emotional Intelligence* (Boston: Harvard Business School Press, 2002).

54. "Managing Diversity" box based on E. E. Fuehr and J. E. Bono, "Men, Women, and Managers: Are Stereotypes Finally Changing?" *Personnel Psychology* (Winter 2006), pp. 815–46; D. Dawley, J. J. Hoffman, and A. R. Smith, "Leader Succession: Does Gender Matter?" *Leadership and Organization Development Journal* (August 2004), pp. 678–90; M. L. Van Engen, R. Van Der Leeden, and T. M. Willemsen, "Gender, Context and Leadership Styles: A Field Study," *Journal of Occupational and Organizational Psychology* (December 2001), pp. 581–99; R. F. Martell and A. L. DeSmet, "A Diagnostic-Ratio Approach to Measuring Beliefs About the Leadership Abilities of Male and Female Managers," *Journal of Applied Psychology* (December 2001), pp. 1223–32; "Are Women Better Leaders?" *U.S. News and World Report,* January 29, 2001, p. 10; and R. Sharpe, "As Leaders, Women Rule," *BusinessWeek,* November 20, 2000, pp. 75–84.

55. "The Secret Skill of Leaders," *U.S. News & World Report,* January 14, 2002, p. 8. See also, L. Gardner and C. Stough, "Examining the Relationship Between Leadership and Emotional Intelligence in Senior Level Managers," *Leadership and Organization Development Journal* (January/February 2002), pp. 68–79.

56. Ibid.

57. See R. Boyatzis and A. McKee, "Intentional Change," *Journal of Organizational Excellence* (Summer 2006), pp. 49–60, and R. Kerr; J. Garvin, N. Heaton, and E. Boyle, "Emotional Intelligence and Leadership Effectiveness," *Leadership and Organizational Development Journal* (April 2006), pp. 265–79.

58. S. Simsarian, "Leadership and Trust Facilitating Cross-Functional Team Success," *Journal of Management Development* (March/April 2002), pp. 201–15.

59. J. M. Kouzes and B. Z. Posner, *Credibility: How Leaders Gain and Lose It, and Why People Demand It* (San Francisco: Jossey-Bass, 1993), p. 14.

60. Based on F. D. Schoorman, R. C. Mayer, and J. H. Davis, "An Integrative Model of Organizational Trust: Past, Present, and Future," *Academy of Management Review* (April 2007), pp. 344–54; G. M. Spreitzer and A. K. Mishra, "Giving Up Control Without Losing Control," *Group & Organization Management* (June 1999), pp. 155–87; R. C. Mayer, J. H. Davis, and F. D. Schoorman, "An Integrative Model of Organizational Trust," *Academy of Management Review* (July 1995), p. 712; and L. T. Hosmer, "Trust: The Connecting Link Between Organizational Theory and Philosophical Ethics," *Academy of Management Review* (April 1995), p. 393.

61. P. L. Schindler and C. C. Thomas, "The Structure of Interpersonal Trust in the Workplace," *Psychological Reports* (October 1993), pp. 563–73.

62. H. H. Tan and C. S. F. Tan, "Toward the Differentiation of Trust in Supervisor and Trust in Organization," *Genetic, Social, and General Psychology Monographs* (May 2000), pp. 241–60.

63. R. C. Mayer and M. B. Gavin, "Trust in Management and Performance: Who Minds the Shop While the Employees Watch the Boss?" *Academy of Management Journal* (October 2005), pp. 874–88; and K. T. Dirks and D. L. Ferrin, "Trust in Leadership: Meta-Analytic Findings and Implications for Research and Practice," *Journal of Applied Psychology* (August 2002), pp. 611–28.

64. R. Zemke, "The Confidence Crisis," *Training* (June 2004), pp. 22–30; J. A. Byrne, "Restoring Trust in Corporate America," *BusinessWeek,* June 24, 2002, pp. 30–35; S. Armour, "Employees' New Motto: Trust No One," *USA Today,* February 5, 2002, p. 1B; J. Scott, "Once Bitten, Twice Shy: A World of Eroding Trust," *New York Times,* April 21, 2002, p. WK5; J. Brockner, P. A. Siegel, J. P. Daly, T. Tyler, and C. Martin, "When Trust Matters: The Moderating Effect of Outcome Favorability," *Administrative Science Quarterly* (September 1997), p. 558; and J. Brockner, P. A. Siegel, J. P. Daly, T. Tyler, and C. Martin, "When Trust Matters: The Moderating Effect of Outcome Favorability," *Administrative Science Quarterly* (September 1997), p. 558.

65. "Weathering the Storm: A Study of Employee Attitudes and Opinions," *WorkUSA 2002 Study,* Watson Wyatt, http://www.watsonwyatt.com.

66. S. Kerr and J. M. Jermier, "Substitutes for Leadership: Their Meaning and Measurement," *Organizational Behavior and Human Performance* (December 1978), pp. 375–403; J. P. Howell, P. W. Dorfman, and S. Kerr, "Leadership and Substitutes for Leadership," *Journal of Applied Behavioral Science* 22, no. 1 (1986), pp. 29–46; J. P. Howell, D. E. Bowen, P. W. Dorfman, S. Kerr, and P. M. Podsakoff, "Substitutes for Leadership: Effective Alternatives to Ineffective Leadership," *Organizational Dynamics* (Summer 1990), pp. 21–38; and P. M. Podsakoff, B. P. Niehoff, S. B. MacKenzie, and M. L. Williams, "Do Substitutes for Leadership Really Substitute for Leadership? An Empirical Examination of Kerr and Jermier's Situational Leadership Model," *Organizational Behavior and Human Decision Processes* (February 1993), pp. 1–44.

67. "Developing Your Trust-Building Skill" box based on F. Bartolome, "Nobody Trusts the Boss Completely—Now What?" *Harvard Business Review* (March/April 1989), pp. 135–42; and J. K. Butler Jr., "Toward Understanding and Measuring Conditions of Trust: Evolution of a Condition of Trust Inventory," *Journal of Management* (September 1991), pp. 643–63.

Chapter 12

1. J. McGregor, "Mining the Office Chatter," *BusinessWeek,* May 19, 2008, p. 54; E. Zimmerman, "Gossip Is Information by Another Name," *New York Times Online,* February 3, 2008; A. Fisher, "Harmless Office Chitchat or Poisonous Gossip?" *CNNMoney.com,* November 12, 2007; S. Armour, "Did You Hear the Story About Office Gossip?" *USA Today,* September 10, 2007, pp. 1B+; "Women Lose Jobs over Office Scuttlebutt," *AARP Bulletin,* July–August 2007, p. 11; G. Cuyler, "Hooksett 4 to Seek Judge's Aid in Getting Jobs Back," *New Hampshire Union Leader,* June 25, 2007; and P. B. Erickson, "Drawing the Line Between Gossip, Watercooler Chat," *NewsOK.com,* June 15, 2007.

2. D. K. Berlo, *The Process of Communication* (New York: Holt, Rinehart & Winston, 1960), pp. 30–32.

3. Ibid., p. 54.

4. See, for instance, "Get the Message: Communication Is Key in Managing Change Within Organizations—Yet Ensuring Its Effectiveness at Times of High Concerns Can Be Tricky," *Employee Benefits* (February 2002), pp. 58–60.

5. Ibid., p. 103.

6. L. R. Birkner and R. K. Birkner, "Communication Feedback: Putting It All Together," *Occupational Hazards* (August 2001), p. 9.

7. L. Hilton, "They Heard It Through the Grapevine," *South Florida Business Journal* (August 18, 2000), p. 53.

8. "From the Past to the Present" box based on S. Baker, "Putting a Price on Social Connections," *BusinessWeek Online,* April 8, 2009; and K. Davis, "Management Communication and the Grapevine," *Harvard Business Review* (September–October 1953), pp. 43–49.

9. M. Fulfer, "Nonverbal Communication: How to Read What's Plain as the Nose . . . Or Eyelid . . . Or Chin . . . On Their Faces," *Journal of Occupational Excellence* (Spring 2001), pp. 19–38.

10. Ibid.

11. P. Mornell, "The Sounds of Silence," *Inc.* (February 2001), p. 117.

12. A. Warfield, "Do You Speak Body Language?" *Training and Development* (April 2001), p. 60.

13. "Information Overload," *Australian Business Intelligence* (April 16, 2002).

14. S. I. Hayakawa, *Language in Thought and Action* (New York: Harcourt Brace Jovanovich, 1949), p. 292.

15. "Jargon Leaves Us Lost for Words," *Australian Business Intelligence* (August 23, 2002); and W. S. Mossberg, "A Guide to the Lingo You'll Want to Learn for Wireless Technology," *Wall Street Journal,* March 28, 2002, p. B1.

16. "Gobbledygook Begone," *Workforce* (February 2002), p. 12; and "Business-Speak," *Training and Development* (January 2002), pp. 50–52.

17. See, for example, M. K. Kozan, "Subcultures and Conflict Management Styles," *Management International Review* (January 2002), pp. 89–106.

18. A. Mehrabian, "Communication Without Words," *Psychology Today* (September 1968), pp. 53–55.

19. "Managing Diversity" box based on J. Langdon, "Differences Between Males and Females at Work," *USA Today,* www.usatoday.com (February 5, 2001); J. Manion, "He Said, She Said," *Materials Management in Health Care* (November 1998), pp. 52–62; G. Franzwa and C. Lockhart, "The Social Origins and Maintenance of Gender Communication Styles, Personality Types, and Grid-Group Theory," *Sociological Perspectives* 41, no. 1 (1998), pp. 185–208; and D. Tannen, *Talking from 9 to 5: Women and Men in the Workplace* (New York: Avon Books, 1995).

20. See also W. L. Adair, T. Okumura, and J. M. Brett, "Negotiation Behavior When Cultures Collide: The United States and Japan," *Journal of Applied Psychology* (June 2001), p. 371.

21. C. H. Tinsley, "How Negotiators Get to Yes: Predicting the Constellation of Strategies Used Across Cultures to Negotiate Conflict," *Journal of Applied Psychology* (August 2001), p. 583.

22. See, for instance, S. P. Robbins and P. L. Hunsaker, *Training in Interpersonal Skills,* 4th ed. (Upper Saddle River, NJ: Prentice Hall, 2006); M. Young and J. E. Post, "Managing to Communicate, Communicating to Manage: How Leading

Companies Communicate with Employees," *Organizational Dynamics* (Summer 1993), pp. 31–43; J. A. DeVito, *The Interpersonal Communication Book*, 6th ed. (New York: HarperCollins, 1992); and A. G. Athos and J. J. Gabarro, *Interpersonal Behavior* (Upper Saddle River, NJ: Prentice Hall, 1978).

23. "Electronic Invective Backfires," *Workforce,* June 2001, p. 20; and E. Wong, "A Stinging Office Memo Boomerangs," *New York Times,* April 5, 2001, pp. C1+.

24. "Right or Wrong?" box based on E. Maltby, "Biz Is Failing: Should You Tell the Staff?" *CNNMoney.com,* March 3, 2009.

25. See, for example, R. R. Panko, *Business Data Networks and Communications*, 4th ed. (Upper Saddle River, NJ: Prentice Hall, 2003).

26. "Virtual Paper Cuts," *Workforce* (July 2000), pp. 16–18.

27. "Technology and the Manager's Job" box based on S. Raposo, "Quick! Tell Us What KUTGW Means," *Wall Street Journal,* August 5, 2009, pp. D1+; and C. Tuna, "Corporate Blogs and Tweets Must Keep SEC in Mind," *Wall Street Journal,* April 27, 2009, p. B4.

28. J. Karaian, "Where Wireless Works," *CFO,* May 2003, pp. 81–83.

29. See, for instance, A. Cohen, "Wireless Summer," *Time,* May 29, 2000, pp. 58–65; and K. Hafner, "For the Well Connected, All the World's an Office," *New York Times,* March 30, 2000, p. D1.

30. J. S. Brown and P. Duguid, "Balancing Act: How to Capture Knowledge Without Killing It," *Harvard Business Review* (May–June 2000), pp. 73–80; and J. Torsilieri and C. Lucier, "How to Change the World," *Strategy and Business* (October 2000), pp. 17–20.

31. See J. Lloyd, "Derailing Your Career," *Baltimore Business Journal* (October 19, 2001), p. 3; H. Johnson, "Soften Up," *Training* (February 2002), p. 20; and M. Langbert, "Professors, Managers, and Human Resource Education," *Human Resource Management* (Spring 2000), pp. 65–78.

32. "Executive Update," *Training and Development* (March 2002), p. 19.

33. "More Than One-Third of People Surveyed Identified Communication Skills or Interpersonal Relationship Skills as the Most Important Quality in a Good Boss," *Training and Development* (February 2000), p. 16.

34. This material is adapted from S. P. Robbins and P. L. Hunsaker, *Training in Interpersonal Skills* (Upper Saddle River, NJ: Prentice Hall, 1996), p. 3.

35. C. R. Rogers and R. E. Farson, *Active Listening* (Chicago: Industrial Relations Center of the University of Chicago, 1976).

36. "And the Survey Says . . ." box based on J. MacIntyre, "Offensive Jargon," *Springfield, Missouri, Business Journal,* October 10–17, 2008, p. 24; "Did You Know?" *O Magazine,* December 2008, p. 172; J. Yang and S. Parker, "Top Managers Don't Appreciate Office Gossip," *USA Today,* December 24, 2008, p. 1B; "Pop Quiz," *Health.com,* October 2007, p. 26; M. Jackson, "May We Have Your Attention Please," *BusinessWeek,* June 23, 2008, p 56; and "Q&A," *Training,* February 2008, p. 15.

37. See, for example, K. Leung, S. Su, and M. W. Morris, "When Is Criticism Not Constructive? The Roles of Fairness Perceptions and Dispositional Attributions in Employee Acceptance of Critical Supervisory Feedback," *Human Relations* (September 2001), p. 1155; and C. A. Walker, "Saving Your Rookie Managers from Themselves," *Harvard Business Review* (April 2002), pp. 97–103.

38. D. Ilgen, C. D. Fisher, and M. S. Taylor, "Consequences of Individual Feedback on Behavior in Organizations," *Journal of Applied Psychology* (August 1979), pp. 349–71.

39. F. Bartolome, "Teaching About Whether to Give Negative Feedback," *The Organizational Behavior Teaching Review* 9, no. 2 (1986/1987), pp. 95–104.

40. K. Halperin, C. R. Snyder, R. J. Schenkel, and B. K. Houston, "Effect of Source Status and Message Favorability on Acceptance of Personality Feedback," *Journal of Applied Psychology* (February 1976), pp. 85–88.

41. Based on P. L. Hunsaker, *Training in Management Skills* (Upper Saddle River, NJ: Prentice Hall, 2001), pp. 60–61.

42. S. Gazda, "The Art of Delegating: Effective Delegation Enhances Employee Morale, Manager Productivity, and Organizational Success," *HR Magazine* (January 2002), pp. 75–79.

43. L. L. Steinmetz, *The Art and Skill of Delegation* (Boston: Addison-Wesley, 1976).

44. Based on Hunsaker, *Training in Management Skills*, pp. 135–36, 430–32; R. T. Noel, "What You Say to Your Employees When You Delegate," *Supervisory Management* (December 1993), p. 13; and S. Caudron, "Delegate for Results," *Industry Week,* February 6, 1995, pp. 27–30.

45. M. Delahoussaye, "Don't Get Mad, Get Promoted," *Training* (June 2002), p. 20; and C. Tinsley and J. Brett, "Managing Workplace Conflict in the United States and Hong Kong," *Organizational Behavior and Human Decision Processes* (July 2001), pp. 360–62.

46. K. W. Thomas and W. H. Schmidt, "A Survey of Managerial Interests with Respect to Conflict," *Academy of Management Journal* (June 1976), pp. 315–18.

47. Ibid.

48. This section is adapted from S. P. Robbins, *Managing Organizational Conflict: A Nontraditional Approach* (Upper Saddle River, NJ: Prentice Hall, 1974), pp. 11–14. Also, see D. Wagner-Johnson, "Managing Work Team Conflict: Assessment and Preventative Strategies," Center for the Study of Work Teams, University of North Texas, www.workteams.unt.edu/reports (November 3, 2000); and M. Kennedy, "Managing Conflict in Work Teams," Center for the Study of Work Teams, University of North Texas, www.workteams.unt.edu/reports (November 3, 2000).

49. See K. A. Jehn, "A Multimethod Examination of the Benefits and Detriments of Intragroup Conflict," *Administrative Science Quarterly* (June 1995), pp. 256–82; K. A. Jehn, "A Qualitative Analysis of Conflict Type and Dimensions in Organizational Groups," *Administrative Science Quarterly* (September 1997), pp. 530–57; K. A. Jehn, "Affective and Cognitive Conflict in Work Groups: Increasing Performance Through Value-Based Intragroup Conflict," in C. DeDreu and E. Van deVliert (eds.), *Using Conflict in Organizations* (London: Sage Publications, 1997), pp. 87–100; K. A. Jehn and E. A. Mannix, "The Dynamic Nature of Conflict: A Longitudinal Study of Intragroup Conflict and Group Performance," *Academy of Management Journal* (April 2001), pp. 238–51; C. K. W. DeDreu and A. E. M. Van Vianen, "Managing Relationship Conflict and the Effectiveness of Organizational Teams," *Journal of Organizational Behavior* (May 2001), pp. 309–28; and J. Weiss and J. Hughes, "Want Collaboration? Accept—And Actively Manage—Conflict," *Harvard Business Review* (March 2005), pp. 92–101.

50. C. K. W. DeDreu, "When Too Little or Too Much Hurts: Evidence for a Curvilinear Relationship Between Task Conflict and Innovation in Teams," *Journal of Management* (February 2006), pp. 83–107.

51. K. W. Thomas, "Conflict and Negotiation Processes in Organizations," in M. D. Dunnette and L. M. Hough (eds.), *Handbook of Industrial and Organizational Psychology*, 2nd ed., vol. 3 (Palo Alto, CA: Consulting Psychologists Press, 1992), pp. 651–717.

52. L. Greenhalgh, "Managing Conflict," *Sloan Management Review* (Summer 1986), pp. 45–51.

53. See, for instance, D. Tjosvold and D. W. Johnson, *Productive Conflict Management Perspectives for Organizations* (New York: Irvington Publishers, 1983).

54. S. P. Robbins, "Conflict Management and Conflict Resolution Are Not Synonymous Terms," *California Management Review* (Winter 1978), p. 71.

55. See E. Van de Vliert, A. Nauta, E. Giebels, and O. Janssen, "Constructive Conflict at Work," in L. N. Dosier and J. B. Keys (eds.), *Academy of Management Best Paper Proceedings* (August 8–13, 1997), pp. 92–96; Robbins, *Managing Organizational Conflict*, pp. 78–89; and S. Berglas, "Innovate: Harmony Is Death. Let Conflict Reign," *Inc.*, May 1997, pp. 56–58.

56. R. E. Walton and R. B. McKersie, *A Behavioral Theory of Labor Negotiations: An Analysis of a Social Interaction System* (New York: McGraw-Hill, 1965).

57. "Negotiation Skills Invaluable in Workplace," *Knight-Ridder/Tribune Business News*, June 23, 2002, p. 1.

58. K. W. Thomas, "Conflict and Negotiation Processes in Organizations," in M. D. Dunnette and L. M. Hough (eds.), *Handbook of Industrial and Organizational Psychology*, vol. 3, 2nd ed. (Palo Alto, CA: Consulting Psychologists Press, 1992), pp. 651–717.

59. Based on R. Fisher and W. Ury, *Getting to Yes: Negotiating Agreement Without Giving In* (Boston: Houghton Mifflin, 1981); J. A. Wall, Jr. and M. W. Blum, "Negotiations," *Journal of Management* (June 1991), pp. 295–96; and M. H. Bazerman and M. A. Neale, *Negotiating Rationally* (New York: Free Press, 1992).

Chapter 13

1. C. Dosh, "Debunking T5 Terror," *Successful Meetings*, April 2009, p. 99; M. Frary, "A Tale of Two Terminals," *Business Travel World*, August 2008, pp. 16–19; K. Capell, "British Airways Hit by Heathrow Fiasco," *BusinessWeek*, April 3, 2008, p. 6; The Associated Press, "Problems Continue at Heathrow's Terminal 5," *International Herald Tribune*, http://www.iht.com (March 31, 2008); M. Scott, "New Heathrow Hub: Slick, but No Savior," *BusinessWeek*, March 28, 2008, p. 11; and G. Katz, "Flights Are Canceled, Baggage Stranded, as London's New Heathrow Terminal Opens," *Seattle Times Online*, http://seattletimes.nwsource.com (March 27, 2008).

2. "Domino's Delivered Free Pizzas," *Springfield, Missouri, News-Leader*, April 3, 2009, p. 3B.

3. B. Hagenbauh, "State Quarters Extra Leaf Grew Out of Lunch Break," *USA Today*, January 20, 2006, p. 1B.

4. T. Vinas and J. Jusko, "5 Threats That Could Sink Your Company," *Industry Week*, September 2004, pp. 52–61; "Workplace Security: How Vulnerable Are You?" Special section in *Wall Street Journal*, September 29, 2003, pp. R1–R8; P. Magnusson, "Your Jitters Are Their Lifeblood," *BusinessWeek*, April 14, 2003, p. 41; and T. Purdum, "Preparing for the Worst," *Industry Week*, January 2003, pp. 53–55.

5. "Right or Wrong?" box based on A. Vanacore, "Cameras Scan Store Lines for 'Sweethearting,'" The Associated Press, *Springfield, Missouri, News-Leader*, May 11, 2009, p. 9A.

6. A. Dalton, "Rapid Recovery," *Industry Week*, March 2005, pp. 70–71.

7. B. Nelson, "Long-Distance Recognition," *Workforce* (August 2000), pp. 50–52.

8. S. Kerr, "On the Folly of Rewarding A, While Hoping for B," *Academy of Management Journal* (December 1975), pp. 769–83; and N. F. Piercy, D. W. Cravens, N. Lane, and D. W. Vorhies, "Driving Organizational Citizenship Behaviors and Sales Person In-Role Behavior Performance: The Role of Management Control and Perceived Organizational Support," *Journal of the Academy of Marketing Science* (Spring 2006), pp. 244–62.

9. "From the Past to the Present" box based on R. Pear, "A.M.A. to Develop Measure of Quality of Medical Care," *New York Times Online*, February 21, 2006; A. Taylor III, "Double Duty," *Fortune*, March 7, 2005, pp. 104–10; C. Bogan and D. Callahan, "Benchmarking in Rapid Time," *Industrial Management* (March/April 2001), pp. 28–33; and L. D. McNary, "Thinking About Excellence and Benchmarking," *Journal for Quality and Participation* (July/August 1994).

10. "And the Survey Says . . ." box based on J. Casale, "Data Breach Threats from Within Growing," *Workforce Management Online*, April 2009; N. Byrnes, "Profiles in Pilfering," *BusinessWeek*, October 13, 2008, p. 16; M. Conlin, "To Catch a Corporate Thief," *BusinessWeek*, February 16, 2009, p. 52; A. R. Carey and S. Ward, "Have a Boss Who Plays Games at Work?" *USA Today*, May 6, 2009, p. 1A; S. L. Mintz, "The Gauge of Innocence," *CFO*, April 2009, pp. 53–57; and "Survey Finds Workplace Violence Is a Top Security Concern," *Facilities Management News*, January 5, 2009, http://www.fmlink.com.

11. H. Koontz and R. W. Bradspies, "Managing Through Feed-forward Control," *Business Horizons* (June 1972), pp. 25–36.

12. M. Helft, "The Human Hands Behind the Google Money Machine," *New York Times Online*, June 2, 2008.

13. B. Caulfield, "Shoot to Kill," *Forbes*, January 7, 2008, pp. 92–96.

14. T. Laseter and L. Laseter, "See for Yourself," *Strategy+Business*, November 29, 2007, http://www.strategy-business.com.

15. W. H. Newman, *Constructive Control: Design and Use of Control Systems* (Upper Saddle River, NJ: Prentice Hall, 1975), p. 33.

16. D. Stout and T. Zeller Jr., "Vast Data Cache About Veterans Has Been Stolen," *New York Times Online*, May 23, 2006.

17. Deloitte & Touche and the Ponemon Institute, "Research Report: Reportable and Multiple Privacy Breaches Rising at Alarming Rate," *Ethics Newsline*, January 1, 2008, http://ethicsnewsline.wordpress.com.

18. B. Grow, K. Epstein, and C-C. Tschang, "The New E-Spionage Threat," *BusinessWeek*, April 21, 2008, pp. 32–41; S. Leibs, "Firewall of Silence," *CFO*, April 2008, pp. 31–35; J. Pereira, "How Credit-Card Data Went out Wireless Door," *Wall Street Journal*, May 4, 2007, pp. A1+; and B. Stone, "Firms Fret as

Office E-Mail Jumps Security Walls," *New York Times Online,* January 11, 2007.

19. D. Whelan, "Google Me Not," *Forbes,* August 16, 2004, pp. 102–104.

20. R. S. Kaplan and D. P. Norton, "How to Implement a New Strategy Without Disrupting Your Organization," *Harvard Business Review* (March 2006), pp. 100–109; L. Bassi and D. McMurrer, "Developing Measurement Systems for Managers in the Knowledge Era," *Organizational Dynamics* (May 2005), pp. 185–96; G. M. J. DeKoning, "Making the Balanced Scorecard Work (Part 2)," *Gallup Brain,* August 12, 2004, http://brain.gallup.com; G. J. J. DeKoning, "Making the Balanced Scorecard Work (Part 1)," *Gallup Brain,* July 8, 2004, http://brain.gallup.com; K. Graham, "Balanced Scorecard," *New Zealand Management* (March 2003), pp. 32–34; K. Ellis, "A Ticket to Ride: Balanced Scorecard," *Training* (April 2001), p. 50; and T. Leahy, "Tailoring the Balanced Scorecard," *Business Finance* (August 2000), pp. 53–56.

21. Leahy, "Tailoring the Balanced Scorecard."

22. Ibid.

23. J. Yaukey and C. L. Romero, "Arizona Firm Pays Big for Workers' Digital Downloads," Associated Press, *Springfield, Missouri, News-Leader,* May 6, 2002, p. 6B.

24. Information on Hoovers Online, http://www.hoovers.com (August 16, 2009); and N. Shirouzu and J. Bigness, "7-Eleven Operators Resist System to Monitor Managers," *Wall Street Journal,* June 16, 1997, p. B1.

25. "Technology and the Manager's Job" box based on D. Searcey, "Employers Watching Workers Online Spurs Privacy Debate," *Wall Street Journal,* April 23, 2009, p. A13; D. Darlin, "Software That Monitors Your Work, Wherever You Are," *New York Times Online,* April 12, 2009; S. Boehle, "They're Watching You," *Training* (September 2008), pp. 23+; S. Shellenbarger, "Work at Home? Your Employer May Be Watching You," *Wall Street Journal,* July 30, 2008, p. D1+; J. Jusko, "A Watchful Eye," *Industry Week,* May 7, 2001, p. 9; "Big Brother Boss," *U.S. News and World Report,* April 30, 2001, p. 12; and L. Guernsey, "You've Got Inappropriate E-Mail," *New York Times,* April 5, 2000, pp. C1+.

26. AMA/ePolicy Institute, "2005 Electronic Monitoring & Surveillance Survey," *American Management Association,* http://www.amanet.org.

27. S. Armour, "Companies Keep an Eye on Workers' Internet Use," *USA Today,* February 21, 2006, p. 2B.

28. B. White, "The New Workplace Rules: No Video-Watching," *Wall Street Journal,* March 4, 2008, pp. B1+.

29. Ibid.

30. P-W Tam, E. White, N. Wingfield, and K. Maher, "Snooping E-Mail by Software Is Now a Workplace Norm," *Wall Street Journal,* March 9, 2005, pp. B1+; D. Hawkins, "Lawsuits Spur Rise in Employee Monitoring," *U.S. News & World Report,* August 13, 2001, p. 53; and L. Guernsey, "You've Got Inappropriate Mail," *New York Times,* April 5, 2000, pp. C1+.

31. S. Armour, "More Companies Keep Track of Workers' E-Mail," *USA Today,* June 13, 2005, p. 4B; and E. Bott, "Are You Safe? Privacy Special Report," *PC Computing,* March 2000, pp. 87–88.

32. A. M. Bell and D. M. Smith, "Theft and Fraud May Be an Inside Job," *Workforce Online,* December 3, 2000, http://www.workforce.com.

33. C. C. Verschoor, "New Evidence of Benefits from Effective Ethics Systems," *Strategic Finance* (May 2003), pp. 20–21; and E. Krell, "Will Forensic Accounting Go Mainstream?" *Business Finance* (October 2002), pp. 30–34.

34. S. E. Needleman, "Businesses Say Theft by Their Workers Is Up," *Wall Street Journal,* December 11, 2008, p. B8.

35. J. Greenberg, "The STEAL Motive: Managing the Social Determinants of Employee Theft," in R. Giacalone and J. Greenberg (eds.), *Antisocial Behavior in Organizations* (Newbury Park, CA: Sage, 1997), pp. 85–108.

36. B. E. Litzky, K. A. Eddleston, and D. L. Kidder, "The Good, the Bad, and the Misguided: How Managers Inadvertently Encourage Deviant Behaviors," *Academy of Management Perspective* (February 2006), pp. 91–103; "Crime Spree," *BusinessWeek,* September 9, 2002, p. 8; B. P. Niehoff and R. J. Paul, "Causes of Employee Theft and Strategies That HR Managers Can Use for Prevention," *Human Resource Management* (Spring 2000), pp. 51–64; and G. Winter, "Taking at the Office Reaches New Heights: Employee Larceny Is Bigger and Bolder," *New York Times,* July 12, 2000, pp. C1+.

37. This section is based on J. Greenberg, *Behavior in Organizations: Understanding and Managing the Human Side of Work,* 8th ed. (Upper Saddle River, NJ: Prentice Hall, 2003), pp. 329–330.

38. A. H. Bell and D. M. Smith, "Why Some Employees Bite the Hand That Feeds Them," *Workforce Online,* December 3, 2000, http://www.workforce.com.

39. Litzky et al., "The Good, the Bad, and the Misguided"; A. H. Bell and D. M. Smith, "Protecting the Company Against Theft and Fraud," *Workforce Online,* December 3, 2000, http://www.workforce.com; J. D. Hansen, "To Catch a Thief," *Journal of Accountancy* (March 2000), pp. 43–46; and J. Greenberg, "The Cognitive Geometry of Employee Theft," in *Dysfunctional Behavior in Organizations: Nonviolent and Deviant Behavior* (Stamford, CT: JAI Press, 1998), pp. 147–193.

40. R. Lenz, "Gunman Kills Five, Himself at Plant," The Associated Press, *Springfield, Missouri, News-Leader,* June 26, 2008, p. 6A; S. Oppermann, "Violence in the Workplace: Is Your Agency Prepared?" *FedSmith,* May 30, 2007, http://www.fedsmith.com; CBS News, "Former Postal Worker Kills 5, Herself," CBS News, January 31, 2006, http://www.cbsnews.com/stories; CBS News, "Autoworker's Grudge Turns Deadly," January 27, 2005, http://www.cbsnews.com/stories; D. Sharp, "Gunman Just Hated a Lot of People," *USA Today,* July 10, 2003, p. 3A; and M. Prince, "Violence in the Workplace on the Rise; Training, Zero Tolerance Can Prevent Aggression," *Business Insurance,* May 12, 2003, p. 1.

41. "Workplace Homicides in 2007," *U.S. Bureau of Labor Statistics Division of Information Services,* August 26, 2008, http://data.blg.gov.

42. J. McCafferty, "Verbal Chills," *CFO,* June 2005, p. 17; S. Armour, "Managers Not Prepared for Workplace Violence," *USA Today,* July 15, 2004, pp. 1B+; and "Workplace Violence," OSHA Fact Sheet, U.S. Department of Labor, Occupational Safety and Health Administration, 2002.

43. "Ten Tips on Recognizing and Minimizing Violence," *Workforce Online,* December 3, 2000, http://www.workforce.com.

44. "Bullying Bosses Cause Work Rage Rise," *Management Issues News,* January 28, 2003, http://www.management-issues.com.

45. R. McNatt, "Desk Rage," *BusinessWeek,* November 27, 2000, p. 12.

46. M. Gorkin, "Key Components of a Dangerously Dysfunctional Work Environment," *Workforce Online,* December 3, 2000.

47. "Ten Tips on Recognizing and Minimizing Violence"; Gorkin, "Five Strategies and Structures for Reducing Workplace Violence"; "Investigating Workplace Violence: Where Do You Start?"; and "Points to Cover in a Workplace Violence Policy," all articles from *Workforce Online,* December 3, 2000.

Chapter 14

1. D. Blanchard, "Lean In for a Smooth Ride," *Industry Week,* January 2008, p. 38; and D. Blanchard, "Blue Bird North Georgia: IW Best Plants Profile 2007," http://www.industryweek.com (January 1, 2008).

2. D. McGinn, "Faster Food," *Newsweek,* April 19, 2004, pp. E20–E22.

3. *World Factbook 2009,* http://www.ocdi.gov/cia/publications.

4. Ibid.

5. D. Michaels and J. L. Lunsford, "Streamlined Plane Making," *Wall Street Journal,* April 1, 2005, pp. B1+.

6. T. Aeppel, "Workers Not Included," *Wall Street Journal,* November 19, 2002, pp. B1+.

7. A. Aston and M. Arndt, "The Flexible Factory," *BusinessWeek,* May 5, 2003, pp. 90–91.

8. P. Panchak, "Pella Drives Lean Throughout the Enterprise," *Industry Week,* June 2003, pp. 74–77.

9. J. Ordonez, "McDonald's to Cut the Cooking Time of Its French Fries," *Wall Street Journal,* May 19, 2000, p. B2.

10. C. Fredman, "The Devil in the Details," *Executive Edge,* April–May, 1999, pp. 36–39.

11. Information from http://new.skoda-auto.com/Documents/AnnualReports/skoda_auto_annual_report_2007_%20EN_FINAL.pdf (July 8, 2008); and T. Mudd, "The Last Laugh," *Industry Week,* September 18, 2000, pp. 38–44.

12. "From the Past to the Present" box based on R. Aguayo, *Dr. Deming: The American Who Taught the Japanese About Quality* (New York: Fireside Press, 1991); M. Walton, *The Deming Management Method* (New York: Penguin Group, 1986); and W. E. Deming, "Improvement of Quality and Productivity Through Action by Management," *National Productivity Review* (Winter 1981–1982), pp. 12–22.

13. T. Vinas, "Little Things Mean a Lot," *Industry Week,* November 2002, p. 55.

14. P. Panchak, "Shaping the Future of Manufacturing," *Industry Week,* January 2005, pp. 38–44; M. Hammer, "Deep Change: How Operational Innovation Can Transform Your Company," *Harvard Business Review* (April 2004), pp. 84–94; S. Levy, "The Connected Company," *Newsweek,* April 28, 2003, pp. 40–48; and J. Teresko, "Plant Floor Strategy," *Industry Week,* July 2002, pp. 26–32.

15. T. Laseter, K. Ramdas, and D. Swerdlow, "The Supply Side of Design and Development," *Strategy & Business* (Summer 2003), p. 23; J. Jusko, "Not All Dollars and Cents," *Industry Week,* April 2002, p. 58; and D. Drickhamer, "Medical Marvel," *Industry Week,* March 2002, pp. 47–49.

16. J. H. Sheridan, "Managing the Value Chain," *Industry Week,* September 6, 1999, pp. 1–4, http://www.industryweek.com.

17. Ibid.

18. S. Leibs, "Getting Ready: Your Suppliers," *Industry Week,* September 6, 1999, http://www.industryweek.com.

19. See, for example, Jusko, "Procurement—Not all Dollars and Cents."

20. See "News Item Future Challenges for the Aromatics Supply Chain," speech given by Nancy Sullivan, vice president Aromatics & Phenol, to the First European Aromatics and Derivatives Conference, London, UK (May 29, 2002), http://www.shellchemicals.com/newsroom/1,1098.71.00.html.

21. D. Bartholomew, "The Infrastructure," *Industry Week,* September 6, 1999, p. 1.

22. G. Taninecz, "Forging the Chain," *Industry Week,* May 15, 2000, pp. 40–46.

23. T. Vinas, "A Map of the World: IW Value-Chain Survey," *Industry Week,* September 2005, pp. 27–34.

24. "Right or Wrong?" box based on M. Boyle, "Wal-Mart Keeps the Change," *Fortune,* November 10, 2003, p. 46.

25. See J. H. Sheridan, "Now It's a Job for the CEO," *Industry Week,* March 20, 2000, pp. 22–30.

26. R. Norman and R. Ramirez, "From Value Chain to Value Constellation," *Harvard Business Review on Managing the Value Chain* (Boston: Harvard Business School Press, 2000), pp. 185–219.

27. S. Leibs, "Getting Ready: Your Customers," *Industry Week,* September 6, 1999, p. 4.

28. See, for example, C. Lunan, "Workers Doing More in Less Time," *Charlotte Observer,* June 1, 2002, p. D1.

29. Leibs, "Getting Ready: Your Customers," p. 3.

30. See, for instance, L. Harrington, "The Accelerated Value Chain: Supply Chain Management Just Got Smarter, Faster, and More Cost-Effective, Thanks to a Groundbreaking Alliance Between Intel and Technologies," *Industry Week,* April 2002, pp. 45–51.

31. Ibid.

32. Ibid; and Sheridan, "Managing the Value Chain."

33. Sheriden, "Managing the Value Chain," p. 3.

34. Leibs, "Getting Ready: Your Customers," p. 4.

35. "And the Survey Says . . ." box based on "First-Hand Accounts," *Industry Week,* July 2008, p. 28; "State of the Workforce Report," *Industry Week,* November 2008, p. 18; "Sustainable Supply Chains," *Industry Week,* December 2008, p. 57; "Taking Charge of Mobile Workforce Costs," *Industry Week,* August 2009, p. 47; and "The Future of Manufacturing," *Industry Week,* November 2008, pp. 51–57.

36. Sheriden, "Managing the Value Chain," pp. 2–3; Liebs, "Getting Ready: Your Customers," pp. 1, 4; and Bartholomew, "The Infrastructure," p. 6.

37. Taninecz, "Forging the Chain."

38. Leibs, "Getting Ready: Your Customers," p. 1.

39. Ibid.

40. Ibid.

41. D. Drickhamer, "On Target," *Industry Week,* October 16, 2000, pp. 111–12.

42. Leibs, "Getting Ready: Your Customers," p. 2.

43. Ibid.

44. "Top Security Threats and Management Issues Facing Corporate America: 2003 Survey of *Fortune* 1000 Companies," ASIS International and Pinkerton, http://www.asisonline.org.

45. Sheridan, "Managing the Value Chain," p. 4.

46. S. Rosenbloom, "Solution, or Mess? A Milk Jug for a Green Earth," *New York Times Online,* June 30, 2008.

47. S. Anderson, The Associated Press, "Restaurants Gear Up for Window Wars," *Springfield, Missouri, News-Leader,* January 27, 2006, p. 5B.

48. D. Bartholomew, "Quality Takes a Beating," *Industry Week,* March 2006, pp. 46–54; J. Carey and M. Arndt, "Making Pills the Smart Way," *BusinessWeek,* May 3, 2004, pp. 102–103; and A. Barrett, "Schering's Dr. Feelbetter?" *BusinessWeek,* June 23, 2003, pp. 55–56.

49. "Technology and the Manager's Job" box based on S. Minter, "What Is Advanced Manufacturing?" *Industry Week,* August 2009, p. 7; J. Bush, "Russia's Factories Shift Gears," *BusinessWeek,* May 18, 2009, pp. 50–51; D. Blanchard, "A Manufacturer for All Seasons," *Industry Week,* December 2008, p. 7; J. Teresko, "Planning the Factory of the Future," *Industry Week,* December 2008, pp. 22–24; and J. Teresko, "Winning with Digital Manufacturing," *Industry Week,* July 2008, pp. 45–47.

50. T. Vinas, "Six Sigma Rescue," *Industry Week,* March 2004, p. 12.

51. J. S. McClenahen, "Prairie Home Companion," *Industry Week,* October 2005, pp. 45–46.

52. T. Vinas, "Zeroing In on the Customer," *Industry Week,* October 2004, pp. 61–62.

53. W. Royal, "Spotlight Shines on Maquiladora," *Industry Week,* October 16, 2000, pp. 91–92.

54. See B. Whitford and R. Andrew (eds.), *The Pursuit of Quality* (Perth: Beaumont Publishing, 1994).

55. D. Drickhamer, "Road to Excellence," *Industry Week,* October 16, 2000, pp. 117–18.

56. Information from *Annual Report 2008,* http://www.iso.org.

57. G. Hasek, "Merger Marries Quality Efforts," *Industry Week,* August 21, 2000, pp. 89–92.

58. M. Arndt, "Quality Isn't Just for Widgets," *BusinessWeek,* July 22, 2002, pp. 72–73.

59. E. White, "Rethinking the Quality Improvement Program," *Wall Street Journal,* September 19, 2005, p. B3.

60. M. Arndt, "Quality Isn't Just for Widgets."

61. For a thorough overview of project management, see S. Berkun, *The Art of Project Management* (Upper Saddle River, NJ: Prentice Hall, 2005); or J. K. Pinto, *Project Management: Achieving Competitive Advantage and MS Project* (Upper Saddle River, NJ: Prentice Hall, 2007).

62. H. Maylor, "Beyond the Gantt Chart: Project Management Moving On," *European Management Journal* (February 2001), pp. 92–101.

63. For additional information on CPM, see W. A. Haga and K. A. Marold, "A Simulation Approach to the PERT/CPM Time-Cost Trade-Off Problem," *Project Management Journal* (June 2004), pp. 31–37.

Photo Credits

CHAPTER 1 Page 3: The Life is Good Company. Page 3: The Life is Good Company. Page 5: Joel Dresang/Newscom. Page 9: Imke Lass. Page 12: AP Wide World Photos/Keith Srakocic. Page 15: Abdelhak Senna/Agence France Presse/Getty Images. Page 17: Brad Swonetz/Redux Pictures. Page 21: Courtesy of Mark Mahaney.

HISTORY MODULE Page 23: Stephen Studd/Stone/Getty Images. Page 23: Plan of the Arsenale, Venice (w/c on paper) (see also 60930), Natale, Antonio (17th century)/Museo Correr, Venice, Italy/Alinari/The Bridgeman Art Library International. Page 23: Transcendental Graphics/Contributor/Hulton Archive/Getty Images. Page 24: Frederick Winslow Taylor Collection, Stevens Institute of Technology, Hoboken, NJ. Page 24: Hulton Archive/Getty Images. Page 25: Newscom. Page 25: Newscom. Page 25: Courtesy of AT&T Archives and History Center, Warren, NJ. Page 26: Bert Hardy/Hulton Archive/Getty Images. Page 26: AP Wide World Photos. Page 26: AFP/Photo Frederic J. Brown/Newscom. Page 27: Newscom.

CHAPTER 2 Page 29: © Brand X/SuperStock. Page 31: Don Emmeert/Agence France Presse/Getty Images. Page 34: AP Photo/Rajanish Kakade. Page 35: LiPo Ching/Mercury News/MCT/Newscom.com. Page 38: AP PHOTO/Paul Sakuma. Page 44: AP Photo/Janet Hostetter. Page 46: Evan Sung/*The New York Times*. Page 55: AP Photo/Michel Euler, File.

CHAPTER 3 Page 57: Branson Airport Marketing. Page 57: Marketing and Air Service Development Branson Airport, LLC. Page 59: © Bob Daemmrich/The Image Works. Page 63: Photo Yahoo!/Newscom. Page 68: Newscom. Page 72: AFP Photo/Lawrence HO/Pool/Newscom. Page 74: Peter Wynn Thompson/*The New York Times*/Rudux. Page 75: AP Photo/Bizuayehu Tesfaye. Page 81: Don Fisher/Allentown Morning Call/MCT/Newscom.

CHAPTER 4 Pages 83–84: Michael Newman/PhotoEdit Inc. Page 84: Habitat For Humanity. Page 87: AFP Photo/Kazuhiro NOGI/Newscom. Page 88: © Ben Bake/Redux. Page 91: © Asian Images Group. Page 92: © Andy Kopra/Redux. Page 94: © Jill Connelly/*The New York Times*/Redux. Page 102: © Ben Baker/Redux. Page 109: AP Photo/Vincent Yu.

CHAPTER 5 Page 123: Greg Ward © Rough Guides. Page 125: © Mario Proenca/4SEE/Redux Pictures. Page 127: AFP Photo/Lightchaser Photography/J. Kiely Jr./Newscom. Page 133: © Chris Mueller/Redux. Page 141: Tangi Quemener/AFP/Getty Images. Page 144: AP Photo/Steven Day. Page 146: AP Photo/Eugene Hoshiko. Page 151: Newscom.

CHAPTER 6 Page 153: Nicole Bengiveno/*The New York Times*/Redux Pictures. Page 159: Getty Images. Page 164: Photo by CNImaging/Newscom. Page 167: Yoshikazu Tsuno/AFP/Getty Images. Page 170: Getty Images. Page 174: John Lund/Age Fotostock. Page 176: AP Photo/Ed Andrieski. Page 183: Tom Dodge, Columbus Dispatch/AP Wide World Photos.

CHAPTER 7 Page 190: Charlie Neuman, San Diego Union-Tribune/Zuma/Press. Copyright 2008 San Diego Union–Tribune/Newscom. Pages 191: Phanie/Photo Researchers. Page 198: © John Loomis/Redux Pictures. Page 202: Liu Jin/Agence France Presse/Getty Images. Page 203: AGE Fotostock America, Inc–Royalty-free. Page 207: Pauline Lubens/San Jose Mercury News/MCT/Newscom. Page 211: AP Photo/Tom Cohen.

CHAPTER 8 Page 213: Steve Ringman/Seattle Times/MCT/Newscom. Page 213: AP Wide World/ Paul Sakuma. Page 215: AP Photo/Junji Kurokawa. Page 218: © Kathy McLaughli/The Image Works. Page 222: B Busco/Photographer's Choice/Getty Images. Page 225: AP Photo/Mike Derer. Page 230: AP Photo/Eric Risberg. Page 234: Fabio Cuttica/Contrasto/Redux. Page 239: Francis Dean/Dean Picture/Newscom.

CHAPTER 9 Pages 240–241: AP Wide World/Frank Augstein. Page 241: © Regis Duvignau/ Reuter/Corbis/All Rights Reserved. Page 243: © AP/Damian Dovarganes. Page 245: © Banana Stock. Page 247: Imaginechina via AP Images. Page 250: Reuters/Jo Yong-Hak/Landov. Page 255: Newscom. Page 258: India Today Group/Getty Images. Page 263: Thomas Strand/Thomas Strand Studio.

CHAPTER 10 Page 264(b): Brian Smith. Page 265(a): Tom Sweeney/*Minneapolis Star Tribune*/MCT/Newscom. Page 271: © Robin Weiner/*U.S. Newswire*/The Image Works. Page 275: © Daisy Daisy/Photographer's Choice/Getty Images. Page 279: STR/AFP/Getty Images. Page 284: Newscom. Page 285: Newscom. Page 291: © Gareth Davies/Getty Images.

CHAPTER 11 Page 293: Courtesy of Citigate Cunningham for HCL. Page 293: India Today Group/Getty Images. Page 296: AP Photo/Paul White. Page 301: Librado Romero/*The New York Times*. Page 303: Robert Prezioso/Stringer/Getty Images, Inc.–Getty News. Page 306: John Keatley/Redux. Page 307: David Leeson II/*Dallas Morning News*/KRT/Newscom. Page 310: WireImage/Getty Images, Inc. Page 312: Mark Peterson/Redux. Page 317: Zuma/Newscom.

CHAPTER 12 Pages 318–319: mm-images/Alamy. Page 319: Cheryl Senter/AP Wide World Photos. Page 322: AP Photo/Ted S. Warren. Page 325: Ben Sklar/© *The New York Times*. Page 329: Suma/Newscom. Page 332: RubberBall/AGE Fotostock America, Inc–Royalty-free. PagePage 334: Michele McDonald/Boston Globe/Landov. Page 340: Gil Cohen Magen/Reuters/Landov. Page 347: Courtesy of U.S. Cellular.

CHAPTER 13 Page 348: PA Wire URN: 6872295 (Press Association via AP Images). Page 349: Steve Parsons/PA Wire URN: 5449420 (Press Association via AP Images). Page 351: Steve Krongard/Stone/Getty Images. Page 354: John Tlumacki/Boston Globe/Landov Media. Page 358: Toru Yamanaka/Agence France Presse/Getty Images. Page 361: Tami Chappell/Reuters/Landov. Page 364: Zuma/Newscom. Page 366: AP Photo/Cedric Joubert. Page 371: Lyle Stafford/Reuters/Landov.

CHAPTER 14 Page 373: Courtesy Blue Bird Bus. Page 375: © Chris Machian/*The New York Times*. Page 378: Getty Images. Page 379: © Ilja C. Hendel/VISUM/The Image Works. Page 383: Getty Images. Page 386: Mark Peterson/Redux Pictures. Page 389: AP Photo/Ng Han Guan. Page 397: Getty Images.

Name/Organization Index